The Prehisto

edited by Colin Renfrew *for Edinburgh Unive*

© Edinburgh University Press 1985, 1990, 1993
22 George Square, Edinburgh

First published in 1985
Reprinted in 1990 with Postscript by Colin Richards
Reprinted in 1993 without former colour plates

Set in Linoterm Plantin
by Speedspools, Edinburgh, and
printed in Great Britain at
The Alden Press, Oxford

British Library Cataloguing
  in Publication Data
The Prehistory of Orkney
1. Man, Prehistoric—
   Scotland—Orkney
2. Orkney—History
I. Renfrew, Colin
941.1´32   DA880.06

ISBN 0 7486 0238 0

Contents

Acknowledgements

The publishers wish to thank the following institutions and individuals for permission to reproduce photographs, as indicated below.

In black and white

National Museum of Antiquities of Scotland: 4.1, 4.2, 4.3, 4.4, 4.5, 4.6, 4.7, 4.8, 4.9, 4.10, 4.11, 4.12, 4.13, 4.14, 7.1, 7.2, 7.3, 7.5, 7.6, 7.7, 7.8, 9.1, 9.2, 9.7, 10.4

Royal Commission on the Ancient and Historical Monuments of Scotland: 6.3, 6.4, 6.5, 8.1, 8.2, 8.3, 8.11

Scottish Development Department (Crown copyright reserved): 3.1, 3.2, 3.3, 3.4, 3.5, 5.2, 5.3, 9.3, 9.4, 9.5, 9.6, 10.1

North of Scotland Archaeological Services: 8.6, 8.8, 8.10, 9 app.1

Nature Conservancy Council: 2.1, 2.4

Hunterian Museum, University of Glasgow: 7.4

British Library: 6.1, 6.2

Kirkwall Public Library: 8.5

Tankerness House Museum, Kirkwall (photo John Brundle): 5.4

University of Durham: 10.2, 10.3

Peter Gelling: 8 app.1, 2, 3, 4, 5, 6

John Hedges: 5.1

Professor Colin Renfrew: 5.6, 6.6, 8.7, 11.1

Drs Anna and Graham Ritchie: 6.7

1 Colin Renfrew **Introduction**

The prehistoric monuments of Orkney are justly famed for the abundantly rich picture they give of man's early past in this area. They constitute a complex which is not surpassed elsewhere in Britain – not even in Wessex, perhaps not even in continental Europe – for the wealth of evidence which it offers. For more than a century the two great stone circles, the Ring of Brodgar and the Stones of Stenness, in their spectacular setting on the Lochs of Stenness and of Harray, have been a romantic tourist sight. The great chamber tomb, Maes Howe, nearby, is one of the finest in existence. And the early prehistoric village at Skara Brae, excavated by Gordon Childe fifty years ago, is one of the few ancient sites whose name is known to a very wide public. From the Later Iron Age, the striking stone towers, the brochs, have always posed something of an enigma to scholars. And from the Viking period come not only the great cathedral of St Magnus and the church on Egilsay where he was martyred, but the foundations, on that rocky peninsula of land known as the Brough of Birsay, of what is often claimed as the Palace of Thorfinn, one of the first Norse Earls of Orkney.

These are just some of the sites which have for many years made Orkney celebrated among archaeologists and lovers of the past. Over the past decade or so, after many years of neglect, there has been a great upsurge of interest in and activity concerning early Orkney. Childe's famous excavation at Skara Brae has been re-opened and the new remains from it meticulously examined using a whole battery of modern techniques. Still older settlement remains have been found on the small and today rather remote island of Papa Westray. The spectacular site of the Stones of Stenness has been carefully examined, yielding new information and allowing for the first time there the application of the radiocarbon dating technique. Tombs of this early period have now been excavated, with the careful recovery of a wealth of new data. For the first time moreover there is now a better indication of what was happening in Orkney in the Bronze Age. For the succeeding Iron Age, the origin of the brochs is now becoming clearer; and the rather obscure period in the early centuries AD, prior to the arrival of the Vikings, is today yielding some information about those enigmatic Picts who were displaced by the Norse invaders. And, at last, systematic and careful excavations of the Viking period, including a re-examination of the Brough of Birsay, are giving a proper archaeological background to substantiate the story told in the Norse sagas.

The present book brings together the initiators of these and other recent projects in the Islands and offers to each the opportunity to give an up-to-date survey of the current state of our knowledge for each period in turn. In some cases the new discoveries have filled major gaps – for instance in the Bronze Age. In others they have served to reverse previously accepted views – that is perhaps the case with the brochs. And in the remainder they have yielded abundant new data which permit of much more detailed reconstruction than has hitherto been possible. It is my role as editor to offer a brief introductory survey, into which the more detailed discussions which follow can conveniently be placed.

THE DEVELOPMENT OF ORCADIAN STUDIES

The development of Orcadian prehistoric studies may be said to begin, in 1772, with the excavations by Sir Joseph Banks on the Bay of Skaill (not so far from the later discoveries at Skara Brae). Banks, after a disagreement about the practical arrangements, had withdrawn from Captain Cook's Second Voyage to the Pacific Ocean, and was instead embarked upon his own voyage of scientific investigation to Iceland. His work on Orkney (Lysaght 1974) may amount to little more than a passing curiosity in the history of archaeology, yet marks the beginning of systematic work in the islands.

Investigation did not advance significantly in the next few decades. The obvious standing monuments first attracted attention. Paramount amongst these were the two great stone circles between the Loch of Stenness and the Loch of Harray. Sir Walter Scott used these as the setting of one of the climactic scenes in *The Pirate* (1821), which is set in Shetland and in Orkney. The other two classes of monument already recognised in those early days were the stone towers or *brochs*, and the chambered constructions set below mounds, which were then termed Picts' Houses, although we today regard them as burial monuments.

At that time, the only obvious source of information was the scanty writings of Roman and later historical writers. The first did little more than mention the Orcades. And, prior to the Vikings, we learn very little of their inhabitants, at that time termed Picts. Adomnan, in his *Life of St Columba*, tells how that saint, while resident at the Pictish Court in north Scotland, sent one of his monks to visit the islands, but this is no more than a fleeting glimpse.

It was perhaps natural, then, that the Reverend George Barry, in his *History of the Orkney Islands* (1805), should regard as Pictish, and dating from around the time of St Columba in the sixth century AD, both the brochs and the Picts' houses. He placed these together in his classification, separating them from the standing stones, and from the earth mounds or tumuli, (most of which are today classed as bronze age). His work is of particular interest because he gives a detailed account and plan of the 'Picts' House' of Quanterness, re-excavated in the past decade and shown to be a splendid chambered tomb, dated to *c.* 3400 BC. He reported:

> So far as can now be discovered, there does not appear ever to have been, in any part of the building, either chink or hole for the admission of air or light; and this circumstance alone is sufficient to show that it had not been destined for the abode of men. The contents were accordingly such as might have been naturally expected in such a gloomy mansion. None of those things, which have been discovered in similar places, were found here; but the earth at the bottom of the cells, as deep as it could be dug, was of a dark colour, of a greasy feel, and of a fetid odour, plentifully intermingled with bones, some of which were almost entirely consumed. And others had, in defiance of time, remained so entire, as to show that they were the bones of men, of birds, and of some domestic animals. But though many of them had nearly mouldered to dust, they exhibited no marks of having been burnt; nor were ashes of any kind to be seen within any part of the building. In one of the apartments, an entire human skeleton in a prone attitude was found; but in the others, the bones were not only separated from one another, but divided into very small fragments.

Despite these evidences, Barry did not identify Quanterness as a tomb, and the distinction between broch and Picts' house was not yet made. It no doubt required a clearer chronological perspective, and this was supplied by the Danish Three Age System, published by Thomsen for the first time in English in 1848 (Ellesmere 1848) and more coherently in the following year by Worsaae (1849). This opened the way for one of the most important, and today underestimated, archaeological works of the nineteenth century, Daniel Wilson's *Archaeology and Prehistoric Annals of Scotland* (1851). Here he correctly identified the so-called Picts' houses as chambered tombs, and set them, along with the great stone circles, into the Stone Age, or Neolithic as it was later termed. He recognised that many of the burials from cists and tumuli should be classified as Bronze Age, and assigned the brochs to the Iron Age. He also successfully distinguished these things from the 'Scoto-Scandinavian relics', today called Viking. These crucial distinctions, with remarkably few modifications, have been followed and built on by nearly all later writers. They underlie the structure of this book.

Excavation was by now a popular pastime, and numerous chambered tombs and brochs were investigated, generally without adequate publication, by a number of enthusiastic antiquaries, amongst whom the most notable was George Petrie. The most striking single event of these years was undoubtedy the opening of Maes Howe in 1861, with the discovery of its remarkably perfect stone interior, and of the extensive runic inscriptions left there millennia after its initial use, by intruding Vikings.

The most impressive publication to arise in the mid-nineteenth century from work in Orkney, however, was a report not of excavation but of survey. It was undertaken by Captain F. W. L. Thomas, commanding a Royal Navy survey ship. Working in all weathers in the winter of 1849 he produced an excellent topographical map of that crucial isthmus of land, between the Lochs of Stenness and Harray, where are located the Ring of Brodgar, the Stones of Stenness and other monuments. He produced detailed plans of these, and of the remarkable chambered cairn on the Holm of Papa Westray. In his account (Thomas 1852) he was careful to distinguish between Picts' houses (i.e. chambered cairns) and Picts' castles or brochs. These distinctions were confirmed by the further excavations, mainly of brochs, conducted later in the century. But the broad outline of Orcadian prehistory had by then already been made clear in the pioneering synthesis of Daniel Wilson, and the survey of Thomas. The great stone circles had thus been recorded and set in their context alongside the chambered cairns (or Picts' houses) in the Neolithic, and the brochs in the Iron Age. Naturally the Norse origin of St Magnus' cathedral and the other early standing Christian buildings had never been in question. The Viking nature of the 'Scoto-Scandinavian' burial finds was now clear.

If the work of the mid-nineteenth century represents the first great phase of Orcadian archaeological research, the second undoubtedly came in the years between the two world wars. The leading figure was the distinguished prehistorian V. Gordon Childe. His excavations at the settlement of Skara Brae, from 1927 to 1931, again drew attention to the great richness of the Orcadian material, and to the excellence of its preservation, arising from the use of stone rather than wood as a building material. Initially Childe dated his finds at Skara Brae as Pictish – meaning Later Iron Age (i.e. the pre-Norse period, in the early first millennium AD). But he soon came to see that this was a serious misunderstanding, and that the appropriate context was Neolithic, nearly two thousand years earlier, as it then seemed. (With the benefit of radiocarbon dating we can now see that Skara Brae is actually three thousand rather than two thousand years earlier than Childe first thought.) Childe successfully corrected this misinterpretation, and went on to investigate several other sites, including two chambered cairns and the neolithic settlement at Rinyo on Rousay. He incorporated the Orcadian material into his two syntheses of the prehistoric period, *The Prehistory of*

Scotland (Childe 1935) and *Scotland before the Scots* (Childe 1946). Important work on the chambered cairns of Rousay was carried out during this period, as well as the excavation of the brochs of Midhowe and Gurness, which resulted in abundant finds but unfortunately only brief or negligible publication. The important excavations at the major Norse site, the Brough of Birsay, likewise remain unpublished, and much valuable information was thus undoubtedly lost in an enterprise which had no more positive outcome than some of the less distinguished antiquarian diggings of a century earlier. Happily the current re-evaluation and re-excavation there opens the way to a fresh and well-documented understanding of this important site (see Curle 1982).

The immediate post-war period saw little archaeological activity in Orkney itself. It did, however, produce three major works of synthesis, which served to consolidate much that had been learned over previous decades. The publication of the Inventory volume for Orkney by the Royal Commission on Ancient Monuments (RCAMS 1946) documented in a scholarly way for the first time the great richness of the material, and this documentation was reinforced for the early period by the publication of the first volume, containing the Orcadian cairns, of Audrey Henshall's great work *The Chambered Tombs of Scotland* (Henshall 1963). In addition Dr F. T. Wainwright's edited volume (1962) *The Northern Isles* gave a balanced overview for both Orkney and Shetland, admirably summarising archaeological and historical knowledge at that time.

The third and current phase of archaeological research in Orkney began in the 1970s and continues with vigour today. It has been characterised by an approach which seeks to ask a whole series of new questions about the economy and society of early Orkney, and which has at its disposal a battery of new techniques to undertake this task. It is the contributors to this volume – together with several other colleagues – who have organised and conducted those various excavation projects which now allow a substantial reassessment of the Orcadian past. In doing so they have been aided by the application of radiocarbon dating, which has confirmed the essential justice of Daniel Wilson's early outline, and allowed the solution of several difficult problems. Those problems were initially made more difficult because many Orcadian sites – such as the mounds of burnt stone – are almost devoid of such artefacts as would allow them to be dated through typological comparison. This was, of course, precisely Gordon Childe's early difficulty at Skara Brae. Indeed one of the happy outcomes of radiocarbon dating in Orkney has been that so many of the broad chronological conclusions set out in the earlier syntheses prove to be essentially correct. The techniques of environmental archaeology have also now been enthusiastically applied (although here too we should note that Childe and his colleagues were precursors). Geomorphological studies and pollen analysis permit the re-

5

construction of the environment of the early inhabitants, and the study of plant and faunal remains allows the reconstruction of many aspects of their diet. The examination of human skeletal remains gives insights into population structure, and documents, among other things, the very short life expectancy during the neolithic period. The important results of recent surveys are mentioned here in the final chapter. All of this ferment of activity has made Orkney one of the most active areas of archaeological research in the British Isles, indeed in Europe. A happy outcome is that the law of diminishing returns has not yet set in. Quite to the contrary, the different projects undertaken have complemented each other, adding up to something very much more than a few disparate excavations. In Orkney, perhaps more than anywhere else in Britain, we have a well-documented picture for most of the phases of our prehistory. Of course there are many gaps, but the outcome of recent work has been to allow us to define much more clearly just where those gaps are.

A BRIEF OUTLINE

By way of introduction to the chapters that follow, it seems appropriate to offer a very concise outline, so that the reader can feel the logic of the development of the book. At the same time a number of the chief current issues can be stressed, for recent work has produced at least as many new problems as it has solved.

The story begins with an unpopulated and apparently treeless landscape. In their discussion of the Orcadian environments, Davidson and Jones survey the evidence from pollen studies and other sources which indicate that after the islands were severed from Scotland before 10000 BC, as a result of rising sea level at the end of the last ice age, the vegetation was one of heathland. The strength of the Orcadian winds seems to have prevented thick forestation, and the cover never became more dense than a scrub of birch and hazel. They go on to document the development of a more open herbaceous landscape in the Late Neolithic, and the onset of colder and wetter weather around 1900 BC. At this time, blanket bog began to form in some areas, and with it peat may have become, for the first time, available as a fuel. There was some further worsening of the climate around 1200 BC, and they suggest a marked deterioration around the beginning of the Iron Age at about 600 BC. It is against the background of these broad changes that the shifts in human settlement pattern must be read. But it is not yet clear to what extent climatic and vegetational change was responsible for the developments in social organisation and daily life which the finds document.

The first settlers seem to have come to Orkney a century or two before 3500 BC. Anna Ritchie in her chapter points out that we have no evidence for any hunter-gatherer population in the islands before the arrival of the first

6

farmers. The earliest settlement which we have at present is her own site, Knap of Howar on Papa Westray, but she stresses that other, perhaps simpler sites may yet be found.

The excavations of Clarke at Skara Brae, which he describes, have added a wealth of detail to the picture first established by Childe. For the first time we begin to have a clear picture of the neolithic economy, which was certainly an agricultural one. Indeed among the most interesting finds in recent years are the plough marks at his site, the Links of Noltland on Westray. The mass of radiocarbon dates now available has however heightened rather than removed one particular problem. The pottery and other finds at Skara Brae form a fairly well defined complex, a recurrent assemblage or 'culture', to use the archaeological jargon. Its most characteristic feature is the pottery, 'grooved ware', found at several sites. On the other hand the pottery found at Knap of Howar and at several other sites is of different form and decoration, and is termed 'Unstan ware', after the site where it was first identified. Previously the Unstan ware assemblage had been thought to be the earlier, but the radiocarbon dates now call the chronological distinction into question, and the explanation for the differences between the finds is not clear. This problem is touched upon not only by Anna Ritchie and Clarke, but by Henshall and Graham Ritchie in the chapters which follow.

The abundant evidence from the chambered cairns is reviewed by Henshall. It is clear now that they are contemporary both with Knap of Howar and its Unstan ware, and with Skara Brae and the grooved ware. The passage graves in the class which Henshall designates as the Maes Howe group are associated with grooved ware, while the long, compartmented cairns like those of Rousay and the recently excavated site of Isbister on South Ronaldsay sometimes have Unstan ware. Whatever the explanation of this distinction, we now have abundant evidence for the burial practices of the time, which, as Miss Henshall describes, in some cases involved excarnation – the deliberate de-fleshing of the bones, whether by exposure or temporary burial, prior to their definitive inhumation within the tomb.

The ritual monuments, most notably the Ring of Brodgar and the Stones of Stenness, are discussed by Graham Ritchie, the excavator of the latter site. The radiocarbon dates, as well as the grooved ware which he obtained, placed the monument close in date both to Skara Brae and to the tombs such as Quanterness which contained grooved ware. This allows him to take issue with my own suggestion that the two great henges represent the culmination, in a sense, of a process whereby the smaller and autonomous social groups of the earlier period, documented by the dispersed distribution of their local tombs, became linked in a more centralised society in the Later Neolithic, in which the great central monuments were conceived as playing a significant and central role.

. . . .

The evidence for the Bronze Age, surveyed by Øvrevik, is still less abundant than for the other periods. But her excavations at Quoyscottie have now documented in detail the somewhat modest burial mounds of the Middle Bronze Age. And from the Later Bronze Age, as radiocarbon determinations now indicate, come the mounds of burnt stone, or burnt mounds, notably Liddle Farm and Beaquoy. They are now seen as domestic sites: cooking places or perhaps permanent settlements.

With the Iron Age and the brochs we are on firmer ground. Hedges is able to draw on the evidence of his important excavations of the brochs at Bu near Stromness and at the Howe of Howe Farm, to suggest that these monuments may have had a local origin within the Northern Isles. The sites of Jarlshof and Clickhimin in Shetland are relevant here, as is the new evidence of the iron age round house outside the neolithic chambered cairn at Quanterness. As Hedges rightly shows, some extravagant earlier ideas of invaders and migrations at this time may now be discounted. Moreover he has shown that the furnishings found within many of the brochs – which like those of neolithic Skara Brae are of stone – are not to be dismissed as later additions, but in some cases at least belong to the primary construction. The picture for this period, and for those which precede and follow it, is usefully supplemented in the appendix by Gelling on his excavations at Skaill in Deerness in the east Mainland of Orkney. It is sad to report that Peter Gelling died while this book was in press.

The period of the brochs merges gradually with that of the Picts. Anna Ritchie rightly stresses that the Pictish period is in the first instance defined historically, by written references dating between the third century AD and the ninth century, at which time the Pictish kingdom of Scotland was assimilated into the new Scottish kingdom. The Picts were no doubt the direct descendants of the broch people, but as the author explains, our knowledge of them has to come primarily from archaeological sources. Her own excavations at Buckquoy is one such source, as are the excavations in the late village surrounding the broch at Howe, described in the appendix by Neil. Now at last we have some solid archaeological material to set beside the rather shadowy historical references to the Picts.

Amongst British prehistorians it is conventional to regard prehistoric times as ending with the Roman period. But of course there was no Roman period in Orkney – despite some Roman imports among the brochs. We have few historical data for the Picts, and even the Norse period in Orkney is known primarily from the Norse sagas. The *Orkneyinga Saga* was written around 1200 AD, and it is to be appreciated (as it was intended to be) as much as a work of literature as of historical documentation. Morris is right, therefore, to remind us that in Scandinavia the Viking Age is generally seen as the last period of prehistory. The Scandinavian approach seems eminently suitable for Orkney, and we make no apology for including the Viking period within this survey of Orcadian prehistory. He is able to draw on his own work in the Bay of Birsay area, including his new excavations on the Brough of Birsay, on Anna Ritchie's work at Buckquoy, mentioned above, and on that of Sigrid Kaland at Westness on Rousay, where there is an important Viking cemetery.

With the Late Norse period in the thirteenth century, and the succession of the Scottish earls, historical records become more abundant. So too, of course, do standing buildings, primarily the great cathedral of St Magnus, founded by Earl Rognvald in 1137 AD and completed over the succeeding centuries. By the time the islands passed to the jurisdiction of the Scottish crown in 1468 they may be regarded as falling within the full light of history.

Acknowledgements. The idea of compiling a volume surveying the prehistory of Orkney was first proposed by Dr Graham Ritchie. This book owes much to his enthusiasm, and to that of Dr Anna Ritchie and of Mr Archie Turnbull, Secretary to the Edinburgh University Press. Dr Graham Ritchie kindly undertook the considerable task of compiling the bibliography. We are very grateful to Mr Turnbull and his colleagues at the Press for the care that they have exercised, notably in bringing disparate contributions together into a coherent whole and in the treatment of the illustrations.

2 D. A. Davidson, R. L. Jones **The Environment of Orkney**

THE PRESENT

Location, Geology and Topography. The seventy or so Orkney islands lie
scattered astride latitude 59°N, within the North Atlantic Ocean, just to the
north of Scotland (figure 2.1). Many of them are very small, some little
more than skerries, so that exact agreement as to their total number (some
authors place it as high as ninety) is difficult. Over one half of the land area
(about 974 km²) of the archipelago occurs on the island called Mainland.
The islands are composed almost entirely of gently-inclined Devonian
(Middle Old Red Sandstone) flagstones and sandstones, together with a
small quantity of volcanic rocks. In addition, there is a restricted outcrop of
younger, probably Carboniferous, sandstones, lavas and tuffs (figure 2.2).

The island group is developed on an undulating plateau tilted north
and east, with a major structural depression in its centre, containing Scapa
Flow, and a residual massif in the south, forming the island of Hoy. There is
a series of depressions in the plateau, from south-east to east, probably
Tertiary river valleys that were subsequently overdeepened by Pleistocene
ice. Inundations, principally in late Tertiary and Flandrian (Post-glacial)
times, have filled these depressions to give the present pattern of islands,
firths and straits. The post-glacial rise in sea level has also buried coastal
peat beds, tombolos and bay-mouth bars or ayres (Mykura 1975). The
legacy of the Ice Age is evident in the rounded configuration of the uplands,
and in a widespread mantle of till at lower elevations. Flandrian deposits
consist mainly of blown sand, which, for example, covers about one-third of
the island of Sanday; and peat, which occurs principally on the eastern
flanks of the west Mainland hills and in central Hoy (figure 2.3).

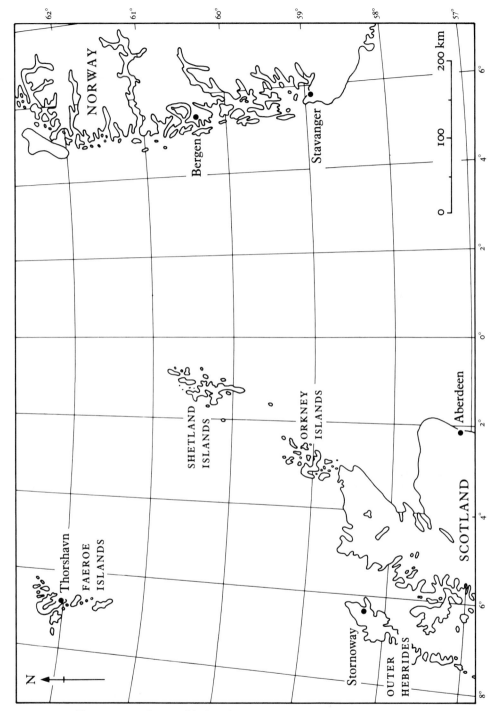

FIGURE 2.1. Geographical setting.

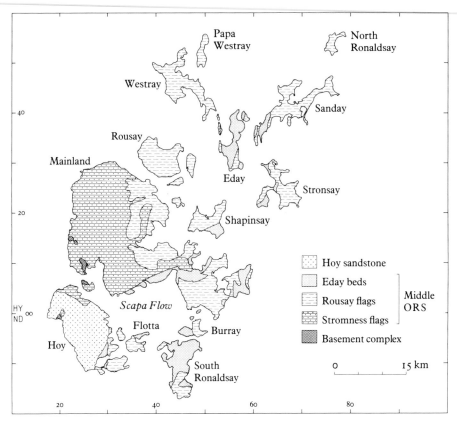

FIGURE 2.2. Solid geology. (From Mykura 1975, reproduced by
permission of the author and the Nature Conservancy Council.)

The geological structure has a distinct effect on land form. The sides of
many hills are stepped, as a result of alternating hard and soft flagstone
strata, a mixture which also explains much varied cliff and rock platform
coastal topography (Mather, Ritchie and Smith 1975). Substantial parts of
Eday, Sanday, South Ronaldsay, and some of eastern Mainland have well-
developed ridge-and-scarp features cut in sandstone (Mykura 1975). Overall, the relief of the archipelago is moderate, considerable tracts of terrain
lying below 150 m OD. Western Mainland, together with much of Rousay, is
hilly, with elevations of up to 275 m OD. The only mountainous country is
located in Hoy where an altitude of 477 m OD is reached (plate 2.1).

Perhaps the most important topographic feature, and one of undoubted significance to early man, is the coastline, whose total length is
about 800 km. The height and steepness of the coastline varies, with high
cliffs, low rocky shores and sandy beaches present in varying proportions.

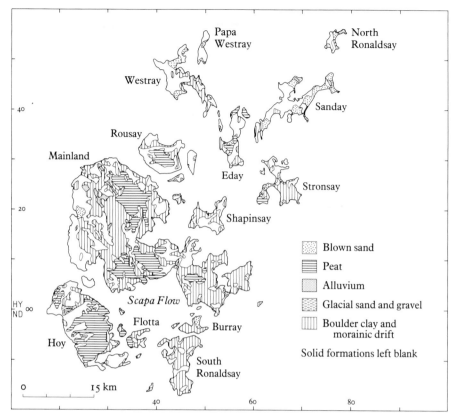

FIGURE 2.3. Surficial deposits. (Based on IGS Quaternary Map UK (North), 1977, reproduced by permission of the Director, Institute of Geological Sciences. NERC Copyright reserved.)

High cliffs, comprising about 20 per cent of the coastline, occur mainly in western Hoy, western Westray and on the west and south-east of Mainland. Sandy beaches (including shingle) make up about 11 per cent and are most common on the north isles. Approximately 70 per cent of the coastline, however, is composed of low rock or boulder clay cliffs and low rocky shores (figure 2.4). In the interior of the archipelago the shelter afforded by nearby land masses gives rise to a low-energy geomorphic environment at the coasts, while, around the fringes of the island group, exposure to the prevailing west and south-west Atlantic winds produces spectacular cliff scenery. Wind action is expressed in the areas of sand-dunes and sand-sheets.

Flora and Fauna. Atmospheric conditions, especially salinity, together with wind speed and frequency, have a significant effect upon plant and

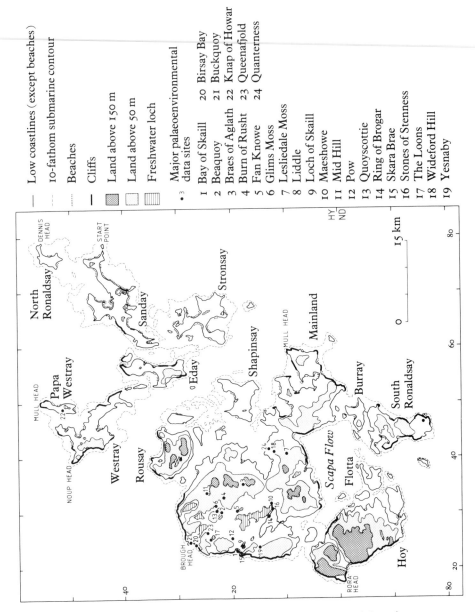

Low coastlines (except beaches)

10-fathom submarine contour

Beaches

Cliffs

Land above 150 m

Land above 50 m

Freshwater loch

Major palaeoenvironmental data sites

1 Bay of Skaill	20 Birsay Bay
2 Beaquoy	21 Buckquoy
3 Braes of Aglath	22 Knap of Howar
4 Burn of Rusht	23 Queenafjold
5 Fan Knowe	24 Quanterness
6 Glims Moss	
7 Lesliedale Moss	
8 Liddle	
9 Loch of Skaill	
10 Maeshowe	
11 Mid Hill	
12 Pow	
13 Quoyscottie	
14 Ring of Brogar	
15 Skara Brae	
16 Stones of Stenness	
17 The Loons	
18 Wideford Hill	
19 Yesnaby	

15 km

FIGURE 2.4. Topography and major palaeoenvironmental data sites. (Coastal types from Mather, Ritchie and Smith 1975, reproduced by permission of the authors and the Nature Conservancy Council. Palaeoenvironmental sites from Bramwell 1979, Caseldine and Whittington 1976, Clutton-Brock 1979, Donaldson, Morris and Rackham 1981, Evans and Spencer 1977, Godwin 1956, Keatinge and Dickson 1979, MacLean 1976, Moar 1969, Ritchie and Ritchie 1974, Sheldon 1979, Spencer 1975, Wheeler 1977, and authors.)

animal distributions. Wind effects are particularly well marked over 150 m OD, and the exposed nature of the islands partially determines the heights at which communities are found.

The last land link with the mainland of Scotland was severed by about 11000 bc, when the sea level in the Late Devensian period rose (A.G. Dawson, personal communication). The Orkney archipelago then became inaccessible to plants and animals unable to disperse across the Pentland Firth. Such physical isolation also meant that migrant prehistoric and historic peoples were forced to make a sea-crossing in order to reach the islands. Amongst the animals introduced by such settlers, was, according to Clutton-Brock (1979), the red deer.

At present, over one half of the Orcadian landscape is utilised in some form of agriculture, the characteristics of which will be examined in the following section. Most of the remainder of the vegetation is semi-natural, and, according to Bullard and Goode (1975), can be grouped into three main categories: grass heath, and tall herb and wetland communities within the agricultural zone; coastal plant communities; and upland vegetation in areas too poor for agriculture.

The degree of exposure is a major constraint on the height at which cultivation is possible. Where some shelter is available, farming may be practised at 100 m OD. Actual cultivation limits, and the extent of improved pasture, vary from locality to locality, a pattern which no doubt also existed in the past. In detail the limit of cultivation and the occurrence of improved pasture are influenced by a set of environmental, economic and social factors, but prime emphasis should be given to the labours of farmers over the centuries.

There is today no semi-natural woodland in the agricultural zone. The native status of many trees is uncertain, and will be discussed later. There are, however, a number of plantations containing a variety of deciduous species, notably where some shelter is afforded. Grass heath occurs mainly on steep slopes in the agricultural zone, and is dominated by grasses, sedges and ericaceous species, together with supplementary herbs. In the upper parts of valleys, tall herb and fern vegetation is encountered, while flushes and mires, many base-rich, occur in similar locations. Extensive areas often occur in the valley mires and in damp patches on agricultural land.

The smaller islands frequently possess a cover of grass heath, of which crowberry (*Empetrum*), thrift (*Armeria*) and sea-plantain (*Plantago maritima*) are important members. Along the coastline, salt-marsh is restricted to sheltered locations at the head of bays and behind ayres. Sand-dunes are likewise not extensive and tend to be of the 'single ridge' type. There are, however, quite widespread areas of dune pasture (machair), known locally as links. This pasture is especially widespread in the north isles and is usually dominated by creeping fescue (*Festuca rubra*), sand sedge (*Carex arenaria*) and carnation-grass (*C. flacca*). In the zone where climatic and soil conditions make cultivation impossible, three main vegetation types exist: first, heath, grassland and subarctic 'fell-field'; second, montane woodland and scrub (localised on Hoy), and consisting mainly of rowan (*Sorbus aucuparia*), birch (*Betula pubescens*), hazel (*Corylus avellana*), aspen (*Populus tremula*) and willow (*Salix* spp.); third, peatlands, divisible into blanket bog which occurs on the higher Mainland hills but is best developed on Hoy, and mires which occur in topographic depressions throughout the uplands. As Bullard and Goode (1975) point out, vegetation restricted to high altitudes further south in Britain is developed at successively lower altitudes northwards because of worsening climatic conditions. Much semi-natural Orcadian vegetation, even at low altitudes, has montane character-istics.

Any analysis of environmental conditions has to take careful account of human agency. Thus, present-day climatic or soil conditions can be evalu-ated in terms of current agriculture on Orkney. Problems arise when any palaeo-environmental assessment is attempted, since data on former en-vironmental conditions and past economies are fragmentary at best. It is conventional in such analyses to describe present-day climatic and soil conditions, and this can be justified on the argument that many of the environmental problems faced by modern farmers have had to be tackled since prehistoric times. Also, the palaeobotanical evidence, to be presented later, suggests that a largely non-wooded environment has been in existence for about 6000 years. This would imply that soil types have not been completely transformed over this period, though it will be shown that some significant changes have occurred.

Comparative environment stability over the last five millennia should not be assumed to indicate an unchanging relationship between nature and man. Major changes have taken place even within the last 200 years. The old agriculture was the run-rig system. The enclosure movement in the early nineteenth century brought consolidated holdings, new agricultural mach-inery, new crops and stock, and a six-course rotation system. In recent decades the amount of land under cereals or roots has been drastically reduced, so that the typical farm is now 88 per cent grass, 7 per cent oats, 3 per cent barley and a mere 1 per cent each of turnips and potatoes (R. Miller 1976). The introduction of new seed mixtures combined with the heavy application of fertilisers give present-day Orkney a very green landscape. These agricultural and associated technological changes mean that the significance of environmental conditions has varied markedly over the last two centuries. Today, new drainage techniques are being applied, so that low-lying, poorly-drained areas are being claimed for agriculture. In con-trast, the use of horses permitted marginal land to be cultivated in the past, which has had to be abandoned when tractors replaced them. The present-day population of Orkney is only a fraction of that of former times. Higher population pressure in the recent historical past meant that more marginal land had to be utilised. It is not enough, therefore, to establish a dynamic relationship between land use, technology and environmental resources; the variable of population pressure must also be introduced into the equation.

Climate. In terms of the physical environment, climate has the greatest impact on the economic life of Orkney, a situation which no doubt also prevailed during prehistory. The salient feature of the climate is the high frequency of strong winds, the effects of which are marked – given the lack of shelter, the overall humid environment with no distinctive wetter or drier periods, and the small annual range of temperature. These characteristics result from the high latitude of Orkney and the strong maritime influence.

TABLE 2.1. Number of days with gusts of 39 mph (17.2 m sec^{-1}) or more at Kirkwall Airport, 10-year means from 1963 to 1972 (from Plant and Dunsire 1974, 73).

JANUARY	15.5	MAY	6.7	SEPTEMBER	8.1
FEBRUARY	12.1	JUNE	4.7	OCTOBER	13.4
MARCH	15.0	JULY	4.8	NOVEMBER	18.0
APRIL	9.7	AUGUST	4.1	DECEMBER	18.3

Total 130.4

In describing the Orcadian climate, one inevitably begins with wind. Anemograph data are available only for Kirkwall Airport and have been analysed by Plant and Dunsire (1974). They note that wind directions are fairly evenly spread around the compass, with the highest frequencies in the quadrant between south and west. An increase in easterly winds is evident in the spring and early summer. Figures for the incidence of gales (over 39 mph/17.2 m sec^{-1}) highlight the dominance of wind in the Orcadian environment (table 2.1). As can be seen from this table, gales are a very frequent occurrence from October until March. Averaged over the year there is a 35.7 per cent chance of a gale on any one day.

The average annual rainfall ranges from *c.* 800 mm in the southern and eastern areas to over 1000 mm on the uplands of Rousay, Hoy and western Mainland (Macaulay Institute for Soil Research, 1978). The monthly and annual totals recorded at Kirkwall Airport are given in table 2.2. The driest period is from April to July. The monthly rainfall totals may not appear very high, but more important is the persistent nature of rainfall in influencing outdoor work. Plant and Dunsire (1974) compute the number of hours during a working day (0700 to 1700 hours GMT) when rainfall is sufficiently intensive to disrupt or prevent outdoor work (table 2.3). These figures, when combined with the incidence of gales, highlight the frequent impossibility of outside work, especially during the months from November to March.

TABLE 2.2 Monthly totals of rainfall (in mm) recorded at Kirkwall Airport, 22-year means from 1951 to 1972 (from Plant and Dunsire 1974, 11).

JANUARY	101	MAY	54	SEPTEMBER	81
FEBRUARY	74	JUNE	57	OCTOBER	112
MARCH	74	JULY	56	NOVEMBER	116
APRIL	52	AUGUST	84	DECEMBER	118

Total 979

A small temperature range, both on a daily and an annual time-scale, is characteristic of Orkney. Figures are given in table 2.4 to illustrate the small annual range of mean daily temperatures on a monthly basis, whilst the differences between the maximum and minimum monthly averages are also small. The small temperature ranges also mean that frost is not common. The average numbers of days with air frost at Kirkwall Airport in January and February are 8.0 and 10.1 respectively. The average date of the first air frost is 20 November and the corresponding date for the last air frost is 23 April for the same station (Plant and Dunsire 1974).

TABLE 2.3. Number of hours of rain falling at some time during the hour at a rate of 0.5 mm hr^{-1} or more between the hours of 0700 and 1700 hours GMT at Kirkwall Airport (from Plant and Dunsire 1974, 21).

10-year mean, 1963-72

JANUARY	56.3	MAY	29.8	SEPTEMBER	41.6
FEBRUARY	38.7	JUNE	24.7	OCTOBER	57.5
MARCH	47.1	JULY	28.6	NOVEMBER	75.0
APRIL	34.6	AUGUST	37.3	DECEMBER	66.7

Total 537.9

10-year mean as percentage of total working time

JANUARY	18	MAY	10	SEPTEMBER	14
FEBRUARY	14	JUNE	8	OCTOBER	19
MARCH	15	JULY	9	NOVEMBER	25
APRIL	12	AUGUST	12	DECEMBER	22

Total 15

The Orkney climate, especially the elements of wind and dampness, places severe stress on agriculture. The present-day absolute emphasis on pasture has reduced the risk of losing locally-grown feedstuffs, but this in turn means that fodder has to be imported. The reduction in hay production in contrast to the rise of silage has also reduced the effect of weather on agriculture. Even so, an unusually wet summer, as in 1979, can cause serious hardship. Before the present 'Green Revolution' as described by Ronald Miller (1976), the traditional mixed type of agriculture would have been more at the mercy of the weather, despite greater diversification. Crop failure, when wet autumns prevented the harvesting of crops or the drying of hay, was endemic in such a physically marginal climate. Presumably such weather fluctuations have existed at least as far back as 1800 BC, when an increase in climatic oceanicity seems likely to have occurred (Keatinge and Dickson 1979). These authors also suggest another climatic change in Orkney about 3800 BC, when onshore winds began to increase. Thus wind may well have presented a serious hazard to farming since neolithic times.

TABLE 2.4. Monthly means of daily maximum temperature, daily mean temperature and daily minimum temperature in degrees Celsius at Kirkwall Airport, from 1951 to 1972 (from Plant and Dunsire 1974, 26, 27, 28). Tables 2.1, 2.2, 2.3 and 2.4 are reproduced by kind permission of the Director-General of the Meteorological Office.

	maximum	mean	minimum
JANUARY	5.3	3.6	1.9
FEBRUARY	5.5	3.4	1.4
MARCH	6.9	4.6	2.3
APRIL	9.2	6.2	3.2
MAY	11.3	8.5	5.6
JUNE	13.9	10.9	7.8
JULY	14.9	12.2	9.4
AUGUST	15.0	12.3	9.7
SEPTEMBER	13.8	11.2	8.7
OCTOBER	11.3	9.2	7.1
NOVEMBER	7.9	6.0	4.1
DECEMBER	6.1	4.4	2.7

Soils. The nature of Orcadian soils can be linked to four factors: the superficial deposits (which are largely glacial tills); the strongly maritime climate; the gently rolling landscape for much of the archipelago; and the influence of man. As described in the previous section, an outstanding feature of the Orkney climate is the effect of a moderate rainfall total of *c.* 800 mm on the lower areas, combined with low evaporation rates. Thus gleying is a dominant soil process in gently-sloping and low-lying areas. Poor drainage also influences extensive areas of hill peat on the uplands of west Mainland, Rousay and Hoy. The incidence of strong winds inhibits the growth of trees. Well-drained forest soils are therefore absent; instead, the norm is for soils to suffer at least some drainage impedance and to be developed under heathland or grassland.

TABLE 2.5. The ten soil associations of Orkney and their parent materials (from Macaulay Institute for Soil Research 1978, 24-5). Table 2.5 and figure 2.5 are reproduced by kind permission of the Macaulay Institute for Soil Research, and the authors.

STROMNESS. Drift derived from sandstones and breccias of the Middle Old Red Sandstone and rocks of the granite-schist complex of the Moinian

LYNEDARDY. Drift derived from flagstones and sandstones of the Middle Old Red Sandstone with rocks of the granite-schist complex of the Moinian

THURSO. Drift derived from strata of the Stromness Flags and the Rousay Flags of the Middle Old Red Sandstone

CANISBAY. Drift derived from strata of the Stromness Flags, the Rousay Flags and the Eday Beds of the Middle Old Red Sandstone

FLAUGHTON. Drift derived from sandstones of the Eday Beds of the Middle Old Red Sandstone

DARLEITH. Drift derived from basic lavas and intrusions

DUNNET. Drift derived from strata of the Upper Old Red Sandstone

RACKWICK. Fluvioglacial sands and gravels derived from strata of the Upper Old Red Sandstone

BOYNDIE. Fluvioglacial sands

FRASERBURGH. Shelly sand

The Soil Survey for Scotland soil maps for Orkney were published in 1982. The survey was executed by Mr F. Dry and the full results of his research are not available at the time of writing. However, an interim report has been published, from which the following description of the soils derives (Macaulay Institute for Soil Research 1978). Superficial deposits cover about 85 per cent of Orkney, with till and peat the most extensive. In areas such as Sanday, North Ronaldsay, and the Bay of Skaill, wind-blown sand is dominant. Rae (1976) interprets the till as being the result of variations in glacier flow over Orkney. The Soil Survey recognise four types of till:

(1) a moderately fine-textured till which occurs throughout the islands, but is most extensive in such areas as east Mainland, South Ronaldsay, Shapinsay, Stronsay, Westray and in particular parts of west Mainland,

(2) a coarse or moderately coarse-textured till which occurs mainly on Hoy,

(3) a moderately coarse or medium-textured till which is common throughout west Mainland,

(4) a morainic till which occurs locally on Mainland.

These tills are further subdivided according to lithological type and age, when linked with the remaining parent materials types (different kinds of sands), provide the basis for the ten soil associations which have been identified. A soil association is a characteristic soil pattern related to parent material and relief.

The Thurso, Canisbay, Dunnet and Fraserburgh Associations are the most extensive, though peat is also widespread (figure 2.3). For mapping purposes, the Soil Survey subdivides soil associations into soil series. These series encompass the following range of major soil groups and subgroups: podzols, peaty podzols, non-calcareous gleys, peaty gleys, brown calcareous soils, oroarctic podzols, calcareous gleys and saline gleys. The first five types are the most widespread.

The spatial pattern of some of these soils is illustrated in figure 2.5. Figure 2.5a presents a topographic extract for the area between Finstown and the outskirts of Kirkwall in the east Mainland. A gently sloping coastal strip along the southern shores of the Bay of Firth gradually rises in an open basin form to Wideford Hill (225 m), Keelylang Hill (220 m), Hill of Lyradale (176 m) and Hill of Heddle (135 m). There is a marked correlation between soil types and drainage conditions. On the upper slopes of these hills, peat is dominant (figure 2.5). Peat also occurs in poorly-drained footslope as well as depressional localities. A hydrologic sequence of soils is evident, for example on the northern slopes of Wideford Hill and Keelylang Hill. Peat on the summit areas is followed by peaty podzols on the upper slopes. Middle slopes may well suffer from an excess of water leading to the formation of peaty gleys, as demonstrated by these slopes on Wideford Hill and Hill of Heddle. Drainage conditions improve on the lower slopes of Wideford Hill – round Quanterness farm. This is reflected in the presence of freely- and imperfectly-drained podzols. The final extensive members of the hydrologic sequence are the non-calcareous gleys which occur in the most low-lying and gently sloping localities. In summary then, the hydrologic sequence is from peat on hill summits, ranging through peaty podzols and peaty gleys on upper and middle slopes to freely and imperfectly drained podzols on the best drained localities. On footslopes or in hollows, non-calcareous gleys and peats predominate. This spatial patterning is evident on much of Orkney, though there are obvious deviations in areas of high relief (for example, Hoy) or where blown sand is extensive. A critical issue is the extent to which soil conditions have changed since prehistoric times.

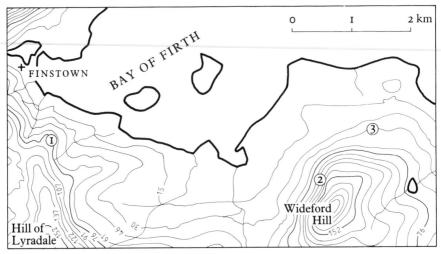

(a)   Chambered cairns: 1 Cuween, 2 Wideford Hill, 3 Quanterness

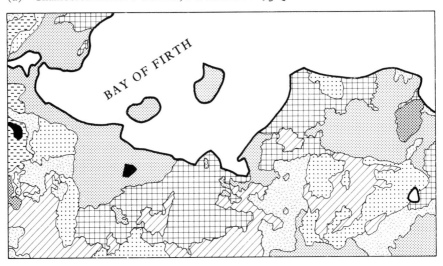

(b)

▦ Freely/imperfectly drained podzols		▨ Peat	
⣿ Peaty podzols		▦ Complex of podzols and gleys	
▢ Peaty gleys		⣿ Complex of shallow podzols and gleys	
▦ Noncalcareous gleys		■ Quarries, etc.	

FIGURE 2.5. (a) Topography and cairn location between Finstown and Kirkwall, Mainland. (b) Soil types in the Finstown–Kirkwall area. (Reproduced by permission of the Macaulay Institute for Soil Research and the authors.)

22

THE PAST

Introduction. During the last dozen years, knowledge of the prehistoric environment of Orkney has increased markedly, chiefly as a result of investigations either at or close to archaeological sites on Mainland. These investigations have been mainly palaeobotanical, with the aim of reconstructing vegetational history, and using the evidence to try to say something about climatic conditions, soil types and the effects of human activity. However, other techniques, such as molluscan analysis, and the examination of bones from archaeological sites, have widened the range of data, and provide an insight into prehistoric resource exploitation and palaeoenvironments. A range of sediments and finds have been dated by radiocarbon, and a detailed chronology built up to accompany the picture of ecological change (table 2.6).

Early Research. Before 1969, when Moar presented evidence of Late Devensian (late last glacial) and Flandrian (present interglacial) vegetation, the only palaeobotanical data consisted of records of tree remains in island peats (Traill 1868); a cursory examination by means of pollen analysis of a number of organic deposits by Erdtman (1924), which revealed woodland sometime during the Post-glacial; and a pollen and macrofossil study of samples obtained from the Maes Howe ditch during Childe's 1955 excavation. The latter were discussed by Godwin (1956), and the results indicate a largely open landscape where human influence was present.

Late Devensian to Middle Flandrian Landscapes. Moar (1969), at Yesnaby and The Loons on Mainland, concluded that the Orkney landscape between about 12000 and 8000 bc, was barren, consisting of open grassland and heath. This became better developed during the climatic warming of Late-glacial Zone II time – the so-called Allerod or Windermere Interstadial (Coope and Pennington 1977). Grasses (Gramineae), sedges (Cyperaceae), juniper (*Juniperus*), least willow (*Salix herbacea*), saxifrages (Saxifragaceae), sorrel (*Rumex*) and crowberry (*Empetrum*) were important constituents of the flora (table 2.6). Moar suggested that the early Post-glacial period was first characterised by an increasing density of heathland as the climate improved. At first, juniper dominated this heathland, then crowberry. Gradually, birch began to colonise, and was joined by hazel, to form scrub vegetation (Pollen Assemblage Zone F III at The Loons) (table 2.6). Pollen of oak (*Quercus*), elm (*Ulmus*) and alder (*Alnus*) were recorded, but these trees were not thought to be native to Orkney, although pine (*Pinus*) may have been present on the islands.

The north-eastern part of the Scottish mainland seems to have been dominated by tall herb communities and birch-hazel scrub in the mid-Flandrian (H.J.B.Birks 1977; Peglar 1979). Remains of birch, hazel and willow are quite widespread in Orkney peats. No oak or alder has been

British Pleistocene stage		Other sub-divisions	Radiocarbon date ad/bc / Calendar date AD/BC	Nature of vegetation	
INTERGLACIAL (FLANDRIAN)		LATE FLANDRIAN (ZN / ZA)	Present	Agricultural land, machair, fen, tall herb and fern communities, dwarf-shrub heath dominated by heather, blanket peat with cotton grass.	Blanket peat formation begins
			1000 ad / 1030 AD		
			0 ad / 60 AD	Pasture land with grasses and ribwort. Arable land with mugwort, crucifers and cereals.	
		MIDDLE FLANDRIAN (ZC / ZLA)	1000 bc / 1250 BC	Heathland dominated by heather. Machair with sea plantain and bucks-horn plantain.	Scrub decline begins
			2000 bc / 2530 BC	Tall herb and fern communities including umbellifers and polypody.	
			3000 bc / 3785 BC		
			4000 bc / 4845 BC		
		EARLY FLANDRIAN (ZI / ZPOST)	5000 bc / c 5900 BC	Birch-hazel scrub. Tall herb and fern communities.	Scrub development begins
			6000 bc		
			7000 bc		
			8000 bc	Denser heathland with juniper and crowberry.	
GLACIAL (DEVENSIAN)		LATE DEVENSIAN LATE-GLACIAL	9000 bc	Open grassland with mugwort. Heathland with crowberry. Denser grassland. Better developed heathland with crowberry and juniper.	
			10 000 bc	Open grassland with sorrel and mugwort. Heathland with crowberry.	

TABLE 2.6. Chronology and vegetation types during the Late Devensian and Flandrian. (Chronological scheme after West 1977. Vegetational and radiocarbon data from Caseldine and Whittington 1976, Erdtman 1924, Godwin 1956, Keatinge and Dickson 1979, Moar 1969, and authors. Radiocarbon/calendar date calibration from Clark 1975.)

24

recovered, and records for pine are dubious.

Also from Mainland, Keatinge and Dickson (1979) have presented detailed evidence for mid-Flandrian vegetation changes. Their earliest pollen assemblages (in Zones GM-1 at Glims Moss and LS-1 at Loch of Skaill), together with radiocarbon assays, confirm and extend Moar's findings, indicating the presence until about 3800 BC of birch-hazel woodland or scrub, with willow, ferns and tall herbs also present. Slight indications of pine, oak, elm and ash are assumed to be the result of long distance transport of grains, from the Scottish mainland and/or Scandinavia. Alder pollen values rise c. 5900 BC and the elm curve declines about 3800 BC (table 2.6). Both trends, and a decline in pine values, are attributed by Keatinge and Dickson to vegetational changes on the Scottish mainland. The decline in pine, for example, may have been a reflection of the reduction in the north-western pine forests around 2600 BC as demonstrated by H. H. Birks (1975).

Initial Replacement of the Scrub. Evidence from Mainland shows that birch-hazel scrub began to be replaced by more open vegetation about 3500 BC. Pollen Assemblage Zones GM-2 and LS-2a at Glims Moss and Loch of Skaill respectively, have high values of Gramineae, ribwort (*Plantago lanceolata*) and a variety of other herbaceous taxa (Keatinge and Dickson 1979) (table 2.6). Keatinge and Dickson point out that such pollen taxa may be representative of the fen vegetation and nearby tall herb and fern communities, but suggest that in view of their substantially increased representation, a more likely explanation is to be found in vegetation disturbance. If such disturbance, involving human clearance of the scrub vegetation, occurred, it would have required less effort than traditional neolithic forest clearance which usually took place in denser woodland. Because of the relatively open nature of the early- and mid-Flandrian Orkney vegetation, where there were many naturally-occurring plants associated with a non-forested environment, it is difficut, on palynological evidence alone, to assert with confidence that the presence of such taxa is a result of human activity, However, when there is well-documented archaeological evidence, as is the case for the Orcadian Neolithic, it is reasonable to infer that high values of grass, ribwort, and a range of their herbaceous pollen taxa including cricifers (Cruciferae) and mugwort (*Artemisia*) reflect agrarian practices, probably of a predominantly pastoral kind. Moar noted that the ribwort pollen curve began to rise as birch-hazel scrub gave way to more open vegetation (Pollen Assemblage Zone F IV), and suggested neolithic agricultural activity as a possible cause.

At the Loch of Skaill, sea plantain and bucks-horn plantain (*P. coronopus*) in the pollen record for about 3800 BC suggest that machair may have begun to develop. Blown sand has been found below occupation layers dated to 3800–3300 BC at Skara Brae (D. V. Clarke 1976a and b). Also,

Keatinge and Dickson report mineral material, whose source may be aeolian, in organic sediments at Loch of Skaill and Pow. Such material may have been a response to increased on-shore wind speeds. The mineral material has a neolithic age, and, if not wind-blown, may be inwash from surrounding slopes, where scrub clearance had taken place.

Molluscs provide corroborative evidence of the replacement of woodland by more open vegetation in the mid-Flandrian. In what is considered to be a neolithic context at Skara Brae and Buckquoy, Spencer (1975) reports that land snails, including *Carychium* and *Discus*, indicative of woodland and occurring in buried soil, are replaced by taxa such as *Vallonia excentrica* and *Pupilla muscorum* in the overlying shell sands. Evans (1977) suggests that the buried soil at Skara Brae is more or less contemporary with the earliest neolithic occupation, and proposes, on molluscan evidence, that it supported a vegetation including grassland and scrub woodland, an interpretation which is consistent with the gleyed nature of this palaeosol. There also seems to have been a degree of neolithic woodland clearance prior to sand accumulation in this locality. At Knap of Howar on Papa Westray, a neolithic settlement contains a midden (dated *c.* 3600 BC), which occurs over a buried soil and under blown sand. Molluscs are present and their ecology, according to Spencer (1975), is consonant with neolithic scrub clearance, which probably gave rise to the blown sand.

It is also possible that a climatic change about 4400 to 3800 BC, referred to earlier, may have been influential in vegetational modification. There is botanical evidence for lower temperatures at this time, a phenomenon also suggested by *Coleoptera* (beetles) (Osborne 1977). If such climatic change meant increased wind speeds, these could have initiated natural, or accelerated human, changes in the vegetation cover, as Keatinge and Dickson suggest, by means of physical damage and salt-spray effects.

The peak of the main Flandrian sea-level rise is recorded by a flooding of the sea into the Bay of Skaill at about 4900 BC. An intertidal reed (*Phragmites*) peat has been identified, which implies that the bay was once a freshwater loch. Invasion by the sea, with the formation of a sandy beach, and the initiation of sand-blow is dated sometime between 4600 and 3800 BC. The deposition of these calcareous sands caused an abrupt change in soil formation and probably had much to do with the formation of considerable areas of open vegetation, perhaps even before the first neolithic settlements.

The Later Neolithic Environment. A number of other sites provide environmental evidence and radiocarbon assays to confirm neolithic activities in Orkney. However, such evidence almost certainly post-dates the initial clearance of birch-hazel scrub, and suggests a predominantly open landscape dominated by herbaceous vegetation, the archaeological context of which is Late Neolithic (table 2.6). At Lesliedale Moss, sediments dated to about 2300 BC have low tree and shrub pollen totals, and considerable herbaceous and dwarf-shrub values, particularly of ribwort, sorrel, members of the rose family (Rosaceae), and heather (*Calluna*), suggesting agrarian, probably mainly pastoral, practices in the locality (Davidson, Jones and Renfrew 1976; R. L. Jones 1979).

Around Maes Howe a similar, virtually treeless landscape is depicted about 2600 BC, a finding supported by pollen analyses at the Stones of Stenness (Caseldine and Whittington 1976). At Maes Howe, Pollen Assemblage Zone MNH-I reflects mixed agricultural practices, probably with a pastoral bias – there is a substantial amount of ribwort pollen, but also that of cereals. At Stenness, oat (*Avena*) and wheat (*Triticum*) pollen, and barley (*Hordeum*) macrofossils (MacLean 1976) have been identified.

At the Quanterness chambered tomb (Renfrew 1979), the earliest radiocarbon date is 3420 ± 110 BC (Q-1294) from the lowest stratum in the tomb. There are bone records of red deer, horse, sheep, ox and pig from neolithic strata which document the pastoral element in the economy at this time. Sheep bones are most frequent, and if their presence is not solely the result of a funerary tradition, their occurrence strengthens the case for the presence of an open and rather sparse vegetation (Clutton-Brock 1979). Bird-bone data from Quanterness indicate that buzzard (*Buteo buteo*) and goshawk (*Accipiter gentilis*), usually woodland inhabitants, were present in the Neolithic (Bramwell 1979). This may support the contention that some areas of scrub woodland survived, although both birds will occupy open terrain if an adequate food supply is available. Frequent birch and willow charcoal of neolithic age have been reported from Quanterness (Sheldon 1979). Fish remains from the same site indicate substantial use of intertidal and deeper water marine resources, in addition to those provided by farming. The fish bones also suggest, notably by the presence of remains of the currently Mediterranean/Atlantic distributed corkwing wrasse (*Crenilabrus melops*), that the Orkney sea temperatures in the Neolithic were slightly higher than those of the present (Wheeler 1979).

Bronze Age Environments. Archaeological evidence of Early Bronze Age dwellers in Orkney is scanty. Pollen diagrams covering this time, for example, Lesliedale Moss and Maes How (Davidson, Jones and Renfrew 1976; R. L. Jones 1979) and Glims Moss (Keatinge and Dickson 1979) reflect a lowering in the scale and intensity of farming which, however, remained mixed. There was also some regrowth of scrub vegetation. Evidence has been obtained from blanket peats at Burn of Rusht, Mid Hill and Braes of Aglath, of renewed agricultural activity which began about 1800 and lasted until *c.* 400 BC, hence spanning the Middle and Late Bronze Age and Early Iron Age (Keatinge and Dickson 1979). At these blanket peat sites, a pre-peat vegetation of open birch-hazel woodland with a well-developed ground flora of tall herbs and ferns, was replaced by grassland, where ribwort, members of the buttercup and daisy families (Ranunculaceae and Compositae) were frequent. The decline in scrub woodland occurs at the peat-soil interface, where carbonised woody material was recorded. Peat began to form at Burn of Rusht, Mid Hill and Braes of Aglath between 1800 and 1300 BC. A similar pollen spectrum is recorded from the base of blanket peat at Wideford Hill (Assemblage Zone WH-1) (R. L. Jones 1979), and although there are no radiocarbon dates for this profile, its age is probably analogous to the other blanket peat sites. Possible reasons for the inception of blanket peat growth have been explored by Moore (1975) and others, and may involve either natural or human factors, or a combination of both. There may have been a colder and wetter climatic phase beginning about 1900 and heightening around 1200 BC, according to Frenzel (1966), which would have favoured peat growth in suitable locations (table 2.6). Moore suggested that tree-felling would have led to an increase in the volume of groundwater, a rise in water-table and the accumulation of organic matter above existing soils. Whatever the cause of blanket peat formation in Orkney, the palynological evidence allows the inference that grazing pressure increased on the Mainland hills around 1900 BC. The blanket bog was probably the first peat to be utilised as fuel – the valley mires were not really suitable for this purpose (Keatinge and Dickson 1979). Hence, prior to the formation of blanket peat, brushwood, or some alternative combustible such as turf or seaweed was likely to have been used as fuel by prehistoric peoples.

Other sites support the notion that Middle and Late Bronze Age times were important agriculturally. At Loch of Skaill, there is a decline in hazel pollen and an increase in indicators of arable farming about 1300 BC. From the Bay of Birsay, a radiocarbon assay of 1606 ± 190 BC (GU-1222) from a midden overlying a buried soil confirms a similar Bronze Age context (Donaldson, Morris and Rackham 1981). Carbonised naked barley, together with a wide range of animal and fish bones at this site reflect a major dependence on the local environment for food.

The preliminary report on the soil survey of Orkney stresses the important role of man in influencing soils (Macaulay Institute for Soil Research 1978). The cultivation and husbandry of widely-distributed natural peaty gley and peaty podzol soils led to the development of a thick topsoil in particular locations. The application of seaweed and farm manure assisted in soil accumulation; and paring, whereby turf first used as bedding for animals was later applied to fields, may also have been important. This process leads to the formation of man-made or plaggen soils, which also occur in extensive areas of north-east Europe (de Bakker 1979). There is evidence to suggest that plaggen formation was already under way in prehistoric Orkney. At the site of Skaill, in Deerness, P. Gelling has identified an intricate pattern of plough marks in a buried soil. Limbrey (1975) has investigated this soil and she describes it as a buried podzol. She suggests that the land surface during the Late Bronze Age, or possibly earlier, had been ploughed and fertilised. The age of this buried soil may have to be revised in the light of radiocarbon dating from the Skaill site. The soil was, however, buried by wind-blown sand before Viking times. Indeed, changes in soils are intimately connected with coastal changes in the Orkneys. A change in sea level of as little as ± 1.0 m would have a marked effect on both the drainage conditions of coastal plains, and on the configuration and extent of lochs, which are at present separated from the sea by a slight drop in elevation. The critical issue is the detailed pattern of sea-level changes during the Flandrian in Orkney, and evidence of these is sparse. As noted earlier, it is generally accepted that the Orcadian coast is one of submergence, with a gradually rising sea level producing the present intricate archipelago. A buried soil at St Peter's Pool, Deerness is mantled by stratified beach deposits at c. 1 m OD (Limbrey, personal communication). If this soil, like that at nearby Skaill, is of Bronze Age date, then a subsequent rise in sea level is suggested. Other tantalising evidence is occasionally present along the shores of some of the lochs, where small, cliff-like notches, about 0.5–1.0 m above OD occur (plate 2.2). Such features are present at Tankerness (HY524093), and Loch of Harray (HY 308139). At Tankerness (Lamb, personal communication), prehistoric structures were discovered during a period when water-level was low in the loch. The obvious implication is that drainage conditions in coastal situations, with feedback along the low-lying loch shores, have deteriorated over the last few millennia.

The other relevant components of coastal change are accretion and erosion. Shingle bars (ayres) have formed at the head of many bays, often impounding bodies of water (oyces) (plate 2.3). The formation of ayres and oyces reflects a gradual lowering of land relative to sea. One effect of ayre formation is to impede drainage in tributary areas, where the extension of peat, and peaty gley or gley soils is thus encouraged.

The other accretionary coastal component is wind-blown sand (plate 2.4). As noted above, sand-blow probably began about 3800 BC. However, it is likely that aeolian deposits in Orkney (figure 2.3) have evolved over a number of time-spans, and not necessarily in a synchronous manner. Such blown sand must, as Donaldson, Morris and Rackham (1981) suggest for the Bay of Birsay, have reduced the coastal agricultural zone where it formed dunes. However, it did also spread as sheets, which provided useful tracts of land for farming, notably pastoral.

A range of archaeological sites provide evidence of Middle and Late Bronze Age environmental conditions. These include Maes Howe, the Stones of Stenness, the 'burnt mounds' of Liddle, Beaquoy and Fan Knowe, and the barrow cemetery of Quoyscottie. At Maes Howe, from

PLATE 2.1. Glacial trough, South Burn, Rackwick, North Hoy.
(Courtesy of the Nature Conservancy Council.)

PLATE 2.2. The eastern edge of the Loch of Tankerness. The loch may
once have had a slightly higher level, as suggested by the small
raised platform currently being eroded. (D. A. Davidson.)

PLATE 2.3. The formation of a shingle bar (an ayre) at the mouth of the Graemeshall Born in Holm has led to the development of a small loch (an oyce). Scapa Flow is in the background. (D. A. Davidson.)

PLATE 2.4. Machair at Mae Sand on Westray. (Courtesy of the Nature Conservancy Council.)

about 2000 BC to the end of the Bronze Age, there is pollen evidence (from Assemblage Zones MHN-2 and MHS-1 of the ditch sequences, together with that from the lower peat layer on the mound platform) of predominantly herbaceous vegetation, although with some limited, temporary resurgences of hazel scrub (Davidson and Renfrew 1976; R. L. Jones 1979). Agrarian activity was varied and included growing. The West Ditch Terminal at Stenness provides a similar sequence of landscape history, with presumed Bronze Age agrarian phases of varying intensity envisaged by Caseldine and Whittington (1976). Thermoluminescence dates signify that the burnt mounds of Liddle, Beaquoy and Fan Knowe, were formed between c. 1000 and 400 BC (Huxtable, Aitken, Hedges and Renfrew 1976). Pollen recovered from soils and peat buried beneath these monuments (R. L. Jones 1975) indicates the local existence of some scrub woodland, a substantial proportion of heather-dominated heathland, and a fairly low level of agricultural activity. As such events pre-date the mounds, they are assumed to represent earlier Bronze Age practices, during which time the landscape was recovering after the rather intensive late neolithic husbandry. The pollen spectra from beneath the barrow cemetery at Quoyscottie are fairly similar to those from beneath the burnt mounds (R. L. Jones 1977). The landscape was open, and there was agrarian activity, including some cereal growing. At Liddle, peat infilling part of the structure has a radiocarbon date of 1185 ± 110 BC (SRR-525) at its base. The pollen record from this peat indicates that human influence was greater than during the time recorded in the buried soil at the site.

In terms of environmental history, the climatic deterioration referred to earlier may be relevant in a Middle and Late Bronze Age context. According to Stuart Piggott (1972), its major impact in Britain may have come around 1300 BC. Cultivation limits were then probably lowered, principally perhaps due to an increased bog and heath cover, which reduced the area available for easy cultivation (S. E. Øvrevik, this volume). Peat seems to have been widely used at burnt mound sites. If, as envisaged earlier, blanket peat formation became widespread around 1800 BC, some would have been available for combustion in the first millennium BC. Alternatively, the resurgence of scrub woodland indicated by the pollen diagrams covering this period could have given a source of fuel. Ritchie and Ritchie (1974) report birch and hazel charcoal associated with a Bronze Age site at Queenafjold, Mainland, which lends some support to this hypothesis. There is evidence of significant heathland clearance around the burnt mound sites prior to the inception of farming. At Liddle, arable farming and disturbed soils are indicated, while grazing was practised too, as part of a mixed economy.

The Iron Age Environment. The agrarian practices of Middle and Late Bronze Age times appear to have continued in the Iron Age, according to various pollen diagrams. A well-documented worsening of climate occurred about 600 BC, when conditions became wetter (Godwin 1975). This must have led to a further restriction of available agricultural land with a corresponding increase in bog and heath vegetation. This is borne out by the pollen record, as also is a fair amount of husbandry. For example, at Glims Moss and Loch of Skaill, peaks in ribwort and mugwort pollen in Assemblage Zones GM-3 and GM-4, and LS-2, may, according to Keatinge and Dickson (1979) represent iron age agricultural activity. The expansion of heather at the start of Pollen Assemblage Zone GM-4 at Glims Moss could have also been a result of widespread heath formation at this juncture, although, as Keatinge and Dickson point out, its local growth on the mire may have been mainly responsible. Assemblage Zone LM-3 at Lesliedale Moss indicates little tree and shrub pollen, and much of dwarf-shrubs and herbs, many of the latter perhaps representing agricultural activity. Similarly, Assemblage Zone WH-2 at Wideford Hill has a majority of heathland and grassland pollens referable to this time period (Davidson, Jones and Renfrew 1976; R.L.Jones 1979).

At the archaeological sites, a number of palaeobotanical and radiocarbon findings relevant to the Iron Age landscape have been made. The upper peat layer on the mound platform at Maes Howe has a heather-dominated pollen assemblage, and contains cereal and other agrarian indicator pollen. At the Ring of Brogar, radiocarbon dates for the basal organic deposit in the ditch have a mean of around 400 BC, and the associated pollen assemblages cover the last part of the first millennium AD. The environmental mosaic was evidently rather different hereabouts. Varied farming activities are portrayed, but there is less heathland pollen, than, for example, at nearby Maes Howe (R.L.Jones 1979). Supplementary environmental data for this period comes from the Quanterness settlement, or 'Round House', whose average age in its first phase is *c.* 700 BC, and in its second phase, about 200 BC. Bones of cattle, sheep and deer were recorded, indicating a subsistence economy, perhaps with a pastoral bias (Clutton-Brock 1979).

The Pre-Norse and Norse Environment. Some of the available palynological data undoubtedly covers the pre-Norse and Norse periods, and a limited amount extends towards the present. However, its collection was not specifically concerned with the environment of historical time. Hence the sampling strategy for pollen analysis tends to mitigate against detailed palaeoecological inferences. General trends at this time may be discerned with reference, for example, to Pollen Assemblage Zone LM-3 at Lesliedale Moss which indicates a further expansion of heathland, very low tree amounts and phases of agricultural activity of a mixed nature. More detail is forthcoming from Pollen Assemblage Zone MHS-2 at Maes Howe. This begins in the Pictish period about 300 AD, and continues beyond 725 AD into

Norse time. It portrays much heathland and a balance of arable and pastoral farmland (Davidson, Jones and Renfrew 1976).

The best pre-Norse and Norse environmental data comes from several archaeological sites in the Bay of Birsay (Donaldson, Morris and Rackham 1980) and from nearby Buckquoy (A. Ritchie 1977). At Birsday, pre-Norse and Norse material has been radiocarbon assayed, mainly to the later part of the first millennium AD. Charcoal of birch, hazel and willow/aspen may indicate the local presence of scrub woodland until Norse time, but molluscan evidence from Buckquoy suggests grassland close at hand (Evans and Spencer 1977). There were plenty of domestic animals, including cattle, sheep and deer at both sites, while Birsay yielded macrofossils of barley and oats, denoting arable farming in the locality. Marine mammals, fish and wildfowl also formed an important part of pre-Norse and Norse diets in this region, according to the bone remains.

CONCLUSION

The Orcadian landscape of today is developed on numerous fairly small islands. Their topography is sculptured in relatively soft rocks, and is generally subdued, principally as a result of Tertiary and Pleistocene geomorphological processes. Save in certain exposed coastal areas, this means that the geomorphic environment is a fairly low-energy one. For instance, there are no major river systems on the islands. The climate of the archipelago is also influenced by the small size of its component land masses, by general maritime features, notably the North Atlantic Drift; and by strong winds which give rise to marked problems of exposure.

The soils are predominantly peaty podzols, peaty gleys and gleys, and there is a substantial extent of blown sand and peat. Within the limit of cultivation, the soils are often drained and fertilised, so that over one half of the islands' area is cultivated primarily for pasture. Most of the remaining vegetation is semi-natural, has many montane characteristics due to the exposure factor, and consists mainly of grass and heath communities, together with wetlands. Trees are conspicuous by their absence.

The palaeoenvironmental record implies that during the tenure of the Orkneys by prehistoric and historic peoples, which began about 3800 BC, a number of major environmental facets have remained substantially unchanged. However, the effects of the successive cultural groups have been considerable, notably in respect of vegetation disturbance and soil change as a result of agricultural practices. Pollen evidence indicates that by c. 5900 BC, a climax vegetation of birch-hazel scrub with an understorey of tall herbs and ferns clothed the islands. Palynological and molluscan data shows that this began to be replaced about 3800 BC by more open vegetation. Such vegetation change was probably brought about by neolithic settlers. It is also possible that an overall climatic deterioration that began about 3800 BC and has continued until the present (aided by means of increased on-shore winds that caused physical damage to plants), intensified salt-spray and initiated sand-blow. By about 2600 BC, in the Late Neolithic, there was virtually no tree cover remaining, and the landscape was one of predominantly herbaceous and dwarf-shrub heath vegetation within which mixed farming, perhaps with a pastoral bias, was being practised. Indeed, by 2600 BC the major semi-natural components of the Orcadian vegetation seem to have begun to resemble those of the present. By about 1300 BC, there would have been even more similarity, as now peat growth became extensive on the uplands, and heathland vegetation covered more areas. Farming was carried on, however, notably in Middle and Late Bronze Age times, and in the succeeding Iron Age and Norse Period, but there is little doubt that the amount of available agricultural land was reduced considerably as climatic deterioration and soil exhaustion rendered much marginal upland unworkable. A number of palaeosols, whose types are similar to present-day soils, have revealed evidence of cultivation and fertilisation, which seems to have begun in neolithic and intensified in bronze age time in selected localities.

Finds of artefacts and bones associated with particular cultures have afforded clues to diet and economy, as well as providing additional environmental data. Imprints of barley on pottery, macrofossils of cereals, bones of oxen, sheep, deer, pigs and goats, together with those of fish and sea birds support the notion of a mixed economy in an open landscape, where arable and pastoral farming, fishing and hunting were tapping a large number of environmental resources as a means of subsistence (Childe 1962; Davidson, Jones and Renfrew 1976). The bulk of the palaeoenvironmental evidence points to the major landscape components of relief, climate, soil type and vegetation cover as having changed relatively little since neolithic time. However, it is clear that successive cultural groups have brought about significant modifications to certain areas, notably by means of agricultural land use in the vicinity of their settlement and funerary sites.

3 Anna Ritchie **The First Settlers**

The islands of Orkney were supporting a permanent human population at least five and a half thousand years ago. These inhabitants had an astounding skill for building in stone, and many of their tombs and some of their houses have survived in remarkable condition. They practised mixed farming, exploited the sea for food as well as transport, made their own pottery and tools and created a self-sufficient economy that remained the basis of Orcadian life down to recent times.

The simple question of exactly when man first came to live in Orkney is frustratingly difficult to answer. Commonsense suggests that the islands must have been explored by people based on the Caithness coast long before anyone took the final step of crossing the Pentland Firth to set up permanent home, but the archaeologist is dependent upon material traces for information and such exploration need leave few tangible clues. Moreover, it is along the Orcadian shores that one might expect to find the earliest evidence of human activity, and those shores have changed dramatically over the last six thousand years; gradual submergence and cliff erosion have combined to destroy the fringes of the early landscape. The tombs and settlements that survive tell us of long-established neolithic communities, not of their pioneering forebears, and we know nothing of the foraging visits by mesolithic fishermen that may have created a store of knowledge about the islands many years before colonisation began.

Claims have nevertheless been made for the presence in Orkney of mesolithic communities (Laing 1974, 25), based on surface finds of flint tools which Lacaille has described as possessing an 'archaic aspect' (1954). This material is insufficient as evidence of a truly mesolithic phase of activity and is best seen, as Lacaille saw it, as an archaic survival in a post-mesolithic context. Mesolithic economy in Scotland is thought to have been based on fishing, plant collection and hunting in that order of importance (Mellars 1976), and, although the fishing was good, the attraction of Orkney must have been marginal for plant collection and non-existent for hunting. A beautiful flaked flint axe found on Fair Isle (Lacaille 1954, 274, fig.121) is almost certainly an imported heirloom. At present the most northerly evidence of mesolithic activity is provided by the flint tools from Freswick Bay in Caithness (Lacaille 1954, 185, fig.72; A. Morrison 1980, 164, fig.7.8). The chronological overlap between mesolithic and neolithic sites indicated by radiocarbon dates (A. Morrison 1980, fig.7.11) provides one aspect of the context in which an intermingling of flint-working traditions could have occurred. Recent studies have emphasised the advantages of a mesolithic life-style, and it is clear that, if their handling of natural resources were efficient, the effort involved in food-production would not necessarily appear attractive to indigenous food-gatherers, and a mesolithic way of life could easily survive alongside a technically more advanced neolithic system. This is particularly true of littoral communities, where the exploitation of fish and shellfish resources is not limited by the seasonal factors governing the availability of most plants and animals (Evans 1975, 105) and where, in the winter months, red deer become an additional local asset (Mellars 1976, 377).

On present evidence, then, it would seem that Orkney presented a virtually empty landscape to neolithic man, empty at least of permanent human settlement, as the earliest neolithic settlers gazed across the Pentland Firth. For Orkney is clearly visible from Caithness, and even from further south on the mainland of Scotland, while Fair Isle is at least sometimes a visible stepping-stone between Orkney and Shetland. It was almost certainly in skin-boats that the first settlers arrived in the Northern Isles, for they are far more seaworthy than dug-outs and more suited to the difficult seas of the Pentland Firth (P. Johnstone 1980, 27, 132), but it is also likely that rafts played an essential role, especially in transporting livestock. There is some evidence to suggest that sea temperatures around Orkney were warmer in neolithic times than today (Wheeler in Renfrew 1979, 149), but even so the sea voyage from Caithness to the islands must have been a cold and hazardous enterprise. It may even have been the local mesolithic fishermen who, in their skin-boats, ferried the early neolithic farmers and their animals across the Pentland Firth (P. Johnstone 1980, 132).

An unusually clear picture has survived of this early period, but there are of course still problems, some very basic and others the more refined questions that result from an already large store of information. The attraction of Orkney as a place to settle and the extent to which the Orcadian environment imposed modification of the settlers' life-style are crucial factors in understanding the process of colonisation. Clark has stressed the importance of fishing as a factor in encouraging sea travel and the discovery of new lands (G. Clark 1980, 99–100). At the same time, appreciation of the various factors is limited by the scant information available about early neolithic settlements on the mainland of Scotland, to provide a yardstick against which Orkney may be measured. Nevertheless, the basic requirements of neolithic man are clear: land suitable for mixed farming, building materials for permanent settlements, natural food resources and a reasonable climate. He was prepared to trade or exchange if necessary for portable goods.

The climate and landscape of Orkney were not only suitable but, in comparison with the northern mainland of Scotland, preferable, and what the islands lacked in timber for building was amply recompensed by the quality of their stone. There was suitable stone for axes, and a supply of beach pebble flint and chert that was adequate, if far from ideal, for smaller tools. Materials for making pottery were to hand. The major drawback is likely to have been the lack of wood, not so much in size and quantity but in variety. Early man is known to have appreciated the different qualities and potential uses of the various woods and wood barks available in the Temperate forest (G. Clark 1980, 42), and the neolithic craftsman in Orkney is likely to have felt frustrated at being unable to obtain locally the ideal woods for his purpose – such as pine for arrow shafts. Supplies of birch and hazel were available, and knowledge of the flexible and water-resistant qualities of hazel bark is demonstrated by its use at Rinyo to line drains (Childe and Grant 1939, 18). Post-sockets for roof-supporting timbers at Knap of Howar indicate posts up to 120 mm in diameter, but there is no way of identifying the wood or of determining whether this timber was home-grown, imported or derived from driftwood.

It is unlikely that the islands were already populated by the larger wild animals; Clutton-Brock has pointed out that any mammals present in Orkney before the arrival of man must either have swum there or have survived from the cold conditions that prevailed before the islands were cut off from the mainland of Scotland (1979, 113). This relict fauna would not have included cattle, sheep, pigs or even red deer, and although the latter are good swimmers it is thought that they too were introduced by man and either kept in a domestic context or released to breed naturally (Renfrew 1979, 120). Once in Orkney, deer could have swum to the smaller islands without human help. The practical difficulties for the early settlers of transporting livestock across the Pentland Firth must have been daunting, even assuming that they would wait for good weather and calm seas before setting out with the young animals lashed to their rafts. From neolithic times onwards, the cattle and sheep of Orkney have differed from those in

Caithness (Noddle 1978), demonstrating the success of early stock-breeding in Orkney. An additional factor in isolating the animal population of Orkney may well have been the increase in wind-speeds around 5000 BP postulated by Keatinge and Dickson (1979), which would have made sea voyages even more difficult.

The earliest radiocarbon dates from settlement sites and pollen diagrams suggest that food-producing communities were fully established in the Northern Isles by about 3500 BC. It is inherently unlikely that developed settlements such as Knap of Howar and Skara Brae should represent the homes of the first pioneering colonists; these sites are the products of a confident farming society. Typological analysis of the surviving pottery from tombs and settlements led Henshall to the conclusion that none belonged to the primary colonising phase, although the immediate origin of the colonists in Caithness is clear from the development of the Orkney-Cromarty class of tomb (Henshall 1963, 61, 117). Sea-level changes and coastal erosion have undoubtedly destroyed some of the evidence of the earliest Orcadians, but the recent discovery of extensive structural remains beneath the sand at Links of Noltland on Westray has demonstrated that there are still sites to be found.

Since we cannot yet identify the very earliest colonists, it is impossible to trace the route by which they arrived on the southern shores of the Pentland Firth, whether by way of the east or west coasts of mainland Scotland. Nor, at this remove, can we give them a name. Their skeletons allow us to picture them as physically very similar to ourselves, their average height only a few centimetres shorter than our own, but their life expectancy much briefer: a recent study of the remains of some 340 men, women and children buried in the tomb at Isbister on South Ronaldsay revealed that few adults had survived beyond their twenties (Hedges 1983a).

Similar figures were obtained from the burials at Quanterness (Renfrew 1979, 162–3) and, if they can be taken as normal, they raise some fascinating questions about neolithic society. What was the status of the few people who reached old age (around 50 years)? There would be enormous problems over transmitting knowledge and organising long-term building projects amongst such a young population, unless the elders wielded considerable authority and were venerated for their experience and wisdom. This point is particularly germane to later neolithic times when projects such as the construction of the great henge, the Ring of Brodgar, or the design and building of Maes Howe chambered tomb, demanded large-scale deployment of labour over a long period as well as sophisticated engineering and architectural expertise.

The earliest settlers need not have been tomb-builders, and there may have been a primary phase, as yet undetected in the archaeological record, during which a very limited range of neolithic activities was practised.

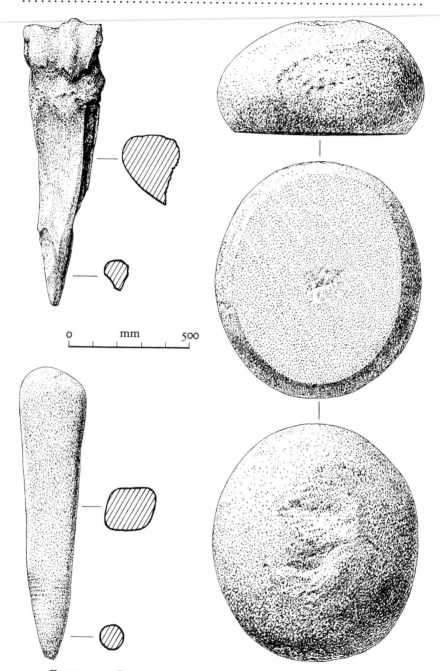

FIGURE 3.1. Bone gouge, stone borer and stone grinder
from Knap of Howar.

There is perhaps a glimpse of this earlier life-style at Knap of Howar, with the unique survival of a tool that is more appropriate to a food-gathering community than to the level of food-production demonstrated by the rest of the economic evidence. This is a stone tool of which three examples were found on the floor of house 2 and which is best interpreted as a seed grinder. It is a circular, fine-grained stone about 90 mm in diameter, with a lower surface ground perfectly flat and a convex upper face bearing a pair of hammered indentations (figure 3.1). The flat lower surface is characterised by a central pitted hollow from 13 to 40 mm across. There are close ethnographic parallels for this tool among food-gathering societies in Africa and Australia, as well as archaeological parallels in the Later Stone Age of southern Africa (R. Inskeep in A. Ritchie 1984; Goodwin and van Riet Lowe 1929, 165–6). In the latter context, the stones were used in conjunction with a larger lower stone of trough-like form, and they relate to the grinding of wild seeds rather than cereals. The purpose of the central pit is to catch the edge of flat seeds and turn them over. D. L. Clarke has emphasised the insignificance of seeds in the mesolithic plant diet of Temperate Europe compared with that of mesolithic communities further south (1978, 30), but Orkney could not match the annual abundance of roots, nuts, berries and fungi of the Temperate forest, and must have presented a local ecology at variance with that of the true forest zone. During the initial human settlement of Orkney, wild seeds may well have made a useful contribution to the plant diet. It has been argued that there were large open areas of herbaceous vegetation already available to the first colonists (Keatinge and Dickson 1979, 604), and these included plants, such as *Rumex*, the seeds of which are known to have been used as food in prehistoric times.

SETTLEMENT AT KNAP OF HOWAR

Knap of Howar lies on the west coast of Papa Westray (NGR HY483518), one of the most northerly of the Orkney islands. The name of the site is tautologous, meaning knoll of mounds, and it is probably a good description of the appearance of the site prior to the first excavations in 1929, when it was covered by sandy hillocks. Coastal erosion had revealed an extensive midden and walling, and excavations by William Traill, the landowner, and William Kirkness uncovered two substantial stone-built houses (plate 3.1). No dating evidence was found and the high standard of the masonry was thought to indicate contemporaneity with Iron Age brochs (Traill and Kirkness 1937, 314). The site was reluctantly accepted into guardianship by the Office of Works in 1937, and its remote location and the lack of information about its date and character made it a little-visited monument. Further excavations were undertaken in 1973 and 1975 by the Department of the Environment in order to obtain dating evidence and to consolidate collapsed areas of walling (A. Ritchie 1984). The basic sequence is simple.

PLATE 3.1. House 1 before re-excavation in 1973.

A layer of midden some 0.4 m thick represents the primary phase of activity on the site but, apart from the remains of stone paving to the south of house 1, there was no trace in the excavated areas of any contemporary building (period I). The two surviving houses were then built on top of the earlier midden, house 1 first and then house 2, and an upper layer of midden some 0.20 m thick was contemporary with their occupation (period II). Both the archaeological evidence and the radiocarbon dates demonstrate that there was no cultural and no significant chronological difference between the two main periods of activity on the site. A series of nine radiocarbon dates places the occupation within the period between about 3700 and 2800 BC. The recent work involved the re-excavation of the interiors of both houses, the dismantling of some 8.5 m of collapsed house wall, the excavation of about 36 m² of midden outside the houses and of 15 test-pits, each 1 m², designed to trace the extent of the midden deposit. Kirkness had taken many photographs during the original excavation (the negatives are now in the National Monuments Record of Scotland), and these were often helpful in determining the extent of that excavation and of subsequent disturbance.

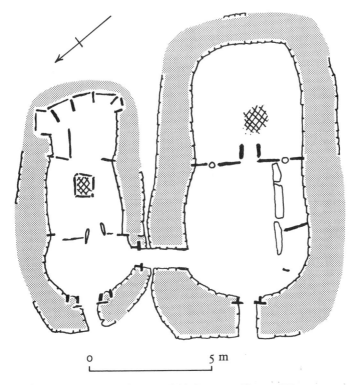

FIGURE 3.2. Plan of the neolithic houses at Knap of Howar.

House I was clearly the main dwelling house and had remained in use throughout period II (figure 3.2). It is rectilinear in plan with rounded corners both internally and externally, and its overall floor-area measures 10 m by 5 m. The wall is 1.5 m thick and was built with an inner and outer drystone facing, one stone thick, and a core of midden material. The inner wall-face was laid directly on the natural subsoil, whereas the outer face was built on top of the period I midden, and it appears that the primary midden cleared from the area within the house was used as core-material for the wall. The wall survives to a height of 1.60 m, and the entrance has survived intact at the W end of the house (plate 3.2). It consists of a paved and lintelled passage, 1.70 m long through the thickness of the wall, with door jambs and a sill stone at the inner end. A second passageway in the N wall leads through the walls of both buildings into house 2, with the door jambs at the latter end. House I is divided into two rooms by a line of four upright

43

PLATE 3.2. The main door into house 1, looking across Papa Sound to Westray.

slabs and, originally, two timber posts. The outer room was paved and furnished with a low stone bench or platform along the s wall, and nothing remained of the original floor deposit except inside the passage connecting the two houses. The inner room had not been cleared as thoroughly in the early excavations, and a thin skin of original floor deposit survived, together with a hearth in a shallow hollow and a massive trough quern. The floor was unpaved and grooving in its surface suggested that a low wooden bench may once have lined its walls. A small aumbry had been incorporated into the N wall (colour plates 1, 2).

House 2 was built immediately alongside house 1, but their walls touched only at the point of the conjoining passage. Although built in the same way with a midden-filled wall, this house is smaller, less regular in plan and appears to have fulfilled a different function. Internally it measures

PLATE 3.3. House 2 as seen from the main doorway, with cupboards
built into the back wall of the innermost room.

7.5 m by 3 m and survives to a maximum height of 1.26 m, and it is divided
by upright slabs into three rooms. The outer room was featureless apart
from the two doorways, one through the s wall into house 1 and the other
through the w end-wall. The latter main entrance consisted of a paved
passage, 1.5 m long, but, although one lintel at least was still in position at
the time of the original excavation, the roof of the passage no longer
survives. The internal wall-face on either side of the main entrance exhibits
a post-and-panel technique not employed at the other doorways. Both
entrance passages had been deliberately and carefully blocked in antiquity.

The small innermost room (plate 3.3) had apparently been used primarily for storage, for built into the wall were five 'cupboards' and three
shelves or aumbries, and there were two pits in the floor. The central room
appears to have been the main working area, for it contained two successive

PLATE 3.4. The middle room in house 2 with its two successive hearths.

hearths and associated floor deposits up to 200 mm thick, undisturbed by the original excavators (plate 3.4). The primary hearth was 0.65 m by 0.70 m with a substantial stone kerb and boulder floor, but the secondary hearth was of the same shallow pit type as in house 1. Although the ash from the hearths was analysed, it proved impossible to identify the fuel; it is unlikely that there was suitable peat for fuel in neolithic times, and timber was scarce, but there would have been plenty of driftwood and local brushwood, and there are good alternatives to wood for burning, including dried animal dung, turf and seaweed.

It is likely that both buildings had a hipped timber-framed roof, perhaps supported by partial corbelling of the walls at eaves level as well as by the tall upright slabs bonded into the walls and the wooden posts in house 1. They were filled with sand when first uncovered, and there does not seem to have been a significant amount of stone slabs in the filling to suggest the sort of flagstone roof-covering still in use on vernacular buildings. A simple covering of turf or thatch must be assumed. Wall foundations and paving found in the early excavations outside the main entrance into house 1 (Traill and Kirkness 1937, 310–11, fig. 1) may represent the remains of a yard or annexe, but erosion had destroyed most of this feature; it does, however, underline the fact that the site may not be as complete and discrete a unit as its surviving remains imply. The missing structures of period I may well have been lost into the sea.

The houses were flanked on either side by midden deposits, not in heaps but spread out to a uniform thickness of some 0.35 m over an area of about 500 m². The lower level of midden belonged to the primary period of occupation, before the surviving houses were built, while the upper level represented the domestic rubbish that accumulated during the use of those houses. The content of the two midden levels was virtually identical, indicating that there had been no change in lifestyle. The midden was rich in artefacts and organic debris, with the important exception of plant remains; one of the effects of spreading out the rubbish instead of allowing it to accumulate in piles was to expose much of it to the air, thus reducing the chances of survival for grain, seeds and even pollen. Wet sieving in the sea yielded a few carbonised grains of hulled barley, but this method was chiefly useful for the recovery of fishbones. A variety of fish were caught, indicating both inshore and offshore fishing. Young saithe, ballan wrasse and rockling were probably caught from the shore, while large saithe, cod, ling and other deep water fish are more likely to indicate line-fishing from boats 2–5 miles out to sea. There was an equally diverse exploitation of shellfish resources in which limpets were predominant but oyster, winkles, cockles and razor shell were also significant; some at least of these shellfish are likely to have been used for human consumption rather than as fishbait, but their contribution as a food source was negligible. The shells were certainly crushed to make a strengthening filler for pottery fabric. Amongst the oyster debris there were noticeably fewer bottom shells than top shells, perhaps because bottom shells are more friable and easier to crush, and, in the 1930 excavation, a pile of ground razor shells was found beside the great trough quern in house 1. Both the shellfish and the evidence from land and freshwater mollusca indicate that there has been considerable change in the environment of Knap of Howar since neolithic times. Today the site lies above a rocky shore and was, prior to the original excavation, covered by almost 3 m depth of wind-blown sand. At the time of its occupation in the late fourth millennium BC, the site appears to have been separated from a sandy shore by an extensive sand-dune system, and it probably lay in pasture-land with small freshwater pools in the vicinity. It is conceivable that Papa Westray was still joined to Westray, for the sound between the two is today very shallow in the Aikerness area. The surviving bird bones include both freshwater and sea species and, although birds were clearly not an important item in the diet, the oil obtainable from birds such as the guillemot, razorbill, puffin and great auk would have been invaluable for domestic use, especially for lighting.

As the evidence survives, Knap of Howar possessed a predominantly pastoral economy based on rearing cattle and sheep, but cultivation of cereal crops may have been more extensive than the record suggests. Soil conditions were distinctly adverse to the preservation of organic material other than bone, and to the few grains of barley found in the midden may be added three pollen grains of wheat from a buried soil horizon broadly contemporary with the site. Two querns found in house 1 may have been used to grind grain among other materials; if so, the grain is more likely to have been grown locally than to have been imported. If they have been correctly interpreted, the seed grinders suggest a methodical approach to the collection of wild plants as a food source, and they may have been used in conjunction with the querns.

Cattle and sheep appear to have been reared in equal proportions and both show evidence of fairly recent domestication: the cattle were large and closely related to the aurochs, and the sheep were a primitive form bearing poor wool. Most animals were killed young as a source of meat, hides and bone for tools. There were a few large pigs. There is little evidence of hunting among the animal bones, only a few deer, and the seal and whalebone are likely to have been derived from carrion.

The faunal evidence suggests a self-supporting farming unit, and this impression is strengthened by an artefact assemblage in which there are no detectable imports, either from outside Orkney or even from outside the Papa Westray–Westray area. The excavations have yielded a large number of artefacts, and these are likely to be a small proportion of the true total; much of the midden and the midden sealed in the house walls remains intact, and it is difficult to estimate how many finds were inevitably overlooked in the early excavations. The largest surviving but perhaps least comprehensible class of material consists of flint and chert, of which about 700 pieces were recovered, one-seventh showing traces of working, including knives and scrapers. This material is derived from the beach, where it is still washed up from marine deposits and, although the nodules can be quite large, the artefacts and debris are characteristically small, often retaining patches of cortex.

The pottery has been studied and drawn by Miss Audrey Henshall, who found parts of at least 78 pots, of which about 13 are Unstan-type bowls, about 41 are simple bowls either plain or bearing restrained decoration and about 9 are bowls with cordons or shoulders. Most are round-based but there is some evidence to suggest a few flattened bases. Unstan ware is named after the chambered tomb at Unstan on mainland Orkney, in which was found a number of very distinctive shallow pottery bowls bearing finely executed decoration. Compared with the tomb pottery, the Unstan bowls from Knap of Howar are small and thin-walled, a feature which Miss Henshall considers to be perhaps of chronological significance. Their decoration is characterised by firm incised or stab-and-drag lines, together with rows of stabs. Such vessels were presumably drinking-bowls. They provide a distinctive cultural context for the site, in which the bulk of the pottery may be seen as plainer domestic Unstan ware, but there are complications. A number of features, especially the cordons and the shouldered vessels, are alien to the classic Unstan tradition and relate more to grooved ware. Moreover, only the cordons relate specifically to Orcadian grooved ware, as distinct from grooved ware generally. The social implications of this pottery evidence are at present difficult to evaluate. Petrological analysis of the pottery together with archaeological evidence of deposits of unfired clay demonstrate that all the pottery was made locally and, although four groups of pottery fabric have been distinguished, none can be correlated with any differences of style in the finished product.

A small polished stone axe, 53 mm long, was found in the primary midden, and analysis of the stone by thin sectioning resulted in its identification as a fine-grained dolomite which, like the clay for the pottery, could have been derived from a local source on Papa Westray. Polished stone axes have been found in several Orkney-Cromarty tombs, including one from Isbister on South Ronaldsay which is very similar to that from Knap of Howar.

The rest of the stone artefacts include two querns and hammerstones derived from beach pebbles, together with two unusual tool-types which may help to identify a characteristic artefact assemblage: the seed-grinders described earlier and a type of borer. There are six of the latter tool, all elongated pebbles 100–172 mm long on which one end shows intensive wear (figure 3.1).

Among the bone artefacts are both common and distinctive tools, from bone awls, pins and a needle to a small bone spoon, a whalebone spatula, a blubber knife and two examples of a unique dimpled bone gouge. Both whalebone and antler were used to make perforated mallets which must be seen as prototype maceheads, an artefact that in stone belongs to grooved ware assemblages (Roe 1968). Many of the bone tools are connected with leather-working, reflecting the importance of animal skins for clothing; at this period, the sheep were too primitive to supply adequate wool for textiles, and garments such as tunics and perhaps trousers would be made from soft calf-skin, while the hairy sheepskins would make good bedding as well as cloaks.

The identification of Knap of Howar as the home of makers of Unstan ware provided the first glimpse in Orkney of the domestic life of the people who buried their dead in stalled cairns. Unstan ware was not a purely funerary type of pottery but was also the fine tableware of the living. The range of associated equipment is predictably wider in the domestic context than among the gravegoods, although few contemporary burials have survived undisturbed. The nearest excavated stalled cairn to Knap of Howar is Holm of Papa Westray North (ORK 21), one of the three chambered tombs on the tiny uninhabited holm off the east coast of Papa Westray; it was partially excavated in 1854, and has recently been re-excavated by the author on the grounds that it is the most likely candidate to have been Knap of Howar's family mausoleum. Study of the material is still in progress: not only human bones but a wide variety of animal and bird bones, with a remarkable emphasis on fishbones and deer antlers that suggests very strongly that there were totemistic ideas behind the way in which the tomb was used. In view of the fact that the only other excavated tomb on the Holm is of Maes Howe type (ORK 22), known elsewhere to have been used by the makers of grooved ware, the discovery of grooved ware outside the newly excavated stalled cairn is of special interest.

There are very close architectural links between Orkney-Cromarty chambered tombs and the houses at Knap of Howar. Upright stone slabs are used to form burial compartments in the tombs and to divide the houses into 'rooms', and low benches furnish both the tombs and the houses, built sometimes in stone and in some cases probably in wood. The internal plan of house 2 is particularly close to that of the tripartite tomb of Bigland Round on Rousay (ORK 2), and there are identical details in their construction; the cairn at Bigland Round was stripped entirely, revealing not only an inner wall-face but also upright slabs set at ground level both radially and concentric to the chamber. Excavation of the wall of house 2 at Knap of Howar, on either side of the entrance, uncovered an inner wall-face and upright radial slabs within the outer casing, the purpose of which was presumably to strengthen the wall (plate 3.5). The entrance had been carefully blocked with stones, and similar blocking has been found at several tombs, including Bigland Round.

ORCADIAN SOCIETY

Knap of Howar on Papa Westray is one of four neolithic settlements in Orkney which are well-preserved and which have been excavated to reveal considerable information about the way of life that they represent: the others are Skara Brae on mainland Orkney, Links of Noltland on Westray and, least well-preserved, Rinyo on Rousay. These last three settlements belonged to people using grooved ware, whereas the decorated pottery from Knap of Howar links the site with the makers of Unstan ware, and this cultural distinction is reiterated, apart from certain basic common elements, in the rest of the associated artefacts, including house-types as well

PLATE 3.5. The entrance in house 2, showing the inner wall-face and
upright slabs within the house wall.

as portable equipment. In chronological terms, Knap of Howar ought not to
be treated separately from the three grooved ware settlements, because the
later radiocarbon dates from Knap of Howar are contemporary with the
earlier dates from Skara Brae. Nevertheless, these settlements represent
two distinct and apparently separate cultural traditions, though not necessarily separate ethnic groups. In his discussion of the problems surrounding
the relationship of the makers of Unstan ware and of Orcadian grooved
ware, Renfrew postulated an evolution of grooved ware from Unstan ware
which began on the mainland of Orkney and then spread to the islands,
although he emphasised that this is a hypothesis that has yet to be proved
(1979, 207). The case for the chronological priority of Unstan ware rests
primarily on the radiocarbon dates. Renfrew discounted rightly (1979, 208)
the late date from Knap of Howar of 2131 ± 65 bc (SRR-452), which is a

re-run on a sample which previously had given an even more aberrant date of 3756 ± 85 bc (SRR-347); neither date can be regarded as reliable, and the acceptable radiocarbon date range for this site is 2820 ± 180 bc (Birm-816) to 2300 ± 130 bc (Birm-815), or about 3700–2800 BC. Although there is overlap, these dates as a group are earlier than those again as a group from grooved ware sites.

A major problem in deriving grooved ware from Unstan ware is, as Renfrew admitted (1979, 207), the existence of comparable grooved ware communities in southern England. D. V. Clarke has, however, argued that the contrasts in the artefact assemblages associated with the northern and southern grooved ware groups are increasing as new material is discovered, and that these contrasts are not explicable in terms of environmental differences (1976b, 240). At the same time, the links within Orkney between Unstan ware and grooved ware in terms of their respective artefact assemblages are also increasing. Stone maceheads are a grooved ware artefact, yet their antler and whalebone prototypes occur in an Unstan ware context at Knap of Howar. There are features in the pottery from the latter site that are alien to the Unstan tradition, particularly the use of applied cordons, but, as this is at present the sole domestic site in Orkney with Unstan ware, such features may be alien only to funerary pottery. Outside Orkney, Unstan ware has been found in a domestic context at Northton on Harris, along with characteristic Hebridean wares and simple undecorated bowls (Simpson 1976, 222), demonstrating that mixed pottery assemblages are possible.

There is a clear need for more Unstan ware settlements in Orkney before there can be any solution to the problem of the relationship between the makers of Unstan ware and of grooved ware. At present the differences between their associated artefact assemblages remain as striking as, and probably more significant than, the differences in pottery styles. None of the characteristic Skara Brae artefacts appears at Knap of Howar, and similarly there are distinctive tool types at present peculiar to the latter site (seed grinders and bone gouges). House-types are a major area of contrast, and it would be helpful to know whether the Knap of Howar houses are truly representative of a type that was built elsewhere in Orkney. If a real change in house-type could be demonstrated, it could help to explain the development of the Maes Howe type of tomb, for the architectural similarities between the Knap of Howar houses and Orkney-Cromarty cairns are so strong as to suggest that tombs were built as houses for the dead, emulating the houses of the living.

There are many details lacking from the impression of life in early neolithic times that survives in the archaeological record, even such basic details as whether flour was made into bread, and yet that blurred impression is familiar. Whatever barbarities existed in social behaviour and tribal ritual of which no trace remains, practical daily life can have been little different from the basic Orcadian pattern that survived until recent times. The economic realities of survival for the small farmer-cum-fisherman in a cold and demanding environment were as much a governing factor in the nineteenth century AD as in the thirty-fifth century BC.

4 D.V. Clarke, Niall Sharples **Settlements and Subsistence in the Third Millennium BC**

Though few in number, some of the known sites of the third millennium are quite exceptional in terms of the quality and range of the material preserved. Most of our information comes from the three villages at Skara Brae on Mainland (Childe 1931; Clarke 1976a), Rinyo on Rousay (Childe and Grant 1939; 1947) and Links of Noltland on Westray (Clarke, Hope and Wickham-Jones 1978). Recent excavations at Pierowall Quarry, Westray, have revealed a badly damaged structure. Chance finds at three other sites on Mainland – Dingieshowe, Sands of Evie (Stevenson 1946, 142–3) and Saevar Howe (Farrer 1864, pl.1.4) – and one on Sanday – Bay of Stove (RCAMS 1980, 16, no.70) – may represent further settlements but no structures have been positively identified (figure 4.1). Of these, Skara Brae is undoubtedly the best surviving prehistoric settlement in northern Europe and the continuing excavations at Noltland suggest that there too the structures will be similarly well preserved.

Before looking at these sites in more detail let us enter a *caveat*. Orkney and its remains form part of a wider province embracing Shetland and the northern mainland of Scotland. Neither of these areas has yet produced structures comparable to those found on Orkney but artefacts found in Caithness at Freswick (L. Scott 1951, 73) and Keiss (unpublished finds in National Museum of Antiquities of Scotland) and at Jarlshof in Shetland (e.g. Hamilton 1956a, 23 and 28, fig.13.3) suggest that such sites might yet be recognised. With only a small number of finds from these two districts, the emphasis naturally falls on the similarity between these objects and examples discovered on Orkney. When we have settlements comparable to Skara Brae and Noltland in other areas of northern Scotland, the differences

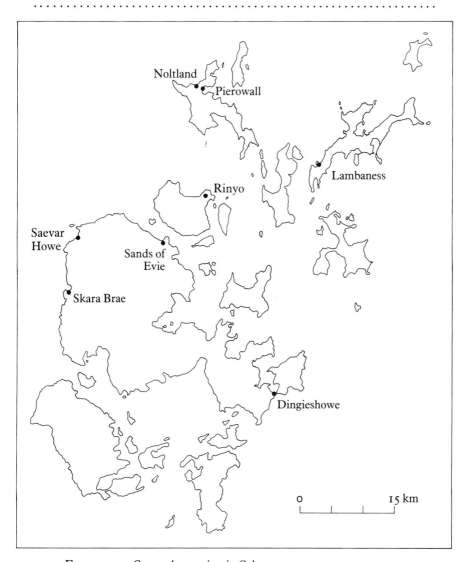

FIGURE 4.1. Grooved ware sites in Orkney.

between the various villages may well assume an equal importance for more general interpretations. This point is relevant to our consideration of the finds from Orkney. In attempting to relate finds from several sites, emphasis is first given to points of similarity and the more we discover the more confident one is that what they represent is membership of a social grouping embracing a number of individual sites. Once this relationship between sites has been established then, by analysing the differences between or within sites, we will begin to gain an understanding of the social systems operating within the larger grouping already defined. No serious study has yet been directed towards identifying, quantifying and explaining such differences in the rich assemblages from Orkney and we will not be able here to offer more than a few unsubstantiated hints. Nevertheless it is important to remember these differences and their potential when reading a chapter such as this one which largely concentrates on points of similarity.

If a concern with similarity underlies any recognition of particular groupings within Orkney, and indeed in contiguous areas, it is harder to place these Orcadian groups in a wider, British context. It has been generally accepted for over forty years that the pottery recovered at sites like Skara Brae and Rinyo forms part of a potting tradition, found throughout Britain and known as Grooved Ware (figure 4.2) (the term is something of a misnomer since much of the decoration, particularly in Orkney, comprises plastic ornament rather than grooving). Within the substantial corpus now available, various styles have been defined (Wainwright and Longworth 1971, 235–44) but the overall unity of the pottery has never been seriously or at least convincingly questioned. What this ceramic tradition means in human terms is, however, far from clear. Earlier views that it indicated a 'culture' (Piggott 1954, 321–46: admittedly involving other material in the description of the culture but wholly dependent on the pottery for the original formulation) have now been modified to a 'sub-culture' (Wainwright and Longworth 1971, 268). The term 'sub-culture' is, we are told, 'normally employed to describe a part of the total culture of a society which is distinctive of a segment of that society, e.g. an ethnic group, a social class group or a regional group'. Whether one adopts the culture or sub-culture view, the evidence from Orkney, other than that of the pottery, is not readily reconcilable with the evidence from farther south. It would be a mistake to suppose that these problems of integration and understanding are in any way restricted to Orcadian material, although this does show the difficulties in their extreme form. Comparable quandaries exist in analysing any of the British evidence for this period (Bradley 1982).

Despite these inherent difficulties in analysis, a great deal of information is available about the grooved ware groups (we retain the term for convenience). The most remarkable and immediate feature is that settlement, as far as we can tell, was concentrated in villages. Villages are today a commonplace in our experience but in third-millennium-BC Britain such settlements were extremely rare – where the evidence exists, the picture is almost entirely that of the single farmstead with ancillary buildings as at Knap of Howar (figure 4.3). Even in areas like Shetland, where the evidence for this period is especially well preserved, the houses, although not particularly distant from one another, nevertheless appear to stand within their own plots of land (Whittle 1980). The Orcadian sites provide a

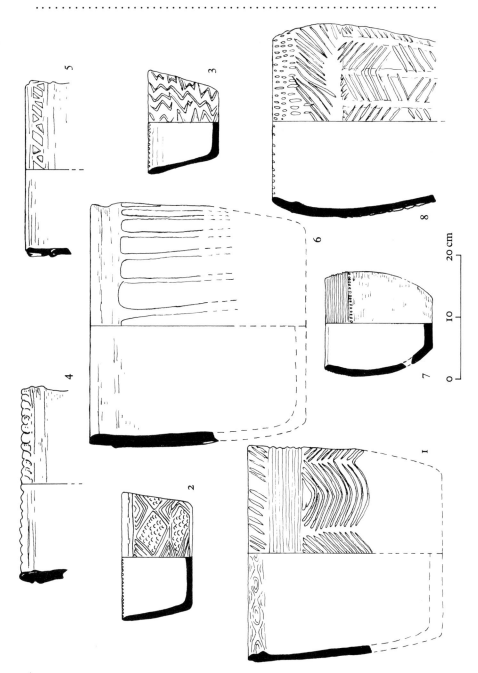

FIGURE 4.2. Grooved ware from Britain: 1 Clacton; 2–3 Greeting
St Mary; 4–6 Skara Brae; 7–8 Durrington Walls.

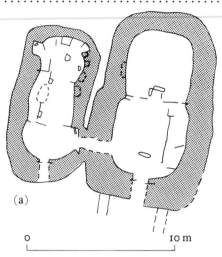

(a)

0   10 m

FIGURE 4.3. Village and farmstead: (a) Knap of Howar;
(b, *facing*) Skara Brae (at same scale).

marked contrast to this image. The houses cluster together, linked by
passages rendered necessary by the semi-subterranean nature of the houses'
construction. Ancillary buildings lie adjacent to but not interspersed
amongst this central nucleus of houses.

THE SETTLEMENTS

This pattern can be best seen at Skara Brae where the fine preservation
of the later-phase village has removed some of the ambiguities associated
with the more ruined remains at Rinyo; at Links of Noltland excavation has
not yet been sufficiently extensive to locate with confidence the domestic
area. The second phase village at Skara Brae consisted of at least six houses
(more may have been lost through coastal erosion), all except one linked by
a main passage running the length of the village. The one exception, house
7, is entered from a separate passage running at right angles to the main
passage.

Each of these houses is closely comparable in terms of construction
techniques, size and internal layout, and all are surrounded by midden
material. This material is not rubbish dumped by the inhabitants of the
houses which it surrounds. The creation of the midden heap is the first stage
in the construction process. Since structures of the earlier village have been
located below these houses this midden material must have been carefully
stored elsewhere for future use; the West Midden at Noltland which
extends over an area of at least 1100 m^2 may well represent material stored in
just this way but never used. The processes involved in constructing the
later-phase village at Skara Brae are complex but in essence they seem to

(b)

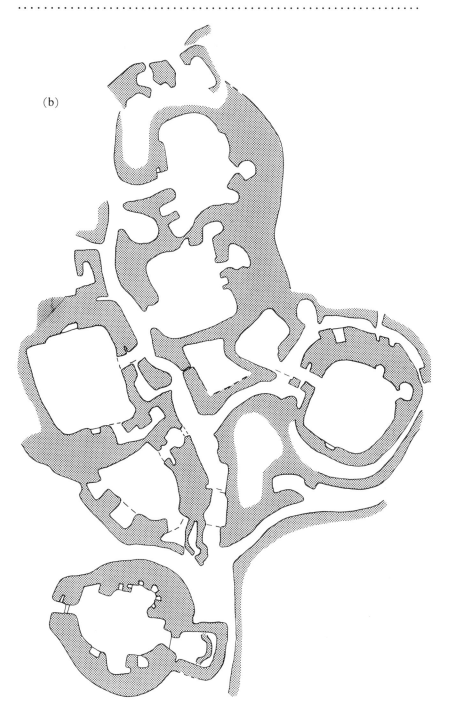

have involved the creation of a mound of midden material which had previously decayed, a period in which this material was allowed to consolidate and finally, the setting of houses into previously left or newly excavated depressions. All the evidence from the recent excavations at Skara Brae points to this basic sequence but we do not know if the midden dome which we can now see is the result of a single major operation or, perhaps more likely, the product of several such operations as additional houses were built. Certainly, the passages, which are similarly set in channels cut or left in the midden heap, were not all built at the same time (D. V. Clarke 1976a, 17). We have no evidence to show whether the houses were similarly constructed in phases though their plans strongly suggest this possibility. There must have been a strong desire for semi-subterranean houses if recourse was made to artificial means in order to create them in the absence of a suitable natural alternative. We see the same processes at the other settlements: at Rinyo the slope of the hillside was cut back and augmented by the use of midden material, and at Noltland a high sand dune was dug into and the hollow lined with midden against which the walls of the structure were set. It is difficult, particularly in the case of the structure at Noltland, to believe that the use of this technique was dictated solely by practical considerations such as improved weatherproofing of the houses. Indeed, structure 8 at Skara Brae, a workshop, is entirely freestanding and shows that a semi-subterranean situation was not thought appropriate for all buildings. Nevertheless, the use of this technique does seem to have produced particularly stable structures, as the preservation at Skara Brae and Noltland shows, and afforded protection to the inhabitants, especially against animals. Whether or not it was a reason for adopting this form of construction, this image of close-set houses linked by passages and surrounded by midden or other material creates a strong impression of a group with a highly developed sense of community.

The individual houses at Skara Brae and Rinyo, by their similarity, do much to reinforce this impression of a close-knit community. All consist of a single room (plate 4.1), square with rounded corners and, although there is some variation in size, 4.5–6 m^2, the differences do not appear great enough for any significance to be interpreted from them. The walls, constructed of drystone masonry with a midden core, have sufficient thickness to accommodate cells entered from the main chamber. Entry to each house was by a single, low, narrow doorway in the wall adjacent to the passage. Inside, the main items of furniture, the skeletons of which survive in stone at Skara Brae, were arranged in the same pattern in each house. In the centre was a large stone-lined hearth (plate 4.2), on the wall opposite the entrance a substantial dresser (plate 4.3) and on both side walls box beds (plate 4.4), originally with pillars to support a canopy. A number of clay-luted stone tanks, about 300 mm^2 and of a similar depth, have been set into the floor

PLATE 4.1. House 1 at Skara Brae.

PLATE 4.2. Stone-lined hearth.

PLATE 4.3. A dresser.

PLATE 4.4. A box bed.

PLATE 4.5. Stone tank, originally luted with clay.

PLATE 4.6. A cupboard.

PLATE 4.7. Interior of a cell.

(plate 4.5). At various points around the walls there are cupboards, the largest generally occurring above the beds (plate 4.6). Finally, each house has a number of cells which vary in size but can be entered only from within the chamber (plate 4.7; colour plate 3).

That we can speak with confidence of the interior arrangements of houses over four thousand years old is remarkable, and depends not only on the unusual quality of the flagstone used in these buildings but also on the preservative nature of the surrounding midden material; in the best preserved houses at Skara Brae the walls still stand to a height of over 3 m. Even so there are some major points for which we have very little evidence, especially the method of roofing the houses. Discoveries in house 1 at Skara Brae, during the early excavations in the middle of the nineteenth century, suggest that it may have had a roof supported on whalebone rafters although no confirmatory evidence was discovered in any of the other houses. Certainly a roof of turf or thatch supported on whalebone or timber rafters seems considerably more likely than a corbelled stone roof but no serious study has as yet been undertaken to determine the range of possibilities. Equally, we should not be misled by the presence of the major items of furniture into believing they represent the whole picture. Some pieces are clearly only the basic frame while others present varied problems of interpretation. The beds, for instance, must be envisaged as containing material such as mattresses made of bracken (cf. Rymer 1976) and bedclothes of animal skins. The canopies above the beds are more difficult since we do not know their purpose; if they were simply designed to protect the bed from water dripping from the roof then animal skins would probably have been sufficient although not necessarily the most practical solution; whereas if they were to increase the storage capacity within the house wood, or less likely stone, would require to have been used. The hearths pose a different kind of problem since there is no difficulty in envisaging their function and appearance. The question is rather what kind of fuel was burnt. Childe, the major excavator of Skara Brae, influenced probably by the present Orcadian situation had no doubt that it was peat but more recent studies suggest that the growth of peat suitable for burning did not begin in this area of Orkney until after the settlement had been abandoned (Keatinge and Dickson 1979). An adequate supply of fuel is, of course, a pre-requisite for subsistence. In Orkney at that time, with peat unavailable and wood only in the form of drift, a variety of materials were probably collected for this purpose. Among the more obvious things are animal dung, still in use until quite recently on northern isles such as Sanday and North Ronaldsay (Fenton 1972), and seaweed (Fenton 1978, 206–9: the glassy, slag-like material known as cramp, found on many Orcadian sites, may well be the accidental product of this use of seaweed) but other items such as whale and seal bone (Heizer 1963, 188) may also have been used. No doubt most fires involved a combination of fuels reflecting only their periodic availability.

Greater speculation is involved in trying to understand the use of the cells and of the clay-luted boxes set into the floors. At first sight the cells seem straightforward enough as providing extra storage space in a unit in which all activities had to take place within a single room. However, there is a considerable variety both in size and form and in the number present in each house. Accessibility to some of them seems to have been made deliberately difficult, a point given emphasis by the discovery, in one in house 1 at Skara Brae, of 2400 beads, pendants, pins and a whale vertebra dish containing red pigment. Others, apparently one in each house, have drains running from them under the floor of the house. These drains are carefully constructed so that those running from individual houses join a main drain carrying the material outside the area of the settlement; at Rinyo traces of a bark lining survived in some sections of the drains. Although not analysed, the material found in the drains is not inconsistent with the use of the cells as lavatories. We can then offer at least three possible uses for the cells as storage areas, as safes and as lavatories. The clay-luted boxes, on the other hand, exhibit such uniformity that a single common purpose may be supposed although there is little to indicate what that purpose might have been. There are generally three or four boxes in each house and the careful luting with clay implies that they were intended to contain water. Perhaps they did no more than enable the household to keep a supply of fresh water

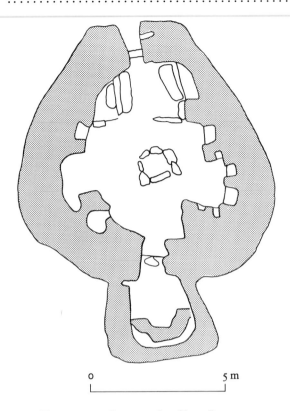

FIGURE 4.4. Structure 8 at Skara Brae.

for domestic purposes within the house even though a single large tank might have met the need better. However, if as seems likely the limpets found in such large numbers on these settlements were collected for use as fish bait the boxes might have had another purpose. Some use of limpet as bait requires that the limpet be soaked for about a week to soften it so that by using the tanks in rotation it would be possible to maintain a supply of fresh bait (D. V. Clarke 1976b, 243–4). These boxes are not closely comparable to the larger tanks found in the burnt mounds of Bronze Age date.

At least two structures however, one at Skara Brae and one at Noltland, do not conform either in plan or in the internal arrangement of their fittings to the pattern seen in the houses. That at Skara Brae, structure 8, is separate from the main village and not surrounded by any accumulation of midden (figure 4.4). Its maximum internal width and length are both 6 m, but in plan it is much more oval than the houses. On the south side there is a porch protecting the entrance through walls over 2 m thick; presumably this remarkable thickness compensates for the absence of a protective midden

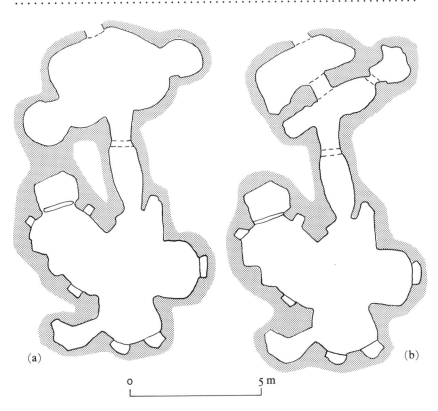

(a)

(b)

0   5 m

FIGURE 4.5. Structure at Links of Noltland.

surrounding it. Although there is a hearth in the centre and cupboards and cells in the walls, the dresser and beds are absent. Instead the walls are deeply recessed and the southern end of the building is largely partitioned off by upright slabs. Childe, in his description of this structure, noted that objects similar to those he had found in the houses were rare but that the partitioned area contained heaps of burnt volcanic stone and that on the floor were numerous small scrapers, cores and rejected flakes of black chert. 'Clearly then', he concluded, 'a flint-knapper had worked in the hut'. Whether or not it was used exclusively for the working of flint and chert, there can be no doubt that we have here a workshop rather than a house. The presence of heat-damaged volcanic stones and an apparent flue in the north end of the structure raises the possibility that the chert was being subjected to heat pre-treatment before being worked. Such a technique is well documented in the ethnographic record and involves the heating and controlled cooling of the chert nodules to improve their flaking qualities, with the use of heated volcanic stone a prime means of attaining the required

67

temperatures. The second building, which is at Noltland, seems also to be set beyond the domestic area but is otherwise not closely comparable to the workshop just described (figure 4.5) Since excavation is not yet complete, interpretation of such matters as its function are clearly impossible but its remarkable nature merits a brief description here, if only to give emphasis to the point that the architectural uniformity already described, while real enough, is unlikely to be anything like a complete picture. It is set into a midden-lined hollow dug into a high sand dune and consists of two rooms of different shape and size linked by a narrow connecting passage some 3.5 m long. Overall the maximum dimensions of the complex are some 12 m long by 7 m broad. The smaller of the two rooms close to the entrance was rectangular with a single cell opening off each side wall. Subsequently one of these cells was sealed off and the room subdivided by a wall across it. Unlike any other Orcadian grooved ware structures, the entrance to this building has been given emphasis by being outlined in the interior with large slabs stuck onto the dry stone walling with yellow clay. The other, larger room has an irregular, lobate plan with the central area surrounded by large recesses. It does not seem to have been modified in any way during its use. The whole structure was subsequently infilled, the smaller chamber, the passage and a cell off the main chamber being packed with midden whereas the larger chamber contained large stone slabs, midden and sand. The whole process was carefully done and involved such things as building an arc of upright slabs to block off the entrance to the large room and the removal and replacement of the roofing slabs of the passage. As well as many artefacts, the midden material contained numerous skulls, a completely articulated skeleton of an otter and large wedges of compacted fish and rodent bone with no midden admixture. Lying on the rubble infill of the main chamber were two cattle skulls and an apparently articulated eagle skeleton. Although, in combination, the overall plan, the use of more than one room and the deliberate infilling find no parallels at other grooved ware sites, many of the individual elements are closely comparable to those found at Skara Brae and Rinyo (colour plate 4).

This wealth of information about the architectural environment of the inhabitants of these settlements can perhaps form a basis for imagining what life was like for an individual, but what can it tell us about the broader social structure? Largely using the evidence of the tombs it has been argued (Renfrew 1976; 1979, 199–223) that we have here the evidence for a 'segmentary society'. This involves groups (i.e. villages in this case) which are clearly defined, operate largely independently and exercise control over their productive resources. None of the groups or segments will be significantly larger than any of the others so that each, despite individual differences, is largely comparable to the others. This structure, however, was, Renfrew argued, modified around 2700 BC by centralising tendencies assuming the form of leadership controlling several groups and reflected in the archaeological record by the construction and use of the henges at Stenness and Brodgar and the monumental tomb at Maes Howe. A more recent study (Hodder 1982, 218–28) is a brief attempt to integrate the settlement and tomb evidence and in particular draws attention to the similarity in the use and arrangement of space in both the houses and tombs, a point which may have some validity notwithstanding the very considerable misuse of the data from which it is argued. With only three partially excavated villages there is not a sufficient base of settlement data by which these hypotheses might be tested. However, while no evidence from the grooved ware settlements is fundamentally at variance with the concept of a 'segmentary society' there is as yet nothing from these sites to support the idea of the emergence of a centralising tendency. Work on constructing the later phase village at Skara Brae was certainly taking place about this time but apart from minor design modifications in the interior fittings no significant changes can be discerned. There is, of course, no reason why the changes in social structure envisaged by Renfrew should be reflected on individual sites. Yet the chronological overlap between Unstan and grooved ware groups (D.V.Clarke 1983) and the marked differences of their assemblages is not explicable in terms of a segmentary society.

Further, the idea of a segmentary society with its implied egalitarianism needs to be treated with caution. Are, for instance, relations between groups to be structured on a different basis in such a society from those within groups? Equally problematic is how disputes between groups were mediated, for the settlements show no evidence of resort to physical aggression, at least in an organised way. Indeed if independent action was largely the norm for these groups, the maintenance of a uniform tradition on an inter-settlement basis for some 500 years or so becomes quite remarkable. It cannot be explained simply in terms of immigrants arriving with a package of traditions and practices already formed which the communities merely perpetuate. The long sequence at Skara Brae creates a firm picture of an innovating and adapting group not unwilling to adopt new practices in changing circumstances. Much of this is irreconcilable with the concept of a segmentary society and it does suggest that the idea will need considerable development to take account of the accumulating evidence from the settlements.

Whatever the generalised nature of the society of which these settlements formed a part, it is possible to make some suggestions concerning the social organisation within the settlements. Most of these will, however, be based on Skara Brae and this dependence on a single site makes them very tentative. There can be no doubt that life was both communal and organised – as the central nucleus of semi-subterranean houses linked by narrow passages would require. But the sense of community was not so strong that

69

it involved a large, shared dwelling-place, such as are found among some early farming groups in continental Europe. Certainly, the domestic area seems to have been particularly well-defined but within that area there was further subdivision based on a family unit. Each of the houses seems best suited to a small group, perhaps involving only two generations, and is certainly not suitable for any kind of extended family grouping. This combination of a sense of community combined with a recognition of separate groups within the community is also reflected in some of the architectural features. The well-constructed doorways at the end of the passages undoubtedly served a very practical purpose but they also emphasise the division between the domestic and non-domestic areas. The presence of similar doors, controlled from within each house, equally acknowledge the presence of separate units within the community. Thus the architectural solutions adopted in the construction of the village can be interpreted as both supporting the cohesiveness of the community and as accepting the need for individual groups to distance themselves from that community from time to time.

It has already been noted that the difference in size between the houses is not particularly great, certainly not enough for a difference of status between the occupants to be inferred with any confidence. Nevertheless, such differences may well have been pointed out in more subtle ways. Anyone entering the houses had their view wholly dominated by the large dresser on the opposite wall (plate 4.8). This piece of furniture, as with modern examples, is designed so that its upper parts have a display area. It is not too fanciful, therefore, to suppose that the objects ranged on the shelves were intended in part as a statement of the status of the occupants. Certainly, the positioning and form of the dresser could not have been better designed for such a purpose. It is interesting to note that the dresser in more recent Hebridean black-houses seems to have had a similar role (Stoklund 1980, 131). Childe, in his discussion of the houses at Skara Brae, drew attention to another parallel with the Hebridean houses involving the arrangement of the beds. He noted that one was always larger than the other and that the larger was always on the right of the fireplace relative to the door. Such an arrangement is found in the Hebridean houses with the larger bed belonging to the man and the smaller the woman. Indeed, the hearth, with its centrally dominant position, was in the Hebrides an important means of demonstrating to the visitor his status in the eyes of the occupants. As the focal point of social activity within the house the seating position around the hearth accorded to the visitor reflected his relationship to the family. Now we know next to nothing about such provisions in the Orcadian houses which we are here discussing but it is interesting that the one item which may reasonably be interpreted as a seat, a large stone block in house 7 at Skara Brae, was positioned in what, on the Hebridean analogies, would

PLATE 4.8. View from the doorway of house 7 at Skara Brae.

be socially the most important position between the hearth and the dresser opposite the door. Of course, these interpretations can be no more than plausible suggestions but they do show that houses cannot be regarded merely as buildings providing protection from the elements but as items reflecting a wide range of economic and social functions some of which have only symbolic forms. Indeed Stoklund concluded 'in many ways the house is a reflection of the society around it. Where we find a very homogeneous building tradition and interior design we can with some certainty conclude that there is a high degree of cultural integration, a harmony regarding the goals, norms and values of life' (1980, 122). Just such a situation as this is found in the Orcadian grooved ware settlements. Moreover, where the scope for variations in the design is small, as in this case, studies of more recent dwellings suggest that the symbolic function is strongest. If then the total integration of these groups is well developed, as the evidence seems to suggest, it is not perhaps surprising that symbols indicating status should prove so elusive in the archaeological record.

THE ECONOMY

In contrast to the structural remains, the evidence for the economy of these settlements can only be interpreted in terms of the whole community. The data come in large measure from the midden heaps in which the rubbish from individual houses cannot be distinguished. Variations within the midden deposits are certainly discernible – at Noltland, for instance, large quantities of beads and bead-making debris have been recovered from one area but such material is almost wholly absent in the other excavated areas – but their significance is still far from clear. We can, then, only provide a broad sketch of the economic activities without much indication of how they were organised. It must be supposed, however, that the highly integrated nature of these settlements is indicative of a considerable degree of co-operation at community level. Certainly, one would expect the differences between these settlements and the isolated farmsteads characteristic of most early farmers in Britain to be reflected in their economic organisations, although it is difficult to distinguish those differences in the evidence available.

Quite the most important feature of the Orcadian settlements is the tremendous diversity of the environment which they could exploit. The land, already largely cleared of trees except for dwarf and isolated examples, was capable of supporting a rich pasture while, in the areas of machair at least, the light sandy soils were easily ploughed. The seas surrounding the islands were rich in many forms of marine life, probably of even greater variety than that found today. Indeed the animal and bird life exploiting this marine environment would have more than compensated for the absence of some land animals brought about by the island situation. Nor need the lack of trees have been as big a disadvantage as might at first appear. The erosion by rivers of the virgin forests of North America would have brought many large trees to the eastern seaboard of that continent and these, having subsequently floated across the Atlantic would provide a ready source of driftwood on Orkney beaches. Some of the wood, which includes actual artefacts (plate 4.9), recovered from a waterlogged midden at Skara Brae has been identified as spruce and this can only reasonably be interpreted as coming from North America. Similar finds have been made at several sites in north and west Scotland and one, at Stanydale in Shetland, provides some indication of the quantities available. There the excavator found spruce in the form of charcoal and, on the basis of the post holes, concluded that some 700 m of dressed timber would have been required to roof the structure (Calder 1950, 192). The richness of the environment and the quantities of material that it could provide is worth emphasising since there is no evidence that the inhabitants of these settlements were involved in any struggle for survival. Indeed, in the one case where we seem to have evidence of a temporary shortfall in the supply of a raw material, namely flint at Skara Brae, they seem to have been able to adapt easily to the use of the locally available, but inferior, chert.

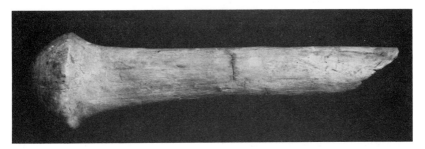

PLATE 4.9. Wooden handle from Skara Brae (203 mm long).

The food supply came largely from agricultural activities although their interpretation is made difficult by the differential survival of the evidence, which is heavily biased towards the products of animal husbandry. In the absence of any evidence to the contrary it has until recently been assumed that grooved ware groups were not involved in cereal production but were instead wholly concerned with pastoralism. Large quantities of carbonised grain, mainly barley, were, however, recovered from the earliest middens at Skara Brae but were otherwise absent in the excavated middens. Not too much is perhaps to be made of this absence since comparable finds remain rare (cf. M. Jones 1980) and a large number of factors are involved in controlling whether such material becomes incorporated in rubbish deposits. Although similar finds have not been recovered at the other settlements, confirmatory evidence in the form of ploughmarks has been discovered at Noltland (plate 4.10). The area so far exposed is small but sufficient to show that the area had been intensively cultivated for some time. The ploughing had been done by a light plough or ard, which scratches rather than turns the soil, but whether the traction involved was human or animal is uncertain. A considerable quantity of domestic refuse has been found in the plough soil and it seems clear that one of the important functions of the community's midden was as a fertiliser on the fields. The use of seaweed is also likely and would not be particularly surprising since its employment as manure is well documented in the recent past for large areas of Scotland, particularly Orkney (Fenton 1974). Insufficient work has yet been done at Noltland for us to be able to judge the size of the fields but in one trench a small length of a boundary ditch associated with the ploughing was exposed. Although it had been re-cut, this ditch went out of

PLATE 4.10. Ploughmarks at Links of Noltland.

use before the ploughing ended, implying that the fields were realigned from time to time. The size of this ditch, which is comparable with one that seems to be associated with the ploughing at Rosinish on Benbecula (Shepherd and Tuckwell 1977), is such that it could only have served to mark off the individual field; it certainly would not have been sufficient to deter animals from entering the field. No indications of a fence were found associated with this ditch and just how animals were kept away from the growing crop remains unclear. However, the fill of the ditch contained a number of large stones, as did that at Rosinish, and these may represent the final traces of a seaweed fence. Such fences were relatively common in the coastal areas of Denmark (Rasmussen 1974, 393–95) and were usually built using a base of heavy stones. Such fences could have a height in excess of 2 m and are reported to have lasted for generations. Incontrovertible evidence of their use would certainly be difficult to recover in the archaeological record, except in exceptional circumstances, so that it cannot at the moment be regarded as anything other than a suggestion. Nevertheless, the problem of protecting the crops was real enough and some solution must have been found.

The animal husbandry seems to have involved roughly equal proportions of cattle and sheep with only a very small number of pigs. Some at least of the cattle were extremely large, with a size rivalling that of their wild predecessor the aurochs, the bones of which might anyway be present amongst the assemblages. On the basis of the bones recovered at Skara Brae, a large percentage of the cattle were slaughtered at the end of their first year. It has often been supposed that such slaughtering represents a lack of adequate supplies of winter fodder but it is possible to reinterpret it as evidence for a dairy based system (Legge 1981, 180). No byres for housing cattle over the winter have so far been recognised among the structures and the construction techniques of the houses preclude the possibility of animals and humans sharing the same accommodation, which was a practice common in the more recent past. The sheep were small, the Soay is perhaps their nearest modern equivalent, and they are unlikely to have produced much in the way of wool; the absence of clearly identifiable weaving equipment among the artefact assemblages perhaps supports this view. The relatively large quantities of sheep present is an unusual feature in the economy of these Orcadian sites. In early farming communities elsewhere in Britain cattle or pigs, either separately or together, would normally dominate the faunal assemblage (Tinsley and Grigson 1981, 225). Only around c. 1000 BC do sheep begin to increase in importance. Clark (1952, 121) has suggested that this is because sheep are more suited to an open environment and whereas in mainland Britain this had to be created, it already existed even before the first settlement of Orkney. Another exceptional feature of Orcadian husbandry practices is the opportunistic relation-

PLATE 4.11. One of the articulated deer skeletons at Links of Noltland.

ship with red deer. At Skara Brae this species accounts for only about 1 per cent of the animal bones recovered and such a situation is best interpreted as occasional hunting. However, at Noltland deer bones are altogether more numerous including the discovery of some fifteen completely articulated skeletons (plate 4.11). Since deer are likely to have been brought to Orkney by man (Clutton-Brock 1979, 113) this bone debris is unlikely to represent the casual slaughter of an indigenous herd. This is not to suggest that the deer were being farmed in the same way as cattle or sheep but nevertheless a herd on an island the size of Westray could only have been viable with man's continuing control and protection. The absence of antler tools in any quantity suggest that the deer were being regularly exploited for food and skins. Presumably the much larger size of Mainland on which Skara Brae is situated prevented the inhabitants there from exploiting the deer in a similar manner.

The other important source of food, as far as we can judge, was collected from the sea in the form of fish and marine molluscs. Large quantities of bones and shells have been recovered in the recent excavations at Skara Brae and Noltland, but understanding exactly what this debris means is more difficult. Limpets are by far the most numerous molluscs at both sites, something which has customarily been interpreted as indicating that they were eaten in large quantities by the inhabitants of these settlements; but their low calorific value and the fact that in the historical past such food has only been resorted to in times of extreme hardship suggests that an alternative explanation should be sought. The most obvious is that they were collected for use as fish bait, such usage being well documented in the recent past in many parts of Scotland. Some shellfish, particularly oysters and crab, would certainly have formed part of the diet but the impression is that they were collected to provide variety rather than as a staple. Fish are likely, however, to have been much more important although again the situation is less straightforward that it might at first sight appear. A preliminary examination of the fish bones suggests that although some are from large specimens most are small and from species living close to the coast. Boats would certainly have been used but it is unlikely that trips were made far from the coast except on rare occasions. Almost no equipment used to catch these fish has been discovered at any of the sites. Yet whether all this fish was for human consumption must be open to question. In the nineteenth-century excavations at Skara Brae a stone mortar was found filled with crushed fish bone suggesting to the excavator that it had once been fish meal. In times of great hardship this has certainly formed part of the human diet in Scotland but its more common use is as feed for cattle.

The problems we have just mentioned concerning the use of fish and shellfish become even more acute in considering the remains of other wild

PLATE 4.12. Bone point made from the humerus of an adult gannet
(128 mm long).

animals and birds, the bones of which are found at these sites. Most if not all could certainly have been eaten, but the desire for other forms of raw material which they could provide may have been an even greater motivation in their capture. The need for skins, oil, feathers and pelts rather than meat may well have been the main reason for hunting whales, seals, seabirds and otters. The bones of all these species have been found in relatively small quantities but there may be a number of factors preventing us from appreciating their real importance. Whale and seal bone which has not been fashioned into artefacts is extremely rare but it has already been noted that such bone provides a good source of fuel and there can anyway have been little incentive to carry bone back from the point where the carcase was beached without some use being made of it. But the relatively small quantities found have caused most observers to suppose that it represents the exploitation of stranded animals. This may well be the case with species such as killer whale and walrus as well as the rorquals which sink once they have been killed (Tønnessen and Johnsen 1982, 6) but other species such as pilot whales are relatively easily caught (cf. Joensen 1976). Equally, adult gannets are almost wholly represented at Skara Brae by humeri which have been fashioned into bone points (plate 4.12). Undoubtedly, this bone has been specially selected for this tool because of qualities which are now difficult to determine but it is unlikely that gannets were caught solely to obtain this bone. The problem is that the vagaries of preservation allow us to see only individual aspects of what is undoubtedly a multi-faceted exploitation of the environment in terms of raw materials. Even with such straightforward material as shell from birds' eggs which must have been collected for food, a question arises with the identification of some of it as probably that of eider duck. These are still numerous in Orkney today but we can only speculate whether the collection of their eggs also involved the obtaining of eider-down.

Most of the objects found at these sites are made from one of three raw materials: pottery, stone and bone. The range of artefact types is considerable but, as we have noted earlier, only the pottery finds ready parallels elsewhere in Britain. The usual explanation for the wide range of other

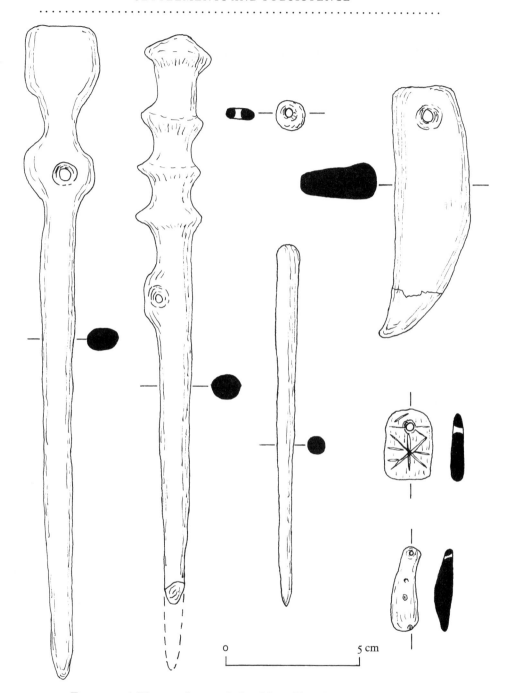

FIGURE 4.6. Pins, pendants and a bead from Skara Brae.

PLATE 4.13. Carved stone objects from Skara Brae.

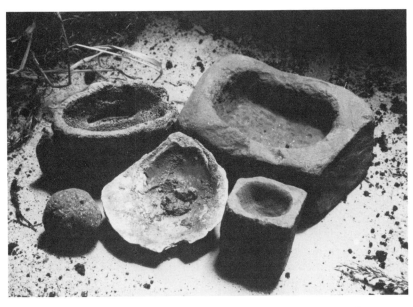

PLATE 4.14. Stone and bone pots containing red colouring matter from
Skara Brae.

artefacts is that they reflect the special environmental conditions found in Orkney, although detailed studies of the objects do not substantiate this view to any great extent. Certainly the flint and chert because of its scarcity had a more restricted use than in other areas of Britain since it was employed solely in the working of wood and bone. In other words, wood and more particularly bone together with larger objects made of the local stone formed the main tool kit. Insofar as we can interpret the function of most of these objects they seem largely to have been employed in the butchering of animals and the processing of their products. The pottery is also to be associated with this group of objects in terms of its use for cooking and storage. There is, however, an equally large group of material including pins, beads, pendants (figure 4.6), some remarkable carved stone objects (plate 4.13) and even bone and stone pots in which red colouring matter was mixed (plate 4.14). The function of this group of objects is much less obviously practical and although bone remains the most important raw material a wider variety, including shell and jet, is utilised than in the case of the tools.

How then can all these strands of information be brought together and what general picture do they provide of the society and economy in the third millennium BC? We are dealing here with communities which, while not unchanging, essentially maintained a stable life-style with its associated traditions for a period exceeding 500 years. This continuity, however, should not be interpreted as backwardness; rather all the evidence suggests that they were groups living in harmony with an environment which they used but did not over-exploit. Apart from rare occasions, this rich and diverse environment was capable of supporting them in a manner sufficiently easy to allow time for a wide range of activities not closely related to survival. The diet was remarkably varied including some items, such as venison and oysters, now regarded as luxuries. This in some ways enviable existence was achieved by small communities, perhaps involving not more than ten or fifteen families, with a considerable measure of self-sufficiency. Presumably the communal sharing of routine tasks which is implicit in the structural integration of these villages provided an opportunity for the development of individual skills of benefit to the community. There is, however, no evidence of craft specialisation in the sense that an individual pursued a task exclusively and depended upon exchanging the products with others in order to maintain himself. Yet the image of independent communities should not be pushed too far. Some raw materials, for example haematite which is only found in Orkney in two veins on the north coast of Hoy, are sufficiently rare in their occurrence for it to be reasonably supposed that they were obtained by contacts with other groups. Regular contacts would anyway be required for the obtaining of marriage partners and without such meetings the remarkable cultural uniformities which we have been describing would be difficult to explain over such a long time-span. Much needs to be done before we can bring this inter-settlement network into clearer focus and begin to understand its social and economic roles. In particular, we need to define more clearly the full range of materials which a settlement might reasonably obtain acting independently within its immediate environment. Only then will it be possible to assess the significance of the wider network. Enough has already been done to show that these aspirations need not be mere pipe-dreams.

5 Audrey S. Henshall **The Chambered Cairns**

Chambered cairns are found in many parts of western Europe, and are the earliest structures still surviving in the landscape. They were built as burial places; essentially they were rooms, normally closed, to which access could be had for burials and other purposes, and they were generally covered by a cairn. Chambered cairns vary greatly in design from one area to another, and some are of astonishing size and elaboration. Until modern times they have generally been objects of awe and superstition, an attitude which has done much to protect them from demolition. The mechanics of the spread of chambered cairns through Spain, France, Britain, Ireland, Denmark, and other parts of Europe, have long been, and continue to be, discussed. It is clear from the diversity of plans, of burial rites, and of the material culture of their users, that it was not a simple matter of emigration and colonisation from a single centre. One of the most intriguing questions is why some early farming communities buried their dead in stone chambers and others did not. The building of even a modest tomb must have entailed considerable physical and economic strain on a neolithic society, and the structures were clearly much more than just burial vaults.

These tombs are known to have been used for very long periods, often many centuries. Their most important functions were probably as foci for social and religious ceremonies concerned with the wellbeing of the communities they served: we may guess at ancestor worship and rituals to ensure fertility of animals and lands. It is ironic that these aspects of the significance of the tombs are, by their nature, those which elude us, for archaeological studies are based on material remains. The tombs may also have served as important territorial markers for the societies that built them.

Nonetheless, in those areas where they were the established burial place, chambered cairns provide a great deal of information about the earliest farmers. Obviously the structures themselves, their plans and building techniques, deserve study. Also their distribution, both on an international scale and in relation to the immediate environment, gives an indication of the early settlement patterns and the lands which were exploited. Then there is the skeletal material recovered from the chambers by excavation, the physical remains of the people who were buried in them and who lived in the habitation sites such as those described in chapters 3 and 4. The pathology of their bones gives an insight into living conditions, and if the material allows, demographic analysis may shed light on social organisation and economics. Faunal remains included in the tombs, by accident or intention, provide evidence on the environment, and on the economy of the communities concerned. It was usual for objects of daily use to be left with the burials or in the filling which finally sealed the tombs. The objects which survive are mainly pottery sherds and stone and flint tools, all of prime importance in any assessment of the origins and contacts of any group of tomb builders, and of their material equipment. Radiocarbon dates taken from bones or vegetable matter can be used, if conditions are favourable, to date the building and period of use, and also the objects within them. As yet only the first steps have been taken in establishing a firm chronology for European tombs and in particular for Orcadian tombs.

The far north of Scotland has a remarkable concentration of chambered cairns, and, for their land area, the Orkney and Shetland Islands have the greatest concentration of all. But the Orcadian cairns are of outstanding interest for other reasons: the variety of size and plan, the elaborate designs and structural excellence, the number which are relatively complete, and the detail with which they have been studied. The earliest tombs are likely to have been built by the first neolithic inhabitants of the islands, and it is clear that they came across the Pentland Firth from Caithness, though the date at which this happened is uncertain, probably in the early centuries of the fourth millennium BC. It is likely that the history of chambered cairns in the islands spans over a thousand years, and during this time a variety of tomb designs developed, partly in ways unique to the islands and partly in response to new ideas reaching the islands from the mainland. The extent to which the culture of the distinctive late neolithic Orcadian grooved ware communities (including the design of their tombs) was due to development within the islands is a matter of debate.

The study of Orcadian chambered cairns really began about the middle of last century with the investigations at a number of sites by George Petrie, James Farrer, R. J. Hebden and F. W. L. Thomas. Following a lull, work began on the Royal Commission's Inventory of the ancient monuments of Orkney in the 1920s and 30s (RCAMS 1946), and in the 1930s there were the series of remarkable excavations by C.S.T. Calder on Eday, and J.G. Callander and W.G. Grant on Rousay. After the war V.G. Childe excavated at two outstanding monuments, Maes Howe and Quoyness, and soon afterwards S. Piggott published his synthesis and interpretation of the information to date (1954, 232–56). A catalogue of sites and their contents, with references, was published in 1963 (Henshall 1963, 183–253, also 1972, 562–3; for Orkney, the code numbers used in these volumes will be quoted in italics, while sites in Caithness and Sutherland also published in Henshall 1963 or 1972 will be prefaced by CAT and SUT respectively). A number of additional sites have been recognised since 1972, and are listed on p.115. There have also been two excavations of outstanding importance in recent years, at Quanterness (43) by C. Renfrew (1979) and at Isbister (25) by R. Simison (J.W. Hedges 1983a).

THE ORKNEY–CROMARTY GROUP

The distribution and architectural development of passage-graves in Scotland was discussed in 1972 (Henshall 1972, 201–6, 257–64). In general terms the earliest small and simple passage-graves of international type, consisting of a circular or polygonal chamber with entrance passage, gave rise, in the Highlands and Islands, to several rather more elaborate plans, the whole group being known as the Orkney–Cromarty group, abbreviated here to OC. One chamber plan had a pair of opposed upright slabs set transversely to the axis to divide an antechamber from the main chamber. An extension of this idea, using a second pair of slabs as a portal to an inner section of the chamber, produced a chamber of three parts. This tripartite chamber plan is common in Caithness, and, the easily quarried sandstones and flagstones providing an excellent building material, the walls of the passage and chamber were of masonry rather than the large blocks of stone usual to the south and west, and quite high false-corbelled vaults were erected over the main part of the chamber. The access passage was on the axis of the chamber, and the whole was generally covered by a relatively small round cairn.

A number of excavated sites in Orkney have this same basic tripartite plan, for instance Bigland (2) (figure 5.1), Kierfea Hill (26), Knowe of Craie (27), all three on Rousay, and Huntersquoy (23), Sandyhill Smithy (47) on Eday. The cairns are of modest size, from about 8 to 12 m in diameter, revetted by a single, or more often a double, wall-face of dry masonry. The passage leads into a chamber some 3.4 to 4.8 m long. All the chambers have lost their roofs but as the surviving transverse slabs are of modest height the roofing is likely to have been about 1.5 to 2.0 m above the floor. The dry-built side walls should probably be envisaged as oversailing in their upper courses above the tops of the upright slabs, and linked by a row of lintels, such as partly survived at Knowe of Lairo (28). This last is a

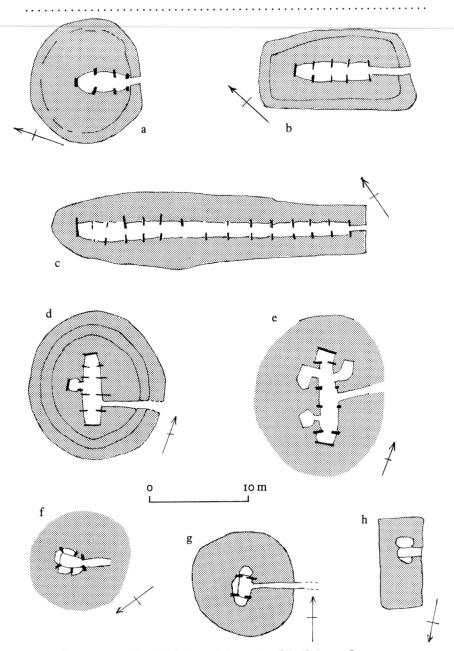

FIGURE 5.1. Simplified plans of the tombs of the Orkney–Cromarty group: (a) Bigland, Round; (b) Knowe of Yarso; (c) Knowe of Ramsay; (d) Unstan; (e) Isbister; (f) Calf of Eday, SE; (g) Huntersquoy (lower chamber); (h) Dwarfie Stane.

large chamber, 5.2 m long, with the paired transverse stones in proportion, 2.1 m high, and the roof 4.1 m above the floor; curiously the chamber and passage are built on a sinuous axis. Among the unexcavated cairns there are similar chambers ranging from small to large, though when incompletely exposed they cannot always be distinguished from stalled chambers. At least one tripartite chamber as large as Lairo is known in Caithness (CAT 70).

A desire for longer chambers led to an increase in the number of compartments. In Caithness only two of these longer stalled chambers are known, but in Orkney the idea was fully exploited leading to the construction of some very remarkable monuments, although a few four-compartment chambers are no longer than the largest tripartite ones. Among the sites with full excavation reports, Knowe of Yarso (32) (figure 5.1) has an interesting chamber plan which is essentially tripartite, the long inner compartment being subdivided in its lower part by a pair of short transverse slabs with a sill stone between them; the innermost section had been divided horizontally by a shelf resting on a scarcement in the side walls.

On a stretch of the south coast of Rousay, only 3½ miles long, there are four other stalled chambers, three of them the longest so far identified. Blackhammer (3), Knowe of Rowiegar (31), Midhowe (37) and Knowe of Ramsay (30) (figure 5.1) in ascending order of size, ranging from seven to fourteen compartments and from 13 to 26 m long. They were described as 'stalled' by the excavators who first revealed this type of chamber, for, even in their roofless state, they do indeed have the appearance of long narrow byres with their series of paired tall transverse stones and the passageway down the centre. At Midhowe (figure 5.3) the best preserved, the tallest transverse stones are over 2 m high, and the side walls still stand 2.5 m high. The innermost compartment is subdivided in the same way as at Knowe of Yarso. The size of these chambers, together with their close distribution, astonishes every visitor. The Rousay stalled chambers, including two unexcavated sites elsewhere on the island, are covered not by round but by rectangular cairns, this change presumably being a practical way to encase the chamber with the minimum of stonework for its support, and to provide a ramp for manoeuvring the lintels into place. At Blackhammer the passage approaches the chamber at right angles to the axis, an arrangement found at a few other sites.

One of the best known Orcadian tombs is Unstan (or Onston, 51), in Stenness (figure 5.1). The chamber of five compartments is of average length, but interestingly is covered by a round cairn. Like Blackhammer, the passage enters the long side of the chamber thus allowing two end compartments both of which have had shelves, and a kerb across their entries. Another feature to note is a cell accessible from the opposite side of the chamber to the passage. The cell is entered between a pair of low portal stones, it has a back-slab but dry-built walls, and is roofed by a capstone at a height of only 1.26 m. When the tomb was excavated in 1884 the finds included sherds of distinctive shallow bowls with decorated collars (a form misleadingly described as carinated in archaeological literature). These became the type-specimens for Unstan Ware, discussed later.

The most recently excavated chamber, Isbister on South Ronaldsay (25, J. W. Hedges 1983a, 1–31, 301–2) (figure 5.1) is exceptional in several respects but closest to Unstan. There are four pairs of transverse slabs giving five segments to the chamber, as the passage enters the chamber from the side. Yet the two middle pairs of slabs project so little beyond the chamber wall that the appearance is more of a large rectangular area with a special area divided off at each end. Access to the end-sections is restricted by the greater projection of the two end pairs of transverse slabs and the positioning of a kerb between them. The difference of the end-sections is emphasised by the side walls at ground level being set back from the line of the main chamber walls, by the flagged floor, and by a flagstone shelf in each. The chamber is also provided with three side cells entered by short passages; the cells are similar to that at Unstan except they are entirely dry-built, and are roofed even lower, at only 1 m. As originally built, the chamber was under an oval cairn of the minimum size to enclose the chamber and cells. The retaining wall of the cairn still reaches a height of 1.9 m at one side, so the cairn seems to have been in the form of a drum with a vertical masonry facing (plate 5.1, colour plate 5).

The quality of the craftsmanship in these cairns induces the greatest respect for their builders. The dry-stone masonry is neat and regular, and at some sites the retaining wall-face of the cairn has been decoratively treated. A projecting basal course is not unusual, and at three Rousay sites the stonework above this is either set slanting in opposite directions on either side of the entrance, to be reversed at the back of the cairn, or set in two bands each slanting in opposite directions and separated by a wide horizontal course, or set in opposed slanting panels reminiscent of the opposed hatched triangles which decorate the collars of some Unstan bowls. The narrowness of the cairn casing in relation to the height of the chambers indicates that a number of sites besides Isbister must once have had vertical retaining walls of considerable height, and these were presumably designed to be seen. The wall-face survived for almost its full height at Isbister because the cairn was covered by an outer rubble mound which sloped down to a boundary wall some 5 to 9 m outside the retaining wall. The large upright slabs forming the ends and divisions of the chambers, the skeletons of the structure, were handled with skill and were so carefully selected and set that they normally remain in position even at badly ruined sites. Often the transverse slabs have slanting upper edges to complement the corbelling of the wall-head above them.

Besides the shelves in some end compartments, some (but not all) of

PLATE 5.1. The chamber at Isbister, showing the south end compartment and, on left, the slab of the passage roof.

89

both the tripartite and the stalled chambers have been found to be equipped with low benches, set along the side walls between the transverse slabs. At Knowe of Craie (27) one of the benches was of solid stone construction similar to those found at one Caithness chamber (CAT 69). Otherwise the benches consist of a slab, bonded into the side wall and supported by stones on edge set on the floor. It is evident that these are original features, but their positioning seems curiously erratic: in two chambers they are along both walls, in one in the inner compartment only, in one long chamber along part of one side only. Failure to identify remains of shelves in some end compartments where projecting stones were clearly intended for their support, as at Knowe of Yarso (32), suggests that some shelves, and some benches too, may have been of wood.

A second variant of the tripartite chamber developed in Orkney, and is named after the cairn at Bookan. At Huntersquoy on Eday (23) and at Taversoe Tuick on Rousay (49) (figure 5.5) the cairns are extraordinary structures with two chambers one above the other, covered by a round cairn, the whole built as a unit. These two-storeyed tombs are sited on slopes, with the upper chamber entered from the uphill side, the flags forming its floor being the capstones of the lower chamber, entered from the downhill side. The upper chamber at Huntersquoy was tripartite in plan. Space for the lower chamber required quarrying back into the clay and underlying rock of the hillside. The plan is based on the tripartite arrangement, but the long axis of the chamber lies along the contour of the hill and thus at right angles to the passage, presumably to reduce effort during construction. Thus the chamber has two end-compartments entered between pairs of transverse slabs, and a central compartment with the low passage entering one side, the 'burial area' lost because of the position of the passage being provided by a recess above its inner end. The lower chamber at Taversoe Tuick is similar, but the upper chamber is irregular, and probably should be regarded, like the miniature chamber outside the cairn which will be mentioned later, as a simplification of the lower chamber plan. The walls of all these chambers are of the highest quality dry masonry, concave in plan between the divisional slabs. All the recesses of these two subterranean chambers have a slab shelf, at each site two of them resting on a solid masonry platform or bench (colour plate 6).

Two separate almost intact chambers, on Calf of Eday (9, 10) (figure 5.1) also belong to this Bookan sub-group, having much in common with the subterranean chambers already described, including round cairns, cutting back into a hillslope, and the provision of benches or shelves in the recesses. However, the divisional slabs projecting from the walls are not strictly paired. The appearance of the terminal compartments at Huntersquoy and Taversoe Tuick is reproduced at Calf of Eday (9) by additional paired upright slabs narrowing the entrance to the recesses, and in one case there is also a kerbstone. The Bookan chamber was a more regular version of this last plan. The surviving roofs of the Bookan group chambers are low, constructed either by large slabs spanning the whole chamber, or by slabs covering each recess and supporting slabs spanning the central area. Although the plans seem distorted and curious, they are ingeniously designed. It is notable too, that, of the variety of chamber plans available in Orkney, it is this type of chamber which appears in Shetland, being the progenitor of the large number tombs in those islands. The reasons may be largely practical, due to the intractable building stone and to the economic difficulties of the early stages of colonisation of those islands.

One extraordinary monument, the Dwarfie Stane (*13*) (figure 5.1), has attracted the attention of visitors and the speculation of antiquaries since the sixteenth century, and indeed its classification as a chambered tomb is periodically questioned. A small chamber has been hewn in a rectangular erratic block of sandstone, itself a remarkable feature lying in a desolate moorland valley on the island of Hoy. The chamber, no more than 0.76 m high, consists of a central passage with a compartment on either side, each marked off with a low sill, one of these compartments being further distinguished by vestigial projecting jambs. The plan appears to be a simplification of the Bookan-type plan, Huntersquoy providing the closest parallel, the idea of carving the chamber out of the solid rock being an extension of the rock-cutting undertaken for four Bookan-type chambers.

At a few sites there are two chambers under one cairn. At the two-storey cairns the chambers, which have been classed respectively as a Bookan and tripartite plan, and two Bookan plans, are strictly contemporary. But the cairn dug by Calder on Calf of Eday (*8*) had a stalled four-compartment chamber and, behind it on a different axis, a small low two-compartment chamber which is best classified with the Bookan chambers. The excavator considered the small chamber was secondary to the large chamber, but the excavation report provides no proof of this assumption and it seems to the writer that the reverse is more likely. On the other hand at Bigland (*1*) on Rousay an unexcavated site gives every appearance of a tripartite chamber being secondary to a long stalled chamber. The close connection of the three varieties of chamber plan so far discussed cannot be in doubt, nor the derivation of the stalled and Bookan plans from the tripartite plan, but the typology suggested by the plans should not be used to construct a chronological sequence, except to note a strong likelihood that at least some small tripartite chambers were the earliest to be built in Orkney.

There are sixty sites which can be identified as certainly or probably tombs of the Orkney-Cromarty group. Of these, fifteen certainly or very probably have tripartite chambers, eighteen have stalled chambers, at fourteen chambers the number of compartments is not known, and seven chambers are of Bookan type (in three cases the cairn covers two chambers). The overall distribution is curious (map 1, p. 116), with a concentration on Rousay and the adjacent coast of Mainland, on Eday and Calf of Eday, and a somewhat less intense concentration on Westray with Holm of Papa Westray. Apart from these islands there are a few tombs on Stronsay, Shapinsay, and on South Ronaldsay with Burray and Swona. Otherwise there is only a scattering of sites on the rest of Mainland, and one each on Sanday and Hoy. The gaps on Mainland and Sanday are filled to some extent by tombs of the Maes Howe group (described below), but there remain some areas where occupation by tomb-builders would have been expected, around Scapa Flow, in other parts of Mainland, and on others of the smaller islands, where no sites have been identified. Within this distribution, the occurrence of tripartite and stalled cairns is, in general terms, similar and widespread except that the longest stalled chambers are all on Rousay, but half of the small number of Bookan chambers are on Calf of Eday and north Eday, with a pair under one cairn on Rousay, and single examples on Mainland and Hoy.

There may be a hint of some difference of function for the Bookan chambers, as the similarity between their compartments and the shelved end-sections of some of the stalled chambers is striking; at Isbister in particular there is the marked structural contrast between the central part of the chamber and the terminal compartments. It may be that this difference led to the building of such terminal compartments as separate tombs, but it must be admitted that evidence from the contents of the tombs is too scanty to demonstrate a functional difference, though at Isbister and Knowe of Yarso (32) the end areas had been particularly intensively used for bone storage.

Long cairns and short horned cairns. Besides the forms of cairns already described, there are also five, possibly seven, long cairns of the type in which the chamber occupies only a small part of the whole structure, the cairn being wider and higher at the end containing the chamber. Long cairns are well represented in Scotland, and have been discussed in some detail (Henshall 1972, 207–40). Their origins were separate from passage-graves, and it is now generally accepted that in northern Scotland they were often (indeed, possibly always) additions to existing passage-graves. In Caithness the forecourt at the wider end was faced with dry-walling, and was sometimes extended by building out long 'horns' from each corner, and this feature may be repeated on a smaller scale at the rear. Only one long cairn in northern Scotland has been excavated this century (CAT 58; Corcoran 1966, 5–22), and another (CAT 12) is presently under excavation. Corcoran showed that, at one site at least, the long cairn post-dated by some time the simple early passage-grave it covered, and in fact masked the tomb entrance so that it could not be used. It is clear that a similar situation existed at other sites in the north mainland, but alternatively the secondary long cairn was sometimes arranged so that the tomb was still accessible, and it is possible that in a few cases the two funerary building traditions merged to produce a chambered long cairn built as an entity. It is worth noting that whereas about a quarter of the chambers in Caithness were covered by long cairns, the proportion in Orkney is only about ten per cent, and it is doubtful if the long cairn tradition ever reached Shetland.

The Orcadian long cairns are similar in size to those in the north mainland, ranging from about 47 to 70 m in length including the horns. All cover, or seem to have covered, OC passage-graves, one being the unusual tripartite chamber already referred to at Knowe of Lairo (*28*), and one a stalled chamber at Point of Cott (*41*). At the former certainly, and at the latter probably, the chamber was accessible from the forecourt. The forecourts vary from a gently concave plan at Knowe of Lairo to a deeper curved plan to front and rear at Head of Work (*18*) and an angled plan at Point of Cott, in each case the cairn being faced by dry-walling. Parallels for all can be found in Caithness. The skew axis of the Knowe of Lairo chamber, and the markedly humped profile at Head of Work, almost certainly indicate a two-period structure. The distribution of these sites is scattered, on Mainland, Papa Stronsay, Westray, and a probable site on Shapinsay.

A more modest embellishment of the exterior of passage-graves is sometimes found in northern Scotland, where round cairns may have forecourts similar to those at long cairns, formed by two pairs of horns projecting at the front and back. Cairns of this plan were first recognised by Joseph Anderson excavating in Caithness in the 1860s (1868, 489–93) who named them 'short horned cairns'. Subsequently another version of the plan was found with a forecourt at the front only, the 'heel-shaped cairns'. Both plans are common amongst Shetland cairns so examples are to be expected in Orkney. It was formerly thought that three such cairns could be identified, but on recent visits to two of them it seemed to the writer preferable to interpret the horns as part of the later structures which certainly exist beside each site. This leaves Burray (*7*) as the only Orcadian short horned cairn, a site destroyed in 1863 and only known from brief descriptions.

A curious addition was made to the oval cairn at Isbister (*25*), for a straight wall abuts its N side, and behind the wall is a deposit of earth and rubble in which were animal and occasional human bones as well as human bones buried deliberately. This structural feature, referred to as a horn-work, has only been partly excavated and both its extent and purpose are obscure (J. W. Hedges 1983a, 23–31, 208–9, 301–2).

THE MAES HOWE GROUP

The second group of chambered cairns on Orkney, the Maes Howe group, contrast both in their design and their contents with the OC group. Whereas the latter are relatively easily recognised when seen in a ruinous state, the former are much more difficult to identify. At present the total of certain MH cairns is only ten, with three probable sites, but there are many cairns with no diagnostic features visible, some of which are likely to cover MH chambers. This relatively high proportion of probable and possible sites would, if verified and excavated, profoundly alter the picture.

In his recent re-assessment of the group following his excavations at Quanterness (43) (figure 5.2) Renfrew has argued persuasively for a revision of the typological arrangement put forward by Piggott and followed by the writer (Renfrew 1979, 201–3; Piggott 1954, 243–6; Henshall 1963, 123–4). If Maes Howe is left aside for the moment, the structures can be described as entirely dry-built with no vertical slabs, the chambers being rectangular (though rather irregular at Vinquoy Hill (53)), roomy and lofty, the walls gently oversailing from a metre or so above the floor. At the ground level there are low inconspicuous openings arranged more or less symmetrically, leading to cells which are roofed at almost the same height as the chamber. The roofing of the chamber, cells, and passage was by flat lintels, or more often by slabs set on edge. The masonry is of excellent quality, most walls in the chamber being bonded at the angles, having massive slabs for the lintels to the cell entries, and frequently one long slab spanning the whole length of the shorter walls.

With the exception of the Holm of Papa Westray (22), the cairns are round but sometimes large, carefully built, with an inner casing of minimum diameter to enclose chamber and cells, and one or two outer casings, all revetted with dry walling. The cairns at Quoyness and Wideford Hill (44, 54) have, since excavation, been left with these walls partly exposed resulting in a curious stepped profile, but there is little doubt that when finished the cairns were either domed in profile with all the revetment walls hidden as at Quanterness (Renfrew 1979, 48), or domed within an exposed outer revetment wall as at Wideford Hill (Kilbride-Jones 1973, 92, 95). At Quanterness a covering mantle of rubble was found, and where best preserved the outermost slabs were deliberately inclined with the slope of the cairn probably to keep the chamber dry (Renfrew 1979, 48). The passages are relatively long, but low, entering the chamber at right angles to its axis. In two cases the outer section of the passage, beyond the inner casing, does not seem to have been roofed but left as an open trench with the side walls rising with the slope of the mound, though in another case the passage was entirely roofed.

Three of the MH cairns, Cuween Hill, Vinquoy Hill and Wideford Hill

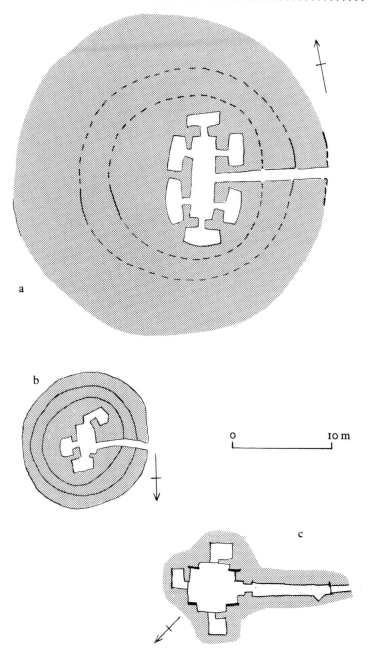

FIGURE 5.2. Simplified plans of the tombs of the Maes Howe group:
(a) Quanterness; (b) Wideford Hill; (c) Maes Howe.

(*12, 53, 54*) (figure 5.2), are similar in points of detail. A sloping site was chosen and the chambers were built level, entered from the lower sde, which necessitated some rock-cutting for the inner part of the structure. The number of cells varies from three to four, and one of them gives access to a subsidiary cell. The cells themselves are irregular in ground plan and, at the first two sites particularly, have been arranged to minimise the amount of excavation into the hillside. Two other cairns, Quanterness and Quoyness (*43, 44*) are on nearly flat sites, and cover larger chambers which are remarkably alike, both having two cells entered from the long sides and one from each end. Those at Quoyness are irregular in plan, but at Quanterness they are rectangular except for bowed outer walls conforming to the curve of the cairn casing. The chamber at this site measures no less than 6.35 m by 1.83 m, by 3.5 m high, somewhat larger than Quoyness. The procedure for constructing one of these remarkable monuments has been analysed by an architect (Renfrew 1979, 66–8).

The tomb on the Holm of Papa Westray (*22*) is an extraordinary structure by any standard. The excessively long chamber measuring in all 20.5 m, has the two ends divided off by cross-walls reaching to roof height, and through these walls are low openings: the remaining central area is 13.5 by 1.5 m. Around the chamber are twelve openings leading to fourteen cells, for two are double. A round cairn to cover this structure would be immense, so the same solution as for the stalled chambers was adopted, an elongated cairn casing.

Maes Howe (figure 5.2) is one of the supreme achievements of neolithic Europe, and stands apart because of its very excellence, but now seems on architectural grounds to be the last and most sophisticated product of the MH tradition of tomb-building. Most of the skills and ideas developed in its design can be found in the chambers already described. The layout of the very spacious chamber is strictly symmetrical, it being square in plan, the passage entering on one side and a cell entry being placed centrally on each of the others. The elevation of these entries together with the cells which lie behind them well above ground level is unique, but a small step up into a cell is found twice at Cuween Hill. The blocking of the entries at Maes Howe by masonry also seems unique, but may reflect a desire to distract attention from them; at other sites the entries were very small and at ground level, here they were disguised. Cells of rectangular plan are found at Quanterness, but at Maes Howe they differ in having low flat roofs. The quality of stonework at the other sites is notable, including bonding of walls, the use of slabs stretching the whole length of a wall, the use of an oblique natural fracture to construct smooth oversailing of the walling below the stepped corbelling (Renfrew 1979, 67), and at two sites there has been restricted use of dressing on the stonework (Childe 1952, 126; Renfrew 1979, 65). But the excellence of the masonry at Maes Howe goes far

PLATE 5.2. The passage at Maes Howe, looking towards the entrance.

beyond that of any other tomb, for the blocks fit extremely closely with occasional fine pinning to bring them into position, occasional rebating to take the corner of an adjacent block, and considerable areas of dressing by pecking and chiselling to achieve a flat surface or to round the edge of the corbelling or the sharp edge of the innermost passage lintel. The way that

97

PLATE 5.3. The chamber, Maes Howe.

massive rectangular slabs have been used is also unique to this site, for some are 5.6 m long and estimated to weigh three tons, and they form the walls, roof and floor of most of the passage, fitting together with unbelievable precision. Vertical slabs, accurately plumbed, are used in the chamber to face one side of each of the four buttresses which fill the corners and support the potential points of weakness, the corners of the oversailing roof. As at two other MH cairns, the outer passage has been an open masonry-lined trench, but only Maes Howe is provided with a recess just within the roofed passage, which contains a block intended to close the entrance when drawn forward against the door-checks (plates 5.2, 5.3, and colour plates 7, 8).

The great domed mound which covers the chamber contains an inner stone casing, but the outer parts of the mound are largely clay and turf with angular stones (Childe 1956, 162–4). The cairns of the three first tombs described were probably partly built from the rock dug to allow construction of the chamber. Limited recent investigation (Renfrew 1979, 31–8) has shown that the shallow Maes Howe ditch encircles only part of the site, for on the NW side it is largely an illusion between the edge of the platform on which the tomb is built and the low bank which encircles the monument. This bank is of two or more periods of construction, the later being modern, an earlier probably being Norse, and a still earlier bank probably being contemporary with the ditch digging. The Ring of Bookan, an enigmatic site which certainly has a wide deep ditch and a ruined cairn within, was formerly considered a parallel to Maes Howe, but this now seems unlikely (see chapter 6).

At Holm of Papa Westray (22) several slabs built into the chamber wall have enigmatic pecked markings and one has 'eyebrow and eye' motifs. A slab with linked spirals and concentric circles was recovered from a destroyed site, probably an MH tomb, on Eday (16), but Pickaquoy (40) which produced a slab with pecked concentric circles is now known to be a burnt mound, not a chambered tomb. A most remarkable discovery in 1981 was the two parts of a decorated stone at a greatly disturbed mound, almost certainly an MH cairn, at Pierowall, Westray (Neil 1981). The intricate all-over design of pecked spirals and concentric circles is of superb quality (plate 5.4).

PLATE 5.4. Carved stone found in the wrecked mound at Pierowall, Westray, almost certainly a Maes-Howe-type cairn.

The Maes Howe tombs, as known at present, are concentrated on Mainland where five are strung across the centre of the island. On Sanday there are two certain tombs, and probably another. There is a tomb each on Holm of Papa Westray, Egilsay and Eday, probably a second on Eday, and probably a site on Westray (map 2, p.117). No sites are known in the southern part of Orkney.

CONTENTS AND RITUAL

When the contents of both groups of tombs are considered, and deductions regarding the builders and users of the tombs are attempted, it is clear that interpretation of the data is beset by the problems common to most groups of tombs. One of the most striking features is the variation in the quantity of material recovered, of durable artefacts and of human and animal bone. Lack of finds may be due to earlier interference with the site, or to indifferent standards of excavation. With bones and other organic deposits there is also the problem of decay, and it is likely that at some sites a large quantity of material has totally disappeared. Finally, there is the possibility of the removal of the contents of tombs for cult purposes during the period of their use. On the other hand, the range and detail of information from the two latest excavations, Quanterness (43) and Isbister (25), reflects the achievement of modern recovery techniques, such as wet sieving, and of detailed scientific study of every aspect of the material recovered.

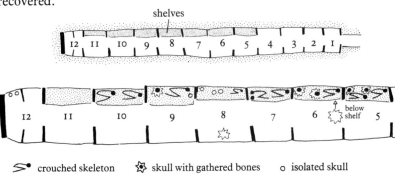

FIGURE 5.3. Diagram of the burials at Midhowe.

As far as the burials go, there is no firm evidence of cremation, for the scorching of bones noted at a number of sites is almost certainly due to the use of fire or embers in the burial rituals in the chambers. All six excavated tripartite chambers, and four stalled chambers, have produced minimal information, whether because of true absence of burials or through other causes is unknown. Bone was reasonably well preserved at Midhowe (37), and the description and photographs make possible a diagram of the burials (figure 5.3, plate 5.5). On the low shelves which had been constructed along more than half of one side of this long chamber were nine articulated crouched skeletons, their backs to the wall, laid on their right or left sides to face the corridor with their heads generally in the corner beside a stall-slab. These burials were more or less complete and undisturbed except that in three cases the skull had been placed upright. In addition, there were remains of fifteen more individuals, incomplete, the bones generally arranged in heaps. Some were represented by 'scanty remains', some by more of the skeleton, but six only by their skulls. Some of the bones were stowed under the shelves. In all there were remains of twenty-five individuals, men, women, adolescents and children. A similar pattern seems to have been found in the smaller chamber at Holm of Papa Westray (21) where at least seven individuals were present, three crouched lying against

PLATE 5.5. The burials at Midhowe, photographed during the excavation in 1932–33.

the wall, two of them with the skulls detached but nearby, also four detached skulls and other miscellaneous bones.

The brief account of the Unstan chamber indicates that there was a considerable amount of bone in all parts of the chamber, the interesting points being several crouched skeletons in the compartment entered by the passage and two in the side cell which was still roofed. But at Burray (7) there were twenty-two or twenty-three skulls and other bones, ten of them in a part of the structure that was probably a side cell (Petrie n.d., 76, 82, 83). The brief description of Korkquoy (34) implies sixty or seventy bodies, some crouched. All that can be said about burials in Bookan-type chambers is that remains of three bodies lay on the benches in the lower chamber at Taversoe Tuick, one of them crouched.

An interest in skulls was obvious at Knowe of Yarso. There were no articulated skeletons, but the bones lay in confusion and almost all were broken. Yet the confusion was not total, for groups of bones in the passage and in the first two compartments were each identified as the scanty remains of an individual, four in total. Thirty adult skulls were counted. All but four were gathered into the end compartment and mainly arranged along the base of the walls, seventeen in its inner section all without lower jaws, eight in the outer section. Other bones were also concentrated in the end compartment, seemingly piled to a depth of 0.5 m; indeed four-fifths of all human bone was in this compartment. A few bones had rested on the shelf which had divided the innermost section horizontally.

Isbister, classified for convenience as a stalled chamber, is an exceptional tomb not least for the extraordinary quantity of human bone it contained and which has been very fully studied (Chesterman 1983; J.W. Hedges 1983a, 20–2, 213–26). Here again there was interest in skulls, many of which were intact and stored in two side cells (the original contents of the third cell are not known), whilst others had been placed against the sides of the chamber along with other bones, some arranged in piles (colour plate 9). Under the shelf in one end-compartment was a jumble of bones but only a few fragments of skulls, and pieces of bone were strewn on the floor throughout the chamber. All the bones were disarticulated, and all the skeletons were incomplete, indeed often only a small part was present. One distinct pile of bones was analysed and found to contain fragments of six individuals ranging in age from adult to infant. J.T.Chesterman estimated that whilst the chamber was in use parts of at least 312 individuals had been deposited there. A quantity of bones which had been placed on the ground before the chamber had been built came from 15 more individuals. Chesterman and Hedges, following the 'excarnation theory' already propounded for the Quanterness material, were of the opinion that very incomplete skeletons had been brought to the chamber which had functioned as an ossuary.

The excavations in the Maes-Howe-type chamber at Quanterness had also produced a large quantity of human bone which was studied in detail by Chesterman and Renfrew and published four years before the Isbister report (Chesterman 1979; Renfrew 1979, 156–72). Twenty per cent of the chamber including five of the six cells was left unexcavated. The total of

12,600 bones or bone fragments were estimated to represent 157 individuals, from which it was calculated that if conditions were constant through the chamber the remains of some 394 individuals had been buried. These figures rest on several assumptions (Renfrew 1979, 158, 162) but if only approximately correct it is evident that the number of bodies involved was as great and probably greater than at Isbister. The age range at both tombs was similar including many infants, children, and adolescents as well as adults, the main difference being that no infants under eight months old were identified at Quanterness whereas newborn babies were present at Isbister. Only slightly more than half the communities survived into adulthood (i.e. reached the age of twenty), few lived beyond thirty and none beyond fifty. The proportion of deaths from infancy to twenty-five years was fairly normal for a neolithic population, but the small number of older individuals, only seven per cent over the age of thirty at Quanterness, is surprising. The bones at Isbister, which were in particularly good condition, showed a high incidence of degenerative disease of the spine, and other abnormalities probably caused by carrying heavy weights, all indications of a very hard life. The ratio of males to females at Quanterness was 32:27, at Isbister 93:38. It appears that all, or nearly all, members of the community were eligible for burial in the tombs.

At Quanterness the floor of the main chamber, cell, and linking short passage was covered by a fairly thin layer of soil with burnt matter, in which were the relatively sparse scattered bones of the first burials. Next, three pits had been dug through this layer and into the bedrock; one pit contained a crouched inhumation with bones from two other bodies, one contained a cist with a crouched inhumation, and the third a cist was not excavated, all three being covered by capstones. Following this the filling of soil, stones and bones continued to accumulate, the stone slabs sometimes laid quite compactly, and the density of the bones increasing nearer the top of the deposit. The upper level was disturbed, and had had a shallow pit dug into it to receive an extended inhumation. The total depth of the bone deposits was about 30 cm. The disarray and fragmentation of the bones suggested that the tomb had been disturbed often during its use, and the sporadic layers of slabs in the bone spreads suggested gradual accumulation, as was indeed confirmed by the radiocarbon dates. The bones lay in total confusion and most were broken into very small pieces (plate 5.6). In a few cases bones of a limb, hand or spine were still in articulation. Most bodies were represented by only a few bones. Observation in the chamber and study of the condition of the bones led the excavator and anatomist to the conclusion that the bones had been in a skeletal, or near-skeletal, condition before they were brought to the chamber, the bodies having been kept elsewhere for a time (perhaps buried in sand as the bones show little gnawing), then exhumed, the missing bones being extracted and the residue of mainly small bones

PLATE 5.6. The main bone spread in one of the cells at Quanterness.

brought to the chamber and scattered on the floor. It was found that some
selection of bones had been in operation, for instance relatively few skulls
were represented and these were broken with most of the pieces missing,
and a relatively large number of neck vertebrae and bones from hands and
feet were present. It is difficult to explain the reasons for this selection. At
Isbister also there was selection of bones, for instance there were few bones
from hands but plenty from feet, relatively few vertebrae and these mostly
from the neck, and as mentioned there were stores of whole skulls.

Although there were similarities between the Quanterness and Isbister
burials, there were also important differences. At the former site the bones
were in very small pieces without any sorting or grouping, and they were

embedded in a continuous filling of earth and stones. In the OC chambers, by contrast, the bones were always accessible until the final sealing of the chamber, and in a number of chambers the bones were sorted or heaped together, and there was especial care for the skulls. At some OC chambers complete crouched bodies were present, sometimes placed on benches which suggests the idea of sleeping on beds. The fact that the benches were original features and occur in all three varieties of OC chamber, taken with the complete burials on benches which presumably belong to the final phase of the use of the tomb (as at Midhowe), suggests that the rites for which the chambers were built did not change radically. The evidence seems to indicate that complete bodies were laid in the tomb, and at a later stage after decomposition the bones were re-arranged and some removed for cult purposes. At Midhowe and Isbister we may be observing the same rite at different stages. Possibly the sparsity of bones in some tombs is complementary to the abundance in other tombs, the bones being moved from one to another: the bones which predated the Isbister chamber must have come from elsewhere.

But the Quanterness rites were not used in other MH tombs. Quoyness (*44*), architecturally so like Quanterness, had a circular shallow cist sunk through the clay floor to the rock below and covered by a capstone, reminiscent of the cists at Quanterness. It contained not a crouched burial, but was full of bones which were fairly intact though lacking skulls. Bones and skulls found in the cells and inner part of the passage represented ten adults of both sexes, and four or five children. At Cuween Hill (*12*) eight skulls and other bones were found. Maes Howe produced only a fragment of skull in one of the cells. In the brief reports of operations at these chambers there is no hint of a bone spread similar to that found at Quanterness, but it may be noted that without wet sieving only a dozen or so bodies would have been reported from that chamber (Renfrew *in litt*).

The situation is further complicated if the seven OC chambers dug by Anderson in east Caithness in 1865–6 are considered (CAT 12, 13, 26, 31, 42, 54, 55), together with two dug earlier by Rhind (CAT 64, 65). There were two distinct layers of burials, of which the upper tallies in general with the Orcadian OC rite, at two chambers there being incomplete articulated skeletons and at two special treatment of the skulls. At other Caithness chambers, as far as can be seen, the rite conforms, and particularly the circumstances found by Corcoran at Tulloch of Assery (CAT 69) where the solid stone benches should be noted. The rite may also be detected as far away as North Uist if the curious 'cist' found in the Unival chamber is in fact a collapsed bench (L. Scott 1948, 12). The lower strata of burials at Anderson's sites were quite different, of compacted earth and stone (the stone sometimes like a partial paving) with bones mixed throughout, the depth being 0.15 to 0.5 m. At three sites it is recorded that the quantity of bone was very great, and mostly it was in small fragments. The descriptions sound like the Quanterness bone layer except that in Caithness fire played a greater part in the rites.

Besides the human bone found in the chambers, the inclusion of animal bone is a widespread practice in Scottish tombs. The relatively moderate amount of such bone at Quanterness was thoroughly studied and it was established that a wide range of animals, many immature or newborn, of birds and of fish, were deliberately introduced at the same time as the burials (Renfrew 1979, 112–49, 153–62). Generally each animal was represented by only one or a few bones, and in the case of a more complete skeleton it could be shown that the remains were widely scattered horizontally in the chamber. Remains of sheep far outnumbered the other species, cattle, red deer, pig, horse, domestic dog, otter and fox, also a very wide range of birds from large to small, and seven species of fish. Studies of the faunal remains from the Isbister chamber showed sheep again to be the main species, with cattle, red deer, otter, dog and pig subsidiary, mainly from immature animals; also thirteen species of fish, two of shellfish, and ten species of birds. Among the last, the most remarkable discovery was at least ten white-tailed eagles, probably introduced as carcases (J. W. Hedges 1983a, 164). A similar range of mammals was identified at some of the stalled cairns though with different species of the larger mammals predominating, as at Knowe of Yarso (32) with parts of thirty-six deer but only a few bones of sheep and one of cattle, or at Midhowe (37) where immature cattle were most numerous. Dog occurred at several sites, as many as twenty-four skulls being found at Cuween Hill (12) and seven at Burray (7). At both OC and MH chambers the animal bones were mixed with the human bones, but they were also in the deliberate filling of the chambers where this existed, notably in quantity at Wideford Hill (54). It is generally assumed that the animal bones represent either the remains of ritual funeral feasts for the living, for there are instances of bones showing cuts or splitting to obtain marrow, or of offerings for the dead as at Isbister where the meat seems to have been introduced as joints but not further butchered. In some cases the extremities of animals, the skulls, antlers and horn-cores, were included; and some of the smaller mammals and birds seem undesirable food. The extraordinary high proportion of white-tailed eagles at Isbister suggests a totemic significance. The dogs may also be a special case, especially where the skulls have been carefully preserved, perhaps explained as the hunters' and herdsmen's best friend.

Like the human and animal bones, the artefacts in the tombs, and particularly the pottery, occur in unpredictable quantity and all stages of incompleteness, and though objects made of perishable materials may have disappeared through decay, this is not the case with stone and pottery. Three OC chambers which have not been disturbed since they were sealed can be compared: Knowe of Yarso (*32*) with at least twenty-nine burials and no neolithic pottery; Unstan (*51*) with an unknown number of burials above five and sherds of at least thirty-five pots; Isbister (*25*) with a very large number of burials and sherds of at least forty-five pots (J.W.Hedges 1983a, 33–43). In the MH group, Wideford Hill with no recognisable burials also had no pottery, Quanterness with a very large number of burials had sherds of at least thirty-four pots. It is generally assumed that the pots came to the tombs as containers, many having been used previously for cooking, and that, having been smashed, sherds were removed haphazardly. At three OC tombs, Calf of Eday, Midhowe and Isbister (*8, 37, 25*), the sherds were in a heap on the floor. At Quanterness the sherds were scattered but their distribution along with other artefacts showed that they had not arrived with the human bones, for no artefacts were found in the cell where the bone was most densely scattered, but the pottery in particular tended to be concentrated in the chamber opposite the end of the passage.

CLOSURE AND SEALING

All chambers, when there were no ceremonies in progress, must have been closed by some temporary but substantial means, and in Orkney this was commonly walling, found in place at one or other end of the passage at five OC sites and one MH site (Henshall 1963, 98, 128). At Maes Howe (*36*) there was the unique arrangement of a block of stone which could be pushed back into a recess in the wall.

A different matter is the deliberate infilling of the chamber and/or passage with earth and rubble as the final ritual act, sealing in the contents of the tomb. At some sites the filling was near total, almost to the roof, at some partial, and at some there was no filling at all. As early as 1849 Petrie found the completely roofed MH chamber at Wideford Hill two-thirds full of debris, above the level of the passage roof. He recognised that the filling, which contained animal bones, must have been deliberately introduced through the roof, and observed a chimney-like construction on the top of the mound which seemed to have been built for this purpose. Petrie was present at the opening of Maes Howe (*36*) and observed that the floor of the passage was covered with rubble to a depth of 0.45 m. The entries into the cells are assumed to have been walled up, using the large blocks of stone found on the chamber floor (Petrie 1861, 355–6). At Quanterness (*43*), on the other hand, it is clear that there was no infilling of either the chamber or passage after the last burials, but at Quoyness and Cuween Hill (*44, 12*) the passage was completely filled. With the OC chambers, because they have lost their roofs, there is often uncertainty in interpreting their fillings, but at three chambers certainly, and probably at others, a deliberate filling was present, containing animal remains, occasional artefacts and human bones. At Isbister (*25*), as at Wideford Hill, the cells were not filled though the chamber was: at other OC chambers there was no filling at all (Henshall 1963, 100–1).

DISCUSSION AND CONCLUSIONS

Two distinct groups of chambered cairn have been described, the origins and development of the OC group being fairly clear, but the origins and development of the MH group still being problematic. The writer's suggestion that they derived from the Irish Boyne tombs was never very satisfactory (Henshall 1972, 268) and even less so now that Maes Howe itself is considered to be late within the group. Yet the discovery of the carved slab at Pierowall with its best parallels amongst the Boyne tombs, points clearly to an Irish element in the culture of the tomb builders. A recent suggestion that the MH tombs developed locally as a variant of the shorter of the stalled chambers such as Unstan in response to a desire for a larger rectangular chamber with a more stable roof (Renfrew 1979, 210, fig.55) seems too simple an explanation. It is true there are some striking architectural similarities between the two types of cairn: the basic rect-angularity of the chambers, the rare occurrence of cells in the one and consistently in the other, the cutting back into the hillside for some chambers in each group, the use of an inner and outer casing for the cairn, the adoption of an excessively long chamber plan with rectangular cairn at one MH site in seeming imitation of the long stalled cairns. Yet the differ-ences are even more impressive: in the MH group the lack of vertical slabs in the chamber, the absence of any shelves or benches, the distinctive way the rectangular corbelling is handled, the high roofing of the cells, the use of lintels set on edge, the occasional appearance of pecked decoration, the retention of round mounds even when the size of the chamber required it to be very large, all contrasting with the practices in the OC group. Alone of all the OC tombs Isbister (25) provides a possible link with the MH group, but the radiocarbon dates show this is a hybrid and not a transitional plan.

The individuality of the two groups of cairns is echoed by the pottery they contained, for, as is well known, the OC chambers have consistently produced round-based bowls, local versions of the widespread early neo-lithic ceramic tradition, whilst only two MH chambers have produced pottery, and this is in the flat-based grooved ware tradition (figure 5.4). If the few sherds of beakers and food vessels are omitted, and the possible grooved ware pots from Bookan (4), the pottery from the OC chambers is of two forms, present in roughly equal numbers. The first is a simple deep bowl which is seldom decorated, but exceptionally at Isbister (25) may bear lugs. The other form is a distinctive wide shallow carinated bowl generally decorated on the collar by incision, stab-and-drag or impressions, and is commonly referred to as an Unstan bowl. Both forms have simple rounded or internally bevelled rims. It is convenient to refer to all this pottery as

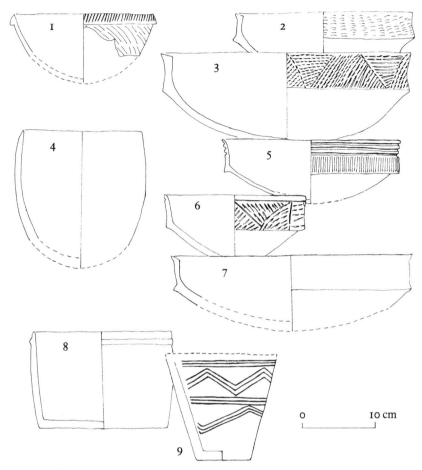

FIGURE 5.4. Pottery from chambered tombs: 1 Sandyhill Smithy;
2 Isbister; 3, 4, 7 Unstan; 5 Midhowe; 6 Taversoe Tuick;
8, 9 Quanterness. Types: 4 simple deep round-based bowl;
2–7 shallow carinated Unstan bowls; 1 open uncarinated bowl;
8–9 grooved ware.

Unstan ware. There is no correlation between either the quantity of pottery, or variations in its form and decoration, and the varieties of OC chambers, except in one respect where three unusual uncarinated open bowls (not to be classed as Unstan ware) were found in three small tripartite chambers, in two cases in or under the clay floor. The implication is that both the tombs (2, 27, 47) and the bowls are of early date. In other cases it has to be realised that most of the pottery is likely to belong to the late use of the chambers, though a few and probably small sherds might relate to earlier phases; the difficulty is to recognise them. Little can be said about the affinities of the plain bowls, but the Unstan bowls, generally considered characteristically Orcadian, are known in small numbers from the Western Isles and north-east Scotland as far south as Deeside (Henshall 1972, 177; Reynolds and Ralston 1979). In Orkney, only one habitation site has produced pottery of this type, Knap of Howar, described in chapter 3.

The grooved ware from Quanterness and the less distinctive sherds from Quoyness (44) (Henshall 1979, 75–9) provide a contrast, for their affinities are with the pottery from the habitation sites discussed in chapter 4 and the ritual monuments discussed in chapter 6. The other artefacts from Quanterness fit into this context, and certainly the bone pin and strange stone objects from Quoyness have good parallels at Skara Brae (Henshall 1979, 79–83; 1963, 130). A further link between the tombs and Skara Brae is provided by the designs pecked on stones of three tombs, and the designs on some stones and some sherds at the habitation site.

In the OC chambers, besides the sherds, there was an undiagnostic selection of flints, bone pins, and stone axeheads; also there were some leaf-shaped arrowheads such as might be expected to accompany round-based bowls. A few diverse but interesting objects are likely to have come from a grooved ware source: ground flint knives, a 'fabricator', a macehead, roughly chipped stone objects, bone points, a perforated ox phalange, and bone beads. In most cases the findspots have not been precisely recorded, but twice these objects appear to have been associated with the burials, and at least once, at Isbister, they were in the deliberate filling of the chamber. Immediately outside the cairn at this last site was a cache of objects, some with grooved ware affinities. It is clear that the makers of grooved ware had an interest in OC tombs, sometimes at a late stage in their use or during the sealing of the chamber, or even later.

Following his hypothesis that the MH chambers evolved from OC chambers, Renfrew tentatively suggested that the two pottery styles which correspond with these tomb groups may be explained in the same way, that grooved ware evolved in Orkney from Unstan pottery (1979, 205–8). There seem to be three major difficulties: the great differences in form and decorative techniques, the long chronological overlap of the two styles, and the necessity to account for the grooved ware in the rest of Britain. Regarding the first, recent work on the pottery from Skara Brae and Rinyo has shown that links between the two styles exist, for D. V. Clarke claims that round-based bowls form a small component of the Orcadian grooved ware assemblage at both Skara Brae and Rinyo, and at the latter site the corky fabric familiar from the OC tomb assemblage was used for a flat base (Clarke 1983, 49, 51). Conversely, the pottery from Knap of Howar includes a few sherds with features of grooved ware derivation. Clarke has also shown that the sequence of Unstan ware preceding grooved ware, long thought to have been established at Rinyo, has no firm basis. The relationship of the two pottery styles is not as clear cut as once it seemed, but on the other hand no substantial evidence for a transition of one to the other can be cited. It seems rather that the two styles ran parallel for several centuries, with some contact between them.

A series of radiocarbon dates is now available for neolithic Orkney (appendix), of which those from Quanterness and Isbister (the latter not available to Renfrew for his recent assessment) alone relate to the foundation of tombs (Renfrew 1979, 200–12; J.W. Hedges 1983a, 61–71, 262–66). Although surprisingly early dates for the building of these two tombs are indicated, it must be admitted that, due to the wide latitude involved in one standard deviation and certain inconsistencies in relating some dates to the stratigraphy, the dates can be applied only in very approximate terms. The probability is that the Isbister chamber was built about 3150 BC and was probably not sealed until about 2400 BC giving a period of use of 800 or so years. The dates from Quanterness indicate that it was probably built before Isbister, for the earliest level is dated about 3400 BC, and the main bone deposits span the period about 3000–2400. Satisfactorily, bones from the Quoyness chamber have been dated to about the middle of this period. It is unfortunate that the early foundation date for Quanterness rests on a single determination, perhaps supported by one early date from the chamber deposits, for if correct they confirm that Isbister could not be a link between the OC and MH chamber designs. The dates, spanning the first four centuries or so of the third millennium, which were obtained from animal bone from three stalled cairns on Rousay, do not relate to their foundation, but are likely to belong to the later phases of the use of the chamber or possibly even to the sealing. All that can be said is that a proportion of the tripartite and smaller stalled chambers are likely to be earlier, indeed probably considerably earlier, than Isbister. This is supported to some extent by the radiocarbon dates from The Ord (SUT 49), an OC chamber in Sutherland which is not typologically early but which was in use more than two centuries before Isbister (Sharples 1981, 53). So a date in the early centuries of the fourth millennium seems likely for the earliest Orcadian OC tombs.

The dating of the MH tombs is even less precise. The only chamber directly dated, Quanterness, is unlikely to be amongst the earliest. Wideford Hill (54) which is geographically close and both smaller and simpler in design, may be expected to be earlier. Typologically Vinquoy Hill (53) and Cuween Hill (12) are close to Wideford Hill. Although Maes Howe (36) is thought to be the latest because of its size and sophistication, and the radiocarbon dates from the bottom of the ditch (averaging about 2700 BC) appear to confirm this, yet in design it is nearer to the simpler tombs; also the relationship of the dated material to the tomb, and the true date of the two radiocarbon assays, are uncertain (Renfrew 1979, 36–7, 206).

The pottery found in the tombs presumably mainly dates from the later phases of the use of the tombs. The Unstan pottery from Isbister may date about 3000 BC, the end of the main period of use of the chamber for burials, or possibly later, up to the time it was sealed; the bulk of the pottery from Quanterness can be no more accurately dated than to the first half of the third millennium. The chronological span of Quanterness and Isbister is roughly the same as Skara Brae and all but the earliest centuries of Knap of Howar. The date of the last burial at Quanterness, about 2400 BC, and the sealing of Isbister at about the same time, have been noted. Late closing dates for chambers are indicated at Calf of Eday (8), Knowe of Yarso (32) and Unstan (51), where sherds of beaker and food vessel, and barbed and tanged arrowheads, were found. At Knowe of Yarso the sherds were certainly in the filling (Callander and Grant 1935, 334), and possibly this was the case at the other sites also.

On the present evidence from the Orcadian chambered cairns it seems necessary to accept that through the later fourth and the first half of the third millennium there were two distinct cultural groups occupying Orkney, however difficult it may be to envisage this in operation in such a restricted area. They could not each live in isolation, and some evidence of the give-and-take has been noted, either the acquisition of objects by exchange or otherwise, possibly the adoption of new building techniques, or even perhaps more fundamental changes in attitudes and beliefs. The distribution of the sites attributable to the two cultures emphasises the complexity of the situation (maps 1, 2), with MH tombs dominant on Mainland and Sanday, OC tombs dominant on Rousay, north Mainland, and the southern islands, and a mixture on Eday, Westray and Holm of Papa Westray. It is also surprising to find the habitation site of Rinyo on the OC-dominated island of Rousay, and the same situation obtained on Westray until the recent discoveries at Pierowall. But the distribution map compresses into one picture events spanning a millennium or so, with no allowance for shifts of population or political dominance.

Two burial rites have been detected in northern Scotland, exemplified by Quanterness and Midhowe-Yarso, as suggested above. It may be assumed that the two designs of tombs on Orkney reflect differences in their use and perhaps their symbolism. The construction of benches seems appropriate for crouched inhumations of the Midhowe rite. The nineteenth-century excavations in east Caithness revealed the Quanterness rite below the Midhowe rite, with an indication at one chamber of yet earlier inhumations. There is no helpful information regarding artefacts from five of the nine tombs and most of the finds from the other four are missing. It may be significant that, besides round-based pottery, objects with grooved ware associations have been found at three chambers, and in one case (CAT 13) there is the rare record that one object (a polished knife) was in the lower stratum. These observations in Caithness seem to indicate interaction between the OC group and representatives (as it were) of a grooved ware/Quanterness rite in an area were MH tombs were not built, with the OC group taking over again in the final phase. The curious chamber at Knowe of Lairo (28) may reflect such changes structurally, in the opposite direction, for the chamber in the OC tradition was lined with secondary walling having niches containing parts of burials, reminiscent of a MH tomb.

These observations regarding the interaction detectable between the OC/Unstan ware and the MH/grooved ware groups still leaves the origin of the latter uncertain, for nowhere else in Britain are the makers of grooved ware involved in building chambered cairns. The undoubted connection with the Boyne tombs indicated by the carvings and perfectly acceptable on chronological grounds, cannot be claimed as particularly powerful as far as the structures go, for the building techniques are purely Orcadian and the design of the tombs have no more than a remote resemblance to Irish passage-graves; nor do the artefacts have much in common with their Irish counterparts. It seems probable that the MH tombs are a largely local development. Investigation of the chamber of the Pierowall site would be the most helpful contribution to assessing the contribution from the Boyne.

The importance of chambered cairns to the communities who built them is self-evident when the time, organisation and the economic surplus needed for their construction are considered. The labour estimate for Quanterness is a minimum of 10,000 man hours, and, because of the distance very large stones had to be brought, the estimate for Maes Howe is of the order of 100,000 man hours (Renfrew 1979, 212–4). This continued, and perhaps changing importance of the tombs is revealed by the long time span through which they were in use, and the embellishment of the exterior of a few with long cairns and horned forecourts. It is quite clear that they became much more than just suitable receptacles for the remains of the dead.

Finally, to pass from matters of mystery to matters of imagination, another possible aspect of the significance of the tombs was explored by Lynch (1973) with regard to Irish passage-graves and their possible use as oracles. Her starting point was the 'roof-box' at New Grange which gave access to the passage through a gap in the roof, the gap being too small to allow physical entry. A similar but less elaborate arrangement seems to have existed at some other Irish cairns. This access may have been used for offerings of a perishable kind, but she suggests the design was for

> 'some form of intangible contact with the spirits of the dead inside the chamber . . . that this narrow slot in a complex hollow stone structure could have been used as some form of oracle. People might seek the advice of their ancestors by asking their questions through the slot and their distorted words would come back to them as an answer, of which they could make what they liked.' (Lynch 1973, 152)

We may just consider whether something similar may have been done in Orkney, for instance at Maes Howe where the block designed to close the passage left an 0.5 m gap below the roof, which at such a sophisticated structure was likely to be a deliberate feature. Again, at Wideford Hill (*54*), the chimney-like opening into the chamber roof has been mentioned already: although it was evidently used to infill the chamber, it is tempting to think it had an earlier purpose and was part of the original design of the chamber.

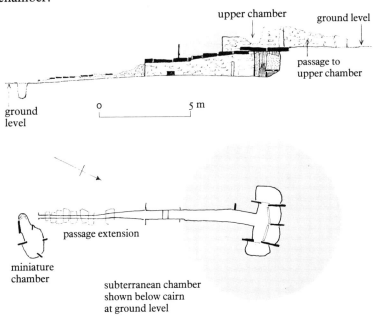

FIGURE 5.5. Simplified plan and section of Taversoe Tuick, a two-storey cairn of the Orkney–Cromarty group.

There are curious arrangements outside the lower chamber at Taversoe Tuick (*49*) (figure 5.5). The lintelled passage projects outwards beyond the revetment of the cairn through a low platform of slabs, the entrance being 1.6 m forward of the cairn edge. Beyond this point the passage walls continue for another 5.8 m, gradually narrowing to only 0.06 m apart at the outer end, with the height of the lintels diminishing from 0.22 to 0.05 m above the floor. The outer end of the passage extension ends at the entry into a subterranean miniature chamber. The entry is a vertical drop, leading to a chamber only 1.5 m across, roofed at a height of 0.9 m, lined with fine masonry, with projecting slabs echoing the Bookan plan. The effect is a half-scale model of a burial chamber. It was intact when found, and contained three complete bowls. Perhaps it was intended for offerings, but it would be possible to crouch in it and speak into the tiny opening of the passage extension. However it was used, it seems obvious the intention was communication with the lower burial chamber, and the miniature chamber was sited in relationship with its outer end. A passage extension once existed at Calf of Eday (9) also, and it could well be that other examples await discovery.

The classification of Orcadian chambered cairns
according to chamber plans (maps 1 and 2)

ORKNEY–CROMARTY GROUP
Tripartite chambers: ORK 1, 2, 5, 6, 11, 23, 26, 27, 28, 42, 47, 56, 62, 67, 70
Stalled chambers: ORK 1, 3, 8, 17, 19, 21, 25, 29, 30, 31, 32, 33, 37, 41, 50, 51, 68, 73
Chambers either tripartite or stalled: ORK 7, 14, 15, 18, 24, 35, 52, 57, 59, 60, 61, 63, 69, 74, 76
Bookan chambers: ORK 4, 8, 9, 10, 13, 23, 49
Sites probably but not certainly Orkney–Cromarty cairns: ORK 34, 39, 46, 58, 64, 65, 78, 79

MAES HOWE GROUP
Certain: ORK 12, 22, 36, 38, 43, 44, 53, 54, 66, 71
Probable: ORK 16, 72, 77

LONG CAIRNS (mapped according to chamber type)
ORK 14, 18, 28, 34, ?41, ?62, 74

Two sites listed in Henshall 1963 are not now considered to be chambered cairns: ORK 40, see comment p.99; ORK 45 is a burnt mound. Four other sites, ORK 20, 48, 55, 75, are unclassifiable and have been omitted from the discussion and the maps.
Sites listed here as ORK 58–79 are additions to the list in Henshall 1963 and 1972 and will be published in Davidson and Henshall *An Inventory of the Chambered Cairns of Orkney* (forthcoming). ORK 58, 59, 61, 62, 64, 67, 69, 70, 75, 77, 78, 79 are included in RCAMS 1946 on the following pages, the inventory number in brackets: 204 (564), 204 (564), 330 (952), 279 (797), 190 (546), 287 (824), 334 (984), 287–8 (827), 332 (967), 172–3 (474), 351–2 (1038), 259 (687). ORK 60, 63, 68, 71, 76 were found by the Archaeology Division, Ordnance Survey, their records are now in the National Monuments Record for Scotland. For the remaining sites the references are: ORK 65, *New Statistical Account 15*, (1845) 54; 66, Bell and Haigh 1981; 72, Neil 1981; 73, Fraser 1980b, 25; 74, Davidson and Henshall 1982.

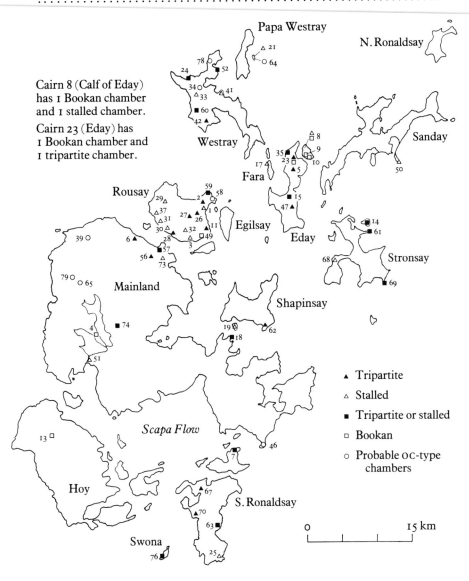

MAP 1. Distribution of cairns with chambers of Orkney–Cromarty type.

MAP 2. Distribution of cairns of Maes Howe type.

6 Graham Ritchie **Ritual Monuments**

The largest of Orkney's inland lochs, the Loch of Harray and the Loch of Stenness meet only at the reedy narrows now spanned by the Bridge of Brodgar and they are separated for the most part by two tongues of land; by far the larger is the NW ridge on which there are the impressive earthworks of the Ring of Bookan (ORK 45), the smaller cairn of Bookan (ORK 4) and the henge monument and stone circle known as the Ring of Brodgar, as well as several groups of burial mounds and standing stones. The smaller and lower promontory to the SE is dominated by the henge monument and stone circle known as the Stones of Stenness, but there are also several other standing stones, and the site of the famous Stone of Odin destroyed in 1814. The chambered tomb of Maes Howe (ORK 36) is some 1.2 km to the E. The superb situation of the Ring of Brodgar, the impressive standing stones both here and at the Stones of Stenness, and the folklore that has accumulated around these sites, have ensured that they have been visited and described by all visitors to Orkney with antiquarian interests since the mid-eighteenth century. Indeed the drawings of Brodgar and Stenness by Richard Pococke, Bishop of Ossory, in 1760 and by the illustrators accompanying Sir Joseph Banks in 1772 are among the earliest representations of northern prehistoric antiquities (Lysaght 1974; plates 6.2, 6.2). George Low, minister of the parish of Birsay and Harray, writing in the 1770s also described and illustrated the stones, although his own account was not published until 1879. The stone circles have retained their fascination for visitors; Sir Walter Scott, for example, used the Stones of Stenness as the location for the climax of his novel *The Pirate*, which was published in 1821. More recently Professor A. Thom has suggested that the Ring of Brodgar

PLATE 6.1. The Stones of Stenness, with the Stone of Odin, the
Watch Stone and, in the background, the Ring of Brodgar:
watercolour by John Cleveley, 1772. (British Library, London,
Add. Ms 15511, f.10.)

and the complex of cairns round it form a lunar observatory.

The Stones of Stenness and the Ring of Brodgar are the most northerly
examples of one of the most enigmatic classes of prehistoric sites – 'henge
monuments'; in general these are circular or oval earthworks comprising a
ditch and a bank, with the latter normally to the outside and composed of
material dug from the ditch. The enclosing earthworks are broken by one or
more entrances to allow access to the central area, and the number of
entrances involved has been used to divide the sites into two main classes:
Class I henges have one entrance and Class II have two or more. Their
distribution is widespread from Cornwall to Orkney, with concentrations in
Wessex and Yorkshire, but such sites are not known on the continent, and
thus represent a peculiarly British response within the social and religious
framework of the third millennium BC (Wainwright 1969). Stone circles are
present in some cases within henge monuments (most notably at Stonehenge, which provides the name for the class of a whole), but they are
exceptional, and the presence of rings of upright timbers for example can
only be demonstrated by excavation (colour plate 10).

Although several campaigns of excavation have been undertaken on
the henge monuments of Britain (particularly at Durrington Walls, Wilt-
shire, at Mount Pleasant, Dorset, at Balfarg, Fife, and at Strathallan,

PLATE 6.2. The Ring of Brodgar: pen and ink wash by Richard
Pococke, 1760. (British Library, London, Add. Ms 14257, f.77v.)

Perthshire) our knowledge of the purpose of such sites is still scanty. As will
be seen later, we have rather fuller information about the chronological
range for their use, while the presence of grooved ware at sites both in the
north and in the south has increased interest in the Orcadian henges because
of their proximity to Skara Brae. The excavations at the Stones of Stenness
and at the Ring of Brodgar in 1973 and 1974 were thus designed to set the
Orcadian henges both within a local framework and within a much wider
context.

In their original form the Stones of Stenness seem to have been a classic
Class I henge with the addition of a central stone circle (Ritchie 1976); the
ditch and bank are approximately circular on plan, measuring about 70 m
overall and enclosing an internal area some 44 m in diameter with the single
entrance to the N. Natural erosion and subsequent ploughing have levelled

PLATE 6.3. The Stones of Stenness: ditch terminal cut into
natural bedrock. (Crown copyright: Royal Commission
on Ancient Monuments, Scotland.)

the bank and all but filled the ditch, but the evidence of early plans and
illustrations, air photographs, geophysical survey and limited excavation
combine to confirm this interpretation. The suggestion that the causeway to
the N is the only one is, however, more tentative; no excavation has been
undertaken in the opposing quadrant, but, on the other hand, there is
nothing in the other forms of evidence mentioned above that would make
the presence of an S causeway likely. The bank survived only as a low clayey
band some 6.5 m wide and 0.15 m in thickness, but the ditch was found to
have been at least 7 m across and over 2 m deep the lowest metre or so cut
into the solid bedrock (plate 6.3). Within these features there was a ring of
twelve standing stones laid out on the perimeter of a circle with a diameter of
about 30 m. Four stones stand today, but two of these were re-erected in
1906–7; the stumps of four others are known, the stone holes of a further
three were recovered in the course of excavation and only the position of the
twelfth remains uncertain. Economy of effort suggests that it is likely that
the stones were set up before the ditch and bank were completed, for the

PLATE 6.4. The Stones of Stenness: central stone setting. (Crown copyright: Royal Commission on Ancient Monuments, Scotland.)

existence of the encircling works would have made the manoeuvring and raising of the stones more difficult. At the centre of the site, excavation revealed a setting of four stones set flush with the ground and enclosing an area measuring about 2.1 m by 1.9 m (plate 6.4). From this setting and running in a line towards the entrance causeway in the N, there were the traces first of a pair of standing stones, although only the stone holes and packing remained, secondly the bedding trench of what may have been a small timber construction, and finally another setting of upright stones. This group of uprights was 'restored' in 1907, and was, with the addition of a fourth stone, made into a 'dolmen' or table tomb; it must be stressed that there is no archaeological evidence for such a construction being an original feature, and the additional stone has now been removed.

The finds recovered during the excavations of 1973–4 include a small amount of pottery which may be compared with that from several sites mentioned in earlier chapters: e.g. Skara Brae, Rinyo and Quanterness. Almost a quarter of a grooved ware vessel was found just above the thin initial silt at the bottom of the ditch in the W terminal of the rock cut ditch. Further sherds of grooved ware were found in the complex of deposits, including cremated bone, within the central setting.

Three radiocarbon dates provide further chronological indication of the use of the site. Determinations of 2356 bc ± 65 (SRR-350), from animal

PLATE 6.5. The Stones of Stenness: general view. (Crown copyright:
Royal Commission on Ancient Monuments, Scotland.)

bones at the bottom of the rock-cut ditch, and 2238 bc ± 70 (SRR-351), from
wood charcoal associated with grooved ware sherds in the central setting,
indicate that activity on the site was under way by the early third millennium BC. A date of 1730 bc ± 270 (SRR-592) was obtained from a small
quantity of decomposed wood from what may have been a small timber
structure. Activity on the site in the mid first millennium AD has also been
discovered, for a pit containing carbonised cereal remains and charcoal gave
a date of AD 519 ± 150 (SRR-352) – a reminder of the wonder that the stones
would continue to generate.

It must be remembered that the excavations at Stenness were on a very
small scale and that other features may exist in the interior, though none was
indicated on the geophysical survey (plate 6.5).

At the Ring of Brodgar, 1.5 km to the NW, excavation has been confined to three trenches, two across the henge ditch and one in an attempt to identify the remains of an outer bank; this site has not suffered the vicissitudes of destruction and reconstruction of its sister circle, and the pattern of its layout is reasonably clear. There were originally sixty stones in the circle, which has a diameter of 103.7 m, and these were surrounded by a rock-cut ditch with entrance causeways in the NW and SE quadrants to form a Class II henge; the evidence for the existence of an outer bank is at best inconclusive (Renfrew 1979, 41–3). It may be that the circle was set out using the standard unit of length identified by Alexander Thom as the megalithic yard of 0.829 m and the circle thus has a diameter of 125 megalithic yards. A geophysical survey of buried features in the interior of the circle did not suggest the presence of any pattern of features, although in the absence of excavation it is impossible to be certain. The ditch was originally some 10 m across and as much as 3.4 m in depth (plate 6.6). Radiocarbon determinations from organic mud in the silted ditch at depths of 0.7 m and 0.6 m below the surface respectively provided dates of 255 bc ± 60 and 375 bc ± 45 (SRR-502 and 503). These do little more than indicate that the ditch would still have been a conspicuous feature by the second half of the first millennium BC. The silting of the ditch does not provide helpful evidence of the presence or not of an outer bank; at both Brodgar and Stenness there is a layer including flagstones and boulders within the earliest levels of the ditch fill, but in both cases such a layer is on the inside of the ditch and must represent material introduced from that side rather than slumped bank material (Ritchie 1976, 11, fig.3; Renfrew 1979, 41, fig.15, layer 16). The similarity of the residual remains of the outer bank at Stenness (a clayey band representing material washed down through what must have been a very stony bank) with the dense hump of clayey soil in the appropriate position at Brodgar (Renfrew 1979, 41, fig.15, layer 3) suggests that there was indeed an outer bank at the latter.

The vessel from the west ditch terminal at Stenness is closely comparable to a pot from the chambered tomb of Quanterness (Renfrew 1979, 79, vessel 2); the triple-line incised slack lozenges or triangles and a series of incised lines below the rim show that the vessels belong to a group which includes pottery from Knappers, Dunbartonshire (Mackay 1950; Ritchie and Adamson 1981, 187, vessel 6), Tentsmuir, Fife (Longworth et al. 1967, 75, 90–1) and Balfarg, Fife (Mercer 1981, fig.43, no.8) but here the decoration is confined to the incised lines below the rim. The comparable radiocarbon dates from Stenness, Quanterness and Balfarg (and the pottery here belongs to a period just predating the earliest, and dated, structures) and the similar pottery styles, may suggest wide-ranging contacts outside Orkney – a possibility that has important implications when we come to consider the origins of the henge monument tradition in Orkney.

PLATE 6.6. The Ring of Brodgar: section across the rock-cut ditch.
(Photo Nick Bradford, courtesy Professor A. C. Renfrew.)

It is possible that deposits within the chambered cairn of Bookan (ORK 4) excavated in 1861, may also have been associated with grooved ware; although the pottery is now lost, the small finds within the tomb are quite clearly described (George Petrie quoted by Henshall 1963, 186). 'At the N end of the central chamber a rude flint lance head was found, with fragments of two rudely fashioned fire-baked clay cups or small vessels on its W side, and also fragments of one or more of the same kind of cups on its E side. A rudely formed raised moulding in a waved form encircled the upper part of one or more of the cups.' Whether or not this is indeed a description of grooved ware, the fact that Bookan is the only example of this class of cairn on Mainland serves to underline the rather special nature of the Stenness-Brodgar area.

The interpretation of the Ring of Bookan, the final site of this group lying 1.6 km NW of the Ring of Brodgar, is not at all certain; what survives at present is a broad flat-bottomed ditch, rock-cut in part, enclosing a flat area measuring about 44.5 m by 38 m (RCAMS 1946, ii, 270, no.732). The ditch itself is about 13.5 m across and at least 2 m in depth. The width of the ditch is certainly greater than the two henge monuments already discussed, and its depth, though less than that of the Ring of Brodgar, is comparable to the Stones of Stenness. There is, however, no sign of a causeway across the ditch, although the E side has been obscured by ploughing, nor is there any trace of an outer bank, but the cultivated ground now comes up to the edge of the ditch. Placed eccentrically within the ditch there is an irregular mound and a number of stones, one of which appears to be earth-fast, but it is not altogether clear whether or not these are the remains of a cairn. Certainly on the surviving evidence the interpretation of the site as a Maes-Howe-type tomb finds less favour with the writer than that as a henge monument with a series of internal stone settings or a cairn. The internal area of the Ring of Bookan is closer to that of the Stones of Stenness (44 m in diameter) than that of Maes Howe (76 m by 60 m); clearly only excavation can solve the problem.

INTERPRETATION

One of the most comprehensive interpretations of megalithic remains is the result of the pioneering research of Professor Alexander Thom following his detailed fieldwork and observation in Scotland, Wessex and Brittany; in a series of books and articles Thom has suggested the use of a standardised unit of length in the construction of many megalithic sites, as well as a knowledge of complex geometry in their layout. He has also postulated that the erection and positioning of standing stones and cairns was designed to allow sophisticated observations of the major celestial bodies including the prediction of eclipses (summarised in Heggie 1981). In 1973 Professor Thom and Dr A.S. Thom suggested that the Ring of Brodgar and the burial mounds around it had served as the backsights from which lunar observations could be made, and in 1978 a fourth sight line was put forward (Thom and Thom 1973; 1975; 1978, 122–37). Indeed they suggest that the position of the Ring of Brodgar and the surrounding mounds was determined by the demands of such observations. The four foresights are the high cliffs at Hellia on Hoy, a notch on Mid Hill, two slopes on Kame of Corrigal and a dip on Ravie Hill. Between about 1600 BC and 1400 BC particular phases of the moon's cycle could be detected when it was in such positions, and the burial mounds are used to line up with the distant horizon in order to make the required observation.

It is clear that the evidence of archaeology cannot be used to disprove the possible use of prehistoric monuments in this way; the sight lines as drawn out by Professor Thom and Dr Thom could conceivably have been designed in the way that they envisage. But we lack information about the dates of the construction of the henge monument and stone circle and of the burial mounds. From the evidence of other sites, it seems likely that the Ring of Brodgar itself was constructed within the third millennium BC in terms of calendar years, but the surrounding mounds may well belong to the period postulated by the Thoms.

In other words one's reaction to such interpretation depends on a personal assessment of the mass of statistical evidence in the light of an equally personal evaluation of the archaeological information about the society of the time. The writer's view is that the engineering skills involved in the quarrying and layout of the circles mean that a common unit of length as described earlier is not unlikely, but that the sophistication of astronomical observation required within the contemporary society as we understand it, albeit very imperfectly, makes the detailed niceties of such interpretations most improbable (Heggie 1981). This is not to deny the likely importance of the sun and the moon in the religious calendar of prehistoric Orkney; the illumination of the rear wall of the chamber of Maes Howe (ORK 36) by the setting midwinter sun is a vivid reminder of the way that prehistoric sites may have been constructed with astronomical happenings in mind (e.g. Brown 1975, 95–6). Maes Howe appears to be the only tomb of its type to be so oriented (Henshall 1963, 130); perhaps the unique arrangement at the entrance to the tomb, where a stone found originally in the passage neatly fits a recess on the N side, could be a blocking stone that could readily have been moved out of position and into the recess when required (Henshall 1963, 220). A further midwinter orientation, in this case of sun rise, has been observed at Newgrange, Co. Meath, where the sun shines through the 'roof-box' over the entrance to the tomb, a sort of dormer window, and along the passage to the central chamber. At Newgrange as the sunlight increased 'various details of the side and end chambers could be seen clearly in the light reflected from the floor' (O'Kelly 1973, 142). The observation of the effects of what must be both deliberate orientation and carefully contrived constructional techniques underline the appreciation of such celestial events by prehistoric man.

The radiocarbon dates and the discovery of grooved ware from the Stones of Stenness mean that the use of the henge monument should not be isolated from any consideration of tombs of Maes Howe type and of the settlements of Skara Brae or Rinyo (D. Fraser 1980a, 6). Renfrew has attempted the most detailed assessment of Orcadian society at this time; he sees Maes Howe, the Stones of Stenness and the Ring of Brodgar as the 'three major works of the later neolithic period, reflecting a labour investment of an order of magnitude larger than that embodied in the other neolithic cairns' (1979, 218). Renfrew envisages a shift in the organisation of Orcadian way of life at this time from one based on an egalitarian society, to which belong the vast majority of chambered tombs and presumably the settlement site of Knap of Howar, to a society based on centralised chiefdoms; to this period may be attributed the henge monuments discussed above and the construction of Maes Howe. This attractive and persuasively argued view-point takes on a particular importance because of the similarity of the sequence of events to that postulated for Wessex at broadly the same period (Renfrew 1983). Clearly the three major monuments under discussion, Maes Howe, the Stones of Stenness and the Ring of Brodgar may all have been constructed rather later than the majority of the Orcadian chambered tombs; the existence of the two main categories of tomb outlined earlier by Miss Henshall means, however, that even at an earlier date it might be possible to envisage the sort of larger social grouping that Renfrew sees as being necessary for the organisation of the building of the three central sites.

Approaches to the interpretation of archaeological evidence differ, one school may see the articulation of social frameworks from the mute testimony of fieldwork and excavation, against which an ever increasing body of archaeological data may be gauged and new frameworks created, as providing the one way forward; thus only the demolition of one hypothesis and the formation of another are permissible intellectual attitudes in such archaeological endeavour. Another approach is to admit that the nature of the evidence is such that wide-ranging theorising is not possible nor indeed constructive; thus the inability to build a theoretical edifice amounts to a positive statement that there may be so many imponderables that planning permission should not be sought. This may be a more constructive, and certainly tactful, approach than to attempt to pick out the foundation stones of such a rickety fabrication as that put forward by Hodder for example (1982, 218–28). Thus, although the construction of henge monuments may indeed indicate a change in the social organisation in Orkney, the contemporary use of chambered tombs such as Quanterness may equally suggest a continuing pattern in burial rituals. There are still remarkably few interlocking pieces of our jigsaw puzzle. In his discussion of the Later Neolithic in Orkney based on the excavations at Rinyo, D. V. Clarke has described the current state of knowledge as 'a beginning in understanding the complexities' of the period (1983, 56). Thus to think of the evidence of pottery, tomb

PLATE 6.7. The Ring of Brodgar: general view.

typology and settlement forms as strands within what may well be a complex society, or succeeding, or parallel societies may well not be far from the mark. Perhaps the work-effort involved in the construction of monuments should not be given more weight in any interpretation of society than the archaeological evidence that implies the contemporary use of the Quanterness and Stenness sites by people using similar pottery. It is wrong to think that the construction of the two henge monuments 'complicates the picture' (Renfrew 1979, 219); the contemporary use of Quanterness and Stenness merely makes it possible to suggest different pictures. In other words the Stones of Stenness must be drawn into 'the pattern of simultaneously functioning sites' outlined by Renfrew (1979, 220), perhaps with a key central location.

Perhaps it is worth re-stating the major questions to which there are as yet no adequate answers – and may well never be! We do not understand the mechanisms by which henge monuments were introduced to Orkney; the absence of any tradition of ditch-digging, partly because of the shallow depth of easily-workable material (and thus the necessity for cutting into the underlying rock), means that the concept of such monuments is indeed likely to have come from the south (plate 6.7; colour plate 11). In his discussion of the monument at Balfarg, Fife, Mercer has, however, raised a chronological problem (1981, 166): the sites at Balfarg and Stenness appear to be earlier in date than those farther south. They are certainly earlier than the large late neolithic enclosures on which recent excavation resources have been concentrated (Durrington Walls, Marden and Mount Pleasant), but early dates have been obtained from henge monuments at Arminghall (2490 bc ± 50; BM-129), Barford (2416 bc ± 64; Birm-7) and Llandegai (2790 bc ± 150; NPL-220) and it may be that imbalance in our knowledge of their date results from excavation preferences. However, the early date for henge monuments, stone circles and indeed grooved ware in North Britain seems assured (Burgess 1980, 41, 48, 339), but what this means in our understanding of Orcadian society is still far from clear. It may well be that henges are a consistent feature of the British Neolithic from at least 3000 BC and that our general picture is unclear because of the small number of radiocarbon windows open to us. Associated with the introduction of the henge-monument tradition from the south is the use of what may just possibly have been a unit of length standard throughout Britain (Thom and Thom 1973; Renfrew 1979, 211). On the other hand, more recent analysis by Heggie has 'found little evidence for a *highly accurate* unit' and 'little justification for the claim that a *highly accurate* unit was in use throughout the area' (1981, 58). Thom's evidence for the possible use of the 'megalithic yard' at Brodgar still seems to this writer at least to be impressive.

Nor do we understand the position of grooved ware pottery, either as far as its floruit in Orkney is concerned, its relationship to Unstan ware in Orkney, or the nature of the relationship between Orkney grooved ware and that from the south. It is worth considering whether the appearance in Orkney of grooved ware need be related at all to the construction there of henge monuments. It is likely, however, that the grooved ware from the settlement sites will provide a more reliable framework for such discussion than will the small number of sherds from ritual or funerary contexts, which may perhaps have been specially selected for such use from a wider ceramic range.

In discussing the Orcadian stone circles in 1814, Sir Walter Scott remarked that the 'idea that such circles were exclusively Druidical is now justly exploded'; in this chapter we have been at pains not to imply that we know more than we do.

7 Sandra Øvrevik **The Second Millennium BC and After**

Social organisation in the Orkney islands in the second millennium and later seems gradually to have evolved along locally autonomous lines, moving away from the centralised organisation which is suggested by the monuments of the Late Neolithic. The burnt mound communities and the barrow cemeteries suggest a dispersed pattern of settlement, with the people represented by these sites having a non-specialist economy based on a combination of hunting, fishing and agricultural activities, perhaps on a semi-nomadic or seasonal transhumance pattern, their few hut circle sites perhaps representing another aspect of this way of life. Evidence of trade is scant, suggesting insular development but not poverty. The artefactual record points to the gradual isolation of the islands. There are few indications of durable wealth, and little evidence of artistic activity. The impression received from the evidence is that the islanders lived in small self-sufficient communities producing little in the way of a surplus to enable the development of a leisured class. Climatic deterioration, and the overuse of the soil in the Late Neolithic, were probably the main reasons for this apparent decline (figure 7.1).

FUNERARY EVIDENCE

Most of our knowledge of Bronze Age society in general comes from studying the funerary monuments which offer most of the site evidence over much of the British Isles. In Orkney, there are over 250 barrows and cairns, alone or in groups (figure 7.2), as well as record of nearly 100 short cists (1946; Ordnance Survey Record Cards), yet our knowledge remains rather patchy. Although a large number of Orcadian barrows or cairns have been

131

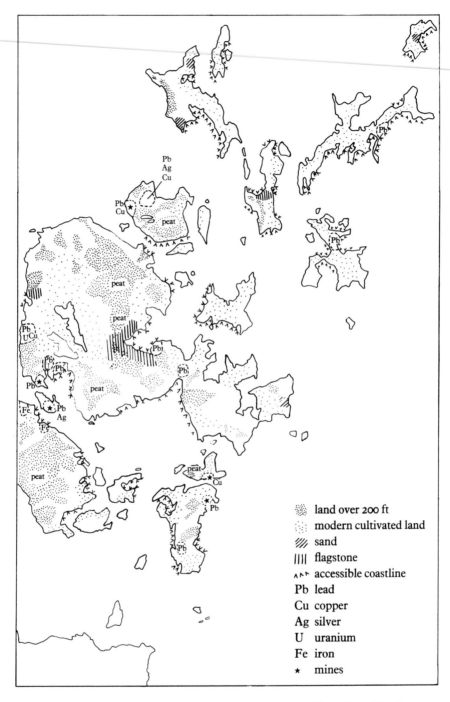

FIGURE 7.1. Distribution of the main resources of the Orkney Islands.

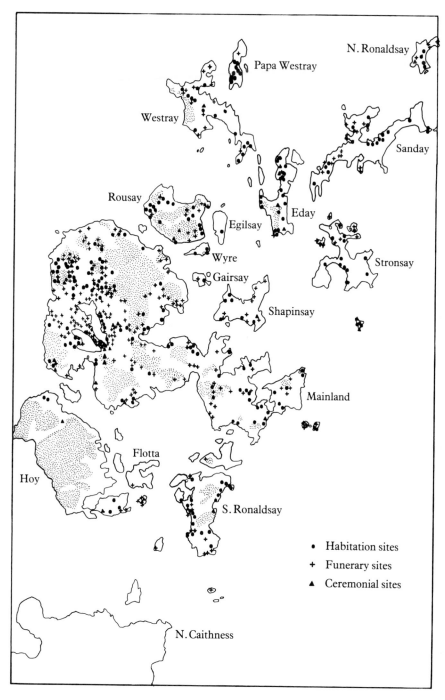

FIGURE 7.2. Distribution of Bronze Age sites in the islands.

The map includes the following labels: N. Ronaldsay, Papa Westray, Westray, Sanday, Rousay, Eday, Egilsay, Wyre, Stronsay, Gairsay, Shapinsay, Mainland, Flotta, Hoy, S. Ronaldsay, N. Caithness

Legend:
• Habitation sites
+ Funerary sites
▲ Ceremonial sites

investigated, few excavations are recent, and there is still only one series of radiocarbon dates for any of the Orcadian barrows (M.E.Hedges 1977). This group, the Knowes of Quoyscottie, is of Middle Bronze Age date. Secondly, burial studies in the islands have been hampered by a lack of dateable associations. In this chapter, chronology is therefore considered in general terms only, except in cases where dates are available: and in a discussion of the bronze artefacts, in the light of John Coles' definitive series of articles on Scottish bronze work (1960, 1964, 1969). Despite a known distribution of about 700 monuments for the period (figure 7.2), based on the records of the Royal Commission and of the Ordnance Survey, absence of recent excavation seriously limits our understanding.

During the Early Bronze Age in the islands, collective burial probably continued in the chambered tombs, and there is certainly evidence of a continuing regard for these monuments. Henshall (1974, 163) concluded her discussion of the Scottish chambered tombs by saying that, although the main period of tomb building was over by the early second millennium BC, they often continued to be used down to the eighteenth and sixteenth centuries BC. There is also Bronze Age evidence of the secondary use of the tombs. For example, Taversoe Tuick (Rousay; ORK 49) had three cists inserted into the infill of the upper chamber (Henshall 1963, 119). The henge monuments, too, became a focal point of burial, as the density of tumuli around the Ring of Brodgar and the Standing Stones of Stenness implies. Graham Ritchie (1976) has demonstrated a continued interest in the Standing Stones of Stenness for 2000 years.

In parallel with the survival of neolithic traditions into the Early Bronze Age, barrow burial and cremation gained in favour. One of the earliest barrow groups in the islands appears to be the Knowes of Trotty, which can be dated on the evidence of the grave goods found in one of the group of twelve. When the largest barrow was excavated (Petrie 1860), it was found to cover a stone cist which contained a cremation deposit together with four gold discs and a number of amber beads (J.J.Taylor 1980, 23, 49) (plate 7.1; colour plate 12). The gold discs may be interpreted as covers for v-bored jet buttons (Coles 1969, 53, 71) and compared to decorated Irish goldwork which is Early Bronze Age. The amber beads included spacer-plate pieces and are comparable with finds from South Britain (Coles 1969, 71). V-bored buttons have beaker associations (D.L.Clarke 1970, 260–5). The only v-bored jet button found in Orkney came from the outside wall of the neolithic tomb at Isbister, where it was discovered with three polished axes, a macehead and a polished flint knife (Henshall 1963, 112, 205, 247), artefacts with both indigenous late neolithic and beaker associations (Roe 1968).

This continuity of late neolithic associations into the Early Bronze Age is also demonstrated by the finding of a beaker in a cist at Birsay close to a disturbed barrow which Hugh Marwick considered may once have covered the cist (1949b, 239–401). It is likely that a number of the short cists which have been uncovered also belong to the Early Bronze Age. About half of these were inserted into natural hillocks or knolls and have been found to contain cremations and inhumations (Ordnance Survey Record Cards). Associated artefacts include polished stone axes, from Dounby and Huan (RCAMS 1946, 38, no.146 and 273, no.770) – a type of artefact not so far associated with barrow burials in the islands.

PLATE 7.1. Amber beads and spacer-plate pieces from
Knowes of Trotty, Orkney.

The concentration of large barrows in the vicinity of the henge monuments might indicate that they were the earliest to be erected in the islands, predating the *groups* of barrows; for there is some evidence to suggest that these latter belong, at least in part, to the Middle Bronze Age. There are some notable distinctions between barrow groups and single barrows, with regard to size and location in particular. In a study of barrow diameters based upon measurements given on the Ordnance Survey Record Cards it was apparent that single barrows tend to have a larger diameter than those in groups. It was also clear that in a number of barrow groups, where sufficient details of dimensions permitted such a study, over half of the sample included one or two barrows in a group, which were considerably larger than the rest. This pattern is demonstrated at the Knowes of Trotty (Petrie 1860). If the suggestion is accepted that large barrows represent Early Bronze Age burials, it may be that these groups represent chronological relationships. Equally, the larger barrows might tend to indicate social superiority, and the grave-goods from the Knowes of Trotty would support this view. But this find is exceptional.

The structural composition of barrows and cairns is not well documented. Petrie (1857), in referring to Farrer's excavation of Plumcake Knowe, does not even consider the nature of its composition, though it is probably a stone cairn. Stone kerbs have been recorded from a number of sites. The cairns on Rousay excavated by Grant in the 1930s at the Geord of Nears and Trumland (Grant 1933; Craw 1934) appear to be examples of kerb-cairns, a form of Bronze Age burial noted in Mainland Scotland (Ritchie and Thornber 1975). Radiocarbon dates from a barrow cemetery with small stone kerbs (M.E. Hedges 1977) all fall in the Middle Bronze Age. The Knowes of Quoyscottie is a group of at least 7 mounds, all apparently small scrape-barrows with diameters less than 9 m, and surrounded by roughly-constructed stone kerbs which were probably not visible when the barrows were completed, a feature noted elsewhere in the islands by Petrie. This barrow group shared a number of features with several other excavated sites in the islands, Queenafjold (Ritchie and Ritchie 1974), Quandale (Grant 1937), Corquoy (McCrie 1881) and Summersdale (Ashmore 1974). It has been suggested that this type of barrow cemetery is typical of the Middle Bronze Age in the islands (M.E. Hedges 1977).

The burial rite was cremation, generally in a neatly constructed flag-stone cist buttressed (as at Quoyscottie and Quandale) or clay luted (as at Queenafjold). Urn burials occurred at Quandale. Partially beneath one of the barrows at Quoyscottie there was a cremation cemetery of over thirty small pits containing cremated bone and pottery sherds. The cremations were not deposited in urns. Slight evidence from Summersdale (Ashmore 1974) and a site on Fair Isle (J. Anderson 1883, 66–7) and another in Shetland (Barron 1895) suggests this was not an unusual pattern in the Northern Isles.

MATERIAL CULTURE

Artefacts from funerary contexts are fairly undistinguished, and ceramics are almost entirely confined to simple urn forms. Petrological analysis of the pottery from Quoyscottie (Williams 1977, 147–8) showed the vessels had been locally manufactured. Steatite vessels have been recovered from cists and barrows on numerous occasions and were probably as popular as clay vessels, although their rate of survival is higher than that of clay. The nearest source of this soft stone is the Shetland Isles. Originally, steatite vessels were considered to be of Viking date (J. Anderson 1874), but in a series of articles on funerary ceramics manufactured from clay, published in the 1930s, Callander (1934 and 1936) suggested the steatite vessels were of Bronze Age date, and of course the contexts in which they have been found now puts the issue beyond dispute, although steatite was also used later by the Vikings. The decoration on steatite vessels is almost exclusively confined to parallel incised lines beneath the rim, and the occurrence in funerary contexts of similar decoration on pottery urns from the islands suggests that it was copied from the stone vessels. This seems to support the idea of indigenous development in funerary ceramics in the islands, and

PLATE 7.2. Incense cup from South Ronaldsay, Orkney.

perhaps indicates a growing insularity in the Bronze Age, even though developments continued along the lines of a wider tradition.

A rather exceptional find from South Ronaldsay was a yellow clay incense cup (plate 7.2); its discovery is not well recorded, but it appears to have come from a barrow (J.A.Smith 1872). D.L.Clarke (1970, 272) suggests north or west Ireland/west Scotland as the probable place of origin of such vessels. In its total isolation among the funerary ceramics from the islands it should probably be regarded as an import and it may represent a further link between Ireland and Orkney in the Early Bronze Age.

Because of poor conditions of preservation, textiles are rarely recovered from Bronze Age contexts. Portions of woollen cloth of different textures were recovered from a short stone cist at Greenigoe, Orphir, in the 1880s. No traces of bone were apparent, but an amber bead and another of opaque vitreous paste were said to have been found with the cloth (PSAS 23, 1888–9, 123–4). A famous fringed hood of twilled fabric from St Andrews Parish was originally regarded as of Viking date (J.Anderson 1883, 103–5), but is also possible that it may belong to the Bronze Age. It was not recovered from a funerary context, however, but was found unassociated in peat moss. In a cist at Arion found in 1966 a skeleton wrapped in woven material was discovered (Ordnance Survey Record Card no.HY21SE23).

A variety of stone artefacts, typical representatives from prehistoric sites throughout the Northern Isles, has been recovered from barrows and cists. They include pounders, hammerstones and rubbers. Agricultural implements have been recently recovered from the Middle Bronze Age cemetery of the Knowes of Quoyscottie (M. E. Hedges 1977), and it is probable that at least some of the crude stone implements referred to by Petrie (1868) as coming from barrows and cists were also agricultural implements. Stone ard shares have come from a variety of domestic contexts in the Northern Isles, including Tougs, Shetland (S. E. and J. W. Hedges forthcoming), and the burnt mounds of Liddle and Beaquoy, Orkney (J. W. Hedges 1975). The stone ard share distribution is so far confined to the Northern Isles (Rees 1977, 145).

Ritual. The ritual associations of Middle Bronze Age barrow cemeteries are indicated in a few different ways. The presence of charcoal and fragments of cremated bone in the mound material at Quoyscottie (M. E. Hedges 1977) and Queenafjold (Ritchie and Ritchie 1975) indicated that cremation was carried out on or very close to the site of the barrows. Animal bones were found together with the primary burial at Queenafjold and one of those at Quoyscottie. The inclusion of animals as burial deposits seems to have its origins in the Neolithic. Henshall (1963, 72) records numerous instances of animal bones from tombs. The bone analysis at Quoyscottie (Young and Lunt 1977, 146–7) reveals a high occurrence of burials of infants and youths. One of the primary burials was that of a small child and another was of a young person. A double cremation pit on the site contained discrete burials, that of a child and of an adult. Multiple burials in cists are fairly common in the islands (Traill 1876; Petrie 1866) and there is slight evidence to suggest that these multiple burials are more often inhumations in flat cists than cremations (though in the past it would have been more difficult to recognise multiple cremation deposits). In a barrow in the parish of Evie and Rendall, described by Petrie (1866), there were two central cists sharing the same basal flag but divided by a central flagstone beneath which was another cist containing two contracted skeletons. These double and treble cists which appear to have been erected simultaneously may represent a family or tribal catastrophe. They are rarely found outside of Orkney. The deposition of agricultural implements in Bronze Age funerary contexts indicates the significance of agriculture to the Bronze Age communities in the islands.

The distribution of Bronze Age burial monuments must be regarded with reserve. J. B. Stevenson (1975, 104–8) has emphasised the problems which hinder any attempts to understand prehistoric settlement patterns. Cultivation has clearly affected the distribution of barrows in the Orkney Islands. Even in the nineteenth century F. W. L. Thomas (1852, 100) was lamenting the adverse effects of agricultural practices on archaeological monuments in the islands. The fact that the larger single barrows and cairns are often situated on flat cultivated land whilst the smaller barrows in

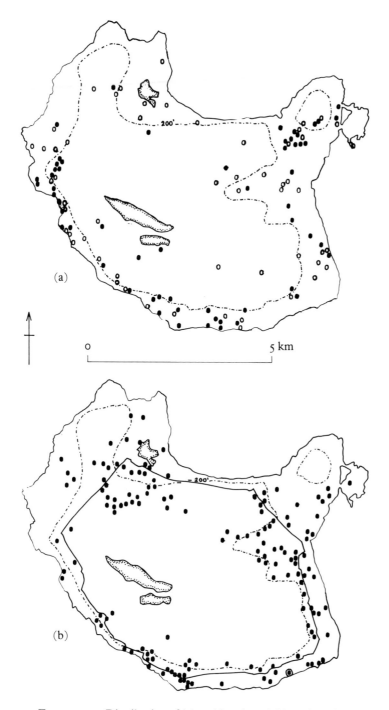

FIGURE 7.3. Distribution of (a) prehistoric and (b) modern sites
in Rousay, Orkney.

groups tend to be in marginal areas is probably as much a result of destruction by cultivation as anything else. Nevertheless it is tempting to suggest that the location of the barrow groups which are probably of Middle Bronze Age date indicates a growing awareness of the value of cultivable land. The close association between agricultural complexes and funerary monuments and the dual purposes attributed to some cairns in the Bronze Age period, particularly in Highland Zone regions, has been demonstrated in Yorkshire (Fleming 1971), and Shetland (Calder 1956). There is certainly some evidence to suggest a close geographical relationship between hut circles and barrows, and the site to the south of Mid Howe (RCAMS 1946, 263, no.706) and recent excavations at Spurdagrove (S. E. Hedges forthcoming) suggest that the hut circles and field systems may be contemporary with at least some of the barrows in the islands.

A study of a selection of barrow groups similar to Quoyscottie by Parry (1977, 151–2) has shown that their distribution may relate to that of the burnt mounds. The tendency of the cemeteries to occupy the junction of arable and uncultivated ground might be taken as an indication that these cemeteries were positioned on the boundaries of territorial zones occupied by the users of the burnt mounds (figure 7.3).

TECHNOLOGY AND TRADE

The number of bronze objects from the Orkney islands is small, but still provides evidence of some trading contacts, and links the Orcadian Bronze Age to the rest of Britain. Because most of the artefacts have been found unassociated, and a good number unprovenanced (Ordnance Survey Record Cards), they do not give us much help in clarifying the chronological relationships of Bronze Age monuments in the islands. Any review such as this is greatly indebted to John Coles' study of Scottish metalwork and its accompanying corpus of Scottish material (Coles 1960, 1964, 1969).

There are a few copper deposits in Orkney (figure 7.1; based on Mykura 1976, 121) and although they are comparatively small, attempts have been made in the past to mine them. Mykura (1976, 119) notes one site in Burray, and another on Rousay, worked in the past. But there is no evidence to date, either in the form of site evidence, or derived from the objects themselves, to suggest that copper ore was mined in the islands in the Bronze Age.

Throughout the Early and Middle Bronze Age periods the Orkneys stand in contrast to neighbouring Caithness in the paucity of metal artefacts. Only two flat axes have been found in Orkney, but Caithness has eight. The reasons for this difference must lie in the growing isolation of the islands, which is evidenced in other aspects of the archaeological record. A flat axe (type Bc), possibly from Orkney (Coles 1969, 84; plate 7.3) may well represent the earliest bronze artefact in the islands. Another Early

PLATE 7.3. Early Bronze Age flat axe, unprovenanced, Orkney.

Bronze Age artefact, found in a peat cutting in Rousay in 1905, is a rather fine dagger with double ribs and rivets and the remains of a horn hilt (Cursiter 1908; plate 7.4). No other metal artefacts which typify the Early Bronze Age are represented in the islands; spearheads, flanged axes and halberds are all lacking, and there is a similar narrowness of range in the types of metal artefacts from Caithness. The paucity of bronze objects in the islands in the Early Bronze Age is particularly characteristic of the north of Scotland generally. Coles (1969, 69) suggests that the first real phase of industrial activity in Scotland commences around the seventeenth century BC.

PLATE 7.4. Bronze dagger with handle of horn, Rousay, Orkney.

A similar situation is seen for the Middle Bronze Age and suggests that Orkney failed to establish itself within the mainstream of developments at this time. The idea of regional insularity is favoured by Coles (1969), though Burgess (1974, 199) disputes the notion. Climatic factors began to affect the British Isles unfavourably in the late second millennium (Burgess 1969, 167), and it is reasonable to assume that areas in the extreme north of

Britain felt the effects earlier and more strongly. Communication routes could have been affected, and this could account for the apparent isolation of the islands during the Middle Bronze Age.

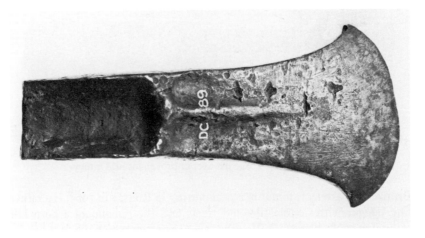

PLATE 7.5. Flanged axe, unprovenanced, Orkney.

Nevertheless, the metal artefacts in the islands reflect sporadic links with other areas of Scotland. A flanged axe (Class II) (Coles 1964, 140; plate 7.5), attributed to Orkney, represents a series of axes which appear to be late on typological grounds; Coles classified it as of the 'Haddington' Group, which is regarded as a local industry probably based in the Forth Valley (Coles 1964, 92). The presence of this axe in the islands indicates contact, possibly conducted along east coast sea routes. A type D spearhead (Coles 1964, 143) found in a peat cutting near Nether House, Firth (H. Marwick 1949b) could have reached Orkney from neighbouring Caithness, for, although this type of spearhead has a fairly general distribution in Scotland and south Britain, a number of moulds have been found in north Scotland (Coles 1964).

A sandstone mould for a flanged axe (PSAS 43, 1908–9, 10) represents half the total for that particular type of axe in Scotland; both moulds were broken. Moulds have generally been taken to indicate manufacture within the vicinity of the find (Coles 1964), but usually only when there is more than one, and, as there is no other evidence to suggest metal-working in the islands at this time, the mould fragment must be regarded as something of an anomaly.

The only associated metalwork for the Middle Bronze Age in the islands is a small double-edged razor with an oval blade and partial midrib on one surface, which was found in a cist inserted into Laughton's Knowe (C. M. Piggott 1947; plate 7.6). It has a tang and appears to have been cast in one piece (Coles 1964). A late second millennium BC date is preferred for this type of razor which compares with radiocarbon dates for burnt mounds and small barrow cemeteries.

PLATE 7.6. Bronze Age razor from Laughton's Knowe, Orkney.

By the Late Bronze Age, however, metal artefacts were clearly more commonly in use in the islands. This is in accord with the increase in production of metal objects which occurs in Scotland at this time (Coles 1964, 129). The relative numbers of metal artefacts in Orkney and Caithness is now reversed, with Orkney having eight, twice as many as Caithness (Coles 1960). The range of bronzes is also greater in the islands, with socketed axes, socketed knives, and razors all represented in Orkney and absent from Caithness. On the other hand, Caithness has two native, Ewart-Park type, swords; a wooden version of this type was found in a peat cutting in St Andrews and Deerness Parish (R.B.K. Stevenson 1958; plate 7.7). During the final stages of the Late Bronze Age a settlement producing locally manufactured artefacts was established at Jarlshof in Shetland. The artefacts produced at this site are consistent with native developments and represent the Adabrock phase of the Scottish Late Bronze Age (Coles 1960). The wooden sword already mentioned is made of yew, a type of tree represented in the pollen from prehistoric sites in the islands. It has been dated to 900–700 BC and is a fairly early copy of the British Hallstatt series of leaf-shaped swords and indicates how rapidly this new type penetrated the British Isles.

Some rather unusual metal artefacts now appear in the islands, unusual because of their distributions. Two socketed knives, one representing part of a personal hoard, have been found at different times in peat in St Andrew's and Deerness parish. They are classified by Coles (1960) as of Thorndon type and their distribution in Scotland is extremely sparse. The one that formed part of a hoard was found together with a bifid, notched, and perforated razor (plate 7.8). Coles (1960) compares the hoard with one from Thorndon, Suffolk, which is dated at around the eighth century BC

and which gives its name to the Thorndon class of socketed knives. The presence of two of this type in Orkney is of some interest in view of their predominantly southern distribution. It is also interesting that they were found in close proximity (C.M.Piggott 1947).

Socketed axes make their appearance in the Late Bronze Age and two have been found in the islands. One, which is now lost, and unclassified, was apparently discovered under a cist (Cursiter 1887). The other axe is described as a facet-type (Coles 1960, 71) and can probably be related to the ribbed axes which have an east Scottish distribution and are attributed to a fairly late phase in the Late Bronze Age (Coles 1960). Other finds from the islands include three spearheads, two of which have rather unusual associations and perhaps indicate the value of these objects to later cultures. A 'pair' of spearheads (Cursiter 1887) were recovered from sites in Birsay. The first, listed by Coles, was found in the top of Saevar Howe, a large sandy knoll known to contain a Viking settlement. The second, according to Cursiter, came from a location a mile or so away from the first and this is presumably the one referred to on the Ordnance Survey card as coming from the Bishop's palace, Kirkwall or Birsay. It was apparently found sticking in a skull. The contexts of both of these are clearly uncertain. The third, a Class IV leaf-shaped spear-head, is comparable to two from Caithness, and Coles assigns them all to the Late Bronze Age although they are of a type which has been found in Middle Bronze Age contexts elsewhere (Coles 1964).

Where associations are known, in three instances they are with funerary monuments. Five artefacts have been discovered in peat cuttings. The reason for this is probably one related to factors of preservation. However, the fact that three of the finds, including the Late Bronze Age hoard, all came from the same peat moss in St Andrews and Deerness deserves consideration. Both of the Thorndon socketed knives and the wooden sword came from this peat moss. It is possible that they represent deliberate depositions, at a time of increasing hard conditions due to climatic deterioration.

Deductions. When the metal artefacts are compared with the ceramics from the islands they seem to indicate an

PLATE 7.7. Late Bronze Age model, in yew, of a Ewart-Park-type sword, St Andrews and Deerness, Orkney.

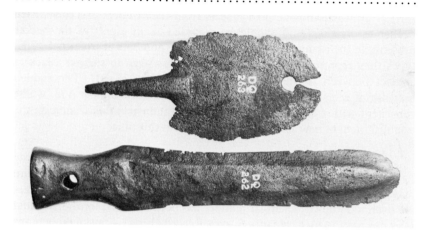

PLATE 7.8. A razor and a socketed knife from a Late Bronze Age hoard, St Andrews and Deerness, Orkney.

absence of any sustained, substantial, contact with the rest of Britain, with the exception of Shetland.

The context and association of funerary ceramics for the Bronze Age in Orkney have already been discussed and apart from a few rather unusual finds, such as the incense cup from South Ronaldsay (Smith 1872), funerary ceramics appear to be the result of local manufacture developed in response to an imported funerary tradition, but displaying little of the variety of form, decoration and fabric found elsewhere in Britain. Funerary ceramics are very simple and there is little display of skill. One of the most interesting features of this pottery is the incised line decoration which appears to have been adopted from that used on steatite vessels. This form of decoration is almost exclusive to vessels from the Northern Isles, both steatite and ceramic. It is interesting to note that steatite has not so far been found in domestic contexts in the Orkney Islands although it does occur on such sites in Shetland. This shows that steatite vessels at least were produced specifically to meet the demands of the funerary traditions. The same cannot really be said for the pottery, although incised line decoration has not been found on domestic ceramics. There does seem to be evidence, largely from the form of decoration, to suggest that funerary ceramics and domestic ware, whilst basically similar in fabric and form, were separate industries.

The presence of metal artefacts and steatite vessels in the islands is a result of outside contacts. The steatite indicates a steady trade, probably with Shetland, and the form of decoration using incised lines is common to both groups of islands. The metal artefacts, particularly in the Early and Middle Bronze Age, indicate sporadic import, rather than trade. The earliest bronzes, and the gold objects from the Knowes of Trotty, have beaker associations and should be regarded as an aspect of the beaker presence in the islands. The differences in the numbers of artefacts and the types they represent in Orkney and Caithness seem to suggest a lack of contact between the northeast Mainland and the islands. The sudden increase of metal objects in the islands in the Late Bronze Age, whilst consistent with trends in the Scottish metal industry, might indicate the establishment of new contacts with Shetland at this time.

DOMESTIC EVIDENCE

Burnt mounds. The best documented and most easily identified group of domestic sites in the Orkney Islands is the burnt mounds, of which there are over 200 known: a similar number has been recorded for the Shetland Isles (RCAMS 1946; Ordnance Survey Record Cards). Considerably fewer have been noted in Caithness and Sutherland (Ordnance Survey Record Cards) but dense distributions are recorded for Wales and southern Ireland (O'Riordain 1953). This general distribution, implying peripheral locations, is belied by the distribution of the sites within the Orkney Islands themselves – where they have been found to occupy the best agricultural land (J.W. Hedges 1975, fig.22). J.B. Stevenson (1975, 104–8) has emphasised the factors of discovery and survival as they affect archaeological site distributions in Britain, and in particular the effect on the proportions of sites in the Highland and Lowland Zones. It is therefore merely speculation to try to reconstruct a meaningful general distribution for these sites at the present time.

The dating of two burnt mounds in Orkney, Liddle and Beaquoy, suggests a range in the Middle and Late Bronze Ages (J.W. Hedges 1975). A series of thermoluminescence dates for a group of burnt mounds in the islands provides a date range of 1000–400 BC (OxTL 189 b–i) (Huxtable 1975, 82–4). However, dating evidence from Ireland, where a number of excavations have been carried out by O'Kelly (1954), indicates a more diverse date range with dates covering the Neolithic and Iron Age (J.W. Hedges 1975, 78, fig.23). Theories as to the purpose of these sites are equally varied. They are connected with a domestic function, and O'Kelly (1954) has suggested that they were temporary hunting camps used for cooking huge joints of meat. Evidence from the excavated sites in Orkney suggest they were used by agriculturalists. A typical burnt mound is characterised by a huge heap of burnt stone and domestic midden. Evidence from the records of the Royal Commission and the Ordnance Survey show that at least forty, or one-fifth of the total, were associated with structures usually in the form of a large, watertight container; walling has also been noted (colour plate 13). Cooking with burnt stones was practised at prehistoric sites throughout Britain but what distinguishes the burnt mounds is the huge size of the mounds and the dominating presence of the cooking trough. It is clear that the sites had a specific function.

The plans of the buildings at Liddle and Beaquoy (J. W. Hedges 1975, 44, 55, figs 5 and 16) (figure 7.4) resemble other domestic site plans in the Northern Isles, particularly Calder's prehistoric houses in Shetland (fig. 74).

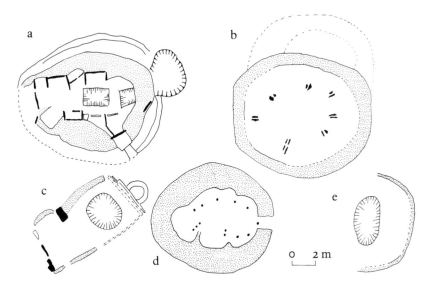

FIGURE 7.4. Some prehistoric house plans from the Northern Isles: (a) Liddle burnt mound; (b) Spurdagrove farmstead; (c) Beaquoy burnt mound; (d) Ness of Gruting, Shetland; (e) Spurdagrove farmstead.

Some of the domestic pottery from the burnt mound sites, Liddle and Beaquoy (J. W. Hedges 1975) appeared to be gritted with burnt stone. This indicates local manufacture and suggests that pottery was produced, at least for domestic purposes, on the lines of a cottage industry.

Ard shares were found at both Beaquoy and Liddle: and bones of sheep or goat, fragments of a quern and the presence of cereal pollen in the records from Liddle all connect the sites to agricultural activities. Shetland has provided more direct evidence. Recent excavations at an agricultural complex at Tougs showed that a burnt mound was contemporary with the other structures. Skeletal remains at Beaquoy, however, included bones of seal or whale and red deer providing evidence of other activities besides agriculture and more readily comparable with O'Kelly's ideas for the Irish burnt mounds.

The problems of function and period of occupation are interrelated. Arguments in favour of permanent occupation can be found in J. W. Hedges

(1975). It is also possible that they were a focal point for small communities and not actually dwellings themselves. The small available floor space in the buildings, suggests that they were not dwellings. Quite possibly a burnt mound served as a cook-house for a small community (figure 7.4). There is no very good evidence to indicate whether or not the communities using the burnt mounds were sedentary or mobile. Higgs and Jarman (1972) suggest that houses and even villages need not necessarily be regarded as indications of a sedentary society.

Field systems. The few known hut circle and field system complexes in the islands provide some further evidence of developments in agriculture. Recent excavations at Spurdagrove (S.E.Hedges forthcoming) showed that, although the visible field system was confined to uncultivated land, there were indications that it had originally extended downhill on to present-day cultivated land. The occupation of a lower slope is repeated at other field-system sites in the islands, notably one on Auskerry, Stronsay. Due to the poor state of preservation at Spurdagrove little environmental material was available for study, but artefactual evidence included a number of implements similar to those found at the burnt mounds and at Quoyscottie. In particular, stone ard shares and other agricultural implements were well represented. Flint was notably absent at Spurdagrove as it was at the burnt mounds and Quoyscottie; a few flints from Beaquoy appear to predate the site. An interesting feature of the 'huts' at Spurdagrove was the use of small field stones in the construction of the walls (colour plate 14). A similar use of small stones was noted at Tougs, Shetland, and seems to have been a good way of using field-cleared stones. The field walls at Spurdagrove had obviously been adopted by later agriculturalists and it was felt that the remaining field shapes were not representative of the original farm. Perhaps the most interesting feature at Spurdagrove was the likelihood that one of the 'huts' was in fact a byre. A series of stone-lined oblong post-holes, 2–3 m apart, formed a radial pattern about 1 m in from the inner wall face; the resulting divisions could have been used as animal stalls (figure 7.4). The pattern is similar to that recorded at the Iron Age site of Alnham, Northumberland (Jobey and Tait 1966). The absence of domestic refuse and of a hearth are also consistent with the interpretation of the building as a byre. The other 'hut' at Spurdagrove had been refloored. The primary floor had contained a large, clay-lined pit of similar size and shape to that at Beaquoy burnt mound. Again there was no evidence of a hearth. At some stage this pit had been filled in, and a new floor laid using stones to produce a cobbling effect. This floor level showed signs of heavy disturbance consistent with it having been trampled by large animals: Bradley's remarks on the devolutionary cycle of uses of buildings may be relevant here (1978, 49).

The disproportionately low number of hut circle sites in comparison with burnt mounds makes difficult any comparison of their relative distributions within the islands. The hut circles appear to favour the lower hill slopes now relegated to pasture, whereas burnt mounds are usually found on agricultural land or in marshy places. Of course, burnt mounds would have a better chance of surviving the onslaughts of agriculture than field systems and hut circles. The field systems survive in so fragmentary and altered a condition that it is not possible to make any calculations about crop sizes or population. The pollen evidence from the burnt mound sites (R. L. Jones 1975) and Quoyscottie (R. L. Jones 1977) suggests an open landscape dominated by *Calluna* heath and small shrubs with indications of cereal production at Liddle and slight indications at Quoyscottie.

CONCLUSION

By the middle of the first millennium BC the Scottish Highland Zone and the Northern Isles appear already to have begun to develop the special character they have today. Population declined as cultivation became impossible at higher altitudes and on poor soils. Encroaching peat and heath resulted in pressure on the best land (Burgess 1974, 167). Apart from the metalwork there is, as yet, no direct evidence for the Late Bronze Age in the islands. The Orcadian earth-houses may, however, provide a missing clue. There are 30 in all in the islands and they form a remarkably uniform group quite distinct in some important aspects from those found in the rest of Scotland. So far they have been regarded as Iron Age largely on the basis of evidence from mainland Scotland and despite the fact that one in Shetland at Jarlshof is of Late Bronze Age date (Hamilton 1956, 38). They are fairly consistent in architectural design, being around about 3–4 m long and extremely low, usually about 1 m in height. They have been sunk into clay or hewn out of rock, and generally lack stone built walls. They were roofed with huge slabs of stone supported on free-standing pillars of stone. The means of entering the chamber was by a short (usually) narrow and low passage. At Upper Cairn on Hoy there were door checks at the inner end of the passage.

Most have been robbed in the past, but half have produced a few finds, usually in the form of domestic midden, animal bones, simple unclassified pottery and simple stone implements: querns were found at a couple of sites. The domestic nature of these sites seems to be attested by the nature of the finds from them (excluding Rennibister which must be given special consideration). Quite possibly they were storage houses (Hamilton 1956, 39). Earth-houses have been interpreted as possible storage rooms for dairy products (Bradley 1978, 51). The apparent desire for concealment has led to the suggestion that they were hiding places used in times of adversity. It is, however, quite possible that some of these buildings were food stores of semi-nomadic groups who occupied the islands towards the end of the Bronze Age.

8 John W. Hedges **The Broch Period**

HISTORY OF RESEARCH

Norsemen in the ninth century evidently knew what brochs were for, since they called them *borg*, a defence (from which broch comes), and they may even have been quite familiar with them, since Mousa on Shetland, at least, was still usable at that time (J. Anderson 1873, cxi). There then seems to follow a period in which the knowledge was lost; Wallace (1700, 57) confused them with burial mounds. Barry, who considered them Pictish, gave a passable account of a broch tower in 1805, but stated it to be based on excavation further south, as the inhabitants of the Northern Isles had more respect for their ancestors than to carry out such investigations (Barry 1805, 96–8).

In spite of Barry's sentiments, there can be no doubt that casual enquiries did continue. The first actual account of an excavation was in 1825, when the son of the parish clergyman dug into the Broch of Burgar (Evie). He found a comb, a deer's horn and a skeleton. In the 1840s the proprietor conducted considerable excavations there, and found a great treasure which he reputedly threw into the sea lest the Crown should seize it (Petrie 1890, 89). In the mid-nineteenth century, Captain F.W.L. Thomas' visit to Orkney resulted in his important and original article on the antiquities, but he was able to illustrate only two plans of brochs: Burgar and Hoxa, neither of which was in any way satisfactory (figures 8.1 and 2). He made a plea for further excavation (F.W.L. Thomas 1852, 119, 210, pl.17): 'though nearly all the Pictish Broughs in Orkney are greatly dilapidated, good service may yet be done by clearing away the rubbish which surrounds the original tower'.

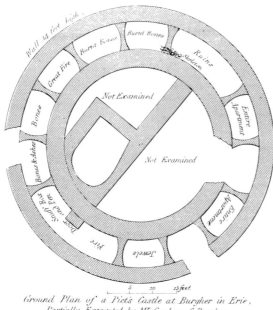

Ground Plan of a Pict's Castle at Burgher in Erie,
Partially Excavated by M. Gordon of Burgher.

FIGURE 8.1. Broch of Burgar, Evie. A cryptic plan exemplifying the
state of knowledge in the early 1840s. (Thomas 1852, pl.17.)

The age of intelligent *antiquarian* enquiry in Orkney is very clearly
defined, only spreading slightly either side of the date bracket 1850–80.
Many individuals were involved, but there are three main characters. Of
these, George Petrie is by far the most important. He was a local man who
worked as factor for an estate. His station in life meant that he was directly
responsible for the exploration of only two brochs; for the most part he just
made rough sketches, with annotations and measurements, of what others
had done.

James Farrer, the second of the trio, was Member of Parliament for
Durham and was on good terms with the Earl of Zetland, the owner of large
tracts of land. During his summer visits Farrer hired labour to dig into a
number of brochs (and other sites). In most instances his work was of the
lowest quality and were it not for Petrie we would have hardly any record of
it. Finally, there is Sir Henry Dryden, the famous architectural illustrator.
His name was connected with the recording of several of the monuments at
the time of their opening or soon after. A large number of his extant
drawings are however based solely on Petrie's sketches which he obtained
after the latter's death.

Up to his death in 1875 Petrie was involved in the recording of some
twenty or more broch sites. Most of these were investigated only in a minor

and uninformative way. We see him first of all in 1847, at Oxtro in Birsay, making notes on the quarrying away of a mound by workmen (Petrie 1890, 76–8, 86–7); here, supposedly 'Bronze Age' cists overlay the broch, relegating it, as he erroneously inferred, to the Stone Age. In 1848 at the Howe of Hoxa (South Ronaldsay), came one of the two widely separated occasions when he was actually in charge of operations; he positively scoured the inside, preparatory to it being turned into an ornamental garden by the owner (figure 8.2) (F. W. L. Thomas 1852, 119–22).

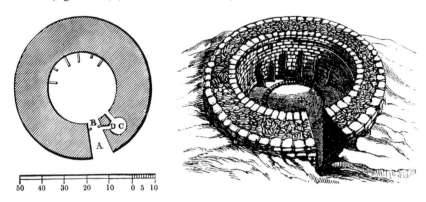

FIGURE 8.2. Howe of Hoxa, S. Ronaldsay. Excavated by Petrie in 1848 when his knowledge of brochs was rudimentary. The interior was scoured; the wall, as shown, is rebuilt; and the entrance plan has been fabricated. (Thomas 1852, 120.)

In 1862 at Burrowston (Shapinsay) Petrie was invited to see the works undertaken by the landowner, and recorded by Sir Henry Dryden. Not only was the broch tower emptied out with some care so that internal structures were preserved, but it was trenched around and a narrow run made out to the sea (figure 8.3) (Petrie 1890, 81–4, 87). In 1865 and 1866 a precisely similar undertaking was carried out by the Reverend Dr Traill at Netlater, Harray (plate 8.1) (Petrie 1890, 78–81, 88). In 1866, perhaps catching the spirit of the times, Farrer worked more systematically in emptying out the Broch of Burrian (Russland), Harray (plate 8.2) (Farrer 1868, 103–5).

The year 1866 is a key reference point, for Petrie then addressed the Society of Antiquaries of Scotland on the subject of Orkney brochs. His paper was not printed until 1874 and was not published for a further sixteen years (1890). It was perhaps as a result of reflections on this summary of work-to-date that Petrie commenced his own large-scale work at the Broch of Lingro (St Ola) in 1870; he was funded both privately and by the Society of Antiquaries of Scotland. Here he had the opportunity of investigating as he wanted to; surprisingly there is no increase in the precision either of the

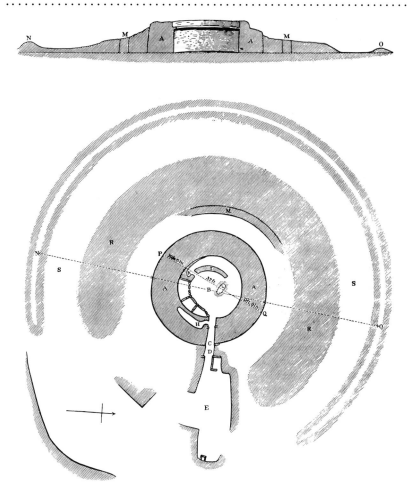

FIGURE 8.3. Broch of Burrowston, Shapinsay. Excavated in 1862; the interior was carefully cleared, the tower trenched around and a barrow run made through outbuildings. (Petrie 1890, fig. 10.)

digging or the recording but Petrie not only emptied the interior with care but had an extensive area of outbuildings around the broch cleared out (plate 8.3) (largely unpublished; J.W. Hedges forthcoming a). The possibility of such outbuildings had already often been suggested by the appearance of structures during trenching operations around broch towers, and in digging out barrow runs.

The impetus continued for a short time after Petrie's death. The Broch of Burrian in North Ronaldsay was investigated by the proprietor of the island in 1870 and 1871 with some help in recording from Dryden (Traill

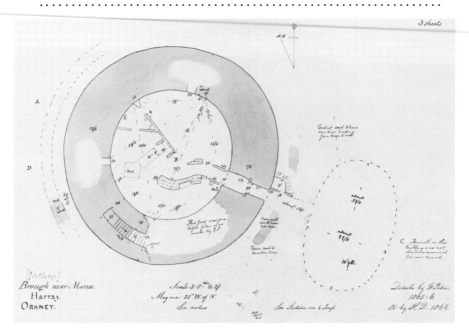

PLATE 8.1. Netlater, Harray. Excavated in 1865 and 1866. (Dryden nd.)

1890, 341–64). The approach taken was unimaginative in the sense that only the interior was cleared, but here two occupations were found and the finds were rigidly separated. This is the first instance of such stratigraphic excavation. In 1881 W. G. T. Watt of Skaill House, Sandwick, commenced operations at the Broch of Borthwick. His work was unsystematic and his publication incomprehensible (Watt 1882), but he did notice two phases of occupation and he not only uncovered some outbuildings but, for the first time, investigated part of the rampart and ditch beyond them. By the end of the main period of antiquarian enquiry a firm outline of what constituted a broch had been drawn. Petrie's paper has already been mentioned; the other major work, which took in Scotland as a whole, was Joseph Anderson's third series of Rhind lectures presented in 1881 and published two years later (1883).

The concept of a broch embodied in Anderson's work has, by and large, stayed with us. A broch is a hollow tower some 17 m in diameter with walls *c.* 4.5 m thick and an enclosed courtyard *c.* 8 m across. Mousa (Shetland) and other less-well-preserved examples indicate that originally the towers may have been up to 14 m high. In order to achieve this and to permit access to the top, the walls were built in two tied skins, between which went a staircase. Sometimes the base of the wall was solid and this was occasionally used to house cells which could be entered from the courtyard.

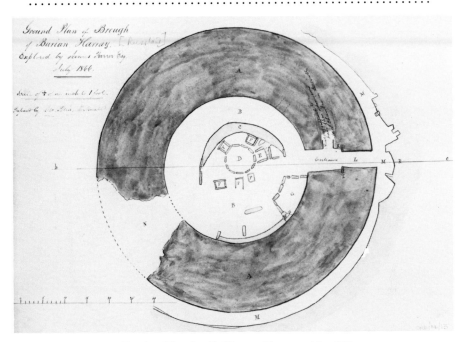

Ground Plan of Brough
of Burian Harray [ ]
Explored by James Farrer Esq.
July 1866.

PLATE 8.2. Burrian (Russland), Harray. Excavated in 1866.
(Petrie nd (a) opposite p.8.)

The only opening to the exterior was the entrance, which was highly
defended by having a recessed doorway often with guard cells behind it.
These towers were thought of as places of refuge standing in isolation; all
the internal furnishings and external buildings were simply dismissed as
secondary usage.

In picking out seemingly broad architectural similarities from a mass of
data of varying worth, the antiquaries defined a type of monument which
has retained its broadly homogenous image. Dating was a problem; they
had been called Danish, Pictish and Stone Age, and their Norse origin was
still being cogently argued (Ferguson 1877). In the Rhind lectures, however, Anderson had them firmly dated to the first and second centuries AD,
on the basis of Roman finds, of which plenty had come from Orkney. After
this the towers were thought to have been dismantled as being of no further
use, and the internal and external features considered to have been created
as shanty dwellings. Ramparts and ditches were even further from the
minds of the excavator and theoretician and attracted little attention. Petrie
in his list of 1872 gives 70 brochs for Orkney (1890, 93–6) a figure later
increased by Graham (1947, 51) to 102 out of a total of some 500 for
Scotland. Close scrutiny of all available documentation suggests there is
evidence for 52 brochs or similar structures in Orkney.

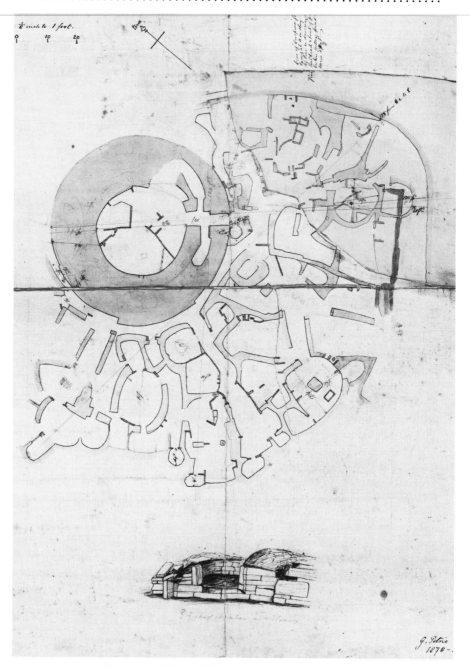

PLATE 8.3. Lingro, St Ola. Excavated by Petrie in 1870 and 1871, the outbuildings being extensively cleared. (Dryden and Petrie nd.)

In the half century after Petrie and his contemporaries very little happened. One James Cursiter was party to the clearing of the wall top of Eves Howe (Deerness) in 1883, and in 1887 was involved in emptying the contents of the halved interior of Green Hill (Hoy) into the sea (1923, 51–2). Cursiter was a little out of the main stream of thought and when he summarised his own views (1898, 10; 1923, 51) he attempted to demonstrate that the brochs came with the Phoenicians *via* a land bridge from Atlantis prior to the last glaciation. After him the only spark of archaeological activity was in 1901 and 1909 when the Loch of Ayre (Holm) was amateurishly trenched into (Graeme 1914). The interior was cleared out badly, but completely, and a few of the outbuildings and parts of the passage between them and the broch revealed. Certainly a few sites may have been damaged or investigated but, by and large, there was a striking gap between 1880 and 1930 when practically no excavation was undertaken and little appeared in print about Orkney brochs except in gazetteer articles (J. Fraser 1923; 1924; 1925; 1927).

Archaeology in general developed markedly in Orkney in the pre-war years when, among other sites, the Brochs of Gurness (Evie) and Midhowe (Rousay) were opened to the public (figures 8.4 and 5; plates 8.4 and 5). Gurness was 'rediscovered' in 1929 and a whole decade of summer seasons embarked upon (largely unpublished; J. W. Hedges forthcoming a); public finance took over from private when the latter ran out. Even after a gap of half a century the approach made and the techniques used had changed little and there is no need to speak separately of this excavation or that at Midhowe. At both, the centre of the broch was emptied, then all the outbuildings and, finally, the ditches and ramparts beyond were excavated. The idea of digging the ramparts and ditches may have come from Midhowe which was smaller, and privately financed, and was finished by 1933 (Callander and Grant 1934; colour plate 15). With the outbreak of the Second World War in 1939 came the end of broch studies in Orkney for another forty years.

So ended a century of fairly intensive work but, by present-day standards, the results of it were very limited. We know little of many of the structures and much only about a few; there are some with many finds, but none is well stratified; there is no reliable dating evidence or evidence relating to environment.

TYPOLOGY

Starting with Graham (1947) or even Petrie (1890), there has been a tendency to analyse attributes of broch towers by simple statistics. This goes to show that they have certain shared traits; granted that, there is wide variability resisting any classification that actually aids understanding. The average broch tower in Orkney has an overall diameter of *c*. 18 m (this and

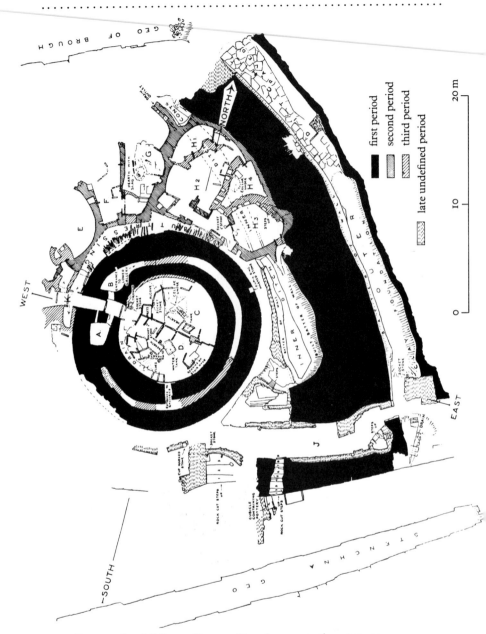

FIGURE 8.4. Midhowe, Rousay. Complete excavation 1930–33 included the outer defences. (RCAMS 1946, fig.273.)

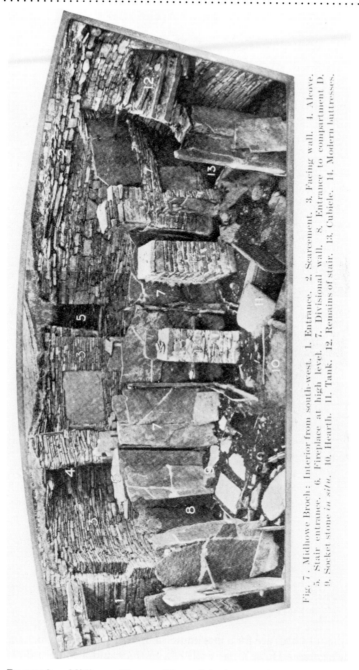

Fig. 7. Midhowe Broch: Interior from south-west. 1. Entrance. 2. Scarcement. 3. Facing wall. 4. Alcove. 5. Stair entrance. 6. Fireplace at high level. 7. Divisional wall. 8. Entrance to compartment D. 9. Socket stone *in situ*. 10. Hearth. 11. Tank. 12. Remains of stair. 13. Cubicle. 14. Modern buttresses.

PLATE 8.4. Midhowe, Rousay. View of the internal furnishings from the south-west. (Callander and Grant 1934, fig.7.)

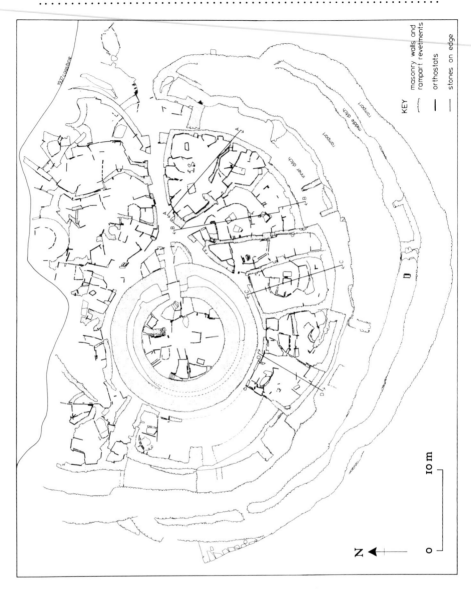

FIGURE 8.5. Gurness, Evie. Completely excavated 1930–39.
(NOSAS, based on original unpublished plans.)

subsequent figures are for a maximum sample of 51 brochs which includes
Bu but excludes Howe), has walls *c*. 4 m thick and a courtyard *c*. 9.5 m
across; the walls occupy 46 per cent of any whole diameter and the floor area
is *c*. 75 m^2. Around these averages is a great deal of variability. Diameters

PLATE 8.5. Gurness, Evie. View of the internal furnishings taken at the
time of excavation. (Thomas Kent collection, Kirkwall Library.)

vary from 12 to 22.5 m, wall thicknesses from 2.75 to 5.2 m and the
diameter of the courtyard from 7.3 to 13.7 m. On any of these counts the
figure for one broch may be double that for another and this applies to the
proportional wall thickness and to the internal area which varies from 28 m²
to 148 m². These variables show little obvious and definite correlation.
There are all sizes of dwelling with most of the range of thicknesses of wall;
large courtyards with similarly thick walls are not easy to document however and may not have existed. Some of the brochs have had their height
preserved quite well; in fact 26 of the 51 are known to have been over 1.5 m
high and seven of these were over 4 m high. There is a tendency for these to
have a below-average floor area, or an above-average wall thickness, or
both.

Both ground-galleried and solid-based brochs are found in Orkney and
the latter sometimes house intra-mural cells. In both types the wall is found
to be used as an access to a higher floor; the stairway usually starts c. 1.8 m
from the floor and winds round to c. 3.6 m where one can re-enter the
courtyard area by a doorway above the scarcement. There are also two
examples where the stair starts at ground level but neither of these has much
height preserved.

The entrances are very variable. The two ground-galleried brochs,

Midhowe and Gurness, have fully fledged ones with jambs halfway along and two guard chambers behind. Some of the solid-based brochs have two guard chambers, some have one and others none at all; several brochs have their guard cells outside the door jambs. In the eight instances where the height of the entrance has been preserved it is *c*. 1.8 m high and over this, where preserved again, there is a cell. The height of the entrance and the floor of the cell above it is that of the access to the intra-mural stairway. At Midhowe the cell itself had the remains of a roof at the height of the scarcement.

Of the 51 Orkney brochs, we have evidence for internal furnishings made of flagstone in 27; of these only 8 have revealed a true floor plan. These internal furnishings, as mentioned, have been dismissed as secondary usage of the towers. They have, however, so many points in common with the structural features of the towers themselves that this is an unfounded assertion. Those floor plans which are clear fall into two types; one-unit dwellings, and those which have been divided. Both would obviously have been installed after the tower had been built and the latter may represent remodelling. In a sense therefore there is no evidence that they are second-ary: and it is now suggested they were used by the original broch occupants.

At Burrian (Russland) in Harray, Farrer revealed a beautiful single-unit floor plan (plate 8.2). More or less central to it was a circular hearth, defined by a kerb of flagstones on edge, and around this was a service area approximately 5.5 m in diameter in which at least five tanks were set in the floor. Around the north part of this hearth and service area a wall was built, and the area between this and the broch wall formed a large bent hall accessible from just inside the broch entrance. Across the other side of the courtyard around the inner wall face were three compartments accessible from the service area. At 5 o'clock in relation to the entrance there is supposed to have been the entrance to an intramural staircase *c*. 1.8 m above the floor but this may have been spurious.

Burrowston (Shapinsay) was similar (figure 8.3) and perhaps more exciting, though the central area was less well preserved; all that remained was the entrance to a well. From 6 o'clock to 9 o'clock the circuit was taken up with three flagged compartments and from there to 2 o'clock by a large bent room which, when found, was actually roofed. On top of this roofed room was an entrance to a stairway which continued up to the height of the scarcement at *c*. 3.5 m where there was another entrance. Bu, which falls within this group of single unit floor plans, is discussed below.

The other five floor plans are examples of the divided type. Midhowe and Gurness are the best of these and demonstrate clearly the relationship between the furnishings and the wall fittings; the others are Lingro (St Ola) (plate 8.3), Loch of Ayre (Holm) and Netlater (Harray) (plate 8.1).

At Midhowe, it is almost as though the single plan were reproduced by binary fission (figure 8.4; plate 8.4). The courtyard was divided east/west into two compartments by a row of large slabs standing over 2 m high and in line with the entrance passage. At the inner end of the entrance passage was a vestibule and on both sides of this a doorway leading into a short lobby from which access could be had to the north and south apartments. Around the peripheral arc formed by their share of the broch wall each had compartments made of orthostats, and centrally placed in each area were rectangular hearths and a cooking tank.

The correspondence between the internal furnishings and the wall fittings was such at Midhowe that it is worth detailing. A floor at the height of c. 3.5 m together with a mezzanine one at the height of c. 1.8 m is suggested by features at other brochs but here, in particular, there is strong evidence. It will be remembered that these measurements were the heights of the floor of the cell above the entrance and the floor of the cell above that; they are also the heights of the beginning of the stair to the scarcement and of the scarcement itself and the entrance over it as well as the intra-mural galleries at both these levels. The furnishings fit very well with this. The entrance to the northern apartment had on its left-hand side an alcove which oversailed the broch wall and on its right a stone press. The alcove was the height of the scarcement; the press was the height of the landing and its roof was fire-cracked and had burnt material on it. Between the press and the alcove was a fitting for a lintel to the entrance to the northern apartment, at a height of 1.88 m. The compartments around the walls were badly preserved but seem to have been roofed at a height of between 1.5 and 1.8 m. In the southern apartment there was an internal stair which went from the top of a compartment to the height of the scarcement.

Gurness, which has so many other features in common with Midhowe, also latterly had a divided floor plan (figure 8.5; plate 8.5), though it is nowhere near as neat and regular. The larger apartment occupies the southern part of the courtyard and contains a hearth, cooking tank and various flagged compartments as well as the access to a landing at 1.8 m (colour plate 16); the well here was actually sealed when the courtyard was divided. The other living area occupied the north-west third of the courtyard and was divided from the larger by an east/west partition. This too had a hearth and peripheral compartments; from it there was an internal flight of steps to the scarcement where it oversailed the interior. The courtyard is complicated at Gurness at the entrance; access to the ground floor is gained by going to the right of this through what must have been a covered passage and over a threshold which has a door jamb c. 1.8 m high *in situ*.

Wells are a common feature of brochs, having been found inside ten of them. One well, at the East Broch of Burray, was on the outside but accessible from the interior. In using a broch well one did not lower a bucket, but instead went down a flight of steps to the water. The well was built by digging a large hole and then facing it with masonry and roofing it.

Outbuildings were found at many brochs during their excavation in the nineteenth century, as the tower was trenched round and a path cleared for spoil. They too were dismissed as secondary and have only been investigated fully at Lingro (St Ola), Midhowe and Gurness, where this stigma has continued to be applied. It seems clear to the author – because of their layout and level with respect to the tower – that they are contemporary with the main broch occupation and they should not be thought separate from it.

Of the three examples, Gurness is the clearest (figure 8.5). There is a passage through the external defences and aligned with the broch entrance itself; at the latter the passage bifurcates and forms a corridor about 1 m wide round the base of the tower. This naturally results in the wall surrounding the broch found in so many old excavations. From it and the main passage to the entrance there are passages to the outbuildings which have rubble-built walls and tend to be wedge-shaped. They share their longitudinal walls and their back ones form a continuous, if irregular, curtain round the settlement. Like the broch interior, these buildings were often subdivided and have in them furnishings made of flagstone; there are fires, cooking troughs, box beds, aumbries, and even a recognisable privy. After subdivision, perhaps 30 or 40 families may have lived at Gurness.

The design at Lingro is very similar (plate 8.3) though Petrie's plan does not show the limits or contents of the buildings; some access to the broch entrance can be seen, as can a corridor 0.7 m wide round the tower from which the buildings were entered. The whole settlement here must have been slightly larger than at Gurness while at Midhowe (figure 8.4) it was smaller. The smaller site is an interesting example of a plan constrained by topographical restrictions.

Because of the method of study, the outer defences have been the least-examined features. They are not uncommon – there are fourteen where identifications have been made – and in almost all the cases outbuildings are known. Purely on typological grounds one may distinguish defences which encircle a broch tower and those which cut off a promontory on which it is situated. Gurness is one of the former type, though coastal, and here the outer defences are entered from the east where the ramparts and ditches incurve on each side (figure 8.5). The outbuildings have a continuous wall round them which goes to the bottom of a surrounding ditch. Beyond this were two ramparts with putative ditches. Midhowe (figure 8.4) and Borthwick (Sandwick) are examples of brochs on promontories, and both are defended by a stout, ditched, wall across with a gate at one end. Some defences are perhaps worthy of note on rather negative grounds; Burrian (North Ronaldsay) for instance, has four ramparts on the landward side and is totally undefended along the low coast.

BU AND HOWE

The century of work on Orkney brochs, which I have summarised, created an unparalleled corpus of information on the subject. Unparalleled though it might be in the context of broch studies it must still be seen as the product of its time and its limitations recognised. One may continually sift through the old material looking for answers to new questions but ultimately the only real way forward is to excavate. It is unfortunate that the very factor that attracted the antiquaries, size, accounts for a lack of recent work due to the limitations of funding. In the last few years, however, there have been two exceptional opportunities to advance our knowledge, both undertaken by the North of Scotland Archaeological Services.

Bu Broch (Stromness) was a salvage excavation carried out during five hectic weeks in 1978 (J. W. Hedges forthcoming, a). During a rescue investigation, a mound of low elevation and unknown content was mechanically trenched prior to destruction. The discovery that it was a broch rather than a cairn meant that, with the time available, a series of objectives had to be defined and rigidly adhered to. If earlier authorities were to be believed, no primary floor plan for a broch in Orkney was known; clearly one should be sought. Secondly, dating for the Orkney brochs had hitherto been on the basis of imported Roman finds with the consequence that brochs could only be dated to the timespan when such imports were feasible; an independent series of radiocarbon dates was desired. Thirdly, the relationship between the broch and any outbuildings and fortification should be sought. Finally, almost unbelievably, there had never been any stratified small finds or environmental material from any Orkney broch and this was a situation that ought to be remedied.

Bu had an overall diameter of 19.5 m with walls 5.2 m thick and a courtyard 9.1 m across; it therefore fits well in the size range for Orkney brochs. Unfortunately, excavation showed the inherent unreliability of such statistics, since the outer 1.6 m of the wall turned out to be an added cladding. Originally the wall had been 3.6 m thick and the whole monument 16.3 m in diameter. The proportion of wall to total thickness thus changed from 44 to 53 per cent. The entrance had been obscured by later re-use but it appears to have been simple, having door jambs halfway along and no guard cells. The wall was only preserved to a height of 1.5 m, depriving us of the opportunity of seeing what, if anything, happened higher up. If the amount of rubble is any indication – and the broch may well have been robbed – then Bu was never very high.

The courtyard bore incontrovertible testimony to the originality of the furnishings found in other brochs and previously described and dismissed as secondary (figure 8.6; plate 8.6; colour plate 17). The floor plan was of the single undivided type, showing great similarity to those at Burrowston

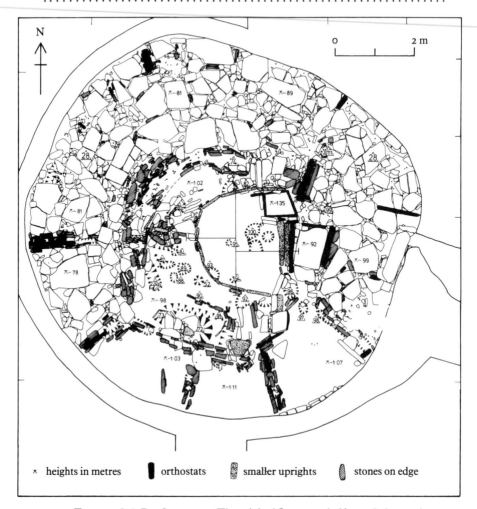

FIGURE 8.6. Bu, Stromness. The original floor revealed in 1978. (NOSAS.)

(Shapinsay) (figure 8.3) and Burrian, Harray (plate 8.2). Centrally placed, and accessible directly from the entrance via a vestibule, was a service area with a massive semi-circular hearth and a cooking tank. This service area had present, *in situ*, a number of kitchen implements, and was covered with carbonaceous material including spent granite pot-boilers. Turning right on entering the broch one would enter a series of three flagged rooms set end-to-end round the inner circumference of the broch wall. The middle one of these was much larger than the outer two and, from the last one, access could be gained to the central area. To the left on entering were the sockets for radial partitions from the wall, suggesting three compartments floored with a mixture of mud and midden. The centre was excavated by means of one trench, while outbuildings and defences were sought by four radial ones. The result was entirely negative; Bu had neither outbuildings nor outer defences; it stood alone. The finds from the broch phase of the site were neither numerous nor exotic but they fitted within what we would call a broch assemblage. Real food for thought came with the radiocarbon dates, three of which put the occupation of the site at *c.* 600 BC: half a millennium earlier than the conventional date.

PLATE 8.6. Bu, Stromness. The original floor revealed in 1978. (NOSAS.)

Old assumptions must now be rethought in the light of Bu. Bu shows clearly, and in spite of theories to the contrary (MacKie 1974, 96–104), that broch-type structures have a long tradition in Orkney and were not brought there either by specialist builders or by dominant incomers during the first century AD. This is corroborated by the finding of the round house at Quanterness, near Kirkwall, which was datable to *c.* 700 BC (plate 8.7) (Renfrew 1979, 194). Bu raises serious doubts about the assumed uniformity of the 52 identified brochs in Orkney (and the many more supposed ones). Hitherto, a broch, once identified, has been tacitly credited with all the attributes of the Anderson stereotype: some may in reality have been as unsophisticated as Bu or even the earlier round house at Quanterness. Bu is

PLATE 8.7. Quanterness, Kirkwall. A round-house belonging to
c. 700 BC in the course of excavation. (Renfrew 1979, pl.22b.)

an example of one type of 'broch' which stood alone and without outbuildings and external defences; it was probably occupied by one family.

The other end of the spectrum is exemplified by Howe (Stromness), a broch whose excavation by the North of Scotland Archaeological Services began in 1978. The interior of the tower has been examined together with a large area outside its entrance. The tower has very Mousa-like proportions, having walls 5.5 m thick and a courtyard only 7 m across; this gives an overall diameter of 18 m and a ratio of wall width to total diameter of 61 per cent. Again, it is clear from excavation that the wall had been widened by 2 m after the collapse of an original thinner one. Originally the broch would have had an overall diameter of 14 m and a ratio of wall width to total diameter of 50 per cent. The wall appears to have a clay core up to the height of 1.5 m and to be solid from there to its maximum preserved height of c. 3 m. At a height of c. 1.5 m at 12 o'clock there is the entrance to the remains of a cell in the wall. The scarcement is not preserved but is suggested by a landing c. 1.5 m from the floor from which steps lead clockwise to the preserved height of the wall. The entrance was not preserved well enough for the lintels to be found in situ; it widened halfway along its length and had no guard cells.

The original floor was destroyed by the laying of a second one after the partial collapse of the wall, and can only be reconstructed from the sockets for its furnishings. This was, however, a typical single-unit layout with a central area, interconnecting flagged rooms to the right from the entrance and unflagged compartments to the left of the service area. The second floor, some furnishings of which reached almost the full height of the wall (plates 8.8 and 9), was very similar. The interconnecting rooms to the right of the entrance were floored with clay and were reduced to two in number; the partition was moved making their width only 1.8 m as opposed to 2.4 m. The central area was proportionally larger and a fragment of its hearth was preserved. The compartments were in particularly good condition, two of them having their lids in place. During the use of both broch floors a souterrain was accessible from a vertical shaft against the wall at c. 12 o'clock.

Excavations outside the broch entrance at Howe have revealed a complex of contemporary outbuildings (plate 8.10). There is a recessed gateway in the external defences from which a passage leads to the broch and around it, giving access to the individual outbuildings. On the outside of these buildings there is a rampart which, at one point where it has been examined, was widened from 1 m in width to 2.7 m and then 3.5 m. Beyond this is very likely to be a ditch and perhaps another rampart and ditch.

Howe has reinforced the conclusion made at Bu that the internal furnishings are original, although they may have been altered and replaced during the use of the tower. Their survival in Orkney is presumably

PLATE 8.8. Howe, Stromness. The replacement floor plan
revealed in 1980. (NOSAS.)

explained by the use of stone there, while wood was used elsewhere. It is
because of this that we can demonstrate the presence of a floor at the height
of *c.* 3.6 m and a partial mezzanine level at *c.* 1.8 m. This discovery adds
greatly to our understanding of broch interiors and should assist in the
interpretation of the slighter traces found in other parts of Scotland. Unlike
Bu, Howe also shows that some broch towers were in effect keeps within a
heavily fortified village which probably accommodated some 250 people.
This major breakthrough in our understanding of what has been found
previously adds a second type of 'broch' which does not fit the stereotype at
all well. Finds from Howe, including Roman ones, suggest that this phase,
at that site, belongs to the first and second centuries AD. This type of
broch-with-settlement is indicative of the development of a form of social
organisation which fits well with the record we have of the Romans making a
treaty with the Orkney chieftains in 43 AD (Laing 1974, 113). It is to be
hoped that this discovery made among the better preserved monuments of
Orkney will lead to the systematic investigation of the immediate surround-
ings of broch towers elsewhere.

REFLECTIONS

In this chapter no mention has been made of the exploitation of the
environment by the people of the broch period, or of the artefact assem-

PLATE 8.9. Howe, Stromness. Elevation showing the replacement furnishings in the west half of the courtyard. (NOSAS/Richard Prideaux.)

blage, while social organisation has only been lightly touched on. Environmental evidence was not sought or kept (in any systematic manner) prior to the Bu excavation of 1978, and the early date of this site together with the very small size of the samples analysed do not form a satisfactory basis for a general statement. The same may be said of the finds, for although an enormous number have been retrieved from Orkney brochs, they have not been from stratified contexts. At Howe occupation continued up to the eighth century and beyond (Hedges and Bell 1980) and this may be the general case with broch sites rather than an exception; the Pictish structures are so poorly built that previous excavators would not have noticed them. The inevitable conclusion is that assemblages, such as that from Gurness (J. W. Hedges forthcoming, b) are likely to represent several phases of occupation, spanning centuries if not a millennium. This situation is aggravated by the lack of change in the basic material culture over the whole Iron Age, so that datable artefacts are the exception rather than the rule. As yet we are ignorant of many aspects of Orkney brochs; only with the conclusion of the large-scale excavation at Howe and its publication will this situation be remedied.

The brochs of Orkney have had so much attention lavished upon them

PLATE 8.10. Howe, Stromness. A sector of the outbuildings excavated in 1980. (NOSAS.)

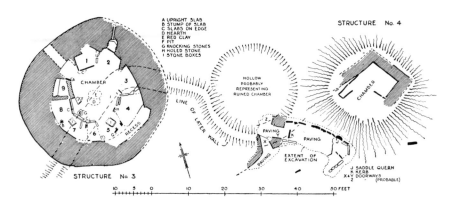

FIGURE 8.7. 'The Potter's Workshop', Calf of Eday.
(RCAMS 1946, fig.124.)

that our view of the Iron Age is very biased in their favour. Conversely the small sites have neither attracted attention nor, when come upon, have they readily been identifiable as belonging to a particular era. It is obvious that there must be Iron Age burials, yet we know nothing about them. There may have been other buildings contemporary with the brochs. The state of our knowledge is poor and the only solution to the dilemma is excavation. Already Quanterness and Bu have given us an insight into the origins of the brochs and their attendant social organisation, while Howe with its continued occupation should help with what follows. Three old excavations should perhaps be mentioned in this context, since they seem to belong to some part of the Iron Age and may indicate the kinds of sites that will be encountered. Calder excavated several buildings on the Calf of Eday in the 1930s (1937; 1939). One of these, the so-called 'potter's workshop', was circular, 12 m in diameter, had a wall 2.25 m thick and a courtyard 7.5 m across; it was entered by a narrow passage with a door jamb near the interior (figure 8.7). Around the perimeter were compartments and in the centre hearths and a cooking trough. The Little Howe of Hoxa (South Ronaldsay) is a truly enigmatic site excavated in 1871 by Petrie (Turner 1872). This was not classified as a broch but was about 13 m in overall diameter and had a wall about 4 m across leaving an inner courtyard only some 5 m in diameter (plate 8.11). The building had a very long protruding entrance and from its sides an intra-mural gallery ran right round the wall at ground level and could be entered from the courtyard at 12 o'clock. Finally, there was a whole complex of buildings excavated at Howmae (North Ronaldsay) by Dr William Traill in 1884 and 1889; one of these was shaped like a wheelhouse (figure 8.8) and the assemblage of artefacts appears to be Iron Age (Traill 1885, 23–32).

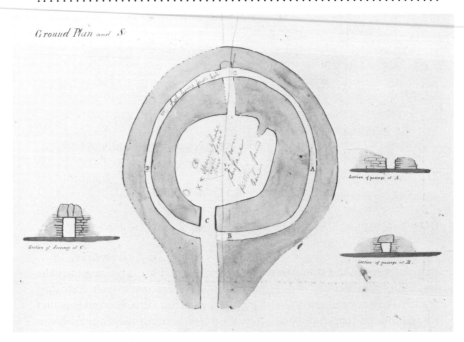

PLATE 8.11. The Little Howe of Hoxa, S. Ronaldsay.
(Petrie nd (b) opposite p.2.)

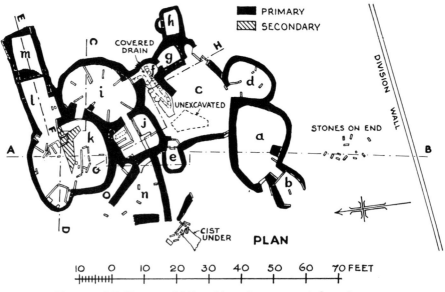

FIGURE 8.8. Howmae, N. Ronaldsay. (RCAMS 1946, fig.93.)

In conclusion, it is hoped that this outline sufficiently indicates the nature and limitations of most of our evidence. Recent excavations have brought some advance in our understanding of the Orkney brochs. Much remains to be learnt, and the broch towers will only be understood adequately when we have a much clearer picture of the Iron Age landscape as a whole.

Acknowledgements. The work briefly reported here has been undertaken in connection with projects carried out for the Scottish Development Department. Patrick Ashmore, the Inspector of Ancient Monuments responsible, is to be thanked for his help and encouragement. The work has been conducted under the aegis of the North of Scotland Archaeological Services; practically all the members, present and past, have made some contribution: a list of individuals would be unduly long. I have been much helped by the staff of the Society of Antiquaries of Scotland Library and of the National Monuments Record of Scotland.

I am grateful to the Royal Commission on Ancient Monuments, Scotland, for providing and giving permission to reproduce figures 8.4, 7 and 8, and plates 8.1, 2, 3 and 11. The Society of Antiquaries of London furnished me with copies of figures 8.1, 2 and 3, and plate 8.4. The North of Scotland Archaeological Services, in collaboration with the Scottish Development Department, provided figures 8.5 and 6, and plates 8.6, 8, 9 and 10, of which plate 8.9 is the graphic work of Richard Prideaux. Professor Colin Renfrew provided plate 8.7 and Kirkwall Library plate 8.5.

Peter Gelling **Excavations at Skaill, Deerness**

Excavations have taken place at Skaill, on the east coast of Deerness, every year since 1963, with the exception of 1966. Three principal sites have been excavated: one Iron Age, another Iron Age/Early Christian, and a third Early Christian, Norse, and later.

Somewhere in the neighbourhood there must be an earlier site than any of these, as underlying ploughmarks were a regular feature. Plate 1 shows some of those found under the Iron Age/Early Christian site. There was a fainter grid of ploughmarks diagonal to the one which shows on the photograph, suggesting that there was no clearly defined field. When sectioned, the marks frequently showed that the plough had been tilted to the left. Stone ard-tips were very common, more so in the earlier than in the later pre-Norse levels, which may reflect an increasing use of iron rather than a decline in cultivation.

The oldest settlement so far found consisted of two sub-circular areas separated by a paved passage (plate 2). The ranging pole lies between the opposed entrances to the two areas. Both were probably roofed, but no evidence for roof-supports was found. The photograph shows the final stage of a fairly complicated structural history. The pottery from this level was exclusively of a plain 'flat-rimmed' variety. Two radiocarbon dates are available: 260 ± 120 bc, and 150 ± 100 bc.

While 'flat-rimmed' ware was still in use, but just about to be superseded, occupation began on a site 160 yards to the north. This may have begun as a ritual site. At one point there was a rough horseshoe of stones enclosing a raised clay floor on which there was a hearth, which appeared to be associated with a pit which had upright stones set just below its lip (plate 3). Nearby, to the left, a second pit, approached by a paved path, and eventually covered by large slabs, contained ard-tips and grain-rubbers.

Subsequently a circular house some 30 feet in diameter was built on this site, with an adjacent enclosure opposite one of its entrances which recalled the figure-of-eight layout of the earlier site. Plate 4 shows this entrance (right foreground) with the wall curving away under the left-hand ranging pole. An enclosing wall can be seen on the left, and it appears again on the left of plate 5, with the house wall well preserved near the opposite

PLATE 1. Skaill: ploughmarks found under the
Iron Age/Early Christian site.

section, but otherwise very fragmentary. The line of both walls had been marked out in advance by deep ploughmarks. A second entrance to the house can be seen in the far right-hand corner of the excavated area. A radiocarbon date of 70 ± 100 bc related to a very early phase of this site. The house appears to have been occupied for a lengthy period, with many reconstructions and alterations, and its exact form at any one time was very hard to determine.

Eventually this house was abandoned and much of its area paved over. The paving can be seen in the section on plate 4. The earliest radiocarbon date so far from this upper level is 530 ± 100 ad, and it may, if only in a chronological sense, be called Pictish. A sample from a deposit which

PLATE 2. Skaill: the oldest (Iron Age) settlement.

PLATE 3. Skaill: Iron Age pit with upright stones below the lip, on the north part of the site.

immediately preceded the paving gave a date of 600 ± 100 ad. At first the paving covered much the same area as the round house, but later it was extended some way to the south, where the occupation belonged exclusively to the Pictish phase.

Quite an extensive building was erected on the paving, consisting of a group of perhaps six oblong rooms, with generally rectilinear walls. The room of which a part is shown on plate 6 measured approximately 13 feet by 11 feet. The pottery from this level was very much finer than anything which had been used previously on the site, with small globular bowls of the characteristic shape. Neither the potting tradition, nor the relatively sophisticated type of building, survived the beginning of the Viking settlement.

PLATE 4. Skaill: entrance (right foreground) to a circular house of
Iron Age date on the north part of the site. The later (Pictish)
paving is seen at the rear in the section.

PLATE 5. Skaill: Iron Age circular house on north part of site. The enclosing wall is seen on the left. One of the entrances is seen in plate 4.

PLATE 6. Skaill, 'Pictish' phase: part of paved floor of room.

9 Anna Ritchie **Orkney in the Pictish Kingdom**

At one time the very title of this chapter would have been considered contentious, for there was doubt not only whether there ever were Picts in Orkney but also whether the islands were inhabited at all when the Norsemen arrived. These doubts arose from lack of positive information and were strengthened by the testimony of the Icelandic historian, Snorri Sturluson, that the Northern Isles were uninhabited (Egil's Saga, IV). This saga was rightly considered to be a more reliable source than the sensational approach of the *Historia Norvegiae* (A. D. Anderson 1922, 330–1), with its notion of pygmies living underground. Pictish studies have, however, advanced rapidly in recent years, both in history and in archaeology, and it can no longer be doubted that Orkney was indeed a flourishing province of the Pictish kingdom throughout its existence. In strict terms, the Pictish period begins with the first mention of the name *Picti*, the Painted Ones, in the surviving historical record, in AD 297, in a Latin panegyric; and it ends with the union of the Picts and Scots under the Scottish king Kenneth mac Alpin, about AD 843. The geographical area of Pictland, determined both from historical sources and from the archaeological record, included all the lands north of the Forth-Clyde line, with the exception (after about AD 500) of Argyll, which had become Scottish *Dalriada*. In practical terms, however, the history of the Picts properly begins with the reign of Bridei, son of Maelchon, in the mid-sixth century. In the archaeological record, the Picts are not incontrovertibly identifiable before the seventh century.

Few artefacts can be attributed specifically to the Picts, rather than to a common cultural tradition shared with contemporary peoples in northern and western Britain, and their identification depends upon the coincidence of their distribution with the geographical and chronological span provided for the Picts by the historical record. Foremost are the carved symbol stones, without which the Picts would barely exist as an archaeological reality. The symbols on the stones can then be used to identify, as Pictish, silverwork and other objects on which they also occur; most notably, heavy silver chains with symbol-decorated terminal rings. Few would date the stones or the related portable objects before the seventh century. The use, for inscriptions, of the *ogam* alphabet must have been acquired by the Picts from the Scots and, to judge by the style of the letters, most of the surviving Pictish ogam inscriptions ought not to be dated before the eighth century (K.H.Jackson 1955, 139). They are identifiable as Pictish rather than Scottish, because they are not written in Gaelic but in the aboriginal non-Indo-European tongue that the Picts used as an alternative to their Celtic language.

Symbol stones and ogam inscriptions are numerically the most important Pictish artefacts, and they show that in archaeological terms the main Pictish period was the seventh and eighth centuries. To this period also belong specifically Pictish house-types and metalwork traditions. Only painted pebbles and nailed timber-laced forts take Pictish archaeology back into the earlier part of the historical Pictish period, for painted pebbles have been found in post-broch contexts (A.Ritchie 1972) and radiocarbon dates from Burghead in Morayshire suggest that that fort may have been built as early as the fourth century AD (Edwards and Ralston 1978).

Though the archaeological reality of the Picts in Orkney is thus well documented by symbol stones, ogam inscriptions, settlements and portable artefacts, confirmation in the contemporary historical record has until recently been lacking. The gap has now been filled, for Dumville (1976) has drawn attention to the relevance for Orkney of the newly discovered *Bern Chronicle,* the text of which is largely a copy of the early part of Bede's *Historia Ecclesiastica,* with some additions and alterations. The entry for AD 46 concerning Claudius and the Orkneys has been recast to include a reference to the Picts: '. . . Orcadas quoque insulas Pictorum romano adiecit imperio, atque inde Romam rediit' [he also annexed the Orkney Islands of the Picts to the Empire, and from there he returned to Rome]. The basic information in Bede's entry about the annexation of the Orkneys by Claudius was presumably derived ultimately from the fourth-century writer Eutropius, and Maxwell has cast serious doubt on the whole episode (1975, 31–5). Nevertheless the Bern addition is of some importance for it shows, as Dumville pointed out, that an Englishman writing in mid-eighth– mid-ninth century considered the Orkneys to be Pictish.

The Picts were not a new ethnic element in the population of Orkney or elsewhere, despite the legends that would have them come from Scythia.

They were simply the descendants of earlier tribesmen who had lived in nucleated villages such as that surrounding the broch at Gurness, or in independent farmsteads such as the wheelhouse on Calf of Eday. According to the *Ravenna Cosmography* (7th/8th c.), the various tribes in the Orkneys had different names for the same island, and Maxwell suggested that this information implies the survival of the aboriginal tongue alongside the Celtic language (1975, 35). It may well be that the older, non-Celtic, element in the population was stronger in the Northern Isles than further south, for Jackson has argued, on place-name evidence, that the main area of Celtic linguistic influence lay in eastern Scotland between the Firth of Forth and the Dornoch Firth (K. H. Jackson 1955, 146–53). The density of ogam inscriptions in the Northern Isles would support the idea of a predominantly non-Celtic population in that area, for more than half the surviving total of inscriptions has been found there, nine in Shetland and six in Orkney. Orcadian place-names are of no help in trying to identify the ethnic make-up of the pre-Norse population (F. T. Wainwright 1962a, 101–7).

Not one Pict from Orkney is known to us by name, unless the reading of an ogam inscription on a bone handle from the Broch of Gurness is correct to take MATS to be a personal name. An Orcadian chieftain appears in Adomnan's account of St Columba's visit, in AD 565, to the Pictish king, Bridei son of Maelchon, but there is no mention of his name. Adomnan uses the term *regulus* to describe this Orcadian ruler, and mentions that Bridei held his hostages; *regulus* is usually translated as 'subject-king' (Anderson and Anderson 1961, 441) or minor king (M. O. Anderson 1973, 144fn). Campbell has emphasised the ambiguity surrounding the use of various terms for minor potentates, in which *rex, subregulus, princeps* and so on were at least in the eighth century interchangeable (1979, 7). The title *subregulus* would appear to be far more commonly used than *regulus*, however, and Adomnan's use of the latter may have been deliberate. If A. Jackson is correct (1971, 128) in identifying the Pictish kinship system as avunculocal, their society would have consisted of several matrilineages, all more or less equal in status. Alternatively, Miller has argued that there were several king-producing patrilineages interlinked by matrilines maintained by the marriages of the royal sisters (M. Miller 1978, 51). In either case, the Orcadian *regulus* may not have been greatly inferior in status to king Bridei. Even though Bede was later to describe Bridei as *rex potentissimus*, a most powerful king, he may not have had direct rule over the whole of Pictland.

In the sixth and seventh centuries AD, Orkney was literally closer to the political and cultural heart of Pictland than in later times. Not only was Bridei's royal residence somewhere near the River Ness, according to Adomnan (both Castle Urquhart and Craig Phadraig are major contenders for the title of Bridei's *munitio* (Alcock 1980, 78–9)), but Isabel Henderson has argued that the practice of carving and erecting symbol-stones originated in the Moray Firth area (1958). Even closer to Orkney, the Golspie area on the coast of Sutherland was an important focus of Pictish settlement (Close-Brooks 1975, 209–10). Alcock has proposed the terms 'Heartland Picts' to describe those living in the eastern lowlands from the Forth to Caithness where symbol stones and *pit*-names are concentrated, and 'Peripheral Picts' to describe those living in the west and north who 'are likely to have borne a diluted Pictish or Proto-Pictish culture' (1980, 62). If it is accepted that the historical and archaeological evidence points to the power centre of sixth- and early seventh-century Pictland being in the Moray Firth area, Orkney was no more peripheral than Angus, although the sea crossing may have made it less convenient. Of the distinctive portable artefacts that constitute Pictish material culture, the Northern Isles lack only the massive silver chain – and seven of the ten surviving chains were in any case found outside Pictland. The mere presence of a great Pictish treasure on St Ninian's Isle need not imply that Shetland was in the mainstream of Pictish cultural life in the eighth century, but moulds from the Brough of Birsay prove that the St Ninian's Isle type of brooch was being manufactured in the Northern Isles (Curle 1974, 302) as well as further south; and sculptured stones from Bressay and Papil demonstrate the strength of late Pictish culture in Shetland.

Regional differences detectable in the archaeological record, and perhaps reflected in the historical record, fit better into the old framework, inherited from Bede, of northern and southern Pictland, in which the Northern Isles are not divorced from the northern Scottish mainland. The distribution of the symbol known as the circular disc and rectangle with square indentation is concentrated in Orkney, Caithness and Sutherland; whatever its meaning, its restricted occurrence would seem to imply that it was special to this area. Painted pebbles have been found only in Caithness, Orkney and Shetland. Burials under kerbed cairns appear to have been a northern Pictish tradition, but Alcock has suggested that their equivalent in stone-free areas of southern Pictland may be the square and circular ditched barrows seen on air-photographs (1980, 65).

SYMBOL STONES

Orkney has yielded eight symbol stones, of which one from Oxtro in Birsay is now lost, four are incomplete, and one from Gurness is so lightly incised on a squat boulder that it is perhaps more likely to be a trial piece than a formal monument. In view of the regularity with which new symbol stones are found on mainland Scotland, it is perhaps surprising that a fragment discovered in 1967 on the Sands of Evie is the only symbol stone to have turned up in Orkney in the last 45 years. It may reflect a measure of the difference in agricultural activity, as most mainland discoveries are made

PLATE 9.1. Symbol stone, Brough of Birsay. (© NMAS.)

PLATE 9.2. Symbol stone, St Peter's Church, S. Ronaldsay. (© NMAS.)

during ploughing. None of the Orcadian stones appears to be later than the eighth century AD and most are likely to belong to the seventh century. Stevenson has demonstrated by typological analysis that the earliest examples of the common symbol known as the crescent and v-rod are those in Sutherland and Orkney (R. B. K. Stevenson 1955, 101–6). It is probable that the stone found in the graveyard on the Brough of Birsay was originally a cross-slab, for its sides appear to be shaped and one face, on which the cross may have been carved, is missing. The cross-slab from the Broch of Burrian bears an ogam inscription and the remains of an incised design which may represent a fish (MacGregor 1974, 96, fig.21); if so, there are two symbol-bearing cross-slabs in Orkney, and they should both be dated to the eighth century AD. The Brough of Birsay stone (plate 9.1) was found in scattered fragments and was not, as previously believed, associated with a triple grave (Curle 1982, 91–2). The surviving face bears four symbols (circular disc and rectangle, crescent and v-rod, 'elephant', eagle) and, executed in shallow relief at the foot of the stone, three warriors in long tunics bearing swords, spears and square decorated shields (colour plate 18).

A stone from St Peter's Church on South Ronaldsay (plate 9.2), where it had been re-used as a window sill, is incomplete and bears a rectangle and a crescent and v-rod on one face and another crescent and v-rod together with a circular disc and rectangle with square indentation on the other face. This last symbol appears to have been of special importance in Orkney, for it occurs on three stones and on a bone phalange from the Broch of Burrian on North Ronaldsay, and it is used only rarely elsewhere. It appears on a stone from Greens on mainland Orkney, in conjunction with a crescent and v-rod and a mirror symbol, and on the Gurness boulder together with two rectangles. A rectangle and a crescent and v-rod are incised on a fragment from Redland, Firth, and a mirror symbol is pecked on the sandstone fragment from the Sands of Evie. The lost stone from Oxtro in Birsay bore an eagle, and another exceptionally fine eagle occurs in combination with a crescent and v-rod and a mirror on the stone from the Knowe of Burrian (detailed catalogue of these stones in J.N.G.Ritchie 1969). The ox phalange from the Broch of Burrian, North Ronaldsay, is incised with a crescent and v-rod on one side and a circular disc and indented rectangle on the other and may have been used as a playing piece (MacGregor 1974, 88, fig.16, no.210). This is the only portable artefact from Orkney bearing Pictish symbols, although a pebble incised with a hexagram and a penta-gram from the same site may be related (MacGregor 1974, 96, fig.20, no.278). Symbols occur on portable artefacts outside Orkney, particularly on fine silverwork, as well as on the walls of caves at Covesea, Morayshire, and East Wemyss, Fife, demonstrating that they could be used less formally than on stone monuments.

Few of the Orcadian symbol stones are securely provenanced and none sheds any light on the function of the stones or the meaning of the symbols. Jackson has drawn attention to the similarities between the Picts and certain tribes in British Columbia who, like the Picts, had a matrilineal society; they were divided into clans each with its own crest, such as an eagle or a fish, which was tattooed on the body and carved on totem-poles to act as house frontal poles, memorial poles and several other functions (A.Jackson 1971, 136–7). It seems very likely that Pictish symbol stones were similarly used in a variety of ways (the interpretations that have been offered are summarised in I.Henderson 1971; A.Jackson 1971). It is clear that, to a passing Pict, the message conveyed by the symbols on a stone monument was clear and intelligible, and the uniformity of symbols throughout Pictland emphasises the political and cultural cohesion of an organised and complex society.

BURIAL AND RITUAL

Very little is known about the pagan religion of the Picts, although some continuity of Celtic ideas and practices may reasonably be expected. A story recorded by Adomnan in which Columba blesses a well sacred to the Picts implies that water spirits were part of the folklore of Pictland as they were among earlier people (Anderson and Anderson 1961, 61b–62a). There are several references in Adomnan to *magi*, a class of pagan priests or magicians the most powerful of whom lived at the royal court, and the 'gods' of the *magi* are contrasted with the one God of the Christians (Anderson and Anderson 1961, 78a–b). Henderson has suggested that some of the figure scenes on symbol stones may represent incidents in Pictish folk-lore (I. Henderson 1967, 67). There are hints in the archaeological record of pagan practices among the Picts. At the Udal on North Uist, deliberate deposits of animal bones, usually lambs, have been found beneath houses of the sixth–eighth centuries and beneath an earlier wheelhouse (I. A. Crawford 1972, 7), recalling a bizarre deposit of 32 ox teeth at À Cheardach Mhor (Young and Richardson 1960, 141) and of red deer jawbones set in an arc round the hearth at À Cheardach Bheag (Fairhurst 1971, 80), both sites being wheelhouses on South Uist. In Orkney, in the central area of the henge at the Stones of Stenness, a group of four pits was found (J. N. G. Ritchie 1976, 15, 22); one of the pits contained charcoal from which a radiocarbon date of ad 519 ± 150 (SRR-352) was obtained, indicating activity, perhaps of a ritual nature, on the site in the mid-first millennium AD.

From about 1000 BC until the Viking Age in Scotland, it is notoriously difficult to identify the burials of a particular people or of a particular period of time, because there was no strong tradition of placing gravegoods along side the dead. Without gravegoods, or a recognisable type of grave structure, an isolated burial can be dated only by radiocarbon analysis of the surviving bones; and many burials were found and the bones subsequently lost before the development of scientific dating methods. Extended inhumations in stone-built long cists were certainly one favoured mode of burial in later prehistoric times in Orkney and some, such as that found close to the seventh–eighth century farmstead (plate 9.3) at Buckquoy (A. Ritchie 1977, 183–4), may contain Picts. The great mound known as Saevar Howe at Birsay was utilised for a cemetery of long cists, perhaps of Viking-age date; it was also the hiding-place, in a small cist, of an ecclesiastical iron bell (RCAMS 1946, 23, no.40; Farrer 1864). It is perhaps

PLATE 9.3. Long cist burial, Buckquoy. (Crown copyright, SDD.)

significant that the pebble incised with a hexagram and a pentacle from the Broch of Burrian, North Ronaldsay, was similarly found in a small stone cist (MacGregor 1974, 70). With the coming of Christianity, long cists became the norm in ecclesiastical cemeteries, and the lower stratum of graves in the churchyard on the Brough of Birsay is thought to belong to the pre-Norse community (Radford 1959, 17).

It is possible that burial in short cists was also practised by pagan Picts (Close-Brooks 1975, 210); symbol stones have been found re-used as cover slabs for such cists, and this mode of burial is unlikely to belong to Viking or later times. The mound covering the ruins of the broch of Oxtro at Birsay was used for a cemetery of cremation burials in short cists, and one of the cist-covers bore the carving of an eagle; the stone is now lost (it is thought to have been incorporated into the wall of one of the farm buildings at nearby Boardhouse), but it was almost certainly a Pictish symbol stone (RCAMS 1946, 11–12, no.11). The symbol stone covering a short cist at Golspie in Sutherland was interpreted as secondary to the burial on the grounds that the cist was empty and the stone too big to have been the original cover-slab (J.M.Davidson 1943), but it is equally possible that this was a cenotaph, and that the symbol stone was over-large as a cover-slab because this was not its primary function. Both here and at Oxtro, the cist-builders are likely to have been re-using symbol stones which had originally been carved for another purpose, perhaps as house-posts displaying the clan crest of the dead. Another possibility is that the 'statement' made by the symbols had been of a temporary nature and the stones had become irrelevant building material.

Recent studies have identified a Pictish type of grave-structure (A.Ritchie 1974, 31–2; Ashmore 1980), in which a long cist is set centrally beneath a low circular or rectilinear cairn with a slab-built kerb. The type-site is Ackergill in Caithness, where a linear cemetery consisted of one circular and seven rectilinear cairns, together with two unenclosed long cists (A.J.H.Edwards 1926; 1927). Examples have been excavated in recent years in Shetland, Orkney, Caithness and Sutherland, underlining the essentially northern Pictish distribution of this type of grave. The cairn at Sandwick, Unst, Shetland most closely resembles the classic rectilinear form at Ackergill, characterised by taller pillar-stones set at each corner and set half-way along the two long sides of the rectangle and by a white quartzite capping to the mound (Bigelow 1978). A radiocarbon date of ad 445 ± 75 (GU-1291) for a sample of bone from the skeleton indicates that the burial is likely to have taken place within the period AD 300–600 (Bigelow forthcoming). The dead person is likely therefore to have been a pagan Pict. Both at Dunrobin, Sutherland (Close-Brooks 1980) and at Ackergill, a symbol stone was found nearby and some form of association between stones and graves is likely though unproven. Radiocarbon dates from the Dunrobin skeleton suggest burial within the period AD 600–900. These dates lend support to the argument that the rectilinear form of kerbed cairn remained in use later than the circular form, enabling Norsemen to adopt this form of burial (A.Ritchie 1974, 31; Ritchie and Ritchie 1981, 175). It is, however, the circular form that has been found in Orkney, on the Point of Buckquoy at Birsay (Brough Road, Area 1, Morris 1979b, 13–14).

PICTISH BIRSAY

The Birsay area was clearly an important focus of settlement in Pictish times. Apart from the symbol stones and burials already mentioned, all but two of Orkney's ogam inscriptions were found in Birsay: one in the domestic settlement at Buckquoy and three on the Brough of Birsay. One of the latter group was found during recent excavations (Morris 1981a, 36), but there appears to be some doubt about the provenance of the two found in earlier excavations. Radford mentions one from the early churchyard (1959, 5) and one from the beach (1962, 174), while Cruden mentions that one was found re-used as a building stone in the complex known as 'Thorfinn's palace' (1965, 25). This re-used stone is the inscription Birsay I in Padel's catalogue of Pictish inscriptions, where he makes the point about both inscriptions from the old excavations that they have a casual, carelessly incised appearance and are unlikely to have been designed as formal, long-lasting monuments (1972, 2, 10–11, 16, 55). He suggests that they are comparable as casual inscriptions with the runic inscriptions in Maes Howe and implies that they should perhaps belong to a ninth-century Viking Age context. None of the Orkney examples is typical of Pictish ogam inscriptions, and none can be given an early date. A cross-slab from the Broch of Burrian, North Ronaldsay, bears an inscription in the letter-form known as bind-ogam, where the strokes representing each letter are joined together (a device that makes reading the inscription infinitely easier); like Birsay I and II, the ogams are incised rather than pocked in the manner of most Pictish inscriptions (Padel 1972, 75–9). There are possible traces of a fish symbol on this stone (MacGregor 1974, 96, fig.21) which, if accepted, make Burrian the sole example in Orkney of association between ogams and Pictish symbols.

The inscriptions from Buckquoy and Gurness are incised on portable objects, a stone spindle-whorl and a bone handle respectively, and Padel has suggested that such chattel inscriptions imply a widespread knowledge of ogams at some point in Pictish history (1972, 3). There are, however, only two other surviving chattel inscriptions, both on bone handles (Bac Mhic Connain, North Uist and Weeting, Norfolk), and it is equally possible that the ogams bestowed a magical or talismanic dimension on these personal belongings and that the cutting of the ogams was done by a special person such as a *magus* or the local midwife. The ogams on the Buckquy whorl are incised in a circle round the central perforation and have been dated to the early eighth century (K.H. Jackson 1977; A. Ritchie 1977, 181–2, 197, fig.8, no.84, 199). The Gurness inscription extends lengthwise down the handle and is likely also to belong to the eighth century (Padel 1972, 98–100). In common with other Pictish ogams outside Orkney, all these inscriptions are characteristically and tantalisingly incomprehensible. If there were a magical connotation to the cutting of ogams, it might help to explain why they were used to convey the older Pictish tongue rather than Celtic, although, by the eighth century, such practices can hardly have found approval in the Pictish church.

To some extent, the importance of Birsay in Pictish times is a reflection of archaeological activity in the area, which has been particularly intensive in the 1970s and 1980s. Nevertheless, the attraction of the Bay of Birsay for boats and fishing and the outstanding fertility of Birsay soils are likely to have made the area a natural focus for settlement in the Pictish period as in later times. The status of the Brough of Birsay is difficult to determine. There was an early Christian cemetery enclosed by a curvilinear wall, and remains of walling beneath the later church may belong to a contemporary chapel (Radford 1962, 167–9); the cemetery included a square kerbed cairn which might belong to the Pictish type of grave-setting identified elsewhere, but the structural evidence from the early excavations has yet to be published. There are traces of earlier domestic occupation beneath the Viking-age buildings, but the extent of the settlement and its nature, whether monastic or secular, are unknown. Radiocarbon dates in the eighth century AD have been obtained from pre-Norse occupation levels (Morris 1981a, 40), and continuing excavations may clarify further the structural sequence. Pre-Norse artefacts include bone combs and pins, the symbol stone and ogam inscriptions already described, and an important assemblage of metalworking material (Curle 1982). The latter includes a lead disc decorated with a trumpet-spiral design which is a pattern for making cast bronze plaques, possibly intended as escutcheons for hanging-bowls (Curle 1974; plate 9.4). The spirals match those on silver hand-pins from the hoards from Gaulcross, Morayshire and Norries' Law, Fife, and the overall design has been described as 'Durrowesque' (R. B. K. Stevenson 1976, 248, 251). There are also clay moulds used in the manufacture of pen-annular brooches (Curle 1974), including the special form identified as Pictish by Wilson in the hoard from St Ninian's Isle in Shetland (Small et al. 1973, 81–105), characterised by stylistic features such as the presence of a panel with curved ends on the hoop of the brooch. This type of brooch belongs to the eighth century, and other examples have been found in Orkney at Pierowall on Westray and from Stromness (Small et al. 1973, 89). Whatever the nature of the Pictish settlement on the Brough of Birsay, it included, temporarily at least, the services of a skilled metalworking crafts-man.

Rescue excavation in the early 1970s of a low elongated mound on the Point of Buckquoy, truncated by coastal erosion of the Bay of Birsay, revealed the remains of a farmstead spanning the Pictish and Norse periods, though without direct continuity between the two (A. Ritchie 1977). The erosion meant that the site was incomplete in all periods except perhaps the last, which was a casual Viking-age burial of the later tenth century, inserted into the mound formed by the ruins of the earlier domestic buildings. Nevertheless, sufficient traces survived to allow the identification of Norse and pre-Norse house-plans and to enable some estimate to be made of the respective life-styles involved. The Pictish phases seem likely to have spanned the seventh and early eighth centuries AD, after which there was a brief interval, perhaps of half a century, before Norsemen began to establish a new farmstead on the site around AD 800 (figure 9.1; colour plate 19).

PLATE 9.4. Lead disc, Brough of Birsay, 58 mm in diameter.
(Crown copyright, SDD.)

The earliest surviving structures were two successive houses of cellular type, in which small cells open off a central area; less than half of house 6 remained intact, with a central slab-lined hearth and three rectilinear cells along one side of the axis of the house. The other side had been destroyed when first house 5 and then house 4 were built. House 5 was very small and its plan-form virtually intact: three rectilinear cells surrounding a central hearth, the entire internal area measuring only 2.75 m by 3.60 m, although the individual cells were not markedly smaller than those in the earlier house 6.

When the Broch of Gurness (or Aikerness) and its surrounding structures were excavated, two separate and distinct buildings were recognised in the uppermost occupation levels, overlying the earlier 'village' surrounding the broch itself (RCAMS 1946, fig.132). One of these buildings was a

PLATE 9.5. Figure-of-eight house, Buckquoy. (Crown copyright, SDD.)

simple oblong structure sometimes assumed to be a Viking-age hall-house, and the other was a cellular house closely similar to those found at Buckquoy. The Gurness example had four cells and was comparable in overall size to house 6 at Buckquoy. This type of house seems not to have been found elsewhere, but the Gurness evidence, together with the seventh-century dating likely for those at Buckquoy, suggests that such houses would be late in any post-broch structural sequence and thus vulnerable to destruction.

Although the interiors of these houses were compartmented, their external appearance was probably a rounded oval; the walls were stone-faced, either by horizontal masonry or by a combination of upright slabs and horizontal walling only on the inside, and an earth and turf backing seems likely. The internal divisions were probably as much a device to alleviate roofing problems as they were a means of separating different areas of the house. In this respect they resemble wheelhouses, where the radial piers not only divided up the interior but also helped to support the roof. The resemblance to the wheelhouse tradition is even more marked in house 4, where the rooms were subdivided by piers of masonry (plate 9.5).

The late Pictish house at Buckquoy, no.4, was larger and more sophisticated in design than its predecessors, but it represents a related type of plan-form, the figure-of-eight house. Here the basic form consists of a large oblong or oval living-hall containing a central hearth and a smaller circular chamber opening off one end. At Buckquoy there was an additional recti-linear room at the opposite end of the living-hall, and beyond it a small entrance vestibule, the whole house forming a linear unit of interconnecting rooms, almost 14 m in overall internal length. A second entrance led straight into the living-hall, and the remains of low stone kerbing along either side of the hall was interpreted as evidence for flanking wooden benches or platforms. The hearth was well-designed: paved and kerbed with stone, one end was left open to allow easy removal of the ash, and there was a pit at the other end in which embers could be kept alight during the night. Post-holes on either side would have held the wooden supports for a spit across the fire. Elaborate hearths are a feature of this period, a reflection perhaps of the stability of Pictish society. The hearth in house 5 was not only open-ended but furnished with a removable slab, notched to fit the side-kerbing of the hearth, which could be used for baking or as a rest for pots. Contemporary and similarly elaborate hearths have been found at the Howe, Stromness (Hedges and Bell 1980, 50–1) and at Calf of Eday (Calder 1939, 175, fig.1, pl.LXVII, 2).

The main part of house 4 was built with walls of horizontal drystone masonry, but the circular chamber was walled with a basal revetment of upright slabs and horizontal masonry above. The chamber was in fact partially underground, and the upright slabs were set against the ruins of the earlier house 6 and against the underlying natural boulder clay. The horizontal walling began only at ground-level. This same labour-saving device was used in Orkney in more recent times, for houses were built partially underground in the seventeenth and eighteenth centuries, and even in the late nineteenth century farm workers would choose to build

PLATE 9.6. Figure-of-eight house, Brough Road Area 3, Birsay.
(C. D. Morris. Crown copyright, SDD.)

against a hillside so that one wall was only a stone facing against the earth (Fenton 1979, 13).

At present there are no very close parallels to the plan-form of house 4 in Orkney. A little to the south of this site on the Point of Buckquoy, a house of related form has been excavated by Christopher Morris (Brough Road, Area 3, in the Birsay Bay Project, Morris 1979b, 16–18, and a possible second house in Area 5, Morris 1980, 27–8). Here the house consisted of two circular rooms of almost the same size, one about 4.50 m in diameter and the other slightly smaller, separated by a central drystone pier. The larger chamber contained a slab-lined hearth and a possible oven. The walls were built of horizontal drystone masonry with a neatly finished inner face and an irregular outer face and an earth and stone core; externally the house was of oval shape (plate 9.6).

Closer in shape and internal layout to Buckquoy house 4 are the buildings belonging to pre-Norse levels at the Udal on North Uist (I.A. Crawford 1973; 1974; Crawford and Switsur 1977). They belong to Crawford's 'Scotto-Pictish' levels, dated to the fourth to ninth centuries AD, and a typological sequence has been identified, showing the development of the house-plan for which the obscure term 'ventral' has been put forward (Crawford and Switsur 1977, 130). The sequence begins with a simple oval house, 5 m by 4 m, with small side-cells, a central slab-lined hearth and a low platform along one side. The second stage, which relates to Buckquoy, consists of a large oval chamber about 6 m long with an oval cell opening off one end, a doorway at the other, a central hearth and flanking platforms on both sides. The final stage sees the addition of more side-cells, and the houses now have fenced yards and small square outhouses. The material culture belonging to these levels is markedly different from that of the preceding wheelhouse occupation of the site (Crawford and Switsur 1977, 129), unlike the situation in Orkney where the basic material culture remained the same throughout the post-broch centuries.

A very small version of the figure-of-eight house forms one of the outbuildings at the Broch of Yarrow in Caithness (J. Anderson 1890, 137, fig. 1). An attempt was made in Ritchie 1974, fig. 1 to produce these various house-plans to the same scale, but mistakenly houses 6, 5 and 4 at Buckquoy, Yarrows F and Gurness were in fact reproduced at twice the size of the rest. The true comparison between Buckquoy 4 and the Udal house n may be seen in Alcock (1980, fig. 4.2).

ENVIRONMENT AND MATERIAL CULTURE

The various Birsay sites are currently the major source of information about the environment and economy of Pictish life in Orkney (Donaldson, Morris and Rackham 1981; A. Ritchie 1977). In general the environment is likely to have been little different in terms of natural vegetation from that of today, though the likely presence of more local pockets of shrub woodland has been stressed. It is clear from documentary sources that cereal crops were more commonly grown in later medieval times than today, especially bere and oats, and the recovery of grains of both these crops from the Brough Road Area 3 of the Birsay Bay Project may hint at the importance of arable agriculture in pre-Norse times (Donaldson, Morris and Rackham 1981, 80). Nevertheless, the emphasis of the archaeological material is upon animal husbandry, and it seems likely that the Pictish economy was predominantly pastoral. At Buckquoy, the animal bones represented about 50 per cent cattle, 30 per cent sheep and 20 per cent pig (Noddle 1977), whereas sheep were predominant in the sample from Room 5 on the Brough of Birsay where there were pre-Norse levels beneath the Viking-age structures. It is possible that Buckquoy functioned as the home farm for the community living on the Brough. These domestic animals were bred primarily for their meat, hides and bone for implement manufacture, and hunting wild animals such as deer and wild cat and birds such as gannet and fulmar was of minor importance. The abundance of bone available from domestic carcases perhaps explains the rarity of whale and seal bones: such mammals would have been butchered on the beach for their skins, meat and blubber and the bones mostly left behind if they were not required.

Marine resources must always have been important in the Orcadian economy. At Buckquoy, fishing appears to have been less important in Pictish times than in the Norse period, but this may be an illusion created by the absence of middens on the surviving area of the Pictish settlement. This factor of partial survival limits many of the conclusions about economic life that can be drawn both from Buckquoy and from most of the Birsay sites. The pre-Norse levels at Buckquoy yielded bones of conger eel, saithe or pollack, ling, cod, hake and ballan wrasse (Wheeler 1977), and cod were also found in contemporary contexts on the Brough of Birsay (Donaldson, Morris and Rackham 1981, 77). This evidence suggests line or net fishing from the shore and line-fishing from boats offshore. Some of the shellfish, predominantly limpets and winkles, from Buckquoy may have been used as fish-bait rather than as food; their meat-weight makes them insignificant as part of the human diet (Evans and Spencer 1977), though a decrease in the size of the limpets from Pictish to Norse samples may suggest an over-collection in pre-Norse times that is not detectable from the surviving numbers of shells. It is possible that, like the modern Faroese and other people who live by the sea (A. Jackson 1977, 50), Picts in the Northern Isles might refuse to eat shellfish on principle. In more recent times, limpets and winkles were eaten only as a last resort in times of famine, though other shellfish such as cockles and razorfish were considered delicacies (Fenton 1978, 541–2). Bede describes the whelk (*coclea*) as a great natural asset to Britain, because its shell was used to make a scarlet dye 'a most beautiful red which neither fades through the heat of the sun nor exposure to the rain; indeed the older it is the more beautiful it becomes' (*Historia Ecclesiastica*, I, i). Dog whelks from which such a useful dye could have been made were the third most common shells found at Buckquoy but not, unfortunately, in the vast quantities necessary for practical manufacture (Evans 1969, 479).

Buckquoy is as yet the only fully published Pictish settlement in Orkney and, unfortunately, the site did not produce a large assemblage of artefacts from the early levels. Once the publication of the Brough of Birsay, Gurness and other sites with Pictish occupation is complete, it should be possible to reconstruct a more detailed picture of the range of Pictish domestic equipment. The first phase of Pictish occupation at Buckquoy included both cellular houses, nos 6 and 5, and the associated artefacts included simple bone skewer pins and a needle, part of a bone mount, a bone spoon and a double-sided composite bone comb. A similar bone mount came from the second Pictish phase, associated with house 4, and they have been interpreted as strengthening plates for the mouths of leather knife-sheaths (A. Ritchie 1977, 179). Carefully made small bone pins were in use in this phase, including one with an animal head, perhaps a cat, and an unfinished example which suggests that such bone pins were manufactured on the site. Pottery vessels were used, including plain large jars, as were iron knives and stone spindle whorls. One of the latter bore an ogam inscription and has already been discussed, and its importance for the site is that it is a specifically Pictish artefact. There was also a painted pebble, well stratified in the primary occupation of house 4 and thus providing a firm chronological context for an intriguing class of object which appears to have been peculiar to the Northern Isles and Caithness. It is a white quartzite pebble, 40 mm long, which has been painted overall with small circles in a dye which has left a brown stain though it may once have been a brighter colour. Twenty such pebbles have survived, all, apart from the Buckquoy example, from broch sites and most belonging to the post-broch period. Although it cannot be claimed as a diagnostic Pictish artefact, the painted pebble was clearly a constituent of material culture in northern Pictland. A variety of curvilinear and dot designs has been used on the pebbles and they are very pleasing objects; unwashed they would be difficult to spot during excavation, and the fact that so many were found even during late nineteenth-century excavations in Caithness suggests that they may have been more common than it appears. It has been argued that painted pebbles were charmstones used to treat sick people and animals by dipping the stones into drinking-water, a tradition that was strong in medieval times and survived in Scotland at least into the late nineteenth century using naturally attractive stones (A. Ritchie 1972). There is even a story recorded by Adomnan about Columba using a holy pebble in just this way at the court of the Pictish king Bridei (Anderson and Anderson 1961, 399–405; colour plate 20).

The Pictish settlement at Buckquoy was succeeded around AD 800 by a Norse farmstead. Although the house-types were distinctly different, and the stratigraphy and chronology of the site indicated that the new buildings were contemporary with the Norse colonisation of the Orkneys, the associated artefacts displayed little evidence of cultural change. The bone combs and pins found in the Norse levels are native in origin, and there is not one indisputably Norse artefact among the finds. The interpretation of this evidence is controversial. It has been argued that there must have been a degree of social integration between the Picts and the incoming Norse settlers during the primary stages of colonisation of the Orkneys in the ninth century (A. Ritchie 1974), in contrast to the traditional view of Vikings inflicting extermination and slavery. An alternative interpretation would have the Norse houses built and the artefacts made under duress by Pictish slaves in the manner to which they were accustomed: 'the Pictish population can only have been subjugated by force' (Graham-Campbell 1980, 69). But the houses were not built according to Pictish custom and, although the Norse takeover of Orkney was indubitably complete in the end, enforced subjugation is not the only answer. The Scots took over the Pictish kingdom on mainland Scotland but no modern historian would suggest that there was wholesale slaughter or slavery there. The political circumstances were different of course, but nevertheless the moral of the comparison is that takeover bids need not be bloody.

Excavations at the Broch of Howe near Stromness have yielded considerable evidence of Pictish occupation (see appendix to this chapter; Hedges and Bell 1980), but assessment of the site must await full publication of the results. The buildings appear to form conjoining units rather than freestanding houses of recognisable plan-form, and the individual components are small in floor area (figure 9.2). The Picts utilised and refurbished earlier buildings in preference to building anew as at Gurness, but the complex sequence of modifications and the quantity of finds argues against any impression of squatter occupation. Pre-Norse structures have also been found at Skaill in Deerness (information Peter Gelling, see appendix to chapter 8, p.176) and at Saevar Howe, Birsay (information John Hedges).

Despite the clear architectural links between house 4 at Buckquoy and wheelhouse tradition, examples of true wheelhouses are rare in Orkney. One was excavated at Calf of Eday, together with later structures which presumably take the site into Pictish times (Calder 1939); the latter include a kerbed and paved hearth with a post-hole on either side for the spit which is virtually identical to the hearth in house 4 at Buckquoy. The spit-supports were made of imported Scots pine probably derived from drift-wood (Calder 1939, 175). Alcock has postulated the existence of two different building traditions, 'the circular and the axial', among the Picts and their immediate forebears, the circular represented by wheelhouses and the axial by figure-of-eight, rectilinear and cellular houses (1980, 74), although he admits that it is difficult to date wheelhouses within the historical Pictish period (1980, 71). That wheelhouses could themselves possess an axial element is demonstrated by the site at À Cheardach Bheag on South Uist, where a large wheelhouse had a smaller wheelhouse opening off it (Fairhurst 1971, fig.3). It seems likely that these various house-types represent inter-related architectural development rather than separate traditions, and the impression given by the existing dating evidence is that the development is linear and sequential from wheelhouses onwards.

Information about the early Christian church in Orkney is disappointingly limited by lack of excavation, although potentially interesting sites have been located by fieldwork (Lamb 1973; 1976). Apart from the early Christian site on the Brough of Birsay, no surviving church or monastic settlement can with certainty be dated prior to the Viking Age, even though it seems likely that the Orkneys were converted to Christianity in the course of the seventh century AD. Corn Holm in Deerness and Castle of Burwick on

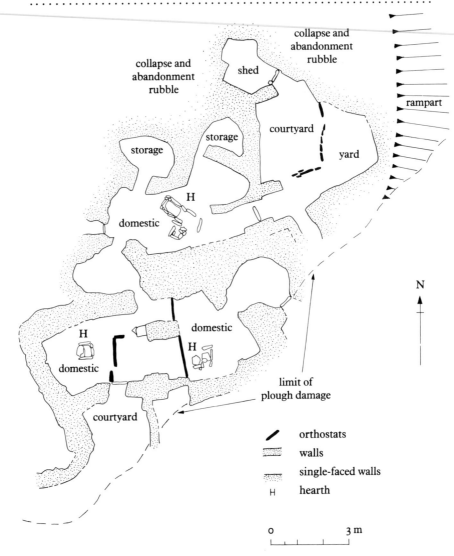

collapse and
abandonment
rubble

collapse and
abandonment
rubble

shed

rampart

courtyard

storage

storage

storage

yard

H

domestic

N

H

domestic

domestic

H

domestic

limit of
plough damage

courtyard

orthostats

walls

single-faced walls

H   hearth

o   3 m

FIGURE 9.2. Howe, Stromness: simplified plan of phase 2
of the Pictish settlement.

South Ronaldsay have been interpreted as eremitic monasteries which may
date from the eighth century through to the tenth and eleventh centuries
(Lamb 1973, 78–82), but there is no evidence for a pre-Norse monastery on
the Brough of Deerness, in fact Morris has suggested that the rectangular
buildings surrounding the chapel may be secular and domestic rather than
ecclesiastical (1977, 70).

Structural evidence for the early Christian church is thus scanty, but there are sculptural and artefactual traces of Christianity from at least the seventh century onwards. The small iron bells from Saevar Howe and the Broch of Burrian mentioned above are normally associated with Irish missionaries and probably date from the eighth or ninth centuries (Bourke 1980), while the 'arm-pit' cross on the Burrian slab is likely to date from the eighth century. The same type of cross appears in considerably more elaborate form on the stone panel from Flotta, which originally formed the front of an altar; the cross is infilled with interlace designs and the piece has been dated to the late eighth century (C. Thomas 1971, 186–8; plate 9.7). The cross-slab from the church of St Boniface on Papa Westray bears an incised cross formed of interlacing segments of circles, and a date in the seventh century has been suggested (Radford 1962, 173).

PLATE 9.7. Altar frontal, Flotta. (Copyright NMAS.)

The Picts were a seafaring nation. They used boats not simply as a means of transport but also as an element of naval power in their armoury. The Pictish threat to late Roman Britain was at least partially sea-borne, and an entry in the Annals of Tigernach for AD 729 mentions the loss at sea of 150 Pictish ships (A. O. Anderson 1922, 226). The great timber-laced fort at Burghead on the coast of Moray must surely have been a Pictish naval base, and Alcock has stressed the coastal distribution of Pictish forts, in two cases coinciding with modern harbours (1980, 80–1). No Pictish forts have yet been identified in Orkney, although they utilised sites defended by the earlier ramparts and ditches associated with brochs, for example at Gurness and probably Borwick on mainland and at Burrian on North Ronaldsay. But there are a few multivallate promontory forts in Orkney, independent of brochs (Lamb 1980, 50–3). There has been virtually no excavation of these forts, and they may belong to the later first millennium BC or to the first millennium AD, but it is possible that some may have been built by the Picts. The Annals of Ulster record that in AD 681 'The Orkneys were destroyed by Brude', and Anderson has interpreted this entry to mean 'the destruction of some fortresses and the taking of hostages' (M.O. Anderson 1973, 175). Certainly something more than the burning of a few farms would seem to be indicated.

There is little evidence to show what sort of boats the Picts used, but Johnstone has concluded that a plank-built rowing-boat is most likely (1980, 152–3). The best documented illustration of a Pictish boat is the carving on the symbol stone at Cossans near Glamis (Johnstone 1980, 152, pl.11.16), but a possible candidate in Orkney is the lightly incised boat beside a Pictish-looking cloaked figure on the stone from Burness in Firth (RCAMS 1946, 99, no.347, fig.72). This resembles the boat carved on a stone disc from post-broch levels at Jarlshof in Shetland (Johnstone, 1980, 153, pl.11.18). The fact that the Jarlshof boat has a sail is worthy of note, for sails appear not to have been used as far north in continental Europe until the sixth or seventh centuries AD.

The Picts have left behind them a personal legacy unparalleled by earlier or later peoples in Scotland: their symbols, potentially a key to their ideas, customs and beliefs. These symbols hint at the social complexities commonplace to the anthropologist but mostly hidden from the archaeologist, simply because so many beliefs are barely if at all embodied in the material debris that remains to be examined. For this reason, and because the Picts are, after all, separated from the twentieth century by little more than a thousand years, their legacy deserves to be studied by every means available. More radiocarbon dates will clarify how useful this chronological tool may be for so restricted a period of time; computer analysis of the combinations and geographical distributions of Pictish symbols ought to allow the archaeologist and social anthropologist together to reach some conclusions about their meaning; and, when the financial climate permits, a programme of controlled but exhaustive research excavation on selected sites would solve many outstanding problems of Pictish archaeology. Despite their historical gloss, the basic elucidation of Pictish society depends not on the historian whose tools for that period are unlikely to increase but on the archaeologist, the collection of whose raw material is at yet in its infancy.

Acknowledgements. I should like to thank Professor Leslie Alcock and Dr Joanna Close-Brooks for their kindness in reading and commenting upon the draft of this chapter, and I am grateful to Nigel Neil and the North of Scotland Archaeological Services for providing the following appendix describing recent work at the Howe, Stromness.

Nigel Neil **Excavations at Howe**

Excavations at Howe, Stromness, begun in 1978 in advance of farm-land improvement, have revealed a series of Pictish farmsteads overlying a broch and associated settlement of several phases. A neolithic chambered tomb underlies the broch tower and the rampart of the broch settlement is currently thought to be neolithic in origin. Work up to the end of the 1981 season has concentrated on the excavation of the Pictish and later broch settlements. No abandonment horizon was present between the late broch buildings and those recognisably 'Pictish' in style, but the broch tower soon went out of use. Aspects of the building techniques employed and the generally 'cellular' plan of the house suggest a degree of continuity. Although the finds have yet to be studied in detail, it is possible to suggest tentatively that use of the tower finally ended sometime in the fourth century. Although there is ample evidence for metalworking – smelting and smithying – in the later broch period buildings, signs of these activities are noticeably absent from the Pictish phases. Recent plough damage has removed parts of some structures but it is impossible to tell whether or not any have been lost entirely; buildings belonging to the undefended broch phases have been found outside the former defences and thus well beyond the surviving limits of the Pictish settlement. With these provisions, the overall impression is one of a small settlement with no more than three domestic areas in use during any of the eight phases and probably only one by the end of the occupation.

The shapes of the earlier Pictish buildings at Howe are governed partly by the re-use of broch period relict structures and partly by the need for support from the collapsed rubble of earlier buildings. Free-standing walls were frequently thick but unstable, except where larger flags were used, perhaps robbed from the broch tower. 'Single-face' walls were of two types – coursed and orthostatic. The latter, generally surmounted by flags, broad-ly resembles the type encountered at Buckquoy (A. Ritchie 1977, e.g. pl. 10). The 'cellular' plan of the buildings at Howe is also reminiscent of Buckquoy, particularly in later phases where there is a tendency towards greater symmetry. Hearths and flagged floors are generally incompatible, cooking areas being floored with earth and ash spreads. The sw building in

PLATE I. Figure-of-eight house (phase 7), Howe, Stromness.
(NOSAS, Crown copyright.)

. . . .

figure 9.2 is a relic of an earlier phase, re-used and modified; it contained six stratified hearths and associated earth floors. The building complex illustrated represents the largest expansion in any one phase and all the cells in it continued to be used for several phases. Eventually, an entrance was cut through the w wall of the sw building as access to a group of flagged rooms; these have been illustrated in an earlier report (Hedges and Bell 1980, 51, left fig.). The building illustrated in plate I lay to the w of those in that report and is approximately contemporary with them. It typifies the tendency towards more regular shapes and exemplifies the trend of having flagged and earth floored areas under one roof; two other cells of similar size were present to the w at the same time, reached by way of an entrance within the building.

A Pictish-Norse transition is not discernible at Howe, either in the finds evidence or in building style. A possible Norse domestic structure is present in an incomplete state as a result of ploughing, but is not linked stratigraphically to any other structure. A glass linen smoother found during nineteenth-century excavations is considered to be securely of Norse date (Grieg 1940, 80–1). Grieg lists it as a grave find and a late but undatable burial was found in the upper fill of the broch tower.

The finds assemblage from the Pictish levels at Howe includes much pottery – generally undecorated, flat-based and finer than earlier wares. Two flagstone gaming boards have been found, and bone and antler artefacts include double-sided combs with iron-riveted spacer plates, a small knife handle with ring-and-dot decoration, and weaving combs. The small number of bronze finds includes tweezers, spiral rings and two penannular brooches with zoomorphic terminals. The better preserved of the latter has been illustrated previously (Hedges and Bell 1980, 50), when a seventh/eighth-century date was offered; they came from near the middle of the building sequence. The post-excavation work on the Pictish settlement at Howe is in progress, and the finds typology has still to be studied.

Acknowledgements. The writer wishes to thank Beverley Smith for her assistance in compiling this report. The line drawing and photograph are by Frank Moran.

FIGURE 9.1. Buckquoy: plan of the Pictish and Norse phases (on next two pages).

Buckquoy,
ORKNEY
1970–71

phases I–II

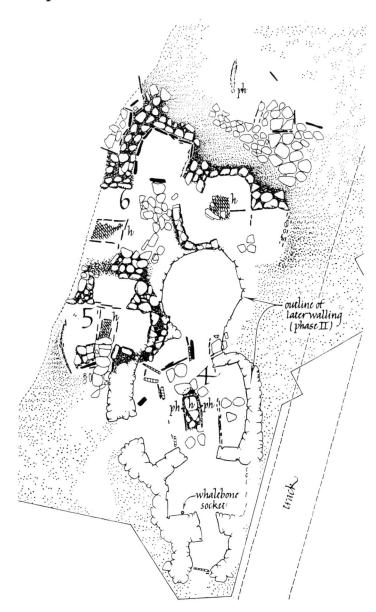

outline of
later walling
(phase II)

6

5

ph

h

h

h

ph · h · ph

whalebone
socket

track

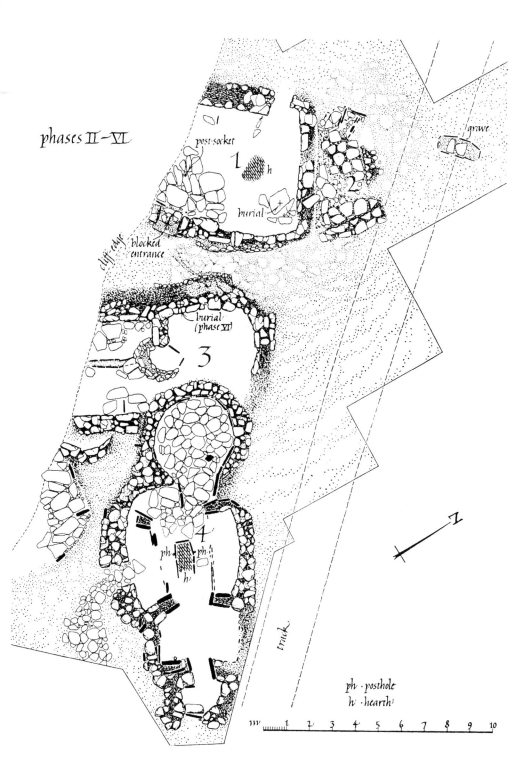

phases II–VI

grave

post·socket

1

h

burial

2

IV

cliff-edge

blocked
entrance

burial
(phase VI)

3

4

ph·

ph·

h·

track

N

ph ·posthole
h ·hearth

m 1 2 3 4 5 6 7 8 9 10

10 Christopher D. Morris **Viking Orkney: A Survey**

RAIDS AND SETTLEMENT

In Scandinavia, the Viking period is generally seen as the last stage of
prehistory: the Late Iron Age, the study of which is fundamentally archaeological. This reflects the lack of contemporary and local historical sources
in Scandinavia; although late sagas often refer back to the Viking Age. In
Scandinavia this period is generally seen as *c.* 800–*c.* 1050, but the terminal
dates are not based on specific events (NAA 1979, Chronological Table,
284). In other parts of Europe it is easier, with fuller written sources, to give
a more exact chronology to the period. In England, for instance, the raid on
Lindisfarne in 793 is often taken as marking the beginning, and the Battles
of Stamford Bridge and Hastings in 1066 the end, of the period. The
accounts in Irish annals of raids in western Scotland and Ireland in the last
two decades of the eighth century have provided a similar starting point for
these areas, but the endings are far from clear. The Norman invasion of
Ireland in 1172 effectively ended Scandinavian predominance, although the
nationalistic school of historians has tended to prefer a date of 1014, with the
Battle of Clontarf. In Scotland, the Battle of Largs in 1263 and/or the
Treaty of Perth in 1266 provide a convenient end-point; while in the Isle of
Man 1266 is the end of the reign of the last Scandinavian king, Magnus.

It is ironic that the records for the Northern Isles of Orkney and
Shetland are so meagre that no single date can be given for the beginning of
the Viking period there, for it was here that Scandinavian influence lasted
longest of all in the British Isles. Formally, they remained under Scandinavian rule until the impignoration of the Isles in 1468–9. However, it is
likely that the succession of Scottish earls in the Orkney Earldom from 1231

began a process of 'Scottification' (F. T. Wainwright 1962c, 190), and, as Barbara Crawford has argued (1977, 113–15), 'by the mid-thirteenth century, Caithness had become to some extent an integral part of the Scottish kingdom'. Although Shetland was linked more directly to Norway from 1195 (B. E. Crawford 1971, 353), in Orkney the main period of cultural influence from Scandinavia had ended by the mid-thirteenth century. Wainwright saw the death of Earl Ragnald in 1158 as a particularly significant stage in the process: this was the end of the Golden Age. Convenience of terminology, rather than strict chronological logic, therefore, maintains the term 'Viking' for the period up to the mid-eleventh century and 'Late Norse' for the following two centuries, when these Isles (and Caithness to the south) were still quite distinctively Scandinavian in cultural (as well as political) orientation.

Such convenience has its drawbacks, in that it cannot easily be maintained for archaeological material. Though the Late Norse period is marked by an increase in documentary source-material for the historian, it is not marked by any fundamental change in the material culture of the inhabitants of Orkney. The problem is compounded by the lack of fine calibration for the dating of artefacts on their own, and the inherent difficulties involved in the dating of distinctive artefact-types or artistic motifs in contexts distant from their source. The inevitable haziness of the chronological distinctions certainly cannot be dispelled, and no attempt to do so will be made here. Nor can the chronological problems be sidestepped by a retreat into a pure, unsullied *pre*-history that ignores the, admittedly sparse, documentary material, and the not-so-sparse institutional and linguistic material. For better or worse, the Viking and Late Norse periods are 'text-aided', and hence *proto*-historic.

The *Orkneyinga Saga*, written *c.* 1192–1206, is a fundamental source for the Late Norse period in Orkney as it gives much detail of the events of the previous century. It also is valuable in that it paints pictures of some of the most powerful men of Viking Britain, such as the Orkney Earls Sigurd the Stout and Thorfinn (for modern translation, see A. B. Taylor 1938 and Pálsson and Edwards 1978). It has provided the basis of some modern historical accounts of the Norse Earldom (e.g. Clouston 1932), as well as giving insights into life in this earldom. However, it has long been recognised that for the Viking period its information is very partial. Indeed, Wainwright's account of the early part of the Viking period in the Northern Isles (F. T. Wainwright 1962b, 126–40) deliberately asserts the primacy of the chronology derived from archaeological and linguistic sources over that of the Saga. More circumstantial evidence of historical references from other parts of Britain is then used to bolster the argument. The present writer would prefer to see archaeology as one of several interconnecting or interpenetrating approaches to the past (see Biddle 1971, 391, 403), with an obligation placed on the student of protohistoric periods to extract the maximum information from each discipline, within its academic limits. Thus, while this chapter will emphasise the material evidence, and not concern itself with the minutiae of evidence from allied disciplines, it should be remembered that this is a matter of convenience, rather than an approach that is, of itself, academically justifiable.

The origin of the Orkney Earldom traditionally lies in a gift from the Norwegian King. The *Orkneyinga Saga* tells of 'vikings (who) used to raid in Norway over summer and had Shetland and Orkney as their winter base', and of how one summer Harold Fine-hair sailed west over the North Sea in order to teach them a lesson. He conquered what amounts to the Northern and Southern Isles, and gave Shetland and Orkney to Earl Rognvald of Möre, who promptly (and probably shrewdly) gave them to his brother Sigurd. Subsequently, Harold gave Sigurd the title of 'earl' (Pálsson and Edwards 1978, 30). A similar account in the *Saga of King (Saint) Olaf* in *Heimskringla* by Snorri Sturluson (Laing and Simpson 1964, 218) tells us that:

> It is related that in the days of Harold Haarfager the King of Norway, the islands of Orkney, which before had been only a resort for vikings, were settled.

Elsewhere in *Heimskringla,* in the *Saga of Harold Fine-hair,* the western voyage of Harold is put after the battle of *Hafrsfjord* (now dated *c.* 890 AD). A further source, the twelfth-century *Historia Norvegiae*, makes the pirates a group related to Jarl Rognvald, who in Harold's day deprived the native Picts of their habitations and utterly destroyed them, subjecting the islands to themselves (quoted by Wainwright 1962a, 99, n.3).

It is of course possible that these saga accounts are untrustworthy. Haakon Shetelig in 1940 discussed the lack of contemporary foreign corroboration for Harold Fine-hair's expedition to the west, and concluded that 'we feel inclined to doubt that the story of Harold's expedition contains any nucleus of historical truth whatever' (Shetelig 1940, 24–5). The information in an Irish source and the *Historia Norvegiae* supports a hypothesis of independent annexation of the Orkneys by the family of the Earls of Möre a full generation before the time of Harold: it would be held, then, not as a fief of the King of Norway, but by means of inherited title from Möre, applied to wherever this dominion was extended. More recently, Professor Peter Sawyer has taken the argument a stage further, noting the absence of references to Harold's expedition in Irish annals, and preferring to see the tradition as 'best understood as a later elaboration, probably modelled on the expeditions of Magnus' (Magnus Barelegs), who led two expeditions in 1098 and 1102 (which are referred to in insular sources). To Sawyer, it would be a sudden and improbable assertion of power by Harold Fairhair late in the ninth or early in the tenth century (Sawyer 1976, 107 and 109).

As far as dating the earlier phases of Viking activities in the Earldom is concerned, scholars have preferred to take the indirect evidence from contemporary insular sources, such as annals referring to Viking raids elsewhere in Britain, to assert that Viking settlement in the Northern Isles must have occurred by the beginning of the ninth century (e.g. Wainwright 1962b, 129–30). Also, the equally indirect evidence of Dicuil, probably referring to the fleeing from the Faeroes of Celtic anchorites and priests *c.* 825 in the face of pirate raids, has been cited (e.g. Wainwright 1962b, 131–2; G. Jones 1968, 269–70). Indeed, the dating of phase I at Jarlshof, Shetland, to *c.* 800 AD is done merely by implication on these bases (Hamilton 1956, 93–4, 106). These are flimsy grounds upon which to date settlements in the north, and, using them, we get no more than the implication that raiding took place in the early ninth century: it does not seem enough to support theories of wide-ranging settlement, even though they support the likelihood of some gradual settlement in certain places. It could be that the saga and other sources may refer to a second, and more formalised, stage in the Viking contact with the north of Scotland.

Much ink has been spilled over the interpretation of these accounts, and play made of the dislocation in date between the saga accounts and the archaeological evidence. Most archaeologists have followed Shetelig and Wainwright in explicitly or implicitly rejecting the saga accounts. Other scholars, perhaps more cautious in their handling of the sagas, have made the point that this material does clearly seem to imply Viking activity before Harold's time, and that it is settlement that is specifically mentioned in them (e.g. Clouston 1932, 6, 20). 'Settlement' in the terms of the author of the *Jarlasaga* (as the *Orkneyinga Saga* was originally called) may very well have meant organisation of the land settled by the new Earl. Alternatively, as both H. Shetelig (1940, 25) and J. R. C. Hamilton (1956, 93) have pointed out (following Steenstrup), an Irish source relates that Raghnall or Rognvald, a Norwegian chieftain, after being driven from home by trouble, was established in Orkney from about 860 AD. The conclusion, therefore was that:

> It is . . . improbable that the Earldom of Orkney was founded by Harold. The Orkney earls certainly belonged to the same family as Earl Rognvald of Möre but appear to have been established in the islands at least a generation before the events related in the Sagas.

THE ARCHAEOLOGICAL RECORD

We need not necessarily be as strict in condemnation of sagas as Wainwright, Shetelig and Sawyer, and we might also be somewhat more cautious as archaeologists over the dating of the artefacts found in graves and settlements. D. M. Wilson's strictures (in reference to England) on the exact dating of artefacts in graves, are apposite:

The grave finds are difficult to date. I am sceptical in the matter of accurate typological dating in the Viking period, believing, with Almgren, that it is difficult to date any object to a period within a hundred years if there is no documentary source to assist the dating. It is easy to classify the swords found in Scandinavian graves, but it is impossible to say whether they represent people buried in the period of the raids or in the period of settlement. (1976a, 397)

We may add that the problem becomes even more acute when the comparison is made between material found in the homeland and in the colonies: is there a time-lag, and if so, how do we assess its length?

The traditional *typological* method of archaeology can offer us only an imprecise tool for the assessment of the origin and dating of Viking settlement in Orkney. It is subject to legitimate query just as the written sources are. Resolution of the problem can come only with some form of independent dating, and in the circumstances this must be archaeological – whether coin-dating or the use of radiocarbon determinations. Such methods have been used elsewhere in Scotland with some degree of success, in the Early Historic period (Alcock 1976), and the beginnings of a chronology exists at the Udal, North Uist (Crawford and Switsur 1977). But in both these cases – and the point is of fundamental importance – the independent dating provided by radiocarbon determinations has been related to the other evidence, whether documentary, artefactual or stratigraphical. If the radiocarbon dates are 'up for trial, or at least for calibration, before the historical dates' (Alcock 1981, 156; cf. Campbell, Baxter and Alcock 1979), they yet provide us with the potential for an advance with a particularly intractable problem, especially if interlocking groups of determinations can be undertaken.

Twenty years ago, Wainwright discussed the nature of the Scandinavian settlement in the Northern Isles as reflected in the archaeological record (Wainwright 1962b, 147–56), and naturally placed considerable emphasis upon the evidence from Jarlshof, Shetland: 'For a picture of a Viking settlement in the Northern Isles we are at present dependent almost entirely upon Jarlshof. Fortunately Jarlshof gives us a very full picture'. Some of the problems he faced are with us still: neither the excavations at Aikerness (Gurness), or the Brough of Birsay excavations, have yet been published, and the difficulties attending the study of pagan Viking graves, while considerably eased as far as Pierowall (Westray) is concerned (Thorsteinsson 1968), are far from resolved. Although Wainwright could enthusiastically assert that 'The material culture of the Scandinavian settlers comes before us most vividly in an archaeological context of graves, houses, hoards, isolated finds and runic inscriptions' (Wainwright 1962b, 147), we are looking at a small sample, the result of work of uneven quality. Considerable resources have been channelled into the archaeological study of

Orkney in the twenty years since Wainwright wrote, but they have not been part of a concerted or co-ordinated research strategy; indeed, much work has been of the nature of 'rescue' archaeology. Given the archaeological wealth of Orkney, it is perhaps inevitable that most excavation work must be of a 'rescue' nature, to record at least part of the disappearing data base: it is not a satisfactory situation and leads to an unbalanced picture. Much of what follows is either unpublished or only partially published in interim or summary accounts. Some could be rendered obsolete by new discoveries.

If in 1962 the picture of settlement in the Northern Isles was dominated by Jarlshof in Shetland, it has remained so since, even though other sites have later emerged. It has provided us with a detailed picture of the growth of the settlement over several centuries from one 'parent' dwelling to a complex which Alan Small has described as a 'township' (Small 1968, 9). The impression of complexity, however, is due as much to the successive building from the early prehistoric period until the post-medieval, as to the nature of the Viking settlement. Even in the Viking period, several phases are superimposed on top of one another. It is quite clear from J.R.C. Hamilton's analysis of the stratigraphy and phasing that at any one time there were probably no more than three families living at this site (see figure in Small 1968, 9). As a nucleated settlement, it could be seen as an early 'township' (cf. Clouston 1920; H. Marwick 1952, 216–23; Fenton 1978, 23–32, 40–8). As for function, the material found here has been interpreted in agricultural terms; and, perhaps surprisingly for a site so near to good fishing, exploitation of the sea's resources appears to have been secondary (Hamilton 1956, 137, 157). There is very little exotic imported material such as might have been expected from a trading-post or town.

A second Viking-age settlement site in Shetland was excavated by Small at Underhoull on Unst, which was a smaller single-building unit, possibly with a second unit nearby (Small 1966). On the basis of these two sites, Small has constructed a model of the ideal basic environmental factors for a settlement of the Viking Age (Small 1971, 75–9). It envisages an economy based on mixed agriculture with fishing also playing an important role. To provide utensils and tools, access to sources of bog-iron and steatite (soapstone) was desirable, and peat would be necessary for fuel. This model for the background to Viking settlement units is valuable in focusing our attention on the key features, but one needs to remember that essentially it applies to Shetland and Faeroe – very different landscapes from Orkney (cf. Brogger 1929, 35). Small himself has mapped the available land for such settlement in Shetland, and environmental factors make a very small percentage of the land mass suitable (Small 1969). Orkney, on the other hand, is very fertile (cf. maps (after O'Dell) in J.W. Hedges 1975, 65), and it need not surprise us if the resulting pattern may turn out to be somewhat different from Small's model for Shetland.

FROM PICT TO VIKING: BUCKQUOY AND BIRSAY

The Viking settlement in Orkney needs to be seen in its own terms, and not as a reflection of settlement elsewhere. In the present state of knowledge, it seems better to look at the particular evidence of Orkney, and await further excavated evidence before proceeding to any generalised statements about the nature of Viking settlement in the northern and western areas of Scotland. The debate over the relationship of incoming Viking to native Pict has been with us for many years, and if it has been given new twists, it is because there has now emerged some new evidence from the particular sites of Buckquoy, Orkney (cf. A. Ritchie 1974); and Udal, North Uist (I. A. Crawford 1981). It is a pity that a contentious tone has entered the debate: Crawford's disparaging remarks upon both the Buckquoy excavations and the wider interpretation of them by Ritchie are as unnecessary as they are misplaced. The value of the Udal excavations for discussion of the wider implications will be the greater when the full range of evidence is fully published, but methodologically it is unconvincing simply to cite this particular case in opposition to the particular case of Buckquoy. It may well be that 'the archaeological evidence cited for the Western Isles is as conclusively in favour of conquest as we are ever likely to get'; but, if it is based solely on the evidence from one site, one cannot accept this generalisation as it stands for the Western Isles, and the following sentence, that 'at present no evidence conflicts with the assumption of a similar pattern for the Northern Isles' (I. A. Crawford 1981, 268), therefore carries no weight at all.

Buckquoy in Birsay, described above (figure 9.1), is the only site in Orkney to have achieved final publication (A. Ritchie 1977). The picture here is one of the replacement of distinctive forms of Pictish period buildings by a rectangular building ascribed to the Viking period, itself replaced successively by two other buildings also ascribed to the Viking period. While the artefact assemblage for the later two buildings (phases IV and V) included some possible Viking artefacts, Ritchie has argued (A. Ritchie 1977, 192) that 'the artefact assemblage from the Norse levels is dominated by native products'. It is also the case that little of the artefact assemblage associated with the earlier, rectangular building was culturally distinctive or easily datable. There will always be a doubt about how earlier material in later contexts is to be interpreted. Few archaeologists will disagree with Crawford that 'disturbance or the retention of spoil could amount for their presence' (I. A. Crawford 1981, 265), but Ritchie's careful distinction for phase III between the finds from the interior of building 3 and those outside that were sealed by later structures (1977, 185) gives authority to her analysis. The ascription to the Viking context is based upon the change of building form from the characteristically cellular houses of the Pictish period. Unless an argument were to be advanced that the buildings of phases III, IV and V were native rather than Viking, it would be difficult to understand the repeated occurrence of native types in association with these rectangular forms other than in terms of continuity of usage of Pictish types. While, in theory, the presence of native artefacts could be the result of repeated disturbance, in the Viking period, of Pictish occupation debris, in practice, the very absence of distinctive Viking types of artefacts in association with the *occupation* of the buildings would seem to argue for the longevity of the native types.

It is unfortunate that the dating of phase III–V of the Buckquoy site is relative to that of a phase VI burial, ascribed to the tenth century, and not based on absolute dating criteria such as coins or radiocarbon determinations. There are other sites in the Birsay Bay area which, like Buckquoy, appear to have been occupied in the Pictish period, and followed by Viking period occupation and/or abandonment. A figure-of-eight shaped building from nearby (Birsay 'Small Sites' Area 3: Morris 1979b, 16–18) also had an absence of distinctively Viking artefacts, as did the fragmentary remains of a building in an adjacent area (Area 5: Morris 1980, 27–8). A second cliff-side site produced incoherent, yet definite, evidence of structural features, together with long-cist burials below cairns, apparently Pictish in character (Ashmore 1980), overlain by midden deposits into which cist-graves, probably Viking in date, were cut (Areas 1 and 2: Morris 1979b, 13–16). The site of Saevar Howe, at the south end of the Bay, has a sequence of Pictish settlement to Viking settlement to long cist cemetery (J. W. Hedges 1983b). Examination of the artefacts from Saevar Howe has demonstrated the existence of a substantial number of pre-Norse or native types of artefact. Although a large proportion of the collection is, in effect, unstratified, some of the native types exist alongside Viking types in the later phases of occupation of the site.

On the Brough of Birsay there is clear evidence from recent excavations in several different areas (figure 10.1) of occupation and structural phases, probably Pictish in date, being replaced by buildings from the Viking period (Morris 1981a, 35–7, 40; Hunter and Morris 1981, 254–7). Earlier excavations had already indicated that the nature of the site had changed from a religious to a secular settlement in the earlier part of the Viking period (Cruden 1958; 1965; Radford 1959). It was also evident in all previous excavations that, in the areas to the east of the chapel on the Brough, Viking period buildings had replaced earlier constructions and midden deposits (Radford 1959, 14–15; Hunter and Morris 1982). Through the building of these structures on a large scale, it has been argued that the site achieved a higher status, being associated with the Earls of Orkney (Cruden 1958; 1965; Radford 1959). Subsequently, by the erection of a church and buildings to the north of it, the site again became essentially a religious one,

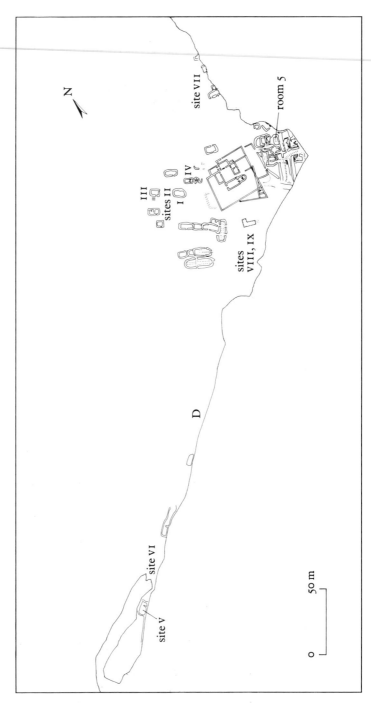

FIGURE 10.1. The Brough of Birsay: overall site survey.
(Crown copyright.)

although its interpretation as Christ Church minster is a matter for debate (see below; colour plate 23).

PLATE 10.1. Beachview, Birsay: 'studio' site. Final photograph 1980.
(C. D. Morris: Crown copyright.)

It is evident that there is much new evidence to be analysed from the Birsay Bay area which has a direct bearing upon the problems of the nature of the initial Viking settlement there (figure 10.2). It is clear that on each of these sites, as at Jarlshof in Shetland, buildings were regularly abandoned and replaced. With plentiful supplies of flagstone on the beach, and the potential for re-use of the stones from earlier buildings, the settlers here could easily adapt the buildings to current needs, or sweep them away and start afresh. This makes for extremely complex archaeological sequences, which are sometimes composed of many fragments of different structural elements (cf. Area IV North: Morris 1982a). However, major changes have been distinguished: Radford and Cruden (Radford 1959, 16–18; Cruden 1965, 26–8) and Hunter (1983) have noted, on the Brough of Birsay, changes in layout and orientation of buildings, and at the recently discovered Beachview 'studio' site (plate 10.1), it appears that the major building discovered so far (Morris 1980, 28–30; 1981a, 38–9) was abandoned and infilled with stones and midden debris which has received an initial radiocarbon determination of 940 ± 55 bp (GU-1191). It was apparently replaced by another building represented so far mainly by the found-

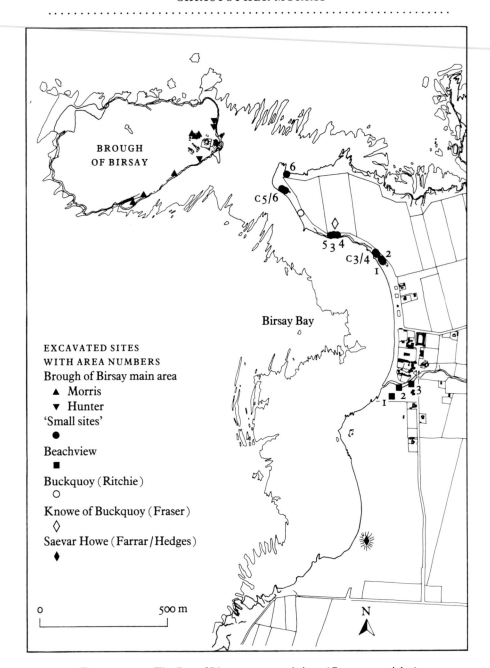

FIGURE 10.2. The Bay of Birsay: excavated sites. (Crown copyright.)

ations of a small circular chamber with central hearth. There were also building remains stratigraphically earlier than the main building. Similarly, on the 'Peerie Brough', at least three major alterations and / or replacements of buildings have been noted (Area V: Morris 1980, 24–5; 1981a, 37–8).

Despite this flurry of excavation on various sites around the Birsay Bay area (for summary see Morris forthcoming) it is not yet possible to generalise about the settlement evolution of the area in the Viking period. Both absolute and relative dating 'markers' will eventually serve to provide chronological limits for each of the various sites, which should then enable statements to be made about contemporaneity, or otherwise, of particular structures and sites. It is a tragedy that so much evidence has already been destroyed, and a sobering thought that the many visible archaeological features on the coast (see Donaldson, Morris and Rackham 1981, fig.5) will appear to give Birsay a picture of dense settlement in contrast to the known evidence from elsewhere in Orkney.

OTHER CURRENT EXCAVATION

Although it is conceivable that, as Birsay was the seat of the Earls of Orkney, a large entourage was attracted there, such evidence as is available from other sites seems to suggest that our present picture of Viking settlement in Orkney is unrepresentative. Dr Ritchie has elsewhere referred to the 'amazingly small body of evidence for such a major phase of Scotland's history' (A. Ritchie 1977, 189), and it can only be put down to a lack of archaeological initiative. Where serious, sustained, work has been undertaken, results have been forthcoming. Peter Gelling's summary of his work at Skaill (Deerness) will shortly be available (Gelling forthcoming and this volume). It is sufficient to note here that, apart from prehistoric occupation, clear excavated evidence has emerged for pre-Norse structures as well as Viking and Later Norse buildings. In the immediate vicinity (figure 10.3) there was also an old church and a hogback monument (Low 1879, 53–5; Lang 1974, 232) and, within a couple of miles in either direction, further secular and ecclesiastical sites ('The Howie'; Brough of Deerness, Morris 1977). There can be little doubt that the position here is likely to be of similar complexity to that in Birsay.

Similarly in Rousay, a major grouping of sites of the Viking period is evident from the area around the Bay of Westness (figure 10.4). A series of excavations is taking place under the direction of Sigrid Kaland. The impetus for the series came from the discovery of a richly-furnished female grave (R. B. K. Stevenson 1968), which has been followed up by examination of the cemetery (Kaland 1973; Youngs and Clark 1981, 183). The indications are that it is a ninth-century cemetery. Nearby are the foundations of two boat-nausts, one replacing the other, and fine stone-built buildings which are later in date than the graves (Wilson and Hurst 1964,

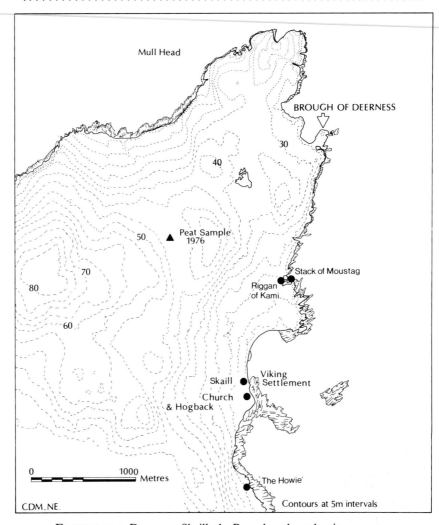

FIGURE 10.3. Deerness: Skaill, the Brough and nearby sites.
(Crown copyright.)

240; Kaland 1973). In the nineteenth century, a Viking sword and shield boss were allegedly found at the Knowe of Swandro, although it is possible that they represent secondary usage (Grieg 1940, 88–90) or may even be from the cemetery (Kaland pers. comm.). The complexity of settlement evolution in this area is further indicated by the place-name Skaill, to the west of the site and now associated with a deserted settlement (H. Marwick 1947, 87) and the probable castle-site known as 'The Wirk' (Clouston 1931, 27–31).

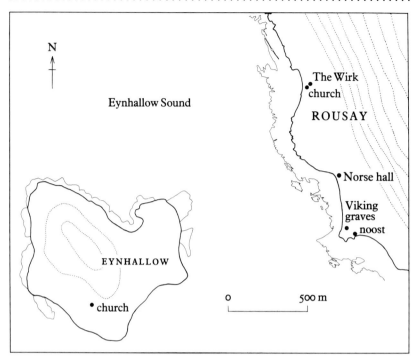

FIGURE 10.4. Norse settlement at Westness, Rousay.

Recent investigation on a more modest scale has indicated that the area of Orphir is likely to be no different. As with other sites, *Orkneyinga Saga* proved a spur to earlier investigators: references (ch.LXVI) to a church and drinking-hall here were well known (Pálsson and Edwards 1979, 112–13). Excavations took place in 1899–1901 and at other times, uncovering walls of buildings, which were generally identified with those of the Bu (Johnston 1903, 22–3). The site of the church was near these (plate 10.2). Work to the north and east of the Bu has investigated other structural remains, notably a tunnel (possibly a souterrain), below midden deposits probably of Viking date. Additionally, it is possible that an industrial site, located at Lavacroon nearby, may date from this period (Batey 1980, 35; 1981, 34), and a Viking grave was found at Greenigoe (Henshall 1952, 17). A runic inscription in Tankerness House, apparently from St Nicolas' Church, and a number of stray finds of steatite and other material, both from Bu Farm and Swanbister nearby, help to fill out the picture (Batey, pers. comm.).

The picture of Viking settlement in Orkney from excavated sites is unrepresentative, not least on distributional grounds, for many areas are unexamined; and intensive examination is the result of particular factors, rather than part of an overall policy to investigate settlement-patterns of the

PLATE 10.2. Orphir, Orkney: Earl's Bu and Round Church.
(C. D. Morris: copyright Durham University.)

period. It is also unrepresentative because four of the sites are high status sites. Skaill (Deerness) and Westness (Rousay) can probably be associated with particular Saga figures, and Birsay and Orphir were directly linked with the Earls of Orkney. Only Buckquoy, and the buildings found on top of earlier Pictish buildings set around Gurness broch (A. Ritchie 1974, 25–6), are as yet exceptions – and the latter has a tenuous archaeological existence as far as published data are concerned (Richardson 1948, 7–8).

VIKING 'CASTLES'

Another group of sites, probably also associated with high-status personages, at least extends the range of site type. There are a number of small fortified or 'castle' sites worthy of note (see Clouston 1926; 1929; 1931; RCAHMS 1946, 49–50; Cruden 1960, 20–1; Talbot 1974). The best-known is undoubtedly that on Wyre, where a small square tower, set within defensive ditches and banks, is reasonably associated with the castle of Kolbein Hruga, mentioned in *Orkneyinga Saga* (Pálsson and Edwards 1978, 139). The site is locally known as 'Cubbie Roo's Castle' (plate 10.3) and both its position on Wyre adjacent to a church and a farm called the Bu of Wyre, and the absence of any other castle site on the island, if circumstantial evidence, is enough to accept the identification (H. Marwick 1928,

PLATE 10.3. 'Cubbie Roo's Castle', Wyre. (C. D. Morris:
copyright Durham University.)

9–11). A second castle site mentioned in the *Saga*, *c.* 1152 (Pálsson and
Edwards 1978, 67) has been associated by J. Storer Clouston and A. B. Taylor with buildings at Cairston in Stromness (A. B. Taylor 1938, 398, n.8),
but later writers have not yet accepted the visible remains as necessarily
indicative of a date consistent with that in the *Saga*, or indeed this place with
Kjarreks-staðir. A third *kastali* is on Damsey, where Swein Asleifsson stayed
overnight in 1136 (Pálsson and Edwards 1978, 113), but such evidence as
there is on the ground has yet to be examined closely. On the basis of the
archaeological evidence from Wyre, the site of the 'Wirk' on Rousay has
sometimes been interpreted as a similar Norse castle (Marwick 1924, 17;
A. B. Taylor 1938, 384, n.5). Comparable to this site is that of Castle Howe,
Holm, which Clouston associated with the Bu of Paplay (see A. B. Taylor
1938, 372–3, no.2). On the other hand, Clouston's interpretation of the site
of *Gernanes*, near Nether Bigging, in Stenness loch, as a Norse castle has not
been universally accepted. The tower at Stenness Kirk, the Castle of Stackel
Brae, Eday, 'Castle' Ellibister (Evie and Rendall), a mound between Langskaill and Netherskaill, Birsay and Harray, and Work, Kirkwall have
all also been put forward as possible candidates for Norse castle status.
Recently, Raymond Lamb has suggested that major structural features
visible in the eroding cliffs near Crosskirk, Tuqoy (Westray) may be
comparable to 'Cubbie Roo's Castle' (Lamb pers. comm., see *The Orcadian*

225

23.7.1981). Excavations in 1982 by Olwyn Owen will undoubtedly clarify the archaeological issues, if hardly bearing on Lamb's further suggestion that these buildings represent the Hall of Haflidi. It is evident in general that a renewed research programme of archaeological excavation would be desirable to assess this group of sites, and the suggestions first put forward with great enthusiasm and persuasion by J. S. Clouston.

Renewed fieldwork has brought to the fore in recent years the potential importance of multi-period mound-sites. The Beachview, 'studio' site, Birsay, mentioned above, has every appearance of being on top of a large mound created by the successive building of structures, and the repeated dumping of midden material in this area. Certainly observation of, and trial excavations in an area of the site to the north, exposed by flooding of the Burn of Broadhouse, have demonstrated this to be the case, and very limited work in a third area of the Beachview site to the north-east produced the same picture (see Donaldson, Morris and Rackham 1981, 74; Morris forthcoming). It seems likely that the mound of Saevar Howe, to the south, was created by continued building and occupation. As emphasised by the excavator, the recent excavations have explored only a fraction of the deposits belonging to the Pictish and Viking periods of occupation, and these may indeed be 'the upper end of a much longer period of occupation than we have evidence for' (J. W. Hedges 1983b). A number of other sites in the islands appear to be the remains of mounds created by this process. Lamb, in his survey of Sanday and North Ronaldsay, has drawn attention to some. The relationship of such very large mounds, possibly covering up to a hectare of ground, to place-names of particular Norse types have been examined, and indicate that the primary Norse occupation was often late in the archaeological history of the mound (RCAMS 1980, 7–8; nos 69–114). Since none has as yet been excavated, it is difficult to attribute specific dating to them, but some sites are probably entirely prehistoric (e.g. Northskaill, Sanday; RCAMS 1980, no.81, 17), while others have produced Norse artefacts (e.g. Pool, Sanday RCAMS 1980, no.84, 18). A number of these sites are subject to violent coastal erosion, and resulting exposed sections, for instance at Pool (Sanday) have proved very valuable for the elucidation of the basic archaeological sequence (J. R. Hunter pers. comm.). Their relationship to adjacent sites is also intriguing, as for instance in the case of Stromness (North Ronaldsay) (RCAMS 1980, no.114, 20), adjacent to the broch of Burrian (MacGregor 1974).

ENVIRONMENTAL ARCHAEOLOGY

It is with sites of this group that a new avenue of research opens, with the application of modern methods of analysis of the palaeoeconomy and palaeoenvironment. In urban contexts these methods are producing valuable results for our understanding of the Viking period (see Kenward *et al.* 1978 and Morris 1982b), and it is already clear that we can expect to place the study of the economy and environment of sites of this period on a more secure basis in this way. Again, the results from Buckquoy, Birsay are the only ones to have reached final publication (A. Ritchie 1977), and a preliminary attempt has been made to integrate results from more recent excavations in the Bay of Birsay to these (Donaldson, Morris and Rackham 1981). As Dr Ritchie has emphasised above (chapter 9), cereal crops, especially bere and oats, were more commonly grown in this area in the past. It is clear from the sampling of the later deposits in Areas 1 and 2 besides the Brough Road, and also from the Beachview 'studio' site, that this was the case in the Viking/Late Norse periods. Their existence was also demonstrated in the Viking contexts at Saevar Howe (Dickson, in Hedges 1983b). There is a hint that, as far as oats were concerned, it was during this period that common oat (*Avena sativa*) was introduced, for only wild oat (*Avena fatua*) is found in earlier contexts – but this will need support from the results of other samples in this area and elsewhere. Some weeds may also have been used in their own right for making bread (Donaldson, Morris and Rackham 1981, 80). Of considerable interest was the occurrence at Saevar Howe, in phase II, of a significant number of examples of seeds of cultivated flax. Flax has been found elsewhere in the early Viking midden at Barvas machair, Lewis, and could as well have been utilised for consumption as for spinning and weaving (Dickson, in Hedges 1983b). As with the Pictish period, it is evident that animal husbandry was fundamental to the economy. At Saevar Howe, cattle, sheep and pig were all found in significant numbers, and there was no major change in the proportion of these between the Pictish and Viking periods. In both periods, sheep outnumbered cattle (Rowley-Conwy, in Hedges 1983b). At Buckquoy, despite the general problems relating to the excavation of middens (A. Ritchie 1977, 191), and to the natural history of waste middens (Noddle 1977, 201), it was clear that cattle, sheep and pig were all exploited. There are some interesting variations between the three Norse phases: for instance, the percentage of minimum number of individuals of cattle varied from 29 per cent in Norse III to 55 per cent in Norse IV, and 47 per cent in Norse V, whereas sheep were 50 per cent in III and V (Noddle 1977, 202, table 1). Miss Noddle is inclined to see 'the availability of livestock [as] dictated by the environment rather than by direct choice' (1977, 202), but it must not be forgotten that Man, to an extent, structures the environment to his choice: it is, for instance, a conscious decision to grow crops, even if the yield is affected by non-human factors, and the same must be true of animal husbandry. Even if we accept that there are several different possible explanations of the presence from Norse III onwards of more bones per individual among smaller genera, that fact alone is significant (Noddle 1977, 202–3). That there are changes in the way in which Man exploits the environment is also evident: there is a much greater range of fish species represented in the Norse phases than in the Pictish (Wheeler 1977, table 12, 212 and 214). It has been pointed out that the importance of fishing in the later Viking periods is observable elsewhere (Donaldson, Morris and Rackham 1981, 77), but on the contrary, no great difference between the fish evidence from the Pictish and Viking periods was seen at Saevar Howe (Colley, in Hedges 1983b).

Judgements such as this must be based on reliable data. The interrelationship of artefacts and eco-facts demand more rigorous analysis in future. The relative importance of fish and cattle at Buckquoy, for instance, cannot be stated in quantitative terms on the basis of the data presented, and the preliminary judgements about this for the 'Room 5' excavation on the Brough of Birsay must, despite the use of wet-sieving, be regarded as indicative of a trend rather than as absolute figures. Here sieving was only conducted down to 5 mm: had sieving been carried out to 1 mm presumably a greater proportion of small bones would have been recovered, and therefore the relative percentages of fish and other bone affected. Both Colley and Rowley-Conwy (Hedges 1983b) have similarly emphasised the implications of partial recovery of fish material at Saevar Howe in relation to the total sample. It is hoped that more reliable quantitative data will emerge from the sampling programme of the deposits on the Beachview sites (Donaldson, Morris and Rackham 1981, 74 and 82). If it is true, as Ritchie has said above (chapter 9), that the 'factor of partial survival limits many of the conclusions about economic life that can be drawn', the factor of selective recovery in the past has limited them even more. If we can at least attempt to recover a reliable cross-section of the environmental and economic evidence, we shall have cut down the number of variables affecting the interpretation of the results and be able to concentrate on the problems of partial survival and partial excavation (see, for example, Carver 1979; Meadow 1980). In analysing the Saevar Howe material, both Colley and Rowley-Conwy (Hedges 1983b) have underlined the need for more refined techniques of analysis of date. In particular, they have emphasised the need to make a distinction not only on the basis of period, but also of type of deposit within a period – for example whether within or outside a structure.

Sites such as Pool (Sanday), Stromness (North Ronaldsay), and Beachview (Birsay), offer the possibility of large-scale recovery and detailed examination of environmental and economic data. This kind of evidence is as fundamental to our understanding of the Viking period in Orkney as is the evidence of particular artefacts; and the design of excavations, whether as responses to threats of destruction of particular sites, or as investigations of unthreatened monuments, must include provision for the examination of this material. It is fundamental because our understanding of exchange networks and the relationships of settlements to an economic system is still at a generalised level (e.g. Small 1968, 7–9). In north Norway, where a similar group of sites has been located, some of these problems are now being faced. Pioneering work was done on these mounds in the 1960s, and a basic chronology worked out for them (Munch 1966). More recently attention has been paid to wider issues, and the observation made that 'Although there is great potential, little work has been done with environmental data' (Bertelsen 1979, 53). It is here, perhaps, that there lies the possibility for fruitful comparison with the mounds in Orkney. Parallel work on these relatively unusual forms of site from two parts of the Viking world ought to provide direct and meaningful insights – perhaps more immediately relevant than the research programme on the Mesoamerican village cited by Bertelsen (1979, 55).

PLACE-NAMES

Of course, this 'new' evidence from environmental archaeology must be related to other material, and cannot exist in a vacuum. Economic factors do not respect the boundaries between academic disciplines, and as relevant here are the insights from the studies of place-names and the organisation of land as reflected in Later Medieval rentals. By their very existence, the large numbers of names in the Isles and certain coastal mainland areas of Scotland carry implications for the understanding of settlement patterns, and the nature of the archaeological record of these patterns.

Wainwright discussed at length work on Orkney place-names prior to 1962, such as the fundamental work by Hugh Marwick (F. T. Wainwright 1962b, 119–26 and 133–40). Marwick's work was largely concerned with the *sequence* of settlement, and he arranged the farm-names into a chronological order (1952, Part III). He based his attempt on the geographical characteristics of the sites in relation to their size, as recorded in fifteenth- and sixteenth-century rentals. He also related it to the *skatting* of land (or imposition of a land tax) which he took to be an event of the end of the ninth century, on the basis of the Harold Fine-hair tradition. However, Professor Sawyer's strictures on this tradition have led him to propose that 'the origin of the skatland should probably be sought in the thirteenth or perhaps the twelfth century' (Sawyer 1976, 109). Though Marwick's use of the absence of skatting to suggest that -*quoy* names were later than 900 AD, and the presence of skat or *land*, *garðr* and *bolstaðr* names to suggest they were pre-900, may well have to be abandoned, his observations on relative chronology may stand, for the argument was not wholly based upon this. He noted that the geographical position of -*quoys* tended to be on the fringes of a *tunship*, as *setr* names, whereas the group of names in *land*, *garðr* and *bolstaðr* were notable for their position on fertile and attractive areas in central positions. However, they appeared still to be secondary to the original settlements, which he saw as represented by some *skaill* names but

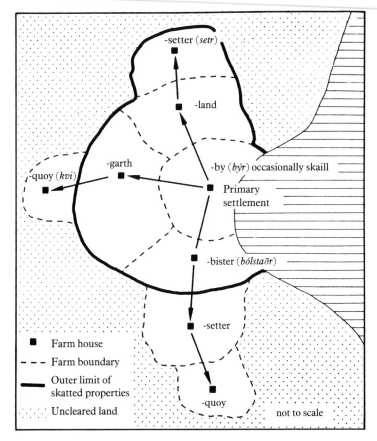

-setter (*setr*)

-land

-garth

-quoy (*kvi*)

-by (*býr*) occasionally skaill

Primary
settlement

-bister (*bólstaðr*)

-setter

-quoy

■ Farm house

- - - Farm boundary

—— Outer limit of
skatted properties

Uncleared land

not to scale

FIGURE 10.5. Orkney place-names sequence: an idealised model.

particularly *byr* names.

This sequence of place-names has been represented graphically by Patrick Bailey (1971, 76): his idealised model (figure 10.5) in fact emphasises the point that Marwick was proposing a *relative* chronology of names on the local level, not an absolute chronology (e.g. H. Marwick 1952, 248). There is no reason why *setr* names in one locality should not in strict chronology come before, say, *land* or *bolstaðr* names in another. Marwick was at pains to emphasise his use of the term 'secondary' as being in relation to geography, and, apart from the argument about skatting, not in absolute chronological terms. His work provides us with a sequence for the spread of settlement at the local level, not a widespread sequence of name-forms tied to an absolute chronology. It would be useful to have other local sequences from other areas, with which to compare this sequence.

On a more general level, Professor Nicolaisen has studied three settlement names, *staðr*, *setr*/*saetr* and *bolstaðr*, in north and west Scotland (Nicolaisen 1976, 85–96). He argued that the distribution of these indicated a relative chronology in the names, and also an expansion of the Viking settlement. He felt that the expanding distribution of *staðr* and *setr* represents the settlement in the earlier and later parts of the ninth century, whereas that of *bolstaðr* supplies 'an overall visual impression of Scandinavian settlement in the north and west when at its most extensive', in contrast to *dalr* which represented the area of influence (1976, 96). As an overall visual impression of the Viking settlement in Scotland, Nicolaisen's maps are very impressive, and, if detailed arguments in favour of the early dates are accepted, then even more important in terms of gauging the scale of this settlement. But, do we have to assume expansion to be constant? In fact, do we not have to reckon with the possibility of fluctuation with periods of contraction as well as expansion? Also, is it possible that the elements may refer to different types of settlement and therefore not be successive, but contemporary? Or, even if a word such as *saetr* refers to a specific sort of settlement, could it as well precede as succeed *bolstðr* in the local sequence? Further work by Nicolaisen is eagerly awaited.

Both the names, and their distribution as small farms, reflect in Orkney the *odal* system of land-tenure (cf. Drever 1933). It is likely that successive generations took into cultivation outlying portions of a landholding, with new farms being established on the margins around the original farm – as is represented graphically in Bailey's model. Marwick has suggested that often these outlying settlements were as productive as the original ones, because of the outfield system of summer-grazing which meant that the constant manuring of the animal fold or *kvi* outside the farm boundary wall (or *garðr*) rendered this area fit for establishment of a new farm which was then given the *-quoy* suffix (H. Marwick 1952, 227–8). The aggregate of the farms growing out in such a way from the original settlement, which would often hold arable and grazing land in common, and have common sources of peat on the moors, became known as *tunships*, and represent nucleated settlements of a form entirely different from the familiar villages to the south (Clouston 1920).

It is clear that such analyses as these of the system of land-holding and settlement-patterns, if subject still to detailed scrutiny, are essential for the understanding of the archaeological material, as the archaeological evidence is essential for the understanding of them. To make an obvious point: the place-name of Buckquoy is an example of a *kvi* (H. Marwick 1970, 60–1) which presumably on Marwick's model would be *relatively* late in the local sequence. But, we may ask, relative to what? Can our archaeological evidence answer this question yet? Dr Ritchie's archaeological sequence at the farmstead on the Buckquoy peninsula is not unbroken and continuous from Pictish to Viking (1977, 181) and so it is conceivable that her site may not come from the primary phase of settlement in Birsay. But, *if* this is the case, where is the primary settlement? Questions such as these are basic, but until there is more direct archaeological evidence it will be difficult to begin to answer them, and to test the models and sequences derived from other disciplines. A similar set of questions arise over the nature of place-names deriving from *skáli*. Clouston (1932, 14–18) and Hugh Marwick (1952, 237–40) both asserted that, despite the apparently humble origin of this name (meaning a hut or shed), places with such names represented early, primary settlements of the Viking period. Clearly the archaeological evidence from Peter Gelling's work at Skaill, Deerness (Gelling forthcoming) will be of very great interest in this connection.

ADMINISTRATION AND EXCHANGE

Other questions arise from study of institutional aspects of the Earldom of Orkney. Fundamental work has been done on such matters by J. Storer Clouston, both in a long series of papers and in his *History of Orkney* (1932). It is abundantly clear from this work that, especially in the social sphere, many features to be found in Orkney, such as the *godings*, the great *bus* and their owners, the *þings* or assemblies, directly reflect arrangements in the rest of the Viking world. The granting of land, the arrangements for collection of *skat* or tax, and some of the administrative features connected with these, such as the provision for defence of the area, have also been examined in some detail, especially by Hugh Marwick, with connections made between the Orkney Earldom and other Viking settlements in the British Isles, notably the Hebrides and Isle of Man (H. Marwick 1935; 1949a). A further detail, that of the *huseby* system – royal administrative farms of a military nature – has been demonstrated by Asgaut Steinnes to have existed in Orkney as in Scandinavia. Four such names still exist, in Birsay, Rousay, Shapinsay and Stronsay; a fifth may be near Braeswick on Sanday, and Steinnes infers that the earl's seat at Orphir was a sixth (Steinnes 1959). It is interesting that, when Thorfinn established himself at Birsay, he appears to have chosen a sea-board site. This may have superseded the *huseby* site, a few miles inland (Steinnes 1959, 46n; H. Marwick 1970, 83–5), but this cannot on present evidence be proved. However, it does seem significant that a site in the west of the mainland should have been chosen by Thorfinn, one can but speculate that it offered him not only strategic advantages in terms of access to the sea, but also possibly economic, in that it was ideally situated to monitor commercial (and other) traffic going northwards and avoiding the unpredictable (and often treacherous) Pentland Firth. To progress in our understanding of this period, it is essential that an attempt be made to relate the archaeological evidence from sites such as Birsay and Orphir to the evidence for institutional arrangements. At present, as with the linguistic evidence, scholars in the different fields have come to conclusions without apparent reference to evidence in the fields adjacent to their own.

At Jarlshof there was little evidence to suggest the status of a trading-post or town. It is the same for Orkney. Small has already observed (1971, 86) that, while Brogger (1929, 121) and A. B. Taylor (1938, 386) identified the *Hǫfn* of the *Orkneyinga Saga* (Pálsson and Edwards 1978, 120-1) with Pierowall on Westray, A. R. Lewis had (1958, 277, note 102) elevated this into the principal Viking port in the Orkneys – for which there is no evidence. Kirkwall seems to have been considered a market town in the early twelfth century (Pálsson and Edwards 1978, 96). Even so, it is said to have had few houses, and it is likely that development of Kirkwall followed the establishment of the Cathedral there (Gourlay and Turner 1977, 2 and 13). There is no clear evidence from elsewhere for a trading-centre, and we must assume that Dublin was the major centre for all northern and western Britain, with routes running north as well as south (Small 1971, 86). There are merchant-graves in the Western Isles (Grieg 1940, 29–30 and 48–61) and Smyth has argued, on the basis of a study of various written sources, for a 'slave-trade' centering on Dublin (Smyth 1977, chs X and XI). In addition, a Hiberno-Manx coinage existed in the Kingdom of the Isles (Dolley 1976b; 1976a, pl.61), and the Hiberno-Norse coinage is well known (Dolley 1966). While such coinages could scarcely have had much value outside their origin centre (Dolley 1966, 121), there is no doubt that commercial transactions took place – perhaps on the basis of units of measure of silver in the form either of ring-money, ingots or hack-silver (Graham-Campbell 1976a, 125; Warner 1976). These units are found in hoards from Orkney, and indeed the arm-rings from Skaill are the earliest dated examples from Scotland (Graham-Campbell 1976a, 125)(plate 10.4).

It would be foolish to explain all exotica and material from other parts of the British Isles, found in Orkney, as the result of commercial contact. There was a considerable period of raiding, of which records in annals and insular material in western Norwegian graves provide incontrovertible evidence (Morris 1979a). It is, however, harder to assess the Orcadian evidence in this context. Even the discovery of the fine insular brooch from Westness, Rousay (R. B. K. Stevenson 1968; colour plate 22) is not con-clusive, for there are various means by which it could have arrived in Orkney: raiding is one, exchange another. Nevertheless, the evidence of hoard material is witness to the political importance of Orkney, and to the considerable wealth owned by certain individuals.

Hoards from Burray and Skaill inevitably dominate the picture (Graham-Campbell 1976a, 119–28). The Skaill hoard probably weighed over 8 kg and Burray 1.9 kg. In both cases, less than 0.5 per cent was in silver coin; the rest was in silver objects and hack-silver. In both, particularly note-

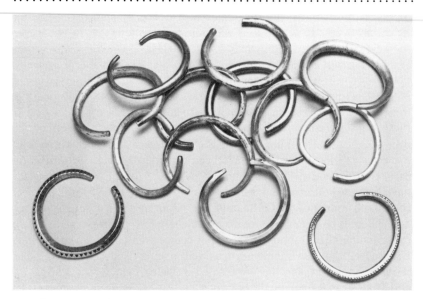

PLATE 10.4. 'Ring-money' from Viking silver hoard, Skaill.
(Copyright NMAS)

worthy were 'thistle' brooches and arm-rings, and the hoards have the appearance of containing both ready units of measure, and material yet to be cut to specific units. This is important, for it lessens Wilson's argument that hoards reflect instability or internecine quarrel (Wilson 1976b, 101). The latest work on these hoards by Olwyn A. Owen (pers. comm.), suggests that their deliberate deposition in particular places might be less related to raiding than to economic activity. Previous work has emphasised the particular position of these two Orcadian hoards in the overall Scottish distribution and the conclusion drawn that 'overseas trade, other than in basic commodities, did not play a central part in the economic life of the Norse settlers in Scotland' (Graham-Campbell 1976a, 115 and 127). It may, perhaps, be worth reiterating the point that the concepts of 'Scotland' and 'Ireland' are largely anachronistic at this time, and that Dublin could well have acted as an economic focus for a hinterland, both within its own island, and along the western seaboard of the Isles. It seems reasonable to interpret the Irish material in terms of the trading connections of the Norse towns in Ireland (Graham-Campbell 1976b), but too great a contrast with material from Scotland should not be drawn (see Morris forthcoming).

Church Building

The wealth of the Orkney Earls is reflected in building projects such as Thorfinn's minster at Birsay, the Round Church at Orphir, and the Cathedral of St Magnus in Kirkwall (all recorded in *Orkneyinga Saga*, Pálsson and Edwards 1978, 71, 113, 118). Each of these buildings is fascinating in its own right as an architectural project. The unusual shape of the Orphir church was undoubtedly inspired, though probably at second-hand, by the Church of the Holy Sepulchre (Radford 1962, 181–2). The minster at Birsay was built following Earl Thorfinn's procession/pilgrimage, and Earl Rognvald went on a two-year round-trip to the Holy Land that was dignified with the description 'crusade' (*Orkneyinga Saga*, chs LXXXVI–XC). If Rognvald, like Thorfinn before, was putting Orkney onto the European political map, he also had brought Europe to Orkney, for he was responsible for the building of the Romanesque Cathedral at Kirkwall (Cruden 1977). At Birsay, too, considerable resources must have been expended on the building of Christ Church minster by Thorfinn. It is at present a matter for debate as to whether this is to be looked for on the Brough of Birsay or on the mainland side of the Bay (Lamb 1974).

Such diversion of resources into church-building projects was widespread in Orkney. Despite problems of chronology, the distribution of mediaeval stone chapels in Orkney is remarkable (figure 10.6). It is generally accepted that many were the private chapels of prominent personages, and that there is a relationship between their foundation and rental districts or *eyrislands*. This organisation of private chapels had been, it may be argued, imposed upon the remnants of an order derived from the pre-Norse, Celtic period, and was itself superseded by a parochial system. Some of the chapels became, with the re-organisation of ecclesiastical arrangements, head-churches of a parish, while others were no longer used (Clouston 1932, ch.XIII; Cant 1973, 1–2, 10–11; 1975, 8–9, 11–13). In addition, Lamb has argued strongly for the existence of a Norse monastic system, as well as the eremitical tradition of the Celtic Church (Lamb 1976).

The archaeology of the church in the pre-Norse and Norse periods, if fascinating, is one that is fraught with difficulties of attribution and chronology. Dr Radford in 1962 brought forward material that he considered related to the Celtic and Norse churches (Radford 1962). Apart from Lamb's important work, the subject in general has hardly advanced since then, and repetition here is not in order. Two particular sites have been excavated since 1962. At Newark Bay, below a sixteenth- or seventeenth-century fortified house, there was uncovered a chapel with an associated cemetery, being eroded at the seashore. The chapel was thought by the excavator, D. Brothwell, to be of tenth century date (on the basis of coins below the flooring), and the skeletons are a very important group from the Viking period. Below the chapel and cemetery were two earth-houses (Brothwell 1977, 182). At the Brough of Deerness, excavations and survey by C. D. Morris on the site traditionally interpreted as a Celtic monastery (Radford 1962, 166–7; C. Thomas 1971, 34–5), raised questions about the

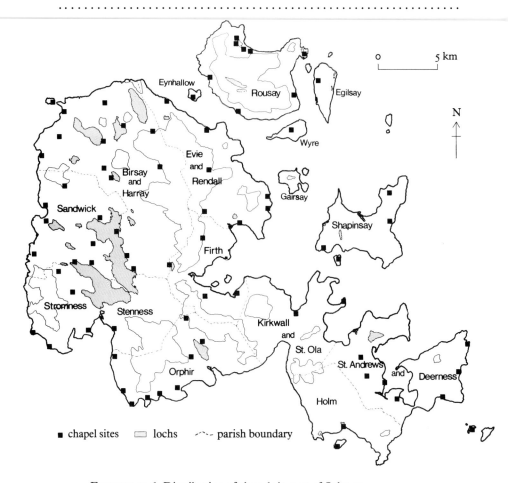

FIGURE 10.6. Distribution of chapels in part of Orkney.

identification. The new survey (figure 10.7) showed a regularity of plan not noted before, which can either be interpreted in terms of a Norse monastery (Lamb 1973, 93–6) or perhaps a secular settlement analogous to the Brough of Birsay (Morris 1977). Excavations showed that there were two major phases of chapel construction, and a very-worn tenth-century Anglo-Saxon coin was found between them. There were very few burials in the churchyard (Morris 1976; 1978). Interesting as these two particular chapel-sites may be, their position within the overall ecclesiastical system of the Viking/Late Norse periods in the parish of Deerness is not immediately clear. The recent survey work by Lamb on North Ronaldsay and Sanday has brought to the fore the urgent need for systematic work on the identification of such sites as a prerequisite for a deeper understanding of the

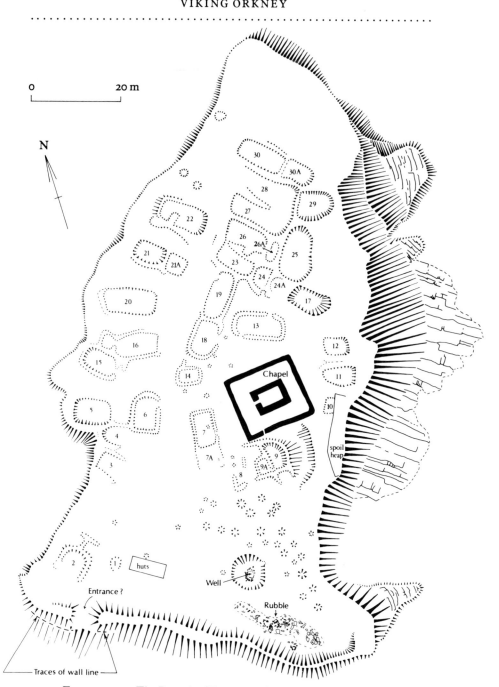

FIGURE 10.7. The Brough of Deerness: site survey 1977.
(Crown copyright.)

church life of mediaeval Orkney (RCAMS 1980, 8). There is an immediate parallel with the situation in the Isle of Man, and current research by Christopher Lowe on aspects of the church archaeology of these two areas of the Norse world should supplement the work of R.G.Cant and the overall survey by Lamb. (Colour plate 24.)

The traditional date for the introduction of Norse Christianity to Orkney is *c*. 995, and is based on a colourful tale in the *Orkneyinga Saga* (Pálsson and Edwards 1978, 39):

> After his return from Wendland, Olaf Tryggvason spent four years looting in the British Isles. Then he was baptised in the Scillies and from there sailed to England where he married Gyda, the sister of King Kvaran of Ireland. Next he spent a while in Dublin till Earl Hakon sent Thorir Klakka out west to lure him away from there.
>
> Olaf sailed east with five ships and didn't break his journey until he reached Orkney. At Osmundwall he ran into Earl Sigurd, who had three ships and was setting out on a viking expedition. Olaf sent a messenger to him, asking Sigurd to come over to his ship as he wanted a word with him.
>
> 'I want you and all your subjects to be baptised,' he said when they met. 'If you refuse, I'll have you killed on the spot, and I swear that I'll ravage every island with fire and steel'.
>
> The Earl could see what kind of situation he was in and surrendered himself into Olaf's hands. He was baptised and Olaf took his son, called Hvelp or Hundi, as a hostage and had him baptised too under the name of Hlodvir. After that, all Orkney embraced the faith.

The tale is also told in *Olaf Tryggvason's Saga* where accounts of the contemporary 'conversions' in Norway and Iceland are also given (Laing and Simpson 1964, chs 32–104 *passim*; G.Jones 1968, 32–5). Jones has suggested that Olaf's motives for his apparent missionary zeal were political and that 'He stands before posterity as one who in his day and place was Christ's best hatchet-man' (1968, 134–5). It is clear that the sagas do not tell the whole story, whether in Norway or Orkney, but it is not as clear, perhaps, as Wainwright would have it, that Christianity had been accepted by 900 (1962b, 158–62). While it may seem inherently likely, the evidence cited in its favour is not unchallengeable. For instance, the argument about the dating of the place-name elements such as *bolstaðr* and *kirkjubolstaðr* by Hugh Marwick (1952, 232–4) is now re-opened with Sawyer's rejection of the skatting theory (see above). Equally, the Bressay stone and Whiteness axe are used in the argument, and it must be axiomatic that generalisations should not be based on single examples. The argument for assimilation or overlap, if suggestive, is no more conclusive here than in other parts of Britain (see Morris 1981b, 233–5), and the dating of both the stone and the axe can hardly be regarded as fixed and secure, being based on typological and stylistic considerations. One might hope, in the future, for clearer dating of chapels, which would throw light on this problem: the evidence from Newark Bay and the Brough of Deerness, when published, will need careful scrutiny.

BURIAL PRACTICES

It is clear that there was a range of burial practice among the pagan Scandinavians of Orkney: burial within existing mounds, burial under new mounds, boat burial, burial under stone cairns, in stone-lined oval graves, in stone-lined rectangular cists, and in simple dug graves. Shetelig, in a pioneering paper (1945) attempted to place the Orkney material in a wider British context. It is now necessary to place them in a longer time sequence in Orkney, for both cist burials and cairn burials are recorded from the Pictish period (see A. Ritchie, chapter 9 above). From the period after the adoption of Christianity, burial necessarily involved the deposition of no grave-goods, and poses problems of association and dating for the archaeologist. However, one cist-grave, unaccompanied with grave-goods, from Sandside, Graemsay, has been C-14 dated to 865–55 bp (J.W. Hedges 1978, 377), and it seems reasonably clear now that the cemetery found by Farrer at Saevar Howe in the nineteenth century (Farrer 1864; 1868) was later than the Viking buildings uncovered recently by J.W. Hedges and is therefore dated to the tenth century at the earliest (Hedges 1983b). With the Pictish period burials from the Brough of Birsay, Buckquoy, Brough Road Areas 1 and 2, and Oxtro broch as well as the Viking and Christian Norse burials from the first three sites and Saevar Howe (see A. Ritchie, this volume), it is clear that, when these sites are fully published, evidence from Birsay will offer a chance for a more detailed understanding of burial practices.

The pagan Viking graves have been discussed by Wainwright, and, quite apart from the general dating problem, have the specific difficulty of poor initial recording (1962b, 148–50; 160–1). His conclusions regarding paganism therefore seem unduly exact, and the argument almost circular when he states that:

> Many more pagan graves will be found, of course, but perhaps not so many as might have been expected a few years ago, for the period of paganism is now being reduced from two hundred years to one hundred or less.

Dr Arne Thorsteinsson has undertaken an invaluable task in disentangling the information from Pierowall, Westray, but his criticism of *Viking Antiquities* is salutary. If he has re-established this cemetery as a major site, it is nevertheless the case that there is an inbuilt limitation to the evidence (1968). It is therefore all the more valuable that a major series of excavations has taken place on the cemetery at Westness, Rousay (R. B. K. Stevenson

1968; Kaland 1973, 93–7, 100; Youngs and Clark 1981, 183). After excavation, there will at last be one complete Viking graveyard recorded to modern standards. It is evident already that in its range of graves it offers examples of types hitherto imperfectly understood, such as the oval grave. If the richest grave remains the one found first, yet the boat-burial recently uncovered goes some way to illumine the defective Pierowall evidence. All graves were unmarked on the present surface, although it appears possible that they originally had some sort of grave-marker (Kaland, pers. comm.). There is in this group the best opportunity for examining Wainwright's statements about the length of usage of the pagan traditions of burial.

Other evidence that has come from pagan graves since Wainwright's day has been of single finds. Dr Ritchie, for instance, excavated a coin-dated late tenth-century male inhumation placed within the ruins of the Phase V buildings at Buckquoy (Ritchie 1977, 190–1). Recent examination of the material from a grave uncovered in 1939 at the Broch of Gurness, has also dated that female grave to the tenth century on the basis of the type of oval brooch represented (Robertson 1969). Similarly, a recently excavated male burial in a cist from Area I, Brough Road, Birsay (Morris 1979b, 14) would be attributed to the tenth century on the basis of the comb type.

A related group of monuments are the house-shaped recumbent monuments known as hogbacks. Their origin lies in Northern England, probably in the tenth century, and this short-lived type was also adopted in particular areas of Scotland (Lang 1974). Five are recorded from Orkney, of which four survive, and all appear to be of a plain, non-illustrative type with tegulation. It is likely that this isolated group is of considerably later date, and the result of late copying of an unusual form of monument normally found far to the south. However, the presence of a low headstone at St Boniface (Papa Westray) (Lang 1974, 211, 230, pl.17a) and late folk-lore traditions (Kirkness 1921, 132; E. W. Marwick 1975, 61) confirm that they were nevertheless still perceived as grave-monuments.

CONCLUSIONS

With the hogbacks, we have moved well into the Late Norse period, rather than the Viking period proper. For that reason, it will suffice to mention the evidence of runic inscriptions such as those from Maes Howe (Liestøl 1968), the Ring of Brodgar, the Brough of Birsay (Marwick 1922) and Orphir (C. E. Batey pers. comm.). They are currently under study by Dr Aslak Liestøl (Liestøl forthcoming). As we move forward in time, so there arises the fascinating subject of the transmission of Scandinavian culture to later periods. At one time, it was thought that Norse building-customs could be detected *in extenso* in later crofts of the Northern and Western Isles (Roussell 1934). More recent work, notably by Fenton, has modified this view (e.g. Fenton 1978, chs 14–15; 1979) and care is needed over cultural assumptions in chronology. However, there are any aspects of the transmission of material culture in which a Scandinavian contribution can be detected, and needs to be weighed against other contributions (see Fenton forthcoming).

It is clear from work in Shetland and Fair Isle that Viking traditions in sea transport continued right up to the modern age (A. Morrison 1973, ch. 3; 1978; T. Henderson 1978). A study of the small boats of Orkney in relation to the Scandinavian tradition is an area of study that needs specialist attention before vital evidence disappears under the impact of modern technology. It is hoped that study currently being undertaken by the National Maritime Museum, Greenwich, on a cast of the small boat from the Viking period graveyard at Westness, Rousay, at one end of the chronological spectrum, will illumine this topic (Youngs and Clark 1981, 183). It is curious that there appears to be less evidence for a Norse ancestry of Orcadian boats than those from Shetland (Lethbridge 1952, 144; Mather 1964).

In comparison to other areas of Scotland, the archaeology of Orkney has fared well in terms of resources allocated and research pursued, and yet much needs to be done, even for the Viking and Late Norse periods. Our picture is at present very partial, and in each particular field of study it is incredible how inadequate our knowledge is. In part, this is due to the fact that some major pieces of work have not yet been fully published, but also to the particularistic nature of the work carried out. The balance of our knowledge is based entirely on the chance of individual initiative or personal interest. Dr Lamb has drawn attention to the vast untapped archaeological potential of the Northern Isles of Orkney, and his Orkney Survey will, in supplementing the work of the Royal Commission, bring to light particularly important sites or areas for these periods. This is already clear from his work on the scattered finds from Sties and on the mound-sites such as Stromness and Pool (RCAMS 1980, nos 132, 84, 114, 248–9). Detailed survey in other areas has done the same: for instance, recently, Kenneth Steedman's survey of Deerness parish brought to light the finds from Quoys, which appear to be Norse in origin (Steedman 1980; pers. comm.). Recent work in Orkney has already added much to our knowledge of these periods, but even if it will not be possible to examine archaeologically even a fraction of all the potential sites, it is essential that the impetus and momentum are not lost. The richness of Orkney's archaeology is comparable to that of Wessex in the Prehistoric period. Viking Orkney was not peripheral: it was a key area of the Viking World.

Acknowledgements. Although brought together in its final form for this publication, the content of this chapter has been in preparation for some time. Parts of it have been presented on various occasions to particular societies and institutions too numerous to list. The invitation from Professor Robert T. Farrell of Cornell University to talk upon this topic within the Cornell Viking Series 1980 provided the stimulus to carry out a more systematic and rigorous study of the topic. Some of the wider implications have been discussed in my paper in the volume edited by Professor Farrell, and will receive further discussion in my projected book on the Vikings in Britain and Ireland. In preparing this chapter, I have benefited enormously from discussion of both detail and general matters with many colleagues and students. In particular, I am most grateful to Dr Anna Ritchie and Dr Sigrid Kaland whose willingness to discuss in detail the results of their excavations in Orkney, as well as more general matters, has been most heartening. To other excavators and researchers who have provided information, and whose names appear in the text, I am indeed indebted. Without open co-operation between scholars working in as compact an academic field as this, progress on the general front would be impossible. In relation to my own work in Orkney, I must acknowledge the considerable support of both the Inspectorate of Ancient Monuments, Scottish Development Department, and of the University of Durham. The results of the Birsay Bay Project would not have been possible without the hard work and support of my Assistant Supervisors, and in particular the enthusiasm of my colleagues, Alison Donaldson and James Rackham, who have widened both the scope of the Project and my own academic frame of reference. The latest stages of bringing this work together – albeit in an interim form – has depended to a great extent on the active support of my wife and colleague, Colleen Batey. Not only has she assisted with the collection and ordering of data, but has also spurred me on to complete the work at a time when it was in danger of being submerged by the obligations of running the Birsay Bay Project.

11 Colin Renfrew **Epilogue**

Yea, hid wis thir lullaby,
The dunder o' the loom, the fleean shuttle i' the skilly haan'
That keepid them a catloup fae starvation.
Here they lived, an' loved an' dee'd.
Bit thoo needsno peety them,
They hid pace i' thir time, an' a trust that teuk them t'row.
They hid fish an' maet fae the ebb,
An' they could mak' a banquet wae a heid o' kail,
An' held Aald Yeul wae snorran keks an' draps o' eel.

From C. M. Costie (1974) 'The Auld Hoose Spaeks'

With the passing of Viking Orkney, the prehistory of the islands comes to an end, although the language was, for many centuries to come, to remain the Norn, the Norse dialect still spoken in the northern islands in the eighteenth century. It lingers today in the lilting intonation and the rich dialect vocabulary of Orcadian speech, admirably captured in the poems of Miss Costie.

In a sense, of course, prehistoric Orkney did not come to an end, for one of the strongest experiences which a visitor to Orkney encounters is an almost overwhelming sense of the continuity of things.

It is still very much less than a century since many of the old ways disappeared with the onset of mechanisation of transport and of farming, the stationing of great fleets in Scapa Flow during two world wars, and now the commercial pressures from the oil installations on Flotta. In his *Reminiscences of an Orkney Parish*, John Firth (1920) described the farming ways and the life in the long houses which, now ruined, still form a prominent feature in the Orkney landscape. In the words of Miss Costie once again:

The waa's aa' blackened,
An' the reuf's faa'n in,
Noo only seelence hings
Whar eence gay laughter bade.

To the student of the past, a visit to one of these houses – or still better to the rural museum at Corrigal – is an illuminating experience. For one sees the very building conventions which were in use five thousand years ago at Skara Brae. The neuk beds (the stone-built beds set in the wall) closely resemble the beds of the neolithic village. And the partitions of sandstone flag in the byres are almost identical to the divisions in the compartmented long cairns, such as one sees clearly today at the cairn of Midhowe on Rousay. This need not be unbroken continuity, of course: it is simply the local sandstone, which fractures into these magnificent flags, being used in a manner for which it is admirably suited. The wonderfully gaunt Standing Stones of Stenness exploit this same property of the stone, which is responsible also for some features of the building style of the chambered cairns of Quanterness type, with their drystone walling, and their long and narrow corbelled roofing (plate 11.1).

The continuities are there, nonetheless, persisting through period after period. The organisation of this book has inevitably focused upon separate time periods, and so has perhaps not sufficiently stressed these elements of continuity, nor considered enough the reasons for the changes which did occur.

The economy of Orkney was essentially based on smallholdings. From the first introduction of farming on to very recent times the basic realities have been corn, livestock and the produce of the sea. That applies as much to Viking as to neolithic times, and other staples today such as kail (cabbage) and potatoes, for instance, are comparatively recent introductions.

ENVIRONMENT AND TECHNOLOGY

There are however some basic changes in environment and life in Orkney which should not be overlooked. In chapter 7 we have seen that during the Bronze Age Orkney underwent a climatic deterioration which may conceivably be associated with the comparative paucity of archaeological finds from that time. Arguably, too, this may have been the time when peat was first widely used as a fuel: certainly the coverage of blanket peat was greatly increased. It is certainly the period of formation of many of the mounds of burnt stone on the islands. Why they came into widespread use then is not yet clear. That one of their chief functions was the boiling of meat in their impressive stone troughs seems to be well documented now. The heat was conveyed to the troughs by hot stones, which were brought to a high temperature in a peat fire. Is it perhaps possible that until that time

PLATE 11.1. Quanterness chambered cairn: a vertical view
showing the oversailing courses narrowing to the roof.

245

there had been sufficient fuel in the form of small trees or shrubs, twigs or driftwood to allow meat to be roasted? It may be that declining wood resources and the simultaneous spread of peat made the technology of trough boiling with peat as the fuel the more effective. Arguably it would not have been superseded until the ready availability of bronze cauldrons in the Iron Age. These would allow water to be boiled (and meat with it) over a peat fire without all the inconvenience and the dirt of heating stones and plunging them into water. In the brochs we no longer see the great middens formed of burnt stone and peat ash, although peat may well have remained the principal fuel. The alleged discovery of its combustible properties by Torf Einar, as related in the *Orkneyinga Saga*, is either apochryphal, or it reflects the rediscovery of a technique which the Pictish predecessors of the Norseman could surely have taught them.

Technologies too certainly changed: most notably, metals were now used. Orkney does not seem to have been rich in bronze: few bronze artefacts have been found and there are no clear signs of metalworking from the prehistoric period. Iron may have been produced locally, but certainly the few items of gold (notably the Early Bronze Age discs from the Knowes of Trotty) and the great quantities of silver from the Pictish period were imports.

The most evident and interesting changes which took place in early Orkney were, however, those in social structure and organisation, and it is to these that we must turn.

Social Change in Early Orkney: External Factors

Despite the relative abundance of finds from early Orkney, the social organisation of the periods in question is far from clear. Still less so are the underlying factors responsible for the transition from one social form to another. In a sense it is still too early to tackle convincingly the problems that are raised by the finds, and I have much sympathy with the cautionary view expressed in chapter 6 by Dr Graham Ritchie: 'not to imply that we know more than we do'. I myself, however, adhere to the first school of archaeological interpretation to which he refers, seeing the deliberate articulation of hypothetical social frameworks as the way forward, while admitting that the evidence is often very thin. Such frameworks are therefore to be seen as devices to aid thought and to further research rather than as claims to reconstruct the past in any definitive way.

This book has been organised in a series of chapters focusing upon separate time periods and partly for that reason there has been in it relatively little discussion of change or of causal factors.

In the archaeology of earlier days it was common to see each change in the material record as the result of the arrival of a new group of people. Immigrants with new technologies and new ideas were seen as the principal

. . . .

agency of innovation. Thus not only were the first farmers of Orkney seen as immigrants – which can hardly be doubted – but so were the builders of the passage graves; the users of grooved ware; the people who built the henge monuments; the Beaker People; those who introduced bronze to the islands; the people first using cremation burial; the broch builders; the Picts and of course the Norsemen. Today this migrationist view is largely discounted, so that while many of these innovations are still accepted as the product of the diffusion of ideas, the arrival of substantial new populations is less willingly admitted.

Only in the case of the Norsemen is large-scale immigration generally accepted. The critic of the current reluctance to accept migrationist views might well comment that in the case of the Norsemen, the anti-migrationist has very little choice, since the advent of the Norse Earls of Orkney is historically well documented. And he might go on to say that what was true of Viking times could well have been true earlier also. But this would be to overlook the special nature of the Viking phenomenon, where the social developments in Scandinavia which created the pressure to sail westwards were accompanied by the necessary developments in ship design and ship building without which such voyages would not have been possible.

The nature and intensity of early Norse settlement in the Orkney Islands is still a matter for discussion. In her chapter on the Picts (chapter 9), Dr Anna Ritchie notes the evidence from her excavations at Buckquoy which suggests that the process of settlement may have been a gradual and fairly peaceful one.

The linguistic evidence, however, remains puzzling. The Orkney Norn, the Norse dialect which became the language of the islands until replaced by Scottish dialect under the Stewart earls, seems to have contained no words clearly derived from the language of the Picts. More surprisingly, the place-names of Orkney are almost entirely Norse, with hardly any toponyms clearly surviving from Pictish times. Why is this? Does it imply a total extermination of the Pictish population, in contradiction to the suggestions of Anna Ritchie? Or can we propose some mechanism by which the incomers would assign to different places in the islands names which had meaning in their own language? There has been, so far as I am aware, very little serious discussion of the precise circumstances in which place-names are either accepted from local inhabitants with a pre-existing system of nomenclature, or created afresh *de novo*. It is possibly true, in general, however, that a new, hierarchically structured society with the incomers as the dominant group, may readily impose the terminology of that group upon the landscape. On the other hand, when the pattern of immigration is one of incomers in small groups, infilling a pre-existing settlement pattern without disrupting it, many place-names in the language of the original population are more likely to survive. In the

. . . .

modern world many nation states seeking to assert their ethnic identity have suppressed place-names of a different ethno-linguistic origin, and perhaps a similar outlook may have operated in Norse Orkney.

On this view, then, it is possible that there are few if any large-scale incursions of new groups of people into Orkney between the initial population by the first farmers and the arrival of the Vikings from the east. The lack of Pictish place-names need not, on the view argued here, indicate a discontinuity in population. Anna Ritchie's view of a more gradual and perhaps peaceful process is equally plausible. Many of the apparent continuities in material culture throughout the first millennium AD could be explained in this way. Raymond Lamb has suggested that the distribution of mediaeval chapels in Orkney, which is itself related to the Norse system of rental districts, may show a continuity with the preceding Pictish tenurial system, and may indeed extend back to the first millennium BC.

VISIBILITY IN THE ARCHAEOLOGICAL RECORD

If we take a hasty and perhaps superficial view of the archaeological record in Orkney, there are three major episodes or phases of very evident building activity which we might be tempted to regard as 'climaxes' in the trajectory of development.

The first of these is a long one spanning the entire period of construction of the chambered tombs, starting with the first, probably well before 3500 BC, and encompassing the building of Maes Howe in around 2800 BC and the two major henge monuments at very approximately the same time. We can consider further below the extent to which this 'cycle' was a single, unitary phenomenon.

Whatever its nature it seems to have come to an end around 2300 BC when the tombs ceased to be used. It is conventional to regard the succeeding period in Orkney, from the end of the construction and use of chambered tombs (which are usually considered as 'neolithic') as assignable to the 'Bronze Age'. This designation, however, while so useful in Scandinavia and in England and southern Scotland, is really rather inappropriate to the Northern Isles, where metal finds are so few. But in any case, the second millennium BC, and much of the first, were until recently very much a gap in the Orcadian record, filled in part by a few earth mounds and some cist burials. The recent increase in our information is reviewed in chapter 7: cemeteries like that of Quoyscottie are now known, and the mounds of burnt stone can be assigned to this period. But, for all this new evidence, we have no public monuments, no major constructions, and very few sites, other than the mounds of burnt stone, which can be considered domestic.

This picture changes dramatically with the construction of the brochs. Their remarkable frequency in Orkney and in Shetland has long been recognised, and they make the earlier part of the 'Iron Age' a period of high visibility in the record, in contrast to the preceding Bronze Age.

For quite how long brochs continued to be built is not yet very clear. Evidently they did continue in use, often as the nucleus of large village structures, for a long time after broch-building had ended – well into the Pictish period. The latter has, like the Bronze Age, until recently been a period of low visibility, although Anna Ritchie's excavation at Buckquoy, and the recent work on the Pictish village at the broch at the Howe of Howe Farm have enhanced our knowledge.

It is not until the Norse period with its conspicuous remains, including the Earl's Palace at Birsay, the round church at Orphir and above all the great cathedral of St Magnus that we again see prominent architectural monuments.

Viewed, then, in rather soft focus, the prehistory of Orkney looks like three periods of high achievement, when the extant monuments allow us to say a good deal, interrupted by two periods (the Bronze Age and the Pictish Iron Age) where activities appear to have been on a more modest scale. Such a division into periods, episodes or phases is, of course, an arbitrary one. We would much prefer to study the various features of society – the demography, the subsistence economy, the social organisation, the belief system – along their trajectory through time without the imposition of such arbitrary divisions. But the changing nature of the record prevents it. In the period of the chambered cairns and that of the brochs, we have sufficient datable sites to prepare distribution maps and to consider the spatial patterns of activity as Fraser (1983) has done for the earlier period. J.W. Hedges (1975) has attempted this for the period of the mounds of burnt stone, but their identification is in many cases less certain. And for the Pictish period, after the brochs, we have observed very few sites: archaeologically they have a very low profile, which is not to say that they are not there.

INTERACTION IN ORKNEY AND IN BRITAIN

While we have accepted that trend of contemporary thought which is cautious in explaining changes in the archaeological record as the result of invasion or immigration, that is not to say that significant contact between different areas was not occurring. And while 'diffusionist' explanations are themselves not currently fashionable, it would not be realistic to discuss the appearance of artefacts of metal in Orkney as anything other than the result of contact with the Scottish mainland. This is one case, given the absence of metal sources in the islands and the paucity of actual finds, where Orkney can be regarded unhesitatingly as the receiver, and the lands to the south as the donor: a relationship where Orkney is in the secondary position. To use the terminology currently favoured by Marxist anthropologists (and others), Orkney was from the standpoint of metallurgical trade and industry at the periphery of a 'world system' whose 'core' lay well to the south. But the simplicities of what some choose to call 'dominance theory', where the world is divided into advanced cores and retarded peripheries, are seldom applicable to societies which are not at a state level of social complexity. Indeed they recall in many ways the old-fashioned diffusionist view which operated on the principle of *ex Oriente lux*, with the Near East as the source of all progress.

Recently a different perspective has emerged where an analysis of change is sought in terms of interactions between neighbouring areas which do not need to be expressed in terms of dominance, or of core and periphery. Often we see changes taking place over a broad area, which clearly embraces many independent social units, or polities as one might term them (without any suggestion that they are urban communities). It is the interactions between these equal-status polities which are often worth studying. This peer-polity interaction approach (Renfrew and Cherry, in press) has recently been applied to a number of cases in prehistoric Europe, and I feel it may be helpful here also.

Let us take the case of the brochs. Many writers, most recently MacKie (1965), have taken the core/periphery view of culture diffusion, with Orkney as the receiver at the fringe, and some other area, in this case south-west England, as the source. The alternative, which some have been tempted to offer, is to see Orkney, or Shetland, or the Western Isles as the source, the focus of innovation. The peer-polity interaction approach would lead one instead to look for parallel developments within many of the localities of the interaction area, including all three insular groups, and Caithness and Sutherland too.

As Hedges rightly stresses, there is now no reason to look for points of origin outside these areas. The early round house at Quanterness (Renfrew 1979, 181) and the structure at the Bu near Stromness (Hedges forthcoming a) allow us to see a possible typological development for early circular structures seen also at Jarlshof in Shetland. And the forts of the Western Isles indicate a background of defensive architecture. The approach invites us to consider the communications and interactions within the area which may have shaped the common developments observed right across it.

Above all we need a clear picture of the social organisation of the time. And to the extent that the brochs were of approximately the same size, and often well spaced in the landscape (rather than placed close together like towers in some larger system of defence), they may be regarded as representing small communities of roughly equal scale and rank (Renfrew 1976). Unless some are much larger and more elaborate than the usual norm, there would seem no case for a hierarchical order, with prominent chiefs or kings controlling large areas from their fortified fastnesses. On the contrary, these seem to be simply the well-defended farmsteads of relatively small rural communities which were the approximate equivalent in territorial scale of the tomb-building groups of the neolithic age.

We begin to see Early Iron Age society in Orkney then as a segmentary society without pronounced personal ranking, in many ways similar to that of the builders of the chambered cairns. The contents of the brochs themselves indicate some disparities in rank perhaps, with objects of fine craftsmanship, but there is none of the wealth during this period which we are to see in the great silver hoards of the next.

What we are apparently seeing in the years up to *c.* 600 BC and to the building of the early brochs is the emergence or consolidation of a society divided primarily into small groups of between perhaps ten and fifty people, usually perhaps extended families. These groups may have had internal ranking in the existence of a prominent household leader. But we have no evidence yet for larger alliances, where a whole number of these households or 'towns' (in the traditional Orcadian sense of the word) would be grouped under a single more powerful leader or chief. To say that we do not see it is not to establish that it did not exist. We can infer alliances, perhaps clan affiliations, such as are present in many segmentary societies, but not yet the concentration of real power into the hands of individuals.

Now one interesting feature of this pattern is that it was a local one, local that is to the area in question in northern Scotland. The rest of the British Isles seems to have functioned in a different way. In most areas around this time there are clear signs of a more centralised society, with a whole hierarchy of 'hillforts' often functioning as tribal centres. This is true for much of Scotland as well as for the south, but not for the more northerly regions where the brochs are found.

The brochs are thus significant in ways going beyond their architectural uniqueness. This is not simply an autonomous architectural tradition, developed perhaps by a process of peer-polity interaction. It represents also a social reality which appears to have differed markedly from that operating further south. Instead, the segmentary societies perhaps represented by the brochs, look, to the modern observer, much more like those represented for us also by the chambered tombs of three thousand years earlier.

We should note also that the society which followed, that of the Picts (who were, of course, quite simply the descendants of the broch builders), although at first sight rather impoverished, does in distinction show signs of more prominent internal ranking. In the first place, we know now that some at least of the Pictish settlements, still centred upon an earlier broch, were very much larger than the original brochs themselves. There were large villages, like that at Howe or Gurness, and more houses, like Buckquoy. Secondly, we have the occasional hoard of silver ornaments, which indicates a fondness for display and conspicuous consumption not hitherto in evidence. And then there are the symbol stones which, although not easy to interpret, may well be making statements claiming or asserting the ascendency of individuals or families over specific territories, just as did the slightly later inscribed stones of the Viking period in Denmark (Randsborg 1980, 131). All of this may possibly belong within a new social order in which local independence was lost, as the Orkneys came within the jurisdiction of the reported Pictish king, whose seat was further south in Scotland. The story of the Orcadian *regulus* (perhaps sub-king) who met St Columba at the Pictish court, as Adomnan relates, may hint at this. But the archaeological record does not yet document the top tier of our proposed hierarchy, and one would need the discovery of the seat of this king, or perhaps of some royal burials in what is now Scotland to illustrate it for us.

NEOLITHIC PROBLEMS

With the autonomous development of the brochs within the northern highlands and islands as a model, we can now turn to some of the more difficult problems of the neolithic period. Here we are no longer faced merely with the old choice between diffusion and local independent invention. We can now consider the role of Orkney within larger areas of intercommunicating polities, within which innovation could occur and be reinforced by competition and by emulation between them.

The beginning of the story – the arrival of the first farmer settlers – seems clear enough, although it would still not be surprising to find that Orkney had been visited or even inhabited on a year-round basis by hunter-gatherer communities without the domesticated plants and animals favoured by the first farmers who subsequently arrived. These earlier groups, concentrating on marine resources, would have enjoyed a way of life generally termed mesolithic. Such a pattern of life is well documented on the Hebridean island of Oronsay around 4500 BC (Mellars 1978). There are just a few indications from surface finds of chipped stone tools, that such communities may have lived in Orkney, but as yet no excavated remains.

In any case, one must regard the first farmers as immigrants, as Anna Ritchie describes, and their way of life is best represented for us so far by her excavations at the Knap of Howar. No doubt other sites as early will be discovered, and one may predict that amongst them will be some chamber tombs of the Orkney–Cromarty type. Of course, it would be possible to argue an extreme 'independent origin' position, and suggest that collective burial in chamber tombs developed independently among the farming communities of Orkney, as it seems to have done in such different parts of Europe as Brittany, Iberia and Scandinavia. But the form of some of the simpler Orcadian cairns compares so closely with those of north Scotland, as Audrey Henshall indicates in chapter 5, that this suggestion seems unnecessary. One may rather suppose that the first agricultural population came to Orkney with a set of beliefs and social or religious conventions which included clear views about the sort of community they belonged to and the manner in which it was fitting to dispose of the dead.

It is after this that the questions arise. Did the Orcadian passage graves like Quanterness and Quoyness simply develop locally from the simple chambered cairns of the first farmers? This is perfectly conceivable, since the flags of Orkney sandstone which are so readily available favour the development of a local architectural style with corbelled roofs over long and narrow chambers, and with numerous side chambers. If there was such a local development in architecture, culminating in the construction of Maes Howe, it may have run alongside a rather different series of developments resulting in the grander stalled cairns such as Midhowe.

Some writers have long argued, however, that the Orcadian passage graves must be related to those of Ireland, notably in the Boyne valley, which show the same feature of a central chamber set in a round mound and reached by a long entrance passage. The Irish passage graves, such as Newgrange, are certainly earlier than the Orcadian examples so far dated. The artefacts in Orkney and the Boyne show little resemblance in general. The carved stone from Pierowall in Westray, recently discovered, may however prove an important clue (plate 5.4), for the style of the carving is very like that of the Boyne tombs – a similarity already hinted in Orkney by the more modest carvings from Eday Manse and the Holm of Papa Westray. This may provide the more convincing indication of the influence upon Orkney of ideas and symbols from the Boyne which is necessary to sub-stantiate the proposed origin for the passage graves. Bradley and Chapman (in press) have recently applied the idea of peer-polity interaction to the later neolithic of the British Isles, and the concept is helpful here. For what one may be seeing here is a convergence of traditions. We may have been wrong to have in mind a 'family tree' model, with a common source for features in different areas followed by an increasing divergence, as develop-ments go their own way and depart increasingly from the common proto-type. Instead there may be an early period with much local variation, followed by the general establishment of beliefs and norms of behaviour over an increasingly wide area, accompanied by the widespread adoption of specific symbols and styles of expression.

On this view it would be perfectly possible for the Orkney passage graves to have begun their development locally, from a starting point in the simpler Orkney-Cromarty cairns, and to have profited during their later development from contacts with the Western Isles and with Ireland.

Such an approach to the question may be necessary if we are to understand the origins of henge monuments and the development of the pottery known as grooved ware – both problems clearly posed in chapter 6 by Graham Ritchie.

Once again, there is so far no evidence of the arrival of new groups of people at this time. Moreover, it should be remembered that in Orkney there is no chronological separation between the building of chambered cairns on the one hand and the construction of henge monuments and the use of grooved ware on the other. In south Britain the long barrows and the Severn-Cotswold tombs belong to an early phase, along with the causewayed camps, while the henge monuments and the accompanying grooved ware are a good deal later. The Orcadian chambered cairns naturally have an origin much later than their southern counterparts, since farming reached Orkney comparatively late. But the two Orcadian henges are as early as most of those of Wessex, and are certainly contemporary with the continuing use of some of the chambered cairns, including Quanterness, Isbister and Maes Howe.

It is again difficult to conceive of so specific a form of ritual monument as the henge originating independently in north and south – especially when the form is effectively restricted to Britain and is not seen in continental Europe. Moreover, as Graham Ritchie points out, the custom of digging circular ditches is not likely to have originated in Orkney where ditches usually have to be rock-cut. There is a convenient prototype in the causewayed camps of the chalklands in the south.

But this does not mean that we must assume a southern origin for the whole ritual complex. The peer-polity interaction approach leads us not to expect a single specifically localised point of origin for the entire ritual complex. Clearly there must have been rather wide contacts at this time, and we may sometimes exaggerate the difficulties of travel. The early radiocarbon dates for the henge at Balfarg in Fife, cited by Graham Ritchie, remind us that Scotland may have played a role in the developmental process. It is possible to argue, too, that the astronomical concepts which may be reflected in the layout of some of the Scottish ritual sites, such as Callanish, may be more at home in the north than in southern lowland England. It might be as valid to see Avebury, for instance, as a southern transformation of the Ring of Brodgar as it would be to assert the converse; yet both may be the product of a process of ritual and architectural development in which the whole of Britain participated. Comparable arguments may be necessary to explain the similarities in the pottery of the time, the grooved ware, which, whatever the local variants, seems evidently related, from Orkney in the north to Clacton in the south.

These may seem somewhat abstract arguments, but they are necessary if we are to set the ritual monuments of Orkney within their broader British context. We do not have to consider them either as derivative, situated at the periphery of some 'world system', nor as a unique point of origin at some notional core. They are better seen as an integral part of a more complex system of interacting parts, making a contribution, although not necessarily a preponderant one, to the evolving belief system.

In human terms this means that we are not necessarily better thinking of distinct stages – an earlier egalitarian phase with chambered cairns and a later, chieftain phase with henge monuments. We can conceive instead of a developing society, in which public ritual was increasingly taking on an important role, and where the religious ideas of one area might have a considerable impact not only on immediately neighbouring communities but more widely.

PREHISTORIC PILGRIMAGES?

Indeed one is tempted to wonder whether there may not have been some *agency of greater mobility* at work in the spread of ritual ideas. Were there perhaps seasonal festivities at many of the great ritual centres and holy places of Britain, which attracted worshippers and adherents not simply from the outlying parts of their own territories, but from much further afield? Is this the underlying human reality behind some of the peer-polity interactions which we have inferred? 'To goon on pilgrimages', as Chaucer puts it in the *Canterbury Tales,* may be a practice of vastly greater antiquity in Britain than the Late Middle Ages.

The notion of the 'periodic central place' is a familiar one for the geographer of the market economy (Skinner 1964), and Isobel Smith long ago suggested something comparable for the causewayed camps of the earlier neolithic of southern Britain (Smith 1965, 19). I have suggested that the great ritual monuments of the south, like Avebury or Durrington Walls, as well as Brodgar and Stenness, may have been the ritual foci of chiefdom societies (Renfrew 1983). Their distribution in space, as the possible foci of quite large territories, supports this idea. But perhaps I have insufficiently stressed that the ritual focus of one territory can exercise a powerful influence upon the inhabitants of *other* regions. The great church of St James of Compostela, for instance, may have been the chief ritual focus for northern Spain in the Middle Ages, but it was also more than that. More relevantly perhaps, the shrine of St Thomas à Becket was undoubtedly the pride of the archdiocese of Canterbury, yet it attracted pilgrims from many lands. Of course, in these cases we are talking about a more developed belief system, a religion of the Book, with an international organisation centred upon Rome. We must not project the religious customs of the High Middle Ages unthinkingly upon the British Neolithic. We are talking here of what we may instead regard as peasant cults amongst totally illiterate populations. And Isobel Smith may also have been right in thinking of medieval fairs and cattle markets – the religious dimension may not, in earlier times, have excluded the practical and economic one. It seems a frequent feature of the behaviour of human societies, or polities (to use the terminology favoured here), that outside and beyond the social and territorial units of political control there are periodic meetings and gatherings. This is true of many hunter-gatherer bands, which occasionally meet together at large gatherings or corroborees, to use the Australian term. It is true also of the ancient Greeks, whose fiercely competitive civic pride was canalised and to some extent overcome at pan-Hellenic festivals, of which that at Olympia is today the most famous. We have mentioned the medieval Christian pilgrimage; and its Muslim equivalent, the visit of the faithful to Mecca, should not be forgotten.

Evidence of very long-distance travel is already available for the British Neolithic. When the polished stone axes, found in the southern counties, were first being examined, and as their sources were identified in Cornwall, at Langdale Pike in Cumbria, etc., it was noticed that some of the causewayed camps had axes from a remarkably wide range of sources (see Smith 1971, 102). No specific human mechanism was offered to account for this, although Grahame Clark (1965) put forward the useful suggestion of ceremonial gift exchange to explain their general widespread distribution. But perhaps we should now add the further religious dimension to the discussion, and suggest that the driving force behind the movement of many of the travellers was the desire to attend the great seasonal religious ceremonies at one site or another. Seasonality is one of the most obvious features in such monuments as Stonehenge, and Thom has suggested that various stone circles of Britain show alignments upon a variety of seasonal solar phenomena. Many of these examples, of course, come from a date after the British Neolithic, but the point may apply to the period of the henges also.

Against such a background of movement – which is securely documented for Scotland (although not yet Orkney) by finds of jade axes ultimately derived from continental Europe (Campbell Smith 1965) – the parallel development of rituals, of monuments, and of symbolic systems in different parts of Britain becomes much easier to comprehend.

From this perspective the development of the Orcadian henges has to be seen as part of a larger British phenomenon. No doubt one aspect of the process was the emergence of more centralised social structures – chiefdoms in modern anthropological parlance. But here I am stressing rather the emergence of what must have been a remarkably powerful body of religious beliefs, with accompanying ritual observances. These are reflected in the notable uniformity of the henges over the whole of Britain, and in the very widespread distribution of grooved ware. Here Orkney, with its still continuing tradition of communal burial, was well equipped to play a part, and this was one of the very few areas where the use and perhaps even the construction of the monuments in the older tradition (the chambered cairns) persisted alongside the new ritual practices in the henges.

SOCIAL TRANSFORMATIONS

In this Epilogue it has been possible to make suggestions about some of the factors underlying the three great cycles of Orcadian prehistory. The development of neolithic ritual, culminating in the two great Orcadian henges, can be seen as part of a religious or ritual movement common to Britain as a whole. I have suggested that it may have been sustained by quite widespread travels of individuals, on what we might imagine as prehistoric pilgrimages.

But why did this tradition come to so dismal an end around 2300 BC? This is a question we cannot yet answer. One might appeal to internal factors: perhaps some agricultural difficulties resulting in population decline (although the evidence for climatic deterioration comes rather later). Alternatively, however, we might note that the whole British ritual complex associated with the henges declined at about the same time. It is now commonly associated with the development of a different set of values, laying more emphasis perhaps on personal prestige (Renfrew 1973; Shennan 1983), seen reflected perhaps in the Beaker burials. Such developments are less marked in the north: indeed it is interesting that it is in the north that the stone circles of the Bronze Age continue some of the old traditions. Orkney, however, was not on any of the trade routes which may have allowed the élites in the south the opportunity of amassing wealth and prestige. Perhaps in this circumstance lies the underlying cause for her decline in the Bronze Age.

The rise in the Early Iron Age of the brochs, whose distribution has been compared above with that of the much earlier chambered cairns, represents a remarkable re-assertion of northern individuality. Once again, Orkney (with Shetland, the Hebrides and the northern counties of the Scottish mainland) produced distinctive architectural forms. It is tempting to suggest that this was again a time of relative autonomy, of isolation even. Certainly in the succeeding Pictish period, when Orkney may have come under the sway of a ruler based in Scotland, the architectural finds are less impressive. Prestige was expressed in other ways again – in silver ornaments, and perhaps by the symbol stones.

The Norse arrival, unlike these other cases, seems to have been an essentially external event, brought about by a mixture of social and technological developments in Scandinavia. The social background to the early Viking raids has been much discussed, and of course they depended heavily on the new technology of the Norse sailing ships. But if the initial shift from Pictish to Norse was essentially an exogenous change, the stability of the new system was a feature of the suitability of the Orkneys for the new exploitation, and of the effectiveness of that system in relation to Orkney.

PROSPECT

One general point indeed emerges as the *Leitmotiv* of the present review: that more work is needed on a number of fronts if we are to reach a really satisfactory understanding of the Orcadian past. This is not a negative conclusion. Quite to the contrary, it is remarkable how far the great upsurge of excavation work in Orkney over the past decade, with which all the contributors of this volume have been associated, has succeeded in giving positive answers to a whole series of questions, as well as bringing to the fore some of the new ones which have been discussed here. The need, of course, is for further work, and here I think we can take comfort from three aspects of the current scene.

The first positive feature in very recent years has been the appointment, by the Orkney Heritage Society, of a resident Orkney Archaeologist. His prime task is rightly seen as one of survey rather than of excavation, and the early results of his work have been nothing less than spectacular. In his survey of two of the north isles of Orkney, Sanday and North Ronaldsay (RCAMS 1980b), Raymond Lamb has brought to light a striking number of new sites, and of new classes of site. In doing so he has documented the extent to which the monuments of rural Orkney are under threat, both from coastal erosion and from the mechanisation and intensification of farming, which today is increasingly departing from the traditional methods which for so long left many sites undisturbed. The survey, moreover, goes beyond the identification of individual sites and moves towards a larger vision of the landscape, the prehistoric landscape, as an object of study. This shift is in keeping with current developments in other areas, and already it has brought to attention some important issues.

When the landscape rather than the individual site is considered the whole question of land use becomes relevant – our attention moves to the fields, rather than focusing solely upon the focal settlements: to whole areas, as it were, rather than to discrete points. And whenever early fields and field systems are studied, whether in Gotland or Wessex or in Dartmoor, field divisions and boundaries take on a new importance. In studying areas, the linear features which divide them are often more interesting than the individual settlement points which they contain. So it has proved in Orkney. Dr Lamb has recognised a class of monument, hitherto largely overlooked in Orkney: the treb dykes. Treb dykes are massive linear earthworks (RCAMS 1980b, 9), and it is Dr Lamb's suspicion, as yet unconfirmed by excavation, that some of them may go back perhaps as far as the Bronze Age. That would certainly harmonise with findings in other areas, such as the impressive Bokerley Dyke system in Wessex. Their study is just beginning, but we can certainly recognise that the investigation of early land use in Orkney is likely to be one of the growth points of archaeological research. This is particularly germane since our earliest systematic records for Orkney relate to taxation in the period of Scottish rule. There is no doubt that many of the land divisions there recorded go back to Norse times, so that there is a potential source of historical information about Norse land tenure to be set alongside the findings of field survey. The great potential of such survey information makes the task all the more urgent, since mechanisation is a constant threat to early field systems, and much has already been lost.

A second encouraging aspect of current research is the contribution now being made by environmental specialists. The work of the pollen analyst formed the basis for many of the observations by Davidson and Jones in their contribution, although much more has yet to be undertaken before we have a full and detailed picture of the vegetational history of the area. The potential contributions of the geomorphologist and soil scientist remain to be fully exploited, not least in the context of the study of land use just discussed. Another interesting topic is the nature of the farm mounds of the north isles. These were again first noticed by Lamb (RCAMS 1980, 7) and are now the subject of study by Davidson (Davidson, Lamb and Simpson 1983). Initial study suggests a resemblance with the 'gardshauger' of Arctic Norway (Bertelsen 1979), and it may be that here we shall have a useful new source of data about early subsistence and settlement.

Finally it is appropriate to refer to the great contributions currently being made by rescue archaeology in Orkney. In Britain in general it has been widely realised, in recent years, that developments within our town centres have been destroying a very high proportion of the evidence relating to early urban development. Such important excavation projects as those of Winchester, York and the City of London have sprung from this realisation – in contrast with Dublin where a terrible desecration has been effected at the Wood Quay site, with the wanton destruction, without adequate prior investigation, of one of the most important Viking sites of Europe. (It should be remarked here that the archaeological potential of Kirkwall itself has not yet been fully appreciated, and a coherent plan for its investigation is much to be desired, for what must surely be the most important Viking settlement in Scotland.) But while British urban archaeology has in general responded to the most pressing threats, this has not been the case with the rural landscape. Whole areas containing a great variety of field monuments have been destroyed in England and in Scotland by deep mechanised ploughing. Happily the problem is rather different in Orkney, since most of the prehistoric settlements and monuments in question are stone-built, and are not so easily eradicated by simple ploughing. Although it is distressing to learn that one of the few single standing stones in Orkney, overlooking the Loch of Stenness, was destroyed by a farmer with a tractor a couple of years ago, and that a broch site, a scheduled Ancient Monument, has been deliberately destroyed by its owner – both these acts being contraventions of the law – such infractions are happily rather rare. The monuments of the past are respected in Orkney. Moreover the Scottish Development Department has responded magnificently to the general situation by sponsoring an organisation, North of Scotland Archaeological Services, whose role it is to undertake rescue excavations in cases where the threat to sites cannot easily be averted.

Several of the important recent excavations in Orkney have been conducted under their aegis, including those at the broch of Bu near Stromness and at the broch at Howe. The latter has been one of the most interesting and rewarding excavations in recent years in the whole of Britain. For in addition to the Pictish remains discussed by Anna Ritchie and the broch mentioned by Hedges, there are earlier or pre-broch remains, and these are now seen to have been constructed upon the site of a neolithic chambered cairn. Of course the full publication of these excavations is now eagerly awaited, but there are encouraging signs that this important enterprise will not go the way of the ill-fated pre-war excavations at the Broch of Gurness and the Brough of Birsay and evade publication altogether. For I have on my shelf an impressive series of well-documented preliminary reports, produced by North of Scotland Archaeological Services for this and other sites, which show that at least the preliminary work has been done, and that this important site is well on the way to publication.

It should be mentioned here also that many of the excavations discussed in this volume were funded either in whole or in part by the Scottish Development Department (Ancient Monuments). The threat to the heritage is as great in Orkney as anywhere else, but the action of the Orkney Islands Council in employing an Orkney Archaeologist and of the Scottish Development Department in supporting North of Scotland Archaeological Services have together succeeded so far in averting disaster.

This is as it should be. For in Orkney, somehow more markedly than in many other areas, the past has the quality of a present reality. The monuments are there, obvious in the landscape, and the evident continuities have a meaning, not just for the archaeological specialist, but for everybody. It is no coincidence, then, that the poets of Orkney have felt and expressed these feelings with great conviction. For Edwin Muir this was one of the deep sources of his poetic writing, and today the work of George Mackay Brown expresses anew the timeless quality of the world of Orkney. The Orcadian today is the inheritor, in this way, of the Orkney of yesterday. And so too, in a sense, are we all who seek to know the heritage of the islands, to the extent that we can gain an understanding of our common early past from a study of prehistory.

The possession of so great a heritage brings with it great obligations, which are not always easy to meet. And that is the thought which Miss

Costie so well expressed in the concluding lines of her poem 'The Auld
Hoose Spaeks', with whose beginning I introduced this chapter and with
whose ending I shall now conclude:

> Peety! Na min, raither thoo should lift thee kep,
> An' say thanks for thee gret heritage,
> . . . .
> An thoo're the culmination o' id aa'
> An' thine's the trust tae see 'id disno dee,
> Bit gets skailled oot amang the folk o' this wir land,
> Tae mak them read, an' see, an' understand.

Colin Renfrew and Simon Buteux **Radiocarbon Dates from Orkney**

In the list which follows, we have set out all the radiocarbon dates currently available from archaeological contexts in Orkney. The dates are given first in radiocarbon years, bc or ad, together with the associated standard error and the laboratory measurement number.

There is as yet no universally agreed procedure for the calibration of radiocarbon dates, which is necessary to express the date in 'true' or calendar years BC or AD. We have used here the procedure proposed by Dr Malcolm Clark (Clark 1975). It should be noted that the accompanying standard error is also modified. The calibrations currently in use are based upon the Californian bristlecone pine, *Pinus aristata*. It is likely that an independent calibration, based on wood samples preserved in Irish bogs, will also soon be available. Current indications are that these figures may not differ very much from those obtained from the bristlecone pine (Ottaway 1983). It is likely, therefore, that further refinements in measurement and calibration will ultimately permit more precise datings (i.e. dates with smaller standard errors). But in most cases such calibrated dates will probably not differ substantially from the calibrated figures set out here. It should be noted however, that to achieve a 95 per cent probability level it is necessary to quote dates with a ±2 sigma range. The range thus lies between the mean date plus 2 sigma and the mean date minus 2 sigma, where the mean date is the calibrated date quoted here, and sigma is the standard error, after calibration, as listed.

Acknowledgement. We wish to thank all the contributors to this volume for supplying the radiocarbon dates listed here, and Dr V. R. Switsur for his advice.

KNAP OF HOWAR

Lab no.	Context	Material	Radiocarbon date bc/ad	Calendar date BC/AD
Birm 816	Lower midden	Mixed animal bone	2820 bc ± 180	3600 BC ± 190
SRR 349	Lower midden	Mixed animal bone	2472 bc ± 70	3205 BC ± 110
Birm 813	Midden filling wall of House 2 (= lower midden)	Mixed animal bone	2320 bc ± 100	2995 BC ± 115
Birm 815	Lower midden	Mixed animal bone	2300 bc ± 130	2970 BC ± 145
SRR 347	Midden filling wall of House 1 (= lower midden)	Mixed animal bone	(3756 bc ± 85)	(4560 BC ± 110)
SRR 452	Re-run of sample SRR 347	Mixed animal bone	2131 bc ± 65	2725 BC ± 110
SRR 348	Upper midden contemporary with House 1	Mixed animal bone	2815 bc ± 70	3595 BC ± 110
Birm 814	House 2, floor deposit	Mixed animal bone	2740 bc ± 130	3520 BC ± 145
SRR 346	House 1, floor deposit	Mixed animal bone	2582 bc ± 70	3350 BC ± 110
SRR 344	Upper midden contemporary with House 1	Mixed animal bone	2501 bc ± 70	3245 BC ± 110
SRR 345	House 1, floor deposit	Mixed animal bone	2398 bc ± 75	3090 BC ± 110

SKARA BRAE

Lab no.	Context	Material	Radiocarbon date bc/ad	Calendar date BC/AD
Birm 795	Occupation deposits on old land surface	Mixed animal bone	2520 bc ± 120	3270 BC ± 135
Birm 480	Occupation deposits on old land surface	Mixed animal bone	2370 bc ± 100	3055 BC ± 115
Birm 794	Occupation deposits on old land surface	Mixed animal bone	2330 bc ± 100	3005 BC ± 115
Birm 637	Beginning of phase I village	Mixed animal bone	2480 bc ± 100	3215 BC ± 115
Birm 638	Beginning of phase I village	Mixed animal bone	2480 bc ± 120	3215 BC ± 135
Birm 639	Beginning of phase I village	Mixed animal bone	2450 bc ± 100	3175 BC ± 115
Birm 636	Beginning of phase I village	Mixed animal bone	2400 bc ± 130	3095 BC ± 145
Birm 790	End of phase I village	Mixed animal bone	2420 bc ± 150	3125 BC ± 160
Birm 789	End of phase I village	Mixed animal bone	2360 bc ± 120	3045 BC ± 135
Birm 791	End of phase I village	Mixed animal bone	2340 bc ± 100	3020 BC ± 115
Birm 788	Beginning of phase II village	Mixed animal bone	2340 bc ± 120	3020 BC ± 135
Birm 786	Beginning of phase II village	Mixed animal bone	2330 bc ± 120	3005 BC ± 135
Birm 787	Beginning of phase II village	Mixed animal bone	2200 bc ± 100	2850 BC ± 115

Lab no.	Context	Material	bc date	BC date
Birm 436	End of phase II village	Mixed animal bone	2090 bc ± 110	2655 BC ± 125
Birm 434	End of phase II village	Mixed animal bone	2070 bc ± 110	2625 BC ± 125
Birm 435	End of phase II village	Mixed animal bone	1920 bc ± 100	2415 BC ± 115
Birm 433	End of phase II village	Mixed animal bone	1880 bc ± 100	2355 BC ± 125
Birm 793	Base of waterlogged layer in midden deposits at periphery of domestic area	Mixed animal bone	2110 bc ± 130	2685 BC ± 145
Birm 477	Base of waterlogged layer in midden deposits at periphery of domestic area	Mixed animal bone	2000 bc ± 100	2520 BC ± 115
Birm 478	Base of waterlogged layer in midden deposits at periphery of domestic area	Mixed animal bone	1900 bc ± 140	2385 BC ± 150
Birm 438	Top of waterlogged layer in midden deposits at periphery of domestic area	Mixed animal bone	2190 bc ± 120	2830 BC ± 135
Birm 792	Top of waterlogged layer in midden deposits at periphery of domestic area	Mixed animal bone	1980 bc ± 110	2495 BC ± 125
Birm 437	Top of waterlogged layer in midden deposits at periphery of domestic area	Mixed animal bone	1830 bc ± 110	2275 BC ± 125

LINKS OF NOLTLAND

Lab no.	Context	Material	bc date	BC date
GU 1429	Secondary ploughsoil immediately preceding main midden deposition in West Midden area	Bone of *Bos*	2265 bc ± 65	2930 BC ± 110
GU 1428	Secondary ploughsoil immediately preceding main midden deposition in West Midden area	Bone of *Bos*	2190 bc ± 65	2830 BC ± 110
GU 1431	Midden around articulated deer skeletons in West Midden	Bone of *Bos*	2000 bc ± 65	2520 BC ± 110
GU 1430	Upper layer of midden deposition in West Midden area	Bone of *Bos*	1910 bc ± 60	2400 BC ± 110
GU 1433	Midden material used to fill in the structure at Grobust	Mixed animal bone	1890 bc ± 60	2370 BC ± 110
GU 1432	Deer butchering site in accumulating sand deposit behind a field boundary in Central Dunes immediately underlying Beaker occupation	Bone of *Cervus elephas*	1772 bc ± 60	2190 BC ± 110

RINYO

Lab no.	Context	Material	bc date	BC date
Q 1226	No context	Animal bone probably *Bos*	1900 bc ± 70	2385 BC ± 110

QUANTERNESS (ORK 43)

Lab no.	Context	Material	Radiocarbon date bc/ad	Calendar date BC/AD
Q 1294	Main chamber, stratum 1	Organically rich soil	2640 bc ± 75	3420 BC ± 110
SRR 754	Main chamber, Pit A, stratum 2 (same burial as Q 1479 and Pta 1626)	Human bone	2410 bc ± 50	3110 BC ± 110
Pta 1626	Main chamber, Pit A, stratum 2 (same burial as SRR 754 and Q 1479)	Human bone	2350 bc ± 60	3030 BC ± 110
Q 1479	Main chamber, Pit A, stratum 2 (same burial as SRR 754 and Pta 1626)	Human bone	2220 bc ± 75	2875 BC ± 110
Q 1363	Main chamber, stratum 3	Human bone	2590 bc ± 110	3360 BC ± 125
Q 1451	Main chamber, stratum 3	Human bone	2160 bc ± 100	2775 BC ± 115
Pta 1606	Main chamber, Pit C, stratum 5 (same burial as Q 1480)	Human bone	2180 bc ± 60	2810 BC ± 110
Q 1480	Main chamber, Pit C, stratum 5 (same burial as SRR 755 and Pta 1606)	Human bone	1955 bc ± 70	2460 BC ± 110
SRR 755	Main chamber, Pit C, stratum 5 (same burial as Q 1480 and Pta 1606)	Human bone	1920 bc ± 55	2415 BC ± 110

ISBISTER (ORK 25)

Lab no.	Context	Material	Radiocarbon date bc/ad	Calendar date BC/AD
GU 1179	Foundation deposit immediately prior to building of tomb	Human bone	2480 bc ± 55	3215 BC ± 110
GU 1178	Foundation deposit immediately prior to building of tomb	Human bone	2295 bc ± 100	2965 BC ± 115
GU 1182	Deposit under intact shelf, Stall 5 (same sample as Q 3013)	Human bone	2530 bc ± 80	3285 BC ± 110
Q 3013	Deposit under intact shelf, Stall 5 (same sample as GU 1182)	Human bone	2425 bc ± 50	3135 BC ± 110
GU 1185	Deposit in undisturbed Side cell 3 (same sample as Q 3016)	Human bone	2470 bc ± 95	3205 BC ± 110
Q 3016	Deposit in undisturbed Side cell 3 (same sample as	Human bone	2410 bc ± 55	3110 BC ± 110

Lab code	Context	Material	Date (bc)	Date (BC)
GU 1180	Deposit on floor of undisturbed Stall 4	Human bone	2470 bc ± 90	3205 BC ± 110
GU 1181	Deposit on floor of undisturbed Stall 4	Human bone	2460 bc ± 130	3190 BC ± 145
GU 1184	Deposit in undisturbed Side cell 3 (same sample as Q 3015)	Human bone	2415 bc ± 90	3120 BC ± 110
Q 3015	Deposit in undisturbed Side cell 3 (same sample as GU 1184)	Human bone	2310 bc ± 55	2980 BC ± 110
Q 3018	Backfill behind hornwork abutting tomb (same sample as GU 1190)	Deer bone	2335 bc ± 45	3010 BC ± 110
GU 1190	Backfill behind hornwork abutting tomb (same sample as Q 3018)	Deer bone	2310 bc ± 55	2980 BC ± 110
GU 1183	Deposit under intact shelf, Stall 5 (same sample as Q 3014)	Human bone	1960 bc ± 80	2470 BC ± 110
Q 3014	Deposit under intact shelf, Stall 5 (same sample as GU 1183)	Human bone	1880 bc ± 50	2355 BC ± 110
GU 1186	Stone infilling sealing tomb (same sample as Q 3017)	Human bone	2090 bc ± 100	2655 BC ± 115
Q 3017	Stone infilling sealing tomb (same sample as U 1186)	Human bone	2080 bc ± 50	2640 BC ± 110
GU 1187	Cist burial inserted in backfill behind North hornwork	Human bone	1300 bc ± 55	1595 BC ± 110

KNOWE OF RAMSAY (ORK 30)

Lab code	Context	Material	Date (bc)	Date (BC)
Q 1223	No context	Animal bone	2390 bc ± 65	3080 BC ± 110
Q 1224	No context	Deer bone	2350 bc ± 60	3030 BC ± 110
Q 1222	No context	Animal bone	2060 bc ± 60	2610 BC ± 110

KNOWE OF ROWIEGAR (ORK 31)

Lab code	Context	Material	Date (bc)	Date (BC)
Q 1221	No context	Cattle bone	2355 bc ± 60	3035 BC ± 110
Q 1227	No context	Deer bone	2055 bc ± 60	2600 BC ± 110

QUOYNESS (ORK 44)

Lab code	Context	Material	Date (bc)	Date (BC)
SRR 753	No context	Human bone	2315 bc ± 50	2990 BC ± 110
SRR 752	No context	Human bone	2240 bc ± 50	2900 BC ± 110

KNOWE OF YARSO (ORK 32)

Q 1225	No context	Animal bone	2275 bc ± 60	2940 BC ± 110

PIEROWALL QUARRY

GU 1582	Material used in construction of structure beside ruined chambered tomb	Bone of *Bos*	2190 bc ± 60	2830 BC ± 110
GU 1583	Secondary occupation of structure beside ruined chambered tomb	Bone of *Bos*	2190 bc ± 60	2830 BC ± 110
GU 1584	Secondary occupation of structure beside ruined chambered tomb	Bone of *Bos*	2080 bc ± 65	2640 BC ± 110

MAES HOWE (ORK 36)

SRR 791	Naturally formed peat layer below bank in North ditch section	Peat	3145 bc ± 60	3930 BC ± 110
SRR 505	Basal organic material above bedrock, 0.70 m below ground level, in North ditch section (same sample as Q 1482)	Silty peat	2185 bc ± 65	2820 BC ± 110
Q 1482	Basal organic material in North ditch section (same sample as SRR 505)	Silty peat	2020 bc ± 70	2550 BC ± 110
Q 1481	Basal organic material in South ditch section (same sample as SRR 524)	Silty peat	1815 bc ± 70	2250 BC ± 110
SRR 524	Basal organic material in South ditch section (same sample as Q 1481)	Silty peat	1495 bc ± 50	1830 BC ± 110
SRR 504	Lower organic layer of two on inner slope of ditch in North section, 0.85 m below ground level	Silty peat	1710 bc ± 45	2110 BC ± 110
SRR 523	Organic mud layers in South ditch section	Silty peat	930 bc ± 45	1145 BC ± 110
SRR 522	Organic layer in South ditch section	Silty peat	ad 265 ± 45	AD 300 ± 70
SRR 521	Uppermost organic layer in South ditch section, 0.46 m below ground surface	Silty peat	ad 715 ± 40	AD 730 ± 70
SRR 792	Burnt material from within secondary bank overlying primary low stone bank in South ditch section	Soil with organic material	ad 905 ± 65	AD 955 ± 80

STONES OF STENNESS

Lab no.	Context	Material	Radiocarbon date bc/ad	Calendar date BC/AD
SRR 350	Basal ditch deposit in main ditch section – organic layer	Animal bone	2356 bc ± 65	3040 BC ± 110
SRR 351	Central setting associated with calcined bone and grooved ware sherds	Wood charcoal	2238 bc ± 70	2895 BC ± 110
SRR 592	Bedding trench of possible rectangular timber setting	Fragments of decomposed wood	1730 bc ± 270	2135 BC ± 275
SRR 352	Pit C	Wood charcoal	ad 519 ± 150	AD 560 ± 160

RING OF BRODGAR

Lab no.	Context	Material	Radiocarbon date bc/ad	Calendar date BC/AD
SRR 502	Basal organic deposit overlying deep silt infill in north ditch section – depth 0.7 m	Organic mud	255 bc ± 60	375 BC ± 80
SRR 503	Lower peat in north ditch section – depth 0.6 m	Organic mud	375 bc ± 45	440 BC ± 70

BEAQUOY (Burnt Mound)

Lab no.	Context	Material	Radiocarbon date bc/ad	Calendar date BC/AD
SRR 1001	In rubble infill of cooking trough of secondary structure	Animal bones and teeth	1677 bc ± 65	2065 BC ± 110
SRR 999	Twigs from silt at base of well-like structure relating to secondary structure	Twigs	511 bc ± 80	615 BC ± 95

POINT OF BUCKQUOY, BIRSAY CUTTINGS 5 & 6 (Midden)

Lab no.	Context	Material	Radiocarbon date bc/ad	Calendar date BC/AD
GU 1222	Carbonised grain from midden deposits associated with structural feature	Carbonised naked barley	1310 bc ± 180	1605 BC ± 190

LIDDLE (Burnt Mound)

Lab no.	Context	Material	Radiocarbon date bc/ad	Calendar date BC/AD
SRR 1000	From base of localised peat deposit over which the structure was built. The date has no connection with the occupation	Peat	2111 bc ± 40	2690 BC ± 110
SRR 525	First peat formed in a flag-lined gully which formed part of the occupational structure	Peat	958 bc ± 45	1185 BC ± 110
SRR 701	Organic detritus from bottom of cooking trough	Organic detritus, mainly heather roots	876 bc ± 75	1065 BC ± 110

KNOWES OF QUOYSCOTTIE

Lab no.	Context	Material	Radiocarbon date bc/ad	Calendar date BC/AD
UB 2161	F 103, cremation deposit cut into natural clay, overlain by clay	Wood charcoal	1195 bc ± 120	1490 BC ± 135
UB 2162	F 64, cremation deposit in Knowe I	Wood charcoal	990 bc ± 85	1235 BC ± 110
UB 2158	F 15, cremation deposit cut into natural clay and concealed by thin layer of clay	Wood charcoal	900 bc ± 40	1100 BC ± 110
UB 2163	F 91, cremation deposit cut into old land surface	Wood charcoal	710 bc ± 85	890 BC ± 100

HOLLAND

Lab no.	Context	Material	Radiocarbon date bc/ad	Calendar date BC/AD
GU 1373	Secondary burial in short cist inserted into primary mound (same burial as GU 1374)	Human bone	995 bc ± 60	1240 BC ± 110
GU 1374	Secondary burial in short cist inserted into primary mound (same burial as GU 1373)	Human bone	930 bc ± 60	1145 BC ± 110

271

Lab no.	Context	Material	Radiocarbon date bc/ad	Calendar date BC/AD
QUANTERNESS ROUND HOUSE				
Q 1465	Primary occupation of round house, prior to wall F	Organically rich soil	620 bc ±85	815 BC ±100
Q 1464	Primary occupation of round house, prior to wall F	Organically rich soil	490 bc ±85	580 BC ±100
Q 1463	Secondary occupation subsequent to construction of wall J and feature w within round house	Organically rich soil	180 bc ±60	185 BC ±80
PIEROWALL QUARRY ROUND HOUSE				
GU 1580	Occupation immediately preceding construction of round house	Bone of *Bos*	560 bc ±80	765 BC ±95
GU 1581	Occupation contemporary with use of round house	Bone of *Bos*	475 bc ±60	545 BC ±80
BU BROCH				
GU 1228	In floor deposits in broch	Charcoal	520 bc ±95	670 BC ±110
GU 1154	In floor deposits in broch	Animal bone	510 bc ±80	615 BC ±95
GU 1152	At base of rubble filling broch interior	Cow's skull	490 bc ±65	580 BC ±80
GU 1153	In floor deposits of earth-house built into disused broch	Animal bone	595 bc ±65	795 BC ±80

SKAILL, DEERNESS

Lab no.	Context	Material		
Birm 413	Occupation of 'Iron Age' site	—	260 bc ± 120	375 BC ± 130
Birm 397	Occupation of 'Iron Age' site	—	150 bc ± 110	160 BC ± 110
Birm 764	Primary context in 'Iron Age/Dark Age' site	—	70 bc ± 100	40 BC ± 110
Birm 763	Primary context in 'Pictish level'	—	ad 530 ± 100	AD 570 ± 110
Birm 762	Primary context in 'Pictish level'	—	ad 600 ± 100	AD 640 ± 110

BROUGH OF BIRSAY, AREA IV, SITE E

Lab no.	Context	Material		
GU 1251	Burnt layer below north wall of Structure E	Charcoal (*Salix/Populus*)	ad 570 ± 55	AD 615 ± 75
GU 1252	Burnt layer below north wall of Structure E	Charcoal (*Salix/Populus*)	ad 670 ± 50	AD 700 ± 70
GU 1253	Burnt layer below north wall of structure E	Charcoal (*Salix/Populus*)	ad 690 ± 50	AD 715 ± 70

BROUGH OF BIRSAY, AREA IV, NORTH OF SITE E

Lab no.	Context	Material		
GU 1254	Charcoal spreads in levelling material sealing features cut into natural clay	Charcoal (*Salix/Populus*)	ad 675 ± 50	AD 705 ± 70
GU 1318	Charcoal spreads in levelling material sealing features cut into natural clay	Charcoal (*Salix/Populus*)	ad 690 ± 50	AD 715 ± 70

BROUGH OF BIRSAY, AREA IV, SITE S

Lab no.	Context	Material		
GU 1319	Burnt layer within blocked entrance, possibly re-used as hearth, of wall in north of area	Carbonised seaweed and charcoal (*Pinus, Quercus*)	ad 795 ± 55	AD 810 ± 75

BROUGH OF BIRSAY, AREA I, SITE N

Lab no.	Context	Material		
GU 1192 & 1195	Features below northern wall of Structure N	Charcoal (*Salix/Populus*)	ad 815 ± 55	AD 835 ± 75
GU 1194	Features below northern wall of Structure N	Charcoal (*Salix/Populus*)	ad 750 ± 85	AD 760 ± 100

BROUGH OF BIRSAY, ROOM 5

Lab no.	Context	Material	Radiocarbon date bc/ad	Calendar date BC/AD
GU 1229	Phase 2b	Charcoal (*Salix/Populus*)	ad 645±55	AD 680±75
GU 1193	Phase 3a	Charcoal (*Salix/Populus*)	ad 955±60	AD 995±80

SAEVAR HOWE

GU 1402	Midden-enriched ground surface contemporary with lowest of three superimposed Norse houses (phase II (a))	Charcoal of spruce	ad 690±60	AD 715±80
GU 1400	Central path of middle one of three superimposed Norse houses (phase II (b))	Charcoal of willow	ad 750±90	AD 760±105
GU 1401	Infill of drain belonging to uppermost of three superimposed Norse houses (phase II (c))	Mixed fish, mammal and shell remains	ad 555±60	AD 600±80

BIRSAY 'SMALL SITES', AREA 3

GU 1230	Rubble and debris fill representing end of use of figure-of-eight building of pre-Norse type	Carbonised grain (*Hordeum vulgare, Avena fatua*)	ad 915±60	AD 960±80

BEACHVIEW 'STUDIO SITE', BIRSAY

GU 1191	Midden post-dating wall and rubble collapse of large building	Carbonised grain (*Avena fatua, Hordeum* etc.) and charcoal (*Pinus*)	ad 1010±55	AD 1040±75

Note: All dates from Birsay are provisional.

SANDSIDE, GRAEMSAY

GU 1067	Skeleton inside long cist	Human bone	ad 1085±55	AD 1140±75

Bibliography

Alcock, L. (1976) A multi-disciplinary chronology for Alt Clut, Castle
 Rock, Dumbarton, *Proc. Soc. Antiq. Scot.* 107 (1975-6), 103-13.
— (1980) Populi bestiales Pictorum feroci animo: a survey of Pictish
 settlement archaeology, *in* Hanson, W. S. and Keppie, L. J. F.,
 Roman Frontier Studies 1979 (= British Archaeol. Reports,
 International Series, no.71), Oxford, 61-95.
— (1981) Early historic fortifications in Scotland, *in* Guilbert, G.,
 Hill-fort studies: essays for A. H. A. Hogg, Leicester, 150-80.
Anderson, A. O. (1922) *Early Sources of Scottish History*, vol.1,
 Edinburgh.
Anderson, A. O. and Anderson, M. O. (1961) *Adomnan's Life of
 Columba*, London.
Anderson, J. (1868) On the horned cairns of Caithness, *Proc. Soc.
 Antiq. Scot.* 7 (1866-8), 480-512.
— (1873) *The Orkneyinga Saga*, Edinburgh.
— (1874) Notes on the relics of the Viking period of the Northmen in
 Scotland, illustrated by specimens in the Museum, *Proc. Soc.
 Antiq. Scot.* 10 (1872-4), 536-94.
— (1883) *Scotland in Pagan Times, The Iron Age*, Edinburgh.
— (1890) Notice of the excavation of the brochs of Yarhouse . . . in
 Caithness, *Archaeol. Scotica* 5 (1874-90), 131-98.
Anderson, M. O. (1973) *Kings and Kingship in Early Scotland*,
 Edinburgh and London.
Ashmore, P. J. (1974) Excavations at Summersdale, Orkney, by F. G.
 Wainwright in July 1960, *Proc. Soc. Antiq. Scot.* 105 (1972-4),
 41-2.
— (1980) Low cairns, long cists and symbol stones, *Proc. Soc. Antiq.
 Scot.* 110 (1978-80), 346-55.
Bailey, P. (1971) *Orkney*, Newton Abbot.

de Bakker, H. (1979) *Major Soils and Soil Regions in the Netherlands,* Centre for Agricultural Publishing and Documentation, Wageningen, Netherlands.

Baldwin, J. (1978) *Scandinavian Shetland. An Ongoing Tradition?,* Scot. Soc. for Northern Studies, Edinburgh.

Barron, D. G. (1895) Notice of a small cemetery of cremated burials, with cinerary urns of clay, recently discovered at Culla Voe, Papa Stour, Shetland, *Proc. Soc. Antiq. Scot.* 29 (1894-5), 46-8.

Barry, G. (1805) *The History of the Orkney Islands,* Edinburgh.

Batey, C. E. (1980) Excavations at Orphir 1979, *Univs Durham & Newcastle upon Tyne, Archaeol. Reps for 1979,* Durham, 33-5 (also *Northern Stud.* 15, (1980), 17-22).

— (1981) Excavations at the Earl's Bu at Orphir, Orkney, *Univs Durham & Newcastle upon Tyne, Archaeol. Reps for 1980,* Durham, 33-5.

Batey, C. E. and Morris, C. D. (1983) The finds, *in* Hedges, J. W. (1983b), 85-108.

Bekker-Nielsen, H., Foote, P. and Olsen, O. (1981) *Proceedings of the Eighth Viking Congress, Arhus 1981,* Odense.

Bell, B. and Haigh, D. (1981) Howe of Howe, *Discovery and Excavation in Scotland in 1981,* 25.

Bertelsen, R. (1979) Farm mounds in North Norway. A review of recent research, *Norwegian Archaeol. Rev.* 12 (1979), 48-56.

Biddle, M. (1971) Archaeology and the beginnings of English society, *in* Clemoes, P. and Hughes, K., *England before the Conquest. Studies in primary sources presented to Dorothy Whitelock,* Cambridge, 391-408.

Bigelow, G. F. (1978) *Preliminary report of the 1978 excavations at Sandwick, Unst, Shetland Islands.*

— (forthcoming) Sandwick, Unst and late Norse Shetland economy, *in* Smith, B., *Archaeology in Shetland,* Lerwick.

Birks, H. H. (1975) Studies in the vegetational history of Scotland. IV. Pine stumps in Scottish blanket peats, *Phil. Trans. Royal Soc. Lond.* B 270 (1975), 181-226.

— (1977) The Flandrian forest history of Scotland: a preliminary synthesis, *in* Shotton, F. W., *British Quaternary Studies: Recent Advances,* Oxford, 119-35.

Bourke, C. (1980) Early Irish hand-bells, *J. Royal Soc. Antiq. Ireland* 110 (1980), 52-66.

Bradley, R. (1978) *The Prehistoric Settlement of Britain,* London.

— (1982) Position and possession: assemblage variation in the British Neolithic, *Oxford J. Archaeol.* 1(1) (1982), 27-38.

Bradley, R. and Chapman, J. (forthcoming) The nature and development of long-distance relations in later Neolithic Britain and Ireland, *in* Renfrew, C. and Cherry, J. F. (forthcoming).

Bramwell, D. (1977) Bird and vole bones from Buckquoy, Orkney, *in* Ritchie, A. (1977), 211-14.

— (1979) The bird bones, *in* Renfrew (1979), 138-43.

Brøgger, A. W. (1929) *Ancient Emigrants: A History of the Norse Settlements of Scotland,* Oxford.

Brothwell, D. (1977) On a mycoform stone structure in Orkney, and its relevance to possible further interpretations of so-called souterrains, *Bull. Inst. Archaeol. London* 14 (1977), 179-90.

Brown, G. M. (1975) *Letters from Hamnavoe*, Edinburgh.

Bullard, E. R. (1975) Orkney habitats: an outline ecological framework, *in* Goodier (1975), 19-28.

Bullard, E. R. and Goode, D. A. (1975) The vegetation of Orkney, *in* Goodier (1975), 31-46.

Burgess, C. (1969) Chronology and terminology in the British Bronze Age, *Antiq. J.* 49 (1969), 22-9.

— (1974) The Bronze Age, *in* Renfrew, A. C., *British Prehistory*, London, 165-232.

— (1980) *The Age of Stonehenge*, London.

Burgess, C. and Miket, R. (1976) *Settlement and Economy in the Third and Second Millennia BC*, (= British Archaeol. Reports, no.33), Oxford.

Calder, C. S. T. (1937) A neolithic double chambered cairn on the Calf of Eday, Orkney, *Proc. Soc. Antiq. Scot.* 71 (1936-7), 115-54.

— (1939) Excavations of iron age dwellings on the Calf of Eday in Orkney, *Proc. Soc. Antiq. Scot.* 73 (1938-9), 167-85.

— (1950) Report on the excavation of a Neolithic temple at Stanydale in the parish of Sandsting, Shetland, *Proc. Soc. Antiq. Scot.* 84 (1949-50), 185-205.

— (1956) Report on the discovery of numerous stone age house sites in Shetland, *Proc. Soc. Antiq. Scot.* 89 (1955-6), 340-97.

Callander, J. G. (1934) The bronze age pottery of Orkney and Shetland, *Proc. Orkney Antiq. Soc.* 12 (1933-4), 9-13.

— (1936) Bronze age urns of clay from Orkney and Shetland, with a note on vitreous material called 'cramp', *Proc. Soc. Antiq. Scot.* 70 (1935-6), 441-53.

Callander, J. G. and Grant, W. G. (1934) The Broch of Midhowe, Rousay, Orkney, *Proc. Soc. Antiq. Scot.* 68 (1933-4), 444-516.

— (1935) A long stalled cairn, the Knowe of Yarso, in Rousay, Orkney, *Proc. Soc. Antiq. Scot.* 69 (1934-5), 325-51.

Campbell, J. (1979) *Bede's Reges and Principes*, Jarrow Lecture, Newcastle upon Tyne.

Campbell, J. A., Baxter, M. S. and Alcock, L. (1979) Radiocarbon dates for the Cadbury massacre, *Antiquity* 53 (1979), 31-8.

Campbell Smith, W. (1965) The distribution of jade axes in Europe with a supplement to the catalogue of those from the British Isles, *Proc. Prehist. Soc.* 31 (1965), 25-33.

Cant, R. G. (1973) The church in Orkney and Shetland and its relations with Norway and Scotland in the middle ages, *Northern Scotland* 1 (1972-3), 1-18.

— (1975) *The Medieval Churches and Chapels of Shetland*, Shetland Archaeol. & Hist. Soc. Lerwick.

Carver, M. O. H. (1979) Notes on some general principles for the analysis of excavated data, *Science & Archaeology*, 21 (1979), 3-24.

Caseldine, C. J. and Whittington, G. (1976) Pollen analysis of material from the Stones of Stenness, Orkney, *in* Ritchie, J. N. G. (1976), 37-40.

Chesterman, J. T. (1979) Investigation of the human bones from Quanterness, *in* Renfrew (1979), 97-111.

— (1983) The human skeletal remains, *in* Hedges, J. W. (1983a), 73-132.

Childe, V. G. (1931) *Skara Brae. A Pictish Village in Orkney*, London.

— (1935) *The Prehistory of Scotland*, London.

— (1946) *Scotland before the Scots*, London.

— (1950) *Ancient dwellings at Skara Brae*, Edinburgh.

— (1952) Re-excavation of the chambered cairn of Quoyness, Sanday, on behalf of the Ministry of Works in 1951-2, *Proc. Soc. Antiq. Scot.* 86 (1951-2), 121-39.

— (1956) Maes Howe, *Proc. Soc. Antiq. Scot.* 88 (1954-6), 155-72.

— (1962) The earliest inhabitants, *in* Wainwright, F. T. (1962), 9-25.

Childe, V. G. and Grant, W. G. (1939) A Stone Age Settlement at the Braes of Rinyo, Rousay, Orkney, *Proc. Soc. Antiq. Scot.* 73 (1938-9), 6-31.

— (1947) A Stone Age Settlement at the Braes of Rinyo, Rousay, Orkney (Second Report), *Proc. Soc. Antiq. Scot.* 81 (1946-7), 16-42.

Clark, J. G. D. (1952) *Prehistoric Europe. The Economic Basis*, London.

— (1965) Traffic in stone axe and adze blades, *Econ. Hist. Rev.* 18 (1965), 1-28.

— (1980) *Mesolithic Prelude*, Edinburgh.

Clark, R. M. (1975) A calibration curve for radiocarbon dates, *Antiquity* 49 (1975), 251-66.

Clarke, D. L. (1970) *Beaker Pottery of Great Britain and Ireland*, Cambridge.

— (1978) *Mesolithic Europe: the economic basis*, London (originally *in* Sieveking *et al.* (1976), 449-81).

Clarke, D. V. (1976a) *The Neolithic Village at Skara Brae, Orkney. Excavations 1972-3: An Interim Report*, Edinburgh.

— (1976b) Excavations at Skara Brae: a summary account, *in* Burgess and Miket (1976), 233-50.

— (1983) Rinyo and the Orcadian Neolithic, *in* O'Connor, A. and Clarke, D. V., *From the Stone Age to the 'Forty Five. Studies presented to R. B. K. Stevenson*, Edinburgh, 45-56.

Clarke, D. V., Hope, R. and Wickham-Jones, C. (1978) The Links of Noltland, *Curr. Archaeol.* 6(2) (1978), 44-6.

Close-Brooks, J. (1975) A Pictish pin from Golspie, Sutherland, *Proc. Soc. Antiq. Scot.* 106 (1974-5), 208-10.

— (1980) Excavations in the Dairy Park, Dunrobin, Sutherland, 1977, *Proc. Soc. Antiq. Scot.* 110 (1978-80), 328-45.

Clouston, J. S. (1920) The Orkney townships, *Scot. Hist. Rev.* 17 (1919—20), 16-45.

— (1926) An early Orkney castle, *Proc. Soc. Antiq. Scot.* 60 (1925-6), 281-300.

— (1929) Three Norse strongholds in Orkney, *Proc. Orkney. Antiq. Soc.* 7 (1928-9), 57-74.

— (1931) *Early Norse Castles*, Kirkwall.

— (1932) *A History of Orkney*, Kirkwall.

Clutton-Brock, J. (1979) Report of the mammalian remains other than rodents from Quanterness, *in* Renfrew (1979), 112-34.

Coles, J. M. (1960) Scottish late bronze age metalwork, *Proc. Soc. Antiq. Scot.* 93 (1959-60), 16-111.

— (1964) Scottish middle bronze age metalwork, *Proc. Soc. Antiq. Scot.* 97 (1963-4), 82-156.

— (1969) Scottish early bronze age metalwork, *Proc. Soc. Antiq. Scot.* 101 (1968-9), 1-110.

Colley, S. (1983) Marine resource exploitation, *in* Hedges, J. W. (1983b), 111-13.

Coope, G. R. and Pennington, W. (1977) The Windermere interstadial of the Late Devensian, *Phil. Trans. Royal Soc. Lond.* B 280 (1977), 337-9.

Corcoran, J. X. W. P. (1966) Excavation of three chambered cairns at Loch Calder, Caithness, *Proc. Soc. Antiq. Scot.* 98 (1964-6), 1-75.

Costie, C. M. (1974) *The Collected Orkney Dialect Poems*, Kirkwall.

Craw, J. H. (1934) A mound containing short cists at Trumland, Rousay, Orkney, *Proc. Soc. Antiq. Scot.* 68 (1933-4), 68-70.

Crawford, B. E. (1971) *The Earls of Orkney-Caithness and their relations with Norway and Scotland: 1158-1470*, unpublished D.Phil. thesis, University of St Andrews.

— (1977) The earldom of Caithness and the kingdom of Scotland, 1150-1266, *Northern Scotland* 2 (1974-7), 97-117.

Crawford, I. A. (1972) *Excavations at Coileagean an Udail (The Udal) N. Uist*, 9th interim report, Christ's College, Cambridge.

— (1973) *Excavations at Coileagean an Udail (The Udal), N. Uist*, 10th interim report, Christ's College, Cambridge.

— (1974) Scot (?), Norseman and Gael, *Scot. Archaeol. Forum* 6 (1974), 1-16.

— (1981) War or Peace-Viking colonisation in the Northern and Western Isles of Scotland reviewed, *in* Bekker-Nielson *et al.* (1981), 259-69.

Crawford, I. A. and Switsur, R. (1977) Sandscaping and C 14: the Udal, N. Uist, *Antiquity* 51 (1977), 124-36.

Cruden, S. H. (1958) Earl Thorfinn the Mighty and the Brough of Birsay, *in* Eldjárn, K., *Third Viking Congress, Reykjavík (1956)*, Reykjavík, 156-62.

— (1960) *The Scottish Castle*, Edinburgh and London.

— (1965) Excavations at Birsay, Orkney, *in* Small (1965), 22-31.

— (1977) The Cathedral and Relics of St Magnus, Kirkwall, *in* Apted, M. R. *et al.*, *Ancient Monuments and their Interpretation*, London and Chichester, 85-97.

Curle, C. L. (1974) An engraved lead disc from the Brough of Birsay, Orkney, *Proc. Soc. Antiq. Scot.* 105 (1972-4), 301-7.

— (1982) *Pictish and Norse Finds from the Brough of Birsay, Orkney 1934-74*, (= Soc. Antiq. Scot. Monograph, no.1), Edinburgh.

Cursiter, J. W. (1887) Notice of the bronze weapons of Orkney and Shetland and of an iron age deposit found in a cist at Moan, Harray, *Proc. Soc. Antiq. Scot.* 21 (1886-7), 339-46.

— (1898) *The Scottish Brochs: their Age and their Destruction. A Theory*, Kirkwall.

Cursiter, J. W. (1908) Notices (1) of a bronze dagger, with its handle of horn, recently found in the island of Rousay, and (2) of an inscription in tree-runes, recently discovered on a stone in the stone circle of Stennis, Orkney, *Proc. Soc. Antiq. Scot.* 42 (1907-8), 74-8.

— (1923) The Orkney brochs, *Proc. Orkney Antiq. Soc.* 1 (1922-3), 49-52.

Davidson, D. A., Jones, R. L. and Renfrew, C. (1976) Palaeoenvironmental reconstruction and evaluation: a case study from Orkney, *Trans. Inst. British Geogr.* 1 (1976), 346-61.

Davidson, D. A., Lamb, R. G. and Simpson, I. (1983) Farm mounds in North Orkney: a preliminary report, *Norwegian Archaeol. Rev.* 16 (1983), 39-44.

Davidson, J. L. and Henshall, A. S. (1982) Staney Hill, *Discovery and Excavation in Scotland in 1982,* 17-18.

Davidson, J. M. (1943) A Pictish symbol stone from Golspie, Sutherland, *Proc. Soc. Antiq. Scot.* 67 (1942-3), 26-30.

Dickson, C. (1983) The macroscopic plant remains, *in* Hedges, J. W. (1983b), 114.

Dimbleby, G. W. (1978) *Plants and Archaeology,* 2nd ed., London.

Dolley, R. H. M. (1966) *The Hiberno-Norse Coins in the British Museum,* London.

— (1976a) Two near contemporary findings of Hiberno-Norse coins from Maughold, *J. Manx Mus.* 7 (1976), 236-40.

— (1976b) *Some Irish Dimensions to Manx History,* Belfast.

Donaldson, A. M., Morris, C. D. and Rackham, D. J. (1981) The Birsay Bay Project. Preliminary investigations into the past exploitation of coastal environment at Birsay, Mainland, Orkney, *in* Brothwell, D. and Dimbleby, G., *Environmental Aspects of Coasts and Islands,* Symposia of the Association for Environmental Archaeology, no. 1, (= British Archaeol. Reports, International Series, no.94), Oxford, 65-85.

Drever, W. P. (1933) Udal Law, *in* Viscount Dunedin, Lord Wark and Black, A. C., *Encyclopaedia of the Laws of Scotland,* vol.15, Edinburgh, 321-36.

Dryden, H. (n.d.) Orkney and Shetland, circles, broughs and etc. Plans, Soc. Antiq. Scot. MS 170, National Monuments Record of Scotland.

Dryden, H. and Petrie, G. (n.d.) The Broughs of Skara and Lingrow, Orkney, Soc. Antiq. Scot. MS 30, National Monuments Record of Scotland.

Dumville, D. N. (1976) A note on the Picts in Orkney, *Scot. Gaelic Stud.* 12 (1976), 266.

Edwards, A. J. H. (1926) Excavation of a number of graves in a mound at Ackergill, Caithness, *Proc. Soc. Antiq. Scot.* 50 (1925-6), 160-82.

— (1927) Excavation of graves at Ackergill . . ., *Proc. Soc. Antiq. Scot.* 51 (1926-7), 196-209.

Edwards, K. J. and Ralston, I. (1978) New dating and environmental evidence from Burghead fort, Moray, *Proc. Soc. Antiq. Scot.* 109 (1977-8), 202-10.

Ellesmere, Earl of (1848) *Guide to Northern Archaeology,* London.

Erdtman, G. (1924) Studies in the micropalaeontology of post-glacial deposits in northern Scotland and the Scotch isles with especial reference to the history of woodlands, *J. Linnean Soc. Bot.* 96 (1924), 449-504.

Evans, J. G. (1969) The exploitation of molluscs, *in* Ucko, P. J. and Dimbleby, G. W., *The Domestication and Exploitation of Plants and Animals*, London, 479-84.

— (1975) *The Environment of Early Man in the British Isles*, London.

— (1977) The palaeoenvironment of coastal blown sand deposits in western and northern Britain, *Scot. Archaeol. Forum* 9 (1977), 16-26.

Evans, J. G. and Spencer, P. J. (1977) The mollusca and environment, Buckquoy, Orkney, *in* Ritchie, A. (1977), 215-19.

Evans, J. G., Limbrey, S. and Cleere, H. (1975) *The effect of man on the landscape: the Highland Zone*, (= Council for British Archaeology, Research Report, no.11), London.

Fairhurst, H. (1971) The wheelhouse site at A' Cheardach Bheag on Drimore machair, South Uist, *Glasgow Archaeol. J.* 2 (1971), 72-106.

Farrer, J. (1857) Notice of a 'Burgh', recently opened in the island of Burray, Orkney, *Proc. Soc. Antiq. Scot.* 2 (1854-7), 5-6.

— (1864) An account of the discoveries at the Knowe of Saverough, *Proc. Soc. Antiq. Scot.* 5 (1862-4), 9-12.

— (1868) Note respecting various articles in bronze and stone; found in Orkney, and now presented to the Museum, *Proc. Soc. Antiq. Scot.* 7 (1866-8), 103-5.

Fenton, A. (1972) A fuel of necessity: animal manure, *in* Ennen, E. and Wiegelmann, G., *Festschrift Matthias Zender, Studien zu Volkskultur, Sprache und Landesgeschichte*, Bonn, 69-75.

— (1974) Seaweed manure in Scotland, *in In memoriam António Jorge Dias*, vol.3, Lisbon, 147-86.

— (1978) *The Northern Isles: Orkney and Shetland*, Edinburgh.

— (1979) *Continuity and Change in the Building Tradition of Northern Scotland*, (= Asa G. Wright Memorial lecture no.4), Reykjavik.

— (forthcoming) Aspects of continuity, *in* Fenton and Pálsson (forthcoming).

Fenton, A. and Pálsson, H. (forthcoming) *Continuity and Tradition in the Northern and Western Isles*.

Fergusson, J. (1877) *Short Essay on the Age and Uses of the Brochs and the Rude Stone Monuments of the Orkney Islands and the North of Scotland*, London.

Firth, J. (1920) *Reminiscences of an Orkney Parish*, Stromness.

Fleming, A. (1971) Bronze age agriculture on the marginal lands of north-east Yorkshire, *Agric. Hist. Rev.* 19 (1971), 1-24.

Fraser, D. (1980a) Investigations in neolithic Orkney, *Glasgow Archaeol. J.* 7 (1980), 1-14.

— (1980b) Redland area, chambered cairn, *Discovery and Excavation in Scotland in 1980*, 25.

— (1983) *Land and Society in Neolithic Orkney*, (= British Archaeological Reports, no.117), Oxford.

Fraser, J. (1923) Some antiquities in Harray parish, *Proc. Orkney Antiq. Soc.* 1 (1922-3), 31-7.

— (1924) Antiquities of Sandwick parish, *Proc. Orkney Antiq. Soc.* 2 (1923-4), 22-9.

— (1925) Antiquities of Birsay parish, *Proc. Orkney Antiq. Soc.* 3 (1924-5), 21-30.

— (1927) The antiquities of Firth parish, *Proc. Orkney Antiq. Soc.* 5 (1926-7), 51-6.

Frenzel, B. (1966) Climatic change in the Atlantic/Sub-Boreal transition on the northern hemisphere: botanical evidence, *in* Sawyer, J. S., *World Climate from 8000 to 0 BC*, Royal Meteorological Society, London, 89-123.

Gelling, P. S. (forthcoming) Excavations at Skaill, Deerness, Orkney, *in* Fenton and Pálsson (forthcoming).

Godwin, H. (1956) Report on the peat samples, *in* Childe (1956), 169-72.

— (1975) *The History of the British Flora*, 2nd ed., Cambridge.

Goodier, R. (1975) *The Natural Environment of Orkney*, The Nature Conservancy Council, Edinburgh.

Goodwin, A. J. H. and van Riet Lowe, C. (1929) *The Stone Age cultures of South Africa*, (= Annals South Africa Mus. 27, 1929).

Graeme, A. S. (1914) An account of the excavation of the Broch of Ayre, St Mary's Holm, Orkney, *Proc. Soc. Antiq. Scot.* 48 (1913-14), 31-51.

Graham, A. (1947) Some observations on the brochs, *Proc. Soc. Antiq. Scot.* 81 (1946-7), 48-99.

Graham-Campbell, J. A. (1976a) The Viking-age silver and gold hoards of Scandinavian character from Scotland, *Proc. Soc. Antiq. Scot.* 107 (1975-6), 114-35.

— (1976b) The Viking-age silver hoards of Ireland, *in* Greene, D. and Almquist, B., *Seventh Viking Congress, Dublin (1973)*, Dublin, 39-74.

— (1980) *The Viking World*, London.

Grant, W. G. (1933) Excavation of a denuded cairn, containing fragments of steatite urns and cremated human remains, in Rousay, Orkney, *Proc. Soc. Antiq. Scot.* 67 (1932-3), 24-6.

— (1937) Excavation of bronze age burial mounds at Quandale, Rousay, Orkney, *Proc. Soc. Antiq. Scot.* 71 (1936-7), 72-84.

Grieg, S. (1940) *Viking Antiquities in Scotland, Viking Antiquities in Britain and Ireland*, vol.2, Shetelig, H., Oslo.

Hamilton, J. R. C. (1956) *Excavations at Jarlshof, Shetland*, Edinburgh.

Hedges, J. W. (1975) Excavation of two Orcadian burnt mounds at Liddle and Beaquoy, *Proc. Soc. Antiq. Scot.* 106 (1974-5), 39-98.

— (1978) A long cist at Sandside, Graemsay, Orkney, *Proc. Soc. Antiq. Scot.* 109 (1977-8), 374-8.

— (1983a) *Isbister: a chambered tomb in Orkney*, (= British Archaeol. Reports, British Series, no.115), Oxford.

— (1983b) Trial excavations on Pictish and Viking settlements at Saevar Howe, Birsay, Orkney, *Glasgow Archaeol. J.* 10 (1983), 73-124.

— (forthcoming a) *Bu, Gurness and the Brochs of Orkney.*
— (forthcoming b) *The Broch of Gurness, Aikerness, Orkney:
A Catalogue of the Finds from the 1930-39 Excavations.*
Hedges, J. W. and Bell, B. (1980) The Howe, *Current Archaeology* 7
(1980), 48-51.
Hedges, M. E. (1977) The excavation of the Knowes of Quoyscottie,
Orkney: a cemetery of the first millennium BC, *Proc. Soc. Antiq.
Scot.* 108 (1976-7), 130-55.
Hedges, S. E. (1980) Spurdagrove, Orkney: a prehistoric farmstead,
Scottish Development Department (Ancient Monuments),
Edinburgh.
Hedges, S. E. and J. W. (forthcoming) Excavations at Tougs,
Shetland; an agricultural settlement in Shetland.
Heggie, D. C. (1981) *Megalithic Science*, London.
Heizer, R. F. (1963) Domestic fuel in primitive society, *J. Roy.
Anthrop. Inst.* 93 (1963), 186-94.
Henderson, I. (1958) The origin centre of the Pictish symbol stones,
Proc. Soc. Antiq. Scot. 91 (1957-8), 44-60.
— (1967) *The Picts*, London.
— (1971) The meaning of the Pictish symbol stones, *in* Meldrum, E.,
The Dark Ages in the Highlands, Inverness, 53-67.
Henderson, T. (1978) Shetland boats and their origins, *in* Baldwin
(1978), 49-56.
Henshall, A. S. (1952) Early textiles found in Scotland, *Proc. Soc.
Antiq. Scot.* 86 (1951-2), 1-29.
— (1963 and 1972) *The Chambered Tombs of Scotland*, 2 vols,
Edinburgh.
— (1974) Scottish chambered tombs and long mounds, *in* Renfrew,
A. C., *British Prehistory*, London, 137-64.
— (1979) Artefacts from the Quanterness cairn, *in* Renfrew (1979),
75-93.
— (1983) The finds, *in* Hedges, J. W. (1983a), 33-59.
Higgs, E. S. and Jarman, M. R. (1972) The origins of animal and plant
husbandry, *in* Higgs, E. S., *Papers in Economic Prehistory*,
Cambridge, 3-13.
Hodder, I. (1982) *Symbols in Action. Ethnoarchaeological Studies of
Material Culture*, Cambridge.
Hunter, J. R. (1983) Recent excavations on the Brough of Birsay,
Orkney Heritage 2 (1983), 152-70, (= Proceedings of the Birsay
Conference, 1982).
Hunter, J. R. and Morris, C. D. (1981) Recent Excavations at the
Brough of Birsay, Orkney, *in* Bekker-Nielsen *et al.* (1981), 245-58.
— (1982) Excavation of Room 5, Brough of Birsay Cliff-top
Settlement 1973-4, *in* Curle (1982), 124-38.
Huxtable, J. (1975) Dating – thermoluminescence, *in* Hedges, J. W.
(1975), 82-4.
Huxtable, J., Aitken, M. J., Hedges, J. W. and Renfrew, A. C. (1976)
Dating a settlement pattern by thermoluminescence: the burnt
mounds of Orkney, *Archaeometry* 18 (1976), 5-17.
Jackson, A. (1971) Pictish social structure and symbol-stones, *Scot.
Stud.* 15 (1971), 121-40.

Jackson, A. (1977) Faroese fare, *in* Kuper, J., *The Anthropologists' Cookbook*, London, 48-51.

Jackson, K. H. (1955) The Pictish language, *in* Wainwright, F. T. (1955), 129-60.

— (1977) The ogam inscription on the spindle whorl from Buckquoy, Orkney, *in* Ritchie, A. (1977), 221-2.

Jobey, G. and Tait, J. (1966) Excavations on palisaded settlements and cairnfields at Alnham, Northumberland, *Archaeol. Aeliana* 44 (1966), 5-48.

Joensen, J. P. (1976) Pilot whaling in the Faroe Islands, *Ethnol. Scandinavica* (1976), 5-42.

Johnston, A. W. (1903) Notes on the Earl's Bu at Orphir, Orkney, called Orfjara in the sagas, and on the remains of the round church there, *Proc. Soc. Antiq. Scot.* 37 (1902-3), 16-31.

Johnstone, P. (1980) *The sea-craft of Prehistory*, London.

Jones, G. (1968) *A History of the Vikings*, Oxford.

Jones, M. (1980) Carbonised cereals from Grooved Ware contexts, *Proc. Prehist. Soc.* 46 (1980), 61-3.

Jones, R. L. (1975) Environment – pollen, *in* Hedges, J. W. (1975), 84-8.

— (1977) Pollen identification, *in* Hedges, M. E. (1977), 149-50.

— (1979) Vegetational studies, *in* Renfrew (1979), 21-8.

Kaland, S. H. H. (1973) Westnessutgravningene på Rousay, Orknyøyene, *Viking* (1973), 77-102.

Keatinge, T. H. and Dickson, J. H. (1979) Mid-Flandrian changes in vegetation on Mainland Orkney, *New Phytol.* 82 (1979), 585-612.

Kenward, H. K. *et al.* (1978) The environment of Anglo-Scandinavian York, *in* Hall, R. A., *Viking Age York and the North*, (= Council for British Archaeol. Research Report, no.27), London, 58-70.

Kilbride-Jones, H. E. (1973) On some aspects of neolithic building techniques in Orkney, *Acta Praehistorica et Archaeologica* 4 (1973), 75-96.

Kirkness, W. (1921) Notes on the discovery of a coped monument and an incised cross-slab at the graveyard, St Boniface Church, Papa Westray, Orkney, *Proc. Soc. Antiq. Scot.* 55 (1920-1), 132-3.

Lacaille, A. D. (1954) *The Stone Age in Scotland*, London.

Laing, L. (1974) *Orkney and Shetland*, Newton Abbot.

Laing, S. and Simpson, J. (1964) Translation of Snorri Sturluson, *Heimskringla. Part One. The Olaf Sagas*, London, revised edition.

Lamb, R. G. (1973) Coastal settlements of the North, *Scot. Archaeol. Forum* 5 (1973), 76-98.

— (1974) The Cathedral of Christchurch and the monastery of Birsay, *Proc. Soc. Antiq. Scot.* 105 (1972-4), 200-5.

— (1976) The Burri Stacks of Culswick, Shetland, and other paired stack-settlements, *Proc. Soc. Antiq. Scot.* 107 (1975-6), 144-54.

— (1980) *Iron Age promontory forts in the Northern Isles*, (= British Archaeological Reports, no.79), Oxford.

Lang, J. T. (1974) Hogback monuments in Scotland, *Proc. Soc. Antiq. Scot.* 105 (1972-4), 206-35.

Legge, A. J. (1981) Aspects of cattle husbandry, *in* Mercer, R. J., *Farming practice in British prehistory*, Edinburgh, 169-81.

Lethbridge, T. (1952) *Boats and Boatmen*, London.
Lewis, A. R. (1958) *The Northern Seas: Shipping and Commerce in Northern Europe AD 300-1100*, Princeton, New Jersey.
Liestøl, A. (1968) The Maeshowe runes. Some new interpretations, *in* Niclasen (1968), 55-61.
— (forthcoming) The runic inscriptions of Scotland, *in* Fenton and Pálsson (forthcoming).
Limbrey, S. (1975) *Soil Science and Archaeology*, London.
Longworth, I. H. (1967) Further discoveries at Brackmont Hill, Brackmont Farm and Tentsmuir, Fife, *Proc. Soc. Antiq. Scot.* 99 (1966-7), 60-92.
Low, G. (1879) *A Tour through the Islands of Orkney and Schetland in 1774*, Anderson, J., Kirkwall.
Lynch, F. (1973) The use of the passage in certain passage graves as a means of communication rather than access, *in* Daniel, G. and Kjaerum, P., *Megalithic Graves and Ritual*, (= *Jutland Archaeological Society Publications*, no.11), 147-61.
Lysaght, A. (1974) Joseph Banks at Skara Brae and Stennis, Orkney, 1772, *Notes Records Royal Soc. London* 28 (1974), 221-34.
Macaulay Institute for Soil Research (1978) *Annual Report*, 1977-8.
McCrie, G. (1881) Notice of the discovery of an urn of steatite in one of the five tumuli excavated at Corquoy, in the island of Rousay, Orkney, *Proc. Soc. Antiq. Scot.* 15 (1880-1), 71-3.
MacGregor, A. (1974) The broch of Burrian, North Ronaldsay, Orkney, *Proc. Soc. Antiq. Scot.* 105 (1972-4), 63-118.
Mackay, R. R. (1950) Grooved Ware from Knappers Farm, near Glasgow, and from Townhead, Rothesay, *Proc. Soc. Antiq. Scot.* 84 (1949-50), 180-4.
MacKie, E. W. (1965) The origin and development of the broch and wheelhouse building cultures of the Scottish Iron Age, *Proc. Prehist. Soc.* 31 (1965), 93-146.
— (1974) *Dun Mor Vaul*, Glasgow.
MacLean, C. (1976) Cereals from Pits A-C, Stones of Stenness, Orkney, *in* Ritchie, J. N. G. (1976), 43-4.
Marwick, E. W. (1975) *The Folklore of Orkney and Shetland*, London.
Marwick, H. (1922) A rune-inscribed stone from Birsay, Orkney, *Proc. Soc. Antiq. Scot.* 56 (1921-2), 67-71.
— (1924) Antiquarian notes on Rousay, *Proc. Orkney Antiq. Scot.* 2 (1923-4), 15-21.
— (1928) Kolbein Hruga's Castle, Wyre, *Proc. Orkney Antiq. Soc.* 6 (1927-8), 9-11.
— (1935) Leidang in the West, *Proc. Orkney Antiq. Soc.* 13 (1934-5), 15-29.
— (1947) *The Place Names of Rousay*, Kirkwall.
— (1949a) Naval defence in Norse Scotland, *Scot. Hist. Rev.* 28 (1949), 1-11.
— (1949b) Notes on archaeological remains found in Orkney, *Proc. Soc. Antiq. Scot.* 83 (1948-9), 236-40.
— (1952) *Orkney Farm-Names*, Kirkwall.
— (1970) *The Place-Names of Birsay*, Nicolaisen, W. F. H., Aberdeen.

Mather, A. S., Ritchie, W. and Smith, J. (1975) An introduction to the morphology of the coastline, *in* Goodier (1976), 10-18.

Mather, J. Y. (1964) Boats and boatmen of Orkney and Shetland, *Scot. Stud.* 8 (1964), 19-32.

Maxwell, G. S. (1975) Casus Belli; native pressure and Roman policy, *Scot. Archaeol. Forum* 7 (1975), 31-49.

Meadow, R. H. (1980) Animal bones: problems for the archaeologist together with some possible solutions, *Paléorient* 6 (1980), 65-77.

Mellars, P. (1976) Settlement patterns and industrial variability in the British Mesolithic, *in* Sieveking *et al.* (1976), 375-99.

— (1978) Excavation and economic analysis of Mesolithic shell middens on the island of Oronsay (Inner Hebrides), *in* Mellars, P., *The Early Postglacial Settlement of Northern Europe*, London, 371-96.

Mercer, R. J. (1981) The excavation of a late neolithic henge-type enclosure at Balfarg, Markinch, Fife, Scotland, *Proc. Soc. Antiq. Scot.* 111 (1981), 63-171.

Miller, M. (1978) Eanfrith's Pictish son, *Northern History* 14 (1978), 47-66.

Miller, R. (1976) *Orkney*, London.

Moar, N. T. (1969) Two pollen diagrams from the Mainland, Orkney Islands, *New Phytol.* 68 (1969), 201-8.

Moore, P. D. (1975) Origin of blanket mires, *Nature* 256 (1975), 267-9.

Morris, C. D. (1976) Brough of Deerness, Orkney, Excavations 1975: Interim Report, *Northern Stud.* 7-8 (1976), 33-7.

— (1977) The Brough of Deerness, Orkney: a new Survey, *Archaeologia Atlantica* 2 (1977), 65-79.

— (1978) Brough of Deerness, Orkney. Interim report on excavations and Survey 1976-7, *Northern Stud.* 11 (1978), 16-19 (also *Univ. of Durham, Archaeol. Reps for 1977*, Durham, 26-8).

— (1979a) The Vikings and Irish monasteries, *Durham Univ. J.* 71 (1979), 175-85.

— (1979b) Birsay, Orkney: 'Small Sites' excavations and survey, *Univs of Durham & Newcastle upon Tyne, Archaeol. Reps for 1978*, Durham, 11-19 (also *Northern Stud.* 13 (1979), 3-19).

— (1980) Birsay: Excavation and Survey 1979, *Univs of Durham & Newcastle upon Tyne, Archaeol. Reps for 1979*, Durham, 22-32 (also *Northern Stud.* 16 (1980), 17-28).

— (1981a) Excavations at Birsay, Orkney, *Univs of Durham & Newcastle upon Tyne, Archaeol. Reps for 1980*, Durham, 35-40.

— (1981b) Viking and Native in Northern England: a case-study, Bekker-Nielsen *et al.* (1981), 223-44.

— (1982a) Excavations at Birsay, Orkney, *Univs of Durham & Newcastle upon Tyne, Archaeol. Reps for 1981*, Durham, 46-53.

— (1982b) The Vikings in the British Isles: some aspects of their settlement and economy, *in* Farrell, R. T., *Viking Civilisation*, Chichester, 70-94.

— (1983) Excavations around the Bay of Birsay, Orkney, *Orkney Heritage* 2 (1983), 119-51, (= Proceedings of the Birsay Conference, 1982).

Morrison, A. (1980) *Early Man in Britain and Ireland*, London.

Morrison, I. A. (1973) *The North Sea Earls*, London.

— (1978) Aspects of Viking small craft in the light of Shetland practice, *in* Baldwin (1978), 57-76.

Muir, E. (1965) *Selected Poems*, London.

Munch, G. S. (1966) Gårdshauger i Nord-Norge, *Viking* 30 (1966), 25-59.

Mykura, W. (1975) The geological basis of the Orkney environment, *in* Goodier (1975), 1-9.

— (1976) *British Regional Geology. Orkney and Shetland*, Edinburgh.

N.A.A. (1979) *Nordic Archaeol. Abstracts 1979*, Viborg.

Neil, N. R. J. (1981) A newly discovered decorated stone from Orkney, *Antiquity* 55 (1981), 129-31.

Niclasen, B. (1968) *Fifth Viking Congress, Tórshavn, 1965*, Tórshavn.

Nicolaisen, W. F. H. (1976) *Scottish Place-Names. Their Study and Significance*, London.

Noddle, B. (1977) The animal bones from Buckquoy, Orkney, *in* Ritchie, A. (1977), 201-9.

— (1978) A brief account of the history of domestic animals in Caithness and Orkney, *The Ark* 9 (1978), 309-12.

O'Kelly, M. J. (1954) Excavations and experiments in ancient Irish cooking-places, *J. Royal Soc. Antiq. Ireland* 84 (1954), 105-55.

— (1973) Current excavations at Newgrange, Ireland, *in* Daniel, G. and Kjaerum, P., *Megalithic Graves and Ritual*, (= Papers presented at the III Atlantic Colloquium, Mosegård, 1969), Copenhagen, 137-46.

O'Riordain, S. P. (1953) *Antiquities of the Irish Countryside*, London.

Osborne, P. J. (1977) Evidence from the insects of climatic variation during the Flandrian period: a preliminary note, *World Archaeol.* 8 (1977), 150-8.

O S Ordnance Survey Record Card (now incorporated with the National Monuments Record of Scotland).

Ottaway, B. S. (1983) *Archaeology, Dendrochronology and the Radiocarbon Calibration Curve*, Edinburgh.

Padel, O. J. (1972) *Inscriptions of Pictland*, Unpublished M.Litt. thesis, University of Edinburgh.

Pálsson, H. and Edwards, P. (1978) *Orkneyinga Saga. The History of the Earls of Orkney*, London.

Parry, G. (1977) Field survey of some Quoyscottie-type barrow cemeteries in Orkney, *in* Hedges, M. E. (1977), 151-4.

Peglar, S. (1979) A radiocarbon-dated pollen diagram from Loch of Winless, Caithness, north-east Scotland, *New Phytol.* 82 (1979), 245-63.

Petrie, G. (1857) Description of antiquities in Orkney recently examined, with illustrative drawings, *Proc. Soc. Antiq. Scot.* 2 (1854-7), 56-62.

— (1860) Notice of a barrow at Huntiscarth in the parish of Harray, Orkney, recently opened, *Proc. Soc. Antiq. Scot.* 3 (1857-60), 195.

— (1861) Notice of the opening of a tumulus in the parish of Stenness, on the Mainland of Orkney, *Archaeol. J.* 18 (1861), 353-8.

— (1866) Notice of a barrow containing cists, on the farm of Newbigging near Kirkwall; and at Isbister, in the parish of Rendall, *Proc. Soc. Antiq. Scot.* 6 (1864-6), 411-18.

Petrie, G. (1890) Notice of the brochs or large round towers of Orkney. With plans, sections, and drawings, and tables of measurements of Orkney and Shetland brochs, *Archaeol. Scotica* 5 (1874-90), 71-94.
— (n.d. a and b) Sketchbooks 5 and 6, Soc. Antiq. Scot. MS 487, now housed in the National Monuments Record of Scotland.
— (n.d. c) Manuscript and notebook, Soc. Antiq. Scot. MS 550, now housed in the National Museum of Antiquities of Scotland.
Piggott, C. M. (1947) A late bronze age 'razor' from Orkney, *Proc. Soc. Antiq. Scot.* 81 (1946-7), 173.
Piggott, S. (1954) *The Neolithic Cultures of the British Isles*, Cambridge.
— (1972) A note on climatic deterioration in the first millennium BC in Britain, *Scot. Archaeol. Forum* 4 (1972), 109-13.
Plant, J. A. and Dunsire, A. (1974) *The Climate of Orkney*, (= Climatological Memorandum, no.71), Edinburgh.
Randsborg, K. (1980) *The Viking Age in Denmark*, London.
Radford, C. A. R. (1959) *The Early Christian and Norse Settlements at Birsay, Orkney*, Edinburgh.
— (1962) Art and architecture: Celtic and Norse, *in* Wainwright, F. T. (1962), 163-87.
Rae, D. A. (1976) *Aspects of glaciation in Orkney*. Unpublished Ph.D. thesis, University of Liverpool.
Rasmussen, H. (1974) The use of seaweed in the Danish farming culture. A general view, *in In memoriam António Jorge Dias*, vol.1, Lisbon, 385-98.
RCAMS (1946) Royal Commission on the Ancient and Historical Monuments of Scotland, *Inventory of the ancient Monuments of Orkney and Shetland*, Edinburgh. References to vol.2, *Orkney*.
— (1980) Royal Commission on the Ancient and Historical Monuments of Scotland, Archaeological Sites and Monuments Series, 11, *Sanday and North Ronaldsay, Orkney*, compiled by R. G. Lamb, Edinburgh.
Rees, S. (1977) The stone implements, *in* Hedges, M. E. (1977), 144-5.
Renfrew, A. C. (1973) Monuments, mobilisation and social organisation in neolithic Wessex, *in* Renfrew, A. C., *The Explanation of Culture Change*, London, 539-58.
— (1976) Megaliths, territories and populations, *in* de Laet, S. J., *Acculturation and continuity in Atlantic Europe mainly during the Neolithic and the Bronze Age*, (Papers presented at the IV Atlantic Colloquium, Ghent 1975), Brugge, 198-220.
— (1978) Space, time and polity, *in* Friedman, J. and Rowlands, M. J., *The Evolution of Social Systems*, London, 89-114.
— (1979) *Investigations in Orkney*, (= Rep. Research Comm. Soc. Antiq. London, no.38), London.
— (1983) The social archaeology of megalithic monuments, *Scientific American* 249 (1983), 152-63.
Renfrew, A. C. and Cherry, J. F. (forthcoming) *Peer Polity Interaction and the Development of Socio-Political Complexity*, Cambridge.
Reynolds, N. and Ralston, I. (1979) Balbridie, *Discovery and Excavation in Scotland in 1979*, 76.
Richardson, J. S. (1948) *The Broch of Gurness, Aikerness, West Mainland, Orkney*, Edinburgh.

Ritchie, A. (1972) Painted pebbles in early Scotland, *Proc. Soc. Antiq. Scot.* 104 (1971-2), 297-301.

— (1973) Knap of Howar, Papa Westray, *Discovery and Excavation in Scotland in 1973*, 68-9.

— (1974) Pict and Norseman in Northern Scotland, *Scot. Archaeol. Forum* 6 (1974), 23-36.

— (1977) Excavation of Pictish and Viking-age farmsteads at Buckquoy, Orkney, *Proc. Soc. Antiq. Scot.* 108 (1976-7), 174-227.

— (1984) Excavation of a Neolithic farmstead at Knap of Howar, Papa Westray, Orkney, *Proc. Soc. Antiq. Scot.* 113 (1984), 40-121.

Ritchie, J. N. G. (1969) Two new Pictish symbol stones from Orkney, *Proc. Soc. Antiq. Scot.* 101 (1968-9), 130-3.

— (1974) Excavation of the stone circle and cairn at Balbirnie, Fife, *Archaeol. J.* 131 (1974), 1-32.

— (1976) The Stones of Stenness, Orkney, *Proc. Soc. Antiq. Scot.* 107 (1975-6), 1-60.

Ritchie, J. N. G. and Adamson, H. C. (1981) Knappers, Dunbartonshire: a reassessment, *Proc. Soc. Antiq. Scot.* 111 (1981), 172-204.

Ritchie, J. N. G. and Ritchie, A. (1974) Excavation of a barrow at Queenafjold, Twatt, Orkney, *Proc. Soc. Antiq. Scot.* 105 (1972-4), 33-40.

— (1981) *Scotland: archaeology and early history*, London.

Ritchie, J. N. G. and Thornber, I. (1975) Small cairns in Argyll: some recent work, *Proc. Soc. Antiq. Scot.* 106 (1974-5), 15-38.

Robertson, W. N. (1969) The Viking grave found at the Broch of Gurness, Aikerness, *Proc. Soc. Antiq. Scot.* 101 (1968-9), 289-91.

Roe, F. E. S. (1968) Stone mace-heads and the latest neolithic cultures of the British Isles, *in* Coles, J. M. and Simpson, D. D. A., *Studies in Ancient Europe*, Leicester, 145-72.

Roussell, A. (1934) *Norse Building Customs in the Scottish Isles*, London.

Rowley-Conwy, P. (1983) The animal and bird bones, *in* Hedges, J. W. (1983b), 109-11.

Rymer, L. (1976) The history and ethnobotany of bracken, *Bot. J. Linn. Soc.* 73 (1976), 151-76.

Sawyer, P. H. (1976) Harald Fairhair and the British Isles, *in* Boyer, R., *Les Vikings et leurs civilisations: problèmes actuels*, Paris, 105-9.

Scott, L. (1948) The chamber tomb of Unival, North Uist, *Proc. Soc. Antiq. Scot.* 82 (1947-8), 1-49.

— (1951) The colonisation of Scotland in the second millennium BC, *Proc. Prehist. Soc.* 17 (1951), 16-82.

Scott, W. (1821) *The Pirate*, Edinburgh.

Sharples, N. M. (1981) The excavation of a chambered cairn, the Ord North, at Lairg, Sutherland by J. X. W. P. Corcoran, *Proc. Soc. Antiq. Scot.* 111 (1981), 21-62.

Sheldon, J. M. (1979) Analysis of charcoal fragments from Quanterness, *in* Renfrew (1979), 29-30.

Shennan, S. J. (1983) Monuments: an example of archaeologists' approach to the massively material', *Royal Anthrop. Inst. News* 59 (1983), 9-11.

Shepherd, I. A. G. and Tuckwell, A. N. (1977) Traces of beaker-period cultivation at Rosinish, Benbecula, *Proc. Soc. Antiq. Scot.* 108 (1976-7), 108-13.

Shetelig, H. (1940) *An Introduction to the Viking History of Western Europe, Viking Antiquities in Great Britain and Ireland*, vol. 1, Shetelig, H., Oslo.

— (1945) The Viking graves in Great Britain and Ireland, *Acta Archaeologica* 16 (1945), 1-55, (reprinted in Curle, A. O., Olsen, M. and Shetelig, H., *The Civilisation of the Viking Settlers in relation to their old and new countries, Viking Antiquities in Great Britain and Ireland*, vol. 6, Shetelig, H., Oslo, 65-111).

Sieveking, G. de G., Longworth, I. H. and Wilson, K. E. (1976) *Problems in Economic and Social Archaeology*, London.

Simpson, D. D. A. (1976) The later neolithic and beaker settlement site at Northton, Isle of Harris, *in* Burgess, C. and Miket, R. (1976), 221-31.

Skinner, G. W. (1964) Marketing and social structure in rural China: Part 1, *J. Asian Stud.* 24 (1964), 3-45.

Small, A. (1965) *The Fourth Viking Congress, York, August 1961*, (= Aberdeen Univ. Stud., no. 149), Edinburgh.

— (1966) Excavations at Underhoull, Unst, Shetland, *Proc. Soc. Antiq. Scot.* 98 (1964-6), 225-48.

— (1968) A historical geography of the Norse Viking colonisation of the Scottish Highlands, *Norsk Geog. Tidskrift* 22 (1968), 1-16.

— (1969) The distribution of settlement in Shetland and Faroe in Viking times, *Saga Book of the Viking Soc.* 17 (1966-9), 145-55.

— (1971) The Viking Highlands, *in* Meldrum, E., *The Dark Ages in the Highlands*, Inverness Field Club, Inverness, 69-90.

Small, A., Thomas, A. C. and Wilson, D. (1973) *St Ninian's Isle and its Treasure*, Oxford.

Smyth, A. P. (1977) *Scandinavian Kings of the British Isles, 850-880*, Oxford.

Soc. Antiq. Scot. (1892) Donations to the Museum and Library, *Proc. Soc. Antiq. Scot.* 9 (1870-2), 356-67.

Smith, I. F. (1965) *Windmill Hill and Avebury, Excavations by Alexander Keiller 1925-39*, Oxford.

— (1971) Causewayed enclosures, *in* Simpson, D. D. A., *Economy and Settlement in Neolithic and Early Bronze Age Britain and Europe*, Leicester, 89-112.

Smith, J. A. (1872) Notice of a cinerary urn, containing a small-sized urn (in which were the bones of a child), discovered in Fifeshire, with notes of similar small cup-like vessels in the museum of the Society of Antiquaries of Scotland, *Proc. Soc. Antiq. Scot.* 9 (1870-2), 189-207.

Spencer, P. J. (1975) Habitat change in coastal sand-dune areas: the molluscan evidence, *in* Evans *et al.* (1975), 96-103.

Steedman, K. A. (1980) *The Archaeology of the Deerness Peninsula, Orkney, unpublished* BA dissertation, University of Durham.

Steinnes, A. (1959) The 'Huseby' System in Orkney, *Scot. Hist. Rev.* 38 (1959), 36-46.

Stevenson, J. B. (1975) Survival and discovery, *in* Evans *et al.* (1975), 104-8.

Stevenson, R. B. K. (1946) Jottings on early pottery, *Proc. Soc. Antiq. Scot.* 80 (1945-6), 141-3.

— (1955) Pictish art, *in* Wainwright, F. T. (1955), 97-128.

— (1958) A wooden sword of the Late Bronze Age, *Proc. Soc. Antiq. Scot.* 91 (1957-8), 191-2.

— (1968) The brooch from Westness, Orkney, *in* Niclasen (1968), 25-31.

— (1976) The earlier metalwork of Pictland, *in* Megaw, J. V. S., *To Illustrate the Monuments*, London, 246-51.

Stoklund, B. (1980) Houses and culture in the North Atlantic islands. Three models of interpretation, *Ethnol. Scandinavica* (1980), 113-32.

Talbot, E. (1974) Scandinavian fortification in the British Isles, *Scot. Archaeol. Forum* 6 (1974), 37-45.

Taylor, A. B. (1938) *The Orkneyinga Saga. A new translation with introduction and notes*, London and Edinburgh.

Taylor, J. J. (1980) *Bronze Age Goldwork of the British Isles*, Cambridge.

Thom, A. and Thom, A. S. (1973) A megalithic lunar observatory in Orkney: the Ring of Brogar and its cairns, *J. Hist. Astronomy* 4 (1973), 111-23.

— (1975) Further work on the Brogar lunar observatory, *J. Hist. Astronomy* 6 (1975), 100-14.

— (1978) *Megalithic Remains in Britain and Brittany*, Oxford.

Thom, A. S. (1981) Megalithic lunar observatories: an assessment of 42 lunar alignments, *in* Ruggles, C. L. N. and Whittle, A. W. R., *Astronomy and Society in Britain during the period 4000-1500 BC*, (= British Archaeol. Reports, British Series, no.88), Oxford, 13-61.

Thomas, C. (1971) *The Early Christian Archaeology of North Britain*, Oxford.

Thomas, F. W. L. (1852) Account of some of the Celtic antiquities of Orkney, including the Stones of Stenness, tumuli, Picts-houses, etc., with plans, *Archaeologia* 34 (1852), 88-136.

Thorsteinsson, A. (1968) The Viking burial-place at Pierowall, Westray, Orkney, *in* Niclasen (1968), 150-73.

Tinsley, H. M. and Grigson, C. (1981) The Bronze Age, *in* Simmons, I. and Tooley, M., *The Environment in British Prehistory*, London, 210-49.

Tønnessen, J. N. and Johnsen, A. O. (1982) *The History of Modern Whaling*, London and Canberra.

Traill, W. (1868) On submarine forests and other remains of indigenous wood in Orkney, *Trans. Bot. Soc. Edinburgh* 9 (1868), 146-54.

— (1876) Notice of two cists on the farm of Antabreck, North Ronaldsay, Orkney, *Proc. Soc. Antiq. Scot.* 11 (1876), 309-10.

— (1885) Notes of excavations at Stennabreck and Howmae in North Ronaldsay, *Proc. Soc. Antiq. Scot.* 19 (1884-5), 14-33.

— (1890) Results of excavation at the Broch of Burrian, North Ronaldsay, Orkney during the summers of 1870 and 1871, *Archaeol. Scotica* 5 (1874-90), 341-64.

Traill, W. and Kirkness, W. (1937) Hower, a prehistoric structure on Papa Westray, Orkney, *Proc. Soc. Antiq. Scot.* 71 (1936-7), 309-21.

Turner, W. (1872) Additional notes on the occurrence of the sperm whale in the Scottish seas (notes from this paper), *Proc. Soc. Antiq. Scot.* 9 (1870-2), 360-6.

Wainwright, F. T. (1955) *The Problem of the Picts*, Edinburgh.

— (1962a) Picts and Scots, *in* Wainwright (1962), 91-116.

— (1962b) The Scandinavian Settlement, *in* Wainwright (1962), 117-62.

— (1962c) The Golden Age and After, *in* Wainwright (1962), 188-92.

— (1962d) *The Northern Isles*, Edinburgh.

Wainwright, G. J. (1969) A review of henge monuments in the light of recent research, *Proc. Prehist. Soc.* 35 (1969), 112-33.

Wainwright, G. J. and Longworth, I. H. (1971) *Durrington Walls: excavations 1966-1968*, (= *Rep. Res. Comm. Soc. Antiq. London*, no.29), London.

Wallace, J. (1700) *An Account of the Island of Orkney*, London.

Warner, R. (1976) Scottish silver arm-rings: an analysis of weights, *Proc. Soc. Antiq. Scot.* 107 (1975-6), 136-43.

Watt, W. G. T. (1882) Notice of the broch known as Burwick or Borthwick, in the township of Yescanbee and parish of Sandwick, Orkney, *Proc. Soc. Antiq. Scot.* 16 (1881-2), 442-50.

West, R. G. (1977) *Pleistocene Geology and Biology with especial reference to the British Isles*, 2nd ed., London.

Wheeler, A. (1977) The fish-bones from Buckquoy, Orkney, *in* Ritchie, A. (1977), 211-14.

— (1979) The fish bones, *in* Renfrew (1979), 144-9.

Whittle, A. (1980) Scord of Brouster and early settlement in Shetland, *Archaeol. Atlantica* 3 (1980), 35-55.

Williams, D. F. (1977) Petrological analysis of the pottery, *in* Hedges, M. E. (1977), 147-8.

Wilson, D. (1851) *Archaeology and Prehistoric Annals of Scotland*, Edinburgh.

Wilson, D. M. (1971) The Norsemen, *in* Menzies, G., *Who are the Scots?*, London, 103-13.

— (1976a) The Scandinavians in England, *in* Wilson, D. M., *The Archaeology of Anglo-Saxon England*, London, 393-403.

— (1976b) Scandinavian settlement in the North and West of the British Isles – an archaeological viewpoint, *Trans. Royal Hist. Soc.* 5th Ser., 26 (1976), 95-113.

Wilson, D. M. and Hurst, D. G. (1964) Medieval Britain in 1962 and 1963, *Medieval Archaeol.* 8 (1964), 231-99.

Wilson, G. V. *et al.* (1935) *The Geology of the Orkneys*, Memoir of the Geological Survey of Great Britain, Edinburgh.

Worsaae, J. J. A. (1849) *The Primeval Antiquities of Denmark*, London.

Young, A. and Richardson, K. M. (1960) A Cheardach Mhor, Drimore, South Uist, *Proc. Soc. Antiq. Scot.* 93 (1959-60), 135-73.

Young, A. and Lunt, D. (1977) Cremated bone and tooth identification, *in* Hedges, M. E. (1977), 146-7.

Youngs, S. M. and Clark, J. (1981) Medieval Britain in 1980, *Medieval Archaeol.* 25 (1981), 166-228.

Indexes

Subject Index. Italicised page-numbers indicate figures, illustrations, plates

Colin Richards **Postscript: The late Neolithic settlement complex at Barnhouse Farm, Stenness**

Orkney is without doubt represented by the most diverse and complete material record of the late Neolithic period in the British Isles. Given this archaeological wealth it is not surprising to see particular areas of the evidence selected for 'social analysis'. Inevitably, however, it is the monuments, both chambered tombs and henge monuments, which tend to provide the basis for such interpretations (Renfrew 1979; Fraser 1983; Sharples 1985; Richards 1988). Although, as Ritchie notes (this vol., 128–9), when the larger henge monuments cannot be slotted into a neat evolutionary sequence of monumentality they become extremely problematic to schemes of social change. A rather more productive line of enquiry involves the integration and comparison of what has been seen as separate areas of evidence: settlement, funerary, and ceremonial (cf. Hodder 1982, 219–27). The same Neolithic people lived in houses within the settlements, participated in or watched various ceremonies and rites of passage, including funerals. Thus, to divide the evidence in such a way as to divorce these areas of human activity creates false distinctions and categories. Moreover it suppresses the richness of the archaeological record in Orkney, particularly the unique occurrence of standing Neolithic settlements.

SETTLEMENT PATTERNS

Taking a broader view of the evidence involves a critical evaluation which extends beyond the remarkable survival of already known late Neolithic settlements. As Clarke and Sharples (this vol., 54) correctly observe these sites are exceptionally preserved; however, they are also exceptionally situated. The distribution of known late Neolithic settlements (figure 4.1), to which may be added Pool and the bay of Stove, Sanday, is essentially coastal with Rinyo, Rousay, providing the only exception. This pattern raises the question of whether all late Neolithic settlement was coastally situated? Alternatively, if it merely reflects differential survival in coastal zones then were the inland sites of similar design and composition? At a basic level these questions would appear to be central to a discussion of social organisation and its change since the architecture and organisation of settlement will relate to the relationships between individuals, families, and entire communities.

An examination of the material presented to the National Museum of Antiquities of Scotland over the last hundred years showed substantial amounts of worked flint and Neolithic stone artefacts to have been collected from the surface of ploughed fields. These were mainly provenanced to inland areas and it became clear that a programme of fieldwalking, as a method of site location, could be effective in discovering a wider settlement pattern. The results of fieldwork undertaken during 1984–6 (Richards 1985) established the presence of several surface scatters of Neolithic flint, stone and burnt bone, all in inland situations (figure P.1). Frequently, however, these surface scatters were situated in close proximity to either the Loch of Stenness or Loch of Harray.

BARNHOUSE

The most interesting discovery was at Barnhouse Farm where a discrete surface concentration of material, including worked flint, polished stone axes, hammerstones and burnt bone, was located on the tip of the Stenness promontory adjacent to the Loch of Harray. Surprisingly, this scatter lay 150 metres north of the Stones of Stenness henge monument (Ritchie 1976, this vol.). Trial excavations revealed a preserved Neolithic land surface directly below the ploughsoil which was being severely damaged through continual ploughing. Consequently, a project of excavation was initiated in 1986 on behalf of Historic Buildings and Monuments.

To date the excavations have revealed an extraordinary settlement complex comprising a long sequence of occupation and a final phase of monumentality. The material assemblage comprises large quantities of Grooved Ware, worked flint and stone. Unfortunately, the bone component is absent due to soil conditions, however, substantial amounts of burnt bone have been recovered. Although a 'Grooved Ware' assemblage the recovered material displays marked differences with the Skara Brae and Rinyo assemblages. Functional differences are clearly represented within the ceramics, yet the decoration is extremely standardised both in technique and design; typically having three parallel grooves forming a wide chevron pattern. This design is identical to the Grooved Ware from the central hearth and ditch of Stones of Stenness henge monument (Henshall 1976,

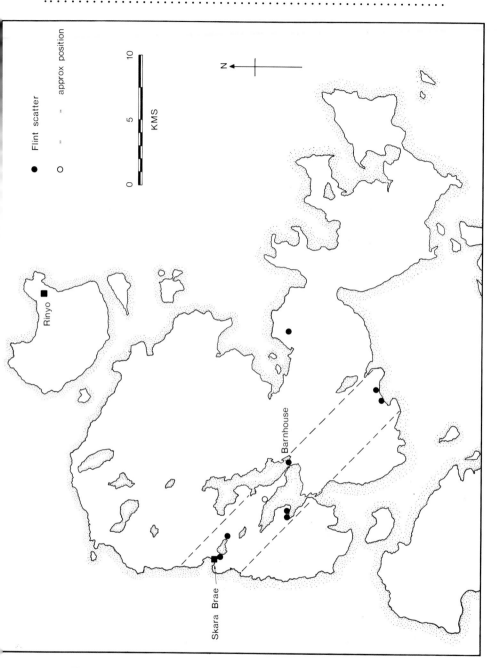

FIGURE P.I. Neolithic sites located through field walking in Mainland, Orkney.

23). However, it should be noted that at Barnhouse distinction is achieved through the occasional addition of dot and circle motifs and serpentine patterns.

The worked flint artefacts at Barnhouse are larger and more numerous than at Skara Brae and many objects of worked stone are unparalleled in other settlements. Of interest is the marked absence of stone Skaill knives; to date, approximately five examples have been discovered at Barnhouse as opposed to several hundred from Skara Brae, Rinyo and Links of Noltland. Materials originating from areas outside Orkney have also been found. Twenty pieces of Arran pitchstone have been discovered in different contexts, including the floors of houses 6 and 10. Besides being the first example of pitchstone found in Orkney this evidence is particularly important in demonstrating that external contacts existed with communities situated along the western Isles and the Atlantic seaboard.

In contrast to the other known late Neolithic Orcadian settlements which are largely undifferentiated in the size and internal organisation of their houses, Barnhouse displays a hierarchical spatial structure. The initial settlement, which in the present absence of radiocarbon dates may be related in time on the basis of its ceramics to the primary settlement at Skara Brae, comprises at least six houses surrounding a larger elaborate house structure (figure P.2). The surrounding houses are of typical circular early Skara Brae – Rinyo design, however, rather than being sunk into sand dunes and surrounded by midden material they are freestanding in an open lochside environment. They appear to have had an outer skin of stacked turves, presumably for extra insulation, and probably had turf rooves (French forthcoming). Like the other late Neolithic settlements an elaborate series of drains and ditches run throughout the settlement linking with drains running out of the houses.

Internally, all appear to generally conform to the arrangement described by Clarke and Sharples (this vol., 60–1) having a square central fireplace being flanked to the left and right by rectangular stone box beds recessed into the walls. At the rear of the houses is situated the so-called stone 'dresser'. The only exceptions to this rule are the adjacent houses 6 and 1 which both have their entrance orientation SSW–NNW as opposed to the normal SE–NW orientation. In the case of house 6, a covered stone lined drain runs from the rear of the hearth centrally out under the rear of the house. No evidence for a stone dresser was found at the rear of this house. House 7, currently under excavation, has a curious split level arrangement in its rear recess with a drain running from the lower level out under the exterior wall. As will be seen in house 2, the side recesses in house 7 are extremely unlikely to have acted as beds.

The larger house 2 is situated in the western area of the settlement. Because of its greater size, centralised position and the open areas to the

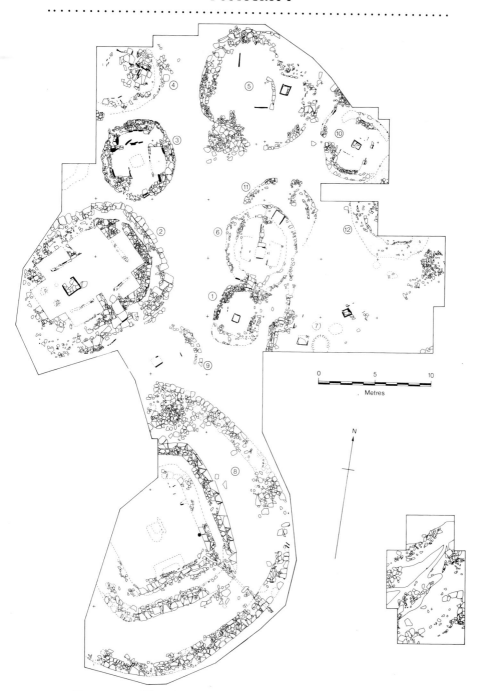

FIGURE P.2. Plan of the Barnhouse settlement complex.

front and side, this house would have acted as a focal point both visually and conceptually. In this way it would have effectively dominated the village. The appearance of house 2 is of particular importance for it fuses the architecture of the house with that of the passage grave. An oval encasing wall with a clay core encircles an inner wall which defines the internal space. Sophisticated masonry techniques, as otherwise seen within the chambered tombs, create internal straight-faced walls which form six recesses (possibly four in a cruciform arrangement in phase 1) through the use of corner buttresses. The only other example of this building technique is within the chambered tomb of Maes Howe which lies in full view 900 metres to the south-east.

In having six recesses bounded from the central area by upright divisional slabs a spatial structure is created within the building which is identical to that seen within Quanterness (Renfrew 1979), and Quoyness (Childe 1952), passage graves. In contrast to these chambered tombs there is no lengthy division between the inside and outside, but after all this is a place for the living. On entering house 2 through a short passage orientated towards the southeast a large and elaborate hearth, flanked by two long upright stones, is seen to the right of centre. Adjacent to the fireplace, left of centre, is set a visible coverstone of a cist or pit dug into the underlying natural ground (plate P.1). Very decayed fragments of bone were found within this otherwise empty cavity. Interestingly, the triangular shape and size of the cover is similar to cist covers located within the central chamber at Quanterness (Renfrew 1979, fig.24).

At a later date the interior of house 2 is re-arranged. The hearth and cist slab are covered and hidden by a new clay floor and a replacement hearth is constructed in the south western area of the house. This effectively removes the activities occurring around the fireplace from direct view when the house is entered. Only when access has been obtained may the events occurring in the left-hand area be witnessed (see Richards forthcoming, a).

HOUSES

Although house 2 is remodelled, creating two distinct periods of use, this phasing cannot be extended to embrace the entire settlement. Instead, a situation of flux appears to exist at Barnhouse where individual houses are built, periodically refurbished, and eventually demolished. This procedure seems to conform to our own experiences of settlement; however, the rules governing the life span of a Neolithic house in Orkney would probably have been quite different due to the different cultural context. One of the interesting features is that at different times virtually every house, with the exception of house 2, is demolished and replaced by another. The newly built house always partially overlies the levelled remains of the older one, but never assumes exactly the same position. Significantly, it is always

PLATE P.I. House 2, phase I (Copyright Controller HMSO).

offset to a varying degree. This disparity is maintained even when a house is replaced up to four times, as is the case with house 5. The open nature of the settlement would not have restricted expansion, nor has any physical settlement boundary been located. Consequently, the pattern of replacement may be attributable to social practices rather than external parameters or population pressure.

A similar pattern of house reconstruction is detectable at both Skara Brae and Rinyo. At Skara Brae the four different phases of construction suggested by Childe (1931, 6) mask numerous smaller episodes of rebuilding. Similar constructional sequences were revealed in the more recent excavations at Skara Brae (Clarke 1976). However, in attempting to compress Childe's four phases into two, Clarke admits that 'one must accept that these two periods each embrace a good deal of alteration and reconstruction much of which cannot be interpreted in terms of the general plan of the site' (ibid, 17). Excavations at Rinyo also revealed the same practice of demolition and rebuilding over earlier houses, which was subsequently discussed in terms of site phasing (Childe and Grant 1939; 1947). Unlike Skara Brae, Rinyo has plenty of space for settlement expansion, therefore, as at Barnhouse, social rules appear to govern house construction. Such consistency in residential behaviour within different 'villages' is of particular interest since the appearance of Grooved Ware, Maes Howe passage graves and large settlements in the late Neolithic may well have a cultural basis (Richards forthcoming, a).

Within this tradition of house replacement we may be witnessing the playing out of particular residential patterns influenced by social rules of inheritance and lines of descent. Moreover, there is also an element of continuity to consider since in building a house over an older one the idea of individual or family descent and continuity assumes concrete expression (Chapman forthcoming). Living on or over the site of an earlier house where ancestors performed the same tasks induces links with the past when undertaking everyday tasks. This is a different manifestation of the intimate relationship between the living and the dead as represented by the chambered tomb.

In fact, the demolition or abandonment of a house may be related to ideas of pollution surrounding the death of a householder rather than the physical disrepair of the structure. Also the house itself would have been symbolically linked to the occupants and their success or tragedies. Houses are built with specific models and ideas of the world in mind, and a variety of constructional rules and rituals to be implemented. Thus the house as an area of habitation also fulfils cosmological requirements within its architecture (Richards forthcoming, a). These wider principles are drawn on through metaphor and analogy in many social circumstances. At a daily level the use of the house involves numerous activities including sleeping, cooking, eating, etc. – therefore at different times within a single day spatial definition and its symbolic meaning change. Over longer periods of time further changes occur with the life cycle of the occupants (Moore 1986, 91). During life the reclassification of the social position of people will effect differences in authority, knowledge, and actions which in turn will alter spatial definitions within the home and may even prescribe changes in habitation. Under these circumstances the lifespan of the house is seen not to be independent from that of the inhabitants and their kinship links.

MONUMENTALITY

The continuity and consistency of settlement revealed in the succession of individual houses at Barnhouse is overshadowed by the erection of Structure 8, a building of 'monumental' proportions. This building is currently under excavation, however, it can on stratigraphical grounds be assigned to a late date in the life of the settlement. Of particular importance is the relationship between monumental Structure 8 and the group of lavish monuments, such as Maes Howe and the Stones of Stenness, which are constructed in the immediate vicinity (Richards forthcoming, b).

Although only the lowest courses of masonry remain intact it is possible to partially reconstruct Structure 8. Essentially, a large square building with rounded corners, based on the architecture of the house, is centrally positioned within a surrounding circular yellow clay platform which is enclosed by a substantial stone wall. In spatial structure the monument is similar to Maes Howe where the main passage grave is surrounded by a clay

PLATE P.2. Entrance to inner Structure 8, Photo: J. Downes
(Copyright Controller HMSO).

platform and enclosed by a ditch. However, Maes Howe is a place of the
dead and is situated away from the settlement. Its entrance passage is
orientated towards the winter solstice, the darkest time of the year, making
a place of cold and darkness. Structure 8 lies within the confines of the
settlement and the living and has an entrance orientated towards the summer solstice, the lightest period of the year.

Unfortunately, the outer entrance through the enclosing wall of Structure 8 is completely eroded. Nevertheless, the surviving stone slots of the
passage into the inner building revealed that it was flanked on either side by
two stone monoliths standing proud of the wall; one of which remained
snapped *in situ* (plate P.2). Between these monoliths, marking the threshold of the entrance was a hearth. A similar arrangement of a hearth lying
between two monoliths was discovered within the Stones of Stenness
(Ritchie 1976, fig.4). Although likely to have been covered by paving slabs
it is significant that a fireplace should lie at the beginning of the route into
the interior. Whether the remnant of an opening or constructional cere-
mony, or a recognisable and active element within the entering procedure,
the presence of a hearth and the action of stepping over fire on a threshold is
a potent form of symbolism embodying purity and transition. A three-
metre-long passage gave access into the interior where a hearth was situated
in the centre of a seven-metre square room. A complete Grooved Ware
vessel was set into the clay floor adjacent to the eastern wall (left side on
entry). The vessel was undecorated except for two horizontal grooves

directly below the rim. Interestingly, the decorated portion was the only visible area of the pot projecting above the floor surface.

Behind the fireplace, adjacent to the rear wall a semi-rectangular slot was cut through the floor. This slot, presumably for stone furniture, assumes the same position as the so-called 'stone dresser' within the house. No further evidence of stone furniture has been located within the interior. The presence of a single 'dresser' in monumental Structure 8 tends to suggest it had greater significance than merely acting as a furniture arrangement for displaying objects denoting status (Clarke and Sharples this vol., 70). In being positioned at the rear of the house it marks the deepest internal space and therefore, a special, if not sacred, area of the house, frequently associated with ancestral spirits and the dead (e.g. Collet 1987).

Several elaborate hearths, pits and remains of stone boxes have been located on the enclosed clay platform outside the large inner building. A quantity of pottery, flint, and stone tools associated with these features has also been recovered. These remains, probably of food preparation and cooking, are restricted to the southern area of the platform, that is the back region (Goffman 1959, 114), which is out of sight of the main performances occurring in the 'front' area. The substantial stone wall bounding Structure 8 would have shielded these activities from external scrutiny.

The overall impression of Structure 8 is that of a large building drawing on certain elements of the house and transforming them into monumental proportions. This recalls Eliade's statement that 'religious architecture simply took over and developed the cosmological symbolism already present in the structure of primitive habitations' (1959, 58). At present it is difficult to be sure if Structure 8 was in use during the later period of settlement at Barnhouse or if it marked the end of permanent settlement. Nevertheless, in architectural form it continues a general movement towards restriction and greater control over the movement of people in the later Neolithic. This concurs with the removal of ritual activities away from the public domain as seen within the internal alterations of house 2 and more generally within Orcadian passage-grave design (Richards forthcoming, b).

CONCLUSION

Although, excavations are still in progress at Barnhouse it is possible in concluding to make some general statements regarding the settlement and the effect its discovery has on perceptions of the Neolithic period in Orkney. The location of a settlement in the centre of what was previously considered a ritual centre or complex forces a critical evaluation of the ritual – domestic dichotomy which is implicit in much archaeological analysis. This problem is crystallised in assessing monumental Structure 8, since it is neither a house, tomb or henge, and yet, appears to incorporate elements of each. A similar problem of definition and interpretation may be identified with house 2. It is not simply a case of one building being influenced by another but rather in architecture we are seeing transforms of similar cosmological themes of order being manipulated in different contexts.

Perhaps related to the presence of Arran pitchstone, and therefore evidence of external contacts, is the inevitable question of political organisation in the late Neolithic period of Orcadian prehistory. On the basis of an elaborate settlement being discovered in the centre of a group of the largest and most spectacular monuments in Orkney it is reasonable to posit the existence of a hierarchical social order. This, of course, could take numerous forms of asymmetrical social relations. However it does suggest that a high degree of authority was exercised by particular social groups (Renfrew 1979, 217).

Things are never that simple and the suspected presence of a social hierarchy does little to interpret the variation noted in the Barnhouse settlement. Indeed the imposition of such categories tends to suppress the complex nature of the archaeological record. If late Neolithic society was stratified how was it maintained and reproduced? We are only just beginning our research into Neolithic Orkney.

ACKNOWLEDGEMENTS

The fieldwalking project was supported over three years by the Society of Antiquaries of Scotland. Louise Austin, Jane Downes and Mike Parker Pearson kindly commented on earlier drafts of this paper. Particular thanks go to Patrick Ashmore and Historic Buildings and Monuments for supporting this project over the last five years. Finally, I am grateful to Colin Renfrew for the invitation to contribute to this volume.

Bibliography (of references not included in the volume)

Chapman, J. (forthcoming) Social inequality on Bulgarian Tells and the Varna problem, *in* Samson, R. (ed.), *The Social Archaeology of Houses*, Edinburgh University Press.

Collett, D. (1987) A contribution to the study of migrations in the archaeological record: the Ngoni and Kololo migrations as a case study, *in* Hodder, I. (ed.), *Archaeology as long term history*, CUP, Cambridge.

Eliade, M. (1959) *The Sacred and the Profane: The Nature of Religion*, Harcourt Brace, New York.

French, C. (forthcoming) The analyses of soil structure at the Barnhouse Neolithic settlement, *in* Richards, C. (ed.), *The late Neolithic settlement complex of Barnhouse*.

Goffman, E. (1959) *The presentation of self in everyday life*, Pelican Books, London.

Henshall, A. (1976) Catalogue of small finds, *in* Ritchie, J. N. G., The Stones of Stenness, Orkney, *Proc. Soc. Antiq. Scot.* 107.

Moore, H. (1986) *Space, text and gender*. CUP, Cambridge.

Richards, C. (1985) *The Orkney Survey Project: interim report*, Glasgow.

Richards, C. (1988) Altered Images: a re-examination of Neolithic mortuary practices in Orkney, *in* Barrett, J. and Kinnes, I. (eds), *The Archaeology of Context in the Neolithic and Bronze Age: Recent Trends*, Sheffield.

Richards, C. (forthcoming, a) The late Neolithic house in Orkney, *in* Samson, R. (ed.), *The Social Archaeology of Houses*, Edinburgh University Press.

Richards, C. (forthcoming, b) Monumental Choreography: Architecture and spatial representation in late Neolithic Orkney, *in* Shanks, M. and Tilley, C. (eds.), *Interpretative Archaeology*. Routledge, London.

Sharples, N. (1985) Individual and community: the changing role of megaliths in the Orcadian Neolithic, *Proc. Prehist. Soc.* 51.

To my mother Şahsine Diken

CONTENTS

ACKNOWLEDGEMENTS

Once more, I am very grateful for the long, creative conversations with Niels Albertsen, who has also read the first draft of the book. It remains a pleasure to 'think with' him.

I am equally grateful for the fascinating, stimulating discussions with Michael Dillon, who commented on many ideas in the book. I will miss our discussions on the eschaton and the katechon.

Carsten Bagge Laustsen, my trusted colleague, has read the first draft and made, as ever, very useful, pointed and helpful observations. I appreciate it very much.

Many thanks, again, to Zygmunt Bauman and John Urry for discussing the project with me and articulating razor-sharp, constructive questions. They remain most inspiring figures.

I am also very grateful to Olga and Sümer Gürel for the marvellous, thought-provoking discussions and to Ebru Thwaites for her immensely valuable comments on the first draft.

I am obliged to the following: Costas Douzinas, Michael Shapiro, Ian Bryan, Mark Lacy, Nayanika Mookherjee, Bruce Bennett, Imogen Tyler, Arthur Bradley, Robert Appelbaum, Esat Ören, Işıl Baysan, Meltem Ahıska, İhsan Metin Erdoğan, Burak Güray, Besim Sağırkaya, Murat Utkucu, Diana Stypinska, Matt Buckley, Joe Rigby, Jack Nye, Sue Sterling, Müzeyyen Pandır and Özge Yaka. I have greatly benefited from their insightful critique throughout the various stages of the book.

Last but not the least, I would like to thank the Leverhulme Trust for granting me a one-year research fellowship, which has meant a lot for the progress of the book.

Bülent Diken
Lancaster, 2011

INTRODUCTION

Life without idea

In a short story published in 1924, 'The Revolutionist', Hemingway tells of the unfortunate destiny of an idealistic young 'comrade' he met in Italy in 1919. A foreigner from Budapest, the young man is travelling alone and with no money. All he has with him is a recommendation from the headquarters of the Communist party and a few reproductions of Renaissance paintings wrapped in a copy of the socialist newspaper *Avanti*. He asks Hemingway: 'How is the movement going in Italy?' Hemingway replies, 'Very badly.' The young man says, 'But it will go better. You have everything here. It is the country that everyone is sure of. It will be the starting point of everything.' To this, Hemingway says nothing (2004: 80). Despite their meeting in Bologna, a Fascist stronghold at the time, the young 'revolutionist' seems to be blind to reality. Hemingway, in contrast, knows that things will not get better, that the Fascists' power is growing aggressively, and this knowledge makes him intensely pessimistic. At the end of the story, the 'revolutionist' parts company with Hemingway, with plans to go to Switzerland, where he ends up in jail.

What one immediately notices in the story is of course the juxtaposition of naïve hope and experienced pessimism. One wonders, however: why does Hemingway resurrect this apparently failed, pathetic figure? Indeed, the sparse prose conveys much more than a realist description of an actual situation. Imperceptibly moving from actual facts to virtual sensations, the story reaches the domain of ideas, conveying a tension between apparently contrasting ideals: faith versus knowledge; hope versus pessimism; demanding the impossible versus being realistic, and so on. This is a tension which is internal to Hemingway himself, since he maintained fidelity to the idea of communism to the end of his life. However, when we come to the story with our contemporary sensibilities, what strikes us most is something else: the very word 'revolutionist', the existence of a figure who openly demonstrates fidelity to a cause, to an idea. Our society, after all, can perceive dedication to a cause only as a lack of reflexivity, as fundamentalism. The 'last man', preoccupied by the thought of ends (of history, of events, of revolutions . . .), cannot imagine a political cause to fight for (Žižek 2002c: 40–41).

Thus, despite its previous carrier as *the* most important concept of politics and critical thought, today revolution seems to have become an obsolete concept. Ours is a post-political society that cannot imagine radical change, a 'one-dimensional' society, in which politics has become hyper-politics. Thus, we are free to politicize anything and criticize everything, but only in a reserved, non-committal way, only in so far as our 'critique' is confined, in a properly fetishistic manner, to what exists. What is more 'untimely' today than the idea of revolution?

Paradoxically, however, everybody today is subjected to the imperative of regular radical change. Populations have grown accustomed to the idea that one constantly needs to adapt to radical transformations, modify one's life strategy in tune with the flexible demands of the market, and be prepared to try new options or start all over again. In this sense, the idea of radical change, of revolution, no longer refers to exceptional circumstances but has become normalized as part of daily life. Ours is a 'culture' of permanent revolution in which constant systemic dis-embedding demands a meta-stable subjectivity in continuous transformation. What is more 'timely' today than the idea of revolution?

'This is a call for revolution.' This is the opening sentence of the Prince of Wales's recent book (2010). Notwithstanding the irony of a 'sovereign' using the term 'revolution', here the word does not fill the world with enthusiasm or horror. Rather, totally deprived of its political and philosophical referents, the idea of 'revolution' is 'trivialized' (see Bauman 2008: 64): hence the interestingly farcical title of the book, *Harmony*. Consensus, not antagonism or refusal, is the essence of trivial revolution. And as such, as banal revolution, the concept is everywhere today. Crucially, however, this banalization occurs against the background of a ban. This ban, the single most important imperative of today's dominant ideology, is encapsulated by Badiou in three words: 'live without Idea' (2009b: 511).

But social life can become a 'problematic', that is, an object of critique and change, only on the condition that people can imagine the possibility of a different society (Bauman 1976: 35–6). 'All . . . events belong to the class of possibilities, which are not present in daily reality in any other way but ideally' (ibid.: 35). 'Idea', in other words, is that which enables us to contemplate our present condition in the prism of the possible, without which social life would turn into bare repetition, into an endless, Sisyphean reiteration of the same.

> Social problems can be grasped only by means of a 'rectification' which occurs when the faculty of sociability is raised to its transcendent exercise and breaks the unity of the fetishistic common sense. The transcendent object of the faculty of sociability is revolution. In this sense, revolution is the social power of difference, the paradox of society, the particular wrath of the social Idea.
>
> *(Deleuze 1994: 208)*

'Life without idea' designates the ambition to suppress this transcendent object which can only be lived 'in the element of social upheaval', in the moments of 'freedom' (ibid.: 193). At the most elementary level, freedom is experimenting with the link between what exists and what is possible. Only in the hour of freedom, of flight from the existing order of things, does there transpire a new sociality that is in excess of what already exists. There can be no social experiment without creativity and no creativity without destroying the current idols: hence the pharmakon-like gift of Zarathustra, fire, or Marx's insistence on the 'leap' that creates 'something that has never yet existed' (Marx 1977: 10).

And then again there is the banal experiment. Burke, the father of the English counterrevolution, had already articulated two opposite senses of social experiment: experiment as revolt or revolution on the one hand, and experiment as reform, as a 'computing principle', on the other (Burke 2004: 153). Burke was condemning the French revolutionaries as 'fanatics', who, without consideration to any interest, 'would sacrifice the whole human race to the slightest of their experiments' (quoted in Toscana 2010: xiv). Similarly, many social theorists today keep condemning fanaticism. They say that we have moved 'beyond Left and Right', that we live in a reflexive society in which even belief needs to justify itself in terms of knowledge. Thus every time a belief insists on its own truth, we are dealing with 'fundamentalism' or extremism – that is, a doctrinaire manner of refusing negotiation, of protecting a principle (Giddens 1994: 85). Yet, on this account, not only Marx and Nietzsche but almost all ethics, all radical politics, all experimental art and all transcendental philosophy could be called fanatic or fundamentalist – none of them, after all, are interested in justifying themselves with reference to opinion, by 'negotiating' existing values. None of them would accept the reduction of belief to knowledge. And all of them would point out that the claim that we live in a society without antagonism (without 'Left' and 'Right') is itself a symptom of nihilism, of an unreflective – 'fanatic' – belief in the existing society, a fetishism of what exists, which negates the domain of possibilities.

> 'Free as a bird', we say, and envy the winged creatures for their power of unrestricted movement in all the three dimensions. But . . . we forget the dodo. Any bird that has learned how to grub up a good living without being compelled to use its wings will soon renounce the privilege of flight and remain forever grounded.
>
> *(Huxley 2004: 152)*

The docile dodo, a flightless bird that is not really a bird, is perhaps a good metaphor for life without idea. In addition, it is also a good metaphor for counterrevolution. After all, the straightforward aspect of all counterrevolutionary thought is its definition of the existing world as an invariant and its direct opposition to ideas that promise another world, its negation of flight. But in a second, more sinister and more interesting sense, counterrevolution signifies the revision or internal perversion of, rather than opposition to, ideas. It designates not merely an external force but a strategic field of formation in which the struggle revolves around appropriating, accommodating and revising ideas and principles. In this second sense, counterrevolution knows that 'life without idea' is an absurd idea. You cannot have a zoo without animals.

In one of Sławomir Mrożek's short stories we come across a zoo director who wants to run his zoo by more cost-effective means. But he is smart enough to know that there can be no zoo without animals. Animals are necessary, especially big ones, like the elephant; 'three thousand rabbits were a poor substitute for the noble giant'. Then he comes up with a plan to obtain an elephant:

> We can make an elephant out of rubber, of the correct size, fill it with air and place it behind railings. It will be carefully painted the correct colour and even on close inspection will be indistinguishable from the real animal. It is well known that the elephant is a sluggish animal and it does not run and jump about. In the notice on the railings we can state that this particular elephant is exceptionally sluggish. The money saved in this way can be turned into . . .
>
> *(Mrożek 2010: 17)*

And so the director and his men make a full-size rubber elephant, filling it with gas. It looks real: an enormous body, huge legs and ears, and of course the unavoidable trunk. Next day, some schoolchildren come to see the elephant. While they look at the animal with admiration, their teacher tells them that the elephant is a herbivorous animal, that it stems from the now extinct mammoth, that a fully grown animal weighs between 9,000 and 13,000 pounds and so on. But suddenly, when a breeze starts, the gas-filled elephant shudders and rises into the air. The story ends here abruptly, stating that those children who witnessed the scene in the zoo 'no longer believe in elephants' (ibid.: 20).

'Life without idea', similarly, is life with 'rubber' ideas. Counterrevolution does not necessarily mean extinguishing creativity and critique as such, but it means docile, gas-filled critique without consequences – until, that is, people 'no longer believe' in ideas.

And so this book is an attempt to retain the belief in three interrelated ideas: revolt, revolution, critique. It asks what these ideas mean and could mean in an age of decaf reality. If there is one thing that unites contemporary radical thought, it is a principled opposition to the imperative of life without idea, to pseudo-experimentation. The social experiment is valuable only in so far as it transcends the actual, the finite, and links us to the virtual, the infinite. It can only have a dissensual, never consensual, relation to the actual. What sustains it is fidelity to the traces of past events and the hope of events to come. Fidelity is resisting the notion of 'ends', insisting that there is an irreducible, ontological possibility of events in this world, a possibility which, for all its repression and trivialization, cannot be eradicated – a real possibility, which persists, always reappears, even when people no longer expect it. This is, indeed, the real concern of the imperative 'live without idea'.

But the concern of those who choose to live with ideas is something else: to find the truths, the events, 'where they are, at their time, and in their element' (Deleuze 1983: 110). That is to say, the relevant question regarding ideas is: where, when, what? Three concepts, in response to this question, are significant for this book: the virtual, *kairos* and singularity.

The virtual

This concept takes us to the heart of the 'paradox' of society which originates in the dual formation of 'society' along two axes, in the form of two series: the actual and the virtual. Everything, and every society, has an actual existence, is stratified and stabilized in one way or another, while at the same time it contains within itself potentialities for change, which links it to the domain of the virtual. But these potentialities are not unreal; rather, they are 'real without being actual' (Deleuze and Guattari 1987: 94). The virtual, as such, is the indicator of the fact that every social relation can become different, can be re-actualized in other ways.

The concept of the virtual is a basic concern of philosophy, often under other names. Derrida (1995), for instance, when he considers the space of the event, returns to a Platonic text, *Timaeus*, more specifically to the concept of *khora*, which signifies 'something' that is real without existing as an actual thing that can be objectively known or recognized. Having no referent, as an amorphous, unformed 'something', *khora* is itself unrepresentable (ibid.: 95–7). As such, however, it is that which 'receives', or 'gives place' to, every representation, to all determinations, without possessing any of those determinations as its own properties (ibid.: 99). *Khora* is the place which gives place to everything, but is itself not existent as an actual place; it is a giving place to taking place of the event. In this sense the place of the event, its topos, is *khora*, or the virtual.

Events, then, are khoratic; things can change because the social world has a virtual dimension. Indeed, in so far as 'society' is reduced to its actual components, represented merely as an actual, recognizable identity or objective reality, the concept of 'society' falls back into the domain of common sense, becomes a 'fetish' (Deleuze 1994: 208). In turn, the event is a break with the fetish, with common sense, and signifies the opening up of the actual to the virtual.

If 'society' is not reducible to its empirical aspects or to virtual ideas alone, what matters then is the 'surface' between the actual and the virtual. This surface, which both joins and separates the actual and the virtual, is the source of a double serialization, which initiates two kinds of events: virtualization and actualization, ideal events and actual events. The two series, however, are 'never equal' (Deleuze 1990: 37). The virtual totality of a society's 'unknown' potentialities is always in *excess* of its actual, 'known' aspect. We do not know, to paraphrase Spinoza, what a society can do. In turn, an actual society is by definition always *lacking* in terms of its knowledge of the potential 'unknowns'. Therefore, the paradoxical relationship between the two series, one presenting an excess and the other a lack, is always a cause for disequilibrium, and it 'is this disequilibrium that makes revolutions possible' (ibid.: 49).

If the two series converge toward a paradoxical element which differentiates both series, this paradoxical element is revolution (ibid.: 51). Revolution is what joins the singularities which correspond to the two (actual and virtual) series, enabling the passage between them. This brings us to the 'element' of the event, to singularity.

The singular

What is the event made of? Let us at this point recall Foucault, who insisted on the singularity of the event, and did so, scandalously, even in the context of the Iranian Revolution. He was, to be sure, alerted to the dangers of theocratic politics, to the religious, xenophobic and sexist excesses of 'the bloody government of a fundamentalist clergy' (Foucault 2005: 265). Yet this was not enough for him to discredit the revolution, for he saw something else in it: 'the spirituality of those who were going to their deaths' (ibid.: 263, 266). His claim was that this possibility, the uprising of the oppressed, is an 'irreducible' possibility which is as real as power (ibid.: 264).

Foucault was severely criticized for his view on the Iranian Revolution. Maxime Rodinson, for instance, an expert on the Middle East, accuses him of being one of those 'high-flying' intellectuals who found a new 'hope' incarnated in the burning 'Muslim Orient' (Rodinson 2005: 267) – a Foucault 'intoxicated' by the successes of the Islamic revolution, ignoring the 'sociological facts concerning religion' and 'the oppressive potentialities' of Islamic political power (ibid.: 267–8):

> The 'political spirituality' that had inspired the revolutionary movement – covering over the more material motives for the discontent and the revolt – had at a very early stage shown that it operated by no means in the humanist sense that had been attributed to it, very naively, by Foucault.
>
> *(Ibid.: 272)*

What is interesting in this criticism is what it misses. Rodinson does not understand Foucault's point, for he understands politics only as a strategic mechanism for interest negotiation and interpretation. His model of politics is the classical 'realist' model according to which pre-given subjects and their interests pre-date political processes and mechanisms. Such a perspective is necessarily blind towards the event and assumes that violent uprisings can emerge only on the basis of the lack of politics understood as interest negotiation. In this sense Rodinson's approach is essentially conservative. When there is no room for the event, everything is referred to what exists; all else is naïve, idealistic, terroristic, fundamentalist intoxication. Foucault, in contrast, is interested in a straightforward ontological reflection: what is taking place in Iran in 1979 is a singular event. Events are singular. There is a political reality to them which is different from other forms of politics, which Foucault does not necessarily dismiss either. The miscommunication between Rodinson and Foucault therefore boils down to a conflict between two understandings of politics:

The strategist is a man who says, 'How does this death, this outcry, or this uprising matter in relation to the needs of the whole and to such and such general principle in the particular situation in which we find ourselves?' It is all the same to me if this strategist is a politician, a historian, a revolutionary, or a partisan of the shah or the ayatollah, for my theoretical ethics are on the opposite side. My ethics are 'antistrategic'. One must be respectful when a singularity arises and intransigent as soon as the state violates universals. It is a simple choice, but hard work: One needs to watch, a bit underneath history, for what breaks and agitates it, and keep watch, a bit behind politics, over what must unconditionally limit it.

(Foucault 2005: 267)

One way of grasping the singular, for which the 'intoxicated' Foucault demands respect, is its sterility or neutrality with respect to the actual. To say that the singular sense of revolution is 'neutral' or 'sterile' is to say that it is indifferent to affirmation or negation, that it is not affected by any proposition which refers to actual, historical qualities, quantities or relations (Deleuze 1990: 32). As such, singularity designates a pre-individual, impersonal world beyond actually existing identities. Singularities are the limits, or 'turning points', at which actual identities differentiate from themselves. For this reason, for it is not an actual or empirical entity, it is impossible to represent singularity. Singularity is that which escapes representation, an irreducible entity at the 'surface' of identities (ibid.: 19).

By the same token, what makes the concept of revolution interesting is not only its actualized forms and structures but also an infinite series of singular potentialities it expresses, not only its 'meaning' produced at the level of commonsensical, scientific or ideological representation but also its 'sense' produced at the level of singularities (see ibid.: 19, 187). And crucially this 'sense' of revolution, its virtual aspect, can never be fully actualized; it remains irreducible, neutral in relation to history. Hence a key figure of potentiality is the potential not to actualize itself, the 'potential to not-do' (see Agamben 1999a: 179–80). In other words, potentiality is also impotentiality. There is a potentiality which 'survives' actuality, which '*preserves* itself as such in actuality' (ibid.: 183). That is, the actualization of the idea of revolution does not mean that the potentiality, the idea, is annulled after being actualized. The power of 'revolution' is the power not to be exhausted in existence.

We must insist on this, for there is always someone who asks: do we not know, on the basis of historical facts, that revolution is not a solution, that revolutions eat their own children, turn out badly? The trouble with this question lies in its assumptions, in its emphasis on 'knowledge', 'actual', 'historical', 'solution', which reduces 'revolution' to an actual, historical category. Yet if 'revolution' is at once actual and virtual, a historical process and an idea, this recurring critique à la mode, never tired of condemning the 'horrors of revolution', confuses two things: 'the way revolutions turn out historically and people's revolutionary becoming' (Deleuze 1995: 171). 'Revolution' is always an event that is separated, distilled from the historical situation. However, through time, it becomes assimilated back into history; it is necessarily 'betrayed'. Following this, pointing out that all revolutions fail is a banal intervention, for the problem is not the future of the revolution but, above all, how and why people 'become' revolutionary (ibid.). No wonder, therefore, that the structural necessity of revolutions to fail does not prevent people from becoming revolutionary. For, even when revolutions fail, the given situation changes, and problems are transformed (Deleuze and Guattari 1994: 177).

But there is another dimension to singularity: even though singularity is an incorporeal, sterile effect that 'subsists' in the virtual, it 'happens to' the actual (see Deleuze 1990: 24). While in its existence and distribution singularity can be understood as neutrality (sterility), in terms of actualization, singularity has a productive dimension, a 'quasi-causality' (ibid.: 109, 125). Thus, in the process of actualization, the surface functions like a 'theatre' where virtual ideas are condensed, that is, actualized, dramatized, as productive singularities (ibid.: 125).

This dramatization brings with it a paradox as well: if revolution as a sterile, singular idea cannot be reduced to its actual consequences, how, then, can we keep alive the tension between the two dimensions of revolution as an idea and as actual reality? In this respect, revolution can be thought of as a 'problem', as what makes us think but does so independently of its solutions (Deleuze 1994: 157). Each actualization, each solution changes, displaces, enriches the (virtual) problem. Revolution, in this sense, is a virtual problem, a social idea, whose varieties are actualized or incarnated in concrete situations which characterize a determinate society.

At the same time, however, it cannot be separated from the actual either. The event cannot take place *ex nihilo*. A problem does not survive without its solutions; it can only express itself in the solutions (ibid.: 163). Thus, the idea of revolution does not bring with it the rejection of the actual as a condition but its precedence. As a problem, revolution is at the same time transcendent, because it belongs to the domain of the virtual, and immanent, because it is embedded in actual relations defined by solutions. Consequently, the concept of revolution can be maintained only as a unity of multiplicities in which different conceptions signify actual diversification. Only on this basis can it be possible to hold a common *concept* of revolution, while everybody can agree to disagree about its different *conceptions*. Only on this basis is it possible to have a common idea of revolution which can be dramatized differently by different actors.

The temporal

Significantly, such actualization requires an 'untimely' intervention, 'acting in a non-present fashion, therefore against time and even on time, in favour (I hope) of a time to come' (Nietzsche, quoted in Deleuze 1983: 107). The virtual 'excess' of revolution cannot find anything adequate to itself in the actual world, and thus can relate itself to the actual only as a 'lack', as what is 'to come'. This is why Derrida (1994), for instance, argues that the spectre of 'revolution' always remains 'to come' while it never really disappears. With a spectre, after all, the question is always to be *and* not to be, actual phenomenality and virtuality, at once (see ibid.: 10–12). In this sense the time of 'revolution' is always 'to come' not because it points to a promise that belongs to the future but because 'it will always remain aporetic in its structure' (Derrida 2005: 86). However, this aporia, the inherent undecidability and uncertainty at the heart of 'society', does not mean that what 'revolution' promises is merely an impossible promise, an unattainable dream, which therefore can be infinitely deferred:

> This im-possible is not privative. It is not the inaccessible, and it is not what I can indefinitely defer: it announces itself; it precedes me, swoops down upon and seizes me *here and now* in a nonvirtualizable way, in actuality and not potentiality.
>
> *(Ibid.: 84)*

Even though the promise of freedom and justice structurally remains impossible, the 'decision' to actualize the promise cannot be deferred. It is absolutely necessary to take a position in actual politics. The 'idea' must be actualized. Thus, to overcome the sterility of revolution ('to revolt'), which can be neither affirmed nor negated, it is necessary to relate the sterility to productivity, to dramatization.

> Having an Idea is this as well. It is as though every Idea has two faces, which are like love and anger: love in the search for fragments, the progressive determination and linking of the ideal adjoint fields; anger in the condensation of singularities which, by dint of ideal events, defines the concentration of a 'revolutionary situation' and causes the Idea to explode into the actual. It is in this sense that Lenin had Ideas.
>
> *(Deleuze 1994: 190)*

'Anger' here has both a creative and a destructive dimension, for it is selective regarding what to negate and destroy and what to affirm and actualize. Hence it is, literally, dramatic: just as each repetition of a play enacts a new interpretation each time it is 'replayed', each actual or historical act is a dramatization that expresses an idea in new ways (ibid.: 10). It is in this sense that revolution is 'the particular wrath of the social Idea'. Dramatic anger establishes a link between the actual and the virtual by completing the work of 'love' (the relation of the idea of revolution to other ideas such as emancipation, equality, justice and so on), a link which makes it possible for the social actors to experience the actual world in a transcendental perspective.

So history is a theatre in which dramatic repetition allows the 'actors' to produce radically new events, in which the virtual idea returns to the actual (ibid.: 10). How then can one repeat? How can one dramatize ideas?

The actual event (dramatization) takes two forms. First, the actor actualizes the event by seizing the moment, by saying '*here*, the moment has come' (Deleuze 1990: 151). This moment is a present at which the past and the future of the event are evaluated with respect to its embodiment (actualization), that is, a 'contracted' present, at which the event is 'grasped' by the actor, made present (ibid.: 150, 152). There is, however, another aspect of dramatization, which goes beyond actualization. The actor, too, is transformed in the process of dramatization. As a result of acting, he deviates from himself, his actual identity, through a process of 'counter-actualization' (see ibid.: 151). Whereas in actualization one seizes the event, making it present, in counter-actualization the event seizes, or 'overwhelms', one, leaving one with no relation to a determinable present or actual identity, 'except an impersonal instant which is divided into still-future and already-past' (ibid.). In this sense, the present of the event is a present in which the past and the future of the event are freed from the limitations of a state of affairs and considered in themselves, in terms of 'sterile' singularities.

On one side, there is the productive part of the event which is realized; on the other, there is the sterile part which cannot be realized. There are thus two accomplishments, actualization and counter-actualization (ibid.: 151–2). The physical actualization of the event in the state of affairs is doubled by the actor through a counter-actualization. And it is precisely through the latter that the actor becomes 'the actor of one's own events' (ibid.: 150), undergoing a metamorphosis, a transmutation. One must be transformed, become intoxicated by the moment while one seeks to seize it. One must 'become worthy' of the event (ibid.: 148). In this way, the two sides of the event, together, give us a full definition of freedom: the 'free man' is the one 'who grasps the event, and does not allow it to be actualized as such without enacting . . . its counter-actualization' (ibid.: 152). And of ethics: 'not to be unworthy of what happens to us' (ibid.: 149).

Revolution, then, is an intervention into time, the present, to change its course, with a view to bringing forth a new future. This intervention always involves a strategic decision, it seeks to 'seize' the moment, but it also necessitates a preparedness to become worthy of the moment, an intoxication which results from being 'seized' by the moment. These, combined with the promise of the new, the 'I hope' above, are what is encapsulated by the ancient Greek word *kairos*.

The 'intoxicated' actor is as necessary as the strategist. This is why 'revolution' is unthinkable from the perspective of 'history', that is, from the perspective of 'objective' facts or interests. Only when people invest their desire in revolutionary becomings, only when they have a desire to become part of an event, to seize and to be seized by an event, does the sense of revolution transpire and people can 'see' the revolution. If there is no enthusiasm, there can be no dramatization. If there is no intoxication, there can be no revolt.

> Progressive liberals today often complain that they would like to join a 'revolution' (a more radical emancipatory political movement), but no matter how desperately they search for it, they just 'don't see it' (they don't see anywhere in the social space a political agent with a will and strength to seriously engage in such activity). While there is a moment of truth in it, one should nonetheless also add that the very attitude of these liberals is in itself part of a problem: if one just waits to 'see' a revolutionary movement, it will, of course, never arise, and one will never see it. What Hegel says about the curtain that separates appearances from true reality (behind the veil of

appearance there is nothing, only what the subject who looks there put it there), holds also for a revolutionary process: 'seeing' and 'desire' are here inextricably linked, i.e., the revolutionary potential is not there to discover as an objective social fact, one 'sees it' only insofar as one 'desires' it (engages oneself in the movement).

(Žižek 2007c: 5)

Those who do not desire it do not see the event. Those who are not seized by it cannot seize the moment. For them, conditions are never ripe for revolt, revolution or critique; the time of the 'untimely' never comes.

About the book

The main idea behind the book is the paradoxical constitution of 'society' through the relationship between the virtual (excess) and the actual (lack). At this structural level, I deal with the three concepts – revolt, revolution and critique – as events that express the paradox of society. Decisive in this context are the complex relations between the three dimensions of the event: spatiality, temporality and singularity.

At a second, thematic level, I focus on the paradoxical natures of revolt, revolution and critique. I emphasize at this level the role of counter-revolt, counter-revolution and counter-critique. The possibility of counterrevolution exists within revolution. Revolution can always, potentially, lead to counterrevolution. Along the same lines, revolt can be appropriated by power; and critique is always prone to becoming a governmental dispositif. This process takes place because revolt, revolution and critique are essentially paradoxical phenomena.

Finally, at a third level, I am interested in the paradoxical characteristics of politics. An implicit argument throughout the book is that politics is always a politics of risk, that any political intervention can end badly. If politics did not have such a paradoxical dimension, it would turn into a technique, into a recipe book for the 'good society'. It would have been reducible to a routine procedure, to a 'politics-light', which merely consists of a struggle within an already established political space. But the political is also that which reconfigures the political space and constitutes a new political scene. The paradox of politics is grounded in this duality between the two senses of politics: politics as business as usual and politics as a break with the given. The book takes issue with this paradox along three lines. In terms of spatiality, it locates politics in the context of the interaction between the actual and the virtual. In terms of temporality, it emphasizes that any political decision must necessarily engage with a paradoxical relationship between what 'has been' and what is 'to come', trying, at the same time, to combine (rational) strategy and (a-rational) intoxication without the possibility of a stable synthesis between them. In terms of singularity, I focus on the simultaneous inclusion and exclusion of singularities in politics as well as on the link between singularity and universality.

The starting point of the book is that revolution is an idea. There is therefore necessarily a utopian streak to the concept, which problematizes a sharp distinction between 'utopian' and 'scientific' approaches to revolution. For the same reason I maintain a relatively close relationship between revolution and revolt. Thus so far I have used 'revolt' and 'revolution' interchangeably, as synonymous concepts. There will, however, emerge significant differences between the two concepts throughout the book.

When necessary, I define 'revolt' in line with historians such as Hobsbawm (see 1965: 1–8) as a relatively unorganized individual or collective upheaval. As such, revolt has a long pre-modern history while at the same time it persists in modernity. Revolution, on the other hand, is a concept of modernity, which is closely related to the development and analysis of capitalism. The promise of revolution is therefore a modern promise; revolution is a modern answer to the ancient problem of oppression and injustice. Thus modernity tends to turn utopia, which was imagined as a non-place even in Thomas More, into an ideal of modernization. But I also illustrate that today, in late modernity, the meaning of the differentiation between revolt and revolution tends to be displaced as revolt increasingly reappears, comes back, both as a figure of pure politics and as a form of relatively spontaneous acting out of political passions.

However, I do not focus on the history of revolt and revolution. Many readers would expect more historical discussion from a book on revolt, revolution and critique. But this book is more focused on social philosophy. Neither do I deal with social philosophy as a discipline. What the book seeks to establish is an undisciplined (rather than disciplinary, cross-disciplinary or post-disciplinary) plane of thought. I must also stress in advance that the book does not deal with revolt, revolution and critique in terms of subjective or objective 'interest'. For this reason, it is distanced to mainstream sociology which perceives politics as interest negotiation as well as a part of the Marxist tradition which insists on the 'objective interest' of the working class in revolution.

Only at certain points, and only relatively, do I consider the concepts in historical terms through brief discussions of actual revolts and revolutions, for example the Spartacus revolt and the French Revolution. I quickly turn to theories that grant revolt and revolution a central place in their structure, that is, theories *of* revolt and revolution. But what I am most interested in is the emancipatory theories that internalize, or identify with, the will to revolt as their own guiding principle rather than considering it as an analytical puzzle, as well as revolutionary theories that seek to participate in radical change. Regarding the first, my focus is, broadly speaking, on a tradition that comprises diverse figures ranging from Nietzsche to Foucault, Deleuze, Agamben, Derrida and Rancière together with the critical theory tradition, which deals with radical change as an 'event' through a synthesis of Marxist and Nietzschean perspectives. Regarding the latter, I focus on the Jacobin, Marxist, Leninist, Maoist understandings of revolution together with contemporary approaches signed by Badiou, Žižek, Hardt and Negri.

The book brings together these diverse theories not in a dialogue but in a 'disjunctive synthesis': as theories which exhibit some similarities in difference or differences in similarities, converge at some points while diverging at others, without seeking to unite them in a dialectic synthesis (see Deleuze and Guattari 1983: 75–83; Badiou 2000: 22). What I am interested in is the way in which these radical theories paradoxically converge, despite significant disjunctions, on some common aspirations (e.g. emancipation), and unite against common enemies (e.g. dominant ideologies). By the same token, I am interested in the ways in which they diverge despite common enemies.

This involves a mapping of the existing perspectives on revolt, revolution and critique. Basically, however, the book is not an introduction to the theorists mentioned above. Rather, it seeks to 'think with' them on revolt, revolution and critique, allowing for both solidarity and confrontations among them in its own framework. What the book is trying to achieve is, in other words, not an exegesis but a thematization (of revolt, revolution and critique).

The main contribution of the book is to articulate the paradox of society and to reconstruct the political via the concept of paradox in the context of revolt, revolution and critique. In this respect I also elaborate on the link between revolt and revolution on the one hand and bio-politics on the other, which is crucial because, especially after the 1960s, the two concepts seem to have moved from the socio-economic field to the bio-political field. Finally, since both revolt and revolution involve the critique of actual reality, the implications of the intimate relationship between revolt/revolution and critique are central to the book. The differentiation between theories *of* revolt/revolution and emancipatory or revolutionary theories is equally relevant in this context.

Unfortunately there won't be a facet list at the end of the book on how one can make the next revolution. Although there will be intimations towards a theory of revolution, what I principally deal with is the concept of revolution as a virtual potentiality. Mine is, above all, an 'enlightenment project' at the end of history. I am asking what the three repressed/revised concepts of our time – revolt, revolution and critique – could illuminate in relation to this 'end'.

The contents of the book

Part I deals with revolt and counter-revolt. The principal question here is the role of revolt in the creation of new values. In Chapter 1, I introduce the concept of revolt and establish its relevance to life, sociality and critical thought. The central figure of revolt in this chapter is repetition. Here I follow Nietzsche and Deleuze, emphasizing the role of revolt vis-à-vis nihilism: in so far as nihilism means that the link between humanity and the world is broken, the problem of revolt is to re-establish this link. In this, revolt exposes a potentiality excluded by the actual. But revolt can become an event only when it involves a counter-actualization of identities.

Chapter 2 relates revolt to politics and temporality through the concept of *kairos*. It discusses the role of *kairos* in mediating the actual and the virtual domains and bringing the new into existence. It insists that *kairos* is not only a matter of 'seizing' the moment; the moment of decision also requires fidelity. Following this, I discuss the 'state of exception' as an instance of counter-revolt. The structural homology between the state of exception and *kairos* is crucial at this point. Then, following Benjamin and Agamben, I differentiate two forms of violence, state violence and revolutionary violence. The chapter ends with a discussion of what is most unbearable to state power, the demand to remain singular, which is at the heart of any radical politics of revolt.

Chapter 3 extends the link between revolt and politics to the question of the subject. It elaborates on subjectivation as an effect which polarizes a historical situation and an extra-historical event. The four main 'subject effects' discussed here are: superego, anxiety, courage and justice. Following this discussion, the chapter argues that revolt against the modern law, which takes the form of superego, necessarily involves a moment of masochism, of counter-actualization. Finally, regarding the question of how revolt can relate itself to politics, the chapter turns to 'pure politics' in Badiou's sense.

Excursus I focuses on Kubrick's film *Spartacus*. In so far as the name Spartacus stands for a gesture of politicization that synthesizes the relationship between the political, the historical and the subjective, the chapter asks whether Kubrick's *Spartacus* is able to demonstrate fidelity to this event-Spartacus. The concept of resurrection is central in this discussion.

Part II deals with revolution and counterrevolution. The organizing principle here is the historical periodizations or sequences defined by the intervention of a political subject (see Badiou 2009a: 92). Chapter 4 deals with the Jacobin politics as a sequence in this sense. The central concept here is democracy. First I discuss the original sense of democracy in the perspective of the French Revolution. Then I turn to contemporary democracy, discussing the way the concepts of freedom, equality and fraternity are 'revised' in modernity. The crucial point at this juncture is how democracy has gradually become a governmental term to manage the infinity of finite cultures and bio-political bodies, without allowing these finitudes to universalize themselves.

Chapter 5 focuses on class as another historical sequence of modern politics. It traverses the memory of the 'proletariat' as a political subject, focusing especially on two different ways of understanding its singularity, as productivity and as negativity, which also give way to two different conceptions of political subjectivation. In both versions, however, the subject of politics remains 'to come' and politics is seen as an activity which produces a new subject rather than representing existing identities. Here I also deal with Marx's understanding of repetition, that is, his theory of revolution based on the relationship between tragedy and comedy or farce. The chapter ends with a critique of pure politics, emphasizing the role of the economy vis-à-vis politics.

Chapter 6 discusses the Leninist sequence, relating it to the concept of *kairos*. The main argument here is that any true political intervention must be able to 'interweave' the two dimensions of *kairos*, strategy and intoxication, in a materialist context. Following Derrida, the chapter insists that the relationship between the two dimensions is best characterized as aporia, not as antinomy. Then I discuss the actuality of fascism and Stalinism as two figures of counterrevolution. What is crucial here is the role of consensus and objective knowledge in Stalinism, which enables Žižek and Badiou to draw an interesting parallel between Stalinism and contemporary liberal democracy.

Chapter 7 takes up the concept of the 'mass' as a political subject and discusses mass politics as the final sequence of modern politics so far. While the Cultural Revolution and May '68 provide examples of mass politics, the figure of counter-revolution which surfaces here is elections. Again, the chapter argues that what was once revolutionary has become a dispositif of power today. Then it dwells on the violent relationship between contemporary liberal democracy and its oriental-ized enemy, Islamic terrorism. In this context I turn to political theology. I con-trast Schmitt's political theology, which seeks to justify sovereignty, with Taubes's revolutionary eschatology, which delegitimizes it. I argue that this polarization is displaced today: while the war against terror, which adopts Schmitt's political the-ology, increasingly looks like a comedy of (t)errors, Al Qaida's terror remains, at the level of ideas, a farcical version of apocalyptic eschatology.

The book is organized in the form of fragments or chapters which move in differ-ent directions. These fragments can be brought together in different ways. In Chap-ter 8 I illustrate my way of synthesizing them. Here I develop a framework to dif-ferentiate revolt and revolution on the one hand and the views on revolution on the other. Central here are the convergences and divergences between two traditions of thought: the philosophy of immanence and the philosophy of transcendence. I emphasize that the relationship between them is best captured as a disjunctive syn-thesis, as an 'agonistic' relation, while they both enter into an 'antagonistic' relation, both on the same side, as against what exists. The main antagonism that proliferates in this chapter is the antagonism between contemporary liberal democracy and the idea of communism, between a world without idea and an idea without world.

Excursus II discusses the continuing relevance of Huxley's dystopic novel *Brave New World*, in which a passive nihilist version of 'happiness' is elevated to the level of a counterrevolutionary political and ethical ideal. Although Huxley's target was Stalinism, *Brave New World* uncannily throws light on contemporary 'democratic' totalitarianism. I discuss this homology in the framework of bio-politics, nihilism and network society.

Part III focuses on critique and counter-critique. Again, counter-critique des-ignates not only the silencing of critique but rather its dissemination as revision. Chapter 9 focuses on a theoretical case, the 'sociology of critique', whose trade-mark is to supplement 'critical theory' with an analysis of the normative conven-tions (regimes of justification) which critique is based upon. I argue that in this endeavour the sociology of critique reproduces the logic of critical theory by taking the sting out of it, by taming its radical edge. What gets lost in this 'reformist' oper-ation is the promise of emancipation. Consequently, the sociology of critique does not seek to transcend but to transform capitalism as capitalism. In response to this, and arguing that critique cannot be reduced to justification, this chapter defines the contours of radical critique and differentiates it from 'reformist' critique.

Chapter 10 takes issue with the essential link between the concepts of revolt, revolution and critique. Critique, following Rancière, always involves disagreement, which is, above all, a disagreement on consensus. The chapter differentiates two forms of radical critique: aesthetic and social. Both posit an idea of emancipation, but do so in different ways, in two different horizons: *poiesis* and *praxis*. Then the chapter returns to the idea of communism as the coincidence of aesthetic and social critique. Discussing this 'coincidence' in terms of a disjunctive synthesis, it elaborates on communism as critique, contrasting it to ontological communism as a paradoxical idea(l).

The Afterword deals with the actuality of communism in the context of the Egyptian revolt. It returns, in this context, to the 'thread' of the event, that is, to the link between the singular, the virtual and the kairological. What is crucial when one is confronted with an event, with the labyrinth of the new, is always a double affirmation. Saying 'yes' to the event must be followed by an 'intervention'.

PART I

Revolt and counter-revolt

1

REVOLT AND REPETITION

> Dissect him how I may, then, I but go skin deep; I know him not, and never will. But if I know not even the tail of this whale, how understand his head? Much more, how comprehend his face, when face he has none? Thou shalt see my back parts, my tail, he seems to say, but my face shall not be seen. But I cannot make out his back parts; and hint what he will about his face, I say again he has no face.
>
> *(Melville 1998: 339)*

This is the way Melville's narrator, Ishmael, describes the impossibility of describing Moby Dick. The inhuman whale, in all its 'white' indifference and indefiniteness, is a monster, a 'Leviathan', which stands for the 'heartless voids and immensities of the universe'. Thus it is sublimated as an unspeaking, silent God with no face, with no promise of meaning, as an already dead God, which therefore cannot be killed (Melville 1998: 175, 310). And in as much as Ishmael cannot describe Moby Dick, Ahab, 'chasing with curses a Job's whale round the world' (ibid.: 167), cannot kill it. With Ahab, Job's biblical rebellion receives a modern twist. It becomes a rebellion against a universal indifference and alienation personified in Moby Dick: an atheist God, a God fit for a time in which 'God is dead'; nevertheless a monster, which constrains freedom and thus provokes revolt (see Friedman 1963: 398–9).

As such, Melville's Moby Dick is a metaphor for the 'absurd', Camus's concept grounded in the perception of an immanent world which does not possess a transcendent meaning or generate authentic values by itself. The feeling of the 'absurd' is born of the contradiction between the human 'longing for happiness' and the indifferent, 'unreasonable silence of the world' (Camus 2005: 26). And Camus declares that the first task of thinking and action in the face of such absurdity is to affirm its existence, rather than denying it. Or, in Nietzsche's words, what is necessary is to accept 'existence as it is, without meaning or aim' (Nietzsche 1967: 35–6). Even if this world had an external, supra-sensual meaning, we would not be able to understand it: 'I don't know whether this world has a meaning that transcends it. But I know that I do not know that meaning and that it is impossible for me just now to know it' (Camus 2005: 49). To think or to act otherwise amounts to nihilism, that is, a lack of strength, an inability to accept the world as it is, resenting the fact that the world is devoid of a goal, unity or meaning. To be able to endure the meaninglessness and the chaos of the world, the nihilist tries to endow it with meaning, imposing an illusionary totality upon it (Nietzsche 1967: 12). Hence, for Camus as for Nietzsche, nihilism is, in its origin, the invention of monotheistic religions, the invention of a transcendent God, in order to escape into a supra-sensory realm beyond earthly life, a realm that promises consolation for the absurdity of the world. As against this nihilism, one must insist on immanence. Ours is a world without an external cause or a final purpose, a world of becoming in which what seems to be ordered is in fact a non-teleological play of absurd chaos. In this world, there can be no eternal categories, absolute truths or timeless facts, and change cannot be reduced to one-directional evolution, to progress (see Nietzsche 1959: 83, 1967: 35–6).

'I *rebel*, therefore we *exist*'

This does not mean, however, that one should resign oneself to the absurd, give up any desire for authenticity. Then how can one approach the contradiction between the human search for authenticity, or happiness, and the absurd? How can one say 'no' to the absurd, negate it, without becoming a nihilist? Revolt, at a first approximation, is the answer to this contradiction. A concept grounded in the problem of nihilism, revolt is a 'leap into flight' out of the absurd, a 'constant confrontation' between the desire for authenticity and the surrounding absurdity, a challenge to the actually existing world, but without succumbing to the illusion of transcendence (Camus 1953: 270, 2005: 52). Revolt is the only form of authenticity, the only hope for certainty one can achieve in the face of absurdity, without surrendering to actual or philosophical suicide.

> I proclaim that . . . everything is absurd, but I cannot doubt the validity of my own proclamation and I am compelled to believe, at least, in my own protest. The first, and only datum that is furnished me, within absurdist experience, is rebellion.
>
> *(Ibid.: 16)*

So revolt is productive; it produces value. In the same way as the Cartesian *cogito* can reflexively construct a minimal certainty on the basis of methodological doubt ('I doubt, therefore I exist'), the rebel creates from absurdity, by folding it, turning it upon itself, a paradoxical certainty, a common ground on which values can be based: 'I *rebel*, therefore we *exist*' (ibid.: 28).

The rebel is a person who draws a limit, a borderline, by saying 'no' to an unjust authority or condition; every revolt necessitates, as Camus remarks, a sense of justice: you have no right to go further. In this sense, revolt starts with questioning the value of existing values. What is at stake here is of a pragmatic nature, the principle according to which values are produced. Therefore 'questioning' inevitably involves a practical destruction, the annihilation of existing nihilistic dogmas. And in so far as violence, the 'hammer', is needed to revolt against nihilistic 'idols', the rebel, who says 'no', is a destructive character.

Is this rebellious, destructive 'no' an irrational gesture? There is, to be sure, a role reason can play in the refusal of what exists. Thus, Marcuse, for instance, posits a direct link between negative reason and rebellion: what is given, the form in which an object immediately appears, is 'negative' in the sense that the object's 'real potentialities' are necessarily not yet actualized. Only in the process of overcoming this negativity, the inherent limitation in the given, does the object attain its truth. The destruction of the given is therefore necessary for truth; reason dissolves, changes the actual, given state of objects, and only through this 'mediation' do objects become adequate to their idea (Marcuse 1955: 26). Since the truth of a thing is made up of its virtual potentialities as well as its actual state, of what that thing is not, the task of critical reason is to intimate, to verify those potentialities hidden by the actual form. Moreover, if the 'negative' indicates the untrue character of a given state of things, which is manifest at the heart of any actual reality, 'nothing that exists is true in its given form' (ibid.: 123). Revolt exposes this 'negativity' and thereby the potentiality excluded by the actual.

However, reason is not the last word on revolt. Revolt needs reason only in so far as the essence of being is conceived as Logos (see Marcuse 1969: 102–05). The real force behind reason is an immanent principle, the will to power, which Nietzsche juxtaposed to God's transcendent judgement. In other words, revolt is also a question of will, of drives and desires. Let us, to discuss this point, revisit Kant's famous example to illuminate the weight of reason to control desire, to transcend the realm of the senses:

> Suppose someone asserts of his lustful appetite that, when the desired object and the opportunity are present, it is quite irresistible. [Ask him] – if a gallows were erected before the house where he finds this opportunity, in order that he should be hanged thereon immediately after the gratification of his lust, whether he could not then control his passion. We need not be long in doubt what he would reply.
>
> *(Kant 2004: 30)*

Here Kant assumes that, thanks to the deterrent, the gallows, the man will not act according to his desire. Nevertheless, there are conditions in which 'it is not impossible for a man to sleep with a woman knowing full well that he is to be bumped off on his way out, by the gallows or anything else' (Lacan 1992: 109). In 'perversion', for instance, passionate excesses move beyond the limits assigned to them by the moderate dialectic between transgression and the law, between the pleasure principle and the reality principle, and reach the register of the real, the place of drives which 'have nothing at all to do with something that may be satisfied by moderation' (ibid.: 110). This is also why revolt is an irreducible potentiality that is as real as power and why people can sometimes risk their lives 'in front of the gallows and the machine guns' (Foucault 2005: 264).

On this account, technically speaking, revolt is a 'perverse' activity that relates to drive, to will, without justifying itself through reason, provided that 'perversion' here is not defined in relation to a pre-established norm, for example as abnormality, following an already existing criterion. Rather, it signifies that which seeks to determine an impersonal, unconscious, virtual field, which is distinct from the actual, empirically existing phenomenon or consciousness: the pervert is 'someone who introduces desire into an entirely different system and makes it play, within this system, the role of an internal limit, a virtual center or zero point' (Deleuze 1990: 304).

As such, as a 'perverse' gesture, revolt is what introduces a virtual dimension into an actual situation. Behind the propositional, rational content of any revolt there is an affective force, an intense desire. And in so far as revolt is a revolt against reactive forces, the affirmation of this affective force is essential for it. Therefore, in the same breath as it says 'no', revolt also says 'yes', confirming that there is something worthy of fidelity. This is why revolt necessarily invokes the question of values for the sake of which the rebel will bracket instrumental reason and risk defeats, even death. 'Not every value leads to rebellion, but every rebellion tacitly invokes a value' (Camus 1953: 20).

These values are not, however, individual values; on the contrary, the rebel feels that they are 'common to himself and to all men', that is, the affirmation involved in revolt 'transcends the individual' (ibid.: 21). The rebel is not alone; he engages with others in a virtual, 'metaphysical' solidarity on the basis of common values. In effect, human solidarity originates in revolt, and revolt 'can only be justified by this solidarity' (ibid.: 27). Revolt has its own (virtual) sense; it has no other (actual) reasons.

> Reasons for rebellion seem, in fact, to change with the times. It is obvious that a Hindu pariah, an Inca warrior, a primitive native of Central Africa, and a member of one of the first Christian communities had quite different *conceptions* about rebellion. We could even assert, with considerable assurance, that the *idea* of rebellion has no meaning in those *actual* cases.
>
> *(Ibid.: 25, my emphasis)*

Each dramatization, each repetition of revolt produces a difference, a creative excess, that is, new values. In this sense, the will to negate is only one side of revolt. Its other side is affirmation, that which pushes out the negative and creates new values. The 'no' cannot be taken to its extreme, brought to completion, without metamorphosing itself into the opposite quality, that of affirmation, which is also a Dionysian transmutation of pain into joy, of hatred into love (Deleuze 1983: 173). The negation of the old is necessary, then, not merely for the sake of destruction as such but because it leads, at least potentially, to the occurrence of the new. 'A given form of existence cannot unfold its content without perishing. The new must be the actual negation of the old and not a mere correction or revision' (Marcuse 1955: 141). Yet, if such hatred cannot transmute into love, if revolt ceases to involve an affirmative moment, the tension between the virtual potentialities and the actual reality can only be resolved into an abstract nothingness. It is as a consequence of affirmation that a given reality differentiates from itself, 'becomes what it is not' (ibid.: 124). Hence there is the test of revolt: the transformation of will into creativity. Then the will is not the last word on revolt either:

> To redeem the past and to transform every 'It was' into an 'I wanted it thus!' – that alone I call redemption! Will – that is what the liberator and bringer of joy is called: thus I have taught you, my friends! But now learn this as well: The will itself is still a prisoner. Willing liberates: but what is it that fastens and fetters even the liberator? 'It was': that is what the will's teeth-gnashing and most lonely affliction is called. Powerless against that which has been done, the will is an angry spectator of all things past. The will cannot will backwards; that it cannot break time and time's desire – that is the will's most lonely affliction.
>
> *(Nietzsche 1961: 161)*

Radical and passive

In so far as revolt is 'redemption' from absurdity, it cannot be based only on will. In the case of such an attempt, there are two dangers that lie in wait for the 'prisoner'. First, the will can release itself in a 'foolish' way, through nihilistic revenge, which is nothing other than 'the will's antipathy towards time': one concludes that, since one cannot undo the past, 'everything deserves to pass away' (ibid.: 162). Ahab, for instance, in his delirious revolt against Moby Dick, is devastated by his own hatred. His 'mad secret', which transforms him into a tragic hero who will risk everything to kill Moby Dick, including his ship and its crew, is his desire for revenge (Melville 1998: 167). Ahab is prepared, 'for hate's sake', to spit his 'last breath' at the whale (ibid.: 507). But his passion for revenge, 'the hot fire of his purpose' to which he sacrifices 'all mortal interests', destroys Ahab himself before Moby Dick (ibid.: 189). What is at issue here is the ambivalence of 'fire'. Fire signifies a search for, a bond with, truth, and this is Ahab the rebel's Promethean aspect as a worshipper of fire. But one can 'burn' with fire as well as 'leap' with it (ibid.: 450). Thus fire, initially the symbol of hope in *Moby Dick*, turns into a symbol of lack of hope, gradually giving rise to a paranoid closure and destroying the ship that feeds Ahab and his men. Ahab stops thinking, goes mad. 'Give not thyself up, then, to fire, lest it invert thee, deaden thee' (ibid.: 380).

But there is a second, equally sinister danger: 'realizing' that no deed can be undone, the will pacifies itself; willing becomes not-willing (Nietzsche 1961: 162). This is the case with Ishmael, the narrator of *Moby Dick*. If Ahab is a 'woe that is madness', Ishmael is the 'wisdom that is a woe' (Melville 1998: 380; see also

Friedman 1963: 451). If Ahab is ready to sacrifice actual existence for the sake of touching the void, the virtual, Ishmael is willing to sacrifice the virtual to be able to open up a space for himself in the actual. Thus, he 'metaphysically' perceives that his own individuality is merged 'in a joint stock company' on the ship, in society, and, on this basis, he can develop a critique of Ahab's spiteful line of revenge (Melville 1998: 287). Yet Ishmael, the only member of the crew who is saved and thus returns to the land, 'does not offer an alternative point of view to Ahab nor succeed in the quest for truth where Ahab fails' (Friedman 1963: 91). For Ishmael, like Nietzsche's 'last man', time is an empty movement just as life is a pointless process, a 'burning ship', moving towards an ultimate catastrophe (Friedman 1963: 86; Melville 1998: 378). And this lack of perspective is also a lack of will. After all, interpretation, the ability to construct a perspective, new values, requires a subject, a personality, that can actively evaluate the world as well as perceive it in a contemplative manner. Yet in modernity God is dead, and action has become impossible. In an indifferent, absurd world, in which he longer can believe, Ishmael turns into an alienated, passive narrator: 'The link between man and the world is broken. Henceforth, this link must become an object of belief . . . Only belief in the world can reconnect man to what he sees and hears' (Deleuze 1989a: 171–2).

In so far as nihilism means that the link between man and the world is broken, the problem of revolt against nihilism is to re-establish this link. If the relationship between the modern, alienated man and the world is to be re-created through the reaffirmation of this world, of 'belief' in it, Ishmael is not able to make this leap of faith. Hence, just as Ahab devalues the actual world, Ishmael devalues values as such. Ahab's leap leads him to (self-) destruction; Ishmael's inability to risk such a leap condemns him to passivity: radical nihilism versus passive nihilism, two inappropriate answers to the question of nihilism, two unsuccessful attempts at revolt.

If, in its origin, nihilism is a will to escape from Nietzsche's 'chaos' or Camus's 'absurdity' to a transcendent, illusory world, with modernity, or with the 'death of God', this originary nihilism divides itself into two: radical and passive nihilism. The first insists on transcendence by taking the negation of *this* world to its logical extreme, the annihilation of the actual; the second, becoming content with the actual world, gives up its virtual dimension: on the one hand, the virtual without the actual; on the other, the actual without its virtual dimension – values without a world versus a world without values. There is therefore a strange symmetry between the two nihilisms, between (Ahab's) willing nothingness and (Ishmael's) annihilation of will: two opposite tendencies juxtaposed to each other in the same social space, paradoxically united in disjunction, disjointed in union.

Thus Nietzsche's definition of a nihilist reads like this: 'A nihilist is a man who judges of the world as it is that it ought *not* to be, and of the world as it ought to be that it does not exist' (Nietzsche 1967: 318). If existing values are devalued while, at the same time, *this* world is preserved, we encounter passive nihilism, or a 'world without values' (Deleuze 1983: 148). For the 'last man', life is devoid of meaning. 'The given reality becomes the only reality; devoid of aim, unity, and truth, and the world 'looks *valueless*' (Nietzsche 1967: 12–13). If, on the other hand, despite realizing that one's supreme values are not realizable, one still desperately clings to them, we confront radical nihilism: values without a world.

'Has been', 'to come'

Revolt, then, must break this deadlock between radical and passive nihilism, and it can do so only on the basis of affirmation. In other words, what is crucial is the passage from the will to affirmation, the central concern of Nietzsche's doctrine of eternal return. Eternal return means imposing 'upon becoming the character of being' (Nietzsche 1961: 330). Since the supreme immanent principle of life is difference, or, in Nietzsche's terminology, the will to power, since the only thing that remains 'the same' in a world of difference, what eternally 'returns', is difference, becoming *is* being (Deleuze 1983).

Thus the essential gesture of the doctrine of eternal return is to propose fidelity to immanence as the source of all values, 'remaining true to the earth' in the face of absurdity (Nietzsche 1961: 42). It is in this context that Nietzsche's demon says:

> This life as you now live it and have lived it, you will have to live once more and innumerable times more; and there will be nothing new in it, but every pain and every joy . . . will have to return to you.
>
> *(Nietzsche 1974: 273)*

This question – 'Do you desire this once more and innumerable times more?' – is the question of eternal return, of affirmation, because only saying 'yes' to all that 'has been' and to everything 'to come' can be an affirmation of immanence to a degree that cannot be surpassed, an absolute affirmation.

> A spirit thus emancipated stands in the midst of the universe with a joyful and trustful fatalism, in the faith that only what is separate and individual may be rejected, that in the totality everything is redeemed and affirmed – *he no longer denies*.
>
> *(Nietzsche 1969: 103)*

True revolt, redemption from nihilism, demands accepting the existing world as a fate, a 'fatalism', which synthesizes Spinoza's *amor fati* (love of fate) with trans-valuation of values. Affirmation is what completes nihilism (Deleuze 1983: 69). Through affirmation, we overcome ourselves, our nihilism. Herein lies the meaning of 'overman': the one who can overcome his own nihilism, go through an act of self-cancellation. The active dissolution of the self, counter-actualization, is the opportunity for another self, another meaning. Thus the overman, the anti-nihilist, is the one 'who wants to perish' (Nietzsche 1961: 44).

We are now in a position to clarify three points. First, even though the 'sense' of revolt is neutral or sterile, that is, indifferent to negation or affirmation, in the moment of actualization affirmation is an essential dimension to revolt. For with actualization (dramatization, repetition) we move from will to eternal return, from singularity to intentionality (Deleuze 1990: 299). However, this is not a move from singularity to a fixed subject.

Hence, second, we can formulate a reservation as to Camus's maxim 'I *rebel*, therefore we *exist*'. True repetition addresses pre-subjective and impersonal singularities, that is, difference, and not established identities. In this sense 'I' is also subject to change. Eternal return involves a counter-actualization of identities. It does not allow the coherence of the subject, of the world or of God to survive (ibid.).

Concomitantly, third, the 'we' that results from revolt can only be thought of as a commonality of singularities or, in the mode of futurity, as a community to come. What is 'common' in the moment of actualization of an event is singularities (Negri 2003: 172). As such, the temporality of revolt promises a redemption which is very different from redemption in its Christian version. This cosmology goes against the monotheistic thesis that time had a beginning and will have an end, that the world was created and will be annihilated on the Judgement Day. In contrast, Zarathustra preaches a world that is in becoming, a world one should return to in order to overcome nihilism (Hass 1982: 224). Therefore the idea of eternal return is a 'substitute for the Christian gift of eternal life' for those 'who do not like to live without danger' (Rosen 1995: 178). For those who do not dream the dream of nihilism: a world without pain, conflict and antagonism. Therefore, while Christian redemption seeks a 'temporalized eternity', an everlasting continuum for the eternal soul, Zarathustra offers an 'eternal temporality' in which historical actors repeat their transitory acts and existence (ibid.: 178). In the doctrine of eternal return, there is no conclusion to historical time.

As a philosophy of history, the temporality of eternal return is fundamentally opposed to the understanding of time as a linear flow, of history as continuous progress. In fact, for Nietzsche, nihilism itself signifies a 'regress' rather than 'progress', a situation in which reactive (passive) forces triumph over the active ones (see Nietzsche 1967: 55). It is the 'same' world, the world of difference and becoming, that eternally repeats itself and gives birth to non-linear change, and what matters in such a world is trying to seize each moment, to be fully present in it, that is, to repeat.

> We produce something new only on condition that we repeat – once in the mode which constitutes the past, and once more in the present of the metamorphosis. Moreover, what is produced, the absolutely new itself, is in turn nothing but repetition: the third repetition, this time by excess, the repetition of the future as eternal return. [. . .] Eternal return . . . concerns . . . only the third time of the series. Only there is it determined. That is why it is properly called a belief of the future, a belief in the future.
>
> *(Deleuze 1994: 90)*

Repetition, the event, requires both a forgetting of the past, a disconnection from the given, and simultaneously a 'belief' in, a connection to, what is to come. We arrive here also at a difference between chronological time and the time of repetition, the time which contains within itself the singularities that have been and will come, the time to begin anew, to create. Thus Nietzsche describes the eternal return as a 'gateway' that connects two opposing paths, two eternities: the past and the future, what has been and what is to come (Nietzsche 1961: 178). The gateway is of course the present moment. Eternal return is about following the two paths 'further and further', until they cease to be in opposition, until the present appears like 'a straight line, limitless in either direction' (Deleuze 1990: 165). Through this movement, the 'future' ceases to be something that can be achieved by going forward in chronological time. Rather, one moves into the future by retracing, reinterpreting the past with a view to raising it to a higher level, through the deconstruction and reappropriation of the past (see Rosen 1995: 188). In other words, the eternal return is intrinsically a process through which time attains a quality on the basis of intentionality or a willed act. Life becomes meaningful only through repetition. The ability to repeat is to mark life with the sign of eternity. 'Was that life? Well then! Once more!' (Nietzsche 1961: 178).

In this sense the creation of value in an 'absurd' world is a matter of choice, of affirmation, without any objective ground. Nevertheless, it is possible to live in a world without values, as the 'last man' does, and be content with it. Therefore the 'last man' is also the one who is most frightened by the idea of eternal return, by the event. Because it lacks a meaning and a goal, the life of the last man is in fact a life 'as it is', a life without the possibility of change or a life of an eternal chain of 'absurdities' (Hass 1982: 216). The 'last man' is the one who lacks the will to revolt, to change his futile life, and maintains its groundlessness. His world is a world in which everything is repeated as bare repetition, without difference or consequence: bare repetition as a 'curse', a sign of resignation vis-à-vis the absurd (Nietzsche 1967: 38). Repetition as eternal return, in contrast, aims at overcoming such bare repetition. It is what enables an anti-nihilist revolt that promises new values.

The art of revolt

The redemption which revolt seeks, then, is possible only by a new vision for the future, by tarrying with the abyssal present of eternal return, the groundless ground on which time becomes untimely. It is 'groundless' in the sense that the idea of eternal return offers no guarantee as to the outcome of repetition; repetition is a matter of chance, 'chance and nothing but chance', of affirming chance, because the relation between the actual and the virtual cannot be confined to the workings of a rational causality (see Deleuze 1994: 40, 50). Thus every repetition is like throwing a dice, each single throw is like affirming chance, that is, insisting on becoming and the being of becoming. And as such, as creative repetition, there is an intrinsic link between art and eternal return: 'We want to experience a work of art over and over again! We should fashion our life in this way, so that we have the same wish with each of its parts! This is the main idea!' (Nietzsche 2006: 241).

Nietzsche perceives art as the originary metaphysical power. Thus he evaluates art higher than truth (Agamben 1999b: 92). The artistic 'will to illusion' is more profound, more 'divine', than the will to truth. Illusions, after all, are necessary to live. Only, illusions must not, as nihilism does, be treated as abstract truths. They must be treated as artistic fictions. Seen in this way our values are necessary illusions or fictions to live, to interpret life, to challenge the actual reality. Our illusions are our values, the ways in which we live/interpret life and life interprets/expresses itself through us. A world without illusion would be a hyper-real world devoid of a virtual dimension. Therefore the real danger is not the disappearance of nihilist illusions, for example the religious illusion of the other, 'real world', but the disappearance of illusion as such (Nietzsche 1969: 41). What is relevant is not opposing reality to illusion, which itself is an indication of nihilism, but rather differentiating illusions, for example as affirming or as life negating (Hass 1982: 90).

Significantly, illusion is something created. Hence for Nietzsche the creation of illusions, art, is the 'highest task' of life, the 'proper metaphysical activity' (1996: iv). Art is the ultimate revolt, the main antidote to the problem of nihilism, because it makes life possible, affirms life. It is 'the only superior counterforce to all will to denial of life . . . antinihilist *par excellence*' (Nietzsche 1967: 452). Yet 'art' here is not merely the production of artworks or art critique. The most significant aspect of art is its relation to life. 'Art is the great stimulus to life: how could it be thought purposeless, aimless, *l'art pour l'art?*' (Nietzsche 1969: 81). Of course, a certain form of art can reproduce and defend old values. True art, however, creates new values, taking on the 'most intolerable burden', the task of redemption (Nietzsche 1961: 160).

Revolt then, ideally, is a work of art 'without an artist' (Nietzsche 1967: 225), an art that cannot be reduced to the institutionalized network of art. Similarly, for Nietzsche, politics for the sake of politics is 'petty politics'. 'Grand politics', in contrast, is a politics that can overcome the nihilistic debasement and enslavement, a politics of revolt. Therefore he likes associating his philosophy with a 'crisis', 'a decision evoked against everything', or a 'dynamite' (2004: 97).

Decisive in this context is, again, the relationship between the actual and the virtual. The 'overman', for instance, signifies a potentiality which cannot be identified with an actual actor, for example the Aryan race (see Nietzsche 1961: 43). Likewise, the value of 'freedom' for Nietzsche lies 'not in what one attains with it, but in what one pays for it – what it *costs* us' (Nietzsche 1969: 92). Freedom is valuable only as long as it is 'fought for', as long as it remains a potentiality. As soon as one declares oneself free the concept turns into a monument of levelling, of nihilism. Thus Nietzsche does not find it desirable 'that the kingdom of righteousness and peace should be established on earth', because it 'would be the kingdom of the profoundest mediocrity' (1960: 343). A democracy, for instance, that declares itself to be a final form, a democracy that cannot question itself, can only be a nihilistic form of government. Therefore the socio-political revolt always must have a metaphysical dimension, which is related to the revaluation of 'all values' as a never-ending process.

Slave revolt

There is, in this respect, an intricate relationship between the virtual and the will to power. Power for Nietzsche is not a condition or a state of affairs; it does not refer to actual physical force or political dominance. Rather, it is an activity, a process of overcoming a resistance. Power is not the final or essential goal of the will. In fact, only the 'slave', the weak, can perceive power in this way. Because he wants to take his master's place, to be recognized by him, the 'slave' can only comprehend the 'master' as a triumphant slave. Thus for him power is a matter of recognition and opinion, of representation. Power as representation is both the product of the 'slave' and his only yardstick for action. Yet the problem with representation is that:

> only values which are already current, only accepted values, give criteria of recognition . . . The will to power, understood as the will to get oneself recognized, is necessarily the will to have the values current in a given society attributed to oneself (power, money, honours, reputation).
>
> *(Deleuze 1983: 81)*

In this sense the 'slave' is not necessarily someone dominated by a master. Slavery is basically a situation in which one's will is dominated by passive, reactive forces rather than active ones. In other words, the 'dominators' can also be the bearers of slave morality. Even 'totalitarian regimes are in this sense regimes of slaves, not merely because of the people that they subjugate, but above all because of the type of "masters" they set up' (ibid.: x). In line with this, Nietzsche is not saying that the weak should merely accept their condition and refrain from the desire to create a better, more just world: the weak can, and should, engage in a struggle for power, but this struggle must be a proper power struggle based on 'grand politics' rather than *ressentiment*. What defines *ressentiment* is precisely the collapse of revolt into a slave revolt. '*Ressentiment* itself is always a revolt; the triumph of the weak *as* the weak, the revolt of the slaves and their victory *as* slaves' (ibid.: 116–17). But true freedom is freedom from *ressentiment*. True revolt seeks resistance rather than revenge: 'Equality in the face of the enemy – first presupposition of an *honest* duel' (Nietzsche 2004: 17). Only then can eternal return become the 'pure Event' which is willed and represented in every actual event, the single Event as the sense of all events.

2

THE PROFANE

Darwin's primal horde, the earliest frame of human sociality, is organized around a paternal despot who holds total control over all females, all life, within the horde, forcing his sons into a life of celibacy. But exclusion from enjoyment provokes violence; brothers band together and, demanding justice, kill the father. As such, the primordial revolt implies an excess, a subtraction, or a flight in relation to existing social determinations. But what happens after the revolt? The Darwinian answer is an endless rivalry and conflict among the sons. Freud, however, suggests another possibility. Being cannibals, the brothers devour the murdered father, whom they hated and envied at once. But now, having satisfied their hatred, another, contradictory affection, hitherto repressed, makes itself felt: they feel guilty. As a figure of guilt, the dead father becomes 'stronger than the living one had been' (Freud 1960: 143). The self-imposed repression takes the place of external repression. The sons seek to annul their deed, the revolt, by a twofold solution: prohibiting the killing of the substitute for their father, the totem, and by renouncing their claim to enjoyment, the incest taboo. With time, the totem animal gives birth to the idea of God, while the social structure develops into institutionalized social and political domination, into the state (ibid.: 150).

The result is a series of enslavements, revolts and counter-revolts (Marcuse 1969: 32). Every revolt gives rise to a potentially victorious moment against domination, but this moment does not last; a constitutive element of the dialectic of revolt and counter-revolt is thus self-defeat and betrayal (ibid.: 83). Freud's primordial clan, for instance, betrays, by reaffirming dominance relations, the promise of their own act, the ideal of freedom, a society without fathers (see ibid.: 66).

Significantly in this respect, classical social theory maintains that 'society' is founded on prohibition (of incest, cannibalism and murder). Whether the law is human or natural, of exchange or of taboos and religions, or related to sovereignty, the origin of the social is posited as a 'distinction' between the law and its outside.

Thanks to the law, humans leave the state of nature in order to enter the social. As such, the law is the background against which revolt is defined, as the desire to transgress a prohibiting law. Following this logic, one can postulate that, without any prohibition, there can be nothing to transgress. Likewise, the rule is known through its transgression, what is normal through the pathological and so on. To understand the social bond one thus has to understand what it excludes.

Only, this ontology presupposes the presence of a normality as the background against which transgression can prove itself to be an exception. However, in contemporary permissive society, in which 'pleasure is the rule' (Foucault 1997: 353), such a background tends to dissolve. When exception (pleasure) becomes the norm, the norm (the reality principle) disappears. When power does not prohibit, the traditional dialectic between the law and transgression is ruptured, and the logic of revolt, in so far as it is understood as transgression, reaches a saturation point (Kristeva 1996: 15).

In its classical, ancient Greek conception, the 'law' does not refer to something primary but rather is viewed, in Plato for instance, with respect to its underlying principles or, alternatively, in relation to its consequences. As such, either the law is the expression of a supreme principle, for example the Good, or, from the point of view of its consequences, it is 'best' to obey the law (see Deleuze 1989b: 81). In its modern conception, however, the law becomes a self-referential, pure form without substance or object. In Kant, for instance, the law neither depends on a superior principle such as the Good nor can be sanctioned by the 'best'; rather, the Good itself is regarded as dependent on the law, which functions without making itself known. The law now 'defines a realm of transgression where one is already guilty, and where one oversteps the bounds without knowing what they are' (ibid.: 83–4). The Kafkaesque problem of revolt in this context is 'the impossibility of entering into the already open, of reaching the place where one already is' (Agamben 1999a: 172). How can one revolt, find an 'outside' vis-à-vis an open door?

One possibility is thinking the 'outside' not as a static, unchanging limit to cross but as a movement animated by 'folds', that is, by forces that bend upon themselves (rather than on other forces) in order to deviate or differentiate themselves from power (Deleuze 1988: 97–8, 1995: 98). Understood in this way, 'transgression' lies not in crossing a line but in folding it (Deleuze and Guattari 1987: 9, 36). In this sense revolt necessitates a free assemblage oriented along a line of flight out of the repressive social machinery. This is what Deleuze and Guattari call a 'war machine', which constitutes 'a pure form of exteriority' vis-à-vis the interiority constituted by the state apparatus (ibid.: 354). The sole meaning of 'war' here is 'a social state that wards off the State' (ibid.: 417). A war machine is that which *deviates*, however slowly, from what exists (ibid.: 371).

As such, the war machine constructs an immanent, 'nomadic' outside in relation to the Law. But power itself is always in relation with an outside. 'The State is sovereignty. But sovereignty only reigns over what it is capable of internalizing' (ibid.: 360). Therefore, sovereignty can always, in principle, appropriate, or 'capture', the war machine. Indeed, it is an essential concern of the state not only to defeat nomadic movements as such but to control their mobility (ibid.: 385). Hence there are the two senses of counter-revolt: defeating the war machine and/or revising, regulating its movements. This is also why Deleuze and Guattari distinguish between absolute speed (of deviation/fold) and relative speed (controlled mobility from one point to another).

'Absolute speed' has nothing to do with physical mobility. As is well known, in Deleuze and Guattari's ontology of becoming, everything is in movement. Everything is a mobile and hybrid (mutable) network, or 'assemblage', a process of interaction and connection between heterogeneous elements. What is significant, however, is that assemblages face two tendencies at once: organization and disorganization. In so far as they constitute the relations that result in stratification, assemblages are part of the strata, that is, of actual, extensive reality. But on the other side assemblages face 'something else, the body without organs', which causes disorganization and disarticulation to the strata (ibid.: 40). The 'body without organs' is, like Spinoza's monist 'substance', an all-encompassing flux, a mutable chaos, from which everything emerges and to which everything eternally returns. As such, it is a concept that refers to 'absolute immobility', to absolute disorganization of 'organs'/assemblages.

In other words, what is at play in this mobile ontology is the dialectic of organization and disorganization, connection and disconnection, stratification and de-stratification. This is why 'de-territorialization', for Deleuze and Guattari, is not reducible to physical linear movement but refers, above all, to disorganization, to a deviation from the strata, through a link to the body without organs. Therefore, at the heart of the production of the assemblages, which create the strata, we also find a tendency of anti-production; at the heart of a mobile ontology, we meet immobility: assemblages 'work only when they break down, and continually by breaking down' (1983: 8). Crucially, however, such immobility is not merely a supplement to mobility (e.g. the airport as the immobile support of mobility), or even a consequence of mobility (e.g. sitting motionless during a flight). Rather, the point is that every mobile assemblage exhibits a paradoxical relation to the body without organs, to 'an immobile motor' (ibid.: 141).

Concomitantly, 'becoming a body without organs' is the highest ethical, political and social ideal for Deleuze and Guattari. It is not the empirical mobility of social assemblages as such but their breaking down, relating to the domain of the virtual, their reaching the level of an 'absolute immobility', that creates the new. The new, or what they call the 'line of flight', is always linked to the body without organs; it always emerges as a subtraction from, as a disorganization of the strata. This is also what 'revolution' means to Deleuze: linking society to its body without organs, to its 'immobile motor', by means of which 'the faculty of sociability is raised to its transcendent exercise' (1994: 208). This idea brings to mind Benjamin's (1999) earlier reflections on modern history as a linear mobility and on redemption as stopping this mobility.

Immobility as cheerful separation

> The whole civilized world has heard of Greenwich. [. . .] 'Yes,' he con-
> tinued, with a contemptuous smile, 'the blowing up of the first meridian is
> bound to raise a howl of execration.'
>
> *(Conrad 1985: 68)*

Benjamin depicts 'history' as a pile of pseudo-events, the indistinct flow of chronological, 'empty' time as a catastrophe. Hence his modernity, understood as mobility and progress, is a mobile hell, the ideal of which is bare repetition, the eternal
recurrence of the same non-events which produce no difference. In turn, 'revolution' to Benjamin is the 'emergency brake' of history, which makes it possible to
arrest the indistinct flow, to break free from the historicist conformism (1999: 252–
4). Historicism cannot grasp revolutionary events, because it is preoccupied with
determining causal, spatial and temporal relations between different chronological
moments. But the time of revolution is never chronological time. Revolution is an
event in which 'time stands still and has come to a stop' (Benjamin 1999: 254).

If official history is the history of the winners, the silenced past of the oppressed
carries within it another temporality, by which history is referred to redemption.
Only redemption can make the 'fullness' of the past possible, can 'fill' time by linking the present to the whole of the past (ibid.: 245). Redemption, revolution, is a
'leap into the past', an act of tearing 'the past from its context, destroying it, in order
to return it, transfigured, to its origin' (ibid.: 253–5; Agamben 1999a: 152). Thus,
if history repeats itself as farce, if in pseudo-history the tragic reappears as comedy,
this is not necessarily a reason for melancholic detachment but rather an occasion
for a joyful separation – history has this course 'so that humanity should part with
its past *cheerfully*' (Marx 1975: 179; see also Agamben 1999a: 154). 'Happiness' is a
cheerful separation from pseudo-history, from bare repetition. It is the affirmation
of an immanent form of life that cannot be captured, or 'sacralized' by the sovereign exception, an 'absolutely profane', autonomous life opposed to sovereignty
(Agamben 2000: 115). Hence there is the essential political question: 'is it possible
to have a *political* community that is ordered exclusively for the full enjoyment of
worldly life?' (ibid.: 114).

Happiness is the idea on which 'the order of the profane' must be erected (Benjamin 1979b: 155). In this context, Benjamin draws a sharp distinction between
the empty time of chronology and the time of the event. The time of revolution
is the messianic time. But he insists that the 'Kingdom of God' is not, as is the case
with messianic eschatology, the *telos* of historical development (ibid.). The domain
of the profane cannot be established on the idea of the Divine Kingdom, for there
is no direct path from theology to the political. Nothing actual can relate to the
virtual by itself, and the actual cannot be constituted on the idea of the virtual. This,
however, does not mean that there is no mediation between the two.

Even though the order of the profane should be built upon the idea of happiness, of free humanity, and even though this idea runs counter to the messianic

'Kingdom of God', there is a solution to the problem. *Kairos* is what mediates the two domains. The moment when the actual world 'touches' the virtual domain, 'when they interlock', is the *kairos* (Taubes 2009: 68). In this sense, the profane (the actual) is necessary for the approach of the Messianic Kingdom (the virtual). Just as in Nietzsche two forces acting in opposite directions increase one another, 'so the order of the profane assists, through being profane, the coming of the Messianic Kingdom' (Benjamin 1979b: 155).

In this sense *kairos*, the time of revolution, is opposed to chronological time. But it is not external to it. Rather, it is an 'operational' time internal to chronology, transforming it from within:

> Whereas our representation of chronological time, as the time *in which* we are, separates us from ourselves and transforms us into impotent spectators of ourselves – spectators who look at the time that flies without any time left, continually missing themselves – messianic time, an operational time in which we take hold of and achieve our representations of time, is the time *that* we ourselves are, and for this very reason, is the only real time, the only time we have.
>
> *(Agamben 2005a: 68)*

Kairos is a 'seized' *chronos*, the time in which 'man' autonomously seizes the moment, 'chooses his own freedom', in opposition to chronological time (ibid.: 69; Agamben 2007: 115). As the temporal dimension of the event, *kairos* signifies the timing of actualization, that is, the recognition, articulation, and decision to seize the moment. It is the moment of opportunity, which can be grasped by a strategic decision, by an untimely intervention, on the basis of reading the symptoms, signs, available in a given situation, 'acting into time to change the course of time' (Dillon 2008: 13; see also Vatter 2000). But why, in the first place, is it necessary to seize the moment? It is necessary because there is a promise involved in *kairos*: the promise of the new. Indeed,

> thinking in terms of creation, time is all-decisive, not empty time, pure expiration; not mere duration either, but rather qualitatively fulfilled time, the moment that is creation and fate. We call this fulfilled moment, the moment of time approaching us as fate and decision, *Kairos*.
>
> *(Tillich 1936: 129)*

It must be emphasized that this promissory aspect of *kairos* is not necessarily messianic in a religious sense; *kairos* is not the Messiah (see Dillon 2008: 14). Messianism is not necessarily a religious experience. Thus, within the communist and democratic traditions there is a messianism which is not reducible to religion through any deconstruction. What is irreducible in this 'messianism without religion' is an experience of the 'emancipatory promise' (Derrida 1994: 74), a promise whose effectivity keeps within itself an 'eschatological relation to the to-come of an event *and* of a singularity, of an alterity that cannot be anticipated' (ibid.: 81). This promise is an 'absolutely undetermined messianic hope', that is, its content is not, in contrast to religion, determined. In this respect there is a crucial difference between religious repetition and the repetition specific to non-religious messianism. In religious repetition a pre-established identity (e.g. the child of Abraham, the resurrected body, the recovered self) returns and does so 'once and for all'; in the eternal return, in contrast, and this is the repetition that pertains to messianism without religion, what returns returns 'for an infinite number of times', without bringing back any ready-made identity, without restoring the self, the world, and God:

> In the circle of Dionysus, Christ will not return; the order of the Antichrist chases the other order away. All of that which is founded on God and makes a negative or exclusive use of the disjunction is denied and excluded by the eternal return.
>
> *(Deleuze 1990: 301)*

In Derrida's words, the 'alterity' of that which returns in non-religious messianism 'cannot be anticipated'. The absolute difference of the event forecloses the return of the absolute as a religious figure, and what is 'to come', the future, remains unpredictable, that is, new. The Last Judgement will not occur. Instead, the messianic return demands a 'messianic opening to what is coming, that is, to the event that cannot be awaited *as such*, or recognized in advance' (Derrida 1994: 81). Non-religious messianism is a 'call', a 'promise' of the new, which always comes in the shape of emancipation, justice and peace, a promise independent of the three monotheistic religions, even when they oppose one another, for it holds to the anti-nihilist belief that 'faith without religion' is possible (Derrida 2004). In such a messianism there is only a paradoxical process of political becoming through which politics is permanently required to revolutionize itself, to refer itself to its groundless ground, to the time of the event.

Concomitantly, there is a significant difference between the present as *kairos* and the 'end of time' understood in terms of chronology. To be sure, the kairological present is coextensive with the chronological present. However, it cannot be reduced to it; it stands in for a momentary leap from the continuum of *chronos*, a contracted moment in which the present, the past and the future merge together, rectifying the past injustices and constituting a different future. In this sense, *kairos* is an indispensable dimension of the event, that which brings the new into existence, which, in turn, expresses it. Therefore it coincides with neither the chronological moment nor the end of chronological time as the 'last moment'. What is interesting regarding *kairos* is not the apocalyptic last day, in which time ends, 'but the time that remains between time and its end' (Agamben 2005a: 62).

Then the question is what is required from the subject in this evental 'moment'. It is crucial in this respect to recall that the decision-making at work in *kairos* is not merely a strategic, rational act; while one 'seizes' the moment, one must also be 'seized' by the moment. Confronted with the potentiality of the event, the 'prom-ise' of the new, one must be able to affirm this potentiality. In this sense *kairos* is an act which forms one's ethos, an ethical act: being in the moment, one is formed by the moment. To use Nietzsche's phrase, you become what you are in *kairos*. In kairological time one 'is always in the position of deciding and being decided' (Dillon 2008: 13). Therefore the problem of *kairos* is never merely an epistemologi-cal problem related to knowing which moment to seize. *Kairos* requires fidelity, too; it demands an appropriate response from the subject, which is, paradoxically, constituted in the very moment of response. Thus what is really at stake in *kairos* is to interweave 'seizing' with 'being seized', strategic timing of the event with fidel-ity to the event, for without such fidelity 'the very opening of the world itself is endangered' (ibid.: 13–14).

The double of *kairos*

> The tradition of the oppressed teaches us that the 'state of emergency' in which we live is not the exception but the rule. We must attain to a concep-tion of history that is in keeping with this insight. Then we shall clearly real-ize that it is our task to bring about a real state of emergency.
>
> *(Benjamin 1999: 248)*

'Power by its mechanisms', Foucault insists, 'is infinite', which does not mean that there is nothing to do against it – the opposite is the case – but the 'rules' that seek to limit power will never be up to this task, will never manage 'to take away from it all the opportunities that it seizes' (Foucault 2005: 266). Can it 'seize' or capture *kairos* too? This is what Benjamin suggests above by juxtaposing two versions of the state of exception: the actual state of exception in which we live and a 'real' one, which can redeem us from the first. There is, in other words, a structural resem-blance between *kairos* (as the time of the event – of revolt) and the state exception (see Agamben 2005b: 2). How does one make sense of this ambivalence? Let us start with sovereignty as an instance of counter-revolt.

Consider Hobbes's two monsters, Leviathan and Behemoth, the gigantic sea monster and the earth monster, both known from the book of Job (see Hob-bes 1985, 2007). Leviathan is Hobbes's early modern, absolutist solution to the problem of revolt: a sovereign state, in which all subjects have the same relation to the sovereign, just as all humans are related to God in the same way. Hobbes's conception of sovereignty is a secularized, political reformulation of the theological relationship between God and his subjects. The state of nature, in which no social bond, no morality and no duty exist, is overcome with the emergence of political order, when all voluntarily surrender their power to the sovereign.

Behemoth, on the other hand, is the harbinger of chaos and serves as an image of a ubiquitous danger of revolt. Thus it is countered by Leviathan, sovereignty. The state, a precondition for society in this perspective, expresses the individuals' free, rational will. But Leviathan also has a mythical capacity to instil fear in its subjects.

The political is created *ex nihilo*, through a formal process of naming, by distinguishing friend and enemy, like a theological 'miracle' that cannot be explained rationally (Schmitt 1985: 36). Yet this *political* theology is secular, for it is the miracle of the sovereign, not of God, that 'creates' the social world.

Hobbes's Leviathan is a reaction to the revolutionary situation in England in the sixteenth century, Schmitt's theory of sovereignty to the chaotic condition of Germany after the First World War. They share a fear of chaos, revolt. Consequently, in both theories sovereignty is what establishes social order and protects it from falling back upon an anomic condition. Schmitt thus emphasizes that Hobbes's state of nature, characterized by envy, hostility and the war of all against all, should not be understood as a chronological period preceding the formation of the society or the law. On the contrary, Hobbes evokes the state of nature, and thus revolt, as a retroactive counter-image to the *polis*, as a potential situation that can be re-actualized at any time (Agamben 1998: 105–06).

This reoccurrence of nature *within* society is the necessary background for political theory. In so far as this recurrence signifies revolt or revolution, order cannot do without the myth of sovereignty, of the conflict between order and chaos. Thus for Schmitt the question of order is *the* question of politics. He identifies order with a *nomos*, a principle of ordering, which does not refer to the law but to what lies behind the law. His core concept in this respect is sovereignty. The sovereign is the one who decides over the exception (Schmitt 1985: 5). Significantly, the state of exception is limited in space and time. In *this* period and within *this* space it is as if the Statue of Liberty has been veiled. Law is, however, not suspended totally, or the state of exception is not a chaos. Rather, in the state of exception the distinction between order and chaos becomes obscure. The violence exercised 'neither preserves nor simply posits law, but rather conserves it in suspending it and posits it in excepting itself from it' (ibid.: 64).

The exception does not subtract itself from the rule; rather, the rule, suspending itself, gives rise to the exception. The particular 'force' of law consists in this capacity to maintain itself in relation to an exteriority (ibid.: 18). Thus the state of exception means that in exceptional circumstances, such as revolt, the law can be suspended (Agamben 2005b: 42). However, this abandonment of the law takes place not in the form of a transgression of the law but rather *instead* of transgression (ibid.: 50). Since the exception has no positive content, what takes place is rather the 'inexecution' of the law, an action whose content is undecidable from the point of view of the law. Therefore the state of exception 'is a zone of anomie in which all legal determinations . . . are deactivated' (ibid.: 50–1).

The law basically displays three characteristics in the state of exception. First, there emerges a zone of indistinction between inside and outside. Since the law suspends itself, it comes, paradoxically, to include what it excludes, its outside, and 'in including its outside . . . it coincides with reality itself' (Agamben 2005a: 105). Following this, second, it becomes impossible to distinguish between obedience to the law and its transgression. The law, in its auto-suspension, is by definition unknowable and unobservable. And third, this unobservability coincides with another impossibility, that of formulating the content of the law. In other words, the law ceases to have the form of a prohibition. As one cannot know or articulate what is legal or illegal, transgression becomes impossible. Or, conversely, when the law functions in terms of rules that are impossible to formulate 'everything' becomes 'possible' (ibid.: 106).

The structural homology between the state of exception and *kairos* is crucial at this point because these three characteristics – the disappearance of the inside–outside divide, the unobservability of the law, and its unformulability – appear in the messianic deactivation of the law too. Paul's messianism is a case in point. Here, the messianic figure of the law, 'the law of faith', which can be rendered as 'justice without law', also suspends the law through deactivation, while this deactivation does not eliminate the law, reducing it to nothing, but preserves it, opening up a space of indeterminacy between the inside and the outside (Agamben 2005a: 100, 2007: 107). The consequence of this is the unobservability of the law, which finds its expression in the radical shortening of Moses' commandment ('Do not desire the woman, the house, the slave, the mule . . . of thy neighbour') by Paul as 'Do not desire' (Agamben 2005a: 108). Since this is not really a commandment, what follows is the Kafkaesque impossibility of observing or formulating a clear prohibition; 'instead, the law is only the knowledge of guilt' (ibid.). And significantly, such unobservability can only be restored by faith. Thus Paul divides the law into two, into a this-worldly law of sin on the one hand and a law of faith on the other, thus rendering it inoperative and unobservable – he 'can then fulfill and recapitulate the law in the figure of love' (ibid.).

Following this, the political task is not to restore the link between exception and the law, reaffirming the primacy of the law, for instance by trying to bring the state of exception back to the domain of the law. The state of exception is not an accidental addition to the workings of power but its central aspect, its fundamental secret. What is necessary is to bring to light this secret, to illuminate the tension between life and the law (Agamben 2005b: 86–7).

> Alongside the movement that seeks to keep them in relation at all costs, there is a countermovement that, working in an inverse direction in law and in life, always seeks to loosen what has been artificially and violently linked. That is to say, in the field of tension of our culture, two opposite forces act, one that institutes and makes, and one that deactivates and deposes. The state of exception is both the point of their maximum tension and – as it coincides with the law – that which threatens today to render them indiscernible.
>
> *(Ibid.: 87)*

Regarding this tension, the contrast between Schmitt and Benjamin is illuminating. Schmitt insists that the distinction between friend and enemy is only a formal, performative distinction, that the sole function of the 'enemy' is the establishment of the political. Therefore, in his political theology, the state (constituted power) and the political (constituting power) do not necessarily coincide. However, since the figure of the 'friend' is the citizen of the state, it comes to attain a more determining role regarding the state than the enemy, and, consequently, the state indirectly becomes the foundation for the political (Derrida 1997: 120). In Benjamin, in contrast, the state is not the starting point. The state of exception concerns not a suspension of the law to safeguard its existence but, precisely, its deactivation.

Here we approach the difference between Benjamin's two exceptions, between the state of exception, in which 'the state continues to exist, while law recedes' (Schmitt, quoted in Agamben 2005b: 31), and revolution, in which both the state and the law recede. Benjamin, in other words, divides the concept of exception into two by juxtaposing to Schmitt's exception another, an exception to exception itself, or 'a real exception'. Whereas Schmitt wants to legitimize state power, Benjamin criticizes it. Schmitt is conservative, Benjamin revolutionary. Whereas in Schmitt exception is the political kernel of the law, it becomes revolutionary or divine violence in Benjamin.

Benjamin differentiates revolutionary violence from the law-preserving violence and the law-making violence. Revolutionary violence is a 'pure' violence in the sense that it exists outside both. It is an absolutely exterior potential that cannot be accommodated, captured or neutralized by Schmitt's state of exception. This is also why Schmitt grounds the necessity of the sovereign 'decision' in the form of a violence that 'suspends' rather than makes or preserves the law (Agamben 2005b: 53–5). In contrast, for Benjamin the question is how to deactivate the law.

> If mythic violence is law-making, divine violence is law-destroying; if the former sets boundaries, the latter boundlessly destroys them; if mythical violence brings at once guilt and retribution, divine power only expiates; if the former threatens, the latter strikes; if the former is bloody, the latter is lethal without spilling blood.
>
> *(Benjamin 1979a: 150–1)*

Mythic violence targets the bare life of *homo sacer*. Divine violence, on the other hand, belongs to the domain of life, whose potentiality is denied by bare life. As such, it opposes the nihilism of the sovereign power by setting 'all life', life as virtual potentiality, as excess, up against the actual, 'bare' physicality of life. Like God's judgement, it strikes the privileged without warning, annihilates without threat, but, in annihilation, also 'expiates' the guilt of bare life, purifying the guilty (not of guilt but) of law as such: 'mythical violence is bloody power over mere life for its own sake, divine violence is pure power over all life for the sake of the living' (ibid.).

Ultimately, while Schmitt understands sovereign violence as a 'miracle', Benjamin 'profanates' political theology, redefining both sovereignty and violence in immanent terms, as profane functions that cannot be depoliticized and contained, as Schmitt wanted, within the domain of the law (Agamben 2005b: 57–64). In this sense, what is at stake in the Benjamin–Schmitt debate is revolt, revolutionary violence, a pure and immediate violence 'that might be able to call a halt to mythical violence' (Benjamin 1979a: 150), provided that 'pure' here is not thought of as a substantial feature of 'pure violence'; rather, the difference between sovereign violence and revolutionary violence 'does not lie in the violence itself, but in its relation to something external' (Agamben 2005b: 61), that is, in its relation to justice and the deactivation of the law.

Is the 'utopia' of revolutionary violence, then, lawlessness? 'Happiness' is not the lack of law as such but a 'new law', a law emancipated from sovereignty and transcendence. It is not a final goal or an ultimate salvation from the law: the 'new', deactivated law is not justice but only that which opens up the possibility of justice. 'What opens a passage toward justice is not the erasure of law, but its deactivation and inactivity . . . that is, another use of the law' (ibid.: 64): 'another use', which 'profanates' the law, turning what is sacred into something common again, into a 'good that absolutely cannot be appropriated or made juridical' (ibid.).

In this sense, revolt or revolution no longer refers to a struggle to control the state. Rather, it becomes the means for a bio-political struggle between the state and the non-state. What matters in this struggle is singularities not (yet) captured by the state. What the state cannot tolerate is, above all, a community of singularities that do not form an identity, singularities which have no claim to the state as such but rather articulate a way of being which cannot be included in the existing order and thus disrupts its system of counting imposed on singularities. As such, regardless of its particular content, the demand to remain singular is at the heart of any radical politics (Agamben 1993: 85–7).

The aporia

But is it possible to completely separate revolutionary or divine violence from sovereign violence? Revolutionary violence, for example the killing of the oppressor, can be rejected with reference to the sanctity of life or to human rights, by maintaining that the 'revolutionary terrorist' values happiness and justice more highly than existence. Benjamin rejects this rejection in so far as 'existence' means bare life, life reduced to its biological determination (Benjamin 1979a: 152). For bare life is not life. However, despite life not being reducible to bare life, 'existence' is indispensable to life. Therefore an aporia is inescapable in the context of divine violence. On the one hand, there can be no pre-existing objective (actual, profane) criterion or measure to account for the violence of the revolutionary act. Yet, on the other hand, although it cannot be reduced to its actual circumstances, to the profane, divine violence can only 'express' itself through the profane. As a revolutionary act that intervenes in the course of time to change time, revolutionary or divine violence involves a radical contingency, for it cannot provide a definitive 'measure' of necessary violence (Dillon 2008: 11). And in the lack of a 'calculus', because it is impossible to draw an absolute line between creative and unproductive violence, revolutionary violence can always, potentially, turn into radical nihilism or appear to do so.

But since there can be no abstract aporia, this aporia, too, must be lived out. At any rate, the violence inherent in *kairos* involves the suspension of the existing order.

Revolt consists in a contingent decision which transcends the actual. Therefore, from the perspective of the actual, that is, in the perspective of the existing laws of the constituted order, such acts necessarily appear as an excess that introduces an irrational, 'impossible' element into the heart of the actual order (Žižek 1992: 44). First afterwards, when a new order is re-established, the act retroactively grounds itself and assumes a positive, determinate character. For this to happen, however, the initial violence is unavoidable: 'there is none the less something inherently "terroristic" in every authentic act, in its gesture of thoroughly redefining the "rules of the game", inclusive of the very basic self-identity of its perpetrator' (Žižek 1999: 377–8). In this sense, revolutionary violence is deprived of any assurance in the existing social order, 'any guarantee in the big Other' (ibid.: 380).

3

REVOLT AS PURE POLITICS

In an amusing scene in Fincher's *Fight Club*, the protagonist, Jack, knocks at his boss's door and enters, standing in the doorway, looking dishevelled. Jaunty, electronic music is playing. His boss is writing at his desk.

'We need to talk,' Jack says.

His boss puts the lid on his pen. 'OK,' he says, taking his glasses off, 'with your constant absenteeism, with your unpresentable appearance, you're up for review.'

Now sitting opposite the boss, and unsurprised, Jack replies: 'Let's pretend. You're the Department of Transportation, OK. Someone informs you that this company installs front-seat mounting brackets that never pass collision tests, brake linings that fail after a thousand miles, and fuel injectors that explode and burn people alive. What then?'

'Are you threatening me?'

'No.'

'Get the fuck out of here. You're fired!'

'I have a better solution. You keep me on the payroll as an outside consultant. In exchange for my salary, my job will be never to tell people these things that I know. I don't even have to come into the office; I can do this job alone.'

The boss looks at him incredulously. 'Who . . . who the fuck do you think you are, you crazy little shit?' He stands up and picks up the phone to call security.

Jack looks down at his hand. It is trembling and flexing, like the mechanical hand of an automaton. It twists and rises, punching him in the face and knocking him off the chair as though no longer his own hand. The boss, still holding the phone, lowers it slightly, looking at Jack in disbelief.

'What the hell are you doing?' Jack says to him before punching himself again and falling back, through the glass coffee table. Mechanically, he sits up. 'Why would you do that?' he says to his boss, who is standing, watching the spectacle. Then Jack shouts, 'My God! No! Please stop,' before grabbing himself by the collar and dragging himself across the room and back. He grabs at his hand with his other hand, as if in mock effect to try to stop it. 'What are you doing? Oh God, no! Please! No!' he says, looking behind himself at the glass shelving. He then throws himself back, crashing through the tiers of glass shelving before reaching the floor. He punches himself again, twice, always with his right hand. Bloodied now, he crawls across the once pristine office, pulling himself along the chairs, towards his boss, who is still standing motionless, disturbed by what he has witnessed. The camera cuts to his boss's appalled expression, his business cards in a box, his name bar on his desk, and between each of these camera movements the image returns to Jack's crawling along the floor. When he reaches the feet of his boss, he grabs at his trousers and begins to pull himself up. 'Look,' he says, as his boss tries to free himself of him, 'give me the pay cheques, like I asked, and you won't ever see me again.'

'And right then at our most excellent moment together . . .' two security guards enter the office and the music stops. Jack drops to the floor, saying 'Thank God. Please don't hit me again.' And already before the image cuts to the next scene, we hear Jack beginning to list, 'telephone, computer, fax machine, 52 weekly pay cheques and 48 airline coupons'. Next we see him wheeling these items out in a trolley bloodied and whistling casually, followed by two security guards. His Fight Club now has 'corporate sponsorship'.

This expertly made comic scene tells a lot about the relation between revolt and subjectivity. There are four obvious dimensions to Jack's subjectivity: his anxiety, its relation to the superego, his courage to stage a masochistic performance, and his determination as to achieving a 'contract' with his boss, which changes the coordinates of his reality.

The source of Jack's anxiety is a disruption in the socio-symbolic space, in 'reality'. In the social context within which the scene is located there is no symbolic authority, only an experience of a flattened, post-Oedipal social space, personified in the dull stupidity of the boss. Jack confronts a void in the place of reality – hence the uncanny sentiment of an uncontrollable disintegration which Jack experiences when his hand starts moving as if it were an 'organ without body' independent of Jack's consciousness or will (see Žižek 2004: 173).

This brings us to the second dimension, the superego, or the law as a self-referential, pure, unknowable injunction, which cannot be translated into an explicit rule set. The superego signifies the non-existence of a 'proper measure', which is why, 'whatever one does, the result is wrong and one is guilty' (Žižek 1999: 394). Hence there is the paradox of the superego: the more one obeys it, the guiltier one feels. This is why the superego is a source of anxiety. Since it is purely formal, the law cannot spell out its content, name an object, without contradicting itself; its repression resides, precisely, in its empty form. Consequently, with the superego, the object of the law and the object of desire overlap: the law is nothing else than repressed desire (Deleuze 1989b: 85). Thus revolt cannot take place only at the level of public social roles; one needs to deal with the libidinal economy which sustains them as well. The servant must confront his own libidinal attachment to the master; Jack must beat himself.

> Even on a purely formal level, the fact of beating oneself up reveals the simple fact that *the master is superfluous*: 'Who needs you to terrorize me? I can do it myself!' So it is only through first beating up (hitting) *oneself* that one becomes free: the true goal of this beating is to beat out that in me which attaches me to the master.
>
> *(Žižek 2002b: 252)*

Since subjection is an embodied relation, one cannot liberate oneself from it only through intellectual reflection; emancipation must be 'staged' at the level of bodily practices as well (ibid.: 253). There are two diametrically opposed strategies in this context: sadism and masochism. Sade's strategy is to attack the law by virtue of a higher principle opposed to it, the principle of Evil, which functions as an obscene superego figure, as a higher law 'placed above the laws' (Deleuze 1989b: 90). In this sense, the sadist is a subject 'reduced to a pure superego', and thus can only find an ego in his victims, experiencing the outside as his only ego (ibid.: 124–5). In masochism, by contrast, the law is not subverted by an upward movement, by ascending from the law to a superior principle. Rather, masochism attempts at demonstrating the 'absurdity' of the law by reducing the law to its consequences:

> The masochist regards the law as a punitive process and therefore begins by having the punishment inflicted upon himself; once he has undergone the punishment, he feels that he is allowed or indeed commanded to experience the pleasure that the law was supposed to forbid. The essence of masochistic humor lies in this, that the very law which forbids the satisfaction of a desire under threat of subsequent punishment is converted into one which demands the punishment first and then orders that the satisfaction of the desire should necessarily follow upon the punishment.
>
> *(Ibid.: 88–9)*

The masochist reverses the relationship between punishment and guilt by turning the first into a condition (rather than a consequence) for the latter. In this sense, masochism is not just the opposite of sadism but has its own function, the destruction of the superego by the ego (ibid.: 125). If the structure of the superego essentially pertains to sadism, masochism, in contrast, is a procedure through which the superego is destroyed. 'Sadism involves a relationship of domination, while masochism is the first step towards liberation' (Žižek 2002b: 253).

The next dimension of Jack's subjectivity is courage. It is through courage that the actor becomes worthy of the event. What is significant here is the structure of the event. First, Jack's act defines the past, the before, in which the event has no place and thus seems impossible or crazy, as is evidenced by the boss's reaction. Second, the act defines a present, the time of a 'metamorphosis' through which Jack becomes capable of the act. And finally, the act defines a future from which the agent himself is excluded (see Deleuze 1994: 89). In a sense, therefore, Jack is a vanishing mediator who performs his own disappearance from the old 'reality', which, in turn, makes a new beginning possible for him. Crucially in this respect, Jack's self-beating is a process of subjective destitution.

> Why is suicide the act *par excellence*? The act differs from an active intervention (action) in that it radically transforms its bearer (agent): the act is not simply something I 'accomplish' – after an act, I'm literally 'not the same as before'. In this sense, we could say that the subject 'undergoes' the act ('passes through' it) rather than 'accomplishes' it: in it, the subject is annihilated and subsequently reborn (or not), i.e., the act involves a temporary eclipse, *aphanisis*, of the subject. Which is why every act worthy of this name is 'mad' in the sense of radical *unaccountability*: by means of it, I put at stake everything, including myself, my symbolic identity; the act is therefore always a 'crime', a 'transgression', namely of the limit of the symbolic community to which I belong.
>
> *(Žižek 1992: 44)*

Yet an act is not reducible to the destruction of reality. Rather it is an involvement with changing its coordinates, with the question of justice (see Žižek 2001a: 167). Thus, in our scene, while demolishing the existing economy of desire between himself and his boss, Jack also opens up the space for another, redefined economy, which finds its expression in a new 'contract', the 'corporate sponsorship'. What is significant here is not the content of the contract but its form, which is indispensable to the masochist gesture. Whereas sadism tends towards the humiliation and destruction of all laws with reference to a superior power, the superego, the specific impulse involved in the masochist gesture is towards creating, generating a new law, even if the law might, in future, impose its own authority upon the contract itself (Deleuze 1989b: 77). What we have in Jack's case is therefore, at a formal level, a redefinition of the value of values as well as their destruction. A new economy is necessary, for there is no escape from the actual symbolic economy: there is no outside, only lines of flight, a moment of revolt that can disrupt the old economy and, hopefully, probably, install a new one. As such, as well as disturbing the underlying fantasy, there is in Jack's masochistic gesture something that affects the symbolic space itself.

Pure politics

How do these four dimensions of the subject (anxiety, superego, courage and justice) relate to politics? To discuss this, let us first turn to Badiou's ontology. Badiou's focus is on the fundamental conflict between being and event, on the irreducibility of the event to history. An event always appears as an excess in relation to its historical context, its situation. At the same time, however, it can only express itself locally, through an actual situation. Thus the situation is a condition, but one to be transcended by the event.

Here, a situation is defined like a set in mathematics, that is, as a collection of multiplicities also called elements or members. In every situation the multiple is 'presented' as a unity, 'counted as one', through an operation of unification (Badiou 2006a: 23). However, in every situation, there remain inconsistent multiplicities which cannot be unified into this 'one'. Hence there is always a gap between the oneness of a situation and the pure multiple that cannot be assimilated into it. This pure multiple is a 'void', a 'nothing' (ibid.: 53, 57). But it is not a non-being; it is real, even though it is not counted. In this sense, the relationship between the situation and the void is homological to the relationship between the 'real' and 'reality' in psychoanalysis (see Badiou 2009a: 37–43). Just as the Lacanian 'real' signifies that which cannot be symbolized in 'reality', the void in Badiou is what cannot be 'placed', what is 'out of place', in the situation. However, the void is constitutive. It makes the presentation of the multiple possible (Badiou 2006a: 69).

> What ontology theorizes is the inconsistent multiple of any situation; that is, the multiple subtracted from any particular law, from any count-as-one – the a-structured multiple. The proper mode in which inconsistency wanders within the whole of a situation is the nothing, and the mode in which it un-presents itself is that of subtraction from the count, the non-one, the void. The absolutely primary theme of ontology is therefore the void.
>
> *(Ibid.: 58)*

To deal with this void, which originates in its own structure, and which remains an inherent source of instability, the situation needs to be doubled. Thus, every situation is 'structured twice', by its own structure and by the metastructure, also called the 'state of the situation' (ibid.: 94). The metastructure ensures that the gap between consistent and inconsistent multiplicities is avoided (ibid.). Two fundamental concepts in Badiou's ontology, belonging and inclusion, are crucial in this regard. While the initial structure guarantees belonging, the metastructure holds for inclusion (ibid.: 97). Therefore 'belonging' to a situation and 'inclusion' in it do not necessarily overlap. A term which is not included in a situation may be a member of it, belong to it. Or a term which is not a member of a situation may be included in it. Thus membership (being presented in a situation) and inclusion (being represented in that situation) are different things. There are, in this context, three possibilities. A term is defined as being 'normal' if it both belongs to and is included in a situation, 'excrescent' if it is included/represented without membership/presentation, and 'singular' if it is present without being represented, a member without being included (see ibid.: 99–100). The 'excrescent' element emerges owing to an excess. Since any present multiplicity can be represented in many different ways, there is always an actual excess of inclusion over membership (Hallward 2003:103–04). Inversely, the 'singular' is present in the situation yet cannot be represented. Thus, from the perspective of the 'state of the situation', the singular does not exist (Badiou 2006a: 97).

In the classical Marxist scheme, for instance, the normal term is the bourgeoisie, which is presented both economically and socially, while it is represented by the state. The singular term is the proletariat, which is present but not represented.

And the excrescent term is the state. Badiou's ontology offers two critical points in relation to this scheme. First, in this scheme, the excrescence of the state does not refer to the 'unrepresentable' void but rather to 'differences in presentation', to the differences between the ways in which the normal and singular terms belong to the whole society. Thus, second, the antagonism between the normal and the singular becomes the foundation of the state. Therefore classical Marxism assumes that, on the basis of the modification of these differences, that is, with the becoming universal of the singular, the state will disappear (ibid.: 109). The problem here is a double reduction as to the void and the excess: reducing the void to the non-repre-sentation of the singular (the proletariat) and the metastructure to an excess that can be eliminated on the basis of the antagonism between normality (the bourgeoisie interests that cannot be universalized) and the singularity (of the proletariat):

> It is not antagonism which lies at the origin of the State because one cannot think the dialectic of the void and excess as antagonism. No doubt politics itself must originate in the very same place as the State: in that dialectic. But this is certainly not in order to seize the State nor to double the State's effect. On the contrary, politics stakes its existence on its capacity to establish a relation to both the void and excess which is essentially different from that of the State; it is this difference alone that subtracts politics from the one of statist re-insurance.
>
> *(Ibid.: 110)*

The contradiction between the event and the situation is based on a purely struc-tural principle. The event always occurs as the scission of the structure, a process in which 'one divides into two' (Badiou 2009a: 14). There is no unity, no political identity that is not split by the minimal difference caused by such scission (ibid.: 6). The primacy of scission means that the decisive contradiction is not between two elements set against each other within the same structure but rather between an element and its place within that structure. The true adversary of the 'proletariat' as a class, for instance, is not the bourgeoisie as another class but the whole bourgeois world. True politics aims at changing the situation as a whole.

The event, in this sense, is a relation to the void. But it also relates to the excess. Since the state of the situation is always in excess of the situation itself, 'representa-tion' is of a higher power than 'presentation'. This excess, which expresses itself as repression and alienation in empirical situations, is not measurable in itself. There-fore one normally relates to the state 'without ever being able to assign a measure to its power' (Badiou 2005a: 144). Only in exceptional situations does the event 'pre-scribe' a measure to this excess 'through the emergence of the subject' (ibid.: 146). Thus, when an event occurs, the state 'reveals itself' (ibid.: 145). What is revealed is not only the excrescent nature of the state, its excessive power, its repression, but also a measure for this excess. 'Politics puts the State at a distance, in the distance of its measure' (ibid.).

Paradoxically, however, this measurement can take place only *after* the event, because from the point of view of a situation there can be no criterion to determine an event. The event can be interpreted and 'named' as an event only retroactively, as the intervention of a decision that gives the event its consistency. Naming interprets and identifies the elements that belong or do not belong to the event.

> When Rosa Parks refuses to give up her bus seat to a white person in Montgomery, Alabama in 1955, this is an event. There were others before her who also refused. What makes her refusal an event is the fidelity to her act by other committed activists. And it is only in retrospect that we realize that hers was an event while the previous refusals were not.
>
> *(May 2008)*

The event is a 'precarious', 'rare' occurrence (Badiou 2005a: 71, 2006a: 344–5). It is exceptional in the sense that it disengages, exempts itself from the prescriptions of the existing situation (Hallward 2003: 27). But this exceptionalism must not be confused with Schmitt's. The event in Badiou is not a finite, once-and-for-all decision based on the sovereign will, but rather a succession of decisions that seek to preserve fidelity to a past event in the light of changing circumstances (Krips 2007: 8–9). Therefore he assigns the possibility of an event 'to the consequences of another event', by placing it within the network of previous decisions. A political intervention is that which 'presents an event for the occurrence of another' (Badiou 2006a: 209). This is why an event is always missed the first time; fidelity always emerges as a 'resurrection', that is, as a repetition (Žižek 2007c: 6, 2008b: 387).

Since the consequences of an event cannot be determined once and for all, only a disciplined procedure can preserve the nature of the event in its consequences. The foundation of the event is fidelity, a discipline of time, which controls and discerns the connection of the event to chance (Badiou 2006a: 211). Fidelity, however, does not mean the closing off of the event to contestation, dogmatism. On the contrary, that the 'decision' to name an event necessarily exceeds the situation implies that any legitimacy of the event is always open to contestation (Callinicos 2006: 102). In other words, fidelity is not conformity to an already established rule; it is sustaining the event in the face of potential contingencies, preserving its infinity through new interpretations (Krips 2007: 6). In this sense politics is a matter of principle, an act of choosing. It consists in fidelity to an axiomatic principle: egalitarianism. But egalitarianism here does not signify an objective, distributive content (e.g. status, income, or egalitarian reforms). Equality is a purely subjective prescription, a 'political maxim' that has nothing to do with the social (Badiou 2005a: 98).

> We have too often wished for justice to found the consistency of the social bond, whereas in reality it can only name the most extreme moments of inconsistency. For the effect of the axiom of equality is to undo the bonds, to desocialize thought, to affirm the rights of the infinite and the immortal against the calculation of interests. Justice is a wager on the immortal against finitude, against 'being towards death'. For within the subjective dimension

of the equality we declare, nothing is of interest apart from the universality of this declaration, and the active consequences that arise from it.

(Ibid.: 104)

Concomitantly, equality must not be judged according to the degree to which it is actualized. It cannot be defined or verified in empirical terms; it can only be affirmed. In this sense, Badiou's is a pure politics, not a mirror, a representation of something else, be it the economy, the state or the society. It is about the constitution of the political subject (ibid.: 22; see also Hallward 2003: 228–9). And this subject has nothing in common with actual individuals or collectivities. Echoing Nietzsche's imperative 'Become who you are', a subject 'becomes' a subject through a decision to become this subject (Badiou 2007a: 100). This is why the subject is not a point of departure; rather, 'we can only *arrive* at the subject' (Badiou 2009a: 279). The subject is 'named', 'found', through a process of deduction or purification:

> When Marx takes it upon himself to listen to the revolutionary activity of his time, to the popular historical disorder, it is a matter of pinpointing in the latter . . . the dialectical form of the political subject as such. The *deduction* of its general activity presupposes only the riots of the nineteenth century. From here it will then be necessary to unfold the complete topology of an order (the capitalist order), to develop the logic of its gaps, and to take the heterogeneous all the way to the end, in order to *name* 'proletariat' that subject which is always not to be found on the anarchic surface of the events.
>
> *(Ibid.: 279)*

The subject is distilled in the event as an effect which polarizes the event and the situation. At this point, we can return to the four main subject effects – superego, anxiety, courage and justice – which are central to Badiou's conception of revolt and revolution.

From anxiety to equality

Let's start with *Antigone*. Creon, the king, orders that the corpse of Antigone's brother, who is condemned as an enemy of the city, remain unburied. But Antigone decides to give her brother a proper burial. When her sister, Ismene, warns her – 'it is foolish to meddle' with the law – Antigone replies by saying that she owes 'a longer allegiance to the dead than to the living'. She would rather disobey Creon than be 'dishonoring laws which the gods have established' (Sophocles 1967: 125). And so Antigone sacrifices her position in the socio-symbolic order. There is of course a kind of sacrifice which mainly aims at securing one's position within a given socio-symbolic order. In this case one sacrifices oneself for the good of a community and in return for this 'heroic' act gets a symbolic place in it. In contrast, Antigone's sacrifice aims at sacrificing this very place within the symbolic. It is a matter of accepting the exclusion from the community. She undertakes a mad, suicidal act by burying her brother.

As such, Antigone stands for a disruptive, suicidal drive, the death drive (Lacan 1992: 281–2; Žižek 2001b: 101). But 'death' here must not be taken literally. The death drive is the force that enables the subject to redefine itself, to be reborn. To use Lacan's phrase, Antigone 'goes through fantasy'. But since beyond fantasy there is only a non-place, the place of death or the impossible real, her decoupling herself from the symbolic initiates a process of violence. This transforms Antigone into the ultimate 'anti-Habermas':

> No dialogue, no attempt to convince Creon of the good reasons for her acts through rational argumentation, but just the blind insistence on her right. If anything, the so-called 'arguments' are on Creon's side (the burial . . . would stir up public unrest, etc.), while Antigone's counterpoint is ultimately the tautological insistence.
>
> *(Žižek 2005: 344)*

In so far as Antigone plunges into the real, is submersed by it, she is the subject of anxiety. Anxiety is basically the excess of the real over the socio-symbolic reality, the sign of a force through which the subject forces a given situation by exposing it to the real (see Badiou 2009a: 146). In other words, the opposition between Antigone and Creon is also an opposition between the superego and anxiety, between the symbolic authority and the real.

Crucially, however, what enables this opposition in the first place is the revolt of Polyneices, Antigone's brother. This originary event sets Polyneices apart from the city. A vanishing mediator, he turns against the city at the cost of exclusion, which, in turn, triggers the development of an unlimited law, an inflated, excessive form of regulation, which reveals the structural excess of state power, its intense pressure on what it represents. Thus Creon, even though he is repeatedly warned that 'no city belongs to one man', that he shouldn't 'offend against justice', and so on, can only answer that disobedience is the worst evil; it is what ruins cities (see Sophocles 1967: 138–41). Consequently, he gives rise to an increasingly formal repression, disclosing the latent superego figure within the law (see Badiou 2009a: 161–2). As the Greek superego, Creon signifies at once a relation to the law and its (self-) destruction. His reaction to the rebel, the non-law, expresses itself as a senseless, purely repressive injunction devoid of any content ('You must!'), as a law, which is itself an excess and thereby destructive (ibid.: 145).

> The internal engine of the tragic comes from the excess of the law over itself, from the figure of Creon. The formless is set on fire only as a reaction, in a second time. As for the figure of the rebel, he cannot be put in any camp. He is simply an algebraic term, an absent cause subtracted from the polis. Those who stand up against one another are the excess of form and the formless, the superego and anxiety.
>
> *(Ibid.: 163)*

What we have is a repetitive chain: the first revolt (Polyneices) is followed by counter-revolt (Creon), which is then followed by another revolt (Antigone). It is in this sense that the 'rebel' is an 'algebraic' term, that is, part of the situation. The situation as an ordered whole, generated by the absent cause, is characterized by an unproductive repetition based on the polarization between the superego and anxiety, between the formal and the formless, both occupying the same political space. This is also why the tragic contradiction has to lead to death, because a tragic situation does not contain any notion of a new law, a new right (ibid.: 163). In the two terms (Creon and Antigone), the unity of opposites prevails in the sense that the resulting subject figure is limited to the already existing structure defined by an infinite debt (revenge, counter-revenge . . .), so that the best the rebel can hope for is a reversal of the game. In other words, in the polarization of the superego and anxiety, a real torsion within the structure, which can lead to the advent of the new, is effectively curtailed. No wonder, therefore, in times of 'decadence', that this unproductive disjunctive synthesis between anxiety and the superego prevails (ibid.: 163).

How can the infinite debt be interrupted and a new notion of right emerge? Badiou's answer is Aeschylus' tragedy *Oresteia*. Here the repetitive cycle of (counter-)vengeance starts when Agamemnon's son Orestes returns from exile to avenge his father. He kills his mother, who has killed his father. However, the cycle is broken when, in the final play, Athena institutes a new law to refer Orestes' case to:

> Now hear my ordinance, people of Athens, who are judging the pleas in the first trial for shed blood. For the future too this council of jurors shall always exist for Aegeus' people; it shall have its seal on this hill.
>
> *(Aeschylus 2003: 103–04)*

With this gesture, the question of justice is no longer secondary to the superego, and subjectivization ceases to occur under the sign of anxiety, and thus death; instead, a new consistency is founded, which alters the previous social order, reinvents the situation as a new situation rather than merely reversing or subverting it (Badiou 2009a: 164). 'Athena's decree produces an egalitarian torsion from whence the new juridical coherence – that of the majority deliberation beyond appeal – once it is apprehended and put into practice, interrupts the mechanical seriality of revenge' (ibid.: 165).

In a sense, therefore, Orestes stands for courage. Like Antigone, he does not accept subordination to the symbolic order and leaps into the real. And in so far as it is based on such an excess of the real, courage is identical to anxiety. However, as a disruptive force within the situation, courage also materializes an inversion of the structure in which it originates: it 'positively carries out the disorder of the symbolic, the breakdown of communication, whereas anxiety calls for its death' (ibid.: 160). Thus, if *Antigone* questions the law with a view to returning to a normality, to a One that circumscribes the antagonism between Antigone's subjectivity on the basis of anxiety and the consistency established by Creon on the basis of the superego, the crucial point in *Oresteia* is the interruption of the One, the originary power, its division with respect to two aspects. First, Orestes' courage transcends anxiety by articulating a 'dispute', demanding a decision on right and wrong. In this sense, Orestes never returns from exile (to the 'old' social order) – courage is 'exile without return'. And second, with Athena, a new order of justice emerges (ibid.: 166–8). On the ground of anxiety and superego, courage and justice articulate a political subject as an effect of the division of the symbolic order by the excess (ibid.: 160).

> This makes clear why a political subject comes into being only by tying the revolt to a revolutionary consistency, and destruction to a recomposition. Such is the real process which bespeaks the fact that for every order and every principle of legal commandment, however stable they may seem, their becoming coincides with their internal division.
>
> *(Ibid.)*

If the subject is what punctuates an existing situation *and* recomposes a new situation, politics must have two dimensions at once: a political 'subjectivization' that interrupts the existing order (revolt) and a 'subjective process' as recomposition (revolution). How are they linked together? The only unity between them, according to Badiou, can be established through the four subject effects (anxiety, the superego, courage and justice). The subject is always an articulation of these abstract effects in varying degrees. But this unity is a split, unstable and open-ended unity.

In the first place, as subjectivization is divided into two, anxiety or courage, the subjective process can relate to either the superego or justice (ibid.: 277). Thus, the question of subjectivization is always how 'anxiety' can become 'courage', the moments of disorder can gain a consistency through systematic political struggle. Likewise, the question of the subjective process is to enable a transition in which the 'superego' gives way to 'justice'.

The failure of the first metamorphosis means that anxiety remains locked into a passive nihilist relationship with the superego: 'passive', because this reactive articulation does not create new values (justice) but merely arranges 'into a discourse the call of anxiety to the superego'; and 'nihilist', because it is based on a 'lack of belief', on 'realism' (ibid.: 328–9). Ultimately, therefore, this vicious circle, in which the lack (which anxiety points towards) and the excess (which the superego structurally produces) constantly reinforce each other, can lead to a police state.

Similarly, the failure of the second transition, from courage to justice, gives way to a radical nihilist dogmatism or fatalism, through which courage falls back upon the superego. The radical nihilist is one who has courage, but lacks the confidence to delimit the superego (see ibid.: 327). Thus, he turns the law into an absolute, dogmatic belief, in the name of which everything can be sacrificed. In so far as justice calls for a relativization of the law, not its absolutization, radical nihilism, too, remains locked into the vicious circle of anxiety–superego. It imagines a clean-cut break with the situation on the basis of its own negative will, which, without recognizing that 'the real of the conditions of possibility of intervention is always the circulation of an already decided event', leads to a Manichaean hypothesis (Badiou 2006a: 210).

As a result, in the first failure, the 'non-law' of justice is reduced to a scepticism, to 'the eternal undecidability of the law', while in the second the law comes to assert an unbreached control over justice and justice becomes a matter of dogmatism (Badiou 2009a: 299). The first concludes that, since God is dead, one can do nothing; the latter claims that, guaranteed by God, one can do anything (see ibid.). In short, then, there is no simple rule to move from anxiety to justice, from revolt to revolution.

> Do you want a simple rule for when anxiety is eating away at you? Look for the courageous act before which you show reluctance, the real that you believe to be impossible, and which is real for this reason. Look for your current indecency.
>
> *(Ibid.: 295)*

Excursus I

THE GHOST OF SPARTACUS

The spirits *are*, insists Derrida. Humanity is a 'series of ghosts' (1994: 138). Since every identity has, beyond its actual existence, a virtual continuity with the past and the future, becoming 'can only maintain itself with some ghosts', certain others, who are no longer or not yet present but nevertheless real (ibid.: xvii). Indeed, any event, any occurrence of the new, carries with it an injunction to remember, to keep up the 'conversation' with the ghosts, even though this conversation lacks reciprocity (ibid.: xviii). Every time one looks beyond the actual, present life, one evokes ghosts. Thus the tangible intangibility of the ghost never disappears; 'a ghost never dies, it remains always to come and to come-back' (ibid.: 99). In this sense all history is repetition, every historical gesture deals with a virtual idea, reiterating, repeating the ghosts of the past, in order to produce difference.

How to repeat, then? How to speak of, with and to the ghost? Kubrick's *Spartacus*, a film which seeks to look beyond its own society in a time in which exception has become the rule, is an interesting case, for it demonstrates, at once, a desire for repetition and its failure.

Quot servi, tot hostes

A Roman proverb warns: your enemies are those who work for you – a warning with good reason, for the slave was what held the Roman Republic together. The slaves 'are always with us, and we are the unique product of slaves and slavery. That is what makes us Romans' (Fast 1960: 39). As such, as the 'irrational' element of a rational totality, the slave is the symptomatic point at which Rome encounters its own unreason.

Thus the film opens with depicting the symptom, Spartacus as an anonymous slave, as *homo sacer*. He is picked up by a Roman businessman, Batiatus, who buys healthy male slaves to train as fighters in a gladiator school in Capua, near Naples.

In the gladiator school, Spartacus meets a black gladiator and asks him his name. 'You don't want to know my name and I don't want to know yours.' Spartacus tells him that he was only asking to be friendly. He answers Spartacus by saying that a gladiator doesn't make friends, for he might have to kill one in the arena. Nevertheless, they do become friends and have to confront each other in the arena, when Crassus, the richest general in Rome, comes to the gladiator school, bringing with him Helena, his lady friend, and another couple, Glabrus and Claudia. The guests ask Batiatus whether he can arrange two gladiator fights 'to the death'. Then, in a rather eroticized sequence, the two patrician ladies choose among the gladiators lined up in the yard two pairs according to their physical appearance, as if, again, they were animals. Galino is set against Crixus, Draba, the black gladiator, against Spartacus.

The first fight, between Crixus and Galino, is shown only from Spartacus' perspective, through the wooden slats of his enclosure. Crixus wins, and Galino's body is dragged away. Spartacus' fight, in contrast, is initially filmed from the elevated perspective of the patrician audience – as if the camera were 'accusing the audience' for the pleasure it subtracts from the spectacle of power (see Cyrino 2005: 107). In the battle Spartacus loses his dagger and is pinned to the ground by the spear of Draba, who looks to the balcony for a signal. Helena gives the sign for death. Draba refuses and instead throws the spear into the balcony, towards Crassus, before attempting to climb up after it, but is killed by a guard's spear. With this self-sacrificial act, Draba reverses his own maxim, 'Gladiators do not make friends', and a possibility, the possibility of solidarity, comes into view. The same evening the other slaves can see Draba's dead body hanging upside down in the garden.

The following day, the gladiators are in the kitchen and Spartacus sees that Varinia, another slave, whom he is in love with, is being taken away. The guard, Marcellus, tells him that she has been sold to Crassus. 'She has been sold?' Spartacus asks. Marcellus responds with cruel pleasure, 'No talking in the kitchen, slave!' Spartacus attacks him. A revolt breaks out. Batiatus escapes to Rome with the wagon prepared for Varinia. The gladiators break free of their compound, beating back the Roman soldiers who try to quash their rebellion, and run to the hills. Augustine writes in *City of God*,

> even historians themselves find it difficult to explain how the servile war was begun by a very few, certainly less than seventy gladiators, what numbers of fierce and cruel men attached themselves to these, how many of the Roman generals this band defeated, and how it laid waste many districts and cities.
>
> *(2005: 3.26)*

Escaped slaves quickly transformed into an 'increase pack' characterized by the 'desire to be more' (Canetti 1962: 107). But they became 'more' not only by adding but also by subtraction, by liberating themselves from their bonds. In other words, they did not revolt *as* slaves – the Spartacus War is not grounded in a 'slave revolt' in the Nietzschean sense, that is, a revolt in which the weak triumph not by creating new values, but simply by reversing, through *ressentiment*, the given power hierarchy, by taking the place of the master.

Therefore, in a scene following the first victories of the slave army, when some soldiers in Spartacus' army enjoy a carnivalesque reversal in which captured Roman soldiers and noblemen are turned into gladiators and made to fight to the death, 'like animals', the former slaves betting to see who will die first, Spartacus stops the spectacle. Seeing this, Crixus jumps into the arena demanding that the battle continue until death. 'What are we, Crixus? What are we becoming? Romans? Have we learned nothing?' The temporality of the carnival, a simple role reversal between the slave and the master, does not threaten the established power relations; rather, it performs a transgression that confirms and completes the rule by reversing it. What the slave needs is not becoming another 'master' but emancipation from slavery as such. 'The goal of *this* liberation, *out* of slavery, cannot be subjugation of the master in turn . . . but, rather, the elimination of the institution of slavery altogether' (Buck-Morss 2009: 56). Perhaps this is why Marx mentions, in a letter sent to Engels on 27 February 1861, Spartacus as a 'noble' personality, a personality that transcends the horizon of the master–slave dialectic.

Revolt as death, death as destiny

Spartacus tells his vision of becoming an army of gladiators, beating the Romans, freeing slaves to join them and escaping by sea. The Silesian pirates have the biggest fleet in the world and they are at war with the Romans. Tigranes, the mercenary, meets Spartacus. They agree the price, but he tells Spartacus that he is going to lose, that battalions are approaching them. 'If you saw the future, your army destroyed, yourself dead, would you continue to fight?'

'Yes', Spartacus responds. 'When a free man dies he loses the pleasure of life; a slave loses his pain. Death is the only freedom a slave knows. That's why he's not afraid of it. That's why we will win.'

Spartacus is a film about death: when Batiatus saves Spartacus from death in the mines, it is only to turn him into a death machine, a gladiator. Later, Spartacus can remain alive because he can kill others or because others, for example Draba, can die for him. And what is slavery if not a life fated to death? Accordingly, when the slave's 'life' as such signifies death, the only reasonable option remains to turn fate into destiny, that is, to choose, to accept death. In the words of Stoic Epictetus, himself an ex-slave: what one should fear is not death as such but the fear of death (see Paz 2007: 196). Since there can be no ethics without freedom, and since freedom necessitates accepting death as destiny, Spartacus' concern is with life, with the fight for freedom – a fight one wins even in defeat.

Thus the plan is set. The principle is exodus. And through the desire for exodus, a collective subject emerges: the army of Spartacus, which forms a 'body', because, instead of disappearing into disorganized packs, the rebels remain faithful to the revolt-event, to the statement 'We slaves, we want to return home' (Badiou 2009b: 51). The subject emerges as an operation through which the new 'body' relates to the event, and it is this relation that regulates the army's strategies of exodus. Through fidelity to the event, the slaves move into a 'new present' in which they are no longer slaves. 'Thus they show (to the other slaves) that it is possible, for a slave, no longer to be a slave, and to do so *in the present*. Hence the growth, which soon becomes menacing, of this body' (ibid.).

The next scene brings us to Rome, to the senate, where we hear how the gladiators are 'ravaging' the countryside, 'forcing' other slaves to join them, 'looting', 'robbing', 'burning' estates. 'Where is Crassus?' one of them asks, looking for a figure of salvation. Through the manipulation of a cynical politician, Gracchus, it is decided that Glabrus should go with six cohorts and that temporary command of the city of Rome should be left to Gaius Julius Caesar.

Crassus, in the meanwhile, arrives at his villa, angry that Glabrus has been sent away from Rome, that Caesar, with his dictatorial tendencies, is now in command of the city of Rome, and that Gracchus is behind it. Awaiting him is a gift of a group of slaves from the governor of Sicily, among them the gifted Antoninus, whom he makes his body servant. We next see Crassus in his bath; Antoninus is washing him. Crassus, trying to seduce him, questions him. Does he lie? Steal? Dishonour the gods? Does he eat oysters? Snails? Is it moral to eat oysters but not snails? Then it is a question of taste . . . They move to the balcony to observe a passing legion of Roman soldiers:

> There, boy, is Rome, the might, the majesty, the terror of Rome; there is the power that bestrides the known world like a colossus. No man can withstand Rome; no nation can withstand her. How much less a boy. There is only one way to deal with Rome, Antoninus. You must serve her. You must abase yourself before her.

When he turns, Antoninus has gone to join the slave army. The next scene flips to Spartacus' encampment, where he is training his army. He meets Antoninus for the first time. As artist/magician Antoninus becomes useful for the army: he reads for the illiterate Spartacus, and entertains the fraternity with his magic, for example 'freeing' birds from eggs, and his songs of exodus: 'Through blue shadow and purple woods, I turn home . . .' What is emerging is a spirited, energetic community.

'However,' writes Camus, speaking of the Spartacus revolt, 'this rebellion introduced no principle to Roman life' (1953: 80). Nothing could be more wrong. The name of Spartacus stands for a generic idea of communism, an image of a world in which there are no slaves and no masters. Thus, apart from Spartacus as an empirical political figure, the name Spartacus signifies a historical becoming, which redefines the past, and a subjective will, signifying the decision to become part of a political event. 'Spartacus' is an egalitarian idea, which synthesizes the relationship between the political, the historical and the subjective. In this sense, Spartacus' politics is a universalist politics *par excellence*, a gesture of politicization, which requires the metaphoric universalization of particular demands, the restructuring of the whole social space (see Žižek 1999: 204–08). In the end, universality exists only in so far as it is incarnated in some particularity. Spartacus can imagine a new world only by focusing on a particular problem, slavery.

And since there is always inequality, there is always a reason to revolt. As such, equality is not merely a goal of politics to be attained in the end but rather 'a point of departure, a *supposition* to maintain in every circumstance' (Rancière 1991: 138). Then Spartacus did not revolt to become equal but because he already was. In this respect his illiteracy has a singular meaning, for the egalitarian maxim must be taken literally: all people are capable of understanding and teaching themselves what others have done and understood, and without masters (ibid.: 139). What causes the excluded to revolt is not necessarily their knowledge of the socio-economic mechanisms that oppress them, nor their self-consciousness as the excluded, but 'their daily encounters with another, better world to which they are denied access': the world of the ruling classes (Jonsson 2008: 184).

Counter-revolt

The Spartacus War deprives Rome of the commerce of all South Italy; half the precincts of Rome are without bread; the city is close to panic. So Gracchus concludes 'We must confirm Caesar as permanent commander of the garrison and assign two legions to intercept and destroy Spartacus at the city of Metapontum.' But there is no one yet to lead the legions. Crassus tries to make a bargain with the senate that he will lead them only if he is made the controller of all the legions and the senate assigns its power to the courts. Gracchus sneers: 'Dictatorship.' 'Order,' Crassus corrects him. Shortly afterwards we see Crassus sworn in at the first council of the Republic as the commander-in-chief of Rome.

Spartacus is a film on Rome's transition from a republic to an empire. 'The age of the dictator was at hand, waiting in the shadows for the event to bring it forth.' That event was Spartacus. Spartacus' revolt made it possible for Caesar (Augustus) to become emperor by ending the Republic. If Romans sublimated order and security, 'if they willingly submitted to dictatorship', it was, partially at least, a response to Spartacus' 'symbolic power' (see Strauss 2009: 189). In this respect *Spartacus* remains 'new' as a pertinent commentary on political subjectivity vis-à-vis the state of exception. According to Schmitt (2004), the state is not only threatened from outside by international war, but also from inside by the 'partisan war', by civil war. With the deterioration of the state's sovereignty, the partisan can practically attain the role of the sovereign and restate the friend–enemy distinction instead of the state. Thanks to Spartacus, the partisan, Crassus could sublimate order, 'the might of Rome', as an absolute value. With Crassus and Caesar, Rome enters into a reactionary state of exception, in which the concern with security – the fear of Spartacus – is elevated above politics, and in which saving the condition of normality, thus avoiding a true exception (the liberation of slaves), becomes the sole purpose of politics. Sovereignty versus civil war; Leviathan versus Behemoth. Hence comes one of the finest details in the film, when Crassus tells Caesar, the coming dictator, that he fears Spartacus 'even more than I fear you'!

In this sense, the Roman war against slaves is an ultra-political gesture that overrides politics, paradoxically destroying what it aims to preserve: the Roman republic. *Spartacus*' Rome is a system which, in order to keep slaves enslaved, brings into being the conditions of everybody's enslavement (Trumbo, quoted in Ahl 2007: 81). For, on the road to dictatorship, security creates its twin: insecurity. To securitize an issue is also to create a danger. Hence, 'this campaign is not alone to kill Spartacus . . . It is to kill the *legend* of Spartacus.' Crassus aims at killing not only the 'body' of the slave army but also an idea, a spirit. So, in the 'exceptional' figure of Spartacus, the slave (body without word) and the spectre (word without body) fully coincide.

In the meantime, Spartacus and the slaves arrive at the sea. We see them planning to board the ships. However, Tigranes brings the news that the Silesian fleet has been obliged to withdraw. Spartacus works out that the Romans paid the pirates just to prevent the slave army leaving. Now, rather than be trapped between two armies in the South, his army must march instead on Rome. Obviously, Crassus wants to fight Spartacus himself to become the saviour of Rome. Spartacus orders Antoninus to set up an assembly. He addresses his people; he tells them of the two converging armies.

> Rome won't allow us to escape Italy. We have no choice but to march against Rome herself, and end this war the only way it could have ended by freeing every slave in Italy. [. . .] Maybe there is no peace in this world for us or anyone else. I don't know. But I do know that as long as we live . . . we must stay true to ourselves. We march tonight!

What speaks here is the faithful subject, its fidelity to the event. Crassus, in turn, is pictured in another assembly, promising 'a new Rome, a new Italy and a new Empire. I promise the destruction of the slave army and the restoration of order throughout all our territories.' This is how the 'obscure subject' speaks, expressing the desire for 'an abolition of the new present, considered in its entirety as malevolent and *de jure* inexistent' (Badiou 2009b: 59). Significantly, however, this is not only a desire for the restoration of a previous order. Rather, a new order is produced under new conditions (the slave revolt) but it is done with the purpose of obscuring and ultimately denying the trace of the revolt-event and suppressing the body, the slave army, in order to replace it with a reified, transcendent body (City, God, Race . . .). In this sense, the action of the obscure subject depends on, is a response to, a prior production of a present by a faithful subject. Thus, within the horizon of subjectivity, 'it is not because there is reaction that there is revolution, it is because there is revolution that there is reaction' (ibid.: 60–2).

The battle is fought, the slave army lost, and Crassus is walking among the masses of the dead. Those captured are told that their lives will be spared and that they will become once again slaves but that the 'penalty of crucifixion has been set aside on the single condition that you identify the body or the living person of a slave called Spartacus'. Spartacus stands and declares 'I am Spartacus.' Simultaneously Antoninus also stands and declares the same, followed by another man and another, until all the men are declaring themselves to be Spartacus. So Crassus cannot identify Spartacus, an enemy he fought without knowing. But he discovers Varinia and her child by Spartacus, and orders that they be conveyed to his house in Rome. And in the senate the victorious Crassus tells Gracchus that 6,000 slaves have been crucified along the road to Rome. Next is the destruction of the ghost:

> So did we destroy Spartacus and his army. So will we in time – and necessarily – destroy the very memory of what he did and how he did it. [. . .] The order of things is that some must rule and some must serve. So the gods ordained it. So it will be.
>
> *(Crassus, in Fast 1960: 153)*

But ideas do not die. Obsessed with Spartacus, Crassus tries to seduce Varinia, but she refuses his love. At the point at which power cannot seduce, the relationship between the slave and the master is inverted. Crassus' miserable attempt at seducing her is reminiscent of his failure to seduce Antoninus at the beginning of the film. In both cases, his desire is dwarfed by the love for Spartacus. Enraged and envious, Crassus comes to Antoninus and Spartacus. Now he can guess who Spartacus is. He orders that they fight now; the victor will be crucified. 'We will test this myth of slave brotherhood.' Spartacus orders Antoninus to let himself be killed, but Antoninus says he won't let Spartacus be crucified. They fight; Spartacus asks for Antoninus's forgiveness as he kills him. Then he turns to Crassus: 'Here's your victory. He'll come back. He'll come back and he'll be millions!' Crassus gives his orders for him to be crucified, 'no grave, no marker'.

Resurrection

> They've never beaten us yet. [. . .] But no matter how many times we beat them . . . they still seem to have another army to send against us. And another . . . It just seems like we've started something . . . that has no ending!

Why, then, did the army of Spartacus ultimately fail after several significant victories? Mainstream historiography explains the defeat with reference to internal reasons, emphasizing that the majority of the slaves could not perceive the disaster waiting for them unless they escaped. Therefore, Plutarch writes: Spartacus' ruin was prepared by his own success, for it 'filled' his army with 'over-confidence' (Plutarch 2007: 237). Spartacus 'lit a fire that he could not put out' (Strauss 2009: 165). At any rate, this is where the reactionary and obscure subjects leave us.

> But they are constantly confusing two different things, the way revolutions turn out historically and people's revolutionary becoming. These relate to two different sets of people. Men's only hope lies in a revolutionary becoming: the only way of . . . responding to what is intolerable.
>
> *(Deleuze 1995: 171)*

One way to repress the event is to reduce it to its historical consequences, allowing its virtual aspect to disappear into actual 'facts'. But there is another, more interesting destination for the subject: repetition in the form of a reappearing, a resurrection. If the faithful subject produces the new present, while the reactive subject refuses it and the obscure subject leads to its occultation, resurrection reactivates the faithful subject in a new context, according to a new logic, 'forgetting' the very forgetting (or failure) of the revolt-event (Badiou 2009b: 65): a procedure which says 'I am Spartacus!', making 'Spartacus' a generic name, common to all those who revolt, like the 'black Spartacus' Toussaint-Louverture, the leader of the insurgent black slaves who escaped from plantations and defeated the Napoleonic forces in Haiti in 1796–1804, or like the 'Spartacist' leaders of the communist revolt in Germany in 1919. 'Ancient Spartacus, black Spartacus, red Spartacus'. . . (ibid.).

Most probably, after all, Spartacus objectively knew that he did not have a chance against the Roman army in the long run, which is why his overall strategy was exodus. For one thing, the majority of the slaves in Italy, especially the urban slaves, had not joined his army; the 60,000 rebels made only 4 per cent of the slave population in Italy (Strauss 2009: 2, 41). The rest took a reactionary position, while the Roman *proletarii* were 'distracted' from the revolt by free bread provision and gladiator fights (see Parenti 2007: 147). Further, his was a cosmopolitan army which consisted of different ethnic groups (Thracians, Gauls, Jews, Greeks and so on), different languages and different sexes and age groups, which constituted, in terms of organization and discipline, a weak spot vis-à-vis the Roman armies (see Badiou 2009b: 51).

Yet Spartacus was obviously not an opportunist; he did not postpone the event with reference to 'objective facts', knowing well that such a position of the objective observer is the key obstacle to the event (see Žižek 2002a: 9). The event, after all, is a 'leap' of faith, and its spectral truth is 'perceptible only to those who accomplish this leap, not to neutral observers' (Žižek 2002b: 187). One cannot feel the 'magic' of the event without already being part of it. This is the meaning of 'I am Spartacus.' And when the 'magic' disappears, when the subject falls back upon 'objective facts', everything changes again. This happens in Monty Python's *Life of Brian*, in the crucifixion scene that has an ironic reference to *Spartacus*: Roman soldiers are approaching Brian to release him from the cross, while all the other crucified prisoners are shouting 'I am Brian'! The difference between the two declarations – 'I am Spartacus', 'I am Brian' – is the difference between fidelity and opportunism. And this difference becomes visible in *Spartacus* not because it sticks to the facts but because it does not (e.g. Spartacus, according to most historical sources, died in battle, not on the cross).

Reactionary . . . and innovative

But is the film *Spartacus* itself not a gesture of redemption, an affirmative attempt to resurrect the name of Spartacus? No doubt, the film attempts this along a parallel between Spartacus' Rome and the cold war American empire. But it has also fallen victim to censorship. Thus, Spartacus' victories and their demoralizing effects on

Rome are almost invisible in the film. In fact, censorship makes itself felt through-out the film, starting with the voice-over prologue:

> In the last century before the birth of the new faith called Christianity, which was destined to overthrow the pagan tyranny of Rome and bring about a new society, the Roman Republic stood at the very centre of the civilized world. [. . .] Yet even at the zenith of her pride and power the Republic lay fatally stricken with a disease called human slavery. The age of the dictator was at hand, waiting in the shadows for the event to bring it forth. In that same century, in the conquered Greek province of Thrace, an illiterate slave woman added to her master's wealth by giving birth to a son whom she named Spartacus. A proud, rebellious son, who was sold to living death in the mines of Libya before his thirteenth birthday. There, under whip and chain and sun, he lived out his youth and his young manhood, dreaming the death of slavery two thousand years before it finally would die.

Why this reference to Christianity? Spartacus was a pagan who believed in Diony-sus (see Plutarch 2007: 234; Strauss 2009: 26, 29–31). But 'his elevation to the cross can have no purpose other than to evoke comparisons with Christ' (Ahl 2007: 80). Thus the film reduces the 'idea' of Spartacus, his spectral aspect, to the framework of Christian theology, producing a Christian drama out of Spartacus. This is the 'creative' touch of the reactive subject, which can turn the slave revolt into a nihil-istic invention of a monotheistic 'god for slaves'. Consider how Camus interprets Crassus' staking out the road from Rome to Capua with crosses:

> The cross is also Christ's punishment. One can imagine that He only chose a slave's punishment, a few years later, so as to reduce the enormous distance which henceforth would separate humiliated humanity from the implacable face of the Master. He intercedes. He submits to the most extreme injustice so that rebellion shall not divide the world in two, so that suffering will also light the way to heaven and preserve it from the curses of mankind.
>
> *(Camus 1953: 81)*

So the slave revolt turns into a victory of *ressentiment*. And the main claim of the event, that the slaves can revolt, undergoes a modification: the slaves can revolt, but only *as* slaves, without 'dividing the world into two'. Yet the event is precisely that which produces a scission, torsion of the social structure. Whenever there is an event, 'one divides into two' (Badiou 2009a: 14). Even in Christian theology, the infinite (God) comes to exist in the finite, actual world by dividing himself into the Father and the Son (God-placed-in-the-actual); that is, God basically occurs as the torsion of the structure, with the consequence that 'the Son is consubstantial with the Father' (ibid.: 15). Through the scission, the virtual expresses, actualizes itself and coexists with the actual. Similarly, when one speaks of an opposition, say, between Rome and Spartacus, one effectively undertakes a political division of the 'people' of Rome alongside two modes of politics, each organizing the 'people' in its own way (ibid.). As such, scission is constitutive of any political identity; there is no unity, no identity that is not split by the minimal difference caused by it (see ibid.: 6). Hence, when Paul insists that 'there are no Jews, no Greeks, no men and women' it is because 'there are only Christians and the enemies of Christianity'. This is what disappears when the film distils a kind of Christian, for whom the two unites in one, from Spartacus, for whom the one divides into two: there are 'only those' who demand freedom '*and* those' who are the enemies of freedom.

However, Spartacus is as much Americanized as Christianized in the film. Spartacus 'dreaming' the death of slavery 'two thousand years before it *would* die' is a particular reference to Lincoln's Emancipation Proclamation (1863). In the end, 'freedom' is a central concept to American self-perception. Interestingly, however, the concept 'began to take root at precisely the time that the economic practice of slavery . . . was increasing quantitatively' and often led to a 'monstrous inconsistency' of defending liberty and owning slaves at the same time (Buck-Morss 2009: 21). This duality of 'liberty' and 'slavery' has been extended to Hollywood in the form of historical epics that typically tell the story of a persecuted, victimized minority, be it Jews, Christians, sometimes slaves, juxtaposed to a tyrannical order, and *Spartacus* follows this tradition (see Winkler 2007: 155–7), with the consequence of depoliticizing and transforming Spartacus the rebel into a Spartacus who 'seems to have risen from his lowly status only to attain middle-class respectability' (Cooper 2007: 43). Even the relationship between Spartacus and Varinia is cut according to this scheme: while in history books she is a Thracian woman 'living with Spartacus', a Dionysian 'prophetess' who is often 'subject to visitations of the Dionysiac frenzy' (Plutarch 2007: 234), in the film she becomes a bourgeois wife who says to Spartacus 'Forbid me ever to leave you', which is answered by Spartacus' 'I do forbid you.'

The spirit and the spectre

But why this reduction which results in a normalized, 'decaf' Spartacus? How can even Ronald Reagan quote Spartacus as 'an example of sacrifice and struggle for freedom' (see Strauss 2009: 4)? How could Hollywood manage to snatch Spartacus from the atheist, communist tradition, converting him 'into a blameless spiritual reformer . . . appropriated by conservatives as just another cinematic configuration of American faith and democracy fighting against oppressive atheist foreign powers' (Cyrino 2005: 115)? What *Spartacus* ironically highlights once more is that critique is open-ended and that it can be accommodated by a power which can turn the critique of business, of the slave trade, into big business.

Yet, despite such displacements, there *is* a remainder which cannot be fully appropriated or assimilated: Spartacus as a symptom. In so far as Spartacus is sublimated in Hollywood as a fantasy–object, it is necessary to go through the ideological fantasy that structures it. Significantly, however, this is not a question of realism. The point is not showing the difference or the distance between the 'reality' of Spartacus and Spartacus as 'fiction'. In fact, it is naïve to suggest that the film merely represents or should represent a profound reality – after all, to confer upon *Spartacus* a realism would be merely to confirm one perspective in the tautological conviction that an image of the revolt 'which is true to its representation of objectivity is really objective' (Bourdieu 1990: 77).

Fictionalizing Spartacus necessarily pushes away or masks some realities, and it is not surprising that there are many historical inaccuracies in the film: for instance, the Roman mines in Libya that the film opens with never existed, just as the figure of Gracchus, the cynical politician, is completely fictional; the armies of Pompey and Lucullus did not join Crassus' army in the final battle; and so on (see Ward 2007: 95–6, 98, 105). What if, however, the representation of Spartacus masks not only a reality – a 'real' Spartacus – but, more importantly, an absence, for example the absence of freedom in the case of today's 'free labour', the slavery that continues to exist after the abolishment of slavery? The secret of *Spartacus* transpires, in other words, when focus is shifted from the dissimulation of an actual existence to the dissimulation of an absence (see Baudrillard 1994: 6). At any rate, the film projects the problem of unfreedom (slavery) to a fantasy space, ancient Rome.

Yet we still live in a society that has the appearance of a realm of freedom and equality, of 'a very Eden of the innate rights of man': both buyer and seller of a commodity participate in the exchange as 'free' persons and they enter into an 'equal' relation with one another (see Marx 1976: 280). But one is *not* free not to sell one's labour power. Hence there is the antagonism between the capitalist society and living labour in capitalism, an antagonism which reflects the bio-political rift between the slave and Rome. It is therefore telling that the first truth that occurred to the ex-slaves in Haiti, the first country in which slavery was abolished, was that the documents granting them freedom were in fact 'empty-handed', for they failed to challenge property rights: even though nobody had a right to force them into work, the ex-slaves still had to work for their maintenance, which in many ways reproduced their status as slaves (see Buck–Morss 2009: 73). Conversely, to the extent it 'violated the rule of property', the Haitian Revolution has been severely disruptive to the existing order and thus has been completely ignored by the Europeans and Americans (see Hardt and Negri 2000: 13).

Recall an interesting detail in Fast's novel *Spartacus*, which disappeared in the film version. Towards the end of the book, Crassus, who himself owns slave-run plantations in South Italy, reveals one of his 'small secrets', his experiment with employing free 'workers' instead of slaves.

'A slave eats your food and dies. But these workers turn themselves into gold. Nor am I concerned with feeding and housing them.'

'Yet', he is interrupted by his interlocutor, 'they could do as Spartacus did.'

Crassus smiles and shakes his head. 'No, that will never be. You see, they are not slaves. They are free men. They can come and go as they please. Why should they ever revolt?' And he goes on to deny the link between the worker and the slave: 'There is no bond between these men and slaves' (Fast 1960: 234).

The film, too, deceives by mystifying this literal bond, by nurturing the ideological fantasy that slavery belongs to another, 'pre-modern' time.

Back to the symptom, to the real that 'returns'. The real that returns has the status of another appearance, another fiction: because of its excessive character, we cannot integrate it into socio-symbolic 'reality' and therefore can experience it only as an uncanny spectre (see Žižek 2002c: 19). Consequently what matters is not only whether *Spartacus* distorts reality by 'fictionalizing' it, but also how reality itself is mistaken for fiction. *Spartacus* also produces an effect of irreality, through which the real itself, the event-revolt, comes to be perceived as a phantasm, while images turn the slave revolt into a simulacrum.

In short, rather than repeating the 'spirit' of the slave revolt, the film 'makes its ghost walk about again' (Marx 1977: 12). It makes the spirit of Spartacus 'disappear by appearing, in the phenomenon of its phantasm' (Derrida 1994: 138). The film convokes the spectre of the slave revolt, but in the same movement as it elevates it to the level of a moral tragedy it also hides, in the phantasm, 'the mediocre content of bourgeois ambition' (ibid.: 140). In other words, the problem with *Spartacus* is that the ghost serves to protect its audience, us, from its own content, the real Spartacus.

It is said that Kubrick himself has sought to disown *Spartacus*, bitterly commenting that the film 'had everything but a good story' (Kubrick, quoted in Cooper 2007: 41). It is sad – the story of the film is fantastic; it is the story of politics as such. But there are other, better reasons to disown the film.

PART II

Revolution and counterrevolution

4

THE INFINITE REVOLUTION

There is no monster hidden in the abyss, there is only fire.

(Houellebecq 2005: 78)

There is an interesting metaphorical relationship between revolution and fire. The French Revolution, for instance, was seen 'as something like an erupting volcano' (Robespierre 2007: 59). But also the fear of revolution is expressed with reference to fire. Thus, towards the end of *The Devils*, Dostoevsky's terrorist/devil, Verkhovensky, modelled on Bakunin's anarchist friend Nechaev, sets the whole town on fire, aiming at 'the systematic destruction of society and the principles on which it is based' (Dostoevsky 1971: 661–2). This fear often coincides with another invariant of modern history, the fear of the crowd. In Canetti's prose, it is 'strange to observe how strongly . . . the crowd assumes the character of fire' (1962: 27). Therefore one of the first reactions to the French Revolution, Edmund Burke's, articulated itself as a fear of the 'swinish multitude' (2004: 173). Like fire, the crowd is an impressive means of destruction, it grows as it spreads, destroys everything hostile and it annihilates 'irrevocably' – nothing after it remains as it was before (Canetti 1962: 20).

And yet the mass is an ambivalent category with more than one meaning. It also signifies a creative force, a line of flight with respect to the existing order. If the ultimate aim of politics is subtraction, putting a distance to the state, the mass is an indispensable concept to politics (Badiou 2005a: 81). After all, non-integration is a necessary condition to become a mass; the mass takes place not by adding but by subtracting, by disorganization in relation to the social strata (Deleuze and Guattari 1987: 149–66). Hence there is a crucial opposition: formal democracy as a figure of the state versus mass democracy as subtraction from the figure of the state (Badiou 2005a: 88–90).

It is in the context of this tension that Rousseau, the philosopher of the first modern revolution, articulated the problem of politics as establishing a form of political association that can defend all its members while they remain free. His solution was the 'social contract', though which individuals transfer their rights absolutely and unconditionally to the political association 'under the supreme direction of the general will': 'The public person thus formed by the union of all other persons was once called the *city*, and is now known as *the republic* . . . Those who are associated in it take collectively the name of *a people*' (Rousseau 2004: 16–17).

Politics exists paradoxically, as a self-founding event which creates its own subject, a 'people'. It can only originate in an event, not in the actual situation, for nothing external, for instance no Hobbesian war of all against all, necessitates the social contract (Badiou 2006a: 345). Since what exists before the contract is only particular wills, the general will is not reducible to an element of the situation before the event. Only after its creation, retroactively, does the general will come to appear as a presupposed element of such constitution (ibid.). The contract, as such, supplements the situation, the state of nature, while 'people' functions as the subject that inserts itself between the void (nature) and itself through the operation of the 'general will' as the sign of fidelity informing this procedure (ibid.: 346).

In this operation, the 'people' splits particular wills, dividing the will of the individual into two: the private will, which has a natural tendency towards 'partiality', and the general will, which inclines towards 'equality' (Rousseau 2004: 26). Since it is indivisible and thus cannot take individual wills into consideration, the general will is inherently egalitarian: 'equality *is* politics' (Badiou 2006a: 347). Democracy is antithetical to political articulations on the basis of particular identities (Badiou 2005a: 93). At the same time, however, the general will cannot be reduced to the metastructure, be represented by the state, for it is what 'frees politics from the state' in the first place (Badiou 2006a: 347). The exercise of the general will 'cannot be represented by anyone but itself' (Rousseau 2004: 26).

As such, Rousseau's politics can retain its singularity only through the intervention of the 'legislator', who belongs neither to the state of nature (for he founds politics) nor to the political state (his role being to declare the laws, he is not submitted to the laws), which makes him a 'quasi-divine' figure who names, distils from the void, a wisdom laying claim to 'a previous fidelity, the prepolitical fidelity to the gods of nature' (Badiou 2006a: 350). Thus for Robespierre, the legislator inspired by Rousseau, punishing a corrupted king politically is not an 'irreligious' act but rather a way of honouring divinity:

> They accuse us of rebellion. [. . .] They call us irreligious: they proclaim that we have declared war on Divinity itself. [. . .] What people ever offered purer worship than ours to the great Being under whose auspices we proclaimed the immutable principles of every human society? The laws of eternal justice used to be called, disdainfully, the dreams of well-meaning people; we have turned them into imposing realities. Morality used to be in philosophers' books; we have put it in the government of nations.
>
> *(Robespierre 2007: 93–4)*

Robespierre opposes virtue to corruption: 'nothing but virtue' can save the society from the evil of corruption (ibid.: 23). Here, 'virtue' is a subjective principle, a purely political prescription that 'refers to no other objective determination', that resists the reduction of politics to interest negotiation or consensus building (Badiou 2005a: 129). But virtue has two faces: in the form of fraternity, as a 'we', it functions as a stabilizer; yet, as a principle of action, of creating equality, it is utterly antagonistic. Thus, in Robespierre's direct moralization of politics, virtue necessarily leads to 'terror', to the violent measures taken by the revolutionary republic to preserve itself against the counterrevolutionary monarchy as a morally united fraternity. He insists that, if justice is to be operative, if the first republic on earth is to be protected against the forces of corruption, terror is necessary. A revolution devoid of its violent substance, a 'revolution without revolution', is not possible (Robespierre 2007: 43; Žižek 2007a: xi). Without virtue, revolutionary terror can only be 'a noisy crime that destroys another crime', but virtue without terror, on the other hand, is 'powerless' (Robespierre 2007: 115, 129–30). This is why revolution can only appear like the eruption of a 'volcano', as the leap of divine violence.

'This jump, however, takes place in an arena where the ruling class give the commands' (Benjamin 1999: 253). Terror positions the event as an excess against the inertia of the existing situation dominated by the ruling class. Therefore Robespierre likens his regime of terror to the 'state of nature' (2007: 59). This state of nature is, like Schmitt's, one that comes after the law, as a state of exception. However, unlike Schmitt's exception, Robespierre's 'terror' has no ambition to preserve normality; its violence does not hand down sentences, condemn kings, but drops them 'back into the void' (Robespierre 2007: 59).

Significantly, this pure violence institutionalized itself in the form of a 'pure', transcendental subject stripped off from its actual identity, a subject born as a process of counter-actualization, through the assertion of its independence from its empirical individuality qua living being (Žižek 2007a: xv).

Countering or revising?

The indifference towards bare life, which is essential to Benjamin's divine violence, is also an indifference towards the actual situation, existing institutions and conventions, or what Robespierre calls 'habit' (see Robespierre 2007: 58). Revolutionaries such as Robespierre are 'figures without habits' who refuse 'realistic' compromises with what exists and reject taking into account the habits that sustain the functioning of the existing order (Žižek 2007a: xix). Inversely, the defence of 'habit' is essential to the counterrevolutionary thought. Edmund Burke, the paradigmatic counterrevolutionary, articulates this:

> Good order is the foundation of all good things. To be enabled to acquire, the people, without being servile, must be tractable and obedient. The magistrate must have his reverence, the laws their authority. The body of the

people must not find the principles of natural subordination . . . rooted out of their minds. They must respect that property of which they cannot partake. They must labour to obtain what by labour can be obtained; and when they find, as they commonly do, the success disproportioned to the endeavour, they must be taught their consolation in the final proportions of eternal justice. Of this consolation, whoever deprives them, deadens their industry and strikes at the root of all acquisition as of all conservation.

(Burke 2004: 372)

Burke, writing in 1790, can perceive the revolution only as a threat against what is inherited. Particularly the revolution's desire to separate the state and the church provokes him, for he sees religion as the 'basis' of society, the source of 'all good' (ibid.: 186). The French Revolution was deliriously attacking this source. But it was not only a question of religion; the 'misfortune' of his age, insists Burke, is 'that everything is to be discussed' (ibid.: 188). And to ward off this 'plague', the event-revolution that threatens everything, he declares fidelity to the situation: 'We are not the converts of Rousseau; we are not the disciples of Voltaire; Helvetius has made no progress amongst us. Atheists are not our preachers; madmen are not our lawgivers' (ibid.: 181–2, 185).

The elementary gesture of all counterrevolutionary thought is its paradoxical definition of the existing situation as an invariant while, at the same time, depicting it as something fragile in face of the danger. Burke deals with this paradox through the idea of reform, which he considers necessary to keep the revolution at bay. One must 'preserve' and 'improve', rather than experiment with radical change (ibid.: 267). As such, reform is a desire for extinguishing not only the empirical danger of revolution, its violence, but also the idea of revolution as such. Three points are immediately significant in Burke's case.

First, he is blind to the nature of political subjectivization. The event, for him, remains unthinkable because he can only think from the perspective of 'history'. But only the 'subjective' perspective, engaged in the event in the first place, can look beyond the situation. Second, he reduces revolution to its empirical consequences, and from the point of view of its consequences every revolution *is*, in many respects, a 'plague'. But revolution is becoming, and becoming is not reducible to history; it is, from the point of view of history, always untimely (Deleuze 1995: 171). As Burke's leftist contemporary Catharine Macaulay insisted, we can gain no insight, 'no light', from history regarding the new – after all, history furnished the French Revolution with no example of a radically egalitarian society (Macaulay 1790: 87–8). Third, in Burke, the revolutionary desire for equality meets its counterpart, the hatred of democracy. He complains that, destroying inherited traditions, the revolution proceeded 'upon the equality of men', which levelled all citizens 'into one homogeneous mass', creating a monster, the mob (Burke 2004: 299–300).

On the basis of these three pillars, objectivism, historicism and the hatred of the mass, every counterrevolution signifies a desire to oppose the event, both before and after it takes place, either through a pre-emptive strategy or by trying to over-turn it, fighting for the restoration of the pre-revolutionary order. As such, coun-terrevolution is a principled reaction against all aspects of revolution, both its idea and its actualization.

Yet the 'idea' of revolution is, precisely, an idea. What is at stake in an idea is never merely the reality of a possibility which already exists inside an actual his-torical situation but rather the possibility of possibility, making the unthinkable possible. In so far as the event is a way of passing beyond the existing situation by creating new possibilities, the counterrevolution is what seeks to delimit those pos-sibilities by (re)defining what is possible and impossible. Therefore the centre of gravity for the counterrevolutionary thought is always what exists. It refers political subjectivity back to the situation, to the existing order, by moving the centre of gravity from the potentiality within a situation to the state of the situation.

This, however, is not a peaceful process. Thus the Thermidorean period, which preached 'against acts of violence', and which turned 'terror' into an unthinkable, isolated, infra-political term, was itself based on terror in that it executed many rev-olutionaries without trial, reinstalled the statist mechanisms in favour of the wealthy and, most importantly, repressed by violent means every possible politics of event that sought a distance from the state (Badiou 2005a: 124–6, 138). Counterrevolu-tion, that is, signifies the end of the event, not necessarily the end of terror.

But it also blocks the subjective process governed by maxims and principles, indexing it to one's calculable 'interests' in the given order (ibid.: 132–3). In this second sense counterrevolution revises, rather than opposes, the principles of the revolution, and makes something else out of them. As such, it constitutes not merely an external, 'counter'-force but a strategic field of formation in which the struggle revolves around appropriating, accommodating and assimilating ideas and principles. This is why the history of modernity is the history of how the founding concepts of modern revolutions, starting with the French Revolution, are appro-priated and revised, thereby suppressed, by capitalism and the state. In this sense, the way the ideas of freedom, equality and fraternity have been captured forms the problematic of contemporary democracy.

Democratic materialism

The Oscar-nominated war film *The Hurt Locker* (2009) provides us with a perfect depiction of contemporary democracy while it recounts the story of a three-man team of US army Explosive Ordnance Disposal technicians based in Baghdad, cen-tring on Sergeant James. James and his men apparently live on borrowed time, a life that consists of a succession of episodes. They can die at any point in Baghdad, a space of abandonment in which the 'citizens' are reduced to figures of exception in which the spectre and the slave, image without body and body without image, coincide (Agamben 1998: 25).

This coincidence is, unsurprisingly, most visible in the Iraqis. On the one hand, they appear in the film as bare life, life that can be killed with impunity. The soldiers' mobile technologies 'scan' and recognize them only as a body. Yet on the other they are orientalized, spectre-like figures devoid of interiority. However, this experience is shared by the American soldiers themselves. For instance, in a telling scene, James sets about disarming a bomb; his men take up position surveying the area. Scanning the surrounding space they spot a man in an apartment block filming them with a video camera and, soon afterwards, several men watching them from a minaret who appear to signal to the man with the camera. The experience of moving through Iraq is, for the soldiers, an experience of being perilously visible, objectified and on display (see Bennett and Diken 2011).

But it is also revealed that this is not a story only about Iraq. This happens in the penultimate scene when James returns home to his wife and child somewhere in the US. Interestingly, however, the return, the family home and the supermarket – synecdochical representations of domesticity and American consumer culture, 'values' typically invoked as justification for the war – are experienced by James as perplexing and uncomfortable. A figure of exception, he is ill equipped to cope with ordinary, 'normal' life. The scene ends with him playing with his infant son in his bedroom, gently explaining to the burbling child that life is a steady process of disillusionment. This is followed by an immediate cut to a shot of Chinook helicopters coming in to land. The episodic narrative concludes with James's rearrival in Iraq, and the final shot, which returns us like a closed circuit to the opening of a narrative, shows James once again strolling down an empty street in protective bomb suit and helmet. This is the beginning of a new rotation with a different company, implying that the task is endless, Sisyphean. No progress, nothing achieved. And no event.

As such, the film spontaneously partakes in 'democratic materialism', the main axiom of which Badiou condenses in a single statement: 'there are only bodies and languages' (Badiou 2009b: 1, 34). In the film we can recognize only bio-political bodies as objective existence, without a virtual, metaphysical dimension to their being. Yet this materialist consensus is also 'democratic', not only in the sense that the soldiers are in Iraq 'to bring freedom' but also because the film recognizes the plurality of languages, cultures. Following this, the vision of *The Hurt Locker* is limited to relations between 'bodies' and 'languages', without any attempt at incorporating in the narrative a political truth. The film refuses the political gesture of depicting the action from alternative perspectives that might challenge those of the soldiers. In tandem, there is no examination of the political, military or socioeconomic purpose of their activities.

Badiou, reacting to the axiom of 'only bodies and languages', insists: 'except that there are truths' (ibid.: 4). 'Truth' always exists as an exception in relation to a given situation and introduces a transcendental dimension to 'bodies and languages'. It refers to an infinity that overcomes the finitude of actual 'bodies and languages' (ibid.: 7–9). This leap is what *The Hurt Locker* cannot achieve. With its insistence upon the materiality of bodies and, incidentally, in its foregrounding of the materiality of the film medium itself, what is striking in *The Hurt Locker* is that there is no attempt at linking to any procedure that can supplement the given situation with an 'event', with a possibility of a change regarding the given. The characters undergo no shift in their subjectivity, never come to regard their lives in a new light or overcome themselves. They are simply locked into their (bio-political) bodies and (spectacular) cultures. In the meanwhile, the film locks its audience into an 'atonic' world in which time collapses into a permanent present, a bare repetition that consists of a succession of disconnected episodes (see ibid.: 121, 420).

And because it refuses to recognize something beyond 'bodies and languages', the film has to maintain at once a bio-political and culturalist conception of its personae, constantly focusing on their fragile mortality. Hence the only passion that proliferates at the level of its narrative is the fear of death. And if the fear of death is lacking, as is the case with James, it never reaches a truth but is narcotized. James, too, obeys the crucial imperative of democratic materialism: that one should 'live without Idea' (ibid.: 511). In short, the world depicted in *The Hurt Locker* is a world that takes the 'the end of ideologies' for granted, which expresses itself as an inability to think the political, a particular blindness towards what is really at stake in Iraq: power and oil (Bennett and Diken 2011).

Freedom, equality, fraternity

This brings us back to the fate of the three concepts – freedom, equality and fraternity – in democratic materialism. Democratic materialism reduces freedom to a negative rule, the rule of what exists, in the sense that one can speak of freedom only in so far as no cultural prohibition prevents individual bodies from actualizing their capacities. Sexual freedom, for instance, a common paradigm of all freedoms today, is grounded on the articulation of bodies and cultural legislations so that one must have the freedom to 'live his or her sexuality', while it is supposed that other freedoms will follow (Badiou 2009b: 34).

To be sure, another, but related, paradigm for freedom today is consumption. The consumer society is one in which the demand for freedom is increasingly absorbed and appropriated by the market (Bauman 1998: 25). As such, consumer freedom makes other forms of freedom look 'utopian', marginalizing and rendering invisible 'all alternatives to itself' (Bauman 1988: 93). Consequently, the interplay of power and freedom takes on a new meaning, and democratic politics, which presupposes a collective interest in the 'good society', is increasingly rendered dysfunctional (ibid.: 70).

What is lost in both versions of 'freedom' is its originary sense in the French Revolution as the desire to govern oneself, the 'intrinsic charm' of freedom, which disappears whenever people seek from freedom anything 'but freedom itself' (Tocqueville 2008: 168). Modern power has always been tempted to fix the meaning of freedom and identify the possibilities of its practice within an order by transforming 'freedom' into a juridical concept of (formal) freedom applied to a technical and strategic conception of power (see Foucault 1977, 1978). As a result, in modernity freedom often appears as an effect of governmentality. Hence it seems that today

> the concept of freedom contains no *immediate* value for seizing because it
> is ensnared in liberalism, in the doctrine of parliamentary and commercial
> freedoms. [. . .] This demands, then, the reconstruction of a philosophical
> concept of freedom through a point other than itself. A free use of the word
> 'freedom' requires its subordination to other words.
>
> *(Badiou 2008b: 173)*

A similar fate meets the concept of equality. Thus the demand for equality is today
understood as a demand for 'more' in an already established system of distribution.
But equality originally means something more radical, aiming at the restructuring
of the whole social space rather than the negotiation of particular interests (Žižek
1999: 204–08). Politics always manifests itself as a disagreement on equality, on
the just distribution of the commons, and this 'just distribution' is never reducible
to arithmetic equality, balancing out what people contribute to and get from the
community, because there exist in the community those who have nothing to
contribute to the common good except their freedom to point out the wrongs, the
inequalities, in the community (Rancière 1999: 6).

> It is in the name of the wrong done them by the other parties that the people
> identify with the whole of the community. Whoever has no part – the poor of
> ancient times, the third estate, the modern proletariat – cannot in fact have any
> part other than all or nothing. On top of this, it is through the existence of this
> part of those who have no part, of this nothing that is all, that the community
> exists as a political community – that is, as divided by a fundamental dispute.
>
> *(Ibid.: 9)*

Further, as the concepts of freedom and equality are internally perverted in contemporary democracies, the concept of fraternity is subsumed under the concept
of community (Badiou 2008b: 148). It, too, has become a governmental term
through which particular communal substances (ethnic, consumptional, sexual,
religious and so on) are constantly classified, mapped and re-mapped (see Rose
1999: 175–7). What is significant here is that governmentality implies an infinite
'plurality' of what is to be governed and perceives what is to be governed as 'specific finalities' (Foucault 1991: 95). In this sense democratic materialism deals with
'bodies and languages' as a matter of managing the infinity of finitudes, without
allowing these finitudes to universalize themselves. As such, 'community' is a sign
of the impossibility of moving from the finite to the infinite, from the particular to
the universal. Its world is 'atonic' in the sense that it is devoid of the transcendental
points at which the agent can confront a truth (Badiou 2009b: 420).

Demanding the infinite

'I am not saying', Foucault emphasizes, that power is 'evil'; 'I am saying that power
by its mechanisms is infinite' (Foucault 2005: 266). The exercise of freedom, therefore, can never be limited to a determinate or finite actual form, to a 'guaranteed

freedom' (Foucault 1986a: 265). What matters is becoming free, not freedom as a state of affairs. Once freedom is institutionalized, when it is 'guaranteed', it turns into a monument of docility. 'The guarantee of freedom is freedom' (ibid.: 245). Freedom can remain freedom only if it can maintain its link to the infinite.

Equality, too, is more than a particular statement to be utilized in 'finite' situations (Badiou 2008b: 173). Rather, going beyond the situation, it links politics to the infinite. Therefore the concept must be separated from the social (e.g. the recognition of cultural differences) or from economic equality (redistribution, equal opportunities and so on). What is decisive is its subjective dimension, which opens it on to the infinite (ibid.).

> What poses a problem is really the definition of democracy. As long as we are persuaded, like the Thermidorians and their liberal descendants, that it resides in the free play of interests of particular groups or individuals, we shall see it deteriorate, slowly or rapidly, according to circumstance, into a hopeless corruption. Genuine democracy, which is what I believe we have to preserve, is a quite different concept. It is equality in the face of the Idea, the political Idea.
>
> *(Badiou 2008a: 91–2)*

Similarly, the concept of fraternity originally designates a relationship between the singular and the universal, indicating the prevalence of the 'infinite' ('we') over a finitude (the individual), an open, infinite 'we', which cannot be historicized as an actual (finite) community (Badiou 2007a: 90–1, 96, 102–04). 'Communism', precisely, stands for this impossibility, the impossibility of community as an identity, a substance or a founding gesture. The 'community' of communism can only be a 'coming community' (Agamben 1993), an immanent 'coming forth' (Badiou 2008b: 148). As such, communism is the real of politics, that which cannot be grasped or represented as 'reality' but can only be encountered as a 'stumbling block' (Badiou 2007a: 108). But, even though it cannot be represented, it can be demonstrated. The 'we' as the real is nothing but its manifestations in which it is both staged and exhausted (ibid.). In this elementary sense, communism consists in insisting on an impossible idea in a democratic materialist world without idea.

What democratic materialism really does, when it revises the concepts of freedom and equality and reduces the idea of community to actual communal substances, is to expel precisely this idea, communism, from the political scene, which is why today 'the only real question is how to open a second sequence of this Idea' (Badiou 2008a: 92).

Political situations are 'infinite', and the main task of politics is to treat this point, to relate itself to 'the ontological infinity of situations' (Badiou 2008b: 172). Democracy is not reducible to the parliamentary system or the legitimate State. Democracy is, before anything else, *the* political mode of subjectification: a process through which the *demos* can attribute to itself 'as its proper lot the equality that belongs to all citizens' and presents itself as the embodiment of the whole society (Rancière 1999: 8, 99, 116, 121).

> Democracy could thus be defined as that which authorizes a placement of the particular under the law of the universality of the political will. In a certain way, 'democracy' names the political figures of the conjunction between particular situations and a politics. In this case, and in this case alone, 'democracy' can be retrieved as a philosophical category, as from now on it comes to designate what can be called the effectiveness of politics, or politics in its conjunction with particular stakes. Understood in this way, politics is clearly freed from its subordination to the State.
>
> *(Badiou 2005a: 92)*

Paradoxically, therefore, true democracy refuses to obey a given constellation of power, including democracy as a representative system. The real meaning of democracy appears in revolt. And in this accurate sense there is a violence that pertains to democracy itself, a violence that suspends the law, takes the form of an explosion of the egalitarian impulse, a violence which functions as a 'terrorist' tendency internal to democracy (Žižek 2007a: xxxiii). This is, to be sure, a violence which is denied by democratic materialism. But does this mean that democratic materialism is itself peaceful?

Violence

Even though democratic materialism denies violence, it is itself violent. Thus, on the one hand, it dictates passive nihilism in the name of tolerance for other cultures and identities, while, on the other hand, this tolerance itself borders on 'fanaticism', for it 'seeks to destroy what is external to it' in the name of human rights (Badiou 2009b: 511). Yet it is impossible to have a concept of humanity without a concept of the inhuman, without dealing with the infinite aspect of the subject which enables it to incorporate itself into the present under the sign of the event: 'The infinite of worlds is what saves us from every finite disgrace. Finitude, the constant harping on of our mortal being, in brief, the fear of death as the only passion – these are the bitter ingredients of democratic materialism' (ibid.: 514).

Let us return to *The Hurt Locker* at this point. Described variously as 'reckless', a 'rowdy boy' and a 'real wild man' by his colleagues, James is motivated by a death drive or a desire to break through numbness or narcosis in search of intense experience. He takes risks, drinks, smokes, listens to heavy metal music at high volume, is uncommunicative and so disliked by the other soldiers that they briefly discuss killing him. His logic builds upon turning risk and sacrifice into a drug, turning renunciation of enjoyment into surplus enjoyment. Hence there is the opening quotation of the film: 'The rush of battle is often a potent and lethal addiction, for war is a drug.' Concomitantly, pain and suffering are necessary to him in order to maintain his subjectivity. As such, he is a perfect instantiation of Nietzsche's radical (or 'suicidal') nihilist. While the passive nihilist or 'democratic materialist' society is obsessed with security, James is addicted to danger. Whereas this society opts for a decaf reality devoid of passions, James is ready to trade off the social bond for his passionate attachment, his addiction. Thus the bomb, the ultimate symbol of terror in a society of fear, is James's only object of fascination (see Bennett and Diken 2011).

Thus in James courage and obsession, risk and responsibility become indistinguishable. Throughout the film his lack of self-control progressively becomes a threat to everybody around him, culminating when he unnecessarily leads his men into the alleys of Baghdad at night on a speculative hunt for some bombers. Despite this, a commentator, Richard Corliss, writes that 'the Army needs guys like James' (Corliss 2008). What if, therefore, James is the new 'Marlboro man': the soldier 'smoking while Iraq burns', an 'icon of American impunity' (Klein 2004)? Significantly in this context, like Kurtz in *Apocalypse Now*, James in *The Hurt Locker* incarnates an obscene enjoyment which does not subordinate itself to any symbolic law (see Žižek 2005). Thus he dares to face the abyss of the real, in the form of war, as a terrorizing *jouissance*. However, while both Kurtz and James are the excesses of the system, the system eliminates Kurtz because he challenges it politically and ethically. In stark contrast, in *The Hurt Locker* the system has nothing against James. Rather, the internal excess is justified and accommodated as for a war hero. Consider the case of the general McChrystal, the man who stayed in charge of the US mission in Afghanistan from June 2009 to June 2010:

> McChrystal . . . fashioned himself a 'bad-ass' early on in life. At the military academy he attended, he cultivated the art of insubordination, and was rewarded for it: when he got 100 hours of demerits, his classmates applauded him as a 'century man'. In the Bush administration, his willingness to go rogue in the name of accomplishing his objectives, and his commitment to ignoring niceties like the chain of command, the truth (he was accused of involvement in the cover-up of a friendly fire incident) or the rules of engagement (he was connected to a prisoner-abuse scandal) were likewise rewarded. He was not disciplined; he was given Afghanistan.
>
> *(Doyle 2010)*

What we get here is a depoliticized picture, in which the lack of antagonistic politics is countered with the inherent excess of the system. In this way, although it seeks to expel violence from its system of values at a surface level, democratic materialism itself produces a paradoxical, ecstatic violence:

> a violence cut off from its object and turning back against that object itself – against the political and the social. It's no longer anarchistic or revolutionary . . . It's not interested in the system's internal contradictions; it targets the very principle of the social and the political.
>
> *(Baudrillard 1998: 66)*

Is James's violence not rooted in this paradox? His violence does not mirror a (political) conflict but the level of consensus; it produces no value, no object and no ends except the reproduction of (addiction to) violence. During James's first call-out to examine a suspected roadside bomb he draws a gun on a taxi driver who tries to race across the cordoned-off street. After a tense stand-off in which James shoots out the windscreen of the car, the driver reverses and is dragged out of his car by soldiers. 'Well, if he wasn't an insurgent', James observes wryly, 'he sure the hell is now.' It is as if the culture of passive nihilism which James hates, its zeal for 'over-protection', leads to the loss of immunity; like redundant 'antibodies' that turn against the organism in which they live, James incarnates an autoimmune pathology about the system (see Baudrillard 2002: 93). And one wonders: if James is saving us from terrorists, who is going to save us from James, from (state) terror which emerges as an excess internal to the system and is normalized as a dispositif?

> To the violent promise of atony made by an armed democratic material-
> ism, we can therefore oppose the search in the nooks and crannies of the
> world, for some isolate on the basis of which it is possible to maintain that
> a 'yes' authorizes us to become the anonymous heroes of at least one point.
> To incorporate oneself into the True, it is always necessary to interrupt the
> banality of exchanges.
>
> *(Badiou 2009b: 422)*

Already Rousseau's philosophy offers a genuine approach to such an interruption. There is though a problem it cannot resolve, which relates to the practical difficulty of the political procedure in which the general will is practised. In Rousseau the principle of politics is legitimized on the basis of majority rule. However, since it is 'indivisible', the general will cannot be determined by majority, by numbers. 'Number itself cannot get its measure' (Badiou 2006a: 354). The reduction of politics to numbers is precisely what happens in representative democracy. On the other hand, the political event becomes accessible only when politics can escape the play of the sheer number, for example voting (ibid.: 353–4). But this does not mean that the number is not interesting for politics: even though the number is not properly political, that is, even though the possibilities within a situation cannot be counted in terms of a finitude, in order to put the state at a distance, politics needs a numericality in order to 'measure' this distance (Badiou 2005a: 145).

Every politics suggests the collective character of the event, that is, the infinite of the situation or presentation, but it convokes, at the same time, another infinite, that of representation or the state of the situation (ibid.: 144). To that excess it gives a fixed measure (see Chapter 3). In this sense, as prescription, 'revolution' is a demonstration of the weakness of the state, the sacrosanct indeterminacy of its excess, by creating a political function that interrupts this indeterminacy (ibid.: 147–8). Only when the state is put at a distance, which is to say measured, can the egalitarian maxim emerge and be deployed. After all, it is the immeasurability of excess that obstructs the egalitarian logic, not the excess itself (ibid.: 149). Hence the cipher of equality is the one: 'to count as one that which is not even counted' (ibid.: 150). The 1 is the number of 'the same', the figure of equality (ibid.).

If freedom is the distance from the state, equality is the move from the infinite to the 1, the production of the one. And on this account democracy is the 'adjustment of freedom and equality' (ibid.: 151).

Rousseau's impasse was determined by the discrepancy between the two meanings of the number. Because he thought of the number only in terms of the majority rule, Rousseau had to see dictatorship, in which the majority rule is suspended, as an appropriate response to exceptional situations where the survival of the state is in question. He could not move to a vision in which the state itself is problematized. His overall concern being the legitimate form of sovereignty, he found in majority rule its empirical form, but could not establish what distinguishes the political procedure itself from its actual, empirical situation. This is an impasse which originates in linking politics not to truth but to legitimacy, and which had to wait for Marx for a solution (Badiou 2006a: 353).

5

NOTHING AND EVERYTHING

Religion, says Feuerbach, takes over the best qualities of humans and allocates them to God, affirming in God what is negated in man (1989: 27). Hence there is the paradox of religious alienation: the more God is valued, the more human life is devalued. Marx repeats the same logic in *1844 Manuscripts*, where he depicts capital as a source of economic alienation: the more wealth the workers produce in capitalism, the poorer they become.

> The less you *are*, the more you *have*; the less you express your own life, the greater is your *alienated* life – the greater is the store of your estranged being. Everything which the political economist takes from you in life and in humanity, he replaces for you in *money* and in *wealth*; and all the things which you cannot do, your money can do.
>
> *(Marx 2007: 119)*

The negation of life is an inbuilt, constitutive aspect of capitalism as a system in which the labourer's own product, the 'life' the labourer confers on the commodity, constantly confronts the labourer 'as something hostile and alien' (ibid.: 70). Concomitantly, revolution designates the desire of humanity to emancipate itself from the dehumanizing effects of alienation.

The process of alienation originates in the economy. In capitalism, labour power is a commodity, a property to be sold in the market. However, it is a 'peculiar' commodity, for its consumption in the production process creates new value, a 'surplus-value' (Marx 1976: 277, 279). Herein lies the 'secret of profit-making' (ibid.: 280), 'secret' because the very 'form' of the relation between the capitalist and the worker mystifies the content of this relation (ibid.: 731). Capitalist production has the appearance of a realm of freedom and equality. Yet, when wage labour is the only form of work available, the worker cannot remain free *not* to sell his labour power: 'the *worker* has the misfortune to be *living* capital, and therefore a capital with *needs* – one which loses its interest, and hence its livelihood, every moment it is not working' (Marx 2007: 84). Likewise, since labour power produces surplus value and thus new capital, the relationship is not equal either; the process of alienation is also, at the same time, a process of exploitation: capital 'realizes itself through the *appropriation of alien labour*' (Marx 1973: 307).

Hence there is the antagonism between living labour and capital. Since capital does not have an essence, a life of its own, it needs the lifeblood of labour, relies on the appropriation of living labour, which is why Marx describes capital as a vampire-like entity (Marx 1976: 716). Capital treats everything, including labour and its creativity, as a commodity, levelling all values to exchange value, the only form of value capital can 'measure'. In other words, capital is an abstract, solipsistic entity which, instead of relating itself to an exteriority, relates itself only to itself.

Yet the notion that capital produces more capital is ultimately an illusion, and this illusion cannot be sustained ad infinitum. It is followed by crises. Therefore the problem with capitalism is not merely its alienating, solipsistic logic but also its disavowal of this logic. The unrestrained movement of capital is ultimately a capitalist fantasy through which capital can disavow its parasitic relation to living labour, the fact that capital does not beget itself but can only reproduce itself through the exploitation of living labour (Žižek 2002b: 283). What crises do is to shatter this fantasy.

Significantly, crises emanate from the internal contradictions of capitalism. In this sense capitalism is its own grave digger. There is, however, a significant tension within Marxism in this respect. *The Communist Manifesto*, for instance, proclaims this role for a political subject: the proletariat (see Marx and Engels 2002: 233). This tension becomes tangible in the context of communism, the idea which Marx initially posits against alienation and its actual form, the reign of abstract capital (Marx 2007: 102). But the antagonism between alienation and communism is not merely a philosophical confrontation between two ideas. The hope that existing social reality can be transformed merely by revolting against ideas, that liberation from ideas will automatically bring with it social change, independently of actual social relations, is itself a product of the existing relations, an ideological expression of the impotence of the idealist ideologies (Marx and Engels 1998: 401). The antagonism can only be resolved in a practical way. 'In order to abolish the *idea* of private property, the *idea* of communism is completely sufficient. It takes *actual* communist action to abolish actual private property' (Marx 2007: 124). If alienation is what breaks the link between man and nature, this link can be re-established only through an actual communist revolution, which can return humanity to itself. And revolution, for Marx, is repetition.

Repetition

In their creative moments, Marx says, people 'anxiously conjure up the spirits of the past to their service and borrow from them names, battle cries and costumes' in order to present the new in a 'borrowed language' (Marx 1977: 10). There is, however, a paradox: one can dramatize the 'spirit', awaken the dead, as part of a new struggle or, alternatively, to 'parody the old', to find once more the 'spirit' of revolution or to 'make its ghost walk about again' (ibid.: 12). On the one hand, therefore, there is a productive repetition that creates 'something that has never yet existed' (ibid.: 10). This is the repetition of an old form to produce something new, a resurrection of the past events. As such, revolution remembers the past (the spectre) in order to forget it (the ghost). And on the other hand, there is the trivial repetition which not only fails to produce something new but uses the very form of the new to perpetuate the old (Zupančič 2008: 151). Reproducing the spectre only in a mechanical way, it only simulates its phantasm, the ghost, the consequence of which is 'farce'.

Thus, 'revolution' appears twice: first as tragedy, as a productive repetition, and then as 'farce', as counterrevolution. Counterrevolution, like revolution, is also a compulsion to repeat. However, its desire to restore, to repeat, takes the empty form of farce, of bare repetition. Therefore, in counterrevolutions we always meet a state returning to its form rather than a society acquiring a new content for itself (Marx 1977: 13).

Marx thinks of tragedy and farce (or comedy) in terms of genres here. In contrast to tragedy, which necessarily causes disharmony and disruption by changing everything, farce builds upon harmony and consensus; it produces non-events within the confines of a given hegemonic discourse. Consider 'bedroom farce': couples get their beds mixed up, rushing in and out of different rooms, constantly connecting to the wrong people, and so on, but in spite of the infinite computation of relations and variables nothing really happens; the outcome doesn't change anything, and, in contrast to tragedy, no change of perspective takes place. In the end, everybody occupies exactly the same position as in the beginning. This is how Marx characterizes the Second Republic:

> alliances whose first proviso is separation; struggles whose first law is indecision, wild, inane agitation in the name of tranquillity, most solemn preaching of tranquillity in the name of revolution; passions without truth, truths without passion; heroes without heroic deeds, history without events; development, whose sole driving force seems to be the calendar, wearying with the constant repetition of the same tensions and relaxations; antagonisms that periodically seem to work themselves up to a climax only to lose their sharpness and fall away without being able to resolve themselves; pretentiously paraded exertions and philistine terror at the danger of the world coming to an end, and at the same time the pettiest intrigues and court comedies played by the world redeemers.
>
> *(Ibid.: 34)*

When the spirit of the revolution is forgotten, what sets in is a passive nihilist society, which falls back upon bare repetition, a society characterized by the absence of events, by a 'bourgeoisie platitude: life, that's all' (Derrida 1994: 137). It forgets that 'it nevertheless took heroism, sacrifice, terror, civil war and battles to bring it into being' (Marx 1977: 11).

But let us note that, for all its pettiness, farce is not a peaceful undertaking. Thus, whenever there is a threat of revolution, the 'civilization and justice of bourgeois order comes out in its lurid light . . . as undisguised savagery and lawless revenge' (Marx 2008: 62). Thus Marx compares the violence of counterrevolution, a 'comedy of conciliation' (ibid.: 61), which followed the Paris Commune, to the time of Sulla, who slaughtered the revolting Roman slaves 'in cold blood' (ibid.: 63).

But for Marx a clean-cut difference between tragedy (the spirit) and farce (the ghost), revolution and counterrevolution, is not enough, for there remains an anachronism: in so far as repetition is a matter of dramatization, of masks, the difference between 'tragedy' and 'farce' seems to reside in 'the difference of a time between two masks' (Derrida 1994: 141). Thus, we first have tragedy and then farce, first revolution and then counterrevolution. It follows that there can be no tragedy without comedy, no comedy without tragedy. And we end up in a vicious circle of revolutions and counterrevolutions, which itself can appear farcical. To get out of this vicious circle, Marx needs a third repetition:

> The social revolution of the nineteenth century cannot draw its poetry from the past, but only from the future. [. . .] Earlier revolutions required recollections of past world history in order to drug themselves concerning their own content. In order to arrive at its own content, the revolution of the nineteenth century must let the dead bury their dead. There the phrase went beyond the content; here the content goes beyond the phrase.
>
> *(Marx 1977: 13)*

The 'social' revolution goes beyond merely political or economic revolution precisely because it can turn aside from the past, stop inheritance. The third repetition is revolution as pure form – the only repetition that can end farce. But this is not a desire to end repetition as such. Revolution is by definition repetition; revolutions 'criticize themselves constantly, interrupt themselves continually in their own course, come back to the apparently accomplished in order to begin it afresh' (Marx 1977: 14). What we have here is a revolution which repeats not an aspect of the past but a configuration that puts the actual and the virtual into interaction, a revolution which occurs when we move from the 'repetition of the necessary' to the 'necessity of repetition' (Zupančič 2008: 153). In this sense, the social revolution is what takes the revolution beyond tragedy and farce, linking it to a society 'to come', to a new people. But to do this the proletariat must abolish the existing society. And in order to abolish existing society, that is, in order to create a society without alienation and exploitation, without the proletariat, the proletariat must 'abolish itself' too. Like Nietzsche's overman who wants to 'perish', Marx's proletariat must counter-actualize itself.

This Marxist–Nietzschean parallel becomes visible in Deleuze's reading of Marx. In Deleuze, as in Marx, there are three stages of repetition. Differently, however, tragedy and comedy are not taken as pre-given genres. Therefore comedy does not follow tragedy; rather, tragedy follows comedy. The repetition of temporal series starts with the comic situation, in which the actor, as in Marx, 'falls short' of creating something new, in which the event is 'too big' to become worthy of it (Deleuze 1994: 89). In this sense, comedy defines the past, which is also the first time of repetition. The second time of the repetition, tragedy, defines a present in which the actor becomes equal to the event and, seizing the moment, throws 'time out of joint'. And the third repetition, in which the future appears, 'signifies that the event and the act possess a secret coherence which excludes that of the self' (ibid.). Here the third repetition is that of eternal return, which does not allow the return of the actor's identity, 'as though the bearer of the new world were carried away and dispersed by the shock of the multiplicity to which it gives birth: what the self has become equal to is the unequal in itself' (ibid.: 89–90). The affirmation of eternal return implies the perishing or abolishment of the actor.

> In all three syntheses, present, past and future are revealed as Repetition, but in very different modes. The present is the repeater, the past is the repetition itself, but the future is that which is repeated. Furthermore, the secret of repetition as a whole lies in that which is repeated, in that which is twice signified. The future, which subordinates the other two to itself and strips them of their autonomy, is the royal repetition.
>
> *(Ibid.: 94)*

Comedy, then, is the condition of repetition. Or, Marx would say, farce is there, history repeats itself, so that man can 'cheerfully' destroy it. The repeater, the proletariat, is necessary, and it is necessary for the proletariat to pass through all the three stages, by repeating repetition itself, by making repetition and revolution a category of the future. This is why the proletariat is a singular subject. Who is the proletariat today, then, if we follow the logic of singularity?

The proletariat as 'minority'

In so far as the basic promise of a communist revolution is that 'people are missing' (Deleuze 1989a: 216), that they are 'to come', politics must be an activity that produces such 'people' rather than representing existing people. In this context we meet the proletariat as a 'minority':

> The difference between minorities and majorities isn't their size. A minority may be bigger than a majority. What defines the majority is a model you have to conform to: the average European adult male city-dweller, for example . . . A minority, on the other hand, has no model, it's a becoming, a process. One might say the majority is nobody. Everybody's caught, one way or another, in a minority becoming that would lead them into unknown paths if they opted to follow it through. When a minority creates models for itself, it's because it wants to become a majority, and probably has to, to survive

and prosper (to have a state, be recognized, establish its rights, for example). But its power comes from what it's managed to create, which to some extent goes into the model, but doesn't depend on it. A people is always a creative minority, and remains one even when it acquires a majority: it can be both at once because the two things aren't lived out on the same plane.

(Deleuze 1995: 173–4)

As minority in this sense, the proletariat is that which escapes, deviates from the majority by subtracting itself from it, because non-integration, disorganization, is the precondition to become a minority. The minor is a line of flight, a 'war machine' (Deleuze and Guattari 1987: 149–66). Its revolutionary aspect consists in its constant self-deterritorialization as a subject position, its refusal to disappear into the dominant codes and axioms (see Thoburn 2003: 111).

The concept of minority enables Deleuze and Guattari to claim that, from the perspective of the capitalist axiomatic, there is only one class, the bourgeoisie, because it is the only class adequate to the capitalist field of immanence, the class that 'leads' the generalized decoding (1983: 253–4). In capitalism everybody, including the bourgeoisie itself, is subjected to, a 'servant' of, the logic of capital. That the decoding bourgeoisie is a servant of capital implies that the capitalist society is a society of *ressentiment*, in which slaves triumph *as* slaves and command other slaves. Then the antagonism is between the bourgeoisie and the others, the minorities, between the slaves of the capitalist socius and those who 'sabotage' it, 'in their basic antagonism at the level of the axiomatic' (ibid.: 255): the bourgeois class versus the proletarian minorities. The subjectivity at stake here is one that is not 'enclosed in a whole bent on reconstituting a self (or even worse, a superego), but which spreads itself out over several groups at once' (Deleuze 2004: 193). A minority is that which makes becoming its aim, and it is in this sense that the proletariat wants to 'abolish' itself. This does not mean that the other aspect of the concept, Marx's determination of the proletarian class on the basis of the extraction of surplus value, is wrong. The problem is to assign a fixed limit between two classes, the bourgeoisie and the proletariat, on the basis of identity, while capitalism constantly displaces its interior limits (Deleuze and Guattari 1983: 255–7).

We find the latest version of a minoritarian politics in Hardt and Negri's political philosophy. Already in Negri's early work, Marx's 'living labour' coincides with Spinoza's multitude, while the law of value is reformulated as what allows capital to capture the creativity of the living labour, to subjugate the singularities of the living labour to an order of measurement (see Negri 1999). Essentially, however, the proletariat as living labour is a virtual excess 'beyond measure'. This productive excess is also a 'constituent power', the power of self-valorization, which demonstrates a creative capacity not only to destroy the transcendent values (e.g. the law of value in Marx) but also to create new values. The multitude is the 'ontological basis of transvaluation' (Hardt and Negri 2000: 359).

In this sense, revolution signifies a virtual potentiality (*potentia*), which cannot be contained within actualized dispositifs or strategies of power (*potestas*). The event, which is immanent in the free praxis of the multitude, is not reducible to the actual structures of the constituted power. Following this, radical politics signifies a struggle between the state and living labour, that is, life. Life is resistance to power. An antagonism which cannot be resolved through an affirmation of the social against the state because, possessing no fixed identity, the global multitude cannot form a society, it is 'pure potential, an unformed life force' (Hardt and Negri 2004: 192). If constituted power functions by capturing singularities and locking them into identities, the multitude designates the refusal to disappear into the apparatuses of capture, an 'exodus' from obedience, from participation in measure: 'do not obey, that is be free; do not kill, that is generate; do not exploit, that is constitute the common' (Negri 2003: 258).

And crucially, the substance of constituent power, of *potentia*, is time. An event 'situates itself in a radical manner on the edge of time, and only there' (ibid.: 235). The politics of the multitude is given immediately, in the immediacy of the event, as an opening to the immeasurable, the virtual. As such, revolution is kairological: it is the 'opportune moment' which changes time by disrupting bare repetition, the flow of chronological time (Negri 2003: 142; Hardt and Negri 2009: 165). So the antagonism between constituted power (the state) and constituting power (the multitude) is fundamentally an antagonism between the chronological time (of measurement) and the kairological (immeasurable) time, the 'time for revolution' (see Negri 2003: 139–59).

The aim of revolution is to institute an immanent, 'absolute democracy'. In this, Hardt and Negri follow Spinoza: democracy cannot be reduced to a social contract. The social contract, whether it is absolutist (Hobbes) or democratic (Locke), has a transcendent character; it transfers, through representation, the power of the people to an external sovereign power, which functions according to a unitary, absolute and transcendent logic (Hardt and Negri 2000: 7). In a Spinozist perspective, on the other hand, the powers of the singular cannot be transferred to a sovereign; democracy must be conceived of as a horizontal continuity, not as a vertical discontinuity (Albertsen 2001: 6). In the perspective of immanence, the multitude is the only absolute sovereign.

. . . and as negativity

However, in Marx the proletariat does not signify only the positive, creative power of the 'living labour'; it is, at the same time, a negativity that cannot be abolished without the actualization of the idea of communism (Marx 1975: 187). The proletariat is both a negative result of the bourgeois society and its negation, that element 'which prevents the totality from ever achieving a closure, for it points, precisely, to the antagonism within the totality' (Kouvelakis 2003: 330–1). Badiou and Žižek, for instance, approach the proletariat from the perspective of this negativity.

For Badiou, there is in every situation one element which does not 'appear' (or 'exist') in a determinate way. In this sense, despite its social and economic existence, Marx's proletariat is, in terms of political appearance, a non-existent, a 'nothing', which, in order to become 'everything', needs to change the whole existing situation (Badiou 2009c: 130–5). The event consists in a 'cut' in the continuum of immanence made by this inexistent element, a 'lack', which then becomes an intense existence, an 'excess' (Badiou 2009b: 384).

Similarly, for Žižek, the socio-symbolic order is inconsistent and the real is located in this gap within its immanence. The event, consequently, is the explosion of the real within the socio-symbolic order. As such, the gap within the immanence involves a 'generative', 'positive notion of lack' (Žižek 2004: 61). Žižek articulates this positivity with reference to Deleuze's sense-event, which is at once a neutral effect and a productive quasi-cause. Since corporeal causality (the socio-symbolic order) is not complete, and since the event is not reducible to this order, 'quasi-cause' is 'a pure, transcendental capacity to affect' which 'fills in the gap of corporeal causality' (ibid.: 27). It is therefore the 'exact equivalent' of *objet petit a*, the immaterial cause of desire (ibid.). Following this, Žižek problematizes the Deleuzian duality of being–becoming from the point of view of Badiou's duality of being-event: we have, at the level of being, the 'multitude of interacting particularities', while the event functions as 'the elementary form of totalization/unification' (ibid.: 28). The gap in being is also the proper domain of politics, for it is this gap that differentiates the real event and the socio-symbolic reality (see also Smith 2004b: 638).

In this way, as negativity, the 'proletariat' still signifies the dissolution of the existing social order. As the class which has nothing to lose and everything to win, the proletariat must abolish the existing social 'bond' (see Badiou 2005a: 75). Hence the proletariat turns the principle of the proletariat, its inclusion in the existing society as negativity, into a political principle: '*I am nothing and I should be everything*' (Marx 1975: 185, 187). The real stake of a proletarian revolution is not the emancipation of the proletariat as such but 'universal human emancipation', for every form of servitude is basically a modification of the relation of the proletariat to production (Marx 2007: 82).

But within the perspective of negativity, there can be only one subject: the proletariat. The antagonism is between the proletariat and the others. Thus for Badiou, the bourgeois class stands for the given, the inertia of representation. It belongs, in other words, to the situation. 'There is one place, and one subject. The dissymmetry is structural in nature' (Badiou 2009a: 130). The true adversary of the 'proletariat' is not the bourgeoisie as a class but the whole bourgeois world of which the proletariat is the principal antagonistic force.

> Why? Because the project of the proletariat . . . is not to contradict the bourgeoisie, or to cut its feet from under it. This project is communism, and nothing else. That is, the abolition of any place in which something like a proletariat can be installed. The political project of the proletariat is the disappearance of the space of the placement of classes. It is the loss . . . of every index of class.
>
> (Ibid.: 7)

The subject is that which cannot be inscribed in the situation except as an excess, and its measure demands the destruction, or the torsion, of the structure in which it emerges (ibid.: 131). This is why the proletariat itself emerges as the torsion of the structure.

The proletariat against pure politics

If politics is an attempt at changing the situation of everybody, of the whole society, it is always a particular (e.g. 'working class') that stands in for the universal ('human'). But the 'proletariat' cannot be reduced to the working class as an actual identity. Marx therefore distinguishes the working class as an objective (actual) social category and the proletariat as an abstract (virtual) subjective position, the class 'for itself', that embodies social negativity. In this context, what made the working class specific for Marxism was its location in an eventual site, in a singular place. Today, however, this 'function of the working class is saturated' in the sense that we can no longer say the emancipation of this class is the emancipation of everybody (Badiou, in George 2008). But the problem remains the same: the move from particularity to universality.

There are today new particular candidates (such as 'immigrant', 'refugee', the 'sans-papiers', and so on) which can potentially fill in the same space once occupied by the figure of 'worker'. Characteristically, these groups stand in the position of an internal exclusion; although they are part of a national whole, the national proletariat, they have no rights in this whole. All the 'immigrant' has, for instance, is a particular sociological identity (see Rancière 1999: 118). A process of political subjectification, on the other hand, would allow the 'inexistent' of what exists to 'abolish' itself as a category, while at the same time developing another vision, another topology of politics which transcends the merely distributive struggle to achieve rights within a given situation (Badiou 2009a: 262–6). What is crucial in this respect is going beyond the idea that politics *represents* particular, objective groups (Hallward 2003: 240–1).

But the potential problem here is the 'totally privileged position' of politics (Badiou 2008b: 160), the distance of 'politics at a distance' not only from actual reality but also from the economy. For Badiou, after all, only a political universalism can challenge the universalism of capital. Hence, as class antagonism gives place to pure politics, Badiou relegates

> capitalism to the naturalized 'background' of our historical constellation: capitalism as 'worldless' is not part of a specific situation, it is the all-encompassing background against which particular situations emerge. This is why it is senseless to pursue 'anti-capitalist politics': politics is always an intervention into a particular situation, against specific agents; one cannot directly 'fight' the neutral background itself. One does not fight 'capitalism', one fights the US government, its decisions and measures and so on.
>
> (*Žižek 2008b: 403*)

Consequently, 'pure politics' comes to seem more Jacobin than Marxist in its neglecting the economy, pushing it out of ontology as if it were a limited empirical, 'ontic' sphere, rather than dealing with it as a transcendental matrix that generates the totality of social and political relations (see Žižek 2002b: 271). However, despite its 'apolitical' appearance, the economy is the 'structuring principle' of politics; the logic of capital is not merely a fact of the particular 'domain' of the economy, but a principle that 'overdetermines' the whole society (ibid.: 332). Or, with Deleuze, the 'economy' is not only an actual entity:

> That is why 'the economic' is never given properly speaking, but rather designates a differential virtuality to be interpreted, always covered over by its forms of actualisation; a theme or 'problematic' always covered over by its cases of solution. In short, the economic is the social dialectic itself – in other words, the totality of the problems posed to a given society, or the synthetic and problematising field of that society. In all rigour, there are only economic social problems, even though the solutions may be juridical, political or ideological, and the problems may be expressed in these fields of resolvability.
>
> *(Deleuze 1994: 186)*

The economy is at the same time virtual and immanent, embedded in actual relations defined by solutions. To deal with the economy, and thus class struggle, only as an empirical, positive category is to ignore its virtuality. If, on the other hand, the economy is treated as a virtual problem, the mediation between the virtual and the actual becomes decisive. This mediation is what disappears in the reduction of the economy to a moment of politics. The pure-political critique of economism must therefore be 'supplemented by its obverse', with the economy, which is '*in its very form*, irreducible to politics' (see Žižek 2002b: 272).

This, in turn, does not mean the reducibility of politics to the economy. Rather, both irreducible, the relationship between the economy and politics is a parallax similar to that of 'two faces or a vase': one sees either two faces or a vase depending on the displacements and shifts of perspective, but never both at once. In this particular sense, there is no relationship between the economy and politics; one cannot 'see' them both at once: one can only choose focusing on the political, which reduces the economy to an empirical domain, or on the economy, which reduces politics to a theatre of appearances (Žižek 2002b: 271–2). In this sense, 'class struggle' designates an impossibility, the lack of a meta-language that can comprehend the two levels from the same point of view despite the fact that they are entwined (ibid.: 272).

The economy as a virtual entity that overdetermines the whole society is correlative to class struggle as the fundamental antagonism of the social, into which all other struggles are condensed (Dean 2006: 59–60). But it never appears as such, as *the* fundamental antagonism, for it is always mediated by other antagonisms such as religious, ethnic or social conflicts (Žižek 2008b: 286). Class struggle rather functions as the number zero, as that which does not have an objective counterpart.

It can be represented only as a lack, as a black hole (see Žižek 2000: 113–14). Just as zero is involved in all rows of numbers even though it is literally not there, class struggle is the zero degree of political order. In this sense, class struggle is 'real', the traumatic core of the social which distorts the social actors' view of it (Žižek 2008b: 287–8). Therefore it cannot be reduced to any form of identity politics. On the contrary, the aim of class struggle is to 'aggravate' differences (e.g. race, gender and class differences) into a fundamental antagonism which functions as the 'structuring principle' of other antagonisms (Žižek 2009b: 161–2). For this reason, class struggle is not focused on the recognition of the other; rather, it seeks to overcome and abolish the other – 'even if this does not mean direct physical annihilation, class struggle aims at the other's sociopolitical role and function' (ibid.: 362).

But class struggle is not a hidden meta-essence that expresses itself through other, for example cultural, struggles. On the contrary, the determining aspect of the economy lies in its being the 'absent cause' of antagonisms (Žižek 2008b: 290). Yet the gap between an antagonism and its absent cause can be dealt with only through politics:

> Politics is thus a name for the distance of the 'economy' from itself. [. . .] there is politics because the economy is 'non-all', because the economic is an 'impotent' impassive pseudo cause . . . simultaneously the hard core 'expressed' in other struggles through displacements and other forms of distortion, and the very structuring principle of these distortions.
>
> *(Ibid.: 291)*

Following this, politics is not merely one type of struggle among others but rather the 'formal principle of antagonistic struggle as such' (ibid.). In other words, politics has no specific content of its own. It is a formal way of dealing with issues involving other specific spheres of life such as the economy, sexuality, welfare services, and so on. This formal aspect also explains why everything *is* potentially political.

After all, if fidelity to the name 'proletarian' only emerges as the result of a contingent political struggle based on the 'naming' of the political subject, such naming depends on an analysis of the actual, contemporary capitalism and its contradictions. The conditions of the communist movement can only 'result from the now existing premise' (Marx and Engels 1998: 57). And today's actual social questions are ecology, intellectual property, new technological developments and the new forms of exclusion (see Žižek 2008b: 428). What is significant, however, is that the antagonisms revolving around these social issues are not of the same intensity. While the first three relate to the 'commons' (e.g. the 'earth' which we all share, the collective values privatized by networks, and so on), which in itself justifies a reference to communism (see Hardt and Negri 2009: 169), there is a qualitative difference between the gap that separates the excluded from the included and the other antagonisms. Here the reference is to the 'proletariat', not only in terms of pure, substanceless subjectivity but also as a figure excluded from the social space, introducing an egalitarian dimension to the discussion of the commons, a dimension without which 'ecology turns into a problem of sustainable development, intellectual property into a complex legal challenge, biogenetics into an ethical issue' (Žižek 2009a: 97–8). In the end, it is logically possible to address any antagonism without challenging the gap between the included and the inexistent (ibid.: 98). This is why we still need concepts such as the proletariat.

> In other words, if one wants an older model, it is rather the trusty Communist formula of the alliance of 'workers, poor farmers, patriotic petty bourgeoisie, and honest intellectuals': note how the four terms are not at the same level – only workers are listed as such, while the other three are qualified ('*poor* farmers, *patriotic* petty bourgeoisie, and *honest* intellectuals'). Exactly the same goes for today's . . . antagonisms: it is the antagonism between the Excluded and the Included which is the zero level antagonism, coloring the entire terrain of struggle.
>
> *(Žižek 2008b: 428)*

6

STRATEGY AND INTOXICATION

> Lenin's wavering between the adventurist utopianism . . . and his own real-
> ism was not accidental. It was one of the manifestations of his split person-
> ality, as it were: he was a man who on the one hand was a visionary and a
> narrow fanatic, and on the other, had his feet firmly planted on the ground.
> It was this combination of contradictory qualities which helped him win the
> hypnotized devotion of both idealists and rogues. The former saw in him
> the Messiah who would lead them to the promised land of democracy and
> socialism. Those were the pure in heart . . . But there were also the not-so-
> pure-in-heart . . . who saw in Lenin a political gang leader of genius.
>
> (Nomad 1961: 320–1)

This is how Max Nomad's *Apostles of Revolution* repeats the standard appraisal of
Lenin: Lenin as the name of the oscillation between two extremes, between utopian intoxication and calculative, instrumental rationality. But does politics need to
choose between these two poles? What if this is a false dichotomy, thereby a false
choice, and therefore a trap for true politics? What if, in other words, the relationship between 'utopianism' and 'strategic calculation' does not necessarily point
toward a 'split', an antinomy, but rather to an aporia intrinsic to the temporality
of the event, *kairos*? After all, *kairos* signifies a double necessity, deciding and being
decided, seizing the moment and being seized by it, at once: two dimensions,
which must be held together in the form of a disjunctive synthesis, without letting
the one collapse into the other. Thus, on the one hand one must transcend the
'vicious circle' of politics as usual:

> *Every* question 'runs in a vicious circle' because political life as a whole is
> an endless chain consisting of an infinite number of links. The whole art
> of politics lies in finding and taking as firm a grip as we can of the link that

is . . . most important at the given moment, the one that most of all guarantees its possessor the possession of the whole chain.

(Lenin 1952: 502)

Confronted with such an 'endless chain' of bare repetition, one must take the risk of a leap; decide and act. This leap is at once incommensurable with the existing situation and immanent to it, for it is 'not a blind leap into the dark' but one based on a strategic analysis of the actual situation, the existing balance of forces, with maximum objective accuracy (Callinicos 2007: 26–7). For the same reason a coherent and disciplined organization of dedicated revolutionaries is necessary. This is what legitimates the party for Lenin. Without a stable organization, no movement can take the 'leap'. And the more the masses are drawn into spontaneous revolts, the more necessary the party is, for it can push the proletarian movement beyond the confines of trade union consciousness. A revolutionary party must establish a distance to economism and differ from other workers' organizations which seek to become as wide and as public as possible. The party must be more restrictive and secretive to be able to combat the tsar's secret service (see Lenin 1952: 375–6, 451–3, 464–7).

What necessitates the Leninist party is the problem of inconsistency: although every particular revolt in one way or another refers to 'communist invariants', for example claims on equality or the critique of private property and the state, this is not enough for a revolution. What is crucial is the formation of a resonance between dispersed revolts. However, the party is not a simple instrument of unification. Just as Marx and Engels conceive of the Communist party in the *Manifesto* not as a 'bond' that represents a class but rather as a mobile platform seeking to 'delimit' the unbound multiplicity of the proletariat's 'excessive' position in the society, for Lenin the party does not stand for the ultimate bond uniting the Bolsheviks – rather it is 'a disparate coalition riddled with all sorts of public disagreements, debates and fractions' (Badiou 2005a: 74–5).

What is decisive for such an organization is the mutual relationship between mass revolt and elite conspiracy (Trotsky 1967, vol. III: 159–64). On the one side, only through mass insurgence can a regime be defeated. A pure conspiracy, even victorious, cannot alter power relations decisively. Therefore the logic of individual terror, for instance, is strictly rejected by Lenin. But on the other side revolution cannot be reduced to insurrection. It must be accompanied by a subject 'strong enough to break (or dislocate) the old government, which never, not even in a period of crisis, falls, if it is not toppled over' (Lenin 1964: 214). To take power, insurrection must be supplemented with strategy, an organization, which seeks to politicize revolts, turning 'blind violence' into political acts (see Žižek 2002b: 225; Dean 2006: 194). In this sense, the Leninist temporal strategy is based on the readiness to seize the moment, 'a state of being available to act in relation to whatever event may arise' (Bensaïd 2007: 159).

This dimension of *kairos*, readiness to decide, on the other hand, is accompanied in Lenin by an absolute decidedness. Consider the April Theses, where he insists on the dissolution of the Russian parliamentary democracy and rejects any patriotic support for Russia's 'imperialist' war with Germany and Austria, arguing instead for the establishment of a militant International. Most importantly, he depicts here the situation of Russia as one that can enable the transfer of power to the working class and the peasants: 'all power to the soviets'. No wonder these theses, when presented at the Tauride Palace, did not exactly make him popular:

> To the majority of those present this was a thunderbolt, a repudiation not only of the previous Bolshevik position, but, it appeared, of Marxism itself. 'Everybody' knew that this was not the moment for a Socialist revolution, but for a bourgeois democratic one. Lenin's theses were a declaration of anarchism, of adventurism unworthy of a Marxist. 'But this is nonsense', shouted one Menshevik, 'insane nonsense.' To others it appeared that surely Lenin was out of touch with real conditions in Russia. [. . .] Triumphantly, the Menshevik leaders concluded that this man was obviously politically dead.
>
> *(Ulam 1965: 432)*

Is it not, especially at a time of war, more 'realistic' to fight for attainable goals, for example better social legislation, better pay, and democratic rights, and wait for better times for the revolution? But Lenin 'is always thinking politically', and this is what strikes his commentators 'as obsessional and repulsive, inhuman' (Jameson 2007: 62–3). What makes Lenin's political thinking 'inhuman' is, precisely, his absolute receptivity, his enthusiasm for the revolution: his willingness to be formed by the moment, his intoxication, which seizes him, as much as his will to seize the moment. And if such a kairological double act seems 'insane nonsense' it is because it neither seeks any 'guarantee' regarding its actual consequences nor tries to hide behind the big Other, behind references to 'objective' facts. If anything, the Leninist kairology transcends such opportunism, which is based on the fear of accomplishing the act, and which therefore reduces politics to pragmatic adjustments, 'realistic' compromises and interest negotiations (Žižek 2002a: 8).

> Here we have two models, two incompatible logics, of the revolution: those who wait for the ripe teleological moment of the final crisis when revolution will explode 'at its own proper time' according to the necessity of the historical evolution; and those who are aware that revolution has no 'proper time', those who perceive the revolutionary chance as something that emerges and has to be seized in the very detours of 'normal' historical development. Lenin is not a voluntarist 'subjectivist' – what he insists on is that the exception (the extraordinary set of circumstances, like those in Russia in 1917) offers a way to undermine the norm itself.
>
> *(Ibid.: 10)*

In so far as the proletariat is not merely a particular class among others but rather a non-class, a singularity that cannot be assimilated into the social structure, and thus becomes the universal class, this universality can emerge only if the normality, the 'vicious circle', which pertains to the regular order of particulars, is disrupted. In this sense, there is no such thing as a 'normal' revolution; each revolution is grounded in an exception (Žižek 2002b: 298). Just as the French Revolution took place because France could not follow the 'normal' English path of capitalist development, the Russian Revolution invented an exception to what Marx saw as 'normal', that only a thoroughly industrialized country could realize the transition to socialism (ibid.). The exception, understood in this way, 'permits, or rather compels, the adoption of whatever is ready in advance of any specified date, skipping a whole series of intermediate stages' (Trotsky 1967, vol. I: 22). This possibility, the possibility of skipping over the stages, was the kernel of the Leninist desire to 'give history a push' (see Ulam 1965: 323).

Paradoxically, it was only because he did not take Marx literally but rather 'betrayed' him that Lenin was able to actualize the first Marxist revolution (Žižek 2002b: 315). After all, a theory can be 'repeated' only through a displacement; repetition always produces a difference, something new, which changes the conditions of the original idea, redefining its terms and coordinates. Thus repeating Marx can only mean 'tearing his theory out of its original context, planting it in another historical moment, and thus effectively universalizing it' (Budgen et al. 2007: 2–3). In this sense Lenin produced novel statements, 'Leninist statements' (Deleuze 2006: 279). Consider this passage in Lenin's pamphlet 'On Slogans':

> Too often has it happened that, when history has taken a sharp turn, even progressive parties have for some time been unable to adapt themselves to the new situation and have repeated slogans which had formerly been correct but had now lost all meaning – lost it as 'suddenly' as the sharp turn in history was 'sudden'. Something of the sort seems likely to recur in connection with the slogan calling for the transfer of all state power to the Soviets. That slogan was correct during a period of our revolution – say, from February 27 to July 4 – that has now passed irrevocably. It has patently ceased to be correct now. Unless this is understood, it is impossible to understand anything of the urgent questions of the day. Every particular slogan must be deduced from the totality of specific features of a definite political situation. And the political situation in Russia now, after July 4, differs radically from the situation between February 27 and July 4.
>
> *(Lenin 1974: 185–6)*

The right slogan, for Lenin, is the one that can identify the moment and name the decisive task at hand, condensing the analysis of the situation (see Lecercle 2007: 276–7). This analysis is always the analysis of an empirical, concrete situation. But it is always, at the same time, a performative statement which constitutes an incorporeal transformation. For instance, Marx and Engels's slogan 'Workers of the world, unite!' extracts from the masses a 'class' *before* the proletariat exists as a body. Repeating the same logic, the Leninist statement extracts the 'party' from the proletarian 'class' (Deleuze and Guattari 1987: 100).

Then, if repeating Marx is not a literal 'return' to Marx, repeating Lenin cannot be a return to Lenin either. To repeat is to accept that such a return is not possible, that the Leninist sequence is over, that Lenin's particular solution to the problem of revolution 'failed', and did so 'monstrously' (Žižek 2002b: 310). But how did this 'failure' take place?

Counterrevolution as Stalinism

> A popular insurrection, by its very nature, is instinctive, chaotic, and destructive . . . The masses are always ready to sacrifice themselves; and this is what turns them into a brutal and savage horde . . . And in moments of crisis, for the sake of self-defense or victory, they will not hesitate to burn down their own houses and neighborhoods, and property being no deterrent, since it belongs to their oppressors, they develop a passion for destruction. This negative passion, it is true, is far from being sufficient to attain the heights of the revolutionary cause; but without it, revolution would be impossible. Revolution requires extensive and widespread destruction, a fecund and renovating destruction, since in this way and only in this way are new worlds born.
>
> *(Bakunin 1973: 334)*

Any radical politics, asserts Benjamin, must 'win the energies of intoxication for the revolution', the energies which have been lacking in Europe 'since Bakunin' (1979d: 236). For reality, in order to transcend itself 'to the extent demanded by the *Communist Manifesto*', an experience of discharge is indispensable (ibid.: 239). Only a politics that can accommodate intoxication, a 'poetic politics', can go beyond the domain of pragmatic calculations and 'bind revolt to revolution' (ibid.: 237). Then strategic thinking must be linked to an intoxication, not as a religious experience ('the opium of people') but as a 'profane illumination' taking place in a materialist context (ibid.: 227).

In other words, any true political intervention must be able to 'interweave' the two dimensions of *kairos*, strategy and intoxication: 'Force of hate in Marx. Pugnacity of the working class. To interweave revolutionary destruction with the idea of Redemption (Nechaev. The Devils)' (Benjamin, quoted in Löwy 1993: 153). Marx the Possessed/Devil; Marx with Nechaev. What fascinates Benjamin in Nechaev is precisely the element of intoxication. After all, 'The Revolutionary Catechism' defines the revolutionary as a possessed person with no personal interest, no property, no name: 'Everything in him is wholly absorbed in the single thought and the single passion for revolution.' The revolutionary is the 'enemy' of every bond the social order represents; he 'continues to live with' these bonds – the laws, morality, traditions and conventions, which he sees only as semblances – only in order to 'destroy them'. 'He knows only one science, the science of destruction.' And he 'despises public opinion' – his logic needs no dialogue (Nechaev 1869). The single invariant in Nechaev's thought, the injunction to be a revolutionary, is a self-referential and self-sufficient maxim; it needs no external justification. No objective, no teleological aim or ethical–practical condition can delimit the reach of this logic, according to which whatever serves the revolution is ethical. In short, Nechaev's 'revolutionary', negating all possible 'relation' to the actual society, and doing so without any compromise, aims at putting an absolute distance to the state.

But since *kairos* means both seizing and being seized, it is easy to fall on either side: trying to seize the moment without being seized by it, or being seized by the moment without a strategy to seize it. There are many variations on both defaults of *kairos*. And these variations define another series of counterrevolutions.

Let us start with *kairos* as strategic calculation, which relates back to the question of sovereignty. If counter-revolt in pre-modernity leads to the constitution of sovereignty (see Chapter 2), the idea of revolution is a modern answer to the problem of sovereignty. This also explains why the idea of revolution, as a modern idea, is so fixated on, fascinated by, sovereignty. Thus one of the fault lines in radical politics is the question of whether a revolution without sovereignty is possible. This question is pertinent because the Leninist model, specifically, addresses the problem of revolution in terms of a counter-power, the vanguard party, which to a high extent mirrors the state power it opposes. And with Stalinism the party turns into an apparatus of sovereignty, bracketing the idea of revolution.

This, however, did not happen on the basis of external factors only. The factors were internal to the Leninist party. Crucially in this respect, a common thread in Lenin's politics is his contention that there persists a separation, a gap between revolutionary insurgencies and their actual stakes, a gap

> between revolution qua the imaginary explosion of freedom in sublime enthusiasm, the magic moment of universal solidarity when 'everything seems possible', and the hard work of social reconstruction which is to be performed if this enthusiastic explosion is to leave its traces in the inertia of the social edifice itself.
>
> *(Žižek 2002a: 7)*

But this separation of the 'event' and the 'work' reproduces an old problem, the collapsing of correlative aspects of revolution into a phase model (Raunig 2007: 39). At the heart of this model there is the distinction between spontaneity and centralism. The party model recognizes spontaneity during a first stage, only to demand the necessity of centralization in the next stage. Thus, even though it is clear that radical politics cannot emerge on the basis of occasional local struggles only, a problem emerges regarding the combination of spontaneity and centralism in a hierarchic way. The Leninist party tends, at this moment, to become a part of the constituted rather than the constituent power, leading to the exclusion of practices not fixated on the state, for example the soviets, the councils, self-management and so on (see Raunig 2007: 30–1). In this sense, although the Leninist model realized 'a real break in historical causality', the price has been 'turning the party, once a modest clandestine group, into an embryonic State apparatus able to direct everything . . . and substitute itself for the masses' (Deleuze 2004: 197). This does not mean that Leninism was essentially, in its nucleus, a totalitarian ideology. But it means that Stalinism – contra Trotsky's repeated claim that Stalinism was an external deviation which had nothing to do with Leninism – was an internal perversion of the Leninist model (Žižek 2007d: 74–5). If it evolved into a dispositif of counterrevolution, it did so mainly for internal reasons.

What is at issue here is, again, the relationship of the revolution with its past, with repetition. If revolution is by definition repetition, Stalinism is a failed repetition of Leninism. This is visible especially regarding the calamity of the very concept of revolution under Stalinism. In Leninism, 'revolution' plays the role of *object a*, an excess of the situation which cannot be represented in the socio-symbolic reality, that is, referred to a subject supposed to know, to a big Other; it is an open-ended situation, a risk-taking endeavor, which may or may not end in success (Dean 2006: 90).

> The Leninist stance was to take a leap, throwing oneself into the paradox of the situation, seizing the opportunity and *intervening*, even if the situation was 'premature', with a wager *that this very 'premature' intervention would radically change the 'objective' relationship of forces itself, within which the initial situation appeared 'premature'*– that it would undermine the very standard to which reference told us that the situation was 'premature'.
>
> *(Žižek 2001a: 114)*

In Stalinism, in contrast, truth is 'objective', not a partisan truth initiated subjectively. Stalinism is a claim on objectivity, a desire for a guarantee in the big Other, in the universal laws of history. The Leninist party knows that there is a gap, that the desire for revolution cannot be grounded in objective knowledge. Therefore it can only understand revolution as a break in gradualness. 'Gradualness explains nothing without leaps. Leaps! Leaps! Leaps!' (Lenin, quoted in Bensaïd 2007: 159). The Stalinist party fills in this gap with fantasy, the illusion that the party *really* knows the object of desire, that its actions are grounded in the objective knowledge of the laws of history, and transforms 'the constitutive leap into a linear story' (Zupančič 2008: 169). In this sense Stalinism is farcical repetition, 'a return to the realistic common sense' (Žižek 2002a: 5). Thus

> the Stalinist period brought a total and implacable ban on all cultural experiments and the elevation of petty-bourgeois commonsense, now dubbed 'socialist realism', to the rank of the dominant cultural idiom. [. . .] The culture of 'socialist realism' was a culture of average taste, and the average tends to abhor and to eradicate the unusual, the novel, the out-of-the-ordinary, the utopian.
>
> *(Bauman 1976: 85)*

The more one is enrolled in common sense, the more one repeats to avoid real repetition. Consider the show trials. Since the Stalinist party is supposed to incarnate the objective truth (e.g. on the essence of capitalism, the development of history, the conditions for revolution, and so on), it cannot, by implication, make mistakes. Hence the result of the trials was always known in advance, which made them look farcical. In the trials, even to claim one's innocence merely confirmed a fundamental guilt, that of prioritizing one's own interests rather than those of the party. A true comrade would sacrifice herself for the party, even when she is 'subjectively' guiltless. To claim innocence thus demonstrated the lack of fidelity, thereby guilt. As such, as a comedy of terror, the Stalinist bare repetition sought to conceal one fundamental fact: the internal perversion of the revolution, a process in which 'confession of guilt conceals the true guilt', the betrayal of the revolution by the party itself (Žižek 2009b: 287; see also 2001a: 128–9).

Interestingly in this context, on several occasions, both before and after the revolution, Lenin explicitly acknowledged that his party stood for organized terror, that organized violence is necessary during times of revolution (see for instance Lenin 1965). But the Stalinist terror was always hidden, functioning as 'the publicly non-acknowledged obscene shadowy supplement of the public official discourse' (Žižek 2002b: 261–2). This obscenity marks a parallel between Stalinism and Nazism. What made both the camps and the Gulag possible is that the perpetuators saw themselves as instruments of an obscene superego figure.

However, Stalinism is not Nazism. For one thing, while truth is objective in Stalinism, it is subjectively grounded in Nazism. Whereas in Stalinism truth is, in principle at least, open to everybody, that is, everybody can learn the objective, universal rules of History, in Nazism truth is seen as the attribute of an identity, the Aryan race. Hence there were no show trials in Nazism. Since the mythical Aryan insight was accessible only to Germans, it would have made no sense to try to make the Jews see it. Thus, whereas the victim of the show trials 'has to participate in his own public degradation, actively forsaking his dignity', the *Muselmann* is simply reduced to a living dead with no interiority whatsoever (Žižek 2001a: 87–8).

In fact, its fixation on objectivity, its reduction of truth to knowledge and the virtual into the actual, not only separates Stalinism from Nazism but also brings it closer, in a rather uncanny way, to contemporary democratic materialism. Both ideologies focus, in dealing with the social bond, on 'objectivity' and speak from the position of 'neutral' knowledge, presenting what is really political as a matter of fact (see ibid.: 139). Both depict their societies in eschatological terms, as the 'end of history' (the 'end' being communism in one case and liberal democracy in the other). Both rely on the denial of a radical, utopian dimension to politics and depict the given reality as the only reality, pushing radical politics to the background. And in both the politics of fear appears as the only remaining way to introduce passion into a pacified, depoliticized society (Žižek 2008a: 34): two societies of fear, one Stalinist, one democratic materialist, each with its own comedy of terror (see also Excursus II on the Stalinist present).

The fascist intoxication

If sovereignty was invented as a response to the pre-modern revolt, and if revolution is a modern response to sovereignty, fascism is a radical re-manifestation of sovereignty in modernity. Therefore it needs to construct itself in the image of a Master, a Führer, who ends the 'chaos' and establishes order. In this, fascism addresses life as a bio-political issue. However, fascism is also a politics of death. Thus the Nazi, for instance, sought to open up not only a Lebensraum for the Aryans, but also a Todesraum for its dehumanized victims. The camps were the epitome of this dehumanization, which culminated in killing. Why? At this point, every rational explanation is necessarily mistaken, for it would mean seeing fascism as a means to something else (see Agamben 1999c: 31–2). What makes the camps disconcerting is really 'their anti-utilitarian function' (Arendt 1994: 233).

This sacrificial aspect allows a parallel between religion and fascism. Fascism is an ideology that desires to become a new religion, to create a perfect community, a paradise on earth in the image of a self-referential sovereignty. Therefore it attracts many: after all, 'the offering to obscure gods of an object of sacrifice is something to which few subjects can resist succumbing, as if under some monstrous spell' (Lacan 1994: 275). But a 'realist' approach to fascism cannot grasp this sacrificial element. Just as it can see only strategic/calculative reason in the place of *kairos*, when, for instance, it makes an opportunist out of Lenin, it cannot perceive the element of desire in fascism. Yet fascism, too, is a desire, an unconscious, rhizome-like movement, '*before* beginning to resonate together in the National Socialist State' (Deleuze and Guattari 1987: 214–15), a desire for intoxication, for being seized by an event. But we must not stop here, for there are different forms of desire. We must identify how the desire for intoxication operates in fascism. For the desire of fascism is a desire which 'desires its own repression' (ibid.: 215). Fascism is 'to desire the very thing that dominates and exploits' (Foucault 1983: xiii). Ultimately, therefore, fascism is a line of death, of 'destruction, abolition pure and simple, the passion for abolition' (Deleuze and Guattari 1987: 229).

Yet, while fascism functions as an 'obscure' religion, there is a fundamental difference between fascism and religion. Let us follow Kierkegaard to illuminate this difference. Abraham is Kierkegaard's hero of faith because his readiness to sacrifice his only son, as an act of madness, exemplifies the essence of faith and confirms the supremacy of God's authority. However, Abraham does not pretend to have understood God's will. God does not reason or negotiate with Abraham: he demands; Abraham obeys. His act of sacrifice 'bridges' the earthly and the divine, the actual and the virtual, without annihilating the distance. In believing, Abraham is certain that God exists. But although he knows that God exists, this knowledge remains partial; uncertainty, too, is absolutely necessary. Kierkegaard's belief thus involves 'fear and trembling', without which the believers would be reduced to puppets in a mechanical universe (1962: 7, 111). Thus faith can 'bridge' the human and the divine only temporarily; it continuously needs to be reaffirmed (ibid.: 51–62). The Nazi terror, in contrast, cancels this very distance between the divine and earthly realms. The Nazi is certain that he has direct access to God's will and perceives himself as the instrument of this willing God. As such, the gap between the actual and the virtual is no longer mediated but traversed as both are reduced to elements on the same continuum. In this sense, the key to understanding the libidinal economy of fascism is enjoyment or, more specifically, the sadistic enjoyment derived from 'doing one's duty', from the self-instrumentalization in relation to a superego figure.

> The obscene jouissance of this situation is generated by the fact that I conceive of myself as exculpated for what I am doing: isn't it nice to be able to inflict pain on the others in the full awareness that I'm not responsible for it, that I am merely an agent of the Other's Will?
>
> *(Žižek 2001a: 112)*

Because fascism incarnates such an obscene enjoyment, its evil is not only 'banal' as in Arendt, but also sadist. In either case, however, it is not possible to offer a precise, objective definition of fascism. Its sense can be approached only through paradoxes and riddles. This is why *Life Is Beautiful*, a wonderful film on camps, defines fascism through riddles. The most interesting riddle in the film is the final one: 'Fat, fat, ugly, ugly. All yellow in truth. If you ask me where I am, I will tell you "quack, quack, quack!" While walking I defecate. Who am I, tell me.' But Lessing, the Nazi doctor who asks the riddle, explains in advance that the answer is not a duck. The riddle is effectively without a solution, an 'anti-riddle' that does not contain the possibility of an objectively correct answer. If one seeks to find an answer, either the rule that riddles ought to have only one correct answer is violated or, alternatively, the correct answer is not verified (Siporin 2002: 350).

In this sense the Holocaust is unspeakable, the limit of language, that which cannot be represented. Yet, that it is unspeakable does not mean that speaking about it should be a taboo. Just as 'normalizing' it, reducing it to history, is not a solution to the riddle of the Holocaust, sacralizing it makes critical reflection impossible. This was after all what the Nazi wanted (see Agamben 1999c). So the paradoxical task is to speak about the unspeakable, to make the aporetic character of testimony the starting point for a radical ethics that can resist the sovereign exception. After all, in relation to bio-politics, a categorical ethics is not sufficient. The crucial question here is not the content of an ethical stance but rather to decide who counts as a subject worthy of ethical concern in the first place, not the content of particular rights as such but the right to have rights.

But how do we move from ethics to a political critique of the present – and from the Holocaust to contemporary fascism? After all, contemporary fascism remains virtually unspeakable in the sense that the word functions like a taboo. There are many who talk and walk like fascists but they cannot be 'named' as fascists. Why? Perhaps because many people expect that, unless a political group literally repeats all the ideological axioms and actions of the Nazi, one by one, and in exact empirical order, we cannot call it fascist. It is as if fascism is defined, once and for all, as Nazism, with the eerie consequence that on this account fascism no longer exists, or exists only as an extreme, archaic phenomenon.

But what if we consider fascism as a creative idea, which cannot be reduced to its actual forms such as Hitler's or Mussolini's fascism? Fascism, like communism or capitalism, is a generic idea, which expresses itself differently in different times and spaces. Also in this sense the riddle above has no solution: fascism is a 'virtual', metaphysical problem that cannot fully actualize itself in concrete 'solutions'. It has therefore a virtually endless repertoire. And if fascism cannot be reduced to Nazism, it is necessary to see its contemporary permutations, its endless resurrections, even when it appears as its opposite.

Therefore it is crucial not to reduce fascism to a 'totalitarian ideology' in Arendt's sense (1973). For one thing, there are significant differences between different ideologies collapsed into this category, between communism and fascism, for instance: whereas communism radicalizes the fundamental antagonism in a capitalist society, class struggle, for the purpose of a political event, fascism disavows it by displacing it on to a racial antagonism. Thus, while communism defines the main antagonism in terms of class, the fascist antagonism appears as one between races or nations. While in communism the 'new' is something to be created, to come, and thus 'resists all categorization', fascism seeks to 'restore' an already given identity in the form of race, nation, blood and soil (Badiou 2007b: 16). As a result, despite its critique of capitalism, and despite its subordination of the economy to politics, fascism is an 'inherent self-negation of capitalism', a desperate effort to 'change something so that nothing really changes' (Žižek 1991: 186). Ultimately, therefore, the difference between communism and fascism is the difference between revolution and counterrevolution. And in so far as it pushes this political difference to the background, the concept of 'totalitarianism' is an apolitical concept, a concept which presupposes an ideological space in which liberal democracy is taken for granted (Žižek 2001a: 3).

The Weberian blackmail

Let us go back to Nechaev. True, his figure of the revolutionary borders on a 'destructive character': a radical nihilist who has 'no vision' but is obsessed with one activity: 'clearing away' (Benjamin 1979c: 157–8). But we must also note, contra the mainstream political philosophy which finds only a senseless violence in Nechaev, that it is not violence in itself that is the problem here. After all, extreme enthusiasm, intoxication and extreme violence often go hand in hand in politics, for what is at stake is the transvaluation of *all* values. The Leninist 'passion for the real', for instance, knows of 'no morality' (Badiou 2007b: 14). Both Lenin and Nechaev juxtapose the real and its semblances; for both, the revolutionary activity is necessarily an activity of 'purification', of 'extracting the real from reality', making the real coincide with its semblance: 'the real as pure event of its transparency' (ibid.: 15). The danger, though, is radical nihilism, a terrorism à la Nechaev, for 'the real as a total absence of reality is nothingness' (ibid.). This is why Benjamin insists, regarding the revolutionary 'intoxication', that the actual must not be destroyed (see Chapter 2). Likewise, Marx warns against the 'conspirators' such as Bakunin and Nechaev who try:

to launch a revolution on the spur of the moment, without the conditions for a revolution. For them the only condition for revolution is the adequate preparation of their conspiracy. They are the alchemists of the revolution and are characterized by exactly the same chaotic thinking and blinkered obsessions as the alchemists of old. They leap at inventions which are supposed to work revolutionary miracles: incendiary bombs, destructive devices of magic effect, revolts which are expected to be all the more miraculous and astonishing in effect as their basis is less rational. Occupied with such scheming, they have no other purpose than the most immediate one of overthrowing the existing government and have the profoundest contempt for the more theoretical enlightenment of the proletariat about their class interests.

(Marx and Engels 1978: 318)

And herein we arrive at the aporia of *kairos*: violence is necessary but there is no calculus as to how much violence is revolutionary violence. *Without* a calculus, the risk is to fall into the trap of radical nihilism, while the danger *with* a calculus is passive nihilism. In other words, both sides of the *kairos* – strategy and intoxication, calculus and conviction, knowledge and faith – are necessary. Strategy without intoxication (passive nihilism) is as useless as intoxication without strategy (radical nihilism).

This is the fundamental problem with conservative theory of revolution: it can think of this aporia only in terms of antinomy. Weber, for instance, approaches the 'split' between strategy and intoxication as an 'antinomy', as a contradiction between 'the ethic of conviction' and 'the ethic of responsibility'. Thus, he claims, confronted with the inherent 'ethical irrationality of the world' (1958: 125), all political action has to make a choice between two 'opposed maxims': *either* it can justify itself with reference to an 'ethic of ultimate ends', to an 'absolute ethic' that does not ask questions regarding consequences – e.g. the dogmatic Christian act 'does rightly and leaves the results with the Lord' – *or*, assuming the burden of decision-making, it 'follows the maxim of an ethic of responsibility, in which case, one has to give an account of foreseeable results of one's actions' (ibid.: 120). This is, as Weber formulates it, also a choice between saying 'my kingdom is not of this world' and 'adaptation' to the sociological reality of modernity, in which case 'all talk of "revolution" is farce, every thought of abolishing the "domination of man by man" by any kind of "socialist" social system or the most elaborated form of "democracy" a utopia' (quoted in Callinicos 2007: 22). Weber's choice is thus ultimately between two renunciations, between renouncing the existing world in the name of an idea or renouncing an idea in the name of the existing world, between values without facts or facts without values, or between radical nihilism and passive nihilism. Whenever the gap between strategy and intoxication is seen as an antinomy rather than aporia, this 'choice' appears as blackmail: either, or.

Therefore it is necessary to insist on 'aporia rather than antinomy' (Derrida 1993: 16). On the one hand, an engagement with the actual, a strategic calculus, is necessary. On the other hand, however, intoxication is equally indispensable to the subject. If you lose faith, there is no point in engaging in radical politics. Both sides of *kairos* are vital. What matters is to keep them in relation. And since this relation cannot be a dialectical relation, since a synthesis is impossible or will result in antinomy, the relationship must be thought of as a disjunctive synthesis, as a parallax of strategy (the economy) and intoxication (pure politics).

But it is not enough, either, to say that this aporia must be maintained, for it will result in the infinite deferral of actualization. Therefore, finally, the aporia must be overcome in praxis, in actual repetition of the idea. In Nietzsche, the figure of overcoming is the eternal return, the only way to get out of the deadlock of radical and passive nihilism, which necessarily involves a self-overcoming, the 'perishing' of the nihilist. In Marx, communism is what overcomes the vicious circle of revolution and counterrevolution, a process which, again, 'abolishes' the subject. Crucially, in both perspectives, what is overcome is false antagonisms and thus false choices. The false antagonisms, in this sense, provide the space for repetition: the false choice between radical and passive nihilism exists so that the nihilist can perish, overcome himself; farce is there so that one can 'cheerfully' destroy it. This is why radical politics always starts with questioning the consensus in a given social space. Free thinking always involves going beyond given questions. 'This is the "Leninist" point on which one cannot and should not concede: today, actual freedom of thought means freedom to question the prevailing liberal-democratic "post-ideological" consensus – or it means nothing' (Žižek 2002b: 168).

7

MASS MOVEMENT, ELECTIONS AND THE MEDIEVAL MAN

> Communism cannot be reached unless there is a communist movement.
>
> *(Mao 2007: 118)*

If Lenin's repetition 'betrayed' Marx by actualizing the revolution in a 'wrong country', in Russia, Mao repeated Lenin by realizing the revolution with the 'wrong class', with peasants (see Žižek 2007b: 2). However, although the status of the peasantry in the Chinese Revolution was a significant departure from the position of the Leninist party, Mao's model was still the party-state, a model which had, at the beginning of the 1960s, started to generate serious problems. Political creativity, for instance, had become unattainable within the party. Thus, reminiscent of his earlier critique of Stalin for focusing on the economy rather than on politics, Mao in this period targets the Chinese Communist party itself, arguing that despite the revolution's success at the level of relations of production many problems remained unresolved at the level of 'superstructure or politics' (Mao 2007: 117–18). Above all, the revolution's ambition to realize the 'end of mankind', to overcome the capitalist subjectivity by creating a new humanity, was not achieved (ibid.: 183).

Thus, in order to invent a new form of politics vis-à-vis a bureaucratized party, in order to repeat the revolution, Mao turned to the forces located outside the party: the students, the workers, the youth and the army. He relied on the masses, hoping that the masses would 'educate' themselves in a revolutionary movement. In this sense, as a mass movement decoupled from the logic of the party, the Cultural Revolution signifies 'a political experience that saturates the form of the party-state' (Badiou 2006b: 292).

Why the masses? Although it is not political in itself, the mass always points toward an eventual site, a crack in the structure of the situation (Badiou 2005a: 72). Its movement is always a potential revolt which interrupts the functioning of the state, opening up new possibilities. But only to the extent that it can undo its 'bond', by affirming singularities as against the consistency of social groups represented by the state, does the mass become politicized (ibid.).

On this account the Cultural Revolution failed because, despite its successful mobilization of the mass, it failed to establish a distance to the state, which became evident when Mao started to worry about the anarchy caused by the rioting students and forced them to recognize the authorities. Mao was himself a 'man of the party-state': he wanted to renew the party, not to destroy it, and had no other hypothesis regarding the state than the line of party reconstruction (Badiou 2006b: 317). Thus he tried to contain the revolts within the very framework of the party-state. As a result, the local rebellions remained diffuse and fragile, unable to translate their particular tactical innovations into strategic political propositions. However, they had a universal success: they showed to the world that the party-state had exhausted itself, that the questions of organization and mass politics could no longer be submitted to the logic of class representation (ibid.: 299).

In other words, the significance of the Cultural Revolution lies in its severing the link between the mass and the party, between political movement and class representation. In the years since the Cultural Revolution, there have been many experiments with a 'politics without the party' (ibid.: 321). May '68 is the most significant one among them.

May '68

May '68 is trivialized today through the stereotypical images of the hedonist hippy, whose self-obsession prefigures the contemporary culture of narcissism, or the abject Maoist militants 'going to the people'. Yet May '68 was neither a depoliticized carnival nor a tale of abjection (Ross 2002: 102–3). The context of May '68 was an anti-capitalist critique coinciding with anti-totalitarian movements, challenging the way society was organized. The stakes were global, and protests took place in many countries.

But it all culminated in Paris, where thousands amassed on the Left Bank, in protest against de Gaulle. Outraged by police violence, many Parisians were sympathetic to the revolt. Students were announcing to the media that they dismissed the capitalist power and refused to obey the Gaullist police. Cobblestones were ripped from the streets and were used, along with railings and burnt-out cars, to erect barricades in the streets against police forces. The Paris stock exchange, a symbol of capitalism, was set alight. France's unions called a general strike in support of the students. It was the largest labour disruption in the history of France, and brought everything to a standstill.

Crucially, therefore, even though it started as a student revolt, May '68 cannot be confined to students alone and their interests, that is, to politics of identity. The emerging political subjectivity was articulated in terms of freedom and equality rather than actual identities such as student, worker and so on (Ross 2002: 11, 57). This opened up a new political space and united intellectual contestation with workers' struggle, which is also the reason why the event quickly took the form of a general strike, gaining its impetus from an ideological refusal of capital and the state. In this sense May '68 signifies a general 'flight from social determinations', a series of displacements and becomings that affected many more than a single social group, students (ibid.: 3–4).

> There were a lot of agitations, gesticulations, slogans, idiocies, illusions in '68, but this is not what counts. What counts is what amounted to a visionary phenomenon, as if a society suddenly saw what was intolerable in it and also saw the possibility of something else. It is a collective phenomenon in the form of: 'Give me the possible, or else I'll suffocate . . .' The possible does not pre-exist, it is created by the event. It is a question of life. The event creates a new existence, it produces a new subjectivity (new relations with the body, with time, sexuality, the immediate surroundings, with culture, work . . .).
>
> *(Deleuze and Guattari 2006: 234)*

In the end, however, the strikes were halted, public transport began again and petrol returned. The cobblestoned streets were covered with tarmac. The event came to an end as quickly as it started. And de Gaulle returned to power in the May election – hence the seemingly strange claim: it is 'beyond question that the election was the essential recourse to dissolve and crush the movement' (Badiou 2008a: 33).

Election as counterrevolution

As a mode of measuring 'opinion', elections are symptomatic for contemporary politics, not because they occupy particular times and spaces in politics but, more importantly, because they function as a 'grid' that frames, and thus delimits, our political perceptions (Deleuze 2006: 144). Consider an example: October 2009, West London, the BBC Television Centre. Inside, the leader of the British National Party (BNP), Nick Griffin, participated in the prime-time British TV programme *Question Time*, watched by 8 million people, together with three other panellists from the three mainstream parties in the UK: the Labour Party, the Conservative Party and the Liberal Democratic Party.

There was much opposition regarding the participation of the BNP in the programme. Many people insisted that the BBC would be doing a racist party the biggest favour in its history. Considering that it was only a few months before the 2010 general election in the UK, this was an important argument. The winning argument, however, was another: since the BNP is a legal party, entitled to fight elections, win seats and receive public funding, it should be able to get time on prime-time television. As Mark Thompson (2009), the BBC's director-general, put it, the public had a right 'to hear the full range of political perspectives'. People must accept that the 'BNP, sadly, are an active part of our democracy, and the BBC was right to invite Nick Griffin on to Question Time' (Denman 2009).

At a first glance, this democracy functioned well on the programme. Griffin did not answer questions directly, trying to spin off every question to irrelevant issues, denying the citations from his former speeches, where for example he had praised the Nazis. When he was asked why he had met Ku Klux Klan leader David Duke, he said Duke was a non-violent figure, triggering off laughter. When asked about whether he had denied the Holocaust, his answer was: 'I do not have a conviction for Holocaust denial.' And then, after characterizing homosexuals as 'creepy', he referred to immigration as a 'bloodless genocide' that destroys the English identity and turns the 'indigenous British' into a minority in their own country. And so on.

Griffin was an easy target for the liberal establishment: remaining at the centre of the debate for most of the programme, he was grilled by the righteous majority around the table (which he called 'a lynch mob') to the extent that at one point, when he was nervously trying to answer the question on the Holocaust, Dimbleby, the presenter of the programme, asked Griffin 'Why are you smiling? It is not a particularly amusing issue.' At another moment, when Griffin was again ridiculed, one of the panellists, Jack Straw, the justice secretary (Labour), dubbed him the Dr Strangelove of British politics, alluding to Peter Sellers's bizarre anti-hero who keeps referring to the US president as Mein Führer.

Nonetheless, there was a very interesting twist in the programme, when, at an exceptional moment, Jack Straw himself was asked by a member of the audience whether it was not the recent immigration policies that had led to the rise of the BNP. After all, Straw was the man who started the British version of the 'debate' about Muslim women's veils. Straw was hesitant and could only try to divert the question, refusing to answer it, while Griffin was smirking. Straw was now receiving his own message in its inverted form, while his own populist attempt at hijacking the issue of immigration from the far right was backfiring. It was therefore 'no small irony that Jack Straw should set himself up as Griffin's opponent' (Younge 2009). This was a strange moment, which did not really belong to the programme. But precisely as such it revealed the truth of the programme, of the election mode: for all the 'debate' it offered its viewers, what *Question Time* really did was to confine the debate within the existing political 'grid', in which the main political antagonism appears to be that between the liberal establishment and the right wing, an ideological blackmail imposing a forced choice, for example a choice between fundamentalism, right-wing populism, racism and so on, on the one hand, and liberal democratic consensus on the other. What *Question Time* really avoided was disrupting this liberal democratic consensus.

There is in this sense a link between elections and repression. Elections are not in themselves repressive, but they are today accommodated by liberal democracy and the parliamentary state (Badiou 2008a: 34). Although they were a radical aspect of the French Revolution, they function today as a counterrevolutionary element in politics.

> In history, competent majorities have legitimated Hitler and Pétain, the Algerian war, the invasion of Iraq . . . There is nothing innocent, therefore,

about 'democratic majorities'. To praise numbers because people came out to vote, independently of the result, and to respect this majority decision in a proclaimed indifference to its content, is another symptom of [a] general depression. [. . .] In actual fact, what we sense here, without people really being able to articulate it, is that elections are at least as much an instrument of repression as the instrument of expression as they claim to be. Nothing produces greater satisfaction on the part of the oppressors than to hold elections everywhere, to impose them, by war if need be, on people who did not ask for them.

(Ibid.: 32–3)

Voting, the main political activity today, is a highly depoliticized practice, for it tends to reduce politics to affects. The rightist populist politics of fear, for instance, boils down all political issues to the 'problem of immigration'. Establishment parties, in turn, articulate their lack of political conviction and goals by trying to manipulate the 'fear of the fear', for example the possibility that their opponents, the rightist parties, will come to power by capitalizing on fears in a populist fashion. Fear against the fear of fear; Griffin versus Straw. Hence the politics of fear borders on passive nihilism – nothing really political happens, and in this sense 'what is lacking in the vote is nothing less than the *real*' (ibid.: 11–12). Consequently, as the difference between the Left and the Right disappears into a dialectic of affects, primarily of fears, the logic of the parliamentary democracy starts to resemble that of the single-party system (ibid.: 28). Consensus turns into an invariant of politics, and most significant issues cease to create scissions, taking the capitalist order, democracy and the market merely as an unquestionable, naturalized background. In a certain sense, therefore, 'Stalinism was the future of parliamentary democracy' (ibid.: 29).

Medievalism

As Deleuze insisted, with an allusion to Nietzsche, since an arrow was shot in space last time, since May '68 it is as if nothing has happened in our society, as if we are passing through a period of desert, characterized by the lack of event (see Deleuze and Parnet 1996). In other words, since May '68 we have been living in a generalized counterrevolution. Significantly in this respect, May '68 was a traumatic event for the establishment. Thus in the 2007 French elections Sarkozy was still promising to 'put an end to May '68' (quoted in Badiou 2008a: 40). This counterrevolutionary period, however, coincided with something else, the general saturation of the fourth, Maoist revolutionary sequence, which followed the Jacobin, Marxist and Leninist sequences, the symptom of which is the difficulty of repetition, of inventing productive and creative forms of revolutionary politics at a time in which 'the idea of revolution is obscure in itself':

Today we have an experimental sequence from the point of view of political practice. We have to accept the multiplicity of experiences. We lack a

> unified field – not only in something like the Third International, but also in concepts there is no unified field.
>
> *(Badiou, in George 2008)*

Badiou concludes that, because of this obscurity, we are today closer to Marx than Lenin, to the nineteenth century than the twentieth. This makes sense, but one wonders whether we did not reach beyond the nineteenth century as well. Interestingly in this regard, since the late 1970s there has emerged a new emphasis in the political discourse on ethics, and especially two figures, human rights and the Gulag/Holocaust, 'came to orchestrate good and evil' (Ross 2002: 12). This discourse was bent on repudiating May '68 specifically and the idea of revolution in general. Later, the same regime of representation found a new ground to articulate the spirit of counterrevolution: the war against terror. The key image of thought in this context is the 'clash', of civilizations and of religions. In this prism, Western power is perceived to be essentially different from and opposed to Islamic fundamentalism. The West is understood either as a secular society obsessed with consumerism (Barber 1996) or as a humanistic version of the Christian faith (Huntington 1997). In both cases, however, it is a civilized, non-antagonistic and non-crusading civilization that counters a barbaric version of Islam. Islamic fundamentalism becomes, in turn, a synonym for chiliastic fanaticism. The new enemy is, in other words, 'an unruly medieval subject in a modern world' (Holsinger 2007: iv). What provokes fear in such a world is the 'failure to be modern' (ibid.: v). And this fear exposes a fundamental inability in the West:

> Two philosophical references immediately impose themselves apropos [the] ideological antagonism between the Western consumerist way of life and Muslim radicalism: Hegel and Nietzsche. Is this antagonism not the one between what Nietzsche called 'passive' and 'active' nihilism? We in the West are the Nietzschean Last Men, immersed in stupid daily pleasures, while the Muslim radicals are ready to risk everything . . . Furthermore, if we look at this opposition through the lens of the Hegelian struggle between Master and Servant, we cannot avoid a paradox: although we in the West are perceived as exploiting masters, it is we who occupy the position of the Servant who, since he clings to life and its pleasures, is unable to risk his life (recall Colin Powell's notion of a high-tech war with no human casualties), while the poor Muslim radicals are Masters ready to risk their life.
>
> *(Žižek 2002c: 40–1)*

To experiment with this idea further, let us recall that there are two 'active' nihilisms in Nietzsche with opposite orientations: while 'perfect nihilism', or anti-nihilism, seeks to transvaluate existing values in order to create new ones, the second, 'radical nihilism', is basically a will to nothingness (see Nietzsche 1996: 67, 119). What if, therefore, our political predicament is rather a false antagonism between radical and passive nihilisms, a 'clash' between willing nothingness and not willing at all, between fundamentalist terror and democratic materialist passivity? Much ideological confusion today stems from this juxtaposition. One obsession in this context is to see in fundamentalist terror the spirit of chiliastic apocalypticism.

Hall (2009) provides a perfect example. His main point is this: although apocalypticism has historically been a strong militant tendency in all three monotheistic religions, in the West, especially through the Reformation, it is 'tamed'. The Protestant ethic brought with it an emphasis on worldly vocations and a religious accommodation of 'rationalized time' (ibid.: 84; see also Weber 2003: 157). Consequently, articulated with chronological time, the time of modern governmentality, the apocalypse was 'secularized' (Hall 2009: 164). But even if the 'apocalyptic tradition', in which figures such as Paul, Müntzer and Robespierre are included, has been generally pacified, some remainders of it still exist today (ibid.: 195). Contemporary Islamic terrorism, like Leftist terror and Marxist guerrilla movements in the twentieth century, is thus seen as an 'apocalyptically structured' ideology that insists on the 'sacred' in a secularized world (ibid.: 164, 173).

Hall's narration is an illustration of how religion and terror are brought together in the horizon of democratic materialism, of a telling blindness towards two decisive issues. On the one hand, it mystifies the content of the 'taming' here, its historical links to counterrevolution. And, on the other hand, it glosses over decisive differences between the apocalyptic tradition and today's fundamentalist terrorism. To discuss these issues, I am tempted to contrast the contemporary katechontic take on the apocalypse, which legitimizes counterrevolution in general and the war on terror specifically, with Taubes's revolutionary theology of apocalypse, which seeks a total delegitimization of power.

Passive nihilism versus the apocalypse

> The very idea that the dawn of the millennial kingdom on earth always contained a revolutionizing tendency, and the church made every effort to paralyse this situationally transcendent idea with all the means at its command.
>
> *(Mannheim 1936: 211)*

For Taubes, the starting point of eschatological apocalypticism is the concept of alienation. In the existing world, injustice is abundant, and both man and God are alienated (2009: 26). Beyond *this* world, there is *that* other world, the world to come, which promises freedom (ibid.: 27). But this difference between *this* and *that* is not a blueprint for nihilistic escapism; rather, it implies a transvaluation in the properly Nietzschean sense. And corresponding to the two sets of values, there are two Gods: the God of creation, of the existing world, and the God of redemption (ibid.: 29). The latter will come by annihilating the existing world. This God to come, who is '*new* to the world', is also a promise of a revolution, a 'turning point': he 'will annihilate the world and then appear in his might' (ibid.: 10).

Since freedom from what exists is its goal, revolution necessarily looks beyond *this* world. It brackets the actual order and existing beliefs, which are the foundations of the actual world. What is significant is that, in this tradition, spanning from the Gnostic theology to the Exodus to Maccabean revolt, the Zealots and Thomas Müntzer, the dialectic between *this* (natural) and *that* (supernatural) world interlock not in the heart of the individual, as a personalized faith, but as two different but interrelated systems, two 'kingdoms'. The 'moment when "this" world touches "that" world . . . is the *kairos*' (ibid.: 68). To be sure, what we have here is a transcendent philosophy which operates with concepts such as eternity (rather than infinity), the God of redemption (rather than the virtual), and so on. But what is significant is its structure, its understanding of revolution as a relation to the virtual infinity and of *kairos* as 'the mystery of the universe' (ibid.).

And this structure can be endorsed from the point of view of power as well. Schmitt, for instance, the 'apocalyptician of counterrevolution' (Taubes, quoted in Ratmoko 2009: xvi), puts *kairos* in the service of power, seeking a theological legitimation of the political. Thus, while the apocalyptic world view seeks redemption in the 'end' of the world, Schmitt advocates *translatio imperii*, that is, the evolution of the Roman Empire into the Holy Roman Empire and the Third Reich. However, this worldly power cannot become 'holy', according to the apocalyptic tradition, for the holy is, precisely, the 'measure' of the God to come: 'The holy is the terror that shakes the foundations of the world. The shock caused by the holy . . . bursts asunder the foundations of the world for salvation' (Taubes 2009: 194).

In this radical sense, the idea of messianic apocalypse cannot be really assimilated by sovereignty. But then how did it gradually disappear? Already in Origen Adamantius (ad 185–254), who brought together the New Testament, the idea of redemption, which in the apocalyptic tradition necessitates the 'end of the world', mutates into an 'individual eschatology', and chiliasm becomes condemned as a Jewish heresy based on 'error and illusion': eventually the Parousia, second coming, becomes redundant, and Christians 'pray for the *end to be delayed*' (ibid.: 77). And once Christianity becomes the official religion of the empire, the Church turns out to be conciliatory to power, and 'any hope for God's Kingdom is snuffed out' (ibid.). Later, especially in Augustine, this reversal becomes sealed.

However, unlike his predecessors, Augustine did not confront chiliasm directly. Rather, he 'reinterpreted' it, taking the eschatological sting out of it and changing its direction. Here the antithesis between the Kingdom of God and the kingdom of the world is still the guiding principle of history, but for Augustine Rome will not be followed by a new world. Instead, the end of Rome will be the end of the whole world (ibid.: 80–1). More importantly, whereas in the apocalyptic tradition the kingdom belongs to the future, is to come, Augustine reverses this futurity by declaring that the Church is already 'the Kingdom of Christ and the Kingdom of Heaven' (ibid.: 80). Stalinism of Christianity? With this move, the messianic promise is definitively excluded from the Church, and starts to appear as 'heresy'.

Ever since Augustine, *individual* eschatology has dominated both the Catholic and Protestant denominations of the Christian Church. Universal eschatology, which bears within it the expectation of the Kingdom, from now on appears within the Christian sphere of influence as *heresy*.

(Ibid.: 80)

Finally, with modernity, the revision is perfected. The Reformation, or 'Copernican Christianity' as Taubes (2009: 108) calls it, is 'modern' in the sense that it takes for granted the loss of heaven, of the idea that there is a heaven above the world in which the new God lives. But 'under an empty heaven', in a world in which the virtual collapses into the actual, to act for salvation becomes irrelevant – when salvation is reduced to the work of grace, which does not necessitate actors' active participation, 'man's fulfillment of the law becomes pointless' (ibid.: 108). In other words, in the apocalyptic tradition, the dialectic between the actual and the virtual, the earth and heaven, is preserved; divine justice must be found, resurrected, in *this* world (ibid.). In Copernican Christianity, by contrast, rebirth (resurrection) ceases to have a power to shape the actual world. When reconciliation is distinguished from redemption, when heaven and earth are separated as two distinct points of view, it becomes possible to envisage 'a secular world in which all spirituality is subordinated to, and defenseless against, worldly power' (ibid.: 109).

Seen in this perspective, a double movement is visible: while it 'sacralizes' power through political theology, modernity also 'secularizes' eschatology, excluding it by accommodating it (Bradley and Fletcher 2010: 2). This tamed, decaf version of eschatological apocalypse, fit for a passive nihilist society, is also the 'blind spot' of contemporary liberal democracy. Consider Fukuyama's neo-evangelistic 'good news' that the 'end of history' has arrived, that all regimes in the world, including dictatorships, now evolve towards liberal democracy (1992: xii–xiii, 212). On the one hand, this thesis sacralizes a particular, actual expression of temporal power, the market, turning it into the *telos* of history (Bradley and Fletcher 2010: 2). But, on the other hand, this divinized liberal democracy is distinguished from its empirical manifestations, arguing that it is a 'trans-historical', that is, an infinite, virtual idea that cannot be reduced to its actual, finite manifestations or delegitimized by use of empirical evidence (see Fukuyama 1992: 139).

> *With the one hand*, it accredits a logic of the empirical event which it needs whenever it is a question of certifying the finally final defeat of . . . everything that bars access to the Promised Land of economic and political liberalisms; but *with the other hand*, in the name of the trans-historic . . . ideal, it discredits this same logic of the so-called empirical event . . . to avoid chalking up to the account of this ideal and its concept precisely whatever contradicts them in such a cruel fashion: in a word, all the *evil*, all that is *not going well* in the capitalist States and in liberalism.
>
> *(Derrida 1994: 86)*

As such, the eschatology-light does not really exclude the dialectic between the actual and the transcendent. Rather, it flattens it so that the 'idea' loses its power of destroying and transvaluating what exists, becoming instead the potentiality of an already sacralized liberal democracy. In a sense, Fukuyama is doing here to the 'trans-historical' idea what Schmitt did to the concept of exception, turning its revolutionary potentiality into a counterrevolutionary justification of the given. His novelty lies in using the tools of passive nihilism as well as political theology in this endeavour. Thus, while he sacralizes the liberal democratic market, he also levels the transcendent ('heaven') and the actual (the 'earth') in such a way that the idea of revolution, of something other than liberal democracy, becomes redundant. His is, in other words, a chiliasm without divine violence.

However, for all its condemnation of violence, this tamed, secularized eschatology is not less violent than the revolutionary eschatology. The difference is not between violence and non-violence but between two forms of violence: the eschaton and the katechon (or, with Deleuze and Guattari, war machine and war). Consider the war against terror, which flirts with the idea of holy or just war, allowing it to enter the public discourse with reference to emergency. The religious emphasis in the war against terror lies on absolute values such as freedom and democracy. 'Freedom is the non-negotiable demand of human dignity; the birthright of every person – in every civilization' (Bush 2002). And the US is the 'vanguard' of freedom and liberty (ibid). The war against terror incarnates 'the collective will of the world' (Bush 2001a). The US acts as a Leviathan 'to rid the world of evil' and so on (Bush 2001b).

Yet, there are significant differences between eschatological apocalypticism and this 'holy' war. While eschatology understands 'freedom' in a mode of futurity, as the freedom to come, the war against terror recognizes it only in a conservative manner, only in terms of existing values, specifically as market freedom. While eschatology negates 'this' world to short-circuit it with 'that' world, the war against terror seeks to sustain 'this' world, with no ambition of overcoming its positivity. While the first is a war of transvaluation, of a non-existent God 'to come', the latter is prepared to sacrifice everything to keep it at bay. Whereas the gaze of eschatology is turned towards the virtual, the war against terror is fixated on the actual (or only acknowledges the virtuality of what already exists). If the first perceives 'terror' as a means of destruction to open up a space for the event, to touch eternity (or infinity in our terminology), the latter turns (state) terror into a dispositif geared towards pre-empting eventualities and governing finite 'bodies and languages'. While the first calls for kairological spirituality, the latter literally protects the time of shopping, claiming that it cannot 'let terrorists achieve the objective of frightening our nation to the point where we don't . . . conduct business, where people don't shop' (Bush 2001c).

It is its counterrevolutionary aspects that make the war against terror farcical, a comedy of (t)errors. Hence it is parasitic on the expectation of happy endings (bringing democracy and so on) and advocates harmony and consensus within the confines of a given hegemonic discourse. The only subject position this comedy allows for is that of 'types' whose actions are a direct outcome of their social positions rather than of singular ('tragic') choices. As Aristotle puts it, 'comedy is . . . an imitation of inferior people' (1999: 9). It is striking, in this respect, to observe the parallel between the infantilized subject of security and the frightened subject of terror, the hostage. The hostage is an anonymous figure, a naked, formless body, which is absolutely convertible: anybody and everybody can be a hostage (Baudrillard 1990: 34–5). Likewise, the politics of security redefines the citizen as a fearful subject to be protected, like a child. Anybody and everybody must be protected. Consequently, both the enemy and the friend are de-subjectified: while the 'enemy' is outlawed as an illegal combatant, the 'friend', the subject of security, becomes infantilized and depoliticized.

Radical nihilism versus the apocalypse

Is Al Qaida a continuation of the eschatological tradition then? Is contemporary Islamic terrorism a 'real' apocalypticism which can be contrasted to the 'tamed' eschatology of Fukuyama or Bush?

Islam, too, shares the foundation of apocalypticism with pre-monotheistic and other monotheistic religions (see Taubes 2009: 31). There are therefore, at first sight, some similarities between the apocalyptic tradition and the fundamentalist Jihad. Al Qaida, too, emphasizes that fidelity to a principle is not enough; something 'more', a radical act, is necessary. And in search of this 'more', it explicitly distances itself not only from unbelievers but also from those 'lukewarm' believers who postpone the apocalypse, the inevitable clash between believers and unbelievers, and let the right moment for intervention pass. True faith urges one, in this perspective, to act on behalf of God and other believers (see Moussalli 1999: 38; Münkler 2002: 70–1).

However, the problem with Al Qaida's ideology, what makes it look like 'Disneyland Islam' (Al-Qattan 2001), is not that it is too radical but that it is, on the contrary, not radical enough. This is for two reasons, one related to religion and philosophy, the other to politics. Regarding the first, Al Qaida's ideology differs from apocalyptic eschatology on a fundamental matter. While the latter draws a distinction between 'this' and 'that', between history and what is to come, it also insists on the dialectic between them:

> The beyond of history . . . is not to be separated from history in a way that distorts the historical foundations. Even the spirit of the world was patient enough to form the figurations of history. The beyond of history is the essence of history, which is closely interwoven with historical foundations.
>
> *(Taubes 2009: 48)*

It is because of this dialectic that there is no direct path from theology to the political, that the actual world 'assists . . . the coming of the Messianic Kingdom' (Benjamin 1979b: 155). That is, the task is to combine the actual with the new, not merely to destroy it in the name of the new. Today's fundamentalist terror, on the other hand, cancels this very distance between the divine and earthly realms, for it is certain that it has direct access to God's will and perceives itself as the instrument of this willing God. Indeed, we arrive here at the concealed complicity between passive nihilism and radical nihilism, democratic materialism and fundamentalist terror: both reduce metaphysical aspects of religion to quasi-empirical statements, belief to knowledge – after all, the fundamentalist 'does not *believe*, he *knows* directly' (Žižek 2008b: 31). As a consequence of this reduction of belief to knowledge, of this certainty, the gap between the divine and the earthly is no longer mediated but traversed.

Where Al Qaida is certain, true believers, though, 'fear and tremble'. Thomas Müntzer, for instance, was insisting during his rebellion that for 'faith to enter the soul' one necessarily goes through an experience of tedium, of emptiness, in such a way that the advent of faith is accompanied by uncertainty, even disbelief; 'faith can only be found with much trembling and tribulation' (quoted in Taubes 2009: 115). Without this experience of uncertainty there can be no faith. Hence there is Kierkegaard's distinction between the ethical and the religious: whereas ethics is given as a taxonomy that can be known through reason, religion means accepting a God whose will remains unknowable. No true faith can persist without accepting this uncertainty as its paradoxical ground, as its own abyss. For this reason, Kierkegaard describes religion as a suspension of the ethical (Kierkegaard 1962: 51–62).

Let us, at this point, turn to the second issue, to politics. In the apocalyptic tradition the concrete particularity of religious sects conceals a desire for 'absolute universality', a desire that historically expressed itself in demands for equality and resistance to worldly power. Müntzer, for instance, establishes spirituality 'for the whole community of God', thus linking the individual's religious life to mass politics (Taubes 2009: 118).

> I am preaching a kind of Christian belief which disagrees with Luther's, but it is to be found uniformly in all the hearths of the elect on earth. And even a Turk would have the rudiments of the same belief. That is the movement of the Holy Spirit.
>
> *(Müntzer, quoted in Taubes 2009: 110)*

'Even a Turk', the greatest enemy of Europe at the time, can belong to the universal community, despite his actual identity. This universalism, the abstraction of 'justice' from the particular desires and interests of particular groups, necessarily points towards an analogy between the (communist) idea of revolution and the (eschatological) apocalypse. Indeed, in so far as liberal political theory articulates this analogy through the concept of 'fanaticism' – the supposedly shared characteristic of all 'apostles of revolution' – it is necessary to emphasize that the decisive aspect of 'fanaticism', what makes it anxiety-provoking from the point of view of the establishment, 'is not so much the psychological character of unyielding conviction . . . but its relationship to abstraction and universality' (Toscana 2010: 239).

Thus, while Luther declares him an 'outlaw, both in the eyes of God and the emperor', Müntzer insists that it is the 'whole community' that holds the 'power of the sword' – 'the princes are not lords but servants of the sword. They should not do as they please, they should act justly' (quoted in Taubes 2009: 112). This is why he affirms his responsibility: 'I must rebel, and intend to do so' (quoted in ibid.).

Is Al Qaida's ideology rebellious in the same way? It cannot be. The apocalyptic principle seeks to combine radical nihilism with a transvaluation, the destruction of what exists with a forming power. If the revolution can point towards 'nothing beyond itself', its movement, however dynamic, will lead into the 'abyss' (Taubes 2009: 11): 'If the demonic, destructive element is missing, the petrified order, the prevailing positivity of the world cannot be overcome. But if the "new covenant" fails to shine through in this destructive element, the revolution inevitably sinks into empty nothingness' (ibid.: 10).

What Al Qaida's thought lacks is ultimately this moment of transvaluation. Thus, while the apocalyptic principle, in Müntzer's rebellion for instance, targets the existing order itself, Al Qaida has nothing against the capitalist system as such. And at a fundamental level, both the American empire and the new terrorism belong to the same nihilistic world:

> All the formal traits of the crime of New York indicate its nihilistic charac-
> ter; the sacralization of death; the absolute indifference to the victims; the
> transformation of oneself and others into instruments . . . but nothing speaks
> louder than the silence, the terrible silence of the authors and planners of
> this crime. For with affirmative, liberating, non-nihilistic political violence
> not only responsibility is always claimed, but its essence is found in claiming
> responsibility . . . The act remains unnamed and anonymous just like the
> culprits. There lies the infallible sign of a type of fascist nihilism. Opposite it
> we find another nihilism for which an old name is appropriate, 'Capital.' *Das
> Kapital*: nihilist in its extensive form, the market having become worldwide;
> nihilist in its felicitation of the formalism of communication; and nihilist in
> its extreme political poverty, that is to say, in the absence of any project other
> than its perpetuation.
>
> *(Badiou 2003: 120)*

Precisely in this sense, Al Qaida's terror is viral; it kills from inside, using radical nihilism as a strategy against passive nihilism, death through suicide attacks against 'life' on offer in the empire: 'Our men are eager to die just as the Americans are eager to live' (an Al Qaeda statement, 10 October 2001). Crucially in this respect, Al Qaida justifies its terror attacks with reference to American hostilities. 'Who-ever has destroyed our villages and towns, then we have the right to destroy their villages and towns . . . whoever has killed our civilians, then we have the right to kill theirs' (Bin Laden 2002). In other words, its actions consist only of 'reac-tions': 'This is a defensive *jihad*' (Bin Laden 2001). Hence an elective affinity exists between 'pre-emptive' war against terror and 'defensive' terror, between reaction-as–action and action–as–reaction (see Diken and Laustsen 2005: 125). In this, just as the war against terror needs the figure of 'evil' terrorism, Al Qaida needs the figure of 'evil' empire. But, as Nietzsche insists, the distinction between good and evil always emerges on the basis of *ressentiment*; the weak can be 'good' only in so far as they can describe an external factor as 'evil'.

Thus today militancy is confronted with a false choice between two forms of activity: non-violence and terrorism. Yet a choice between a passive nihilist fantasy of 'purity from violence', in which all forms of violence are considered inherently unjust, and suicidal strategies of terrorist nihilism is no choice at all. Since violence is part of life, the right, the just and the good cannot be conceptualized independently of the exercise of power: this could result only in the negation of life and our power, and indeed such *ressentiment* is 'precisely what links nonviolence with terrorism, casting it together with what it so adamantly tries to oppose' (Hardt and Negri 1994: 292). Consequently, the question is how to differentiate the violence of radical nihilism, of passive nihilism and of revolutionary, anti-nihilist transfiguration.

8

ANTAGONISMS AND DISJUNCTIVE SYNTHESES

We have so far focused on two dialectics in the context of revolution, between the actual and the virtual, on the basis of repetition, and between revolution and counterrevolution. The first suggests that there is a constant interaction between the virtual and the actual aspects of the concept, an interaction which also problematizes a clean-cut distinction between 'utopian' and 'scientific' approaches to revolution. Yet the idea of revolution can only be actualized in history. But how precisely this actualization can take place is an issue in itself. Significantly in this respect, revolution is quintessentially a modern concept. Whereas 'revolt' has a longer historical range than modernity, the concept of revolution is a modern answer, *the* answer of modernity, to the question of inequality, injustice and irrationality. And, as a modern concept, 'revolution' requires a human capacity to act in history in order to change its course, a modern subject defined as 'the agent of history' (see Arendt 1965: 53). Concomitantly, the emphasis on the subject invites in modernity the prioritization of 'revolution' over 'revolt'.

Along the same lines, the production of such capacity for action requires discursive, material and affective apparatuses, or dispositifs, without which the subject can govern neither itself nor the revolution. Hence, in order to actualize the idea of revolution, the four different periodizations or subjects discussed in the previous four chapters (pure politics, class, the party, mass politics) also articulate different modes of governance with different properties. Even when they fundamentally converge on assuming a necessity, that the subject is to be produced, this production refers, in each case, to different processes of political subjectivation, which also enable different problematizations of the correlation between the actual and the virtual.

Under certain circumstances, however, the differences among these problematizations disappear or move to the background. The reason for this, which takes us to the heart of the matter, is the differential relationship between revolt and revolution. While revolt is always *a* revolt, a singular logic among logics, revolution always points towards a specificity, a specific temporality that interrupts history, which is then universalized: hence *the* French Revolution, *the* October Revolution and so on. As such, *the* revolution becomes a yardstick, a model for other revolutions, which is why for Badiou, for instance, all revolutions seem to be measured up against the French Revolution, while for Žižek the universal model remains the party, and for Hardt and Negri it is the mass movement of the multitude. As a desire to discern and bring the universal (which is by definition not historical) into history, or to bring transcendence into multiplicity, by materializing the universal, *the* revolution is always already also a desire to end revolt (which signifies an inconsistent multiplicity) and all other revolutions (which are reduced to revolts, e.g. the American Revolution for Badiou).

> The age of revolution has constituted a gigantic effort to acclimate uprisings within a rational and controllable history. 'Revolution' gave these uprisings a legitimacy, sorted out their good and bad forms, and defined their laws of development. For uprisings, it established preliminary conditions, objectives, and ways of bringing them to an end. Even the profession of revolutionary was defined. By this repatriating revolt into the discourse of revolution, it was said, the uprising would appear in all its truth and continue to its true conclusion. This was a marvelous promise. Some will say that the uprising thus found itself colonized by *realpolitik*. Others will say that the dimension of a rational history was opened to it. I prefer the question that Horkheimer used to ask, a naïve question, and a little feverish: 'But is it really so desirable, this revolution?'
>
> *(Foucault 2005: 264)*

Here, the division between the virtual and the actual reappears at the level of actors, as a division between the political spirituality of event and *realpolitical* rationality which 'colonizes' it. But this identification of revolt with the virtual or 'spiritual politics' as opposed to that of revolution with the actual or strategy reproduces a problem: it turns the event into 'a purely formal feature, indifferent towards its historical content' (Žižek 2008b: 113). The risk here is, once more, the return of a dichotomy between strategy and spiritual intoxication, or the separation of the two sides of *kairos* from one another. In other words, a dichotomy between revolt and revolution does not cover the entire field at hand:

> if it were so, then we would remain stuck forever in the opposition between emancipatory outbursts and the sobering 'day after' when life turns to its pragmatic normal run. From this constrained perspective, every attempt to avoid and/or postpone this sobering return to the normal run of things amounts to terror, to the reversal of enthusiasm to monstrosity.
>
> *(Ibid.: 116)*

Therefore what is really at stake in a revolutionary process is the question of how to open up a space for the virtual idea within the actual, 'how to transpose the political emancipatory outburst into the concrete regulation of policing' (ibid.). One could insist here, with Badiou and Žižek, that the true difference between an authentic event and a pseudo-event, for example between communism and fascism, lies precisely in the creation of a new positivity, a transvaluated order. This can be thought, of course, as a matter of taking control of the state, but is not limited to it. What matters is articulating singularities into a consistent political subject that can 'make insurrection lasting and stable' (Hardt and Negri 2009: 239). Such continuity cannot be provided by existing institutions, for this can result only in the neutralization of the scission opened by the revolt. What is necessary, therefore, is an institutional process that does not negate but develops such scission by remaining 'open' to internal and external conflicts, by affirming revolt as well as collective practices that designate a 'form of life' (ibid.: 356–7). As such, 'institutions form a constituent rather than a constituted power' (ibid.: 359).

But since such openness logically means that the positive order is also prone to external and internal perversion, exposed to counterrevolution, such an undertaking is essentially aporetic, which, in turn, requires thinking revolt and revolution together, in the form of a disjunctive synthesis, for if revolt without revolution is an impotent act revolution without revolt can always be 'colonized' by *realpolitik*.

Historically speaking, anarchism has theorized revolt as a singular act of subtraction or non-relation. Revolution, on the other hand, aims at breaking down institutions to collectively re-establish new ones. The first prioritizes the politics of flight, while the latter understands the political in the classical sense, as something transcendent to the social. What is necessary, and challenging, is to think both gestures together, without replacing the one for the other, in an ambivalent zone 'between the line of flight as a gesture of revolt and a purely political line' (Agamben 2004: 121). The task, in other words, is to bridge singularity and collectivity, presentation and representation. Politics (the 'party', the 'agora', etc.) is necessary to transcend singularity and, by the same token, singularity ('class', 'flight', etc.) is indispensable in order to translate 'social' problems into a 'political' language (ibid.; see also Bauman 1999: 87).

This brings us to our second dialectic, the one between revolution and counterrevolution. Although all revolutions operate in terms of a desire to break out of the circle of history, they all fail; a revolution 'must devour its own children' (Arendt 1965: 57). One reason is structural, for the virtual idea of revolution cannot fully exhaust itself in the actual. But there is also a political reason: when 'political' revolution is not supplemented with a 'social' revolution, for example when the 'slave' takes the place of the 'master' without abolishing the institution of slavery itself, the socio-symbolic order remains intact. For these two reasons, it is always necessary to repeat, to think revolution in ever new fields.

Thus the movement from sequence to sequence (e.g. from the French Revolution to the classist mode to the Leninist Party and so on) signifies the necessity of permanent change in political practice, which implies both new thinking and the rethinking of the new. To be able to transcend the impasses confronted within each sequence, one needs to think the platform differently. This is, for instance, what happened when Lenin created the Bolshevik party, or when Mao moved 'revolution' to the domain of culture, both creating a new, different subject which is not given in the two-classes (dual) scenario. Here, political creativity involves a desire to move beyond the framework of thesis–antithesis, revolution–counterrevolution, a desire to affirm transfiguration. In this particular sense, the grid of sequences (Robespierre–Marx–Lenin–Mao) is also a vicious cycle in which the notion of revolution is caught. At this point, the pertinent question for any theory is how to transcend this vicious cycle by inventing a new sequence, a fifth evental sequence, for as long as politics remains within the cycle it can only take the form of 'progress' or temporal continuity.

This is, however, not only a theoretical-epistemological or political-strategic question. Revolutionary politics emerges only as a desire to transcend the continuity of the sequences of revolution and counterrevolution. *The* revolution is also a desire to end (the continuum of) history, for, if *the* revolution wants to bring transcendence into history, doing this, bringing the universal into multiplicity, would stop history. In this utopian sense, *the* revolution is the 'end of the world', a final, redemptive act. Or the desire for *the* revolution is a desire for the disappearance, or the end, of politics, a desire for a society in which revolutions are no longer necessary. This is why communism is the only genuine revolution for Marx, a reference to *the* revolution that stops the cycle of revolutions, a utopian, impossible desire for a revolution without an antithesis, for revolution without counterrevolution. As such, *the* revolution is also the apolitical kernel of politics.

No doubt, that this desire is 'impossible' means that one should get rid of the fantasy of the Last Judgement, of salvation.

> Communism is thus not the light at the end of the tunnel, that is, the happy final outcome of a long and arduous struggle – if anything the light at the tunnel is rather that of another train approaching us at full speed.
> (*Žižek 2009a: 149*)

The idea of revolution, rather, calls for the disruption of bare, farcical repetition, for the 'emergency brake' of history. But more importantly, the recognition of impossibility here also entails the recognition of the virtual aspect of revolution. In this sense, as a desire for the impossible, communism signifies the search for the possibilities offered by the impossible, which is not to be confused with the possibility of the impossible, of salvation. For in so far as the impossible is impossible to exist, remains 'to come', what matters is to stick to the idea of immanence, resisting the temptation to turn the hope of redemption into transcendent salvation. Herein we face the necessity of recognizing the inevitably utopian dimension of the concept of revolution, the 'coming revolution', vis-à-vis the vicious cycle of history.

Yet, while 'to come' is an essential dimension of revolution in general, while it is the dimension that links the concept to the future, it does not allow itself to be located within the four sequences. However, to the extent the four sequences are saturated (for it is perfectly possible that each sequence still has relevance to a certain degree, intersecting with other sequences in different relations and combinations), this does not entail the end of fidelity. What matters rather is to continue experimentation, to improvise, obtaining 'something like a fidelity to the fidelity' (Badiou, in George 2008). One can only open oneself in relation to what is to come, try to become 'worthy of the event', even when one cannot say anything concrete about it. Hence there is the paradox: the necessity of being prepared for something inherently unexpected, unpreparable. There *is*, nevertheless, a great difference between being prepared and not being prepared in relation to the unexpected, which is the difference that 'fidelity to fidelity' makes. In this sense the question of revolution today is not only a problem related to the lack of a new sequence or a new theory of revolution focused on the sequences of the political subject. It is also a question of illumination, of remembering the origin in Benjamin's sense – not only remembering, for instance, the 'history' of the French Revolution, but imagining how our own society would look from the prism of the French Revolution. What is interesting, in other words, is not so much what people say about Marx or Nietzsche today, but what Marx and Nietzsche would say about them.

What, then, must be 'remembered' from the four sequences? How can we testify to something 'to come', and how can we link the testimony and the virtual together? Or how can we observe the paradoxical nature of society, the paradox of testifying to what is 'to come'? Figure 8.1 illustrates my line of thought to deal with such questions.

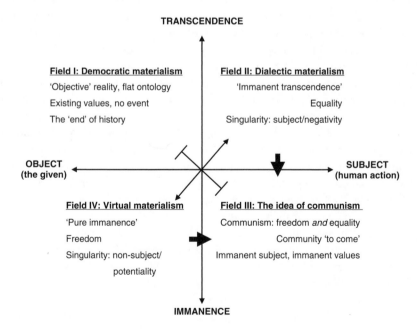

FIGURE 8.1   Dynamics of revolt and revolution

As a hermeneutical device, Figure 8.1 enables one to question and interpret the dynamics and the relations suggested by the theories mentioned so far without being captured within their own schemas. Its intention is not to 'position' the theories or concepts as such but to discuss them from the point of view of the book, focusing on the intensities and tendencies they produce. In other words, the figure seeks to construct a perspective on the paradox of society by illustrating a dynamic field of forces.

The figure is based on two orthogonal axes: a vertical continuum between transcendence and immanence and a horizontal continuum between the object (the given) and the subject (human action). It operates with an *a priori* understanding of the event as both non-subjective (Deleuze) and subjective (Badiou). This idea serves as the horizontal axis of the figure, where the relationship between the two poles is that of a continuum, a process of subjectivation. The same logic applies to the vertical axis, that of transcendence and immanence: the relationship between them is not given in advance but is thought here as a process or continuum. This approach allows for a differentiation between two understandings of transcendence: on the basis of the given or existing values and as an achievement of the eventual subject. That is, transcendence is not identical to the conscious action of the (human) subject, just as immanence is not identical to the lack of subject. Consequently, we have four 'ideal-typical' vanishing points: 'objective reality' in which what exists is elevated to the level of transcendent factuality (Field I); the event as a subjective, active transcendence of what exists (Field II); the event as a non-subjective, passive involution of the given (Field IV); and, finally, the immanent subject of communism as it is originally formulated by Marx (Field III).

Thinking and action within Field I suggest a flat ontology, a 'one-dimensional society' that lacks a virtual dimension. Concepts such as post-politics or democratic materialism, and prophecies like the 'end of history' or the 'end of revolutions' belong here. Also, in so far as it refers to what already exists (e.g. given norms and values, 'objective' reality or actual identities such as 'fatherland', 'family' and so on) any figure of transcendence belongs to this field. For instance, when Stalinism declares communism to have arrived, reducing it to the level of actual reality, or when the concept of 'proletariat' fully coincides with the 'working class' as an actual identity, the 'transcendent' falls back upon Field I. Following this, it is important that the distinction between the virtual and the actual is not subsumed under the distinction between transcendence and immanence. 'Transcendent factuality' signifies an inability to deal with the virtual. The only conception of the virtual possible in Field I is thus statistical probability, an ersatz transcendence which dictates that we should treat probability as God.

Field II signifies the first line of politics which cannot be contained within Field I. It is the domain in which the radical contestation of what exists, of capitalism and the state, takes place with reference to the conscious action of a subject that transcends existing reality. Reality is thought of here as something which is not immediately transparent; thus its way of functioning must be uncovered in order to change its structure. In this context singularity, for example the 'proletariat', stands for negativity.

'We are nothing, let us be all.' That is the very definition of Revolution: a non-existent uses its being-multiple in order to declare that it will exist in the absolute sense. And for that to happen, we have to change the world of course, change the world's transcendental.

(Badiou 2009c: 141)

Here the primary concept is revolution, and revolt is seen through the prism of revolution. This emphasis coincides with another, the emphasis on equality (whether the concept is directly related to the critique of capitalism or, stripped off from its economic determinants, mainly refers to justice), while freedom is contemplated in the horizon of equality.

In Field IV the most relevant adversary is alienation, the lack of freedom. Concomitantly, here one is primarily focused on freedom, while equality is seen in the perspective of freedom. Hence there is the conceptual series that defines this field: alienation–revolt–freedom. As in Field I, what we have here is a flat ontology in which everything is already given, a Spinozist–Deleuzean surface with no transcendence, with no hierarchy, no depth, and no pre-established subject. Ultimately, therefore, freedom is 'not a matter of human liberty but of liberation *from* the human' (Hallward 2006: 139). In stark contrast to Field I, however, on this immanent surface the actual and the virtual coexist and interact. 'Virtual materialism', characteristic of thinking within this field, considers events as the results of immanent processes of actualization and virtualization. And so here singularity is thought of as a pre-subjective potentiality rather than as subjective negativity.

In Field III things come together. Here two demands, freedom and equality, coincide (but are not necessarily united) in the idea of communism. Significantly, in Marx the commodity form is not only about exploitation. The commodity is also that which separates itself from, turns against, its producer as something 'alien'. Hence the idea of communism is as much related to the reappropriation of the means of production as to the demands for equality. This reappropriation not only refers to a relation of property but rather designates the transcendence of both private and public property, thereby the emancipation of human creativity. In this sense, as the coincidence of freedom and equality, communism signifies a utopian 'society to come', a virtual idea, in the light of which one can act upon the actual world in ways that are fundamentally different from pragmatic politics.

Communism, as such, is the ground zero of politics, that which makes politics possible. For the same reason, it also signifies the destruction, or rather the self-overcoming, of the figure. Hence Field III is the field in which dichotomies (e.g. freedom–equality, subject–object) disappear and the two forms of radical politics (libertarian and egalitarian) make sense together. Most importantly, in the idea of communism the dichotomy of transcendence–immanence is deconstructed. Accordingly, this field makes it possible to think immanence and the subject together. When singularity is viewed as negativity (the part of no part) and potentiality (creative multitude) at once, it turns into an immanent, experimental identity which seeks to 'overcome' (Nietzsche) or 'abolish' (Marx) its actuality.

The main antagonism

As a whole, what is significant in Figure 8.1 is the way the fields relate to and differ from one another, which constitutes its dynamic aspect. In this respect revolt and revolution appear as movements, events, which destabilize Field I. In turn, counter-revolt and counterrevolution are stabilizing gestures. Further, different movements across the fields generate different types of relations. Thus, one can imagine conflicting but mutually supportive relations among elements of the different fields, where different thoughts, actions and desires derive meaning from each other in spite of mutual conflicts and disputes. In this sense, the relation between Field II and Field IV can be characterized as a disjunctive synthesis. This disjunction is 'agonistic' rather than 'antagonistic', that is, it designates an us–them relation in which the two sides of the relation are not 'enemies' but 'adversaries' who share a common ground, even though they can acknowledge that 'there is no rational solution to their conflict' (Mouffe 2005: 20).

But there can also emerge directly antagonistic relations where the different fields seek to dominate, over-code or simply ward off one another. The relationship between Field I and Field III is antagonistic in this sense. Thus, even though dialectic materialism (Field II) and virtual materialism (Field IV) do engage in agonistic conflicts with one another as 'adversaries' (e.g. freedom versus equality, revolt versus revolution, the immanent non-subject versus the transcendent subject, and so on), they also converge against their common 'enemy', democratic materialism (Field I), in relation to which both are unconditionally antagonistic. In this way, the main antagonism in the figure is between democratic materialism and the idea of communism, between a world without idea and an idea without world.

It is because of this fundamental antagonism that the opposition between Field II and Field IV is secondary, and takes the form of a disjunctive synthesis.

Disjunctive syntheses

The disjunctive relation between Field II and Field IV can be qualified through a comparison between Badiou and Deleuze. Badiou himself stresses on several occasions that, despite significant differences (see Badiou 2000), he shares with Deleuze some basic philosophical and political aspirations, that they are on the same side against what exists (see Badiou 2009c: 115–18). Both systematically resist the thought of 'ends' (the end of history, the end of revolutions, of metaphysics, of ideology, etc.). Second, both value and prioritize the role of dissensus. In both lines of thought, what matters is never consensus or shared values but 'separation' (Badiou) or 'disjunction' (Deleuze). Third, both philosophies are focused on infinity in the context of the event. While for Deleuze philosophy is about inventing concepts 'at infinite speed', for Badiou the aim of philosophy is to make it possible to live 'like immortals', fighting the idea of finitude through an affirmative principle: 'trust only in the infinite' (ibid.: 118). Fourth, both Deleuze and Badiou put a distance to language, to representation, trying to replace 'judgement' with experience and becoming. And finally, in both perspectives, nothing, including critique, is as valuable as affirmation, as 'finding the integral affirmation of the improbable and doing so . . . without any negation of any kind, trusting – involuntarily – in becomings' (ibid.: 117).

But this 'relation' includes significant disjunctions, too, especially regarding the concepts of immanence, event and subject. To start with, Badiou's set theory is an atheistic theory that can do without a transcendent instance, without theology. As mentioned before, for Badiou the truth-event is not transcendent to the situation but emerges as its immanent 'supplement', as a 'cut' in the continuum of becoming. But in Deleuze's perspective the event is the immanent consequence of becoming, without any possibility of a 'cut' or 'lack' in immanence. There can be nothing beyond, no 'supplementary' dimension to immanence. 'Immanence is immanent only to itself and consequently captures everything, absorbs All-One, and leaves nothing remaining to which it could be immanent' (Deleuze and Guattari 1994: 45). Therefore, seen from Deleuze's perspective, what Badiou wants is to 'think transcendence within the immanent', expecting a 'breach' from immanence (ibid.: 47; see also Smith 2004b: 640). It is this breach that materializes Badiou's four truth procedures (politics, science, love, art).

Most importantly, Badiou proceeds from the set as a single multiplicity, as a neutral base in relation to the actual and the virtual. He 'draws up a line that is single . . . on which functions and concepts will be spaced out' (Deleuze and Guattari 1994: 152). The keyword here is 'single': according to Deleuze and Guattari, all lines are actual and virtual at once. Hence, there 'must be at least two multiplicities, two types, from the outset' (ibid.). The two types (actual and virtual) of multiplicities are not distributed on a single line but continuously interact in the form of actualization and virtualization (ibid.). Then the problem with Badiou's ontology is that it abolishes the 'problematic' interaction between the actual and the virtual from ontology by presenting being only in terms of the actual (Smith 2004a: 92). In a Deleuzean perspective, in contrast, an actual 'state of affairs' cannot be disconnected from the virtual:

> This is what we call the Event, or the part that eludes its own actualization in everything that happens. The event is not the state of affairs. It is actualized in a state of affairs, in a body . . . but it has a shadowy and secret part that is continually subtracted from or added to its actualization: in contrast with the state of affairs, it neither begins nor ends but has gained or kept the infinite movement to which it gives consistency. It is the virtual that is distinct from the actual, but a virtual that is no longer chaotic, that has become consistent or real on the plane of immanence that wrests it from the chaos – it is a virtual that is real without being actual, ideal without being abstract. The event might seem to be transcendent because it surveys the state of affairs, but it is pure immanence that gives it a capacity to survey itself by itself and on the plane. What is transcendent . . . is the state of affairs in which the event is actualized. But, even in this state of affairs, the event is pure immanence of

what is not actualized or of what remains indifferent to actualization, since
its reality does not depend upon it. The event is immaterial, incorporeal,
unlivable: pure *reserve*.

(Deleuze and Guattari 1994: 156)

Since Badiou presents the event in an axiomatic form, his truth procedures, the
affirmation of the event, its naming and articulation cannot take place in ontology
but can only be based on the subject's decision which is separated from ontology.
Thus Badiou needs the duality of 'Being' and 'Event', of ontology and the truth-
event, which can only 'supplement' ontology by interrupting it, opening up a 'cut'
in its fabric, while for Deleuze, in contrast, truth (and axiomatics itself) originates in
'problems' which are not subjective but ontological (Smith 2004a: 92–3).

It is interesting in this respect that, although he draws a sharp distinction between
theology and philosophy, although his philosophy is radically a-theological, or
immanent, Badiou insists on making use of categories which are fundamentally
the categories of the philosophy of transcendence (e.g. truth, eternity). Therefore,
while Badiou can convincingly show that his transcendence is really immanent,
one may wonder, from a Deleuzean perspective, what the difference between
immanent transcendence and transcendent transcendence is. Regarding this difference, Žižek's Badiou-inspired theory of the event is illuminating.

For Žižek, immanence has two meanings. First, it is a kind of bare repetition,
a normality or continuum. Transcendence occurs when the continuum of immanence is 'ruptured' and rendered 'inconsistent'. However, as a gap within immanence, transcendence does not refer to a beyond. On the contrary, it emanates from
within immanence itself. The gap is an 'absolutely immanent gap', which is similar
to Badiou's 'void' within immanence (Žižek 2004: 60). 'The tension between
immanence and transcendence is thus also secondary with regard to the gap within
immanence itself: "transcendence" is a kind of perspective illusion, the way we
(mis)perceive the gap/discord that inheres to immanence itself' (ibid.: 65).

Through the redoubling of immanence into a normality and its rupture, a second form of immanence, an 'immanent transcendence', appears through immanence (Žižek 2001b: 99). In this sense the subject, too, is transcendent in its
capacity to overcome becoming (desire), relating itself to the real (drive), to the
'immanent transcendence which pertains to drive as such' (ibid.). Functioning as an
excess, death drive disturbs the tautological order of the symbolic order, indicating
a dimension 'beyond' immanence as bare repetition, beyond ordinary 'biological
life' (ibid.: 102, 104). And it is this excess that the subject must assume in order to
repeat, to produce the event as immanent transcendence:

> Was Nietzsche right, then, in his claim that Christ was the only true Chris-
> tian? By taking upon himself all the Sins and then, through his death, paying
> for them, Christ opens up the way for the redemption of humanity – how-
> ever, by his death, people are not directly redeemed, but given the *possibility*
> of redemption, of getting the rid of the excess. This distinction is crucial:

Christ does *not* do our work for us, he does not pay our debt, he 'merely' *gives us a chance* – with his death, he asserts *our* freedom and responsibility, i.e. he 'merely' opens up the possibility, for us, to redeem ourselves through the 'leap into faith', i.e. by way of choosing to 'live in Christ' – in *imitatio Christi*, we *repeat* Christ's gesture of freely assuming the excess of Life, instead of projecting/displacing it onto some figure of the Other.

(Ibid.: 105)

To open a parenthesis here, in the Nietzschean tradition we find a different version of such immanent transcendence. Late Simmel, starting from a tragic conflict in all culture, a contradiction between 'life' and 'form', discusses that the formal structure of all sociality is a continuum between two limits. Form is antithetical to life, for it objectifies it. But life needs form. Yet, even though it needs forms, life cannot be contained in forms; it exceeds or transcends form. The flow of life denies permanent structures. So life is both 'more-than-life', life that needs an actual form, and 'more-life', the creative self-overcoming of life that can destroy its actual forms (Simmel 1971: 368–9). Thus, for Simmel, as for Nietzsche, what defines a human being is its capacity to overcome itself. Although each human being is constituted within determinate actual boundaries, without which life would be devoid of meaning, these limits can be overcome, while, at the same time, each overcoming creates new boundaries (ibid.: 354). Therefore, the essence of humanity is best expressed though a paradox: 'we are bounded in every direction, and we are bounded in no direction' (ibid.). 'Life' includes both the boundaries and transcending of the boundaries, both actual forms and lines of flight. And in this sense '*transcendence is immanent in life*' (ibid.: 363).

Where does this discussion leave us? While both philosophies unite in the idea of immanence, they diverge in their understandings of immanence. Thus, on the one hand, it is not possible to accept the idea of 'immanent transcendence' for Deleuze because it invites us to 'think that immanence is a prison (solipsism) from which the Transcendence will save us' (Deleuze and Guattari 1994: 47). But on the other hand Deleuze's radical immanence itself tends to become a transcendent category (Albertsen 1995: 136). Thus Badiou sees the Deleuzean event as 'the becoming (-One) of (unlimited) becoming' (2009b: 382). He can neither accept the idea that the event is coextensive with the actual (that the virtual does not differ ontologically from the actual even though it cannot be reduced to it) nor settle with an interpretation of the event as a single Event, as the eternal recurrence of the same. Badiou's event, in contrast, signifies the 'decomposition' of situations by 'multiple event-sites'; just as the event produces a distinctive 'present', it also separates itself from other events (ibid.: 385).

'Immanent transcendence' versus 'transcendent immanence': this disagreement in agreement, disjunction in relation, means that the polarity here is not a neat polarity but rather a continuum based on the concept of immanence. This viewpoint is further justified by the fact that they have common enemies and shared aspirations. If their common enemy is democratic materialism, their shared aspiration is the thinking of the immanent event. This is also why whenever they accuse each other it is mainly because the other falls back into Field I. Thus, sometimes Badiou's Deleuze looks like the grammatician of democratic materialism (ibid.: 34–5, 381–7); at other times Deleuze's Badiou is accused of doing 'royal science' (Deleuze and Guattari 1994: 152).

There are, however, significant implications of this disjunctive synthesis. Consider the concepts of freedom and equality. Although Field II prioritizes equality, it tries to incorporate freedom into its framework (see Chapter 4). Likewise, Field IV is not insensitive towards the problem of injustice although it values freedom more than equality (see Chapter 1). In both cases, that is, one concept remains irreducible, while the other concept is not negated but derives its meaning from the first. It is this irreducibility that condenses the separation of the two fields from each other.

A similar situation is obvious regarding the question of the subject. In both fields the grounding concept is singularity, which transcends the time and space operative in Field I. But whereas in Field II singularity is thought of as negativity, as a transcendent, incalculable and immeasurable excess which cannot be ordered, in Field IV it appears as positivity, as a given, irreducible power of difference located in the 'Body without Organs' and thus cannot be commanded in strategic, rational terms. Therefore in Field IV the insistence is that, if you institute singularity as a body, it will lose its pre-subjective, impersonal quality, that is, stop being a singularity. In contrast, seen from within Field II, singularity is a figure of transcendence, of that which cannot be ordered. It is an 'Organ without Body', the part of no part. Hence the drive here is to 'embody' singularity, to give it a body, to turn it into a subject. The subject is that which needs embodiment, to be made. Along the same lines, *kairos* becomes the moment to embody singularity, the moment in which the subject is formed.

A dialectic synthesis between Field II and Field IV seems, against this background, difficult to achieve. But if, on the other hand, one totally separates the two fields, the disjunctive synthesis ceases to be operative. What is necessary from the point of view of the disjunctive synthesis is therefore to maintain the tension between the two fields while avoiding the reduction of one to the other or their complete separation. To discuss this further, we first need to deal with the concept of critique, which is the topic of Part III.

Excursus II

HUXLEY'S *BRAVE NEW WORLD* – AND OURS

'Our dreams', says Agamben, 'cannot see us – this is the tragedy of utopia' (1995: 74). What makes utopian dreams so disappointing is their distance from what we are, their inability to 'see' our present alienation and unfreedom. But our nightmares are closer to us. In contrast to dreams, fear provokes weariness, an indispensable element of all dystopias, including *Brave New World*, which projects our civilization 'along the lines of its own teleology to the point where its monstrous nature becomes immediately evident' (Adorno 1967: 98). It interrogates a society in which time and *eo ipso* all potentiality have stopped making sense. Thus Lenina, who stands for the spontaneous ideology of the brave new world, asks: 'what's time for?' (Huxley 2007: 77).

Brave new world is the end of history. It is what is left in a society when you take away the possibility of revolt, revolution and critique, a world in which radical change is rendered not only impossible but also undesirable. And 'yes, everybody is happy now' (ibid.: 65). Yet this 'happiness' is one reduced to sheer consumerism, just as 'politics' in the brave new world is degraded to conformism. More tellingly yet, the only alternative set in the book against this sterile, suffocating civilization is religious fundamentalism. Therefore John, the fanatic, the passionate miscreant in the novel, is the only person who can look beyond what exists (see Attwood 2007). Hence there is a crucial similarity between the brave new world and ours: both take themselves for granted and know of only one enemy, fundamentalism; both offer the same false choice: between post-politics, politics without belief, and fundamentalism, belief without politics.

The 'happiness' of stability

The novel opens in 'A.F. 632', 632 years after Ford. And we are immediately introduced to the brave new world's maxim, which consists of a revision of the French Revolution's ideals: 'Community, Identity, Stability'. The setting is a global welfare state. The main political instrument is biological engineering. As biology and politics coincide, people are no longer born from natural parents, which is considered 'obscene' (Huxley 2007: 31), but raised in 'hatcheries' and 'conditioning centres' to fill predetermined positions in the biological class structure: on top the Alphas, 'perfected' by eugenics, at the very bottom Epsilons, 'sub-human' products of dysgenics, workers who are, like everybody else in the world state, distracted from politics by drugs and entertainment, embodying the fantasy generated by any control society: slaves who cannot (even think of) revolt.

In this utilitarian world, everybody has to be 'socially useful' (ibid.: 63). Thus spending time alone is considered suspect. In a highly networked society the desire for solitude signals a danger of unbonding. Concomitantly, art and philosophy are banished. If people need 'distraction', they get it by 'soma', a drug that provides 'a holiday from reality', an ersatz religious experience: 'Christianity without tears – that's what soma is' (ibid.: 210). With soma, the pursuit of bodily pleasures is an ethical imperative. Sex, for that reason, is no longer repressed but is a prescribed activity. Thus, as 'everyone belongs to everyone else', the body becomes a networked public property (ibid.: 34). One 'ought' to be promiscuous and have 'fun' (see ibid.: 36, 81). In this sense *Brave New World* is an allegory of regressive evolution. It is a society in which 'to be infantile' is a 'duty' (ibid.: 84). So the governmental imperatives in the brave new world are the same as those of the nursery: play, learning, stability and happiness.

'Play' coincides with hedonistic consumption. As consumption is sublimated as a virtue, under-consumption becomes a danger to the social bond. Everything must justify itself with reference to consumption. And consumption, like children, cannot wait. 'Never put off till tomorrow the fun you can have today' (ibid.: 81). The most 'horrible' fate in the brave new world is being 'compelled to live through a long time-interval between the consciousness of a desire and its fulfilment' (ibid.: 38). The fear of the 'interval', of time, is also the fear of desire. And to extinguish passion the brave new world adopts applied science as the cornerstone of its materialism. Every specialized caste 'learns' to be happy on the basis of its own ideological prejudices. Since everyone is bred to do their own job and ideologically conditioned to be happy with this, there are no class antagonisms; 'all men are physico-chemically equal' (ibid.: 63). As such, as a lack (of antagonism), 'happiness' becomes the bedrock of socio-political stability.

And of course freedom in such a world can only be a freedom from conditioning. Bernard Marx, a key figure in the book, articulates this desire as he wonders 'what passion is', what it would be like to be subjected to pain with no soma, and so on (ibid.: 81, 89). As he questions the value of dominant values, he also materializes a discontent, which is, nevertheless, fuelled by his 'complexion', a bio-genetic mistake in his hatching. He is also the first who develops a taste for solitude, which frightens Lenina, who never questions her society:

> Lenina was crying. 'It's horrible, it's horrible,' she kept repeating. 'And how can you talk like that about not wanting to be a part of the social body? After

all, everyone works for everyone else. We can't do without any one. Even
Epsilons.'

'Yes, I know,' said Bernard derisively. '"Even Epsilons are useful"! So am
I. And I damned well wish I weren't!'

Lenina was shocked by his blasphemy. 'Bernard!' she protested in a voice
of amazed distress. 'How can you?'

In a different key, 'How can I?' he repeated meditatively. 'No, the real
problem is:

How is it that I can't, or rather – because, after all, I know quite well why
I can't – what would it be like if I could, if I were free – not enslaved by my
conditioning.'

'But, Bernard, you're saying the most awful things.'

'Don't you wish you were free, Lenina?'

'I don't know what you mean. I am free. Free to have the most wonderful
time. Everybody's happy nowadays.'

He laughed, 'Yes, "Everybody's happy nowadays". We begin giving the
children that at five. But wouldn't you like to be free to be happy in some
other way, Lenina? In your own way, for example; not in everybody else's
way.'

'I don't know what you mean,' she repeated.

(Ibid.: 78–9)

The more a society becomes its own justification, the more it brands as blasphemy
every suspicion 'against the notion that what is, is right – just because it exists'
(Adorno 1967: 101). This accord with what exists, which adopts the actual as its
norm, paradoxically restores the mythic power in the form of a new taboo, and
disagreement only provokes *ressentiment*: 'I don't know what you mean.' What
such 'freedom' excludes is the insistence that what exists 'cannot be true' (Marcuse
1964: 122–3). The virtual idea of 'freedom' cannot be fully actualized; people can
have certain liberties, but these concrete liberties cannot embody the idea of freedom as such. Since an idea 'denotes that which the particular entity is, and is *not*',
the idea of freedom comprehends, at once, 'all the liberty not *yet* attained', as well
as those liberties attained (ibid.: 218). Hence what looks like 'freedom' to the brave
new world is not, cannot be, much more than voluntary servitude (see Marcuse
1969: 12–13).

But in what sense, precisely, is the brave new world a totalitarian society? In this
respect a comparison to Orwell's *1984* is an obligatory point of passage. As Huxley himself points out, whereas *1984* portrays a totalitarianism that seeks control
through fear, through punishment, the brave new world controls its citizens by
rewards, in non-violent ways (see Huxley 2004: 5). In this, 'science' is supported
with a permissive, sexualized ethics. Thus, while in *1984* people are compelled
to conform to a puritan ethics, permissiveness is what guarantees the brave new
world against destructive (and creative) passions. It humiliates its subjects through
pleasure, not pain.

> Orwell feared those who would deprive us of information. Huxley feared those who would give us so much that we would be reduced to passivity and egoism. Orwell feared that the truth would be concealed from us. Huxley feared the truth would be drowned in a sea of irrelevance. Orwell feared we would become a captive culture. Huxley feared we would become a trivial culture.
>
> *(Postman 1985: vii–viii)*

Huxley himself links this change of scene to the trajectory of totalitarianism in the Soviet Union, where, already at the end of the 1950s, Stalin's '*1984*-style dictatorship' was evolving into a system that sought to control part of its population, especially the high-ranking professionals, through rewards, granting them certain liberties to think and act, while, at the same time, imposing conformity on the masses through the fear of punishment (Huxley 2004: 6). Effectively, the Soviet Union looked like a system that combined discipline and seduction, *1984* and *Brave New World* (ibid.: 6). Certainly, there is also a certain dose of anti-Americanism in *Brave New World*: hence its critique of commercial joviality. However, while Huxley sees totalitarianism as a natural line of development for the Soviet Union, he considers it only as a potential danger for the West (ibid.: 15). He overlooks two issues here.

First, the duality between 'fear' and 'reward' is not specific to Stalinism but pertains to sovereignty in general. Thus, although Huxley is adamant that in the brave new world power is exercised by granting freedoms, not through restrictions, a restrictive aspect nevertheless transpires. As Mond, the ruler, says: 'as I make the laws here, I can also break them. With impunity' (Huxley 2007: 192). What we have here is sovereignty, the 'law beyond the law' (Agamben 1998: 59). In this sense *Brave New World* cannot be structurally separated from, but contains within itself, its own *1984*. Sovereignty is always a parallax of *1984* and *Brave New World*. It is because it can be exercised by both restricting and granting freedoms that sovereign power is by definition arbitrary, intimately bound to the exception.

And second, if totalitarianism is identified with Stalinism, the concept starts to function as an ideological fantasy, allowing one to dream away from the malfunctions of one's own society. Nonetheless, if we detach the concept of totalitarianism from this ideological function, using it minimally to designate a society that cannot question itself, it can uncannily link the former totalitarian society of the East with that of the contemporary West, aided by thought control, entertainment industries, manipulated masses, bio-genetic sciences and so on. After all, there is a structural homology between obeying the iron laws of the capitalist 'market' and the iron laws of Stalinist 'history'.

The tourist's reservation

The brave new world is not one world; there are vast areas, 'savage reservations', which its network bypasses. Everything it has sent to the 'bunk' of history, for example religion, family relations, primitive passions, violent rituals, and so on, continues to exist here, where people are still born and raised by biological parents.

As such, the reservations stand for what is abandoned, for what 'has not been worth the expense of civilizing' (Huxley 2007: 141). But there are organized tours to reservations, which resemble today's favela tourism. Incidentally Bernard and Lenina go to a reservation for a 'holiday', a holiday which signifies a search for experience in a society in which everything is a simulacrum (ibid.: 146). The *mise-en-scène* of the brave new world is, in other words, the disappearance of experience; the subjects undergo, but never have, experiences. And the hysteria of such a world is the production of the real (see Baudrillard 1994: 23).

> 'I don't like it,' said Lenina. 'I don't like it.' She liked even less what awaited her at the entrance to the pueblo, where their guide had left them while he went inside for instructions. The dirt, to start with, the piles of rubbish, the dust, the dogs, the flies. Her face wrinkled up into a grimace of disgust.
>
> *(Huxley 2007: 94)*

Bianca Freire-Medeiros, an expert on favela tourism, reports that the most commonly photographed object by the favela tourists is rubbish (2009). Similarly, for Lenina, for whom 'civilization is sterilization' (Huxley 2007: 94), the reservation *is* rubbish. She is like Hegel's 'beautiful soul' who engages with the social world without recognizing her own active role in its production, disavowing the fact that the reservations are a necessary outcome of an order-building process and economic progress, through which the brave new world produces a surplus population of *homines sacri*.

The 'main problem' of our society, says Luhmann (1994: 4),

> is indifference and neglect . . . We will have, apparently, in the next century a large mass of, say, bodies which have to survive somehow on their own, and not so much as kind of parts, or kind of persons used for whatever purpose in function systems.

But this exclusion, the reduction to 'bodies', takes place not outside, but from inside, the world society; it is a manifestation of sovereignty. The reservations are instances of the camp in so far as they emerge as an expression of 'untying' (see Agamben 1998: 90). Thus in their very exclusion they are also included in the bio-politics of the brave new world. The favela/reservation is hierarchically placed qua power relations, which, by the same token, 'includes' it in a broader context, that of the bio-political capitalist economy.

However, the 'reservation' functions in *Brave New World* as an orientalist image of a chaotic space, an archaic state of nature beyond 'our' space and time, and therefore beyond our responsibility, a space of secret enjoyments (rituals, 'obscene' family ties, passionate encounters and so on) or of despotism (violence, repression and so on), like the 'rogue states' of our time. But this dichotomy breaks down if we consider the reservations as a symptom of the brave new world itself. In the end, *homo sacer* is at the heart of the brave new world in which eugenics and dysgenics together reduce its citizens' lives to bare life. Hence the first intimation to revolt occurs when Bernard recognizes a bio-political dimension in the culture of hedonism, as he hears two male characters talking about Lenina 'as though she were a bit of meat', only to find out later that she, too, 'thinks of herself that way. She doesn't mind being meat' (Huxley 2007: 39, 80).

As is well known, Huxley himself made references to eugenics before and during the period in which he wrote *Brave New World*. He went as far as defending it to prevent 'the rapid deterioration . . . of the whole West European stock' (quoted in Bradshaw 2007: xxii). After the Holocaust, however, when eugenics started to lose its appeal for the liberal democratic intelligentsia, Huxley, too, was warning against domination by technological means. Thus, revisiting *Brave New World* in 1958, he writes:

> The Nazis did not have time . . . to brainwash and condition their lower leadership. This, it may be, is one of the reasons why they failed. Since Hitler's day the armoury of technical devices has been considerably enlarged. [. . .] Thanks to technological progress, Big Brother can now be almost as omnipresent as God.
>
> *(Huxley 2004: 52)*

Indeed, as Esposito (2008) argues, even though Nazism was militarily and politically defeated in the Second World War, it has won a cultural victory in the sense that its emphasis on bio-politics, its focus on the body as a political category, has now become a commonplace in Western liberal culture. If 'man for Nazism is his body and only his body' (ibid.: 13), 'man' in our culture tends to become one who possesses his own body as an individual property, can use it, buy and sell it, as if it were a commodity. It is telling, therefore, that today's 'liberal eugenics', which describes its project as improving human well-being, can only distinguish itself from the Nazi eugenics by insisting on state neutrality (eugenics must be practised on the basis of liberal individual freedoms, without state intervention) and by distancing itself from biological reductionism, by claiming that it does not suppose an essential 'norm', for example the Aryan as an 'ideal type', that can serve as a criterion to evaluate individuals (Mills 2007: 198). Notwithstanding the plausibility of such arguments, they inevitably entail a propensity for increasing bio-political regulation of potential life through legal and technological intervention (ibid.: 201).

Seen in this perspective, the real function of dystopia is to project real problems into a future temporality, a fantasy space. Books like *Brave New World* deceive not by presenting what is fiction as true but by creating the illusion that what is true (bio-politics, inequalities, unfreedom and so on) is fiction (see Žižek 2002c: 19).

Violent disjunctions

In their tourist escape, Bernard and Lenina meet a woman, Linda: originally from the brave new world, she came to the reservation years ago, as a tourist, but, becoming pregnant, a catastrophic fate in this world, she could not go back. Thus, without hope and without soma, her life in the reservation has been excruciatingly hard, the life of an outcast, also because her promiscuity was hated by the savages. Hence she is excited to meet Bernard and Lenina, to see their 'civilized' faces and clothes. But with her missing teeth, her obesity, her wrinkles, the filthy blanket over her head, and so on, she cuts a disgusting figure in Lenina's eyes (Huxley 2007: 102–3). And as much as Linda is nostalgic about the brave new world, her son, John, is curious about it. John is also an outcast; although religious, he is excluded from the religious rituals of the reservation. So Bernard, the outcast of the brave new world, arranges a special permit for Linda and John to visit the brave new world, presenting the idea to the authorities with reference to scientific purposes: analysing savage life.

When they arrive, John immediately becomes a celebrity, a noble savage. Lenina, too, with whom John fell in love at first sight, comes to like him. The repulsive, toothless, old and fat Linda, however, is isolated and escapes into a 'permanent soma holiday'. In the meanwhile, John gradually tires of the new world, which appears to him more and more trivial. He is also 'distressed' by his mother's abandonment, her permanent holiday. But he refuses to take soma. Even in relation to Lenina, his feelings turn ambivalent; while still loving her, he detests her promiscuity. The tipping point comes when Linda dies alone in a hospital. Her death like a *homo sacer*, unmourned, provokes John to violence (ibid.: 139–42).

At this point, Mustapha Mond, the ruler, has a conversation with John, which is the most interesting part of the book, for it reveals the stakes of the confrontation between the two worlds. Mond articulates the brave new world's philosophy, its fixation on stability, which results in a fear of time and change. It comes to light that what is most frightening to the brave new world is the possibility of an event. It is for this reason that the brave new world sacrifices philosophy and art, to 'shift the emphasis from truth and beauty to comfort and happiness' (ibid.: 201). When John insists that religion is necessary to 'compensate' for the miseries of the world, Mond answers that religion is uncalled for in the brave new world. In so far as the idea of God is grounded in human beings' suffering and pain, society can get rid of it, if it can provide another solution to the problem:

> And if ever, by some unlucky chance, anything unpleasant should somehow happen, why, there's always *soma* to give you a holiday from the facts. And there's always *soma* to calm your anger, to reconcile you to your enemies, to make you patient and long-suffering. In the past you could only accomplish these things by making a great effort and after years of hard moral training. Now, you swallow two or three half-gramme tablets, and there you are. Anybody can be virtuous now.
>
> *(Ibid.: 209–10)*

The idea of God, in the end, is not compatible with scientific ideals. But Mond's enlightened rejection of religion does not amount to a consistent atheism; the brave new world merely replaces monotheistic religions with an earthly, decaf deity, soma. Or rather, since soma is a commodity, with 'capitalism as religion' (see Benjamin 1996). Responding to the same fears, for example pain, weakness and mortality, soma functions as a pure cult religion, without a specific dogma and theology, and celebrates permanent duration, to the point at which God himself is included in the logic of capital.

Towards the end of *Thus Spoke Zarathustra*, we meet some of Zarathustra's guests, who all think they have 'unlearned' from Zarathustra the religious sentiment, the despair that follows from feeling weak in this world and prompts humans to imagine a transcendent heaven in which pain and antagonism no longer exist. Thus, they are in the carnival mood. Yet Nietzsche makes it clear that killing God is not enough to get rid of him. A materialist, hedonist world is prone to new, this-worldly illusions, even new gods and idols. At one point in the carnival, therefore, the noise abruptly stops and, precisely when they think they have overcome it, the crowd falls back upon a religious mood. 'They have all become *pious* again, they are *praying*, they are *mad*!' (Nietzsche 1961: 321). But what they worship is a this-worldly God: an ass. They explain that the ass carries their burden, he is patient and never says no, indeed he never speaks, and so on. 'Better to worship God in this shape than in no shape at all' (Nietzsche 1961: 322). In *Zarathustra*, it is the 'ugliest man', the passive nihilist, who has murdered God and delivers the tribute to the ass that has 'created the world after his own image, that is, as stupid as possible' (ibid.). In the brave new world, too, 'providence takes its cue from men' (Huxley 2007: 208). The ass is embodied in utilitarianism, and the desire for change, for transfiguration, has disappeared into the cry of the ass.

Against this pseudo-religion, John sustains that 'tears are necessary' (Huxley 2007: 210). He wants God, poetry, freedom – and sin. 'In fact,' Mond replies, 'you're claiming the right to be unhappy.' 'All right then,' John says insolently, 'I'm claiming the right to be unhappy' (ibid.: 211–12). He chooses religion, self-denial and chastity. Then he isolates himself to a hermitage in search of purification, starting to mourn his mother. Yet his religious ritual, his 'hitting himself with a whip', becomes a sensation when the media rediscover the whereabouts of the 'mystery savage' (ibid.: 219–21). His self-flagellation, now a spectacle exposed to the public gaze, attracts more and more 'tourists' to his hermitage. Even Lenina comes to see him one day, mixing with the crowd chanting 'Whip, whip, the whip!' (ibid.: 225). But at the sight of Lenina, and unable to notice her tears, John loses control and attacks her, whipping her 'like a mad man' (ibid.: 227). Something interesting follows. Fascinated by pain and impelled, from within, 'by that habit of cooperation, that desire for unanimity and atonement, which their conditioning had so ineradicably implanted in them', the members of the crowd begin to 'mime' John's passionate gestures, everybody striking at one another in a mass orgy of soma, sex and violence (ibid.: 228). The same night, as a last attempt to escape the brave new world, John commits suicide.

Let us, at this point, note the symmetry between Mond's and John's positions. If Mond is obsessed with the eternal present, John is crippled by his traumatic past; whereas Mond is fearful of the future, John, realizing that he cannot realize his ideals in the brave new world, dreams of another, idealized future (see Baker 1990: 133). Both characters have an aversion to time, and this aversion finds an outlet in the hatred of the feminine excess: as Mond loathes the female, which he associates with the 'obscene' temporality of natural birth and mothering, John's obsession with self-denial as a religious gesture finds a concrete target in Lenina's promiscuity (ibid.: 132).

Mond's ethical disorientation (passive nihilism) and John's despair (radical nihilism) are homological positions that have a shared origin in religious nihilism. This shared origin is revealed when Mond's state ideology ultimately sides with religion, banning a scientific paper, declaring pure science an 'enemy' – 'Yes, even science' (Huxley 2007: 198). Here, Mond is compelled to quote Cardinal Newman, a nineteenth-century British theologian: 'independence was not made for man' (ibid.: 204–5). Nonetheless, this shared origin does not mean that the two existential strategies coexist peacefully. In John, therefore, we find an instinctual revolt, almost a 'biological hatred', through which 'the energy of the human body rebels against intolerable repression' (Marcuse 1969: 16), an open-ended energy, which can seek political channels or, becoming suicidal, can lead to self-destruction and terror.

In this sense, the uneasy relationship between the brave new world and John's fundamentalism is visionary regarding the contemporary 'war' between post-politics and fundamentalist terror. It makes sense, therefore, to emphasize that John is 'not really a savage' (Baker 1990: 138) – he is a hybrid, or the brave new world's own shadow, which has fallen out in the reservations but, as in Hans Christian Andersen's fable *The Shadow*, returns to take his revenge on his old master by forcing him to follow his shadow, turning him into a shadow of a shadow. John's radical nihilism, like an 'anti-body', turns against the organism that created him. But his radicalism is also a nihilism, which cannot create new, immanent values, and which reconciles him to what he rebels against. John's suicide ultimately confirms the brave new world's ultimatum: 'it is impossible to live while questioning society' (Britto 2007: 63).

Yet radical nihilism is not the only route to violence in the brave new world. What is interesting in the whipping scene is that the body is metamorphosed, through the orgy, into an instance of pure enjoyment and excess, into a potlatch, in which individuality is totally 'dis-possessed' (see Bataille 2001: 17–18). Thus, the crowd experiences a kind of abandonment, a metamorphosis into bare life, which comes in an unexpected way, as a sadist orgy.

> Sade's modernity does not consist in his having foreseen the unpolitical primacy of sexuality in our unpolitical age. On the contrary, Sade is as contemporary as he is because of his incomparable presentation of the absolutely political (that is, 'biopolitical') meaning of sexuality and physiological life itself. Like the concentration camps of our century, the totalitarian character of the organization of life in Silling's castle – with its meticulous regulations that do not spare any aspect of physiological life (not even the digestive function, which is obsessively codified and publicized) – has its root in the fact that what is proposed here for the first time is a normal and collective (and hence political) organization of human life founded solely on bare life.
>
> *(Agamben 1998: 135)*

While the political and the biological become interchangeable, the bed takes the place of the agora (see Lacan 1990). The significance of the whipping scene lies in this swap. Thus the Sadean maxim of unconstrained enjoyment ('I have the right to enjoy your body, and you have the equal right to enjoy mine') is adopted by the brave new world: 'everyone belongs to everyone else'. In this sense the book takes issue with the valorization of transgression in our culture. If the idea of a 'culture' of transgression, a generalized transgression, is impossible to sustain, it is not only because this would mean the becoming rule of transgression, but also because the pleasure principle cannot be sustained without the reality principle. The pleasure of eroticism consists in breaking a taboo, which is, in turn, acknowledged in breaking; the rule works because it is broken. Therefore, transgressing the norm is not an emancipatory move in itself. But then for whom is this orgy staged? For the big Other, the anonymous machine which works independently of human will, like Orwell's Big Brother or the authority that Kafka's K searches for but never finds, or for the brave new world's dead God 'that manifests himself as an absence' (Huxley 2007: 206). At any rate, the orgy is staged for an imaginary father figure, and precisely as such conceals the fact that there is no big Other which commands us to obey or, of course, to enjoy – the system is us.

To put it differently, in the brave new world perversion is père-version, the version of the father: a society in which the dominant mode of subjectivity is no longer the disciplinary subject of normalization but the 'polymorphously perverse' subject following the command to enjoy (see Žižek 1999: 248). This is why the sexualized, naked body does not disturb the existing order. After all, what makes sexuality disturbing is not the sexual act itself but the 'mode of life' related to it, which 'can yield a culture and an ethics' (Foucault 2001: 298, 300). The 'body' itself is already a bio-political body which is not outside the reach of power (Agamben 1998: 187). The sexual 'freedom' of the brave new world is what opens up the very space for extending the range of the bio-political paradigm. Hence the regular orgies and the frequent partner swapping become a boring, 'official sexual routine', which 'turns pleasure to fun and denies it by granting it' (Adorno 1967: 104–5).

The lack of lack

The brave new world is a control society in which everything is commodified; all sociality is filtered through the logic of businesses. Its passive nihilism is thus in perfect harmony with the cynicism of capitalism, in which morality ceases to be a register for critical reflection (see Deleuze and Guattari 1983: 225). However, cynicism is not merely a matter of 'false consciousness'. The cynic is aware of the distance between the ideological mask, 'soma holiday', and the social reality; but he insists upon the mask. He knows that what soma provides is merely an illusion, but he enjoys it. It is in this gap that cynicism, the lack of affect, paradoxically becomes an affect, not as a direct position of immorality but rather as a morality that serves immorality (see Žižek 1989: 29–30).

In this perspective the brave new world is close to our reality. After all, one of the defining characteristics of contemporary capitalism is the commodification of experience. Our culture increasingly 'exists in the form of commodified experiences' (Rifkin 2000: 154). What is crucial in this respect is the ownership of not material but immaterial property, for example copyrights and brands, which ground experience (Žižek 2002b: 289): hence the emerging split between the economy of spectacles, based on the commodification of experience, and its 'real' base, material production, which is 'transfunctionalized into the supporting mechanism for the stage production' (ibid.: 289), a world in which work, 'not sex, appears as the site of obscene indecency to be concealed from the public eye' (ibid.: 289).

This obscenity of work, while sex is normalized, is grounded in *Brave New World* through a subtraction, that of needs: 'People are happy; they get what they want, and they never want what they can't get' (Huxley 2007: 194). But Huxley, reducing 'need' to a biological notion, ignores the fact that human needs are 'historically mediated' through praxis (Adorno 1967: 109). In a capitalist society, this mediation takes place through the link between commodity and fetishism. Further, it is because commodities are desired, as well as needed, that the capitalist economy has an inbuilt totalitarian tendency, that the world of commodities can 'indoctrinate and manipulate' (Marcuse 1964: 12). However, instead of dealing with the paradoxes of commodity fetishism, Huxley chooses to naturalize capitalism, making 'a fetish of the fetishism of commodities' (Adorno 1967: 113).

Yet the 'satisfaction of needs' does not really weaken the hold of fetishism in the brave new world. When it is decoupled from its material use value, the fetish becomes even more pervasive. Soma, for instance, signifies a pure fetish value completely separated from its material stand-in. This total emancipation of fetish value from use value is the 'ecstasy' of the commodity form, a movement through which the commodity disappears into the simulacra by multiplying itself infinitely 'in order at every moment to make up for a reality that is absent' (Baudrillard 2005b: 224).

> This, of course, compels us to reformulate completely the classical Marxist topic of 'reification' and 'commodity fetishism', insofar as this topic still relies on the notion of the fetish as a concrete object whose stable presence obfuscates its social mediation. Paradoxically, fetishism reaches its acme precisely when the fetish itself is 'de-materialized', turned into a fluid, 'immaterial' virtual entity.
>
> *(Žižek 2002b: 287–8)*

Thus, the danger is not only forgetting that there are real people and social relations behind the logic of capital. Such a critique of commodity fetishism, adopted by Adorno above, must be supplemented with the point that the 'abstraction' at work here is not only a misperception of a social reality but also a process through which reality itself attains the status of a spectre, a fiction, while its concrete effects become even more overwhelming (ibid.: 287). This is the status of economy in *Brave New*

World. Thus, despite revealing a world in which everything and everybody are subjected to the logic of capital, Huxley avoids problematizing the economy itself, which 'strengthens the reified situation Huxley cannot tolerate: the neutralization of a culture cut off from the material process of production' (Adorno 1967: 108). Combined with this, the lack of mediation between material and spiritual needs allows Huxley to sidestep the question of justice, which is intrinsically linked to the fulfilment of material as well as spiritual needs. Thus, he criticizes mass culture for diminishing the predisposition for metaphysics, overseeing how mass culture, precisely as a form of metaphysics, contributes to inequality and alienation:

> Full of fictitious concern for the calamity that a realized utopia could inflict on mankind, he refuses to take note of the real as a far more urgent calamity that prevents the utopia from being realized. It is idle to bemoan what will become of men when hunger and distress have disappeared from the world.
>
> *(Adorno 1967: 116)*

Without a politics, an exit route from the deadlock of the two nihilisms, Huxley oscillates between them. On the one hand, while he laments the loss of idealism, passing a negative judgement on the brave new world's passive nihilism, his saviour becomes, in a liberal democratic spirit, the individual. Yet, on the other hand, he elevates John's fundamentalist view on happiness to the level of a real alternative, creating the impression that 'the happiness produced by the transgression of taboos could ever legitimate the taboo' (ibid.: 104). The choice remains between two already reified categories: the bourgeois individual versus the prohibition, both confirming a fetishized present. Huxley paradoxically condemns the totalitarian new world while, at the same time, glorifying the individualism which created it, 'curses' the imaginary future with reification 'without realizing that the past whose blessing he invokes is of the same nature' (ibid.: 106, 114). This, then, is what Huxley leaves us with: the disjunctive synthesis the novel imposes on the reader, the struggle between Mond and John, is a false antagonism against the background of a dominant ideology which forecloses the event. Therefore, a radical politics in the brave new world would, first and foremost, seek to subtract itself from this dualism. Likewise, in our world,

> the hegemonic ideological field imposes on us a field of (ideological) visibility with its own 'principal contradiction' (today, it is the opposition of market-freedom-democracy and fundamentalist-terrorist-totalitarianism – 'Islamo-fascism' etc.), and the first thing to do is to reject (to subtract from) this opposition, to perceive it as a false opposition destined to obfuscate the true line of division. [. . .] The true antagonism is always reflective, it is the antagonism between the 'official' antagonism and that what is foreclosed by it.
>
> *(Žižek 2007c: 4)*

What Huxley does not do is think the social field beyond the disjunctive synthesis of the prohibition and the logic of the market. This is also what gives its totalitarian twist to the novel. There Is No Alternative. In the brave new world there is no line of flight that can escape the continuum of the disjunctive synthesis, no truly antagonistic praxis that can confront and change the system.

However, there is an internal, logical limit to the totalitarian tendency. 'Totality' is unachievable because the virtual possibilities of a society can never be contained within an actual structure. Because it is open, history always gives rise to becomings. In this sense totalitarianism 'does not exist' (see Badiou 2009a: 12, 92). There is always something that escapes the social organization (Deleuze and Guattari 1987: 216). Even in *Brave New World*, a line of flight materializes behind its protagonists' backs: for all the effort Huxley puts into emphasizing Lenina's unerotic effect on John, and on the reader, Lenina's artificial promiscuity, against the author's intentions, produces a 'highly seductive' effect 'to which even the infuriated cultural savage succumbs at the end of the novel' (Adorno 1967: 105–6).

New spirit, old spectre

One of the most intriguing aspects of *Brave New World* is its interpretation of sexual freedom as something that leads to debasement. In the brave new world, when the conjugal bond is abolished and sexual freedom is legalized, sexuality becomes subsumed within the system, which 'over-organizes' all aspects of life (see also Huxley 2004: 34–5). Consequently, that 'everyone belongs to everyone else' refers for Huxley to a sexual communism, which leads to the disappearance of individuality along with other prohibitions. But why does Huxley insist on this trajectory, on that everybody's 'belonging' to everybody else necessarily leads to lack of freedom? And what does 'belonging' mean here?

Huxley, a liberal, perceives 'belonging' as a property relation. Correspondingly, sexuality is socialized in the brave new world only in the sense that the body is no longer private property but becomes a public property, a property of the state. As erotic drives are institutionalized, the body is captured by the system and functions as an instrument of regulation and domination, or as a dispositif, as a 'sacred' object untied from the domain of the common, which is why it is 'blasphemy' not to allow one's body to 'belong' to everyone else. In this sense the 'profanation' Huxley describes has a meaning only in relation to private property.

> But you Communists would introduce community of women, screams the whole bourgeoisie in chorus. The bourgeois sees in his wife a mere instrument of production. He hears that the instruments of production are to be exploited in common, and, naturally, can come to no other conclusion than the lot of being common to all will likewise fall to the women.
>
> *(Marx and Engels 2002: 240)*

However, a true 'profanation' of the body, that is, its untying from the domain of the law, would take place only in so far as the sacralized body ceases to be a private *or* public property, and becomes 'common' again. The communist utopia is thus a system in which property as such, as a dispositif, is destroyed, a situation in which 'belonging' would attain a communist meaning, as 'the free development of the individual is the condition for the free development of all' (Marx and Engels 2002: 244). This is what is unimaginable for Huxley. The tension he describes, that between private and public property, between capitalism and socialism, excludes the idea of communism. And in so far as true 'happiness' is profanation, the deactivation of the law, it is fair to say that Huxley's 'anger at false happiness sacrifices the idea of true happiness as well' (Adorno 1967: 103–4). It is even imaginable that, in a world without (private and public) property, 'pure fungibility', which Huxley is so alarmed by, 'would destroy the core of domination and promise freedom' (ibid.: 105).

Having said this, is there not, however, a truth in Huxley's diagnosis in relation to contemporary, post-Fordist network society? Given that *Brave New World* describes a Fordist dystopia, a 'solid modernity' which sacrifices authenticity, difference and creativity in the name of 'stability', it does not, at first sight, have much to offer to the understanding of contemporary society. In 'liquid modernity', speed, not stability, is the major factor of domination (Bauman 2000: 150–1). Thus, whereas the brave new world found its inspiration for the cult of stability in Henry Ford, the inspiration for the 'liquid' brave new world is Bill Gates, who 'has the ability to let go' (Sennett 1998: 62).

Huxley's dystopia requires a commitment, defined in Fordist terms, to a common good: 'happiness'. But what would be the common good in a rewritten *Brave New World* with Bill Gates as its deity? In *The New Spirit of Capitalism*, Boltanski and Chiapello (2007: 169) discuss how, because capitalism is a world without value, an inherently 'absurd' system, it is constantly in need of justification. And justification, they claim, can come to it only from outside. Following Weber, this external source which justifies participation in capitalism is the 'spirit' of capitalism: a set of values and beliefs which helps to justify it as an order and can provide people with moral reasons for engaging with it. While the first spirit, the 'Protestant ethic', focused on the nineteenth-century image of the bourgeois entrepreneur, the second, consolidated especially between the 1930s and 1960s, was centred on the figure of the director/manager responsible for the workings of the big-scale Taylorist, bureaucratized firm. Needless to say, this is also the spirit *Brave New World* reacts to. And today we are entering a new, globalized phase, in which the 'new spirit of capitalism' finds a new 'hero' in the figure of the 'network-extender', who justifies his or her actions with reference to creativity, difference and mobility (see ibid.: 16–20, 356).

The third spirit values 'projects' as a general form of activity (ibid.: 107). Hence the activity of the mediator in establishing and extending networks is becoming 'a value in itself', irrespective of the specific goal or substantial character of the mediated entities (ibid.). 'In a connexionist world, a natural preoccupation of human beings is the desire to *connect* with others, *to make contact*, so as not to remain *isolated*' (ibid.: 111). And for this purpose, one must be '*adaptable*, physically and intellectually *mobile*' (ibid.: 112). A stable habitus à la Bourdieu is no longer desirable. Rather, today's grand person is the one who is able to distance himself from his own environment and immediate circle of relations. The connexionist man is a 'nomad' (ibid.: 122).

Consequently, a networked world is a complex world of interdependencies in which 'everyone belongs to everyone else'. But is it another brave new world? What is decisive here is an essential open-endedness that pertains to networks, for the competencies such as mobility, adaptability and connectionism can always, potentially, be used in an individualistic, egoistic way. This opportunism, however, is not justified in the new spirit of capitalism: one should be acting in search of the 'common good', that is, in order to engage with others, inspire confidence, be tolerant, respect differences and pass information to others, so that everyone in a network can increase their 'employability' (ibid.: 115). In this sense the new capitalism has an ethical scheme of evaluation. Accordingly, to 'belong' in networks does not mean belonging in Huxley's sense. In networks everything 'belongs' to everything else, 'everything may be allied to everything else', but 'nothing can be reduced to anything else, nothing can be deduced from anything else, everything may be allied to everything else' (Latour 1988: 163). 'Belonging' here is an 'irreductionist' affair which cannot be thought of in functionalistic, systemic terms. And as such Huxley's mode of 'belonging' is antithetical to the logic of networking; 'network' is not only relations between people and things in terms of property but all kinds of associations.

However, there is a potential link between the two types of belonging. This link corresponds to the difference between what Boltanski and Chiapello call the 'network-extender' and the 'networker'. Whereas the first acknowledges debts contracted with others participating in the same network, the latter engages in opportunistic behaviour, making a selfish use of the networks – the networker is, as such, an emblematic figure that stands for a 'network world that is not subject to the control of the projective city' (2007: 356, 378). In a certain sense, then, that 'everyone belongs to everyone else' can have two very different meanings within networks too. Moreover, the 'networker' reduces others in the network to a commodity. In so far as the pursuit of profit remains the fundamental horizon of networks, that is, in so far as the distinction between 'disinterested' sharing in the interest of the 'common good' and the strategic utilization of network relations is blurred, the intermediaries start to behave as if they have 'a property right over the person of the one whom he puts in contact with a third party, who anticipates an advantage from this liaison' (ibid.: 456), as if, in other words, 'everyone belongs to everyone else' in Huxley's sense.

And such commodification fully coincides with exploitation in its strongest, bio-political sense, which involves an 'offence against the very dignity of human beings' (ibid.: 364, 365). Indeed, if Fordism conferred 'an official form on the commodification of human beings' by reducing them to machine-like appendices to the assembly line, the post-Fordist logic of networking penetrates 'more profoundly into people's interior being', transgressing once more the moral (and partly legal) imperative not to commodify human beings (ibid.: 464–5).

So the risk of networking is falling back upon bio-politics. And since this risk is an inbuilt, structural risk, the world of networks is always prone to become a world in which 'everyone belongs to everyone else' in Huxley's sense. This tendency is accentuated by a paradox internal to the new spirit of capitalism, a paradox which becomes visible if we consider Spinoza as the grammatician of the new, post-Fordist spirit of capitalism because most of his themes (anti-teleology, anti-dialectic, multitude, the plane of immanence occupied by bodies and souls, power as potentiality, the destruction of the subject, and so on) converge with the characteristics of this new capitalism (Illuminati 2003: 317; Albertsen 2005: 80). Further, in network society, Spinoza's pragmatic ethics tends to become a norm, a normative injunction. In this sense, 'post-Fordism is the communism of capital' (Virno 2004: 111). The paradoxical logic here consists in including and excluding immanence in the same movement, transforming immanence into a transcendent rule (Albertsen 1995: 136). It is also this logic of indistinction (between immanence and transcendence, capitalism and communism, and so on) that generates a coincidence between yesterday's brave new world and today's network society, as the two meanings of 'everyone belongs to every else' are blurred.

Critique?

To end with, let us turn to the fate of critique in *Brave New World*. Its trajectory in the book follows three stages: discontent, reconciliation, exclusion. Thus we meet Bernard first as a sceptic. Then he experiences bringing John Savage to the brave new world as intoxicating 'success', which makes him popular among the high society and transforms him into a reconciled conformist. However, he still rides on the narcissistic privileges of critique, constantly parading 'a carping unorthodoxy' (Huxley 2007: 136–7). Finally, when John stops attending his parties, Bernard falls from favour too, and metamorphoses back into an outcast. At this point power avenges his vanity. But since the rulers have no wish to cut throats while they can silence dissent in other ways, they exile him to an island:

> That's to say, he's being sent to a place where he'll meet the most interesting set of men and women to be found anywhere in the world. All the people who, for one reason or another, have got too self-consciously individual to fit into community-life. All the people who aren't satisfied with orthodoxy, who've got independent ideas of their own. Every one, in a word, who's any one.
>
> *(Ibid.: 199–200)*

Here we have the intellectual as a stranger, 'a skeptically compassionate caricature of a Jew' (Adorno 1967: 106). However, attributing Bernard's revolt to his inferiority complex, charging him with vulgar snobbism and moral cowardice, Huxley participates in a long-established bourgeois tradition: 'unmask anyone who seeks to challenge things as both the genuine child and the perverse product of the whole which he opposes' (ibid.: 106–7). Is this not still the fate of critique in today's post-politics, which welcomes critique but only by reducing it to something without consequence, confining it to pragmatic negotiations and strategic compromises, and thus rendering politics in the sense of a radical questioning of the social impossible? As such, *Brave New World* is an early demonstration of the crisis of critique, which, in contemporary society, continues in the form of a deepening gap between *vita contemplativa* and *vita activa* (see Bauman 2000: 43). People know more, become more reflexive, even more critically disposed, but, as the distance between knowledge and action increases, their critique turns out to be 'toothless'; exceptional freedoms coincide with exceptional impotence (ibid.: 23). And if radical critique still persists, refuses to disappear into the simulacra, it can always be 'unmasked' as the perverse child of post-politics. Are we not all part of the system?

Are we?

PART III
Critique and counter-critique

9

CRITIQUE OF CRITIQUE OF CRITIQUE . . .

In so far as the contemporary regime of governmentality is bio-political, bio-politics constitutes the problematic of critique today – with one qualification though. Bio-politics does not only mean the reduction of 'life' to the biological life of the species, to bare life; it also writes bodies, turning them into codes, images and passwords (see Deleuze 1995: 180). Thus the bio-political subject emerges as an exceptional figure, as the coincidence of the body without word, the slave, and the word without body, the spectre, of presentation without representation and representation without presentation (Agamben 1998: 24–5).

To discuss the predicament of critique in this context, I focus on a theoretical case, the 'sociology of critique' as it is formulated by Boltanski and Thévenot (2006) and developed by Boltanski and Chiapello (2007). This sociology is critical of critical theory. It claims that, while critical theory seeks to 'dig beneath' the consciousness of social actors in order to 'unmask' the role of hidden structures which determine their actions, it remains indifferent to the values of the actors, the normative principles and risks involved in action, and reduces social action to 'the realization of potentialities inscribed in structures' (Boltanski and Chiapello 2007: x–xi). Consequently, the sociology of critique endeavours to supplement critical theory with a 'theory of critique', with a pragmatic analysis of the normative values that inspire intentional action. In order to be critical, it insists, one must first understand what critique is.

Aesthetic and social critique

Critique has its basis in social change. In this regard the sociology of critique focuses on the transformations of capitalism. Capitalism, it maintains, is an 'absurd' system whose axiomatic logic is indifferent to moral concerns and categories (Boltanski and Chiapello 2007: 8). Hence it constantly generates critique. Historically, capitalism has been criticized along two basic lines: as a source of alienation and oppression, because it subordinates human freedom, creativity and autonomy to the market; and as a cause of inequality and poverty, with destructive effects on the social bond, for it encourages egoism and opportunism. The sociology of critique refers to the first type of critique as 'artistic critique' and to the latter as 'social critique' (ibid.: 37).

The artistic critique has its origin in the works of bohemian artists such as Baudelaire, and has culminated in the French post-structuralism of the 1970s. Social critique, on the other hand, has been rooted in the leftist movement of the nineteenth century and emphasized the consequences of exploitation. While the artistic critique put emphasis on freedom, social critique prioritized the demand for equality. But they had in common a desire for 'total revolution' (Boltanski 2002: 6). In contrast to the artistic critique, however, the social critique has contained within itself also 'reformist' agendas, which, rather than opposing the capitalist mode of production as such, sought to minimize exploitation through socialist and social democratic strategies (Boltanski and Chiapello 2007: 39).

Significantly, however, neither artistic nor social critiques are the 'grave diggers' of capitalism. Boltanski and Chiapello insist that capitalism 'needs' both forms of critique. Their Weberian concept 'spirit' is vital in this respect. Because it is an 'absurd' world without value, capitalism cannot justify itself. Its moral lifeblood, its 'spirit', must come to it from outside, that is, among other things, from critique. What makes capitalism a robust system is its paradoxical ability to find moral support in what criticizes it, to absorb and accommodate what opposes it (ibid.: 27).

In a certain sense, therefore, critique of capitalism comes *before* capitalism. Thus the sociology of critique claims that, just as industrial capitalism had partially incorporated the social critique through Fordist welfare-state arrangements, there is emerging today a new spirit of capitalism through the assimilation of the artistic critique. We have been witnessing, since the late 1960s, a transfer of competences from leftist radicalism toward network capitalism, which absorbed and re-coded past critique into present justification (see ibid.: 107). Crucially in this respect, the '68 revolts were characterized by the coincidence of artistic and social critique of capitalism, by the simultaneous demands for 'autonomy' and 'security' (ibid.: 169, 171; see also Boltanski 2002: 8). The response of capitalism, however, was selective. While it 'recognized' the first demand, it 'sidestepped' and silenced the other (Boltanski and Chiapello 2007: 190, 199). The artistic critique has received more recognition, but this 'success' meant its assimilation into capitalism. The new spirit thus took shape by accommodating the artistic critique, especially its emphasis on autonomy and creativity, while ignoring the social critique and its demands. 'Transcending' both itself and the anti-capitalist critique, capitalism developed a 'new, liberated, and even libertarian way of making profit', a 'leftist capitalism' (ibid.: 201–2).

So capitalism actively responds to critique through its vampire-like, everrenewed 'spirit'. Thus today's radical critique, too, will turn into a capitalist norm tomorrow. Is critique useless then? Should one drop it, or is it necessary for critique to radicalize itself even more, to run even faster than capitalism? Or should critique, inversely, function like an 'emergency brake' of this mobile system? The sociology of critique opts for a pragmatic solution, 'reformist' critique, insisting on the attainability of a normative position in the contemporary world, and formulates its task as to 'constrain' the excesses of the new system (ibid.: xiv–xv, 41). It emphasizes, in this context, that the 'spirit' of capitalism not only legitimizes the accumulation process but also constrains it; indeed, 'it can legitimate it only because it constrains it' (ibid.: xx). The internalization of the spirit by social agents enables them to feel indignation and to criticize the system, which, in turn, forces capitalism to incorporate 'some of the values in whose name it was criticized' (ibid.: 25, 27–8). That is, the 'spirit' of capitalism is what makes critique possible. Critique is based on justification.

Justification, displacement and categorization

As such, critique operates at two levels. People engage in critique in particular situations, but critique can take place only if they can 'transcend the particularities' and establish general equivalences across different situations (ibid.: 527). They achieve this transcendence by referring to some already established, generalized 'conventions', that is, to the 'regimes of justification'.

To be sure, justification is not the only mode of action available to actors. But it is the only mode of action which enables 'disputes in which violence is excluded' (Boltanski and Thévenot 2000: 361, 366). Justification/critique can take place only in the form of a peaceful conflict, as a conflict between equals. The other situations in which people act differently, without a sense of justice based on a notion of equivalence, are 'love', 'violence' and 'familiarity' (ibid.: 359). Violence is a mode of action beyond any principle of equivalence, a mode of action at the 'limits' of critique, for it does not seek to justify itself (ibid.: 361). Likewise, 'love' (agape, friendship) is a mode of action in which symbolic exchange, the gift without the expectation of return, transcends the principle of equivalence; it is the sphere of peace without dispute. Finally, 'familiarity' refers to a mode of action based on 'tacit agreements', in which critique is not activated (ibid.: 362–3).

As such, as frameworks of peaceful conflict, the regimes of justification function as 'tests' through which what belongs to a given situation is decided. Tests are 'events' in which social actors put themselves against one another and, as in an arm-wrestling match, 'reveal what they are capable of and, more profoundly, what they are made of' (Boltanski and Chiapello 2007: 31). Tests are always tests of strength. But when the situation is subject to justificatory constraints that are respected by protagonists the test of strength is regarded as legitimate, as a 'test of status' internal to a regime of justification (ibid.). In this case critique will take the form of 'corrective' or 'internal' critique, which aims 'to improve the justice of the test – to make it stricter – to increase the degree to which it is conventionalized, to develop its regularity or legal supervision' (ibid.: 33). But critique can also relate itself to the exteriority of a given regime of justification by referring to an alternative world view. In this case, what is at issue is no longer 'corrective' but 'radical' critique, which problematizes the validity of the test itself. 'From this second critical position, the critique that aims to rectify the test will itself often be criticized as *reformist*, in contrast to a radical critique that has historically proclaimed itself *revolutionary*' (ibid.: 33).

Against this background, the sociology of critique shows that capitalism systematically seeks to reduce the importance assigned to the established 'corrective' tests by searching for new paths of profit rather than confronting the established tests (ibid.: 34). Such 'displacements' are the moments at which justification dissolves into violence and the test of legitimacy is transformed into a pure test of strength (ibid.: 35). Displacement can escape the normative evaluations enabled by the regimes of justification, for it is a mode of action 'deployed on a single plane' (ibid.: xxv). In other words, displacement involves the deconstruction of the two-tier space of justification. Now, having 'only one level' to operate in, one can no longer refer to transcendent conventions (ibid.: 320). In this sense, displacement presents itself as a Deleuzean 'plane of immanence', in which the question of justice and critique cannot be posed, because such a horizontal plane 'knows only differentials of force whose displacements produce (small) differences, continual variations between which there is no hierarchy, and "complex" forms of repetition' (ibid.: 107, 454).

There is, however, the possibility that there emerges a new transcendent principle of justification, a new set of values or a new 'plane of transcendence', from this flat, one-tier plane of immanence (Albertsen 2008: 70). Boltanski and Chiapello call this possibility 'categorization': the attempt at identifying the nature of displacements in order to facilitate the exclusion of violence and revert to the domain of justification in which established tests again have the last word in conflicts. As such, categorization is an intervention that transforms the 'test of strength' into a 'test of status' (Boltanski and Chiapello 2007: 318). So the 'paradox of critique' is grounded here: critique has to confront the consequences of displacements in the mode of categorization (ibid.: 322). This is what is emerging today with the 'new spirit': a new discourse, a new regime of justification, within which network capitalism can be criticized through new interpretative schemas, identifying the new problems caused by displacements (ibid.: 107).

> In this sense, the formation of a new city [regime of justification] might equally – and just as validly – be regarded as an operation of legitimating a new world and the new forms of inequality or exploitation on which it is based; and as an enterprise aiming to make this world more just by reducing the level of exploitation it tolerates and, consequently, limiting the profits that those it favours can expect. Once a city is established, a more ordered world, comprising great men and little people, replaces a chaotic universe, with its strong and its weak.
>
> *(Ibid.: 522)*

Following this, Boltanski and Chiapello need an immanent concept of critique adequate for network capitalism. And since the artistic critique is already assimilated, they return to social critique, attempting to resurrect the concept of exploitation.

In today's society, they argue, exploitation has its roots in the divide between the 'network-extender', who works for the common good, and the 'networker', who exploits networks in an opportunistic manner, without recognizing the contribution of others to the networks in which he participates. However, there is in networks a structural and substantial link 'between the good fortune of the strong (great men) and the misery of the weak (little people)' (ibid.: 360). In so far as the contribution of the latter is made invisible, the fortune of the first 'remains a *mystery*' (ibid.: 361). What 'the weak' contribute to the networks is their immobility: 'some people's immobility is necessary for other people's mobility' (ibid.: 361–2). The immobile stabilize the world in which others travel light. And to the extent that this productive role is not acknowledged in a 'fair' way in networks, the immobile are exploited (ibid.: 363).

Regarding 'fairness' here, Boltanski and Chiapello distinguish between legitimate and illegitimate exploitation, between exploitation in the 'weak' and 'strong' senses (Albertsen 2008: 72). In the weak sense, exploitation relates to how the contribution of the 'weak' is neglected in the production of profits. In the strong sense, exploitation assumes an intense bio-political form that commodifies human beings and thus 'affects vitality itself' (Boltanski and Chiapello 2007: 365):

> Critique relies here on the principle of dignity, in the sense of the impossibility of consigning people once and for all to a single form of status: someone who is a little person in one respect must always have every opportunity to be great in another. To diminish a human person so that she is no longer in a position to demonstrate her worth in any sphere is thus to attack what constitutes her dignity as a human being.
>
> *(Ibid.: 364–5)*

Back to mimesis

Critical theory had operated on the basis of a mimetic principle with two interlinked assumptions: first, the 'unmasking' of what is hidden, of the reality behind appearances, leads to enhanced understanding; and second, this understanding leads to action, to praxis (Rancière 2009a: 27). The sociology of critique no longer wants to take this link for granted. On the contrary, it seeks to abolish the critical procedure, avoiding the discussion of hidden structures or the role of ideology. Paradoxically, however, this 'critique of critique' itself practises a form of critical theory and reproduces its logic. Thus the sociology of critique has its own social critique, focusing on exploitation, and its own aesthetic critique, emphasizing the accelerated commodification of human beings in networks (Albertsen 2008: 77). Moreover, it grounds the relationship between capitalism and its critique on a typically critical-theoretical reflection on the nature of capitalism as an omnipotent, homogenizing force which captures every critical gesture, making a farce out of critique and a commodity out of farce – which is a standard critical-theoretical gesture, just as the argument that the immobility of the immobile is a necessary condition for the mobility of the mobile is (ibid.). And in all this the crucial moment of critique remains the moment at which the 'spectator' is, on the basis of indignation and critique, transformed into an 'actor', a transformation which is 'the political moment par excellence' (Boltanski 1999: 31).

In a way, therefore, the sociology of critique brings out the same mimetic effects as critical theory. It criticizes critical theory only to reproduce its logic (see Rancière 2009a: 30–1): 'But something . . . has changed. Yesterday, these procedures still intended to create forms of consciousness and energies directed towards emancipation. Now they are either entirely disconnected from this horizon of emancipation or clearly directed against this dream' (ibid.: 31–2). The sociology of critique reproduces the logic of critical theory by taking the sting out of it, taming its radical edge. What gets lost in this 'reformist' operation is the promise of emancipation. Crucially in this respect, emancipation is not merely an epistemological-critical problem; it does not come from critical knowledge. Its main referent, its mode of expression, is the event. Therefore emancipatory critique starts from another assumption: 'the incapable are capable' (ibid.: 48). Here 'equality' is not a measurable goal to be attained in a given system of distribution but is the condition of possibility for radical critique, thus a principle 'to be maintained in all circumstances' (Rancière 1991: 138).

As such, radical, emancipatory critique begins when we suspend mimesis, when we stop presupposing a mimetic relation (e.g. between 'unmasking' and 'action', between the 'spectator' and the 'actor') and thus avoid the regression (critique of critique of critique . . .) which has its origin in this presupposition. For in critical procedures there is something else that takes place: 'a shift from a given sensible world to another sensible world that defines different capacities and incapacities, different forms of tolerance and intolerance' (Rancière 2009a: 75). In so far as an actual, hierarchic social order, or a 'police order' as Rancière calls it, is characterized by a propensity towards consensus, towards a harmonious framework in which everyone knows their place, the principle of equality is that which introduces dissensus into this order by demonstrating a 'gap in the sensible itself' (2010: 38).

> What 'dissensus' means is [. . .] that every situation can be cracked open from the inside, reconfigured in a different regime of perception and signification. To reconfigure the landscape of what can be seen and what can be thought is to alter the field of the possible and the distribution of capacities and incapacities.
>
> *(Rancière 2009a: 49)*

The 'indignation' which the sociology of critique articulates in relation to network capitalism never assumes the form of a critique in this sense. Rather, it emphasizes that radical critique is today assimilated by the new spirit of capitalism and subordinates critique to the logic of capital and its law of equivalence. Hence its implicit claim is this: what is supposedly a radical denunciation of the system, a gesture of revolt and revolution, is in reality governed by its logic. For all its pretension to make a difference, radical critique is just another supply for the vampire-like capital, a 'reality' which is supposedly 'hidden' to critical theory! Indeed, radical critique survives, in this horizon, only in the form of an illusion, the illusion of 'total revolution' (see Boltanski 2002).

Communism

The structure of its tamed critique becomes particularly visible when the sociology of critique deals with exploitation in the 'weak' sense. Thus, in contrast to the Marxist theory of exploitation based on the labour theory of value, Boltanski and Chiapello offer no criterion to measure the merits which favour the 'grand men' of network capitalism (Albertsen 2008: 73; see also Bidet 2002: 216–17). Instead, the notion itself appears as a category of justification, which the sociology of critique is happy to admit, claiming that critique legitimizes what it criticizes. But then it becomes difficult to see how network capitalism, which calls for a new, intensified round of commodification, including the bio–political commodification of human affects, can be criticized without critique coming into conflict with the new spirit of capitalism itself (Callinicos 2006: 72).

Indeed, as it reduces all critique to reformist critique, the sociology of critique operates with a capitalist concept of exploitation in the sense that it is not interested in alternatives to capitalism but in the potentialities of capitalism. Its critique seeks not to transcend but to transform capitalism *as* capitalism, a form of critique which, naturalizing capitalism, moderates itself as a revisionist activity. The regimes of justification are, after all, capitalism's own answer to critique. Hence there is another paradox: on the one hand, the sociology of critique distances itself from 'fatalism', arguing that the displacements of capitalism are not 'inevitable', but on the other it posits that they cannot be radically questioned (Albertsen 2008: 77). It rather melancholically tells us that capitalism has displaced the terrain for critique, that we are soaked up to the system even when we criticize it.

Interestingly in this respect, although it diagnoses two temporalities of critique, one which comes *before* capitalist displacements (social and aesthetic critique) and one which proliferates *afterwards* (in the form of the 'spirit', as justification), a distinction that corresponds to the distinction between 'radical' and 'reformist' critique as well, the sociology of critique is silent about what happens to social and aesthetic critique after it is 'accommodated' by capitalism. Are they, for instance, fully captured or is there a rem(a)inder? Or do ideas die? There are two points to note in this context. First, radical critique itself has always been preoccupied with how critique is assimilated by capitalism. Consider, for instance, Deleuze and Guattari's reflection on the new capitalism:

> the more shameful moment came when computer science, marketing, design, and advertising, all the disciplines of communication, seized hold of the word *concept* itself . . . Philosophy has not remained unaffected by the general movement that replaced Critique with sales promotion . . . Certainly,

it is painful to learn that Concept indicates a society of information services and engineering.

(Deleuze and Guattari 1994: 10)

Yet this does not lead Deleuze and Guattari to giving up the 'concept': the more critique is absorbed into the system, the more it is 'driven to fulfil the task of creating concepts that are aerolites rather than commercial products' (ibid.: 11). The more critique fails, the more it is compelled to find new lines of flight. Moreover, every event contains a part that is irreducible to its social network, to any social determinism, for it is essentially a break with this causality, 'an unstable condition which opens a new field of the possible' (Deleuze and Guattari 2006: 233). Therefore, 'an event can be turned around, repressed, co-opted, betrayed, but there is still something there that cannot be outdated' (ibid.). Genuine critique, in other words, remains new.

Second, when Boltanski and Chiapello suggest that the aesthetic-critical demand for 'creativity', 'flexibility' and 'autonomy' in the workplace is assimilated into the new spirit of capitalism, one cannot but agree with Rancière:

> In itself, the thesis is pretty flimsy. There is a world of difference between the discourses of managerial seminars . . . and the reality of contemporary forms of capitalist domination, where labour 'flexibility' signifies forced adaptation to increased forms of productivity under the threat of redundancies, closures and relocations, rather than an appeal to the generalized creativity of the children of May '68. As it happens, concern for creativity at work was foreign to the slogans of the 1968 movement. Quite the reverse, it campaigned against the theme of 'participation' and the invitation to educated, generous youth to participate in a modernized and humanized capitalism that were at the heart of 1960s neo-capitalist ideology and state reformism.
>
> *(Rancière 2009a: 34–5)*

In short, there is more to social and aesthetic critique than the sociology of critique allows one to see. And this 'more' cannot be grounded within the regimes of justification. As Boltanski and Chiapello mention, the idea of communism, for instance, unites the (aesthetic) critique of alienation, the demand for freedom, and the (social) critique of exploitation, the demand for equality (2007: 171). But the communist idea of equality is not articulated in terms of a critique of exploitation in the 'weak' sense, as a question of distribution. Marx's proletariat does not want to participate in an existing system of distribution. It wants to change the rules of distribution as such. Likewise, it does not seek to remain what it is but wants to 'abolish' itself. This critique, which seeks to move beyond capitalism, cannot be contained within the regimes of justification. As Boltanski and Chiapello themselves note, the idea of communism points toward an emancipation that transcends the domain of justification; 'communism' itself is not a regime of justification but a critique of justification as a mode of action (ibid.: 172; Albertsen 2002: 60,

2008: 74). Indeed, the idea of communism constitutes a line of flight regarding justification. But Boltanski and Chiapello do not follow this line; for them, 'communism' basically signifies a threat, that of 'demanding a world without tests' (2007: 172).

This brings us to a crucial difference between Weberian and Marxist conceptions of capitalism. Whereas in Weber the spirit of capitalism must be found outside capitalism, in Marx the ideology (spirit) of capitalism is generated by capitalism itself: if the world of commodities is characterized by consistent relations of exchange among commodities, which is made possible by a common measure of equivalence, money, this 'immanent' relation between value (the equivalence of commodities) and money is itself grounded on a 'transcendent' element, the abstract human labour, which is common to both value and money but does not exist on the plane of immanence (Albertsen 2008: 78–9). This immanent transcendence then functions as the ground for a radical critique of what exists and what ideologically mystifies it.

The sociology of critique flattens, precisely, this idea of transcendence. Its critique, to be sure, is supposed to operate at 'two levels', so that the 'conventions' which the regimes of justification refer to enable the actors to 'transcend the particularities' of actual situations (Boltanski and Chiapello 2007: 527). But these conventions are, like Durkheim's 'norms', historically generalized value systems (ibid.: 520). Thus the transcendence at issue here is a socially and historically produced transcendence which 'relies on existing categories' and which is 'inscribed in the past' (ibid.: 323).

This empirically observable transcendence brings to mind a paradox, which Foucault called the 'empirico-transcendental doublet' (1992: 322). The modern category of 'man', for instance, is supposed to be an *a priori*, transcendent figure outside history, while it is in reality a product of power/knowledge, that is, belongs to history.

> This is because we are so blinded by the recent manifestation of man that we can no longer remember a time – and it is not so long ago – when the world, its order, and human beings existed, but man did not. It is easy to see why Nietzsche's thought should have had, and still has for us, such a disturbing power when it is introduced in the form of an imminent event, the Promise-Threat, the notion that man soon would be no more – but would be replaced by the superman.
>
> *(Ibid.: 322)*

Similarly, the sociology of critique holds that critical intervention into the course of history to change history is possible because there exist some *a priori* values (the 'grandeurs' of justification) on the basis of which history can be rectified. These factors, moreover, can be accessed rationally, via critical reason. Yet, on the other hand, these 'transcendent' values turn out to be historical. Transcendence, which is supposed to be ahistorical, is thereby reduced to the historical. In this sense, the sociology of critique understands normativity only in terms of already existing values rather than transvaluation. It does not ask any questions regarding the value of (existing) values. Rather it operates as a 'collector of current values':

> The image of the philosopher is obscured by all his necessary disguises, but also by all the betrayals that turn him into the philosopher of religion, the philosopher of the State, the collector of current values and the functionary of history.
>
> *(Deleuze 1983: 107)*

What matters for radical critique, on the other hand, is the question of where the new values come from, which requires more than justification or 'corrective tests'. The sociology of critique demonstrates this in relation to capitalist displacements, which, as 'tests of strength', transcend the bounds of justification. But the question is whether one can imagine the same possibility, that of displacements, from the point of view of opposition to capitalism as well. *This* is what is foreclosed in the sociology of critique. Thus, we end up with a curious, 'flat' transcendence, which can relate a particular situation only to the generalities which the regimes of justification allow for.

This flat transcendence, however, must not be confused with the Spinozist–Deleuzean 'surface', the horizontal plane of immanence. The two 'flat' ontologies are diametrically different. Most importantly, whereas the sociology of critique operates with particularity (and the general), the latter focuses on singularity (and the universal). And the difference singularity makes is, of course, the event, which signifies infinitely more than the 'tests' of the sociology of critique.

Counter-critique

This relationship between the particular and the general brings us back to democratic materialism and its bio-political governmentality based on the regulation of the 'infinity of finite things' (Dillon 2011). What bio-politics does is, precisely, to reduce singularities, which refer to infinity, to finite particularities, to 'bodies and languages' only. Significantly in our present context, bio-political governmentality does not oppose but asks for constant critique. In a knowledge-based 'control society' one never finishes learning; on the contrary, 'continuous assessment' becomes an imperative (Deleuze 1995: 179). Thus everybody is invited, encouraged and forced to continually assess and revise their particular, empirical position in this society. Permanent critique and thus permanent revision are dispositifs of bio-political governance.

In this sense, what is 'assimilated' by the new spirit of capitalism is not so much radical, emancipatory critique, but rather the revisionist critique which flattens transcendence, reducing singularity to particularity, universality to generality, and dissensus to a dispositif that generates consensus. The internal perversion of critique, critique as continuous revision, revision as disseminated critique – this is what counterrevolution means in the context of critique. It is the becoming adequate of what is supposed to be inadequate, which also explains why 'critique' paradoxically consolidates what exists, why nothing really changes, while everything or anything is constantly criticized in our society.

Obsessed with the question of distribution and particular identities, democratic-materialist governmentality is preoccupied with 'critique'. Therefore 'critique' has not disappeared today; rather, it has slid into a world in which the critique (of critique of critique . . .) of the system is a component of the system itself. Moreover, this 'critique', or rather counter-critique, tends to become pre-emptive in the sense of emptying out the emancipatory core of critique in advance. Thus, if critique is a demonstration of the 'inconsistent' element within a particular order, counter-critique functions like the recent police tactic 'kettling': a device to contain within barriers the mobility of a demonstration, preventing its massification. Likewise, in 'continuous' critique one is continuously 'kettled'; one's critique never reaches the dimension of a universality but rather remains organized, regulated, and controlled in its own particularity, in its own compartment in a society held together by 'critical' kettles.

Then there are two immediate options. One can either drop critique altogether, go somewhere else, or take critique somewhere else, reappropriating its radical core, the promise of emancipation. In either case, though, what is necessary is a certain withdrawal from the existing apparatus of critique. Critique cannot be content with what exists, do without the promise of the new. 'To criticize without creating' is always a sign of *ressentiment* (see Deleuze and Guattari 1994: 28). In a 'world without ideas' shaped by the aspirations of democratic materialism, critique can have meaning only if it can side with infinity, with the event, by keeping a distance from power and retaining fidelity to the event:

> This is the story that philosophy is always telling us, under many different guises: to be in the exception, in the sense of the event, to keep one's distance from power, and to accept the consequences of a decision, however remote and difficult they may prove.
>
> *(Badiou 2009d: 13)*

If critique is to be more than an academic dispositif, to count for something in 'life', it must function like a 'knot' that ties together the event, separation and fidelity (ibid.: 16). Critical thinking emerges only as an exception to what exists. Hence its fundamental task is to illuminate the gap between potentiality and actuality, between thought (the problem) and being (solution), a gap which is also the space of the event. Critique, in other words, seeks to restore 'the dimension of potentiality to mere actuality' (Žižek 2009b: 78).

Take Walter Benjamin's notion of revolution as redemption-through-repetition of the past: apropos of the French Revolution, the task of a true Marxist historiography is not to describe the events as they really were (and to explain how these events generated the ideological illusions that accompanied them); the task is, rather, to unearth the hidden potentialities (the utopian emancipator potentials) which were betrayed in the actuality of the revolution and in its final outcome (the rise of utilitarian market capitalism).

(Ibid.)

Critique points toward a spectral, virtual aspect in all sociality. In this sense critique implies a critical decision, a choice marked by the irreducible gap of the event (ibid.: 79). If it cannot choose sides, it is reduced to an element of the situation. And in so far as it sides with the event, it must separate itself from the given situation. The essence of critique consists in disturbing the consensual arrangement of the situation. Critical intervention is what opens up a space for the event by separating it from the situation. There is therefore 'no common measure' between the situation and the event (Badiou 2009d: 7). In so far as critique seeks to preserve a link to the infinite, it must oppose the infinity of truths to the finitude of 'bodies and languages'. Thus critique is 'effectively incompatible with democratic debate' (ibid.). What matters for it is to create new concepts, inventing new 'problems', and to 'dramatize' the inherited concepts in creative ways, and it can do so only if it can avoid the imperative of democratic dialogue: 'Philosophy has a horror of discussions. It always has something else to do. Debate is unbearable to it' (Deleuze and Guattari 1994: 28–9).

There is no 'normal' criterion, no routine procedure for emancipatory critique. Critique is 'abnormality par excellence' (see Žižek 2009c: 69). The critical gesture consists in questioning the actual social order from the point of view of what it excludes, subtracting itself from prevailing consensus. Hence, from the perspective of the existing social order, radical critique is necessarily an excess: it forces the limits of the given, introducing a singular, paradoxical element, into the heart of consensus. In this sense, the real problem of radical critique is a parallax shift between subtraction and emancipation. Herein lies the attraction of Melville's *Bartleby*, the passive clerk who answers his boss's demands systematically by saying 'I would prefer not to' (see Agamben 1993: 35–8, 1999b: 243–74; Deleuze 1998: 70–87; Baudrillard 2005a: 90; Žižek 2008a: 182–3).

As he prefers 'not to', Bartleby appears as a figure of negation as to the given constellation of power and its order-words. In his refusal of the orders, however, he does not merely negate something (e.g. by saying he does *not* want to do . . .) but affirms something else (he *prefers* not to do . . .) – that is, 'opens up a new space outside the hegemonic position *and* its negation' (Žižek 2009b: 381–2). After all, any critique which is supported only by 'negation' is parasitic upon and thus legitimizes what it criticizes by participating in its framework. In contrast, Bartleby's critique functions as a 'gesture of subtraction at its purest', the equivalent of Benjamin's pure violence that produces an empty space through withdrawal (ibid.: 382).

The test of critique is this capacity to affirm, through separation, the promise of emancipation. Herein lies, too, the significance of fidelity. In his recent work, Boltanski juxtaposes the given 'reality' to 'world', a difference which is similar to that between the actual and the virtual. Thus 'world' refers to a fundamentally paradoxical and unstable domain of possibilities, which is bigger and richer than the given reality. Following this, Boltanski attempts to think sociality from the perspective of 'world'. Referring to Derrida's conception of justice as an 'appeal' for justice, as an impossible justice to come, he redefines sociality as an impossible 'appeal for sociality' (Boltanski 2009: 236). In other words, Boltanski tells us that both radical meta-critique and the pragmatic sociology deal, at the end of the day, with the same impossibility. Interestingly, however, while this impossibility grounded in the question of to be *and* not to be, in the unity-in-disunity of the actual and the virtual, compels Derrida to remain faithful to the radical critique of what exists, it turns Boltanski to the 'power of institutions' with a view to stabilizing this impossibility via 'critique'. This is a perfect illustration of how one can approach radical critique from the point of view of its pragmatic double and, by the same token, of how one can separate meta-critique from its radical content, referring it back to what exists and blocking its revolutionary gestures. In this sense the sociology of critique is doing to meta-critique what Fukuyama did to messianic eschatology. For this reason, perhaps, both perspectives are obsessed with the thought of 'ends'. And, for the same reason, what critique needs today more than ever is fidelity to fidelity, to its emancipatory core, 'preferring not to' rather than restlessly producing more of the same (critique-as-dispositif, dispositif-as-critique). It is like the Inuit dealing with a cold snap:

> When an Inuit becomes lost, he will make himself comfortable and conserve energy, perhaps building an igloo, perhaps sitting with his back to the wind, moving around only occasionally to keep himself from freezing, sleeping if possible. Then, when the storm has passed and he can see again, he will carry on to his destination. A European, by contrast, will instinctively thrash on, building up a sweat with his exertions. As he exhausts himself, the sweat generated will turn to ice, which in all likelihood will kill him.
>
> *(English 2010)*

Every storm tells something about the person who confronts it; every society reveals something of the nature of critique stuck within it.

10

CRITIQUE AS COMMUNISM, COMMUNISM AS CRITIQUE

> . . . *the categorical imperative to overthrow all relations* in which man is a debased, enslaved, forsaken, despicable being . . .
>
> *(Marx 1975: 182)*

Critique always involves disagreement, which is, above all, a disagreement on consensus. 'Consensus', however, is not only the avoidance of conflict. At a deeper level, it is an agreement regarding the terms of disagreement (see Rancière 2010: 144). That is, it allows one to have different opinions, to disagree, criticize, but only in a given framework of sensibility, which is effectively justified each time such permitted critique takes place. The true target of radical critique, in turn, is this framework itself: not playing a given game, indulging in its officially recognized transgressions, but changing the game itself. Critique is a process of separation, of dis–identification, vis-à-vis a given framework of the sensible. To criticize is to juxtapose sense to sense, to contrast another sensibility to 'the police distribution of the sensible' (ibid.: 212), to open up a space for what can be said, seen and thought otherwise. 'The point of critique' is, in short, 'not justification but a different way of feeling: another sensibility' (Deleuze 1983: 94).

But this other sensibility is not performed in a uniform way. Social critique and aesthetic critique animate it differently, with different tools. This chapter focuses on this differentiation, relating it to the idea of communism which signifies the coincidence of the two forms of critique.

Social critique

Since it exists only in so far as it disturbs the consensus which sustains the police order, politics is by definition dissensual. Dissensus, or critique, is what brings 'politics into being by separating it from the police' (Rancière 2010: 36–7). It is a form of *praxis*, an intervention into a given order of the sensible. This is why Marx starts his critique of political economy by demonstrating that it is obsessed with one sense of equality, the question of distribution in a given world, and juxtaposes to this sense another sense, equality as an egalitarian maxim. Thus the difference between 'interpreting' and 'changing' the world is ultimately grounded in the difference between the two senses of equality (see Marx 1998: 569).

A critique that wills something cannot be content with describing its object in a 'disinterested' manner but aims to intervene in it. Neutral description is always 'false', for it always involves a form of consensus; true critique 'affects its object' by describing it from the paradoxical point of view of its potentialities (Žižek 1996: 208). Hence, while critique traverses what 'is' it also turns to what 'is not', relating itself to the empirical (reality) and the transcendental (utopia) at once. Critique is the thought of 'what is not what there is' (Badiou 2009d: 15). What is relevant to it is not deducing what we can do and know from what we are but in separating out, 'from the contingency that has made us what we are, the possibility of no longer being, doing, or thinking what we are, do, or think' (Foucault 1986b: 46).

This is why the crucial distinction for critique is not between 'utopian' and 'scientific' but rather between different utopias, that is, between different becomings (Deleuze and Guattari 1994: 110). Critique can be critical only if it is critical of its own (historical) present, and it can do so only relating itself to another (utopian) time. Critique is against its epoch, its time, and practised in the opposition between the present and non-present, between 'our time' and 'the untimely' (Deleuze 1983: 107). The 'untimely' is, precisely, the time of what is to come.

> Thinking depends on certain coordinates. We have the truths we deserve depending on the place we are carrying our existence to, the hour we watch over, and the element that we frequent. There is nothing more false than the idea of 'founts' of truth. We only find truths where they are, at their time, and in their element. Every truth is truth of an element, of a time, and a place.
>
> *(Ibid.: 110)*

Critique is a relation to another place (the virtual), another time (*kairos*) and another element (singularity), that is, a relation to the event, which is also to say that critique is not for the sake of critique; it wants something else, a better 'life', a society 'to come'. But we do not seek the 'truth' only consciously; we do not think 'unless we are forced to' (ibid.). For this reason Marx relates *praxis* to drives and passions, to will:

> When the conscious character of praxis is degraded – in the *German Ideology* – to a derived characteristic, and understood as practical consciousness . . . or immediate relationship with the surrounding sensuous environment, it is will, determined naturalistically as drive and passion, that remains the sole original characteristic of praxis. Man's productive activity is, at bottom, vital

> *force*, drive and energetic tension, passion. The essence of praxis, the genetic characteristic of man as a *human* and historical being, has thus retreated into a naturalistic connotation of man as *natural* being. The original container of the living being 'man', of the living being who produces, is will. Human production is praxis. 'Man produces universally.'
>
> *(Agamben 1999b: 85)*

If the essence of life is *praxis*, the highest level of *praxis* is political action (Arendt 1958: 97). However, although it initiates, like politics, a process of separation from the police order, critique is not reducible to politics. Its singularity is grounded elsewhere. Critical thought has its own politics, which cannot be cut down to its political consequences. While political separation aspires to transforming collective situations, to political militancy, conceptual *praxis* conceives of its task, even when it directly engages with politics, as proposing new 'problems' addressed to anyone and everyone (Badiou 2009d: 22). Consequently, what may be significant for politics may not be so for critical thought, and vice versa (ibid.: 22–3).

What is the audience, the address, of critique then? Further, how is it transmitted and inscribed in the world it intervenes into? The 'address', the specific subjective position relevant to conceptual *praxis*, can only be an 'empty' position in the sense that there is no actual person or community addressed by a concept. What matters to critique is not establishing dialogue but articulating a 'question' which signifies the absence or 'void' of the address (Badiou 2008b: 28). Likewise, the 'transmission' of critical thought is not necessarily a matter of 'public' debate. What is more important is fidelity, the work of the 'disciple' who undertakes the transmission of the concept (ibid.: 28). Inscription, in turn, is necessary to transform the void of the address into a persistent mark. While the addressee is nobody (the void) and the transmission requires some (the finite), the inscription, a book for instance, is open to all and thus designates a relation to the 'infinite' (ibid.: 29).

The point of conceptual *praxis* is to maintain this link. Without the infinity of an inscription (the book) a new disciple would not be able to reach the empty place; without the address it would not be possible for the disciple to 'suture' her finiteness to the infinite; and without the transmission, the address and the book could not be related together, 'since a book cannot be written except from the disciple's standpoint' (ibid.: 29) or, as Deleuze would say, except by dramatizing a virtual or infinite idea. Apart from maintaining this link, critical *praxis* has no determinate goals or aims, only an 'imperative of continuation' (ibid.: 27). For the fundamental choice for it is between the event, belief in the future, and an inability to confront an open future. But this is a retroactive choice which can be articulated only in paradoxical terms:

> Here we should invert the existentialist commonplace according to which, when we are engaged in the present historical process, we perceive it as full of possibilities and ourselves as agents free to choose among them; while from a retroactive point of view the same process appears as fully determined and

necessary, with no opening for alternatives; on the contrary, it is the engaged agents who perceive themselves as caught in a Destiny, merely reacting to it, while, retroactively, from the standpoint of later observation, we can discern alternatives in the past, possibilities of events taking a different path.

(Žižek 2009b: 79)

'Freedom' here is not the free will of a liberal subject. Freedom comes only after the decision to side with the event, which retroactively determines one's thought and being. Depending on our choice as to the time, the place and the element, we arrive at 'the truths we deserve'. That is, we become worthy of the event, determine what determines us, and 'continue' – continue to repeat the idea of emancipation, trying to restore its utopian excess that survives its past defeats (see Žižek 2008b: 209), to repeat not what earlier critique did but, paradoxically, what it failed to do:

> At its most radical, theory is the theory of a failed practice: 'This is why things went wrong . . .' One usually forgets that . . . the greatest Marxist accounts of revolutionary events are the accounts of great failures (of the German Peasants' War, of the Jacobins in the French Revolution, of the Paris commune, of the October Revolution, of the Chinese Cultural Revolution . . .). Such an examination of failures confronts us with the problem of fidelity: how to redeem the emancipatory potential of these failures through avoiding the twin trap of nostalgic attachment to the past and of all-too-slick accommodation to 'new circumstances'.
>
> *(Ibid.: 3)*

It is through fidelity of the subject, its courage to 'continue', that the thought of the event paradoxically attains its being as a 'thought-practice' (Ashton *et al.*2006: 10). As such, conceptual *praxis* is fidelity, 'the courageous work of a *free* man under the condition of a truth against the state' (ibid.: 10) – 'against the state', for critique can relate to the social only through separation. Even though it emerges from the social, critique is not of the social, not reducible to it. It is not what can be sustained within the social, for example in the form of 'communication' or 'dialogue', but what sustains the social, supplementing it with the possibility of events. In other words, social critique is not something 'social' actors do – they do it by subtracting themselves from the 'social'.

Aesthetic critique

In *The Will to Power*, Nietzsche mentions a kind of art without artist, a 'work of art where it appears without an artist' (1967: 225). For him, the essence of art is something else than art itself, the will to power. Because it can be identified as becoming, as the eternal self-generation of the will to power, art can detach itself from both its creator, the artist, and the sensibilities of its spectator (Agamben 1999b: 93).

Defined as such, the 'artist' is anybody who 'reframes' reality, changes the given frames of the visible by rupturing the meanings attached to it and 'creating new relations between hitherto unrelated things and meanings' (Rancière 2010: 140–1). The aesthetic 'fiction', in other words, is an illusion in a specific sense, not merely an irreality or non-reality but rather, as in *il-ludere* in Latin, a *play* upon, a challenge to, actual 'reality' (Baudrillard 1993: 140). The aesthetic illusion is creation, putting something into play, inventing the 'modes of appearance of things' (ibid.: 59).

This brings us to the concept of *poiesis*, which the ancient Greeks distinguished from the two other modes of human action: *praxis* and *work*. *Work* meant to them a submission to necessity, an immediate relation to biological life, which 'made man the equal of the animal' and which was, for the same reason, an activity reserved for slaves (Agamben 1999b: 69). *Praxis* was positioned higher than work in this hierarchy and meant, as already mentioned, willed action. Finally, *poiesis* signifies creativity, bringing something into being, producing values as an end in itself. It is that which opens up a space for *praxis*, the 'foundation of the space of truth' (ibid.: 72). As such, *poiesis* necessarily involves critique or dissensus, a break with established forms of representation and sensory experience. And in so far as human beings are tied together by a sensory fabric, in so far as what is 'common' is 'sensation', such aesthetic critique is about the transformation of the *sensus communis* (Rancière 2009a: 57).

> Whether through words, colors, sounds, or stone, art is the language of sensations. Art does not have opinions. Art undoes the triple organization of perceptions, affections and opinions in order to substitute a monument composed of percepts, affects and blocs of sensations that take the place of language. The writer uses words, but by creating a syntax that makes them pass into sensation that makes the standard language stammer, tremble, cry, or even sing: this is the style, the 'tone', the language of sensations, the foreign language within language that summons forth a people to come.
>
> (*Deleuze and Guattari 1994: 176*)

Aesthetic critique distils a dissensual element from an actual, given framework of sensory experience. A writer, for instance, 'seizes hold of' the language, makes it 'vibrate', in order to extract (singular) affects from (particular) emotions, (virtual) sensations from (actual) opinions in view of a promise, 'in view . . . of that still-missing people' (ibid.). Art tells of the 'suffering' of (actual) people, their protests and struggles, to the missing (virtual) people to come (ibid.: 176–7). Art's significance lies in this passage between the actual and the virtual. Yet the artwork 'does not actualize the virtual event but incorporates or embodies it: it gives it a body, a life, a universe' (ibid.: 177). 'Universe' here is neither actual nor virtual: it is 'possible' (ibid.). Just as the actualization of an event signifies 'the reality of the virtual', the artwork embodies the 'reality of the possible' (ibid.).

This is why an artwork rejects a disappearing into the actual, 'persists' in it, calling for a 'people who refuse to remain in their situation' (Rancière 2010: 170).

It calls for, in other words, 'nomadic' people who can 'deviate' from their actual identities (Deleuze and Guattari 1987: 371, 381). What makes nomads nomadic, after all, is not their physical movements but their singularity; 'they become nomads because they refuse to disappear' into places assigned to them in a given social order (Deleuze 1995: 138).

Pragmatic . . . and docile

We can, at this point, return to Figure 8.1 and rearticulate it in relation to critique. Both social critique and aesthetic critique posit an idea of emancipation, but do so in different ways, through *praxis* and *poiesis*. In this, social critique seeks to unite indignation with political subjectivation as a figure of transcendence, while aesthetic critique combines indignation with becoming on a plane of immanence (see Albertsen 2008: 74).

In Figure 10.1 social critique belongs to Field II. Thinking here is grounded in the tradition of critical theory, in the conception of capitalism as a system and the understanding of revolution as a radical alternative to it. Since capitalism is not immediately transparent, its mode of functioning must be uncovered so that one can change it. This, however, is not merely a theoretical problem, or rather the theoretical problem can be solved only in *praxis*, through the constitution of a political subject, which pushes social critique towards the idea of communism, towards Field III. This link between critique and *praxis*, and thus the transcendence or 'immanent transcendence' of the subject, is an absolute condition for social critique. Without this link, critique falls back upon Field I.

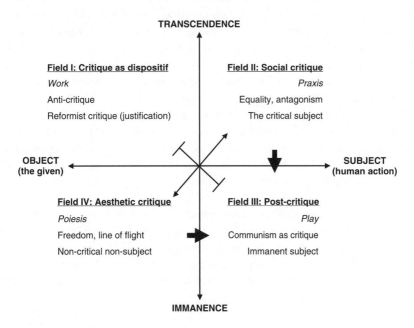

FIGURE 10.1   Dynamics of critique

What we have in Field IV, in contrast, is not a critical subject, but a non-critical non-subject: 'non-critical', because critique emerges here as a paradoxical outcome of subtraction or withdrawal from a norm, as a 'line of flight', rather than as confrontation; and 'non-subjective', because this form of critique, aesthetic critique, operates at the level of sense and affect, not consciousness or meaning. Thus what matters here is the construction of not a re-presentable subject but a community of sense, an 'encounter' among singularities which can only be sensed (Deleuze 1994: 139). As such, Field IV presents us with a horizontal ontology, in which difference and repetition, singularity and universality, interact on a plane of immanence. Here critique seeks 'to acquire a consistency without losing the infinite' (Deleuze and Guattari 1994: 42), that is, to link the actual to the virtual.

Field I, on this account, is characterized by a 'flat' transcendence, for what it considers 'transcendent' is really historical. If critique exists in this field, it exists only as pragmatic, or reformist, critique. This pragmaticization leads to the separation of critique from the domain of the virtual, and thus from the idea of emancipation as well as the desire for revolt and revolution. In other words, the pragmaticization of critique and the disappearance of the link between critique and revolt/revolution are one and the same process. Thus, whereas both social and aesthetic critique seek to 'counter-actualize', Field I is characterized by a propensity towards what might be called counter-virtualization. The truth of 'pragmatic critique' is what exists. It has no operational conception of *praxis* or *poiesis*, and it dismisses radical critique as 'utopian'.

Radical critique *is* utopian; it seeks to transcend the existing order of things and is therefore 'incongruous with the state of reality within which it occurs' (Mannheim 1936: 192). But there are different forms of utopia. One of them is the conservative utopia itself, which 'merges the spirit, which at one time came upon us from beyond and to which we gave expression, with what already is, allowing that to be objective' (ibid.: 236–7). The conservative experience 'justifies' what exists, the 'is', because for it 'everything that exists has a positive and nominal value merely because it has come into existence slowly and gradually' (ibid.: 235). *This* utopia is what is concealed in the critique of radical critique as 'utopian'. Reformist or pragmatic critique itself has a utopian dimension, a 'utopian' belief that it is possible to achieve real change within the framework of existing reality, within contemporary capitalism. In this sense, pragmatic sociology speaks the language of 'the utopia in power, masking itself as pragmatic realism' (Žižek 2009a: 77–8).

> After denouncing all the 'usual suspects' for utopianism then, perhaps the time has come to focus on the liberal utopia itself. This is how one should answer those who dismiss any attempt to question the fundamentals of the liberal-democratic-capitalist order as being themselves dangerously utopian: what we are confronting in today's crisis are the consequences of the utopian core of this order itself.
>
> *(Ibid.: 79)*

Along the same lines, what is significant regarding 'flat' critique is not only its denial of radical critique but its revisionist aspect in the sense that it often appears as a 'decaf' derivation of another, more radical tradition of thought. Consider, for instance, the actor-network theory and university Marxism as domesticated versions of post-structuralism and Marxism.

The actor-network theory, one of the most popular theories in today's academia, insists that action must be understood in terms of 'mediation' in a continuous network of associations (Latour 1996a: 237). Society consists only of networks: 'there is nothing but networks' (Latour 1996b: 370). The social is a 'flatland' which is 'only made of lines' (Latour 2005: 172). Therefore, at first sight, the actor-network theory seems to be close to Deleuze, who also insists that 'lines are basic components of things and events' (1995: 33). But whereas Latour's lines are only actual, 'actualized virtualities' (2005: 59), for Deleuze there are always two kinds of lines, actual and virtual, which constantly interact to produce virtualizations of the actual as well as actualized virtualities, without the virtual becoming fully actualized.

Latour has a concept that is similar to the virtual: 'plasma', which signifies the necessary but incomplete and open-ended background, the 'outside', for every networking activity (ibid.: 242–3). As that which is 'not yet measured, not yet socialized . . . or subjectified' (ibid.: 244), plasma cannot be captured by concepts of actuality. Thus the concept affirms the significance of the virtual, or testifies to the fact that there is more to the world than networks. Indeed, 'plasma' could be seen as a potential line of flight internal to the actor-network theory. Crucially, however, this concept is not really operationalized, and visibly remains a residual category, a kind of ersatz virtuality in the actor-network theory. In this sense Latour's ontology is a revisionist ontology, the formula of which could be: Deleuze minus the virtual – a 'practical metaphysics' (ibid.: 50) without concepts like the 'body without organs'.

Unsurprisingly, therefore, Latour insists regarding the idea of emancipation, the 'infatuation of social sciences', that it cannot mean 'freed from bonds' (ibid.: 52, 218). It cannot be attained, as Deleuze and others suggest, through separation or unbonding, for 'the more attachments' the subject has 'the more it exists' in the world of networks (ibid.: 217). One cannot be more distanced from any insistence on infinity. The actor-network theory is not interested in singularities (which are linked to the infinite) but instead is obsessed with the facticity of particularities, with following the (actual) lines. One cannot but wonder: is the point at which Latour (2004) declares that critical theory 'has run out of steam' not also the point at which the pragmatic critique itself has turned into a dispositif for governing the infinity of finite 'lines' in a world in which everything is in constant movement, and constantly assessed, but nothing really changes in any radical sense, a world so nuanced that it cannot be evaluated from any other point of view than that of 'mediation'? Perhaps Badiou is right: 'The modern apologia for the "complexity" of the world . . . is really nothing but a desire for generalized atony' (Badiou 2009b: 420). The infinite nuancing of the 'associations' between particular, finite bodies and languages (and, of course, 'things') is what sustains democratic materialist governmentality today.

A similar reduction can occur in relation to Field II. What Derrida calls 'university Marxism' is interesting in this context, for, as a depoliticized Marxism, it reduces Marx's philosophy to scientific knowledge by neutralizing its political imperative in analytic exegesis, 'by silencing in it the revolt' (1994: 38).

> Marx is OK – today, even on Wall Street, there are people who still love him: Marx the poet of commodities, who provided perfect descriptions of the capitalist dynamic; Marx of Cultural Studies, who portrayed the alienation and reification of our daily lives.
>
> *(Žižek 2002a: 3)*

But this 'return' of Marx is acceptable only because 'the *revolt*, which initially inspired uprising, indignation, insurrection, revolutionary momentum, does not come back' (Derrida 1994: 38), only as a dwarfed Marx, as a Marx without philosophy or Shakespeare, and only as a decaf Marxism without its spectral, malignant content: the revolt.

But, despite these revisions, the point is that radical social and aesthetic critique cannot be fully assimilated. Its actual forms can be emptied out, turned into lifeless refrains, but there always remains an irreducible singularity. History can come to terms with radical critique only by taking this sting *out* – precisely because it cannot be assimilated. Revision means, by definition, the impossibility of assimilation.

Communism: disjunctive and/or ontological

The real antagonism in Figure 10.1 is, again, between Field I and Field III: between the absence of critique or critique as dispositif on the one hand and the idea of communism on the other, which is ultimately a polarization between the (finite) actual and the (infinite) virtual. In turn, the different forms of critique emerging from within Field II and Field IV form a disjunctive synthesis. In both fields critique is considered interesting or relevant in so far as it is linked to *praxis* or *poiesis*. When this link is not sustained, both forms of dissensus dissolve into a dispositif. It is in response to this danger that social critique and aesthetic critique insist on the necessity of separation. Within Field II, this is performed as the active subtraction of the subject from the situation; within Field IV, it is performed as a non-subjective, passive synthesis between singularities in *sensus communis*.

The insistence on the subject within Field II means that not everything is political; here politics is understood as a rare, exceptional event. Within Field IV, in turn, everything is political in so far as a link between the actual and the virtual is established. Thus, within Field II different domains such as art and politics seek further differentiation, more purification. While politics tends to become pure politics, art produces its own truth procedures, its 'own artistic truths' (Badiou 2005b: 12; see also Rancière 2009b: 63). In contrast, within Field IV art and politics tend to become undifferentiated, and the specificities of both political intervention and artistic invention are tied to 'one and the same suprasensible sensible experience' of the virtual (Rancière 2010: 182).

However, the two fields share the idea of emancipation. While social critique offers a conceptual framework to deal with it, aesthetic critique stages a conflict between different regimes of sense, focusing on affects and sensations rather than concepts. But concepts and sensations constantly pass into each other, for 'there are sensations of concepts and concepts of sensations' (Deleuze and Guattari 1994: 177). Therefore 'social emancipation is simultaneously an aesthetic emancipation' (Rancière 2009a: 35). In so far as politics is viewed as a stage, as the manifestation or appearance of 'the part of those who have no part', there is an aesthetic dimension to politics. This dimension, the 'aesthetics of politics', enables the framing of a 'we', a subject, by reconfiguring the distribution of sensations in the process of political subjectivation (Rancière 2010: 141–2). Likewise, there is a 'politics of aesthetics', which, instead of giving a collective voice to the anonymous element, the part of no part, 're-frames the world of common experience as the world of a shared impersonal experience' (ibid.: 141).

Thus aesthetics (of politics) and politics (of aesthetics) are inseparable. They can, however, produce effects only 'under the conditions prescribed by an original disjunction' (ibid.: 142). In other words, there is no mimetic relationship between aesthetic critique and social critique, between art and politics. No causal relationship exists between the community of sense and the community of the subject. Although the idea of emancipation relates aesthetic critique to social critique, the relationship is disjunctive, and thus cannot be formalized:

> The problem is therefore not to set each back in its own place, but to maintain the very tension by which a politics of art and a poetics of politics tend towards each other, but cannot meet up without suppressing themselves.
>
> *(Ibid.: 183)*

Concomitantly, the price of cancelling out this tension is either purification of each domain or their disappearance into one another.

What happens if we move to Field III? Even though there is no determinate relationship between aesthetic critique and social critique, there is, after all, a promise which unites them: the promise of a fraternity to come in which the freedom of each and the equality of all do not contradict each other, in which politics and art unite in the affirmation of life. Marx called this utopian hope communism; Nietzsche called it play. If utility or *work* is what conditions the absence of critique and the critical dispositif (Field I), and if social and aesthetic critique both oppose this with reference to *praxis* (Field II) and *poiesis* (Field IV), what grounds Field III is *play*, the overcoming of 'work'.

As Nietzsche puts it, confronted with the world of false idols, of conservatism and buffoonery, in which 'all values have already been created' (Nietzsche 1961: 55), the ultimate task for the critical spirit is to create new values. This creativity can take place only through 'play', the symbol of which is the child. Free play is an expression of the useless as opposed to 'work', God's 'childlikeness' (Nietzsche 1967: 410). Ultimately, therefore, the promise of critique is profanation, turning the law into something 'common', into something to 'play with':

> One day humanity will play with law just as children play with disused objects, not in order to restore them to their canonical use but to free them from it for good. What is found after the law is not a more proper and original use value that precedes the law, but a new use that is born only after it. And use, which has been contaminated by law, must also be freed from its own value. [. . .] This liberation is the task of study, or play. And this studious play is the passage that allows us to arrive at that justice that one of Benjamin's posthumous fragments defines as a state of the world in which the world appears as a good that absolutely cannot be appropriated or made juridical.
>
> *(Agamben 2005b: 64)*

As a utopia, such 'play' implies peace, that is, the lack of (the necessity of) critique. Therefore, in a certain sense, the utopia of communism (Field III) signifies the self-overcoming of critique. But is this peace not also a form of consensus? To this question there are two different answers with two different implications regarding the idea of communism. The first focuses on the purely virtual aspect of communism; the other insists on its ontological, both actual and virtual, character. Thus for Rancière communism becomes another name for the disjunctive synthesis between politics and aesthetics (between Field II and Field IV), which implies an infinite deferral of its actualization, while Deleuze's ontological communism designates a real, ontological metamorphosis.

For Rancière, in so far as the promise of politics is a 'common' world, equality, the implementation of this promise can only take the form of dissensus. The stages where politics appears are 'not the foundations of a solid world of institutionalized equality. Politics will always fail to deliver on promises to implement freedom and equality integrally' (Rancière 2010: 80). In fact, in its origin, the aesthetic idea of communism (as a community of sense) was a response to this political failure. The failure of the French Revolution prepared the ground for a new type of revolution, a social revolution, which indicates the reconfiguration of the lived world in accordance with the forms of freedom and equality found in the aesthetic sphere (in the Kantian 'free play'). But this sensual community, which emerges on the basis of a social revolution, was too often imagined as a consensual community in which the 'common' is embodied in the material sensorium of lived experience. Consequently, communism designated an actual state in which the hitherto differentiated spheres (aesthetics, politics, economics and so on) are reunified; art and life are brought together. 'Unfortunately, however', this idea of total revolution 'never resulted in a free and equal society' (Rancière 2010: 82).

If the 'actuality of communism' is the sign of an impossible consensus, the dissensual community, in contrast, starts from the premise of the '*inactuality* of communism' (ibid.). It is '*a-topian*' in the sense that there can be no 'objective' communism, that the principle of unconditional equality can function 'only in a world in which communism has no actuality' (ibid.). There can be no 'actuality' of communism, only 'the actuality of its critique', which is also, by definition, the critique of actuality as such (ibid.: 83). Indeed, if communism actually existed, 'and if it was a good one, capitalists would buy it and exploit it as they saw fit' (ibid.).

As such, Rancière's communism seems to function like a Kantian 'regulative idea', as an idea which enables phenomenal inquiry, critique, but can never be realized (see Kant 2003: 292–301). One can juxtapose to this 'transcendental' communism another: 'ontological' communism. For Deleuze, too, communism is relevant only in so far as its virtual aspect is not exhausted, in so far as it remains 'inactual'. But for him the 'inactuality' or the virtuality of communism is as real as its actuality. And there is a passage from the virtual to the actual, from the sensory to reality. Thus the 'vibration' the artwork produces promises not only a people to come but also its reality, a new way of inhabiting, not a finite territory but the deterritorialized, infinite 'universe' of the possible (Deleuze and Guattari 1994: 180). The promise is a promise of real transformation, of a real sensory becoming, becoming-other.

But Deleuze insists that, for a real transformation to happen, the artist must expose himself to the power of the virtual, become seized by it. And in so far as the artwork is the result of this intoxication, in so far as art expresses the experience of the virtual, the community of sense cannot be only a matter of 'actualizing' forms – it is, more importantly, a matter of counter-actualization. As such, the present of communism is the present of the 'actor', of counter-actualization (see Deleuze 1990: 168). The significance of 'communism' lies in counter-actualization, in metamorphosis, more than in actualization. This is why the artwork is not in vain, although suffering is eternal and the 'actuality' of the revolution is always its betrayal:

> But the success of a revolution resides only in itself. [. . .] The success of a revolution is immanent and consists in the new bonds it installs between people, even if these bonds last no longer than the revolution's fused material and quickly give way to division and betrayal.
>
> *(Deleuze and Guattari 1994: 177)*

In this sense, the actuality of communism cannot be infinitely deferred. The paradox must be lived out. 'What is excessive in the event must be accomplished, even though it may not be realized or actualized without ruin' (Deleuze 1990: 168). After all, the only way for art to exist is to create new percepts and affects on the basis of exposure to something more important than itself, the anti-nihilist belief in life, in the virtual, in the inhuman power of life, which is unintelligible but sensible. Art thus enjoys, on the basis of this intoxication, a 'sensory transcendence', which is opposed to the suprasensory, religious transcendence (Deleuze and Guattari 1994: 193). Or, as Rancière is quick to note, the price for this intoxication becomes 'the reintroduction of a kind of transcendence in the thought of immanence'

(2010: 180). But perhaps communism is, above all, the name of this indistinction between immanence and transcendence. It is, at any rate, the will to actualize communism that sets seemingly opposing concepts such as 'immanent transcendence' or 'transcendent immanence' into motion and relates them to each other in unexpected ways.

One thing is sure: whether it is infinitely deferred or is taken as an ontological given, 'communism' is never the 'end', never the Last Judgement as a historical realization. To insist on redemption is not to insist on salvation in a religious sense, on a fantasy of the Last Day based on consensus. Communism means the possibilities offered by the impossible (the full actualization of a virtual idea). It means potentiality: a sign of the fact that we do not know what a society can do. Thus it remains, since Marx's original formulation, a paradoxical concept (e.g. the condition for the freedom of one is the freedom of all).

AFTERWORD

De te fabula narratur!

> . . . what are you laughing at? Change the name and you are the subject of
> the story.
>
> *(Horace 2005: 5)*

When much is written about a phenomenon, when it appears to occupy a central
position in thought, it is often a sure sign that that phenomenon is about to vanish,
illuminating, like a dead star, in the very process of disappearing. When I started
to write this book, in 2009, the opposite was the case: I was not writing about a
phenomenon which was about to vanish but about one that seemed to have faded
away already. At that time, the concept of 'revolution' did not appear in the public
sphere or in popular culture any more. Many thought it would never reappear.
The concept was equally absent in the philosophical and social scientific discourses,
except, that is, in the works of a few Leftist philosophers such as Badiou, Negri,
Rancière and Žižek. Did their efforts not signify the last, cramp-like movements
of a dying concept? This was, at any rate, the view of mainstream philosophy and
social science – at that time.

The paradox, at that time, was that we were living, as ever, in a world saturated
with enormous conflicts and misery, that there was all the more reason to criticize
existing and emerging forms of oppression and injustice. After all, if we look at the
contemporary world through the prism of classical Marxist theories of revolution,
what we see is precisely a more or less permanent 'revolutionary situation' characterized by the coexistence of extreme poverty and extreme wealth. What needs to
be explained in such a world is stability rather than destabilizing tendencies: why
nothing happens, or why the counterrevolution has been so stable and so strong.

Yet that which has disappeared often returns. Hence we are constantly witnessing that phenomena considered to be far away, 'historical' or even dead knock on
our door, catching us unprepared and perplexed. Were we not told, for instance,

more than a few times, that modernity means increasing secularization, that it inevitably brings with it the disappearance of religion from the political, social and cultural scene? But seen in the prism of contemporary troubles, if there is anything that has not disappeared, it is religion, to the extent that our 'civilization' today defines itself with reference to religion, accepting it as the main yardstick to differentiate itself from others. Never say never.

Yet this book was not written to prophesy the return of revolt or revolution. This does not require a prophecy. Ideas do not really disappear. They have the habit of not dying, although they never reappear in the same ways they have appeared in the past. Thus, at the beginning of 2011, when I was about to finish this book, the world woke up to four revolts, in Egypt, Tunisia, Bahrain and Libya. They were completely unexpected, especially to the West. The West first supported the dictators in the name of stability. Tony Blair articulated this shameful instant in his exemplary rhetoric when he described the Egyptian dictator, Mubarak, as 'immensely courageous and a force for good', warning against the possibility that a revolt might bring the Muslim fundamentalists to power (Blair, in McGreal 2011). The question, for him, was how these countries were going to 'evolve and modernise, but do so with stability' (Blair, in Sparrow 2011). This is ironic, outrageous and hypocritical: Blair is one of the few who legitimized the Iraqi war with the promise of 'bringing democracy', that is, on the basis of an assumption that a revolution cannot come from below in the Muslim Orient. And precisely at the moment it came, in 2011, the first thing Blair did was instinctively to support the dictator.

But this is half the story. Gradually, the response of the establishment shifted from reacting to revising, to mystifying the spirit of the revolts. Thus it quickly translated the reason of the revolts into its own language: people's fight for 'democracy' under 'totalitarian' regimes and so on. This was the moment when the 'international community' seemingly gave its support to the revolts, trying, as always, to 'teach these savage populations the basics of democracy' (Badiou 2011). In this process the event was orientalized: the totalitarian despots versus their victims. This victimization is too familiar in the repertoire of counterrevolution. Recall the liberal protagonist in Conrad's *Under Western Eyes*:

> . . . in a real revolution the best characters do not come to the front. A violent revolution falls into the hands of narrow-minded fanatics and the tyrannical hypocrites first. [. . .] The scrupulous and the just, the noble, humane, and devoted natures; the unselfish and the intelligent may begin a movement – but it passes away from them. They are not the leaders of a revolution. They are its victims: the victims of disgust, of disenchantment – often of remorse. Hopes grotesquely betrayed, ideals caricatured – that is the definition of revolutionary success.
>
> *(Conrad 1957: 117–18)*

But those the counterrevolutionary discourse victimizes think and live differently: 'Those who risk their life most often think in terms of life, not death, not bitterness, and not morbid vanity' (Deleuze 2006: 144–5). The truth is that those rebels, which the liberal-Orientalist discourse depicts as duped, because they didn't yet grasp what liberal democracy is, have showed us what democracy really is. If victimization means one thing it is contempt for this truth. 'What a distressing persistence of colonial arrogance! Given the miserable political situation that we are experiencing, isn't it obvious that it is us who have everything to learn from the current popular uprisings?' (Badiou 2011).

Sadly, however, the uprisings gradually turned into a symbol of a deficit, of the eternal lack of democracy in the Orient. And the concept of 'revolution' metamorphosed into a sign of underdevelopment, as if it is something that can happen only in the 'totalitarian' Muslim Orient. Perversely, therefore, revolution 'there', in the Orient, started to legitimate the absence of revolution 'here', in the West. Here, after all, we have 'democracy' and things are not nearly so bad. This culture of content had made Marx consult Horace's satire:

> If, however, the German reader pharisaically shrugs his shoulders at the condition of the English industrial and agricultural workers, or optimistically comforts himself with the thought that in Germany things are not nearly so bad, I must plainly tell him: *De te fabula narratur!*
>
> *(Marx 1976: 90)*

'The tale is told of you.' The universal lesson of the four revolts, open to each and all, was that the event is possible. It was this possibility that shocked the establishment.

> One cannot but note the 'miraculous' nature of the events in Egypt: something has happened that few predicted, violating the experts' opinions, as if the uprising was not simply the result of social causes but the intervention of a mysterious agency that we can call, in a Platonic way, the eternal idea of freedom, justice and dignity. The uprising was universal: it was immediately possible for all of us around the world to identify with it, to recognise what it was about, without any need for cultural analysis of the features of Egyptian society.
>
> *(Žižek 2011a)*

It is easy to recognize in this universality the thread of the event, the link between its singularity, its moment and its place, which has been the central topic for this book. What made the revolts singular was the fact that they relied on the free association of people which did not restate some particular, familiar demands. As Badiou noted, the word 'democracy', for instance, was 'practically never mentioned'; instead, the demonstrations operationalized new demands, opening up a 'new field' of possibilities (Badiou 2011). It is this singularity that disappears in the attempt at orientalizing the event.

In the same attempt, the temporality of the event is referred back to chronological time and rearticulated as a demand for progress, to 'evolve and modernise' on the arrow of time. If anything, however, the time of the revolts was another time, *kairos*, the moment at which everything seems possible. The revolts offered a moment of decision, a choice: the event or the state. The demonstrating masses seized this moment and were seized by it. In the event, the monads of *kairos* joined together, transforming themselves into a 'common name', exposing themselves 'to the void indicated by the arrow of time, thus constructing the to-come' (Negri 2003: 171).

Social theory had long told us that there is no place for revolution in late modernity. Luhmann, for instance, one of the most sophisticated names in contemporary social theory, declared that there is no centre in modern world society to take care of the societal integration of functionally differentiated, autopoietic systems. 'There is no aim, no objective, no centre, or no top of the system . . . which you could eliminate and then you would have a good society' (Luhmann 1994: 4). But did Tahrir Square not, precisely, become such a 'centre'? To be sure, there is no physical centre of the modern capillary power which is everywhere and nowhere. But the point is, precisely, that the topological space of the event is not reducible to the empirical space.

> Once a certain threshold of determination, obstinacy and courage has been passed, a people can indeed concentrate its existence in one square, one avenue, a few factories, a university. [. . .] In the midst of an event, the people is made up of those who know how to solve the problems that the event imposes on them. It goes the same for the occupation of a square: food, sleeping arrangements, protection, banderols, prayers, defence fight, all so that the place where everything is happening, the place that has become a symbol, may stay with its people at all costs. These problems, at a scale of hundreds of thousands of people who have come from all over the place, may seem impossible to solve, especially since the state has disappeared in that square. Solving unsolvable problems without the help of the state, that is the destiny of an event. And it is what determines a people, all of a sudden and for an indeterminate period, to exist, there where it has decided to gather.
>
> *(Badiou 2011)*

The miracle of the event is exactly to transcend the empirical space, to condense a place into a khoratic, virtual 'centre', a space of spacing, into a space in which new possibilities emerge, the unthinkable becomes reality or, to use a metaphor dear to Nietzsche, into a 'labyrinth of the future' (1967: 3). This space, to repeat, is neither Oriental nor Muslim; it is the space of creation. It must therefore be emphasized that one of the most significant dimensions of the Egyptian revolt was its irreducibility to religious motives. Thus it was frequently called by its own militants an 'Allah-free' revolution, a revolt grounded in secular universal demands for freedom and justice: 'The most sublime moment occurred when Muslims and Coptic Christians engaged in common prayer on Cairo's Tahrir Square, chanting "We are one!" – providing the best answer to the sectarian religious violence' (Žižek 2011a). Along the same lines, affected by 'a row of Christians standing in order to keep watch over the Muslims bent in prayer', Badiou saw in Tahrir Square all the traits of communism in a 'pure form', 'the purest since the commune of Paris' (Badiou 2011).

But there remains one issue to be clarified. What are we to do with this slogan, also chanted in Tahrir Square: 'Ya Rab [O God], ya Allah, free Egypt from tyrants. Can't Mubarak hear us?' Such slogans were part of the revolt as well. Should we not, then, recognize the 'Muslim' presence in the square as well? This question, I suggest, is a trap: to speak of communism in Tahrir Square has another dimension than describing the event, a performative intervention, which is also the ultimate affirmation of the event. Let me, to end with, discuss this.

What is interesting in the slogan above is that it sets Allah (*that* world) against the sovereign (*this* world). In this sense it is structured in eschatological terms. The revolt, after all, could be likened to the Day of Judgement from the perspective of Mubarak, a day the crowds were absolutely unwilling to negotiate and insisted on his unconditional overthrow.

> When President Obama welcomed the uprising as a legitimate expression of opinion that needs to be acknowledged by the government, the confusion was total: the crowds . . . did not want their demands to be acknowledged by the government, they denied the very legitimacy of the government. They didn't want the Mubarak regime as a partner in a dialogue, they wanted Mubarak to go. They didn't simply want a new government that would listen to their opinion, they wanted to reshape the entire state. They don't have an opinion, they are the truth of the situation in Egypt. [. . .] Either the entire Mubarak power edifice falls down, or the uprising is co-opted and betrayed.
>
> (*Žižek 2011b*)

The slogan points towards two Allahs: one which has served Mubarak, the other which has brought him down. This eschatological dimension is what the establishment, both in the West and in the Orient, is really afraid of. Therefore, every time it meets it, it seeks, impulsively, to reduce it to Al Qaida's Disney-Islam. This 'Allah', which exists only in the event, signifies, partially at least, the popular will and speaks the language of Paul's universalism. The question is, then, how a communist can deal with it.

One example is the way of Nazım Hikmet, a Turkish communist poet, who, in one of his poems from the 1930s, resurrected the spirit of an Islamic heretic: Sheikh Bedreddin. In 1417, under Ottoman rule, Bedreddin started a revolt which united Muslim peasants, Greek sailors and Jewish tradesmen against the sultan. Ideologically, Bedreddin was refusing both religious and political authority, insisting that the only sovereign is God, and that this God must not be turned into an institution on earth. Further, he was preaching that everything on earth was common. This attack on private property, together with his principle that presupposes the equality of intelligence ('God appears in all'), meant that one could not be a servant to anybody else than God (see Bedreddin 2010: 309, 314; Eyüboğlu 2010: 175, 247–8). The revolt, on this basis, was universalist in orientation; it constructed no dichotomy between Muslims and other believers. The insurrection itself was led by Bedreddin's disciple from contemporary West Turkey, Börklüce Mustafa. It lasted three years and was finally crushed by the sultan. Concomitantly, Muslim theology, in both Ottoman past and Turkish present, has always been contemptuous of the revolt. Nazım, in contrast, distils its communist aspect in his epic poem:

> . . .
>
> Turkish peasants from Aydın,
> Greek pilots from Chios,
> Jewish tradesmen,
>
> ten thousand heretic comrades of Börklüce Mustafa
> plunged like ten thousand axes into the enemy forest.
> Their standards crimson and green,
> their shields inlaid, their ranks of bronze helmets
> were all laid low, but
> as the sun sank in pouring rain, by evening
> of the ten thousand only two thousand remained.
>
> Ten thousand gave eight thousand of their men,
> so they might all together sing their songs,
> and all together haul the nets from the waters,
> and all together work the iron like embroidery,
> and all together plough the earth,
> all together eat the honeyed figs,
> and all together say they share in everything,
> Everywhere,
> except their beloved's cheek.
>
> They were defeated.
> . . .

(Hikmet 2002: 64)

What comes to the foreground is the relation of the singular to the common: 'sharing in everything'. This was what was seen as 'blasphemy' by the rulers. Thus, at the end of the poem, we see Bedreddin for a last time, hanging on a tree:

> . . .
>
> Rain falls softly.
> In Serez artisan market
> across from a coppersmith's stall
> my Bedreddin hangs on a tree.

Rain falls softly.
Late on a starless night,
swinging on a leafless bough
wet with rain,
the stark naked body of my Sheikh.

Rain falls softly.
Serez market is dumb,
Serez market is blind.
In the air the cursed grief of the speechless and unseeing,
and Serez market hides its face in its hands.

Rain falls softly.

(Hikmet 2002: 72)

This defeat of the Muslim Spartacus, and many other similar defeats, is the necessary background against which a victory took place in Tahrir Square. In this respect
Nazım Hikmet's position could be likened to Derrida's messianism without a messiah. Thus, in a short fragment which follows the Epic, somebody asks a contemporary follower of Bedreddin: 'This belief of yours is like the Christian belief. They
too say that the prophet Jesus will come again to the world' (Hikmet 2002: 75). To
this, Bedreddin's follower answers: 'Bedreddin will be resurrected without bones,
without beard, without moustache – he will be resurrected like the gaze of the eye,
the word of the tongue, the breath of the bosom. This is what I know' (Hikmet
1987: 265, my translation).

Many squares, like Serez Square, had to 'hide their face' before in the grief of
counter-revolt. This is what makes Tahrir Square an eventual space. But what does
this victory say about the difficult relationship between communism and Islam?
This brings us to the second part of the slogan: 'Can Mubarak hear us?' How does
the ear, itself an old symbol of the labyrinth, hear the event, the 'labyrinth of the
future'?

The thread of our labyrinth in this book, the event, is the link between the
untimely, singularity and 'a goal in the future', a link to what is to come (Nietzsche
1967: 220). Life itself is this thread; and to spin on it 'in such a way that the thread
grows ever more powerful – that is the task' (ibid.: 349). And there is no escape
from this labyrinth, from the New. The labyrinth of the event is 'not the lost way
but the way which leads us back to the same point, to the same instant, which is,
which was, and which will be' (Deleuze 1983: 188). The labyrinth of the event is
one in which the new eternally returns.

This thread is the first way to 'hear' the event: affirmation. But one can also
deny, even despise the truth of the labyrinth. This second thread is to the negative, to *ressentiment* (ibid.: 188). It is to those despisers of the event that Nietzsche
says: 'And we, we beg you earnestly, hang yourselves with this thread' (Nietzsche,
quoted in ibid.: 110). And yet there is still time for affirmation. Affirmation can

take place in the time that remains. This is one meaning of the labyrinth. More importantly, however, the labyrinth, the event, signifies becoming; affirming the event is affirming becoming (ibid.: 188). But, and herein lies the whole point, affirmation is not only something to be 'heard'. Therefore in the Greek myth:

> Dionysus not only asks Ariadne to hear but to affirm affirmation: 'You have little ears, you have my ears: put a shrewd word there.' The ear is labyrinthine, the ear is the labyrinth of becoming or the maze of affirmation. The labyrinth is what leads us to being, the only being is that of becoming, the only being is that of the labyrinth itself. But Ariadne has Dionysus' ears: affirmation must itself be affirmed so that it can be the affirmation of being. Ariadne puts a *shrewd word* into Dionysus' ear. That is to say: having herself heard Dionysian affirmation, she makes it the object of a second affirmation heard by Dionysus.
>
> *(Ibid.)*

Similarly, the slogan above is not only something to be heard. One must also put a shrewd word into the ear of the intoxicated, Dionysian crowd; one must intervene. It is significant in this context that monotheistic messianism (up to Bedreddin, Müntzer and so on) had arisen in the shadow of a declining paganism, including the first known messianic sect, Zoroastrianism. In modernity, in contrast, especially with Marx and Nietzsche, 'Prometheus arises in the shadow of Christ' and, 'in the kingdom of Prometheus, Antichrist becomes a title of honor' (Taubes 2009: 89). I believe, contra Taubes, we must insist that this 'honor' deserves fidelity: no critique is possible, even today, without the critique of religion.

Mubarak, and many others, cannot 'hear' the crowd in an affirmative way. But those who can 'hear' it must affirm it a second time, through an intervention, a shrewd word. That shrewd word, this book suggests, is communism.

REFERENCES

Adorno, T.W. (1967) *Prisms*, Cambridge, MA: MIT Press.

Aeschylus (2003) *Oresteia*, Oxford: Oxford University Press.

Agamben, G. (1993) *The Coming Community*, Minneapolis: University of Minnesota Press.

Agamben, G. (1995) *Idea of Prose*, New York: SUNY Press.

Agamben, G. (1998) *Homo Sacer: Sovereign Power and Bare Life*, Stanford, CA: Stanford University Press.

Agamben, G. (1999a) *Potentialities: Collected Essays in Philosophy*, Stanford, CA: Stanford University Press.

Agamben, G. (1999b) *The Man without Content*, Stanford, CA: Stanford University Press.

Agamben, G. (1999c) *Remnants of Auschwitz: The Witness and the Archive*, New York: Zone Books.

Agamben, G. (2000) *Means without End: Notes on Politics*, Minneapolis: University of Minnesota Press.

Agamben, G. (2004) 'I Am Sure that You Are More Pessimistic than I Am', Interview with Giorgio Agamben, *Rethinking Marxism* 16(2): 115–24.

Agamben, G. (2005a) *The Time that Remains*, Stanford, CA: Stanford University Press.

Agamben, G. (2005b) *The State of Exception*, Chicago: University of Chicago Press.

Agamben, G. (2007) *Infancy and History*, London: Verso.

Ahl, F. (2007) '*Spartacus*, Exodus, and Dalton Trumbo: Managing Ideologies of War', in M.M. Winkler (ed.), *Spartacus: Film and History*, London: Blackwell, pp. 65–86.

Albertsen, N. (1995) 'Kunstværket – en sansningsblok under evighedens synsvinkel: Spinoza, Wittgenstein, Deleuze', in N. Lehmann and C. Madsen (eds), *Deleuze og det Æstetiske*, Århus: Århus Universitetsforlag, pp. 135–62.

Albertsen, N. (2001) 'Spinoza, imperiet og kapitalismens nye ånd: Til fornyelsen af den sociale og æstetiske kritik af kapitalismen', Paper presented at the seminar 'Globalisering, Kunst, Fællesskabsfølelser og Offentlighedsformer', Center for Tværæstetiske Studier, Aarhus University, 3 December.

Albertsen, N. (2002) 'Retfærdiggørelse i byen', *Distinktion* 4: 45–61.

Albertsen, N. (2005) 'From Calvin to Spinoza', *Distinktion* 11: 171–86.

Albertsen, N. (2008) 'Retfærdiggørelse, Ideologi, Kritik', *Dansk Sociologi* 2(19): 66–84.

Al-Qattan, O. (2001) 'Disneyland Islam', *Open Democracy*, www.opendemocracy.net

Arendt, H. (1958) *The Human Condition*, Chicago: University of Chicago Press.

Arendt, H. (1965) *On Revolution*, London: Penguin.

Arendt, H. (1973) *The Origins of Totalitarianism*, New York: Harcourt, Brace & Company.

Arendt, H. (1994) *Essays in Understanding 1930–1954*, New York: Harcourt, Brace & Company.

Aristotle (1999) *Poetics*, London: Penguin.

Ashton, P., Barlett, A.J. and Clemens, J. (2006) 'Masters and Disciples: Institution, Philosophy, Praxis', in P. Ashton, A.J. Barlett and J. Clemens (eds), *The Praxis of Alain Badiou*, Melbourne: re.press, pp. 3–12.

Attwood, M. (2007) 'Everybody Is Happy Now', *Guardian*, 17 November.

Augustine (2005) *City of God*, Christian Classics, Ethereal Library, http://www.ccel.org/ccel/schaff/npnf102.iv.III.26.html

Badiou, A. (2000) *Deleuze: The Clamor of Being*, Minneapolis: University of Minnesota Press.

Badiou, A. (2003) *Infinite Thought*, London: Continuum.

Badiou, A. (2005a) *Metapolitics*, London: Verso.

Badiou, A. (2005b) *Handbook of Inaesthetics*, Stanford, CA: Stanford University Press.

Badiou, A. (2006a) *Being and Event*, New York: Continuum.

Badiou, A. (2006b) *Polemics*, London: Verso.

Badiou, A. (2007a) *The Century*, London: Polity.

Badiou, A. (2007b) 'One Divides Itself into Two', in S. Budgen, S. Kouvelakis and S. Žižek (eds), *Lenin Reloaded: Towards a Politics of Truth*. Durham, NC: Duke University Press, pp. 7–17.

Badiou, A. (2008a) *The Meaning of Sarkozy*, London: Verso.

Badiou, A. (2008b) *Conditions*, New York: Continuum.

Badiou, A. (2009a) *Theory of the Subject*, New York: Continuum.

Badiou, A. (2009b) *Logics of Worlds: Being and Event*, vol. 2, New York: Continuum.

Badiou, A. (2009c) *Pocket Pantheon: Figures of Postwar Philosophy*, London: Verso.

Badiou, A. (2009d) 'Thinking the Event', in A. Badiou and S. Žižek, *Philosophy in the Present*, London: Polity, pp. 1–48.

Badiou, A. (2011) 'Tunisie, Egypte: Quand un vent d'est balaie l'arrogance de l'Occident', http://www.versobooks.com/blogs/394-alain-badiou-tunisie,-egypte-quand-un-vent-d'est-balaie-l'arrogance-de-l'occident

Baker, R.S. (1990) *Brave New World: History, Science, and Dystopia*, Boston, MA: Twayne.

Bakunin, M. (1973) *Bakunin on Anarchy: Selected Works by the Activist-founder of World Anarchism*, ed. S. Dolgoff, London: Allen & Unwin.

Barber, B.R. (1996) *Jihad vs. McWorld: How Globalism and Tribalism Are Reshaping the World*, New York: Ballantine Books.

Bataille, G. (2001) *Eroticism*, London: Penguin.

Baudrillard, J. (1990) *Fatal Strategies*, Paris: Semiotext(e)/Pluto.

Baudrillard, J. (1993) *Baudrillard Live: Selected Interviews*, ed. M. Gane, London: Routledge.

Baudrillard, J. (1994) *Simulacra and Simulation*, Ann Arbor: University of Michigan Press.

Baudrillard, J. (1998) *Paroxysm*, London: Verso.

Baudrillard, J. (2002) *Screened Out*, London: Verso.

Baudrillard, J. (2005a) *The Intelligence of Evil or the Lucidity Pact*, London: Berg.

Baudrillard, J. (2005b) *The System of Objects*, London: Verso.

Bauman, Z. (1976) *Socialism: The Active Utopia*, New York: Holmes & Meier.

Bauman, Z. (1988) *Freedom*, London: Open University Press.

Bauman, Z. (1998) *Work, Consumerism and the New Poor*, Buckingham: Open University Press.

Bauman, Z. (1999) *In Search of Politics*, London: Polity.

Bauman, Z. (2000) *Liquid Modernity*, London: Polity.

Bauman, Z. (2008) *Art of Life*, London: Polity.

Bedreddin, Ş (2010) 'Varidat', in I.Z. Eyüboğlu (2010) *Şeyh Bedreddin Varidat*, Istanbul: Derin, pp. 299–350.

Benjamin, W. (1979a) 'Divine Violence', in *One-way Street*, London: Verso, pp. 132–54.

Benjamin, W. (1979b) 'Theologico-political Fragment', in *One-way Street*, London: Verso, pp. 155–6.

Benjamin, W. (1979c) 'The Destructive Character', in *One-way Street*, London: Verso, pp. 157–9.

Benjamin, W. (1979d) 'Surrealism', in *One-way Street*, London: Verso, pp. 225–39.

Benjamin, W. (1996) 'Capitalism as Religion', in M. Bullock and M.W. Jennings (eds), *Selected Writings*, vol. 1: *1913–1926*, Cambridge, MA: Harvard University Press, pp. 288–91.

Benjamin, W. (1999) *Illuminations*, London: Pimlico.

Bennett, B. and Diken, B. (2011) 'The Hurt Locker', *Cultural Politics* 7(2): 165–88.

Bensaïd , D. (2007) 'Leaps! Leaps! Leaps!', in S. Budgen, S. Kouvelakis and S. Žižek (eds), *Lenin Reloaded: Toward a Politics of Truth*, Durham, NC: Duke University Press, pp. 148–63.

Bidet, J. (2002) 'L'esprit du capitalisme: Questions à Luc Boltanski et Eve Chiapello', in J. Lojkine (ed.), *Les sociologies critiques de capitalisme*, Paris: Presses Universitaires de France, pp. 215–33.

Bin Laden, O. (2001) 'Muslims Have the Right to Attack America', *Observer*, 11 November, www.observer.co.uk

Bin Laden, O. (2002) 'Full Text: Bin Laden's "Letter to America"', *Observer*, 24 November, www.observer.co.uk

Boltanski, L. (1999) *Distant Suffering: Morality, Media and Politics*, Cambridge: Cambridge University Press.

Boltanski, L. (2002) 'The Left after May 1968 and the Longing for Total Revolution', *Thesis Eleven* 69: 1–20.

Boltanski, L. (2009) *De la critique: Précis de sociologie de l'émancipation*, Paris: Editions Gallimard.

Boltanski, L. and Chiapello, E. (2007) *The New Spirit of Capitalism*, London: Verso.

Boltanski, L. and Thévenot, L. (2000) 'The Sociology of Critical Capacity', *European Journal of Social Theory* 2(3): 359–77.

Boltanski, L. and Thévenot, L. (2006) *On Justification: Economies of Worth*, Princeton, NJ: Princeton University Press.

Bourdieu, P. (1990) *In Other Words: Essays towards a Reflexive Sociology*, Stanford, CA: Stanford University Press.

Bradley, A. and Fletcher, P. (2010) 'The Politics to Come: A History of Futurity', in A. Bradley and P. Fletcher (eds), *The Politics to Come*, New York: Continuum, pp. 1–12.

Bradshaw, D. (2007) 'Introduction', in A. Huxley, *Brave New World*, London: Vintage, pp. xvii–l.

Britto, S. (2007) 'Negative Morality: Adorno's Sociology', Ph.D. thesis, Department of Sociology, Lancaster University.

Buck-Morss, S. (2009) *Hegel, Haiti, and Universal History*, Pittsburgh, PA: University of Pittsburgh Press.

Budgen, S., Kouvelakis, S. and Žižek, S. (2007) 'Introduction: Repeating Lenin', in S. Budgen, S. Kouvelakis and S. Žižek (eds), *Lenin Reloaded: Towards a Politics of Truth*, Durham, NC: Duke University Press, pp. 1–4.

Burke, E. (2004) *Reflections on the Revolution in France*, London: Penguin.

Bush, G.W. (2001a) 'Presidential Address to the Nation', 7 October, www.yale.edu/law-web/avalon/sept_11/president_035.htm

Bush, G.W. (2001b) 'Washington DC, The National Cathedral', 14 September, www.yale.edu/lawweb/avalon/sept_11/

Bush, G.W. (2001c) 'America Strikes Back: Bush's Press Conference Runs on Themes', CNN Live Event/Special, aired 12 October, http://transcripts.cnn.com/transcripts/0110/12/se.04.html

Bush, G.W. (2002) 'Bush's National Security Strategy', *New York Times*, 20 September.

Callinicos, A. (2006) *The Resources of Critique*, London: Polity.

Callinicos, A. (2007) 'Leninism in the Twenty-first Century? Lenin, Weber, and the Politics of Responsibility', in S. Budgen, S. Kouvelakis and S. Žižek (eds), *Lenin Reloaded: Towards a Politics of Truth*, Durham, NC: Duke University Press, pp. 18–41.

Camus, A. (1953) *The Rebel*, London: Penguin.

Camus, A. (2005) *The Myth of Sisyphus*, London: Penguin.

Canetti, E. (1962) *Crowds and Power*, London: Phoenix.

Conrad, J. (1957) *Under Western Eyes*, London: Penguin.

Conrad, J. (1985) *The Secret Agent*, London: Penguin.

Cooper, D.L. (2007) 'Who Killed the Legend of Spartacus? Production, Censorship, and Reconstruction of Stanley Kubrick's Epic Film', in M.M. Winkler (ed.), *Spartacus: Film and History*, London: Blackwell, pp. 14–55.

Corliss, R. (2008) '*The Hurt Locker*: A Near-perfect War Film', http://www.time.com/time/arts/article/0,8599,1838615,00.html

Cyrino, M.S. (2005) *Big Screen Rome*, London: Blackwell.

Dean, J. (2006) *Žižek's Politics*, London: Routledge.

Deleuze, G. (1983) *Nietzsche and Philosophy*, New York: Columbia University Press.

Deleuze, G. (1988) *Foucault*, Minneapolis: University of Minnesota Press.

Deleuze, G. (1989a) *Cinema 2: The Time-image*, London: Athlone Press.

Deleuze, G. (1989b) *Coldness and Cruelty*, New York: Zone Books.

Deleuze, G. (1990) *Logic of Sense*, New York: Columbia University Press.

Deleuze, G. (1994) *Difference and Repetition*, London: Athlone Press.

Deleuze, G. (1995) *Negotiations*, New York: Columbia University Press.

Deleuze, G. (1998) *Essays Critical and Clinical*, London: Verso.

Deleuze, G. (2004) *Desert Islands and Other Texts (1953–1974)*, Cambridge, MA: MIT Press.

Deleuze, G. (2006) *Two Regimes of Madness: Texts and Interviews 1975–1995*, New York: Semiotext(e).

Deleuze, G. and Guattari, F. (1983) *Anti-Oedipus: Capitalism and Schizophrenia*, Minneapolis: University of Minnesota Press.

Deleuze, G. and Guattari, F. (1987) *A Thousand Plateaus: Capitalism and Schizophrenia*, vol. II, Minneapolis and London: University of Minnesota Press.

Deleuze, G. and Guattari, F. (1994) *What Is Philosophy?*, London: Verso.

Deleuze, G. and Guattari, F. (2006) 'May '68 Did Not Take Place', in G. Deleuze, *Two Regimes of Madness: Texts and Interviews 1975–1995*, New York: Semiotext(e), pp. 233–6.

Deleuze, G. and Parnet, C. (1996) 'Gilles Deleuze's ABC Primer, with Claire Parnet', http://www.langlab.wayne.edu/CStivale/D-G/ABC3.html

Denman, T. (2009) Reader comments, *Guardian*, 23 October.

Derrida, J. (1993) *Aporias*, Stanford, CA: Stanford University Press.

Derrida, J. (1994) *Specters of Marx*, London: Routledge.

Derrida, J. (1995) *On the Name*, Stanford, CA: Stanford University Press.

Derrida, J. (1997) *The Politics of Friendship*, London: Verso.

Derrida, J. (2004) 'For a Justice to Come', Lieven De Cauter's interview with Derrida, http://archive.indymedia.be/news/2004/04/83123.html

Derrida, J. (2005) *Rogues: Two Essays on Reason*, Stanford, CA: Stanford University Press.

Diken, B. and Laustsen, C. (2005) *The Culture of Exception: Sociology Facing the Camp*, London: Routledge.

Dillon, M. (2008) 'Lethal Freedom: Divine Violence and the Machiavellian Moment', *Theory and Event* 11(2): 1–22, http://muse.jhu.edu/login?uri=/journals/theory_and_event/v011/11.2.dillon.html

Dillon, M. (2011) 'Specters of Biopolitics: Finitude, Eschaton and Katechon', *South Atlantic Quarterly* 110(1): 782–94.

Dostoevsky, F. (1971) *The Devils*, London: Penguin.

Doyle, S. (2010) 'Gen McChrystal and the Myth of Macho', *Guardian*, 26 June.

English, C. (2010) 'A Brief History of Snow', *Guardian*, 7 January.

Esposito, R. (2008) 'Totalitarianism or Biopolitics?', Paper presented at the conference 'Italian Thought Today: Biopolitics, Nihilism, Empire', University of Kent, 5–6 April.

Eyüboğlu, I.Z. (2010) *Şeyh Bedreddin Varidat*, Istanbul: Derin.

Fast, H. (1960) *Spartacus*, London: Panther.

Feuerbach, L. (1989) *The Essence of Christianity*, New York: Prometheus Books.

Foucault, M. (1977) *Discipline and Punish*, London: Penguin.

Foucault, M. (1978) *The History of Sexuality*, vol. 1, New York: Vintage Books.

Foucault, M. (1983) 'Preface', in G. Deleuze and F. Guattari, *Anti-Oedipus: Capitalism and Schizophrenia*, Minneapolis: University of Minnesota Press, pp. xi–xiv.

Foucault, M. (1986a) 'Space, Knowledge, Power', in P. Rabinov (ed.), *The Foucault Reader*, London: Penguin, pp. 239–56.

Foucault, M. (1986b) 'What Is Enlightenment?', in P. Rabinov (ed.), *The Foucault Reader*, London: Penguin, pp. 32–50.

Foucault, M. (1991) 'Governmentality', in G. Burchell, C. Gordon and P. Miller (eds), *The Foucault Effect*, Chicago: University of Chicago Press, pp. 87–104.

Foucault, M. (1992) *The Order of Things*, London: Routledge.

Foucault, M. (1997) *Essential Works of Foucault 1954–1984*, vol. I: *Ethics*, ed. P. Rabinow, Harmondsworth: Penguin.

Foucault, M. (2001) 'Friendship as a Way of Life', in C. Kraus and S. Lotringer (eds), *Hatred of Capitalism*, New York: Semiotext(e), pp. 297–302.

Foucault, M. (2005) 'Is It Useless to Revolt?', in J. Afary and K.B. Anderson, *Foucault and the Iranian Revolution*, Chicago: University of Chicago Press, pp. 263–7.

Freire-Medeiros, B. (2009) 'Touring Poverty', Paper presented at Lancaster University, Department of Sociology, 2 December.

Freud, S. (1960) *Totem and Taboo*, London: Routledge.

Friedman, M. (1963) *Problematic Rebel: An Image of Modern Man*, New York: Random House.

Fukuyama, F. (1992) *The End of History and the Last Man*, New York: Free Press.

George, N. (2008) 'Interview with Alain Badiou', http://www.16beavergroup.org/mtarchive/archives/002641.php

Giddens, A. (1994) *Beyond Left and Right*, London: Polity.

Hall, J.R. (2009) *Apocalypse*, Cambridge: Polity.

Hallward, P. (2003) *Badiou: A Subject to Truth*, Minneapolis: Minnesota University Press.

Hallward, P. (2006) *Out of This World: Deleuze and the Philosophy of Creation*, London: Verso.

Hardt, M. and Negri, A. (1994) *Labor of Dionysus: A Critique of the State-form*, Minneapolis: University of Minnesota Press.

Hardt, M. and Negri, A. (2000) *Empire*, Cambridge, MA: Harvard University Press.

Hardt, M. and Negri, A. (2004) *Multitude*, London: Hamish Hamilton.

Hardt, M. and Negri, A. (2009) *Commonwealth*, Cambridge, MA: Belknap Press.

Hass, J. (1982) *Illusionens filosofi: Studier i Nietzsches første manuskripter*, Copenhagen: Nyt Nordisk Forlag.

Hemingway, E. (2004) 'The Revolutionist', in *The Snows of Kilimanjaro*, London: Arrow Books, pp. 79–80.

Hikmet, N. (1987) 'Ahmed'in Hikayesi', in N. Hikmet, *Benerci Kendini Niçin Öldürdü?*, Istanbul: Adam, pp. 263–5.

Hikmet, N. (2002) 'The Epic of Sheikh Bedreddin', in N. Hikmet, *Beyond the Walls: Selected Poems*, Trowbridge: Anvil, pp. 51–72.

Hobbes, T. (1985) *Leviathan*, London: Penguin.

Hobbes, T. (2007) *Behemoth, or the Long Parliament*, London: Elibron.

Hobsbawm, E. (1965) *Primitive Rebels*, New York: W.W. Norton.

Holsinger, B. (2007) *Neomedievalism, Neoconservatism, and the War on Terror*, Chicago: Prickly Paradigm Press.

Horace (2005) *Satires and Epistles*, London: Penguin.

Houellebecq, M. (2005) *The Possibility of an Island*, London: Weidenfeld & Nicolson.

Huntington, S.P. (1997) *The Clash of Civilizations and the Remaking of World Order*, London: Simon & Schuster.

Huxley, A. (2004) *Brave New World Revisited*, London: Vintage.

Huxley, A. (2007) *Brave New World*, London: Vintage.

Illuminati, A. (2003) 'Postfordisten Spinoza', *Agora* 2(3): 317–29.

Jameson, F. (2007) 'Lenin and Revisionism', in S. Budgen. S. Kouvelakis and S. Žižek (eds), *Lenin Reloaded: Toward a Politics of Truth*, Durham, NC: Duke University Press, pp. 59–72.

Jonsson, S. (2008) *A Brief History of the Masses: Three Revolutions*, New York: Columbia University Press.

Kant, I. (2003) *Critique of Pure Reason*, New York: Dover.

Kant, I. (2004) *Critique of Practical Reason*, New York: Dover.

Kierkegaard, S. (1962) 'Enten Eller', in *Samlede Værker*, vols II and III, Copenhagen: Gyldendal.

Klein, N. (2004) 'Smoking while Iraq Burns', *Guardian*, 26 November.

Kouvelakis, S. (2003) *Philosophy and Revolution: From Kant to Marx*, London: Verso.

Krips, H. (2007) 'The Politics of Badiou: From Absolute Singularity to Objet-a', http://white-headresearch.org/occasions/conferences/event-and-decision/papers/Henry%20Krips_Final%20Draft.pdf

Kristeva, J. (1996) *The Sense of Non-sense and Revolt*, New York: Columbia University Press.

Lacan, J. (1990) 'Kant with Sade', *October* 51: 55–75.

Lacan, J. (1992) *The Ethics of Psychoanalysis 1959–1960*, book VII, London: Routledge.

Lacan, J. (1994) *Four Fundamental Concepts of Psycho-analysis*, London: Penguin.

Latour, B. (1988) *The Pasteurization of France*, Cambridge, MA: Harvard University Press.

Latour, B. (1996a) 'On Interobjectivity', *Mind, Culture and Activity* 3(4): 228–45.

Latour, B. (1996b) 'On Actor-network Theory: A Few Clarifications', *Soziale Welt* 47: 369–81.

Latour, B. (2004) 'Why Has Critique Run out of Steam? From Matters of Fact to Matters of Concern', *Critical Inquiry* 30: 225–48.

Latour, B. (2005) *Reassembling the Social*, Oxford: Oxford University Press.

Lecercle, J.-J. (2007) 'Lenin the Just, or Marxism Unrecycled', in S. Budgen, S. Kouvelakis and S. Žižek (eds), *Lenin Reloaded: Towards a Politics of Truth*, Durham, NC: Duke University Press, pp. 269–82.

Lenin, V.I. (1952) 'What Is to Be Done?', *Collected Works*, vol. V, Moscow: Progress Publishers, pp. 352–520.

Lenin, V.I. (1964) 'The Collapse of the Second International', *Collected Works*, vol. 21, Moscow: Progress Publishers, pp. 205–59.

Lenin, V.I. (1965) 'The Lessons of the Moscow Uprising', in *Collected Works*, vol. 11, Moscow: Progress Publishers, pp. 171–8.

Lenin, V.I. (1974) 'On Slogans', in *Collected Works*, vol. 25, Moscow: Progress Publishers, pp. 185–92.

Löwy, M. (1993) *On Changing the World*, Atlantic Highlands, NJ: Humanities Press.

Luhmann, N. (1994) 'The Idea of Unity in a Differentiated Society', Paper presented at the XIIIth Sociological World Congress 'Contested Boundaries and Shifting Solidarities', Bielefeld, Germany.

Macaulay, C. (1790) *On Burke's Reflections on the French Revolution*, London: C. Dilly.

Mannheim, K. (1936) *Ideology and Utopia*, New York: Harcourt.

Mao Tse-Tung (2007) *Mao: On Practice and Contradiction*, ed. S. Žižek, London: Verso.

Marcuse, H. (1955) *Reason and Revolution*, London: Routledge.

Marcuse, H. (1964) *One Dimensional Man*, London: Routledge.

Marcuse, H. (1969) *Eros and Civilization*, London: Sphere Books.

Marx, K. (1973) *Grundrisse*, London: Pelican.

Marx, K. (1975) 'Contribution to the Critique of Hegel's Philosophy of Law: Introduction', in Karl Marx and Frederick Engels, *Collected Works*, vol. 3, London: Lawrence & Wishart, pp. 175–87.

Marx, K. (1976) *Capital*, vol. I, London: Penguin.

Marx, K. (1977) *The Eighteenth Brumaire of Louis Bonaparte*, Moscow: Progress Publishers.

Marx, K. (1998) *Thesis on Feuerbach*, in K. Marx and F. Engels, *The German Ideology*, New York: Prometheus Books.

Marx, K. (2007) *Economic and Philosophic Manuscripts of 1844*, New York: Dover.

Marx, K. (2008) *Writings on the Paris Commune*, St Petersburg, FL: Red and Black Publishers.

Marx, K. and Engels, F. (1978) *Collected Works*, vol. 10, New York: International Publishers.

Marx, K. and Engels, F. (1998) *The German Ideology*, New York: Prometheus Books.

Marx, K. and Engels, F. (2002) *The Communist Manifesto*, London: Penguin.

May, T. (2008) Book review (of N. Hewlett, *Badiou, Balibar, Rancière: Re-thinking Emancipation*, Continuum, 2007), *Notre Dame Philosophical Reviews*, http://ndpr.nd.edu/review.cfm?id=12443

McGreal, C. (2011) 'Tony Blair: Mubarak Is "Immensely Courageous and a Force for Good"', *Guardian*, 2 February.

Melville, H. (1998) *Moby Dick*, Oxford: Oxford World's Classics.

Mills, C. (2007) 'Biopolitics, Liberal Eugenics, and Nihilism', in M. Calarco and S. DeCaroli (eds), *Giorgio Agamben: Sovereignty and Life*, Stanford, CA: Stanford University Press, pp. 180–202.

Mouffe, C. (2005) *On the Political*, London: Routledge.

Moussalli, A.S. (1999) *Moderate and Radical Islamic Fundamentalism: The Quest for Modernity, Legitimacy, and the Islamic State*, Gainesville: University of Florida Press.

Mrożek, S. (2010) *The Elephant*, London: Penguin.

Münkler, H. (2002) 'The Brutal Logic of Terror: The Privatization of War in Modernity', *Constellation* 9(1): 66–73.

Nechaev, S. (1869) 'The Revolutionary Catechism', *Anarchist Library*, http://theanarchistlibrary.org/HTML/Sergey_Nechayev__The_Revolutionary_Catechism.html

Negri, A. (1999) *Insurgencies: Constituent Power and the Modern State*, Minneapolis: University of Minnesota Press.

Negri, A. (2003) *Time for Revolution*, New York: Continuum.

Nietzsche, F. (1959) *Nietzsche: Unpublished Letters*, ed. Karl F. Leidecker, London: Peter Owen.

Nietzsche, F. (1960) *Joyful Wisdom*, New York: Frederick Ungar Publishing.

Nietzsche, F. (1961) *Thus Spoke Zarathustra*, London: Penguin.

Nietzsche, F. (1967) *The Will to Power*, New York: Vintage.

Nietzsche, F. (1969) *Twilight of Idols*, London: Penguin.

Nietzsche, F. (1974) *The Gay Science*, New York: Vintage.

Nietzsche, F. (1996) *On the Genealogy of Morals*, Oxford: Oxford University Press.

Nietzsche, F. (2004) *Ecce Homo*, London: Penguin.

Nietzsche, F. (2006) 'Notes from 1881', in K.A. Pearson and D. Large (eds), *The Nietzsche Reader*, London: Blackwell, pp. 238–41.

Nomad, M. (1961) *Apostles of Revolution*, New York: Collier Books.

Parenti, M. (2007) 'Roman Slavery and the Class Divide', in M.M. Winkler (ed.), *Spartacus: Film and History*, London: Blackwell, pp. 144–53.

Paz, F.J.T. (2007) '*Spartacus* and the Stoic Ideal of Death', in M.M. Winkler (ed.), *Spartacus: Film and History*, London: Blackwell, pp. 189–97.

Plutarch (2007) 'Crassus (8–11)', in M.M. Winkler (ed.), *Spartacus: Film and History*, London: Blackwell, pp. 234–9.

Postman, N. (1985) *Amusing Ourselves to Death*, London: Methuen.

Prince of Wales, Juniper, T. and Skelly, I. (2010) *Harmony: A New Way of Looking at Our World*, London: Blue Door.

Rancière, J. (1991) *The Ignorant Schoolmaster: Five Lessons in Intellectual Emancipation*, Stanford, CA: Stanford University Press.

Rancière, J. (1999) *Disagreement*, Minneapolis: University of Minnesota Press.

Rancière, J. (2009a) *The Emancipated Spectator*, London: Verso.

Rancière, J. (2009b) *Aesthetics and Its Discontents*, London: Polity.

Rancière, J. (2010) *Dissensus*, New York: Continuum.

Ratmoko, D. (2009) 'Preface', in J. Taubes, *Occidental Eschatology*, Stanford, CA: Stanford University Press, pp. xi–xxiii.

Raunig, G. (2007) *Art and Revolution: Transversal Activism in the Long Twentieth Century*, Los Angeles: Semiotext(e).

Rifkin, J. (2000) *The Age of Access: How the Shift from Ownership to Access Is Transforming Capitalism*, London: Penguin.

Robespierre, M. (2007) *Robespierre: Virtue and Terror*, ed. S. Žižek, London: Verso.

Rodinson, M. (2005) 'Critique of Foucault on Iran', in J. Afary and K.B. Anderson, *Foucault and the Iranian Revolution*, Chicago: University of Chicago Press, pp. 267–78.

Rose, N. (1999) *Powers of Freedom: Reframing Political Thought*, Cambridge: Cambridge University Press.

Rosen, S. (1995) *The Mask of Enlightenment: Nietzsche's Zarathustra*, Cambridge: Cambridge University Press.

Ross, K. (2002) *May '68 and Its Afterlives*, Chicago: University of Chicago Press.

Rousseau, J.-J. (2004) *The Social Contract*, London: Penguin.

Schmitt, C. (1985) *Political Theology: Four Chapters on the Concept of Sovereignty*, Cambridge, MA: MIT Press.

Schmitt, C. (2004) 'Theory of the Partisan: Intermediate Commentary on the Concept of the Political', *Telos* 127: 11–78.

Sennett, R. (1998) *The Corrosion of Character*, New York: W.W. Norton.

Simmel, G. (1971) *On Individuality and Social Forms: Selected Writings*, Chicago: University of Chicago Press.

Siporin, S. (2002) '*Life Is Beautiful*: Four Riddles, Three Answers', *Journal of Modern Italian Studies* 7(3): 345–63.

Smith, D.W. (2004a) 'Badiou and Deleuze on the Ontology of Mathematics', in P. Hallward (ed.), *Think Again: Alain Badiou and the Future of Philosophy*, New York: Continuum, pp. 77–93.

Smith, D.W. (2004b) 'The Inverse Side of Structure: Žižek on Deleuze on Lacan', *Criticism* 46(4): 635–50.

Sophocles (1967) *The Complete Plays of Sophocles*, New York: Bantam Classics.

Sparrow, A. (2011) 'Blair Says Leak of Palestine Papers "Destabilising" for Peace Process', *Guardian*, 28 January.

Strauss, B. (2009) *The Spartacus War*, London: Weidenfeld & Nicolson.

Taubes, J. (2009) *Occidental Eschatology*, Stanford, CA: Stanford University Press.

Thoburn, N. (2003) *Deleuze, Marx and Politics*, London: Routledge.

Thompson, M. (2009) Reader comments, *Guardian*, 22 October.

Tillich, P. (1936) *The Interpretation of History*, New York: Charles Scribner's Sons.

Tocqueville, A. de (2008) *The Ancien Régime and the Revolution*, London: Penguin.

Toscana, A. (2010) *Fanaticism*, London: Verso.

Trotsky, L. (1967) *History of the Russian Revolution*, vols I and III, London: Sphere Books.

Ulam, A.B. (1965) *Lenin and the Bolsheviks*, Glasgow: Fontana Library.

Vatter, M. (2000) *Between Form and Event: Machiavelli's Theory of Political Freedom*, Dordrecht: Kluwer.

Virno, P. (2004) *A Grammar of the Multitude*, Los Angeles: Semiotext(e).

Ward, A.M. (2007) '*Spartacus*: History and Histrionics', in M.M. Winkler (ed.), *Spartacus: Film and History*, London: Blackwell, pp. 87–111.

Weber, M. (1958) 'Politics as Vocation', in H.H. Gerth and C.W. Mills (eds), *From Max Weber: Essays in Sociology*, New York: Oxford University Press, pp. 77–128.

Weber, M. (2003) *The Protestant Ethic and the Spirit of Capitalism*, New York: Dover.

Winkler, M.M. (2007) 'The Holy Cause of Freedom', in M.M. Winkler (ed.), *Spartacus: Film and History*, London: Blackwell, pp. 154–88.

Younge, G. (2009) 'When You Watch the BNP on TV, Just Remember: Jack Straw Started All This', *Guardian*, 21 October.

Žižek, S. (1989) *The Sublime Object of Ideology*, London: Verso.

Žižek, S. (1991) *For They Know Not What They Do*, London: Verso.

Žižek, S. (1992) *Enjoy Your Symptom!*, London: Routledge.

Žižek, S. (1996) *The Indivisible Remainder*, London: Verso.

Žižek, S. (1999) *The Ticklish Subject: The Absent Centre of Political Ontology*, London: Verso.

Žižek, S. (2000) 'Class Struggle or Postmodernism? Yes, Please!', in J. Butler, E. Laclau and S. Žižek, *Contingency, Hegemony, Universality: Contemporary Dialogues on the Left*, London: Verso, pp. 90–135.

Žižek, S. (2001a) *Did Somebody Say Totalitarianism?*, London: Verso.

Žižek, S. (2001b) *On Belief*, London: Routledge.

Žižek, S. (2002a) 'Introduction: Between the Two Revolutions', Introduction to V.I. Lenin, *Revolution at the Gates*, Selected writings of Lenin from 1917, London: Verso, pp. 1–14.

Žižek, S. (2002b) 'Afterword: Lenin's Choice', Afterword to V.I. Lenin, *Revolution at the Gates*, Selected writings of Lenin from 1917, London: Verso, pp. 165–336.

Žižek, S. (2002c) *Welcome to the Desert of the Real*, London: Verso.

Žižek, S. (2004) *Organs without Bodies: On Deleuze and Consequences*, London: Routledge.

Žižek, S. (2005) *Interrogating the Real*, New York: Continuum.

Žižek, S. (2007a) 'Introduction: Robespierre, or, the "Divine Violence" of Terror', in M. Robespierre, *Robespierre: Virtue and Terror*, London: Verso, pp. i–xxxix.

Žižek, S. (2007b) 'Mao Tse-Tung, the Marxist Lord of Misrule', in Mao Tse-Tung, *Mao: On Practice and Contradiction*, ed. S. Žižek, London: Verso, pp. 1–28.

Žižek, S. (2007c) 'On Alain Badiou and *Logiques des mondes*', http://www.lacan.com/zizbadman.htm

Žižek, S. (2007d) 'A Leninist Gesture Today: Against the Populist Temptation', in S. Budgen, S. Kouvelakis and S. Žižek (eds), *Lenin Reloaded: Towards a Politics of Truth*, Durham, NC: Duke University Press, pp. 74–100.

Žižek, S. (2008a) *Violence*, London: Profile Books.

Žižek, S. (2008b) *In Defense of Lost Causes*, London: Verso.

Žižek, S. (2009a) *First as Tragedy, Then as Farce*, London: Verso.

Žižek, S. (2009b) *The Parallax View*, Cambridge, MA: MIT Press.

Žižek, S. (2009c) 'Philosophy Is Not a Dialogue', in A. Badiou and S. Žižek, *Philosophy in the Present*, London: Polity, pp. 49–72.

Žižek, S. (2011a) 'For Egypt, This Is the Miracle of Tahrir Square', *Guardian*, 10 February.

Žižek, S. (2011b) 'Why Fear the Arab Revolutionary Spirit?', *Guardian*, 1 February.

Zupančič, A. (2008) *The Odd One In*, Cambridge, MA: MIT Press.

INDEX

In this index figures are indicated in **bold** type.